HISTORICAL ATLAS OF CANADA

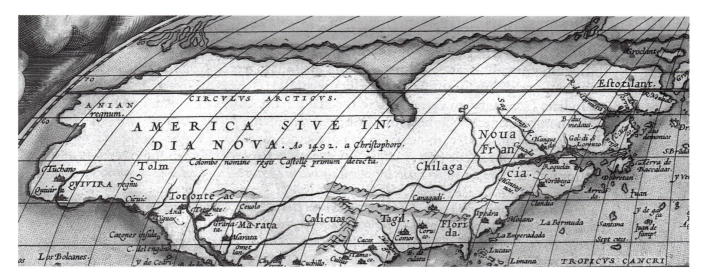

Historical Atlas of Canada

Canada's History Illustrated with Original Maps

Derek Hayes

Douglas & McIntyre
Vancouver / Toronto
University of Washington Press
Seattle

Douglas & McIntyre Ltd.
2323 Quebec Street, Suite 201
Vancouver, British Columbia V5T 4S7

National Library of Canada Cataloguing in Publication Data

Hayes, Derek, 1947–
    Historical atlas of Canada

    Includes bibliographical references and index.
    ISBN 1-55054-918-9

    1. Canada—Historical geography—Maps.
    2. Canada—Discovery and exploration—Maps.
    I. Title.
    G1116.S1H39 2002   911′.71   C2002-910288-x

Published in the United States of America by
The University of Washington Press,
P.O. Box 50096, Seattle, Washington 98145-5096
ISBN 0-295-98277-2

Design and layout by Derek Hayes
Copy editing by Naomi Pauls
Jacket design by Val Speidel
Modern photographs by Derek Hayes
Printed and bound in Hong Kong, P. R.C., by C & C Offset
Printed on acid-free paper

We gratefully acknowledge the financial support of the Canada Council for the Arts, the British Columbia Ministry of Tourism, Small Business and Culture, and the Government of Canada through the Book Publishing Industry Development Program (BPIDP) for our publishing activities.

To contact the author:
www.derekhayes.ca
derek@derekhayes.ca

> For Carole,
> And my first-generation Canadians,
> Neil and Ross

Acknowledgements

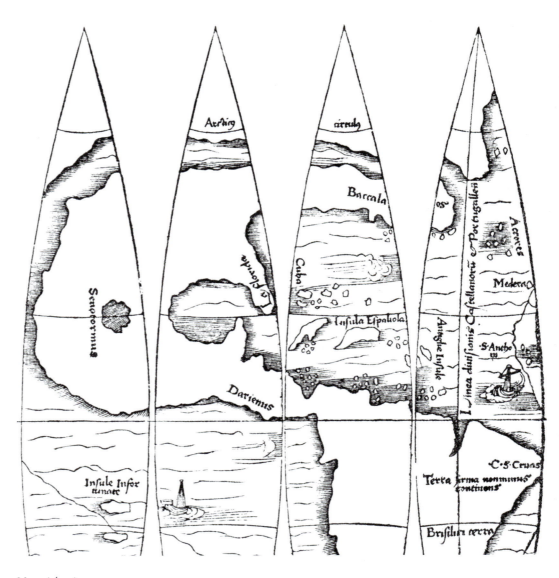

MAP 2 (*above*).
Probably the earliest cartographic representation of Canada with three coasts is this map dated about 1530. The segments are globe gores, which would fit together when formed on a globe. This is all that is left of a so-called Ambassadors' Globe depicted in a painting of ambassadors at the court of Henry VIII done by Hans Holbein in 1533. The Northwest Passage so clearly shown, giving Canada an Arctic coastline, may have been drawn from a voyage—or claimed voyage—of Sebastian Cabot, son of John Cabot, in 1508–09; he may have sailed through Hudson Strait into Hudson Bay, believing the latter to be the South Sea. There is, however, no first-hand evidence of Cabot's voyage, and many historians doubt it occurred, in which case the geography on this map would have been merely an extremely good guess.

MAP 1 (*with book title, previous double page*).
Part of a map depicting the second fall of the French fortress town of Louisbourg, on the east coast of Cape Breton Island, in 1758. In this scene, British troops are seen landing from their transport ships anchored in Gabarus Bay, south of Louisbourg. They are then advancing (to the right) towards the fortress. This stylized map, a panoramic depiction of the fall of Louisbourg, was drawn by a French admiral named Bockoune, about whom we unfortunately know very little. The map is shown in full on pages 96–97.

Encouragingly, a very high proportion of the maps in this book come from the superb cartographic collections of the National Archives of Canada, in Ottawa. I have to thank Ian Wilson and his staff at the National Archives of Canada, without whom the book could not have been created. In particular, Louis Cardinal and Jeffrey Murray were very helpful, allowing me direct access to the National Archives' storage vaults in Gatineau and thus cutting my search time—to find the right maps—by a huge amount. They spent days with me in the cold and sunless environment of the vaults assisting me in my searches, and some of the maps chosen for inclusion were suggested by them. Jean Matheson and others at the Specialized Media Consultation desk were tremendously helpful, and patient, in dealing with my numerous requests for photographic reproductions, many of them for new photography.

A large number of maps illustrating Canadian history were of course created by French, British, American, Spanish, and other European explorers or mapmakers, and most native maps survive only as copies made by Europeans. Thus the historical maps of Canada are widely scattered throughout the archives and libraries of the world.

In particular I should like to thank Andrew Cook, Tony Campbell, and Lynn Osborne and Debbie Hall at the British Library; Tammy Hannibal, Marie Reidke, and Debra Moore at the Hudson's Bay Company Archives, Winnipeg; Edward

Redmond, Geography and Map Division, Library of Congress; Carol Urness, James Ford Bell Library, University of Minnesota; Robert Karrow and Pat Morris, Newberry Library, Chicago; Sjoerd de Meer, Maritiem Museum Prins Hendrick, Rotterdam; Celine Villeneuve and Monique Lord, Archives nationales du Québec, Québec; Lindsay Moir, Glenbow Museum Library, Calgary; Robin Harcourt-Williams, Hatfield House, U.K.; Catherine Hoffmann, Bibliothèque national de France, Paris; Alec Parley, Beach Maps, Toronto; Don Stewart, MacLeod's Books, Vancouver; Christine Bourolias and Carolyn Gray, Archives of Ontario, Toronto; Jo-Anne Colby, Canadian Pacific Railway Archives, Montréal; Garry Shutlak, Provincial Archives of Nova Scotia, Halifax; Joel Sartorius, Rare Book Division, Free Library of Philadelphia; Susan Danforth, John Carter Brown Library, Providence, Rhode Island; Donald Hogan, McGill University Library, Montréal; Alan Walker, Special Collections, Toronto Reference Library; Eileen Meillon, Stewart Museum at the Fort, Montréal; David Jones, University of Alberta, Edmonton; Sharon Nichol and Adrian Webb, United Kingdom Hydrographic Office, Taunton, U.K.; Frances Woodward, Special Collections, University of British Columbia; Georg Zimmermann, Sächsische Landes-bibliothek, Dresden, Germany: and Sarah Toulouse, Bibliothèque municipale de Rennes, France.

I would also like to thank the staffs of the following institutions: Archivo General de Indias, Sevilla, Spain; Archives

nationales, Paris; Archives d'Outre-Mer, Aix-en-Provence, France; Biblioteca Apostolica Vaticana, Vatican City; British Columbia Archives, Victoria; Biblioteca Estense, Modena, Italy; Beinecke Rare Book and Manuscript Library, Yale University, New Haven, Connecticut; Bayerische Staatsbibliothek, Munich; City of Vancouver Archives, Vancouver; Det Kongelige Bibliotek, Copenhagen; Huntington Library, San Marino, California; Museo Naval, Madrid; United States National Archives, Washington, D.C.; Newfoundland Museum, St. John's; National Maritime Museum, Greenwich, U.K.; New York Public Library, New York; Oregon Historical Society, Portland, Oregon; Public Record Office, London; Service historique de la Marine, Vincennes, France; Musée de la civilization, Québec; Vancouver Public Library, Vancouver; Provincial Archives of Alberta, Edmonton.

Thanks to my wife, Carole Hayes, for numerous translations and ongoing encouragement. Also Chris Sparling, John Crosse, Bruce Ward, Nick Doe and Ed Dahl for discussions and clarifications. I thank my editor, Naomi Pauls, who laboured tirelessly, it seemed to me, to improve the text. I know the book is a better one for her efforts. Val Speidel designed the jacket and made useful typographical and design suggestions. Managing editor Susan Rana coordinated production. Finally, thanks to Scott McIntyre, my publisher, for his commitment to publishing Canadian history.

Contents

Acknowledgements / 4

Introduction / 7
Saint Brendan and Other Early Navigators / 9
The Norse Voyages / 10
Pre-Columbian Apocryphal Voyages / 13
Out of the Mists—Canada / 15
Early Explorations of the Coasts of Canada, 1500–1527 / 20
Early French Explorations / 24
Jacques Cartier—the Foundation
    of the French Claim to Canada / 25
Early English Attempts to Find a Northwest Passage / 34
Probing the Northern Seas / 38
Early English Colonization Attempts / 45
Samuel de Champlain—the Mapmaker
    Who Founded New France / 49
The Founding of Montréal / 57
Jesuits and the Fur Trade—French Exploration to 1700 / 58
The Defence of New France to 1713 / 70
The Seigneurial System / 76
The Coming of the English—the Hudson's Bay Company / 77
The British Attempt to Find the Northwest Passage
    in the Eighteenth Century / 80
The French Fur Trade Empire / 85
France Explores Westwards—the La Vérendryes / 86
The Fall of Louisbourg in 1745 / 88
Jacques-Nicolas Bellin's Atlas / 90
The Founding of Halifax / 92
The Acadian Deportation / 95
The Battle for a Continent—the French and Indian War / 96
The Fall of Québec—and an Empire / 99
James Cook's Maps of Eastern Canada / 106
James Murray's Map / 112
Québec under the British / 114
The American Attack on Québec / 116
Prince Edward Island / 118
The Coastal Surveys of Des Barres / 120
The Demise of the Beothuk / 122
Defining Canada, 1783 / 124
The Coming of the Loyalists / 126
Perceptions of the West / 132
An Inland Journey / 136
Alexander Henry's Great Map of the West / 138
The Maps of Peter Pond / 140
Alexander Mackenzie Crosses the Continent / 143
The Hudson's Bay Company Moves Inland / 146
The Hudson's Bay Company's Great Surveyors—
    Philip Turnor and Peter Fidler / 147
Native Maps / 152
The First Map of the West Coast / 156
James Cook—Defining the Width of Canada / 158

West Coast Exploration and Trade / 159
Spanish Explorations of the West Coast / 160
George Vancouver Surveys the West Coast / 163
Defining the West—David Thompson / 166
Early Toronto / 169
A Mere Matter of Marching—the War of 1812 / 172
The Selkirk Grant and the Red River Settlement / 178
Fixing the Forty-ninth Parallel Boundary Line / 180
The Rideau Canal / 181
The Canada Company / 182
Arctic Exploration 1818–1859 / 184
Westward Expansion of the Fur Trade / 197
The Rebellions of 1837 and the United Province of Canada / 200
Linking the Lakes / 201
Drawing the Line—the Webster-Ashburton Treaty / 202
The Founding of Fort Victoria
    and the Colony of Vancouver Island / 203
The Forty-ninth Parallel Extends to the Sea / 204
A Pioneer Road Map of Canada / 205
British Columbia Discovers Gold and Becomes a Colony / 206
Henry Hind's Expeditions / 207
The Palliser Expedition / 208
The Coming of the Railway / 210
Confederation and the Intercolonial Railway / 212
The Riel Rebellion of 1869 / 213
Manitoba Becomes the Fifth Province / 214
British Columbia Joins Confederation / 215
The North-West Rebellion, 1885 / 216
The Canadian Pacific Railway—the Settlement of the Prairies
    and the Linking of a Nation / 218
Winnipeg—Gateway to the West / 227
Edmonton—Gateway to the North / 228
Calgary—from Police Post to Oil Capital / 230
The Discovery of Oil / 232
The Art of the Bird's-Eye / 233
Vancouver—Pacific Terminus / 236
Ottawa—the Nation's Capital / 238
Toronto in the Nineteenth Century / 240
Montréal after the Fall of New France / 242
Gold in the Klondike / 244
The British Dominion / 246
The Canadian Arctic and the Northwest Passage Achieved / 248
Fire Insurance Maps / 251
The Boundary with Alaska / 252
The Evolution of Provincial Boundaries / 253

Map Catalogue / 257
Notes / 264
Bibliography / 265
Index / 268

MAP 3.

Bearing the date 1541, this is part of a world map by Dieppe mapmaker Nicolas Desliens. It may be the earliest surviving map to use the name *Canada*. The map has none of Jacques Cartier's names from his third voyage in 1541, but nevertheless, on the basis of geographical evidence elsewhere, it is now thought possible that it was created later, perhaps 1555. If so, then the earliest map with the name *Canada* is the Harleian map (MAP 28, page 26). Cartier understood the name to be applied to the site of present-day Québec, also called Stadaconé. In his account of his voyages, Cartier listed native words with their meanings; *kanata*, he wrote, meant "town." Whether from *Canada* or *kanata*, the name *Canada* soon appeared on many other maps.

This map is in the collection of the Sächsische Landesbibliothek in Dresden, Germany, and was badly damaged by water used to fight fires created from bombing during the Second World War. The shape of North America—with south at the top, as it was in many of the maps of the time—is strange to modern eyes, but reflected the reality of European geographic knowledge in the sixteenth century; the east coast was imperfectly known, the west coast almost totally unknown. The entire north and west coasts of what would one day become the nation of Canada are marked *Terre Septentrionale Inconnue*, "Unknown Northern Land."

The new name *Canada* appears on the "middle peninsula" in a position roughly corresponding to the coasts of Labrador or Baffin Island, far away from the position of Cartier's Canada, on the shores of the St. Lawrence. The latter river is shown as far inland as Québec, with the Île d'Orléans (the unnamed black-coloured island) at its western end. Desliens's map is thought to have been a practical map intended for navigation, and detail on this map stops at Québec likely because it was essentially the limit of westward navigation for ocean-going ships. But the French knew of the land beyond; Cartier made it as far inland as the Iroquois village of Hochelaga, site of today's Montréal (see page 28).

The lower peninsula, *Terre du labrador*, is Greenland; the top peninsula, *Terre des bretons*, is the region stretching from Gaspé to Nova Scotia. Detail of this map is shown on MAP 29, page 27.

Introduction

This historical atlas of Canada is the first to be published using only historical maps rather than modern redrawn ones. It is intended as a history illustrated with maps rather than a carto-bibliography.

An attempt has been made to gather together original maps illustrating progressive geographical knowledge of the country and important events in Canadian history. The selection of maps is purely personal, although I have done my best to ensure that all maps significant to the history of Canada are included. The reader may judge whether I have been successful in this regard. But maps have also been included for their artistic merit, interest, or even because they were so far out in geographical understanding as to hold a fascination to us today.

Topics have been selected based on their historical importance, geographical significance, and the availability of surviving maps. It is, of course, difficult to cover the entire sweep of Canada's long history in a single book, and some may find the text too short, probably a fair criticism. But I have deliberately tried to include as many maps as possible, and maps at a size where details are clearly visible, at the expense of text, feeling that there are plenty of Canadian histories available but few with these maps, and certainly none in which they have been collected together in an atlas format.

There are many French and British maps, as one would expect, since these two countries supplied much of the colonizing force of early Canada. But there are also maps of Spanish, Russian, American, Portuguese, Danish, and other origins. These nations had varying degrees of influence in extending geographical knowledge—or competing with the French and British for what is now Canadian territory.

In addition, many native maps have been included, but perhaps not as many as some might like, because native maps were generally ephemeral, drawn on birchbark or on the ground, and were usually not intended to last. Hence they often survived only when others transcribed them onto paper or took them home with them. Because maps had to survive to be available here, this book may appear to some to emphasize the European presence in Canada at the expense of the native. This is unfortunate and unintended, but I have of course had to work with the maps that still exist, and the fact that one type of map tended to perish should surely not preclude the study of others that survived.

It is also true that many maps depict explorations by Europeans, and show what to them was discovery. Others are an imperial gesture of conquest of land and a record of political domination. There is no doubt that European nations of old considered it their right to claim for themselves whatever land was not occupied or claimed by other Europeans—and sometimes land that had been—without regard to the native occupants. But often these same geopolitical maps showed emerging geographical knowledge of Canada, knowledge that could be added to the map of the world.

Here are maps of the seizing of an empire and the settlement of the prairie, of war and wanderlust, battles and boundaries, forts and fur trade, river communications and railway surveys; explorers' maps and defence plans; native maps of Beothuk, Blackfoot, and Cree; maps of rebellion; maps of the search for a Northwest Passage from the sixteenth to nineteenth centuries; gold rush maps; early maps of all the major cities; and Indian Treaty maps. There are maps drawn for governors, kings, princes, and the Empress of Russia; panoramic maps; bird's-eye maps; and three-dimensional maps. Many of the maps are artistic, some utilitarian, but all are included for their historical significance and the story they have to tell.

Canadian history has been profoundly influenced by its geography. What better way to explore the nation's history than through maps drawn at the time? The result, I hope, will be a better understanding of Canada's past, and from a new perspective.

English ships head for Canada in this illustration from a map drawn by Hessel Gerritz in 1612. The map was based on one by Henry Hudson. See Map 46, pages 38–39.

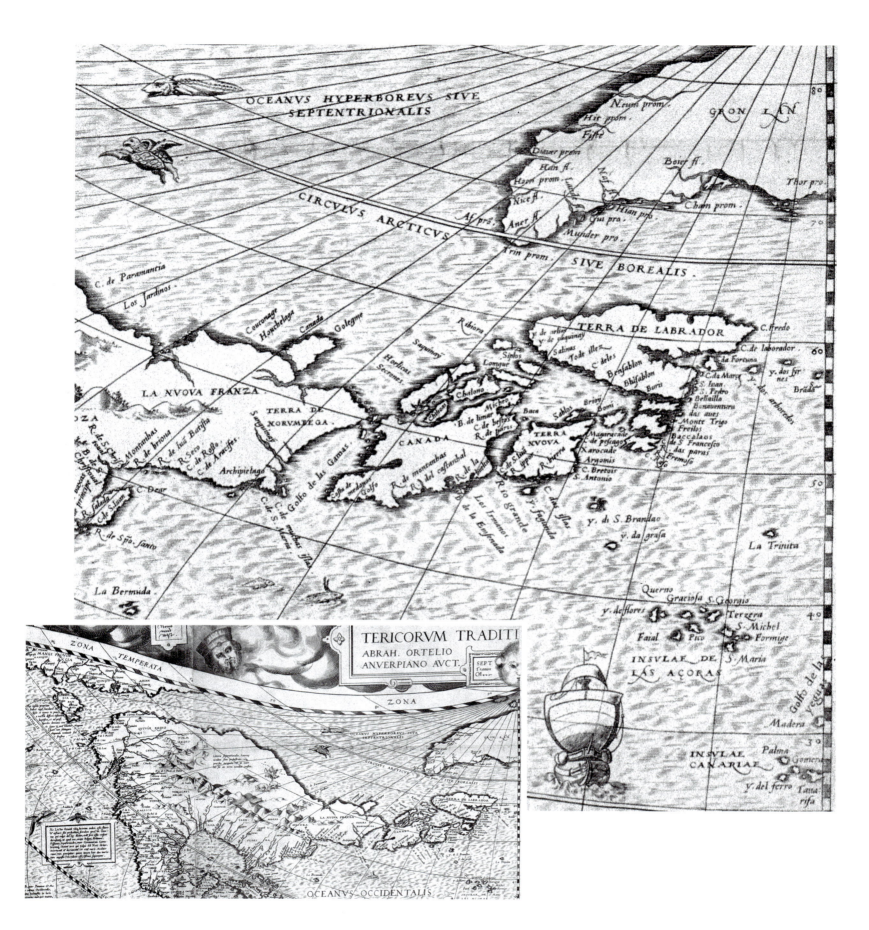

Map 4.

At first glance, Canada seems to be missing altogether from this map of North America taken from Abraham Ortelius's world map published in 1564. But wait! What is that small island on the eastern side? Yes, it's Canada. The result of misinterpretation of information from explorers, this sort of error easily crept into maps of this era. Many places have at one time or another been depicted as islands—the most famous was California—but this is the only map of "Canada as an island." There are a few others, but all are copies of this map by Ortelius, and they persisted even after Ortelius had fixed the error on his own maps. Every place Jacques Cartier looked for a strait, Ortelius has shown one, even if Cartier reported none (see page 25). This map would have appealed to Europeans in the sixteenth century, for it showed an easy route to the riches of the east—and no Canada in the way.

Golfo de las Gamas is an early depiction of the Bay of Fundy. *Honchelaga* (Hochelaga), Cartier's Montréal, is marked on the north coast of the continent, along with another mention of *Canada*. *Terra Nvova* (Terra Nuova) is Newfoundland, and *Terra de Labrador* is Labrador, a name which migrated from Greenland (here *Gron Lan*) in the first half of the sixteenth century. The name had first been applied to Greenland by João Fernandes (see page 20). The smaller map shows all of North America, while the larger is a detail of the northeastern portion.

Saint Brendan and Other Early Navigators

People migrated from Asia into the land that is now Canada at least as early as 9500 B.C., leaving archaeological evidence in the form of stone spearheads and arrowheads.

Chinese and Japanese sailors may have arrived on the coasts of British Columbia by design or accident from perhaps 200 B.C. on, but there is no direct evidence of this until the seventeenth century. Later maps seemingly "document" such voyages (see Map 185, page 134, and Map 222, page 156), but they are based on no better evidence than that available today. Likewise, as early as the sixth century, voyages were made by Irish monks towards the west; but there is no evidence any reached Canadian shores.

The most celebrated of the latter voyages is that of Saint Brendan, which is documented in an Irish saga called the *Navigatio Sancti Brendani Abbatis*. More than a hundred copies of this manuscript survive, some from as early as the eleventh century. It must have been considered a good read by many for it to have been so copied in a day when all books had to be reproduced by hand.

The *Navigatio* says that Brendan was the abbot of the Monastery of Clonfert in Galway, Ireland, who constructed a skin-clad boat around 570 and embarked on a series of voyages to fantastic places to the west, including the *Terra Repromissionis Sanctorum*, the "Land Promised to the Saints." Some of the details do have a ring of truth about them—tales of coagulated seas (pack ice), volcanoes (in Iceland?), and icebergs—but other events, like the celebration of Mass on the back of a friendly whale, as shown here, are clearly exaggerated. One story even has Brendan landing on the shores of North America to be greeted by an old man wearing no clothes, but covered by pure white hair and beard. In reality, it is very doubtful that Brendan ever reached North America. However, this did not stop John Dee, in 1580, from including St. Brendan's voyage—together with that of John Cabot and even the legendary King Arthur—in a defence of the English title to North America. Imaginary St. Brendan's Islands are often found in the Atlantic Ocean on old maps.

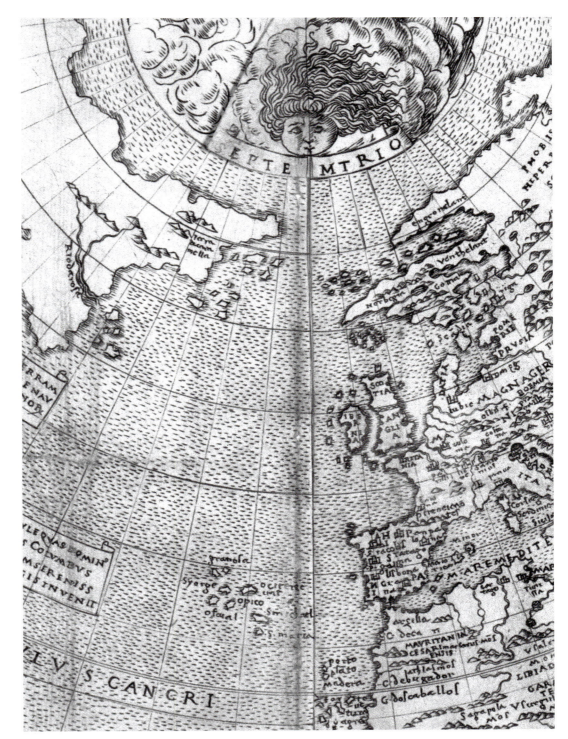

MAP 5.
Part of a world map by Giovanni Contarini, 1506. It shows the shores of Newfoundland, then assumed to be a peninsula of the Asian continent, bounding the western Atlantic. In between this continent and Europe lie many islands, imagined or assumed, fed by tales from Saint Brendan on. In particular the ring of islands on the west coast of Ireland could well be derived from an interpretation of the *Navigatio*. But there was real land out there in the far Atlantic—Canada. A larger section of this map is shown as Map 16, page 16.

An improbable scene with cartographic pretensions showing Saint Brendan celebrating Mass on the back of a mid-Atlantic whale, from a twelfth-century rendering of the Brendan saga, printed in the early seventeenth century. The Fortunate Isles and a Saint Brendan's Island are shown, but there is no hint of land farther to the west. Although Brendan would have sailed in a skin-covered boat, all the vessels shown here are clearly wooden.

In 1976 and 1977, a voyage from Ireland to Newfoundland via the Faroe Islands and Iceland was made by historian and explorer Tim Severin, to prove that it was possible for a skin-covered boat, a *carraugh* such as Brendan would have constructed, to sail across the Atlantic. His 36-foot-long leather boat, *Brendan*, just made it. Unfortunately, proving that a voyage is possible does not prove that it actually happened.

There is plenty of evidence that Chinese or Japanese junks reached the west coast of Canada, but no one knows how early the first arrival might have been.

The Norse Voyages

The Norse voyages to North America are told in early Icelandic history books called sagas. These were written by early historians at the beginning of the thirteenth century and later rewritten. They were written in all probability without reference to maps, and indeed it seems that Old Norse, the language in which they were written, did not even have a word for "map"; Norse navigation did not use or make charts.

From the sagas come stories of the Vikings' discovery of the coasts of Canada, to which they sailed from their settlements in Greenland. The Norse had arrived in Greenland in 983 after successively establishing settlements in the Shetland Islands, the Orkneys, the Faeroes, and Iceland.

The farther north one goes in Davis Strait, between Greenland and North America, the narrower it becomes, and at about the latitude of the Arctic Circle the distance from Greenland to Baffin Island is only about 320 km. So a sailor would not have to go very far offshore from Greenland before the tops of the mountains on Baffin Island would be visible. It follows, then, that this may have been the place where the crossing to North America was first made.

The sagas tell us that Leif Eiriksson (or Ericsson) retraced a voyage made in the late tenth century—in 985 or 986—by Bjarni Herjolfsson, who had been blown westwards in a storm to a land which was forested. Eiriksson set out about 1001 to find this land. Baffin Island is today thought to have been Eiriksson's first landfall, which he named Helluland, or "Slab-Land," after the nature of the rocks on the coastline. This not being the forested land described by Herjolfsson, he continued southwards until he came to such a forested region, with sandy beaches, which he named Markland, or "Forest-Land." This is generally thought to be the coast of Labrador south of Hamilton Inlet, where the forested area would likely have extended to at this time.

Eiriksson then sailed farther south still, to the land he named Vinland. There is less agreement as to the location of Vinland, or even why he gave it this name, but the consensus is for Newfoundland. "Vin" could have meant "green meadow" but is now almost universally assumed to mean "wine." Despite a warmer climate at the time, it seems unlikely that wild grapes grew in Newfoundland; however, as late as the 1530s Jacques Cartier recorded finding grapes on the shores of the St. Lawrence, so perhaps it is possible grapes grew also in Newfoundland. A more likely explanation is that the Norse settlement at L'Anse aux Meadows, at the tip of Newfoundland's Northern Peninsula, was a collection place for products, including grapes, from

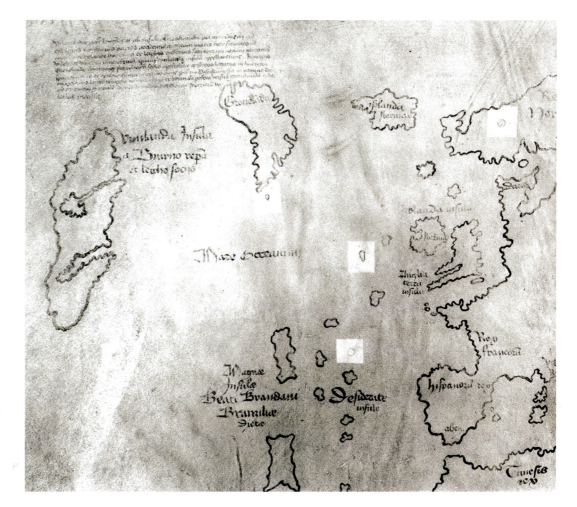

MAP 6.
This is the famous Vinland Map, claimed to date from 1440. What could possibly be the very first surviving map of any part of Canada, or America for that matter, is a story unto itself. No map has ever generated as much controversy as this map. Held in an undisclosed private library in Europe up to 1957, the map was then acquired by Yale University and revealed to the world in 1965, accompanied by a large book on the map and its accompanying document, called the *Tartar Relation*. The book itself was a best-seller which was reprinted several times, and was even a Book-of-the-Month Club selection, such was the interest in it. A second edition appeared in 1996. Scholarly conferences were held to discuss the map, and much of the discussion revolved around whether it was genuine. Indeed, right from the day the book was published, this was what generated the most discussion—is it genuine?

In 1974, a laboratory analysis of the ink used for the map determined that some components of the ink might have been twentieth-century in origin, and this seemed to establish that the Vinland Map was indeed a forgery. In 1986, a much more sophisticated test was applied to the map by physicists at the University of California, Davis, involving subatomic particles in a new piece of equipment called a cyclotron. The test was non-destructive and thus could be applied to the entire document, not just a chip of the ink. This apparently established once again that the map could be genuine, because the components of the ink were found to be entirely characteristic of a fifteenth-century document.

Today some scholars consider the map genuine, while others are sure it is a fake, with the recent balance of opinion favouring the latter verdict. However, whether or not this particular map is genuine, the fact that there is much other evidence for Norse voyages to North America must not be forgotten; it is the map, not the voyages, that is in question. And if the map *is* a fake, it is a very clever one, and a deception that will go down in history as one of the most magnificent historical hoaxes of all time. Even as a possible forgery, the map is reputed to be worth some $24 million.

The legend beside the large island is *Vinlanda Insula a Byarno repa et leipho socijs*, or "Island of Vinland, discovered by Bjarni and Leif in company." It seems to apply the name "Vinland" to the entire region. Many newly discovered lands in the period from the Norse voyages to the mid-sixteenth century were referred to as islands, and indeed many headlands reported by explorers often appeared to be islands when viewed in passing from the sea, and were recorded as such. In the earliest written record of Vinland, that of Adam of Bremen, about 1070, it is referred to as an island. On the Vinland Map, Greenland is, most interestingly, shown as the island it really is, but one is hard-pressed to believe that this could have been anything more than a guess by the original maker of the map, for Greenland was not proven to be an island until 1892, when Robert Peary trekked to its northernmost extent.

The text above Vinland and Greenland translates as follows:

By God's will, after a long voyage from the island of Greenland to the south toward the most distant remaining parts of the western ocean sea, sailing southward amidst the ice, the companions Bjarni and Leif Eiriksson discovered a new land, extremely fertile and even having vines, the which island they named Vinland. Eric [Henricus], legate of the Apostolic See and bishop of Greenland and the neighbouring regions, arrived in this truly vast and very rich land, in the name of Almighty God, in the last year of our most blessed father Pascal, remained a long time in both summer and winter, and later returned northeastward toward Greenland and then proceeded [home to Europe?] in most humble obedience to the will of his superiors.

farther afield. The evidence for this is that butternut or white walnut wood has been found at the site, and this tree has never grown north of the St. Lawrence and northeastern New Brunswick. If this was gathered and brought north, so could grapes.

Other locations farther south have also been claimed as Vinland; a recent claim was for the Chegoggin River, just north of Yarmouth, Nova Scotia, but the absence of any archaeological evidence, such as has been found at L'Anse aux Meadows, makes these claims less compelling.

Maps 7 (*right, top*), **8** (*right, bottom*), and **9** (*overleaf*).
The three surviving Norse maps, drawn during the seventeenth century in Iceland or Denmark, are copies of earlier Norse maps.

Some of the maps of Icelandic origin drawn in the early sixteenth century were derived from written records made by Norse sailors who frequented the waters of Iceland, Greenland, and eastern Canada from the tenth to the fifteenth centuries. These sailors learned to find their way by knowing landmarks on the coasts and the stars in the sky, without the help of maps, and are thought not to have actually produced any maps themselves; there is no Norse cartographic tradition.

Since the maps shown here claim to have used earlier Icelandic maps as their source, it seems likely that they used earlier versions of maps which are now lost. There was at this time an attempt to locate the lost Norse colonies in Greenland, which inspired a search of Icelandic archives and this redrawing of old maps. At the begining of the seventeenth century, the king of Denmark sent out three expeditions to attempt to locate his lost subjects in Greenland, and, it seems, hoping to find silver and gold in the process. He was also trying to reassert the sovereignty of Denmark following the publication of the account of John Davis's voyages of 1585–87 in the 1589 edition of Richard Hakluyt's *Principall Navigations* (see page 36).

What appears to be evidence of continuing Norse voyages to Canada in the thirteenth century, a strand of yarn dated to that time, was found near Pond Inlet, Baffin Island, in 1985, although it was not dated and recognized for what it likely was until 1999. Inuit who lived in the region did not spin wool or weave cloth, and thus this yarn points to Norse origins. Other items of Norse origin have been found on Ellesmere Island. This does not necessarily mean that Norse voyagers reached this far north, as the items could have been traded anywhere and later transported to another site.

All three of the Danish or Icelandic maps show the entire North Atlantic, and all in varying degrees show land on the western side of the ocean—Canada. The problem with all three is that since they were redrawn after the European discovery of North America, it is possible their creators added knowledge from later maps to those they were copying. Certainly some later-known features have been added. On the other hand, if the mapmakers were adding later knowledge to "update" the maps, there is a lot more geography that they surely knew that is *not* on these maps. It all makes for an intriguing and ongoing mystery.

Map 7 (*right, top*).

This is the Sigurdur Stefánsson map, of Icelandic origin. It was copied in 1670 from an earlier one probably made in 1590, not 1570, as shown in the cartouche. It tends to support the location of Vinland in Newfoundland; the peninsula named *Promontorium Winlandia* is tantalizingly similar to the Northern Peninsula of Newfoundland, and is approximately correctly shown in latitude relative to England, and in distance and direction from Greenland. Eiriksson's Helluland and Markland are also shown, this time as projections from a North American continent. Note that North America is almost attached to Europe, with Greenland as a peninsula from this northern connecting landmass. This is a feature repeated in all three of these "Norse" maps.

Map 8 (*right, bottom*).

The map drawn about 1640 by Icelander Jón Gudmonson. He was thought to have been working from earlier maps that are now lost. Impossibly near to a recognizable England and Ireland, part of America, *America pars*, is named. South of this is a large, unnamed bay, likely the Strait of Belle Isle, and south of this is land which seems to be Newfoundland, but which is labelled *Albania* (shown just to the east of *Terra florida*). This was a named claimed by some to recognize earlier settlement by the English, or Albans. The original source is dated to some time before the twelfth century, after which the name Albania was assumed to be generally replaced on Icelandic maps by the name Vinland, following the Eiriksson voyage. Another interesting little curve ball in the continuing mystery of who reached North America first! Greenland has assumed massive proportions here, and stretches across the North Atlantic. The imaginary island of Frisland from the probably fraudulent Zeno map (Map 12, page 14) is shown, and this clearly demonstrates that at least some knowledge that was later than the Norse voyages has been added. If the strait at bottom left is Hudson Strait, the spiral symbol probably represents the "whirling and overfalling"—probably a tide rip—reported by John Davis in 1587 and pursued by Henry Hudson in 1612, thinking that it meant there was a through passage to another sea.

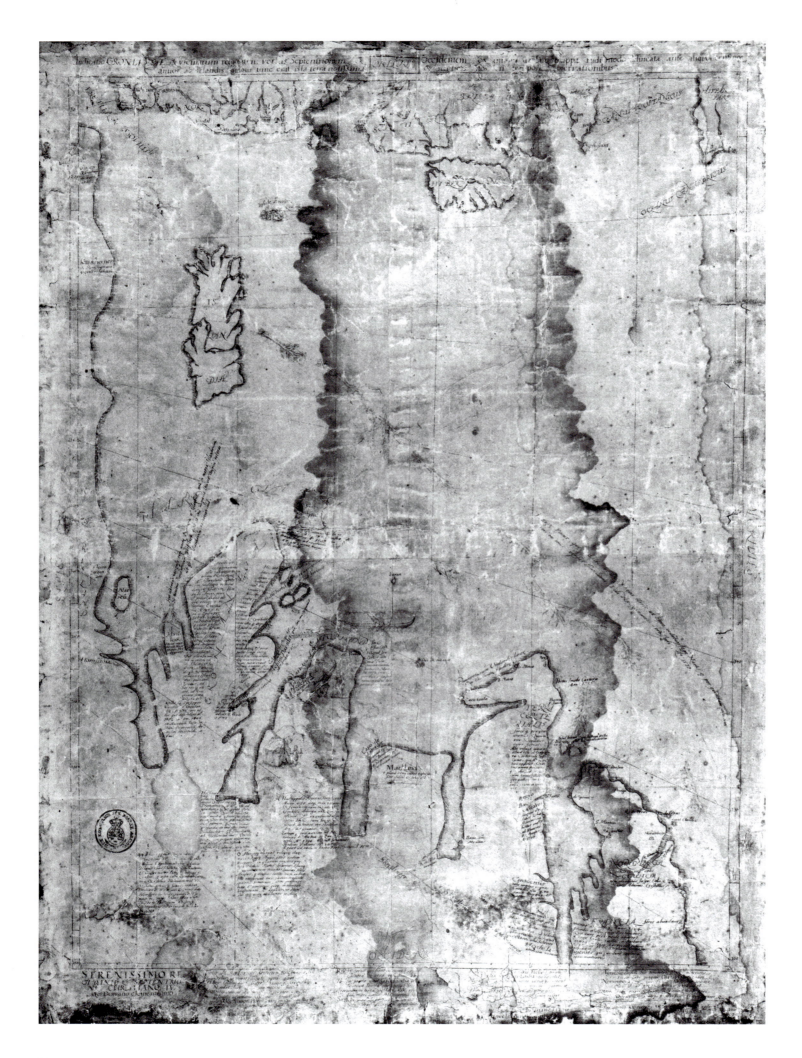

MAP 9.

This map by Bishop Hans Poulsen Resen was drawn in Copenhagen in 1605, citing ancient Icelandic maps "some centuries old" as sources. He also incorporated knowledge derived from information and maps available at the time he drew it, most notably some information which appears to come from Gerhard Mercator's map of 1569 (MAP 10, page 13). The map has been drawn with east at the top. *Nova Francia* is noted as well as *Helleland* (Baffin Island); *Markland* (Labrador), with *Capo de Labrador* (Cape Chidley, at the northern tip of the coast of Labrador); and *Promontorium Vinlandia Bona, Terra Corte Rialis,* and *Regio Bacalearu* (all Newfoundland). The large peninsula marked *Gronland* is Greenland; *Islandia* is Iceland. This map is in by far the worst condition of the three "Norse" maps, all of which are now in the Royal Library in Copenhagen. Two bad stains on the map (the vertical lines that have a cliff-like three dimensional appearance) are easy to confuse with drawn coastlines.

Pre-Columbian Apocryphal Voyages

A number of voyages from Europe to the land that is now Canada are sometimes advanced as having been made after the Norse settlement in Newfoundland but before the voyage of John Cabot in 1497. Lacking much hard evidence, investigators have from time to time deduced tracks of voyages based largely on hearsay or circumstantial evidence. In medieval Europe documents had to be written out longhand, and copied the same way, so even documents considered very important in their day may have only ever existed as two or three copies. Thus it was very easy for them to become lost, and few maps from this period survive. In addition, of course, the arts of navigation and mapping were not developed, so even if an intrepid mariner did get to North America he might not have been able to document his journey.

Ecclesiastical historian Adam of Bremen wrote about 1075 of a voyage made perhaps to Greenland and Vinland, but his conception of where these lands lay was to the east of Iceland, north of Asia. Who is to say if his work relates to North America, as some claim, for perception of distance and direction was much different in Adam's day.

A possible voyage to the east coast of Canada was undertaken by another cleric, Nicholas of Lynn, around 1360. Some authors attribute to him a voyage to the northern part of Ellesmere Island and right down the coast of Canada to beyond Nova Scotia, but again, there is little hard evidence to go on. Nicholas is more important in the annals of the early European discovery of North America because of a book he may have written, *De Inventio Fortunata*, "The Discovery of the Fortunate Islands." We know that a copy was presented to the English king, Edward III, about 1360, and five copies of the book were in existence between 1360, when it was written, and 1570, but none survive today. The book is nevertheless significant, because a Flemish author named Jacob Cnoyen either copied a map from the Nicholas work or made one up based on its descriptions. This was eventually reproduced by perhaps the most influential and copied mapmaker of the sixteenth century, Gerard Mercator, who included the map as an insert on his seminal world map of 1569. This view of the Arctic regions, which Nicholas or Cnoyen could have derived from a description by Aristotle, has four large islands surrounding the North Pole, an inflowing sea, and a clear Northwest Passage (and, indeed, a clear passage around the pole in any direction). It influenced explorers and mapmakers for a long time thereafter. Mercator's map was updated by his son Rumold in 1595 to incorporate the discoveries of Martin Frobisher and John Davis

(MAP 42, page 36). These navigators likely knew of the 1569 Mercator map configuration, as the map conforms to their expectations.

There is one other documented but unverified account of a voyage to North America by a European navigator before Columbus and Cabot: that of Prince Henry Sinclair to Nova Scotia in 1398. The sole authority for this voyage is an account published in Venice in 1558. It was based on family documents from a voyage by Nicolo and Antonio Zeno, who, shipwrecked on the island of "Frislanda"—conceivably the Faeroe Islands north of Scotland—in 1380, met a local prince they named "Zichmni." He in turn was identified with Prince Henry Sinclair, a real Scottish Earl of Orkney and Caithness. Whether they were one and the same is the stuff of controversy to this day, but the Zeno narrative tells of a voyage to a place they called "Estotiland," perhaps Labrador or Newfoundland. Some maintain that a landfall may also have been

made near Stellarton, Nova Scotia, because the narrative tells of a "great fire at the bottom of a hill" and "a spring from which issued a certain substance like pitch, which ran into the sea." Above Stellarton, at a place named Asphalt, was a spring of pitch which did flow to a tidal part of the East River, and there seems to be no other location with this characteristic and unusual feature on the whole east coast of North America. Nevertheless, the evidence is still only circumstantial.

More significantly, the Zeno narrative contained a map (MAP 12, page 14) which confused mariners for centuries, including Martin Frobisher in 1576–78 (see page 34), and Estotiland found its way onto quite a few maps of the period. Hence although the Zeno narrative and map are probably completely fictitious, they are still important for their effects on others, for the Zeno geography was certainly believed to be true in the sixteenth century, and

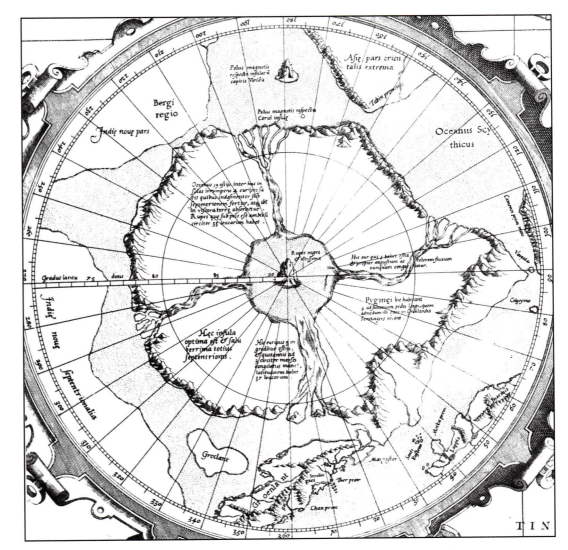

MAP 10.
An early concept of the Arctic, published by Gerard Mercator in 1569. The Arctic is shown as four islands, an idea derived from medieval texts. The Arctic coast of Canada is shown, with an indentation that may have given rise to the "prototype Hudson Bay" shown on later maps (see MAP 47, page 39). This map was updated by Mercator for the 1595 edition (part is shown in MAP 42, page 36). Mercator had to have this map as an inset on his world map, for on his 1569 map using his new projection the poles were unmappable, since they stretched to infinity.

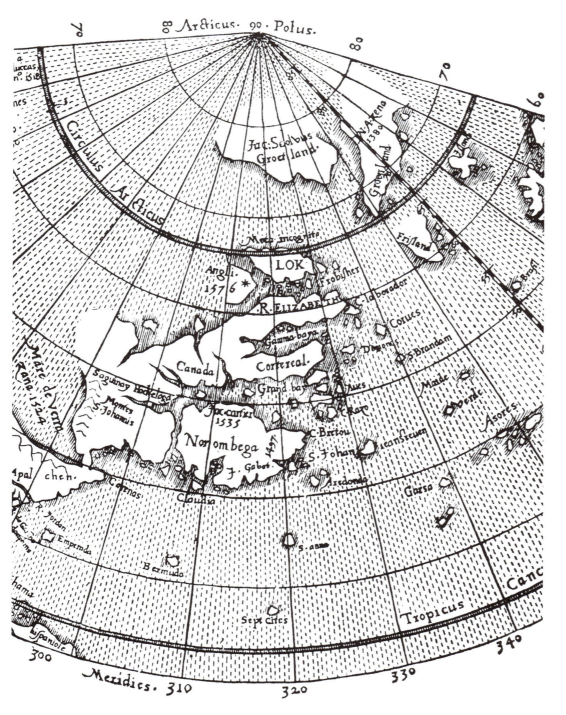

several navigators carried the map with them. Frobisher, using the Zeno map, believed that the southern point of Greenland, Cape Farewell, was Frisland, and it followed that the east coast of Labrador and Baffin Island were thought to be the eastern coast of Greenland. Thus maps for a long time showed Frobisher's straits as cutting through the southern part of Greenland as, for example, on John Seller's map published in 1698 (MAP 58, page 44).

A number of other probably apocryphal voyages prior to Cabot and Columbus had some influence on mapmakers and hence on later explorers. A perhaps Polish mariner named Johannes Scolvus Polonus was attributed with the second discovery of America in 1476 by Cornelius Wytfliet, who in 1597 produced the first printed atlas of America. Scolvus was reported to have "penetrated the Northern Strait under the very Arctic Circle, and arrived at the country of Labrador and Estotiland."

An English promoter of the Northwest Passage concept, Michael Lok, published a map in 1582 (at left) that shows "Jac. Scolvus Groetland" on an island to the west of Greenland. But then, Lok's map was hardly notable for its accuracy.

João Vaz Corte-Real, the father of Gaspar and Michael Corte-Real (see page 20) is claimed by many in Portugal as being the real discoverer of America. He is said to have reached Newfoundland in 1472, with Scolvus as a pilot.

These voyages remain unsupported by any real evidence; they all derive purely from secondary sources, which although written within a century after they supposedly occurred, were also written in an age when historical accuracy, critical analysis, and scientific proof were largely undeveloped.

MAP 11 (above).
Part of Michael Lok's intriguing map, published in 1582. The entire map shows his idea for a Northwest Passage, based loosely on the concepts of Giovanni Verrazano (see page 24), whose sea is seen at left (*Mare de Verra zana*). The map also incorporates information brought back by the recently returned Martin Frobisher (see page 34). Frobisher's "confirmation" of the position of the Zeno *Frisland*, actually the southern part of Greenland, is shown on this map, as is his "strait," just marked *Frobisher*, immediately south of *Lok* island. Michael Lok, a London merchant, was the principal backer of Frobisher's voyages and a long-time promoter of the idea of a Northwest Passage. Note the reference to Johannes Scolvus on the unidentified landmass in the north.

MAP 13 (below).
A map by Cornelius Wytfliet, published in 1597, shows the location of the supposed land of Estotiland, perhaps somewhere in Labrador. Many maps of this period show Estotiland, which was based on the Zeno narrative and map. This map is one of several published in the first atlas of the Americas; another is MAP 47, page 39.

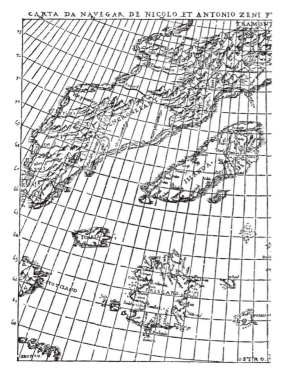

MAP 12 (left).
The western part of the Zeno map, published in 1558 and said to refer to the voyage of Prince Henry Sinclair to Nova Scotia in 1398. There are many supporters of the validity of this account, although today it is widely thought of as a fraud, designed to show that Venetians preceeded Genoans to the New World—the Zenos were from Venice, Christopher Columbus from Genoa. Of much more significance, however, is the influence this map had on other mapmakers, and on explorers such as Martin Frobisher, who naturally expected to find the lands shown on the map.

Out of the Mists— Canada

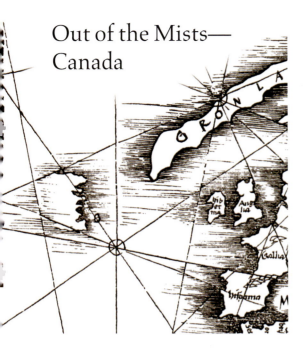

Map 14.
Part of Martin Waldseemüller's *Carta Marina* of 1513, showing Cabot's Newfoundland seemingly rising from the sea. Only the east coast is defined.

In fifteenth-century Europe, preserving food was difficult if not impossible, and much food had to be eaten after it had gone bad. In order to make this bad food at least somewhat palatable, spices were in high demand, but they were scarce, and very expensive. Much of the spice trade was in the hands of Arab traders, who supplied Europe from the Moluccas, or Spice Islands, by sea and over land. However, in 1453 Constantinople, today's Istanbul, fell to the Ottoman Turks and cut off the supply of spices to Europe.

Alternative routes to the Spice Islands were sought. In 1487–88 the Portuguese explorer Bartolemeu Dias rounded the southern tip of Africa, and in 1497, Vasco da Gama reached India. In 1492, Christopher Columbus set out to prove his theory that the Spice Islands and the Indies could also be reached by sailing westwards. He sailed to the Bahamas and Hispaniola, and thought he had indeed reached the Indies. But they were the West Indies.

John Cabot was a Genoese explorer-merchant who, unable to interest either the Spanish, who had Columbus's discoveries newly under their belt, or the Portuguese, who were more interested in exploring the southern and eastern route, went to England in 1495 to see if he could find some enthusiasm there.

Cabot went to Bristol, which at that time was the leading English trading port. There is considerable evidence that well before Cabot, ships from Bristol had set out to try to discover the Isle of Brasil or Hy-Brasil—not today's Brazil, but either Newfoundland or a mythical island nearer to Europe. Maps of the fifteenth century often show the Atlantic full of mythical islands, and Brasil (Isle of the Blest) was a perennial favourite. A rock off Cape Sable, Nova Scotia, is named Brazil Rock to this day. Fishing vessels from Bristol may have been visiting

Newfoundland's Grand Banks from about 1480 on; fish was a very significant feature of the diet at this time, with the Roman Catholic Church mandating about a third of the days as meatless. In addition, tensions were high following a trade war of sorts between England and the Hanseatic League, a cartel of Baltic merchants. Thus the trade of Bristol ships with Iceland, where they had traded for cod for some time, was tenuous, and as a result, the Bristol merchants were keen to find an alternative source for cod.

Into this environment came John Cabot and his sons. They found support amongst the Bristol merchants and petitioned the king, Henry VII, for royal permission to seek out new lands in the name of the English Crown. Having turned down a similar proposal from Bartolomeo Columbus on behalf of his brother Christopher in 1488–89 only to see the Spanish king sponsor the latter's voyage, widely regarded as successful, Henry was not about to lose out this time, and granted the petition of Cabot and his sons on 5 March 1496. They were "upon their own proper costs and charges to seek out, discover, and find whatsoever isles, countries, regions, or provinces of the heathen and infidels, whatsoever they be, and in what part of the world soever they be, which before this time have been unknown to all Christians."

It is now believed that John Cabot first attempted to sail to his Indies in 1496, but was unsuccessful. This information only came to light in 1955 through the discovery in a Spanish archive of a letter from an English trader or spy named John Day. He sent a letter to the Grand Admiral of Castille after Cabot's second voyage in 1497, making a clear reference to this first and unsuccessful voyage.

The voyage for which Cabot is famous was made in 1497. He set sail in his ship the *Matthew* in May 1497, and made a landfall on 24 June 1497. The consensus is that he made his landfall in Newfoundland, but there is no real evidence for this; it could have been Nova Scotia. The site chosen for the 1997 re-enactment of the *Matthew* voyage was Newfoundland's Cape Bonavista.

Contemporary documents record that Cabot found the sea to be swarming with fish, so dense in the water that they could be caught with a weighted basket. This was certainly news

that would have pleased his financial backers in Bristol. King Henry was also pleased with Cabot's efforts, and it is recorded that he awarded £10 from his privy purse "to hym that found the New Isle."

Cabot certainly made maps of his discoveries, but they have unfortunately been lost. A letter from the Milanese ambassador to England, Raimondo de Raimondi de Soncino, to his ruler the Duke of Milan, dated 18 December 1497, records, "This Messer Zoane [Cabot] has the description of the world in a map, and also in a solid sphere, which he has made, and shows where he has been."

Convinced that he had reached the "land of the Great Khan"—Asia—Cabot thought he was on to a good thing and, no doubt using the visual aids described by the ambassador, set about persuading his financial backers and King Henry to allow another voyage. Cabot seems to have thought that Cathay was on the other side of the land he had discovered in 1497, and his likely intention was to sail through some assumed passage and find himself in Cipango—Japan.

This was a persuasive argument. Receiving more letters patent from King Henry in February 1498, Cabot sailed with five ships. He took priests with him, significant because they could perform a ceremony of possession. The Milanese ambassador recorded Cabot's intentions. "Messer Zoane," he wrote, "proposes to keep along the coast from the place at which he touched [on his 1497 voyage] more and more towards the East, until he reaches an island which he calls Cipango, situated in the equinoctial region where he thinks all the spices of the world have their origin, as well as the jewels."

Early on in the voyage, the ships encountered a storm, causing one ship to return to port; but the other four continued. That was the last ever heard of John Cabot.

There is some evidence, however, that Cabot may have made a landfall in Newfoundland, then ranged southwards along the entire east coast of North America. Some of that evidence is cartographic. First, in 1500, two years later, the Portuguese explorer Gaspar Corte-Real (see page 20) visited Newfoundland, and took back to Portugal a number of native people. In the possession of the natives was found a broken sword hilt apparently from Venice, and one of the boys was wearing two silver earrings

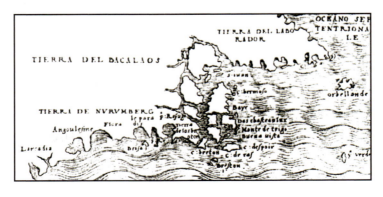

Map 15.
This map by Giacomo Gastaldi, printed in 1548, shows the Newfoundland area as a collection of islands, a concept derived from the early accounts of Cabot's voyages. Note *L'arcadia*, placed farther south, following Verrazano (page 24); it would migrate northwards until it became the French name for Nova Scotia. This was the first *printed* map to show any detail of the Atlantic coast.

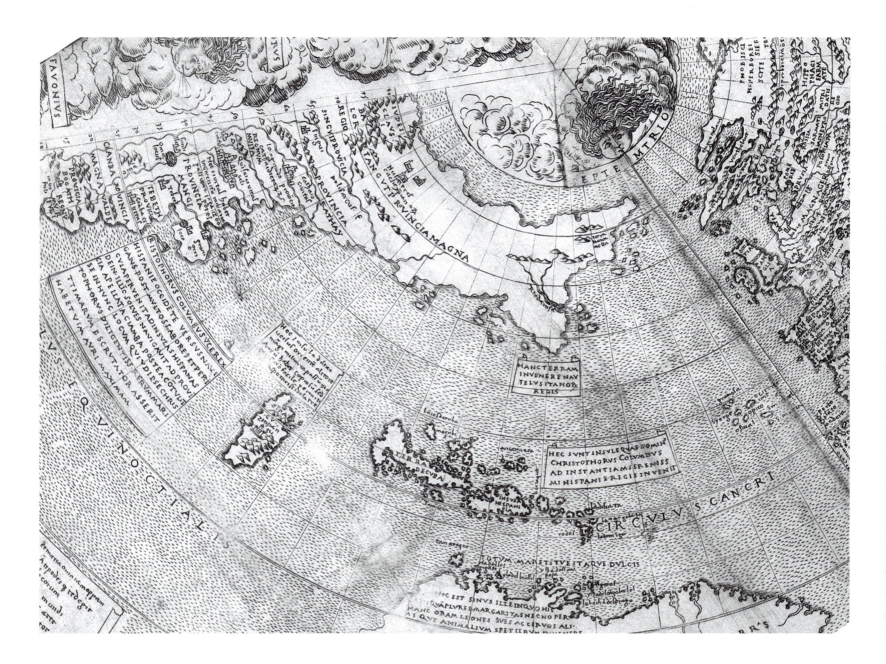

which again seemed to have been made in Venice. Many historians view this as evidence of Cabot having reached Newfoundland in 1498, because in 1497 he had had no contact with native people. The only other alternative, in fact, would seem to be that another European mariner landed in Newfoundland before Cabot—itself an intriguing proposition.

The second piece of evidence is the map (MAPS 19 and 20, pages 18–19) of the Spanish cartographer Juan de la Cosa, a pilot who had sailed with Columbus on his second voyage in 1493 and, significantly, also with the Spanish explorer Alonso de Hojeda, who visited the Caribbean in 1499. The only information about the coasts of Canada derived from John Cabot's two voyages seems to be shown on this famous map of the world. On that part of the coast which represents Labrador, Newfoundland, or Nova Scotia, La Cosa placed a line of English flags starting at the southern end with the inscription *Mar descubierta por ingleses* ("Sea discovered by the English"), and ending at the northern end with *Cauo de ynglaterra* ("Cape of England"). None of the names are in themselves sufficient to determine the locations of Cabot's actual landfalls.

The depiction of the coast of North America and even parts of the Caribbean west and north of the farthest points that Hojeda attained showed up on Juan de la Cosa's map, which he drew in 1500 or very shortly thereafter. It seems that the only way La Cosa could have been in possession of this information at that date was if he had acquired it from Cabot. There is even further corroborating evidence for this supposition. Hojeda was known for his brutality to native peoples and even other Spaniards. In 1501, when he was about to set out on another voyage, he obtained a patent from his king and in it he was given a gift of land in Hispaniola for "the stopping of the English." Again, it is possible that some other English expedition was on the east coast of America at that time about which history has left no trace, but this seems unlikely. Given Hojeda's record of violence, this strongly suggests that the English who were "stopped" were the Cabot expedition. Certainly the two expeditions could have been in the Caribbean in 1499.

Cabot is not accepted by everybody as the first European explorer of the North American mainland. Some historians consider that the fact Cabot's pension was drawn in 1498 and 1499

points to his return to England, but it is likely that his widow would have drawn the pension in his name in any case. If he had returned to England it is probable that his maps would have been shown to King Henry and his court, and would certainly have been noted by the Spanish ambassador and passed on to Spain, and thus La Cosa. But it also seems likely that if this is what had happened, some documentation would have been preserved. Unless more evidence turns up in an archive somewhere, we shall have to be content with Juan de la Cosa's map, which does seem to point to John Cabot.

MAP 16 (*above*).
Cabot's concept of the world as illustrated by Giovanni Contarini in 1506. The body of North America is not here, but a wide strait leading to the riches of the east. The island at the centre is Cuba, and the island to the left of centre is Zipangu—Japan. Newfoundland is at the tip of the southeasternmost peninsula of the Asian landmass; the northeastern tip is Greenland.

MAP 18 (*right, bottom*).
Part of a world map by Florentine mapmaker Francesco Rosselli, drawn in 1508. This map clearly demonstrates the idea that Newfoundland was an arm of Asia some distance from Cathay, with nothing bar islands blocking a voyage to the riches of the East. With this concept in mind, it is not surprising that Cabot would have cruised south along the coast he encountered.

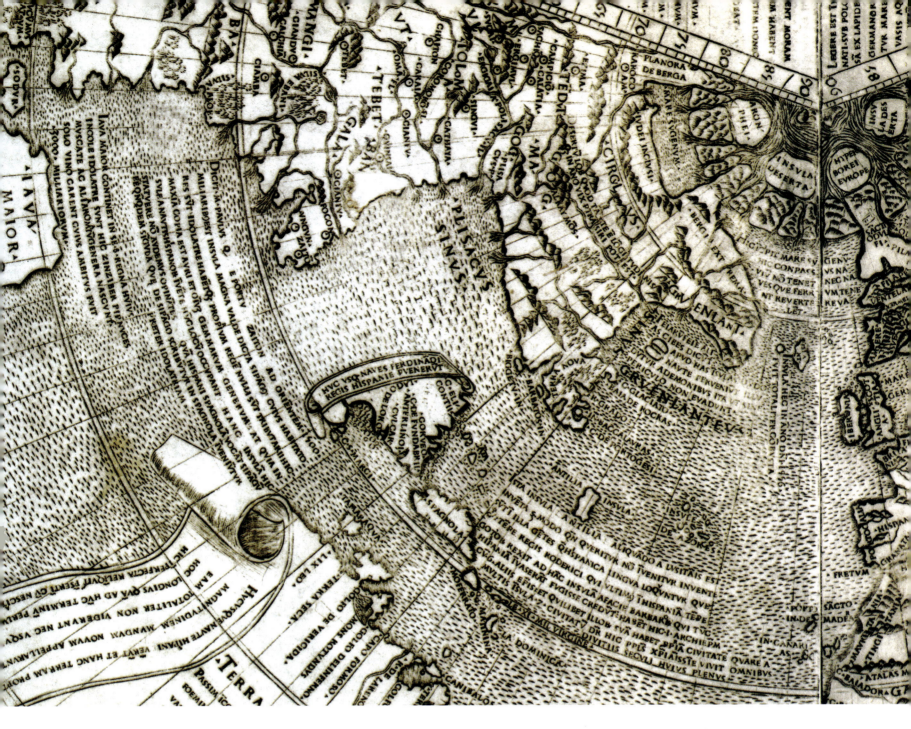

MAP 17 (above).
Part of a "Map of the Known World," published by Johann Ruysch in Rome in 1507 or 1508. It also shows North America as part of Asia, and illustrates the concept of a direct westerly route to Cathay embraced by Cabot. Greenland is shown connected to this Asian landmass. Much more detail of Newfoundland is shown than on the Contarini map opposite. Ruysch may have sailed on an English ship to Newfoundland, shown as *Terra Nova*, sometime in the period 1500–1507. C[ape] *Glaciato* is Newfoundland, C[ape] *de Portogesi* may be Nova Scotia, and *In*[sula; island] *Baccalauras* may be Cape Breton Island. This map is bound in a book and has a blank separation strip between its two halves. For clarity, it is shown here without that separation.

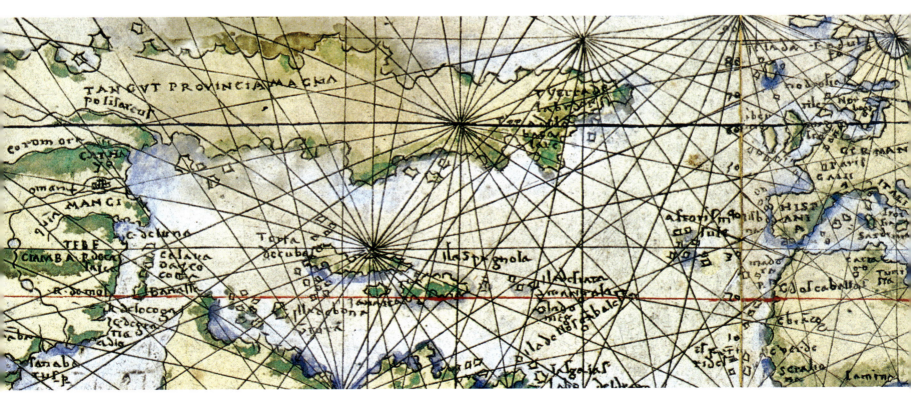

Map 19 (*above*) and Map 20 (*right*).
Parts of Juan de la Cosa's world map of about 1500. Map 20 shows the western half of the whole map, Map 19 shows
a detail of the so-called English Coast, probably the coast of Newfoundland. This was the first map to show the eastern
outline of the coast of North America, indeed, the first to show any part of the continent. It is drawn and coloured on the
prepared surface of an ox-hide measuring 1.67 x 0.9 m. The map, rather badly damaged, was discovered in a Paris bookstore
in 1832 by the Dutch ambassador to France, and it was authenticated by Alexander von Humboldt, the German naturalist.
The map was sold at auction in 1853 and was bought by the queen of Spain. Thus it arrived at the Museo Naval in Madrid,
where it is now kept. The map has been backed on a sheet of leather, and it is this that shows through the holes in the map.
The larger map has been reproduced with the edges of this leather backing, shown pinned down, while the smaller portion,
above, is shown with just the map, except for the holes. The waviness of the parchment hinders the sharp reproduction of the map.

Some experts, notably the American historian Samuel Morison, have suggested that the western part of the La Cosa map was finished
later than 1500, perhaps 1505. Certainly the map is in two sections, but 1505 is not universally accepted as the date for the western half.
Nevertheless, it was undoubtedly drawn at some time close to 1500. The information shown on other regions of the map, including South
America, only covers explorations to 1500, so it seems unlikely that later information would have been used for only the northern part. Even
if this were the case, it is not clear where information on the eastern coastline of the United States came from, if not Cabot, as there are no other
recorded voyages during this period that covered the area south of what are now the Maritime provinces of Canada.

On the map, the location of the easternmost flag, the point nearest to England, is on the same latitude as Bristol, and would logically be the landfall of
a ship sailing by keeping on the same latitude, which was the prevalent method of long-distance navigation in Cabot's time. This point is labelled *Cavo
de Yngleterra* ("Cape of England") and is most commonly considered to be Cape Breton, but there is no general agreement about its identity, just as there is
no agreement as to Cabot's landfall. Morison wrote that it "may as well be Cape Bauld or Cape Race or Cape Cod." Morison considered the line of flags "if anything
more than a whimsy" to represent a later voyage by a Bristol-Portuguese syndicate, but there is no evidence for this view. Morison was unable to accept anything more
than, as one contemporary English historian wrote in 1512, Cabot "founde his new lands only on the ocean's bottom." But most modern historians accept the view that this
map does present information derived from John Cabot. The orientation of the "English Coast," so-called because the five flags have been identified as English,
is east-west, and this does not fit the actual coast. But we know that the different magnetic declination on the east coast of Canada, as compared with Europe, was not allowed for until
Samuel de Champlain (see Map 70, page 52), and this may explain the discrepancy. A separate "oblique meridian" on Pedro Reinel's map of 1504 attempted to rectify this
problem (see Map 23, page 22).

Regardless of its exact date or how the information it depicts was found by Juan de la Cosa, this map stands as one of the most significant to cartographic history
because it was the first to show both of the Americas as a continuous continental landmass. It does not show the Americas as part of Asia, although, of course, by not showing
a western coastline, it leaves the extent and possible western connections of the continent open to speculation.

Early Explorations of the Coasts of Canada, 1500–1527

One historian has called the period immediately after Cabot's disappearance on his 1498 voyage "a dark period in the history of North American discovery, faintly and doubtfully illuminated by old maps." Although this is perhaps a bit of an overstatement, certainly there is little documentation of voyages from Europe to the northern part of North America before Jacques Cartier in 1534 (see page 25). The spotlight was on voyages to the Caribbean and South America. Pedro Alvares Cabral discovered Brazil for the Portuguese, and this held out far more promise from a European perspective than did a land of trees and cod.

In 1513 the Spaniard Vasco Núñez de Balboa crossed the Panamanian isthmus and sighted the Pacific Ocean, and in 1519 his compatriot Ferdinand Magellan sailed around the southern tip of South America and into that ocean, which he named. It seemed more likely that these explorers were on the right track for gold and spices.

In October 1499, João Fernandes, from the Azores (colonized by the Portuguese earlier in that century), was granted letters patent by King Manuel of Portugal to search for islands. They were to be in the Portuguese half of the world, east of a line at about 46° W, decided by the Treaty of Tordesillas in 1493 to be the dividing line between Portuguse and Spanish dominions.

Fernandes was a *lavrador,* the Portuguese name for a small landowner. In slightly changed form, this was destined to become the name of part of modern Canada, for Fernandes sailed to the northwest Atlantic, found Greenland, and named it *Tiera de Lavrador* because Fernandes was reputedly the first to sight land. It was not until later, after Martin Frobisher (see page 34) tried to call it "West England," that mapmakers revived the old Norse name Greenland, and shifted the name "Lavrador," now Labrador, to the land on the other side of Davis Strait.

Terra Laboratoris is shown as a narrow insular Greenland on Map 21, below, the so-called King-Hamy map of 1502, which is the earliest known map to connect João Fernandes, the *labrador* or *lavrador* from the Azores, with Greenland.

When he returned to the Azores, Fernandes learned that the Portuguese king had granted new letters patent to his countryman Gaspar Corte-Real and it seemed unlikely he would favour Fernandes again. Fernandes sailed to Bristol, much as John Cabot had done a few years before, to see if he could interest the English in voyages to find new lands. We know that Fernandes was granted letters patent by Henry VII in March 1501, and we know that a voyage of what has been termed the "Anglo-Azorean syndicate" was made out of Bristol in 1501–02, but there is no record of Fernandes, although it seems logical to assume he was on board. Three more voyages of this syndicate were made in 1503–05.

It is thought that Gaspar Corte-Real had also attempted to sail to the coasts of Newfoundland before 1500, but, like Fernandes, had not succeeded. We know this only because in the letters patent granted to him by the Portuguese King Manuel in 1500, there is a reference that he "formerly did make great efforts, of his own free will and at his own cost, with vessels and

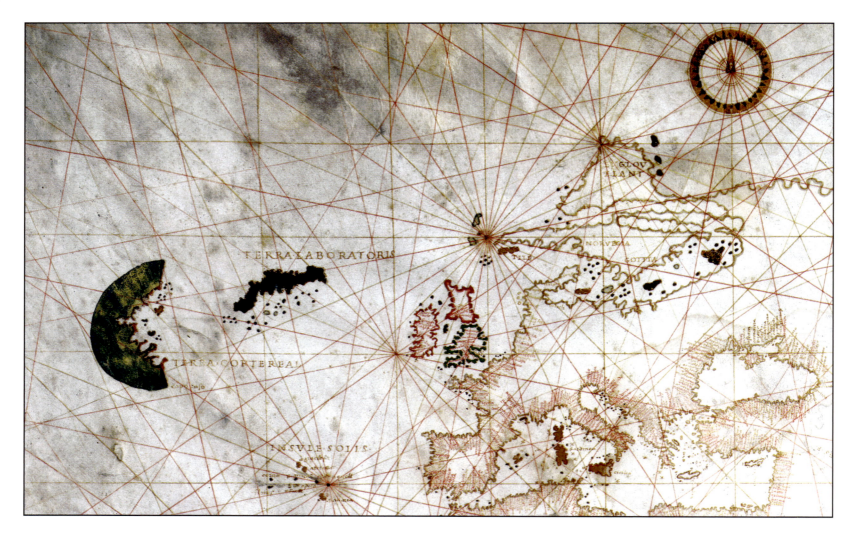

Map 21.

This is part of an anonymous world map of about 1502, commonly known as the King-Hamy map, after its first finder and first publisher, respectively. It is not only the first map to show evidence of the Fernandes voyage, but also the first map to depict Newfoundland with a place name. Here, on the southernmost point of *Terra Cortereal* is *Capo Raso,* still today Cape Race. *Terra Laboratoris* refers to Greenland. The map is perhaps Italian, since the *p* in *Capo* is neither Spanish nor Portuguese.

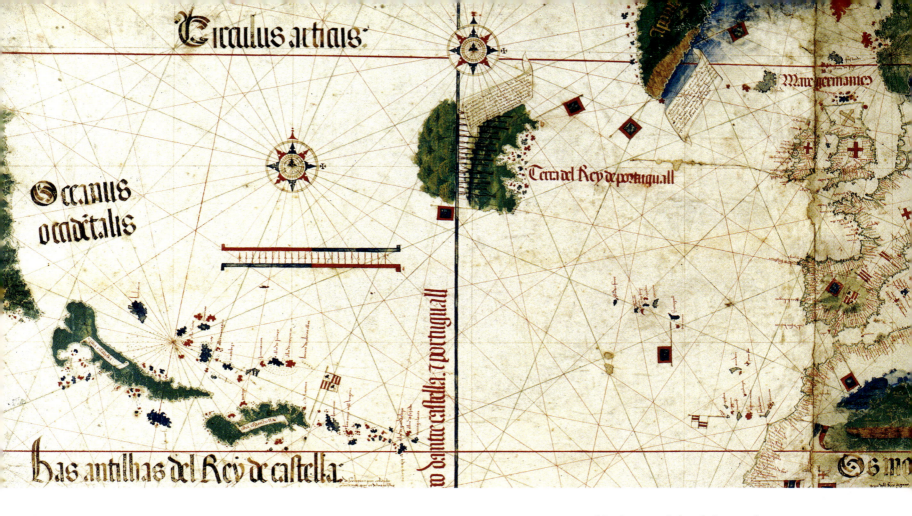

MAP 22.
The oldest map which mentions the Corte-Reals is a map now called the "Cantino planisphere," made in Lisbon for Hercules d'Este, Duke of Ferrara, in 1502. It was commissioned by Alberto Cantino, the duke's envoy to the Portuguese court, and accompanied an account of Gaspar Corte-Real's second voyage sent by him to the duke. The map can thus be considered as intended to illustrate the discoveries of Gaspar Corte-Real. To the west of Greenland just south of the *Circulus articus* and, notably, shown just east of the Tordesillas line (so that it would be in Portuguese territory) is *Terra del Rey de portugall*—the "Land of the King of Portugal." At the north end of this land is a Latin inscription which, translated, reads: "This land was discovered by order of the Most High and Excellent Prince Dom Manoel of Portugal. It was found by Gaspar Corte-Real, one of his noblemen, who, upon discovering it, sent [back] a vessel with men and women of that country. He remained with the other vessel but never returned [home], and the belief is that he was lost. That country contains much mast-timber." This refers to what happened to Corte-Real in 1501.

men, spending his fortune, and at the peril of his life, to discover islands and a continent; and that, hoping to succeed, he desires at present to continue." Indeed, Gaspar's father, João Vaz Corte-Real, has been credited by some Portuguese historians as the first discoverer of Newfoundland, in 1472, although this is not widely accepted outside of Portugal.

It is not known where Gaspar Corte-Real made his landfall in 1500, but it seems likely that it was in Newfoundland. Virtually all the maps of the early sixteenth century that show a *Terra de Corte-Real* place it between 39° and 55° N, which corresponds to a region from the middle of Newfoundland to a little less than halfway up the coast of Labrador.

Corte-Real may have tried to sail northwards during 1500. In 1501, he again sailed to the Newfoundland coast, but is thought this time to have cruised southwards. He sent his accompanying ships back to Portugal and thus to tell the tale, but Gaspar and his ship were never seen again. Gaspar's brother Miguel set out in 1502 to look for him, but he also never returned.

After the Corte-Reals, Portuguese ships are known to have continued to visit the coasts of Canada, fishing for cod. As early as 1506, the volume was such that a tax was levied by the Portuguese Crown on cod from Newfoundland.

There is some evidence that about this time both Portuguese and Spanish ships sailed along the coasts of Labrador, Newfoundland, and farther south searching for the strait that they believed would lead them to the Spice Islands. They must have formed some knowledge of the coast of Nova Scotia or even further south, because a map from about 1504 already appears to show a part of that coastline in addition to the knowledge from Gaspar Corte-Real. This is the "Map of the Atlantic" of Pedro Reinel (MAP 23, overleaf).

In England, four explorer-merchants, Hugh Elyot, Thomas Asshehurst, Francisco Fernandes, and João Gonsalves, the latter two former associates of João Fernandes, formed a new syndicate called the Company of Adventurers into the New Found Lands in 1502, and were granted new letters patent by the king for trade purposes as much as to search for a strait to the Spice Islands. Surviving records show that at least some of these voyages came back to Bristol laden with fish from Newfoundland. Although Elyot's syndicate appears to have fallen apart after 1505, considerable evidence suggests that other merchants continued to make what were essentially fishing trips to the rich banks off Newfoundland's coasts.

Sebastian Cabot, the youngest son of John, had by his own account (which is not very reli-

able) been with his father on his 1497 voyage to Newfoundland. In 1508–09 he may have sailed in search of the elusive passage to Cathay that his father could not find. Later medieval historians tell of a voyage to latitude 55° N, where, discouraged by great masses of ice, he turned southwards, passed Newfoundland, "the Land of the Baccalai," and sailed south to Cuba. Sebastian was a recognized self-promoter so it is far from certain that such a voyage actually occurred. The Ambassador's Globe, MAP 2, page 4, was perhaps produced using information from Cabot's voyage, or his claims to a voyage. Yet Sebastian produced a beautiful map in 1544, which showed the voyages of Cartier (MAP 35, page 32) but failed to show his own claims. The map is, however, probably one of the most artistic of all the early maps of North America.

Around 1520, a Portuguese adventurer named João Alvares Fagundes obtained from his king letters patent giving him seigneury over "isles and lands which he should discover beyond the Atlantic." He then sailed to eastern Canada, perhaps with colonists, with the intention of setting up a cod fishery. He is thought to have sailed into the Gulf of St. Lawrence, perhaps beyond Anticosti Island, and along the coasts of New Brunswick and Nova Scotia. He found and named the group of islands that is today St. Pierre and Miquelon, naming them *Ilhas do arcepelleguo da onze mill virgeens,* after a legend about eleven thousand sea-going virgins. Miquelon still has a Virgin Cove.

Fagundes returned to Portugal and petitioned the king to grant him the lands he had discovered. In 1521 the Portuguese king, in more letters patent, conveyed previously unknown islands and parts of the mainland to him.

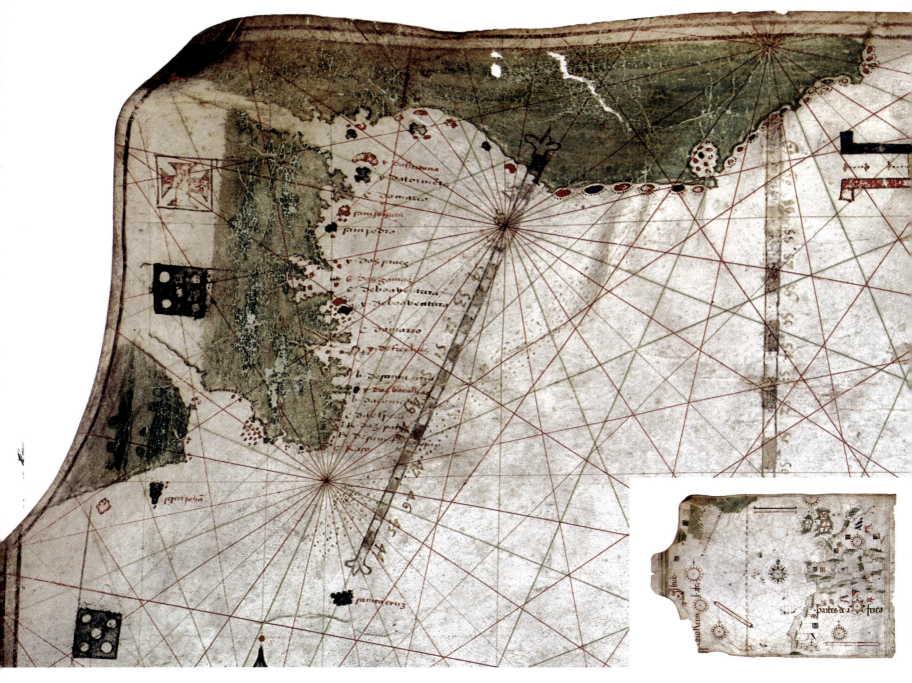

MAP 23.

Part of the "Map of the Atlantic" by Portuguese mapmaker Pedro Reinel, drawn on an animal skin about 1504. It shows information from Gaspar Corte-Real and is also the first map to show the coast of Nova Scotia (bottom left). The east coast of Newfoundland is the middle large mass, while Labrador is at the top. Some modern names, in Portuguese of course, show up on Reinel's map for the first time. These include *y dos bacallaos* (Baccalieu Island), *b de conceicān* (Conception Bay), and *c de espera* (Cape Spear). Also shown is *c Raso* (Cape Race). The inset shows the shape of the whole map.

European kings, it seems, were adept at giving away lands that didn't belong to them, although the king's rationale would likely have been that the land was (or he hoped it was) somehow east of the Tordesillas line, and thus Portuguese by edict of the Pope.

Fagundes sailed again soon after, this time with colonists, with the intention of setting up a shore-based fishery. They settled on a bay on Cape Breton Island, probably at Ingonish, near the northern tip of the island. However, it seems that a turf war broke out. Breton fishermen, who had fished in the seas off the island for some years by this time, cut the Portuguese fishing lines and burnt their houses, making life difficult for Fagundes's colonists. By 1526, with no help from Portugal, they gave up and sailed back to Portugal, thus ending the first documented settlement of Europeans in North America after the Norse.

Some later maps derived from Portuguese models that show places named by Fagundes include the Dieppe maps, the 1542 Harleian map (MAP 28, page 26), the 1550 Desceliers map (MAP 31, page 29), and Sebastian Cabot's 1544 map (MAP 35, page 32).

In 1524 Estévan Gomez sailed to North America for the Spanish king. Gomez was a naturalized Portuguese sailor who had changed his name from Estêvão Gomes when he entered the service of Spain. He had been a pilot on one of Ferdinand Magellan's ships, had mutinied in the Strait of Magellan, and had been jailed on his return to Spain. After the return of Magellan's decimated expedition in 1522, the Spanish king decided Spain should also search for a better route to the Pacific, and Gomez, probably to save his skin, said he could find one. Thus he was released and appointed captain of a new expedition put together in haste to try to forestall the French expedition of Giovanni Verrazano (page 24), about which the Spanish now knew. As it happened, despite the efforts to hurry, Gomez's expedition did not sail until two months after Verrazano had returned.

Gomez sailed from Corunna, in the northwest corner of Spain, which is the same latitude as Sable Island, Nova Scotia. Gomez intended to

reach America by staying in the same latitude, sailing north on finding land to try to find his promised strait. The tactics adopted suggest that Gomez was aware of the possibility of a strait in the vicinity of today's Gulf of St. Lawrence, a possibility that could have been derived from Fagundes or others.

Gomez did make his landfall close to where he planned, on Cape Breton Island, and entered the Gulf of St. Lawrence. This was in February 1525, unfortunately for him, because he decided that there was too much ice for this to be a practicable route to anywhere. He saw Prince Edward Island, which he named St. John, found the Gut of Canso, then sailed southwards along the coasts of Nova Scotia and Maine, trying the Penobscot River as a possible strait. Finding no strait, and no gold either, he kidnapped natives for slaves and returned to Spain, where his exploits met with derision and the slaves were set free.

A beautiful map drawn in 1529 by the Spanish mapmaker Diogo Ribiero shows the discoveries attributed to Gomez, along with Portuguese and English information from earlier voyages. *Tiera de los bretones* (Cape Breton) is shown, but not the Gulf of St. Lawrence, a surprising omission given that the

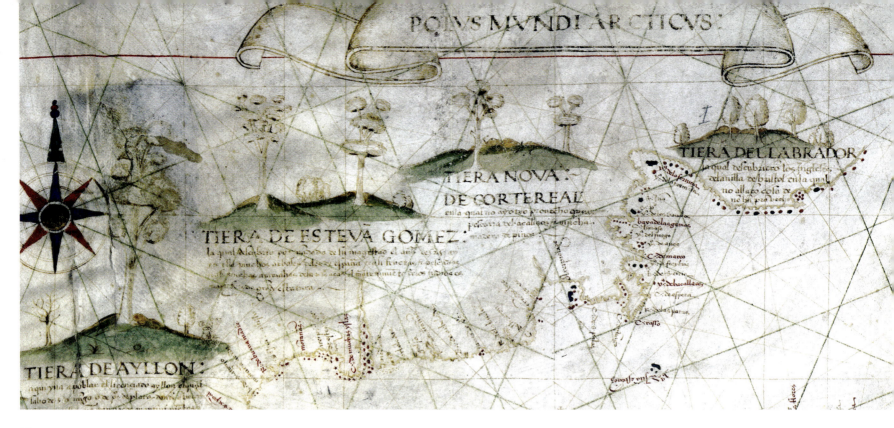

MAP 24.

Part of a world map drawn in 1529 by Diogo Ribiero. On *Tierra de Labrador* is written *Esta tierra descubrieron los Ingleses no ay en ella cosa de prouecho* ("This country was discovered by the English, and there is nothing there worth having"). On Newfoundland there is this legend: *Tierra de los Bacallaos laqual descubrieron los corte reales y aquy se perdieron—hasta aora no an allado cosa de prouecho mas de la pescaria de bacallaos que son de poca estima* ("The Land of Codfish discovered by the Corte Reals, and where they were lost. Up to this time nothing of value has been found there, except the fishing of codfish, and these do not amount to much"). On what is now New England is *Tierra de Estevam Gomez, laqual descubrió por mandado de su mag[estad] el año de 1525 ay en ella muchos arboles y fructas de los de españa y muchos Rodouallos y salmones y sollos non han allado oro* ("Country of Estevam Gomez, which he discovered by order of His Majesty. It contains numerous trees and fruits of Spain, much rodovallo [fish], salmon, and soles. No gold has been found"). The legend farther south refers to Luís Vasquez de Ayllón, another Spanish explorer, who sailed north along the eastern shore of the United States from Hispaniola in 1525–26 with five hundred would-be colonists. He only got as far north as North Carolina; Ayllón died and his colony dispersed.

map specifically presumes to show the "Land of Estévan Gomez." Ribiero's Newfoundland is still a peninsula attached to Nova Scotia. Gomez's discoveries are also noted on the 1542 Harleian map (MAP 28, page 26).

After the English king Henry VII died in 1509, the English interest in exploration waned. It was not until 1527 that another English voyage to Newfoundland was planned, other than fishing trips.

Robert Thorne was a Bristol merchant who lived in Seville, Spain; he claimed that the true discoverers of Newfoundland were his father, Nicholas Thorne, and Hugh Elyot (from the Anglo-Azorean syndicate voyages of 1501–05). Thorne had perhaps a wider view of the world than most at this time; he proposed in 1527 that a ship could sail northwards across the North Pole and into the Pacific Ocean, thus making a relatively short voyage to the Spice Islands. He of course did not believe the Arctic Ocean to be icebound. Henry VIII was interested in his proposal. While the idea of crossing the pole was not supported, the idea that there was nevertheless a Northwest Passage going somewhat in the same direction seemed reasonable to the king.

King Henry had two ships fitted out. One was lost, but the other, commanded by John Rut, sailed to the Newfoundland or Labrador coast. Going northwards, Rut was discouraged by the appearance of "Ilands of Ice" and did not get very far. This was a rather pathetic effort, by all accounts, in light of the later attempts that would be made to find a Northwest Passage, but Rut's voyage seems to have been the first recorded probe of the anticipated strait.

Rut turned southwards, and in August 1527 entered the harbour at St. John's, finding there some ten fishing vessels, from France and Portugal. The significance for England was that Rut missed two chances to enter the Gulf of St. Lawrence *before the French*—Jacques Cartier—did so, eight years later.

In 1527, as part of his communications with the English government, Robert Thorne sent a map of the world to Edward Leigh, the English ambassador to the Spanish court. It was engraved on wood and showed Labrador and Newfoundland as part of a large continental mass (MAP 25, below). This original wood engraving has been lost, but a copy was reproduced in Richard Hakluyt's book *Divers Voyages touching the discouverie of America and the Ilands adiacent into the same*, published in London in 1582.

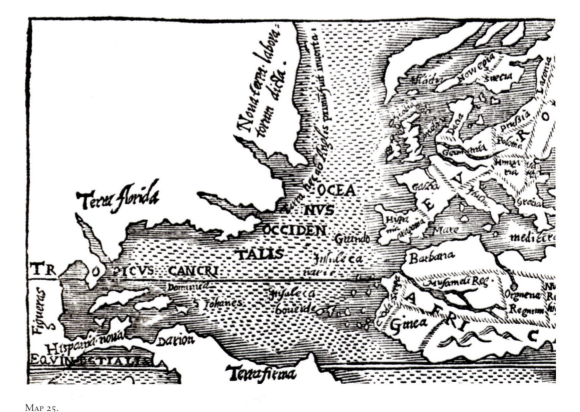

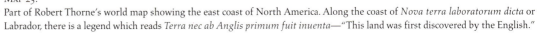

MAP 25.

Part of Robert Thorne's world map showing the east coast of North America. Along the coast of *Nova terra laboratorum dicta* or Labrador, there is a legend which reads *Terra nec ab Anglis primum fuit inuenta*—"This land was first discovered by the English."

Early French Explorations

The first documented French voyage to North America was in 1504, for fishing, and in 1508 France sent *La Pensée*, which sailed from Dieppe under the command of Thomas Aubert. The region now known as Nova Scotia was known to fishermen from Brittany by 1520; the name of Cape Breton Island is from a Portuguese map of that year, and French fishermen are thought to have harassed the Portuguese under João Alvares Fagundes about 1521 when the latter attempted to set up a settlement in Cape Breton to dry fish (see page 22). But the French did not explore.

Then, in 1523, all this changed. The Spanish and English kings had used Italian explorers—Columbus and Cabot—so why not the French? In 1523, a Florentine navigator, Giovanni Verrazano, was commissioned to "discover Cathay" for the French. The effort was prompted by the return of the Spaniard Juan Sebastián del Cano after his momentous first circumnavigation of the world. This was the voyage begun in 1519 by Fernão Magalhães, better known as Ferdinand Magellan, who found the Strait of Magellan, a route to the Pacific Ocean and the Spice Islands. Now the French wanted to find a more accessible strait many were convinced must exist to somehow "balance" the one at the other end of the continent.

Verrazano sailed from the Portuguese Madeira Islands in January 1524 in his ship *La Dauphine* and made a landfall at Cape Fear, at about 34° N. After a short jog south in search of a harbour he couldn't find, Verrazano sailed north along the Atlantic coast of today's United States. On the way he made his famous misjudgement which led him to believe he had found the "eastern sea"—the Pacific Ocean and the passage to Cathay—when he looked over offshore islands on the North Carolina coast at Cape Hatteras and saw water beyond. This legendary error is shown on his brother Girolamo's map, below (MAP 26).

Farther north, perhaps at Kitty Hawk, the site of the Wright brothers' first powered flight in 1903, Verrazano encountered a hilly section of coast "full of very tall trees," which, because of its beauty, he named Acadia, after the Greek philosopher Virgil's concept of an ideal landscape, Arcadia. The significance of this from the Canadian point of view is that later mapmakers tended to place Acadia farther and farther north until it ended up becoming L'Acadie, the French name for Nova Scotia and New Brunswick.

Verrazano continued northwards, exploring the approaches to New York; the entrance to New York Harbor is today called the Verrazano Narrows. He missed the Bay of Fundy and most of Nova Scotia by being too far offshore, but sailed along the east coast of Newfoundland before heading back to France. Portuguese place names are used on Verrazano's map in Newfoundland, perhaps a clue that Verrazano had a Portuguese map with him; he did not claim any new discovery there.

Giovanni Verrazano led another expedition to the New World in 1528, landing on an island in the Caribbean. He was attacked by Carib natives and killed, being eaten on the spot according to contemporary accounts. His brother Girolamo narrowly escaped, returning to Europe and drawing his map the following year.

Giovanni had found no new strait to the Pacific, although he thought he had. Nevertheless, it was six years before the French dispatched their next expedition, that of Jacques Cartier, and he did not sail to the place where Verrazano had located his apparent passage, but into the Gulf of St. Lawrence—to Canada.

MAP 26.
Map of the voyage of Giovanni Verrazano, drawn by his brother Girolamo in 1529. The "Sea of Verrazano" opens up westwards from North Carolina. The map locates *la macra*, a misspelled L'Acadia. More clearly marked is *c. de bretton* (in red ink), beside which is a nascent Cabot Strait, the southern entrance to the Gulf of St. Lawrence. North of the strait the coast represented is that of Newfoundland. Farther north still, the fainter large peninsula marked *Terra Laboratoris* is Greenland.

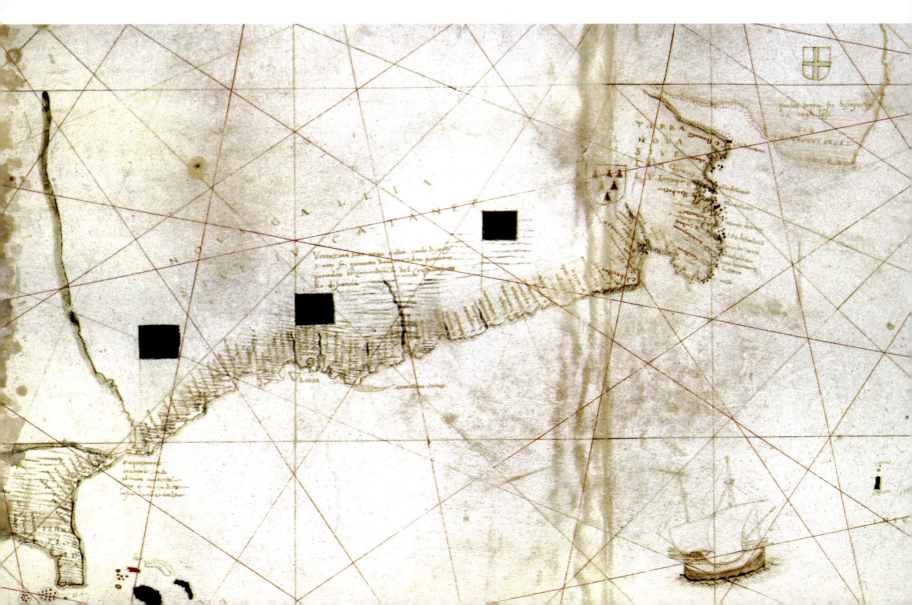

Jacques Cartier—the Foundation of the French Claim to Canada

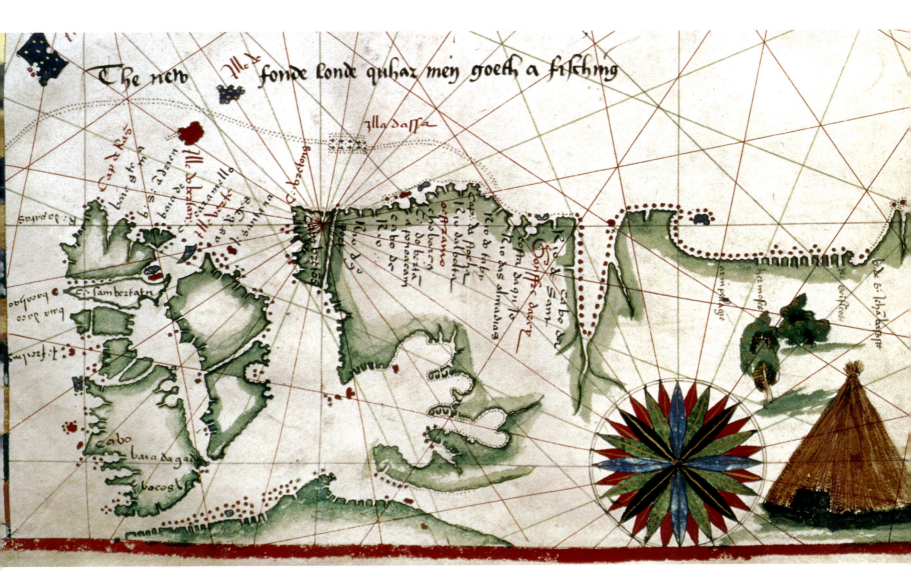

The new fonde londe quhar men goeth a fisching

Map 27.

This beautiful map was drawn about 1534 or 1535 by Dieppe mapmaker Jean Rotz, using only information from Jacques Cartier's first voyage in 1534. South is at the top. The map is drawn in pen and ink, with watercolour and gilt, and shows clearly the coastlines Cartier saw, and how the Îles de la Madeleine (Magdalen Islands) were thought to be part of the mainland, as was Anticosti Island. The depiction of the latter island as part of the peninsula of Gaspé and the former as part of Cape Breton positively shows that this map only records information from Cartier's first voyage, since on his second he determined the insularity of these islands. The map does not, however, note any places named by Cartier from his first voyage, though the map shows many other place names on the Atlantic side of Nova Scotia and the southern shore of Newfoundland. The latter is now shown as a complex archipelago following a cartographic trend from about this time (see, for example, the map of Giacomo Gastaldi, Map 15, page 15). The double dashed line in the Atlantic represents the Grand Banks, and the note about fishing is in English, as Rotz made this map for the English king, Henry VIII. The first European illustration of a native wigwam is at bottom right.

Giovanni Verrazano had whetted the French appetite for finding the way to Cathay and its supposed riches, and in 1532 the king, François I, found the man to continue the effort in Jacques Cartier, a master mariner from the northern French port of St. Malo.

The Treaty of Tordesillas, which as far as the Catholic Church was concerned divided the world into only Portuguese and Spanish spheres of influence, was effectively broken in 1533. King François persuaded the Pope to declare that Tordesillas applied only to lands discovered by Spain and Portugal to that date, not to those found by other countries such as France. This was the green light for the continuing French search for a passage to Cathay. The search for gold and other precious metals was also a motivation; Verrazano had stated, without justification, that these were to be found in northern regions.

So the decision was taken to mount an expedition, led by Cartier, to Newfoundland, and from there to try to find the passage to Cathay. After a long period of preparation, Cartier sailed with two ships in April 1534.

The French must have known of the existence of a strait in the vicinity of Newfoundland, probably from fishing captains, though they did not know where it might lead. This likelihood is borne out by the fact that Cartier made a beeline for that location right away. An order for Cartier's first voyage authorized him to sail "beyond the strait of the Baye des Chasteaulx," the French name for the Strait of Belle Isle, between Newfoundland and Labrador. French fishing vessels had been fishing on the Grand Banks for some time, and the way there was fairly well known to Cartier, who may have previously been to Newfoundland. At any rate, Cartier made a fast passage of only twenty days to a landfall at Cape Bonavista in early May.

Cartier stayed ten days in a bay here, hoping to avoid the many icebergs that frequent this coast at that time of year. Then he sailed northwards, rounded Cape Bauld at the northern tip of Newfoundland, and entered the Strait of Belle Isle. He sailed westwards along the southern shore of Labrador and what is now the eastern tip of Québec, to which he gave his oft-quoted moniker "the land God gave to Cain," on account of all the bare rock he saw.

Cartier then cruised southwards along the west coast of Newfoundland, and crossed the Gulf of St. Lawrence via the Îles de la Madeleine (Magdalen Islands), which he thought were part of the mainland. Near Île Brion, the northernmost of the Magdalen group, he observed that

TERRE DV LABOVREVE

MAP 28.
Part of the so-called Harleian map of the world, dated about 1542–44 and named after a former owner, Edward Harley, Earl of Oxford. The name *Canada* is prominent on this map, and it may be the first use of the name on any surviving map (see MAP 3, page 6). The embellishments show a bearded figure, presumably Cartier, meeting natives. The map is possibly by Jean Rotz or Pierre Desceliers, both members of the "Dieppe school" of cartographers. As far back as the twelfth century, Dieppe, on the northern coast of Normandy, was noted as a place from which maritime expeditions departed. In the sixteenth century, Dieppe was one of a select group of French ports that were bustling with maritime trade. One of the most influential merchant families, that of Jean Ango (father and son), owned a fleet of merchant ships and was a financier of the voyage of *La Pensée* to Newfoundland in 1508, Giovanni Verrazano's 1524 voyage, and the voyages of Jacques Cartier. Kings may grant permission for such voyages, but it was the merchants of places such as Dieppe and Bristol who paid for them! As a centre of trade and exploration, mapmaking and navigation, Dieppe was home to a group of some of the premier mapmakers of the time, many of whose maps are illustrated here.

the tides were very strong, and from this he correctly deduced that there is a passage between Newfoundland and Cape Breton. He noted that this would yield a great saving in time and distance in future if they found a strait to Cathay.

Continuing southwards they came to the north coast of Prince Edward Island and landed briefly near Cape Kildare, which they called Cap d'Orléans (and where there is today Jacques Cartier Provincial Park). Cartier was the first recorded European to visit the island, which he described as "low and flat but the finest land one can see and full of beautiful trees and meadows," a description which would still be true enough today. Rounding North Cape, Cartier's Cap de Sauvaige, they sailed southwards down the west coast of Prince Edward Island, and crossed Northumberland Strait to the mainland. Not realizing that Prince Edward Island was an island, they named Northumberland Strait Baie de St. Lunaire.

Proceeding now northwards along the New Brunswick coast, they found Miramichi Bay and sailed into a bay on the southern side of the Gaspé Peninsula, naming it the Baie des Chaleurs for its warmth. Here in this deep bay,

over 100 km long, Cartier hoped he had found his strait to Cathay. For that reason, he named the north point of Miscou Island at the bay's entrance Cap d'Espérance—Cape of Hope. But it was not to be. On 10 July they reached the end of the bay, and realized it was not the path to riches after all.

In the Baie des Chaleurs Cartier and his men had their first encounters with the native Mi'kmaq people, who wanted to trade—a likely sign that they had been "discovered" by Europeans before Cartier's arrival.

Continuing northwards, Cartier anchored in Gaspé Bay. Here he met about two hundred Laurentian Iroquois, with their chief, Donnacona, on a fishing expedition from their base at Stadacona, which was destined to become the city of Québec. Many gifts were exchanged, and Cartier erected a cross, taking possession of the country for the king of France. This act has been seen as the birth of French Canada. Donnacona naturally enough seemed to object to this and made Cartier understand that the land in this region belonged to him. Cartier managed to persuade him that the cross had only been set up as a landmark. Then he "persuaded" Donna-

cona to allow him to take his two sons with him, on a promise that they would be returned. The degree of willingness on Donnacona's part is uncertain; Cartier's narrative of his second voyage makes references to his "captives," but on the other hand Donnacona's control of the St. Lawrence region downstream of Stadacona was at the time being challenged by another native group from Maine and hence he may have initially viewed Cartier and his men as allies to cultivate.

Leaving Gaspé Bay and sailing northwards, Cartier mistakenly thought that the south channel of the St. Lawrence River between Anticosti Island and Gaspé was a bay and, instead of following the riverbank westwards, unknowingly sailed across the river to Anticosti Island, which of course he did not recognize as such. The ships ranged along the coast of Anticosti, turning westwards finally along the north coast of the island. Here they ran into such strong headwinds and currents that they had to resort to their longboats, which could be rowed. Progress soon became difficult even for rowing, and Cartier with a few of his men took to the shore to reconnoitre the way ahead. They found the land trending southwestwards at the western end of Anticosti Island. In the meantime the ships had drifted eastwards.

At this point, Cartier held a meeting of his officers to determine what should be done. They were concerned that if they waited until the wind changed they might not be able to return through this relatively narrow channel, which they named Destroyt (Détroit; Strait) Sainte

Pierre after the saint's day it was when they arrived there. Appropriately enough, today it is named Détroit Jacques-Cartier. On 2 August they decided nothing more should be done that season, and that they would return to France. This they did, passing through the Strait of Belle Isle once more and reaching St. Malo on 5 September 1534, another speedy passage.

Cartier undoubtedly made maps of his first voyage, and his second and third, but they have been lost, as have the original journals of all of his voyages, although one extant manuscript of the second voyage could be Cartier's. The accounts of the first voyage that survive were first published in Italian in 1565, in English in 1580, and in French only in 1598.

The maps we do have which show Cartier's voyages all derive from the Dieppe school of mapmaking which flourished in the mid-sixteenth century. Only one map shows the discoveries of Cartier's first voyage alone, and since his second was the following year, 1535, this map presumably must have been drawn in 1534 or 1535, although it was not made public until 1542, as one map in an atlas. The map (MAP 27, page 25) is that drawn by Jean Rotz, who, although French and of the Dieppe school, was at the time in the employ of the king of England, Henry VIII. The atlas he presented to the king was called the *Boke of Idrography* (Book of Hydrography). In the same atlas is a map of the world which shows updated information based on Cartier's second voyage, but the map in question, a map of eastern North America and the Caribbean, stands unique as showing only the results of Cartier's first voyage. It is ironic that the only surviving map that shows Cartier's first voyage is a map drawn for the *English* king.

One other map shows part of eastern Canada as Cartier found it on his first voyage. This is the map commonly referred to as the "Harleian Mappemonde" (MAP 28, left, top). Although most of this map records information from Cartier's second or third voyages, the Gulf of St. Lawrence region is much the same as the 1535 Rotz map, and in particular shows the Îles de la Madeleine (Magdalen Islands) as part of the mainland. Anticosti, however, is shown as an island, which was a discovery of the second voyage.

The king of France obviously thought it likely that a strait to Cathay, just like the Strait of Magellan discovered by the Spanish in the south, lay farther along the passage Cartier had found when forced to turn back by winds and currents and the time of the year, his Détroit Sainte Pierre. Thus Cartier received his commission for a second voyage very quickly, less than two months after arriving back in France. He was "by royal command, to conduct, lead and employ three ships equipped and victualled for fifteen months, for the perfection of the navigation of lands by you already begun to discover beyond les Terre Neufes."

MAP 29.
Perhaps the earliest known *dated* map—1541—to show Cartier's voyages, drawn by Nicolas Desliens of Dieppe. Some scholars now consider that it may have been drawn later, despite the date. It shows no names from Cartier's third voyage, which supports the 1541 date, but other geographical evidence from elsewhere in the world—though nothing specific—suggests a date of about 1555. If this map dates from 1541 it contains the earliest use of the name *Canada* on a map. The whole of North America is shown as MAP 3, page 6. Names, which are difficult to read, include *R. de Sagnay* (Saguenay River), *b: de Challeur* (Baie des Chaleurs), *c: breton* (Cape Breton), and, barely visible due to water damage, at the tip of the "Newfoundland archipelago" is *c. do Raz* (Cape Race), and, just below it, *S. jehan* (St. Jehan, St. John's).

On 19 May 1535, Cartier sailed from St. Malo for Newfoundland with three ships—his flagship, *La Grande Hermine*, *La Petite Hermine*, and *L'Émerillon*—and 112 men. This time the Atlantic crossing took seven weeks. No time was to be wasted searching for a passage; they headed directly to Détroit Sainte Pierre—the St. Lawrence. Because of the later start and the much longer Atlantic crossing, it was in fact slightly later in the year that Cartier reached the most westerly point he had reached the year before. But this time he intended to stay over the winter, and the winds were favourable, so this did not concern him.

On 10 August, on the north side of his passage, he found a good harbour which he named *La baye sainct Laurens*, because it was the feast of St. Lawrence, a Roman martyr. This was the first time the name "St. Lawrence" had been used. It would eventually be applied to the gulf, the river, and to a mountain range, the Laurentides.

Three days later, rounding the western end, he recognized the insularity of Anticosti Island, and named it *L'Isle de l'Assomption*. From this time on, Anticosti would be shown on maps as an island. Consulting the two natives, Donnacona's sons Domagaya and Taignogny, that he was bringing back home, Cartier wrote, "It was told us by the two savages whom we had *captured* on our first voyage, that this cape formed part of the land on the south which was an island, and that south of it lay the route to Honguedo [Gaspé], where we had *seized* them when on our first voyage, to *Canada*; and that two days' journey from this cape and island be-

gan the kingdom of the Saguenay, on the north shore as one made one's way towards this *Canada*" (italics added). This passage not only reveals that Donnacona's sons may have been forced to go with Cartier the year before, but it is also the first mention of the name "Canada." Cartier used the name to apply to the north shore of the St. Lawrence from about Grosse Island in the east, by the northern tip of Île d'Orléans, to about midway between Québec and Trois Rivières, and it is shown on several maps in that location.

After some searching to ensure that a passage to Cathay did not exist along the north shore of the St. Lawrence, Cartier continued upriver, which he now began to call La Grande Rivière or La Rivière de Hochelaga. At the Saguenay River the expedition made contact with natives who knew Donnacona's sons, and on 7 September they arrived, recorded Cartier, at "the point where the province and territory of Canada begins."

Cartier named the Île d'Orléans, with an eye to his patronage, after the son of the French king. There, where the Saint Charles River enters the St. Lawrence, was Stadaconé, or Stadacona, the village of Donnacona. Cartier's ships anchored in the Saint Charles, which he named the "Ste Croix."

Domagaya and Taignogny had apparently promised Cartier that they would pilot him to Hochelaga, which he had learned was a major native settlement yet farther upriver, but now they stalled; Donnacona did not want Cartier to form any alliances with other tribes. Cartier resolved to go without them, and, taking only

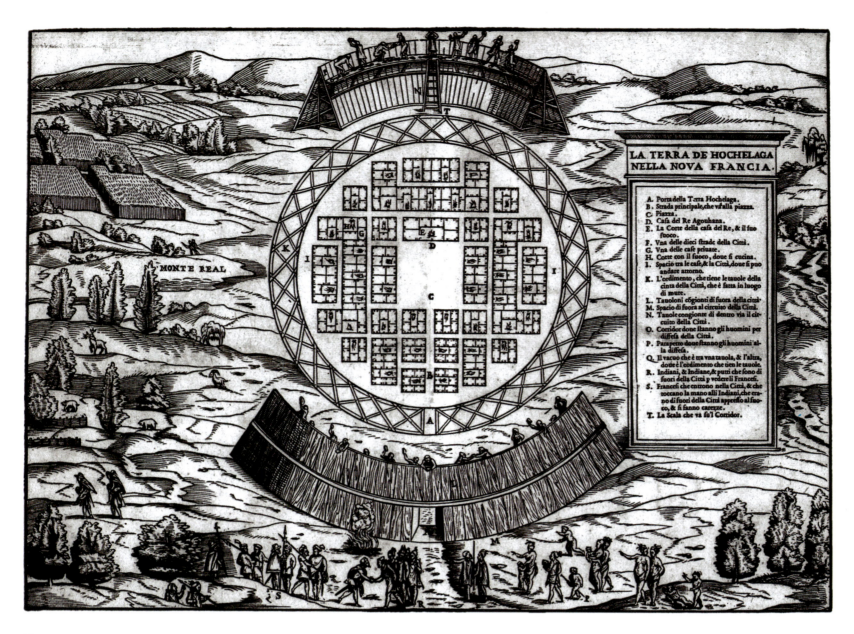

MAP 30.

A view of Hochelaga drawn in 1556 by Venetian mapmaker Giacomo Gastaldi. Opinions vary as to the accuracy of this well-known town plan, the first of Montréal, or indeed of any settlement in North America. It is supposed to be based on Cartier's own plan drawn in 1535 or 1536; his own description states that the town was protected with wooden walls and two towers, as the plan shows. Some fifty dwellings were inside the walls, though probably not laid out regularly as Gastaldi's plan shows. One writer has said that his plan "seems to be based more closely on Italian renaissance ideals than on New World reality." Note the name *Monte Real*, the first cartographical mention of what would later become Montréal.

his smallest ship, *L'Émerillon*, and towing the longboats of the other ships, he managed to make his way upstream. The river was at or near its lowest flow of the year, and it took nine days for them to travel about 116 km to Lac Saint-Pierre, where they left the ship and proceeded the final distance in the ships' longboats. On 2 October 1535, Cartier arrived before Hochelaga, a large fortified Iroquois settlement, and the site of Montréal. MAP 30 is a plan of Hochelaga by the Venetian mapmaker Giacomo Gastaldi that ranks as the first plan of any settlement in Canada. Since it seems to agree with the descriptions in the written accounts we can assume it was based on those, or on a sketch brought back by Cartier, though it is doubtless idealized. The settlement was protected by a wooden wall with two redoubts "garnished with rocks and stones, for defense and protection." Fifty dwellings were inside the wall.

On 3 October, Cartier put on his dress cloak and with his gentlemen volunteers and twenty sailors armed with pikes marched towards the settlement. Reaching the settlement, they found it close to a hill that Cartier named Mont Réal, later Montréal.

Cartier and his men were well received, probably because the natives had not seen Europeans before and thought they were gods of some sort; many disabled natives were brought to him to be touched. "One would think that God had come down there to cure them," wrote Cartier. Certainly Cartier tried to impress; he later had trumpets and other musical instruments sounded, which had the desired effect.

Climbing to the top of his newly named Mont Réal, Cartier could see some distance in every direction, and could also see that he could go no farther, for there, just above where he had left his boats, were the Lachine Rapids. The rapids were not, however, as is sometimes supposed, named by Cartier as being the nearest he got to La Chiné—China or Cathay—although they were indeed as far westward as he got. They were named 134 years later by René-

Robert, Cavelier de La Salle, who also travelled inland looking for China; he descended the Mississippi in 1682, and claimed the whole of Louisiana for France.

In an episode that would later prompt another entire voyage by Cartier, some of the natives had indicated that after passing these rapids there was another river (the Ottawa) that flowed into the St. Lawrence from the north. By touching Cartier's whistle chain, which was made of silver, and a gilt dagger handle that looked like gold that belonged to one of the sailors, they made Cartier believe that these metals came from up this river.

Cartier and his men now retraced their tracks to Stadaconé, where the rest of his expedition had been left. In Cartier's absence, his men had built a fort beside where the ships were anchored. Here, at what they called the harbour of Ste. Croix, they prepared to spend the winter. They salted down fish and meat, and Cartier recorded many essentially anthropological details about Donnacona's tribe. By mid-February of 1536, scurvy had affected both the natives and Cartier's men, but tragedy was averted by the use of the bark of the arborvitae tree, which the natives showed Cartier how to use.

MAP 31.

The beautifully illustrated but increasingly fantastic work of Pierre Desceliers reached a culmination with his 1550 map of the world. "Illuminated" would be a better word to describe this map. Ostrich-like birds, unicorns, and turbaned human figures combined to produce a map which was intended to entertain as well as to inform. There is an inscription which says the king of France sent "the honest and clever gentleman M. de Roberval with a great company of intelligent people, both gentle and common, and with them a great company of degraded criminals to people the country." The map also states that Jacques Cartier discovered this country and that its *"austerité, intempérance, et petit proffit"* led to its abandonment again. *Canada* is named four times, and *Ochelaga* and *Sagne* (Saguenay) are shown. The Atlantic Ocean is called the *Mer de France*. The American historian Samuel Morison, referring to the illustrations on this map including a whale with two blowholes, which "does not create much confidence in the cartographer's pictorial accuracy," says "Desceliers had quite an establishment, and I suspect that he did the actual cartography himself and told some clever boy to put a ship here and a whale there, to fill up space." This map was made for presentation to the French king, Henri II. One of the prized possessions of the British Library, this huge map (215 x 135 cm, or 7 x 4½ ft) on thick parchment (or vellum; it is an untanned sheet derived from the inner layer of animal hide, and is quite tough) is kept loosely rolled on a specially made acrylic tube, itself in a specially made long cased box complete with a brass title plate on the top.

The labels visible on the map include:

Circulus arcticus ... *Circulus arcticus*

Hoc fluuio facilior est nauigatio in Saguenai

Saguenai

Saguenay flu:

Noua Fran   Canada

Ci   a

Chilaga

Moco fa

Hochelaga

Hochelay

Honguedo

Sinus S. Laurentij

Golfam de Merofro

Terra Corte realis

Nor   om   bega

C de Breton

Dobretan

Arredonda

Terra de bacal

Ilha Bacailo

Map 32.
Gerard Mercator's pivotal world map of 1569, the first to use his Mercator projection, where lines of constant bearing are shown as straight lines on the map, of immense utility to navigators. The map incorporated much information from the Cartier voyages. Because the map was engraved and printed rather than simply remaining as a single drawn manuscript copy, it had a significant and lasting influence on the cartography of eastern Canada. Ironically, given this fact, it was not as accurate in this region as some of its predecessors. Newfoundland, *Terra de bacal*[laos], is fragmented, though not outrageously so. *Estroit de St. Pierre* is shown on the wrong side of Anticosti, and *Honguedo* is incorrectly shown on the north shore of the St. Lawrence. *Canada* is shown both as a settlement and as the area around it, and the whole region on both sides of the river is *Nova Francia. Sinus St. Laurentii* appears for the first time—Mercator took the name Cartier had given to a small bay on the north side of the St. Lawrence and applied it to the entire gulf, as it is still called today.

Probably aiming to cultivate Cartier's friendship, Donnacona embroidered tales about a fascinating Kingdom of Saguenay, where there were large amounts of gold and precious stones; this of course interested the French, and Cartier hatched a plan to kidnap Donnacona and take him to France, so that he could personally relate these tales to the French king. Abandoning *La Petite Hermine* because by now he only had enough men to handle two ships, he set sail for France on 6 May 1536.

After some delays due to an east wind, they sailed up the St. Lawrence and through the Détroit de Honguedo, the passage to the south side of Anticosti Island which Cartier had considered to be just a bay on his first voyage. This time he resolved to use what he felt sure by this time was a strait to the south of Newfoundland leading to the open Atlantic. They landed on Île Brion and sailed around the Îles de la Madeleine (Magdalen Islands), which he had thought were part of the mainland when he first saw them in 1534. Touching Cape Breton at Cape St. Lawrence, then the south coast of Newfoundland, Cartier sailed eastwards to Les Îles de St. Pierre, where on 11 June he met several French fishing boats. St. Pierre and Miquelon is today the only part of North America still under the sovereignty of France. From there, after one last stop in a bay on the Avalon Peninsula, Cartier finally sailed for France, reaching St. Malo on 16 July 1536.

Captured and taken to France by Cartier, Donnacona seems to have enjoyed a position as a bit of a celebrity, or at least a curiosity, and became adept at feeding the French court with the information he cleverly perceived they wanted, promoting his "Kingdom of Saguenay." He slowly added embellishments to his story so that Saguenay became a land of gold and riches where oranges and pomegranates grew, as did the spices so keenly sought at this time: pepper, nutmeg, and cloves. Stories of strange people, from unipeds to winged men, also were included in his stories.

Before long it was resolved to launch a third voyage to this rich land, which was now seen as a northern land similar to those farther south that had been conquered by the Spanish; Hernan Cortés had defeated the Aztec empire in Mexico in 1519, and Francisco Pizarro the Inca empire in Peru in 1533. A war between France and Spain for the two years ending in 1538 delayed the venture somewhat, but then preparations began. They were relatively complicated this time and the expedition did not finally get going until 1541. Donnacona, the expedition's booster, died in the meantime.

The idea now was not to find a passage to Cathay, but to found a colony in the glorious Kingdom of Saguenay to exploit its untold riches and send them back to France. With this objective in mind, François I appointed a French nobleman, Jean-François de La Roque, Sieur de Roberval, as the overall commander of the expedition and also appointed him governor of the new lands. With several hundred colonists and five ships, including *La Grande Hermine* and and *L'Émerillon*, Cartier set sail from St. Malo on 23 May 1541, ahead of Roberval, who was not yet ready. Hence Cartier effectively controlled his expedition again. The plan was that Roberval was to follow Cartier to Canada.

Three months later, Cartier anchored at Stadaconé, where the new chief, Agona, understandably enough seemed unconcerned that Donnacona had not returned. Cartier decided to build his settlement a short distance upriver from today's Québec at Cap Rouge, which he named Charlesbourg-Royal. The colonists collected quartz crystals, which they thought were diamonds, and iron pyrites, which they thought were gold, and two of the ships were sent back to France with these. Cartier built a stockaded settlement and then, with a few men, proceeded upriver to search for Saguenay, but he only got as far as the Lachine Rapids. Native guides drew Cartier a sort of map with sticks that showed the rapids which would have to be overcome, and Cartier decided not to risk it. The natives could have directed him up the Ottawa River, but they did not, perhaps because they were deliberately trying to discourage him.

Cartier returned to Charlesbourg-Royal and found that the natives had become increasingly unfriendly, probably as they had come to realize that the French meant to stay. He overwintered, losing in the period some thirty-five men to native attacks. Hopelessly undermanned,

as Roberval had not turned up, Cartier sailed back to France. He did find an outward-bound Roberval in the harbour at St. John's, Newfoundland, on the way, but ignored his order to follow him back to Canada.

Roberval had in fact not sailed from France until April 1542, almost a year after Cartier, with three ships and a company of his gentlemen friends and more colonists. Continuing on after his encounter with Cartier in St. John's, Roberval sailed to the site of Charlesbourg-Royal. On the way he marooned his own niece or cousin, Marguerite de La Roque, on one of the Harrington Islands (on the north coast of the Gulf of St. Lawrence, near the Strait of Belle Isle) for getting too amorous with one of his men. Her lady's maid was sent with her, and her amour jumped overboard to join her. Neither of them survived, but Marguerite did, eventually being picked up by a French fishing boat and returned to France, where her story entered the realms of French classic literature.

Landing in Canada, Roberval built a new settlement, which he named France-Roy. The

map of Nicolas Vallard (MAP 38, overleaf) is beautifully illustrated with what is thought to show France-Roy; the number of ladies and gentlemen and soldiers seems unlikely to be a depiction of Cartier's party. The bearded figure is presumably Roberval. Despite almost certainly knowing of the arborvitae cure for scurvy, some fifty of Roberval's company died of the disease that winter. In June 1543 Roberval belatedly began his search for Saguenay. One party led by Roberval followed Cartier's track upriver, but again did not get further than the Lachine Rapids, turning back after one boat was lost with eight people.

A pilot with Roberval, Jean Alfonce, explored the Saguenay River. In an account he published later, Alfonce wrote of the Saguenay River that "inside the entrance, the river widens after two or three leagues, and begins to take on the character of an arm of the sea, for which reason I estimate that this sea leads to the Pacific Ocean or even to la mer du Cattay." Clearly Alfonce did not get to the Chicoutimi rapids, or he would likely have experienced the

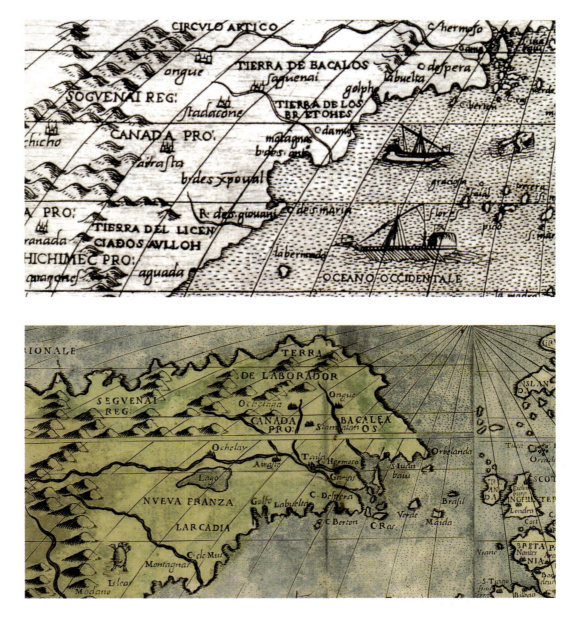

MAP 33 (*top*) and MAP 34 (*bottom*).
Two editions of a world map by Paolo Forlani, about 1560 (MAP 33) and 1565 (MAP 34). Although not incorporating the geographical discoveries of Jacques Cartier very accurately, these maps are noteworthy as the first *printed* maps on which his name *Canada* appears. Forlani is not very clear about its position, as Canada moves from one edition to the other!

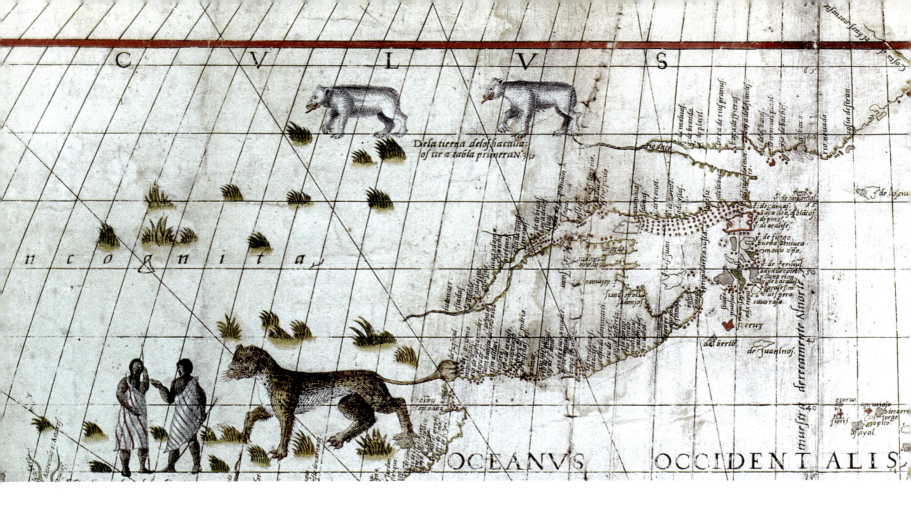

MAP 35 (*above*).

Canada *Incognita*. One of the most beautiful maps of the sixteenth century was the world map drawn, or at least supervised, by John Cabot's son Sebastian in 1544. The map is engraved, and huge, 120 x 180 cm. Although engraved, only a single copy of this map is known to exist today, the copy found in the library of a Bavarian curate in 1843 and now in the Bibliothèque nationale in Paris. The map was drawn in Seville, Spain, where, as chief pilot of Spain, Sebastian Cabot was in charge of the *padron real*, or standard government chart from which others were copied, and in this position he had access to the information required to draw a map of the world. This one was actually a commercial production, not a government one; it was not intended to be used for navigation (which is just as well, considering its size!). Because of this, it is beautifully illustrated, so that it could be sold to wealthy merchants for decoration; hanging maps were quite the fashion, if you could afford them.

The section reproduced here is based to a large extent on the discoveries of Jacques Cartier, but also incorporates information from Cabot's own voyages. Of particular significance is the inscription against Cape Breton's North Cape: *prima tierra vista*, "land first visited," which purports to show his landfall with his father. A legend states: *Esta tierra fue descubierta por Joan Caboto Veneciano, y Sebastian Caboto su hijo; anno M.CCCC.XCIIII a veinte y quatro de Iunio por la mannana*, ("This land was discovered by John Cabot and Sebastian Cabot, his son, 24 September 1494 [1497]"). This was the first and only recognition that Sebastian Cabot ever gave to his father. It is also the inscription which fixed John Cabot's landfall on Cape Breton rather than in Newfoundland for centuries, although the majority of historical opinion now seems to favour the Newfoundland landfall. The map is similar to that of Nicolas Desliens (MAP 29, page 27), and Sebastian may well have seen it; he may well have had a poor recollection of the "northward-facing cape" that he attributed to his father's landfall and from the Desliens map thought North Cape was a good guess. It is also possible that placing the landfall on Cape Breton was intentional, to support English claims to eastern Canada against the French. We will probably never know the truth.

same problems that Roberval ran into and realized that this was no strait of the sea. Alfonce drew a map of his explorations, which is shown here (MAP 36). It shows Lac Saint-Jean, the river's source (though many other rivers flow into it), but he may have been told about it by the natives. Alfonce's map does not agree very well with his narrative. Nevertheless, the map is one of the earliest surviving maps of a local region of what is now Canada.

For Roberval, the Lachine Rapids were the last straw; he had seen enough. This was plainly not the rich land Donnacona had described, and in July 1543 Roberval left for France, thus ending the first French attempt to establish a colony in Canada.

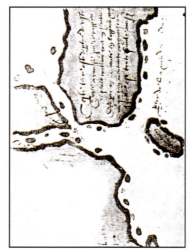

MAP 36 (*above*).

One of the maps by Jean Alfonce, drawn about 1544, from his guide to the world, *La Cosmographie*. This shows the Gulf of St. Lawrence. The island is Anticosti—Cartier's *Isle de l'Assomption*—and the St. Lawrence River flows in from the west. The river on the north side—more a strait, really—is the Saguenay River, and it is shown opening to another sea, *La Mer du Saguenay*, that Alphonce thought would lead to Cathay. In reality it was Lac Saint-Jean, the source of the river.

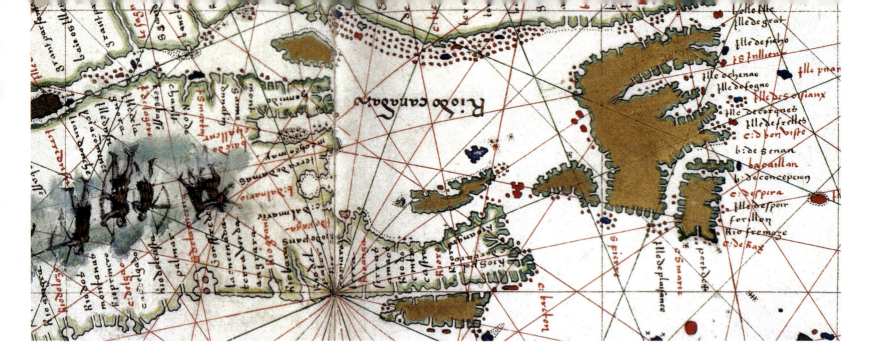

Map 37 (*above*) and Map 38 (*below*).

Perhaps the most beautiful of all the Dieppe maps is the map known as the Vallard. The name, Nicolas Vallard, and the date, 1547, are prominently shown on the map (not on the parts shown here), but Vallard was quite possibly the person for whom the map was drawn rather than its maker. The map almost has more illustrations than map, reflecting the fact that little was known of the interior, but mapmakers did not like blank spaces. *Rio do Canada* and some other place names are, strangely, in Portuguese. Newfoundland is here shown as a single large island, except for the Avalon Peninsula, which is forgivably almost insular anyway. The coast south from Cape Breton follows Ribiero's map of 1529 (see Map 24, page 23). The map has south at the top (as Map 38, below); the detail above (Map 37) has been reversed to put north in its more conventional place and allow easier reading of names. The outline geography is quite recognizable, and there are many recognizable names, including *b: de concepcion* (Conception Bay), *ille de plaisance* (Placentia), *s pierre* (St. Pierre, which with Miquelon remains French to this day), *c: Breton,* and *baie de challeur.*

Early English Attempts to Find a Northwest Passage

The concept of a passage to Cathay was still very much alive in Europe despite failure to find one in the St. Lawrence or through Central America. Magellan had found one around the southern extremity of South America in 1520, and it was inconceivable to many sixteenth-century minds that there should not be a northern one to "balance" the one in the south. Cartographers, lacking the real one, invented their own, and these maps in turn convinced many that a Northwest Passage existed. An active promoter of the idea in the period 1565 to 1583 was Humfrey Gilbert. Gilbert's book *A Discourse of a Discoverie for a New Passage to Cataia* was written in 1566, though not published until 1576, to promote the company formed to send Martin Frobisher to find this elusive Northwest Passage.

Frobisher himself had been an advocate of a Northwest Passage for some time, and was keen to prove his theory. He was to lead no less than three voyages to Canada.

Frobisher sailed from England with three ships, *Gabriel, Michael,* and an unnamed smaller ship, a pinnace, in June 1576. After a tempestuous voyage in which the pinnace was lost, they sighted the east coast of Greenland, which Frobisher thought was the island of Frisland, a mythical land shown on the Zeno map (MAP 12, page 14), which he carried with him. The master of *Michael,* distrusting the pack ice, deserted the expedition and stole away home, leaving Frobisher on *Gabriel.* After further stormy sailing in which the ship lost one of its masts, they sighted Resolution Island, off the southeastern

cape of Baffin Island. "Hee hadde sighte of a highe lande," wrote George Best, one of Frobisher's officers, in the wonderful and still comprehensible English of the time, "whyche hee [Frobisher] called Queene Elizabeth's Forlande." Then, "sayling more northerlie alonst the coast he descried another forlande with a greatte gutte, bay, or passage, deviding as it were, two mayne-lands or continents asunder." Frobisher thought he had found the strait to Cathay, "wherefore he determined to make profe of this place to see how far that gutte had continuance." Sailing "fyftie leagues" to the west, Frobisher decided that he had indeed found his strait and that America lay to the south, Asia to the north (as in MAP 2, page 4). "This place he named after his name Frobisher's Streytes," following Magellan's naming of the southern strait after himself as the discoverer. He had found Frobisher Bay, at the head of which today stands Iqaluit, the capital of Nunavut.

Returning to the mouth of this bay, Frobisher landed on a small island, which he named Hall's Island, after his sailing master Christopher Hall. Here five men were lost to Inuit with whom they attempted to trade, so now, with only thirteen crew left, Frobisher decided to return to England. First taking possession of the land for England, they picked up stones as souvenirs or tokens of possession. One stone they brought back to England was a black stone which seemed to be metallic. Two assayers declared it to be iron pyrites, which it was, but a third assayer, perhaps bribed by someone hoping to make a killing in a stock promotion, decided it was gold

ore. This was what England wanted to hear, whether it was true or not. The Spanish had found gold in America; why not the English?

Now the pace picked up. Others joined the original financial backers of Frobisher to form the Company of Cathay, an informal joint-stock venture in which Queen Elizabeth herself invested £1,000.

A new ship, *Aid,* much larger than *Gabriel* and *Michael,* was purchased, and the three ships, with 120 men, were stuffed with supplies for another voyage. Thirty of the men were miners. To his credit, despite bad weather Frobisher was able to guide his fleet back to Hall's Island. The summer of 1577 was spent trying to find their five lost men, which they did not; fighting off Inuit attacks and attacking the Inuit themselves, and loading their ships to the gunnels with the black stone they thought was gold ore, dug from an island Frobisher called Countess of Warwick's Island after the wife of a patron, today's Kodlunarn Island. Then they sailed back to England, arriving in September 1577.

Still assayers claimed that the 200 tons of rock Frobisher had brought to England was indeed gold ore. It seems that some skulduggery was going on, for two assayers came to the same conclusion; however, whatever the reason, the Company of Cathay sent Frobisher off again the following year, 1578, to gather yet more of the "gold ore." Now with a fleet of fifteen ships, more than three hundred miners, and men and provisions to establish what was planned to be the first English colony in North America,

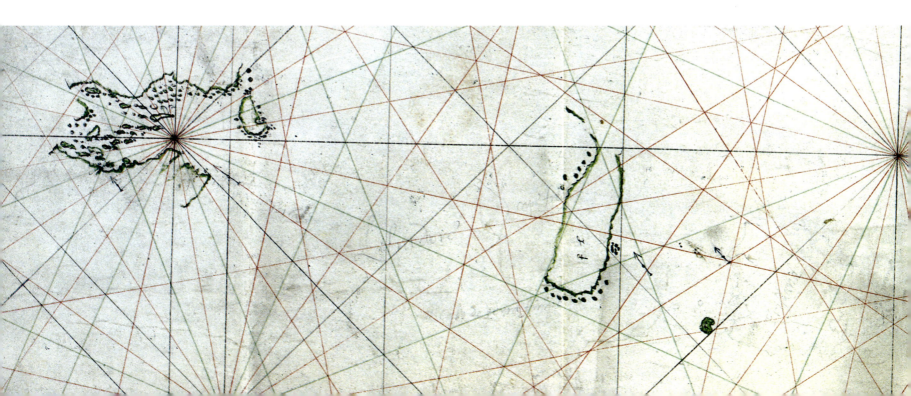

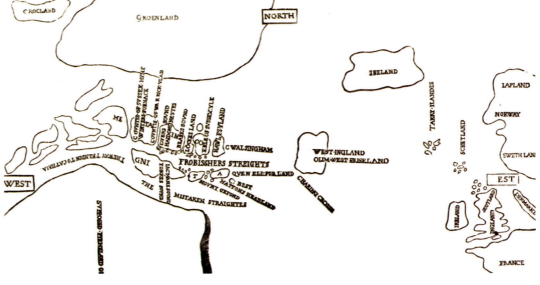

MAP 40.
A map by James Beare showing Frobisher's discoveries and ideas. His *Mistaken Straightes* were the least of Frobisher's mistakes; the straits were in fact Hudson Strait, and did indeed lead to another sea—but Hudson Bay, not the South Sea.

Frobisher again set sail at the end of May 1578. This time he was not so lucky at finding his strait. Frobisher found himself, with twelve of his ships, on the wrong side of Queen Elizabeth's Foreland, sailing westwards in what he named "the Mistaken Straightes," shown clearly on MAP 40, right. This was Hudson Strait. Observing that the flood tide ran for three hours to the ebb tide's one hour, he was convinced that *this* was the route to Cathay. Future maps would note a "furious overfall" at the entrance to this strait, and this may well have led Henry Hudson to explore this strait as the *real* way to Cathay a few years later (see page 38). Frobisher seriously considered continuing to sail west, which he did for twenty days, but then he decided he had better follow his instructions and mine rocks for the Company of Cathay, which, after all, had financed the whole affair.

Frobisher's men began mining on Kodlunarn Island on 1 August and also obtained rocks from other sites nearby that were easier to dig out. Other mine sites are marked on MAP 40. In all, 1,350 tons of rock was loaded and taken to England. The backers of the Company of Cathay tried desperately to find ways to extract gold from the rock Frobisher had brought back, spending yet more money in the process. Needless to say, when all the dust had settled, the Company of Cathay was bankrupt, and the rock was used to pave roads and build walls.

An account of the expenses of the first voyage, in 1576, shows that Frobisher took a number of maps with him. The accounts include £ 5 for "a very great carte of navigation" and £ 1.6s.8d for "a great mappe universall of Mercator in prente." This was the great Mercator world map of 1569, which incorporated considerable information for the North Atlantic from the Zeno map (MAP 12, page 14) and reinforced Frobisher's misconception that Greenland was the non-existent "Frisland." An additional £2 was spent for "6 cartes of navigation written in blacke parchment whereof 4 ruled playne & 2 rounde," one of which is shown here (MAP 39, left).

One of Frobisher's captains, George Best, had rushed an account of the voyages into print on his return to England; published in 1578, his book contained two maps. One, MAP 41 (below), was a map of the world which shows the way

the passage to Cathay was visualized at the time. The Northwest Passage shown on this map is labelled "Frobusshers Straightes." Meta Incognita, a name Queen Elizabeth gave to the southern shore of Frobisher Bay, which is still named as such, is shown on this map as a group of islands. The islands are shown more clearly on the other map from Best's book, a woodcut print attributed to James Beare, another of Frobisher's officers (MAP 40, above). Here are *The Mistaken Straightes*—Hudson Strait—and, of course, *Frobishers Streights*, plus *Hawles Ysland* and the *Countis of Sussex Myne*; even rock mining sites were named after sponsors! West of the Mistaken Straightes, sounding more like a line from a modern song, is marked *The Way Trendin to Cathaia*.

The confusion Frobisher had had in mistaking Greenland for the mythical Frisland, caused by the Zeno and Mercator maps he carried and his inability to measure longitude, further confused mapmakers for centuries afterwards. Many maps (for example MAP 58, page 44) were drawn showing Frobisher's Straits cutting through the southern tip of Greenland.

In the England of the 1570s, excitement over the push to find the Northwest Passage was in overdrive. One particular enthusiast, already mentioned, was Humfrey Gilbert. His 1576 book advocated setting up an English colony in North America as well as finding a Northwest Passage. In 1577, the year of Martin Frobisher's second voyage, the English mathematician and astrologer John Dee published a memorial on navigation in which he coined the term "British

Empire." This was the same year Sir Francis Drake sailed from England for the Pacific and what would become the first English circumnavigation of the world.

The following year, 1578, Gilbert obtained a charter from Queen Elizabeth which allowed him "to discover, searche, finde out and viewe such remote heathen and barbarous lands . . . not actually possessed of any Christian prince or people," make a settlement with any English subjects willingly accompanying him, and enjoy viceregal powers of government.

Gilbert had nine ships under his command in September 1578, but lost three just one day before sailing due to infighting between himself and his captains; the rest of his fleet never got any farther than Ireland. Intending to leave again the next year, he was forbidden to do so because one of his ships had turned to piracy. It would be five years until he could sail again.

Gilbert intended, it seems, to found a colony in Norumbega, today's New England. He finally set sail again on 11 June 1583 with five ships and about 260 men, including craftsmen. They made a landfall not in New England but in Newfoundland, anchoring in St. John's Harbour. There, on 5 August 1583, they planted a wooden pillar on the shore with the "Armes of England ingraven in lead," and Gilbert announced to the men of thirty-six Spanish, Portuguese, French, and English fishing boats anchored in the harbour that they were now under English sovereignty. This is regarded by many as the birth of the British Empire. However, Gilbert did not put settlers on the shore. Two of his captains refused to go farther, so he replaced them and sent the ships back to England. Gilbert continued southwards, sailing in the smallest vessel, a pinnace called the *Squirrel*, so as to more easily be able to explore shallow waters. It was not to be. One of his remaining ships was wrecked off Sable Island, and eighty-five men drowned. With so few men left, Gilbert decided to wait until the following year to found his colony and sailed for England. Running into bad weather, his small ship foundered, and he was drowned.

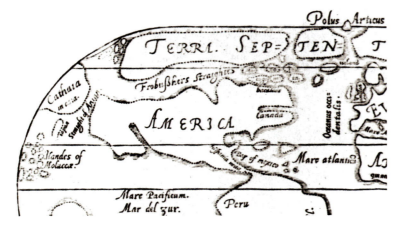

MAP 41.
This part of George Best's world map of 1578 shows a clear Northwest Passage to Cathay and the Spice Islands.

Before Gilbert left England in 1583, cosmologist John Dee completed a map for him, labelled *Humfray Gylbert knight his charte* (Map 43, right). It may well have been essentially a promotional piece to advance interest in his upcoming voyage of colonization. The map shows Dee and Gilbert's conception of a Northwest Passage and also the St. Lawrence flowing from the Atlantic to the Pacific. The sea of Verrazano also opens to the Pacific. Newfoundland is depicted as three large islands, and *estotiland*, taken from the Zeno map, is an island off Labrador. Features derived from Cartier are also shown, most notably the name *Canada*.

Humfrey Gilbert's brother Adrian had received a patent similar to his brother's from Queen Elizabeth to explore and colonize lands to the west. Part of this group of promoters for a Northwest Passage was John Davis, who in three separate voyages would be responsible for extending geographical knowledge north into the strait between Canada and Greenland which now bears his name.

Davis embarked on his first voyage in 1585, with two ships, the delightfully named *Sunneshine* and *Mooneshine*, and forty-two men, a relatively modest effort after the failures of Frobisher and Gilbert.

Sailing north into Davis Strait, they found a large inlet they called Cumberland Sound, which, of course, they thought was the passage to Cathay. The drowned glaciated valleys on the east coast of Baffin Island are by their nature very deep, and this convinced Davis that the sound was open at the western end, as did the sighting of whales. However, with the season advancing, he did not wish to be frozen in for six months, so retreated to England for the winter.

The next year, 1586, Davis tried again. He had written of Cumberland Sound: "The northwest passage is a matter nothing doubtful, but at any tyme almost to be passed, the sea navigable, voyd of yse, the ayre tolerable and the waters very deep." With this kind of promotion, financial backers were persuaded once again.

This time four ships sailed, but two were to investigate a supposed "over the pole" route, advanced by John Dee, up the eastern side of Greenland; Dee correctly thought that no land would intervene, but could not conceive of a whole ocean being frozen. Naturally, this did not work out the way Dee thought it would.

Davis could not find Cumberland Sound this time, although he must have passed its entrance. He sailed southwards but missed Hudson Strait also, finding only the coast of Labrador. After a whole season he had found virtually nothing. He sailed back to England in September.

But the search for the passage was not to be given up easily. The amazing thing is that Davis was still able to find financial backers. There seemed no question that the passage was there; it was just a matter of finding it. Davis wrote to William Sanderson, a major financial backer: "I now have experience of much of the Northwest part of the world, & have brought the passage to that likelihood, as that I am assured it must be in one of four places, or els not at all. And further I can assure you upon the perill of my life, that this voyage may be performed without further charge, nay with certaine profite to the adventurers."

The persuasion must have worked, for the following year, 1587, Davis tried yet again. Now with three ships, Davis this time had to deal with a near mutiny, as the sailors on two of his ships decided they would rather spend their time fishing than exploring. Davis thus released two ships and continued alone, in a small pinnace.

Davis now wanted to explore to the north, where he expected to find a better passage, and sailed as far north as 72° 46′, to high cliffs on the coast of Greenland which he named *Sanderson his Hope*, after one of his most persistent financial backers, William Sanderson. Today it is Upernavik, Greenland. It was just as well for Sanderson that he had a headland named for him, for this was all he was to get for his money. Ironically, Lancaster Sound, which is the real entrance to the Northwest Passage, lies in the

same latitude, but on the west side of what is now Baffin Bay.

Davis crossed Baffin Bay, encountering pack ice and at one point nearly becoming trapped. Finally he found *the Streights* again, Cumberland Sound. This time he sailed "threescore leagues," about 275 km, to the west up Cumberland Sound. Then, Davis wrote, "Wee ankered among many Isles in the bottome of the gulf," finally realizing that this was not a passage to Cathay or anywhere else after all.

Continuing south, Davis now found Frobisher Bay, but did not recognize it as Frobisher's discovery because cartographers had already placed Frobisher's Straits at the southern tip of Greenland, confused by Frobisher's identification of the mythical island of Frisland with the real Greenland, resulting from the fiction on the Zeno map. Davis named Frobisher Bay *Lumlies Inlet* after Lord Lumley, an important person at Queen Elizabeth's court.

Davis encountered "whirling and overfalling" as he came out of Frobisher Bay, passing by "a very great gulfe, the water whirling and roaring as it were the meeting of tydes." This was the eastern entrance to Hudson Strait. Davis offered no explanation for not investigating this more likely "passage"; such exploration would have to wait a few more years, for Henry Hudson.

Davis sailed southwards, past Hudson Strait. He named the northern tip of Labrador *Chidleis cape*, today Cape Chidley, after a friend of his. He then sailed south along the Labrador coast almost to the Strait of Belle Isle, at which point he gave up and returned to England. Davis himself clearly had not given up, as he wrote to William Sanderson on his return: "I have bene in 73 degrees, finding the sea all open, and forty leagues between land and land. The passage is most probable, the execution easie, as at my comming you shall fully know." This time Sanderson was not impressed; there were to be no more voyages for Davis.

The account of Davis's voyages in the 1589 edition of Richard Hakluyt's *Principall Navigations* was read by the king of Denmark, who decided that he had better assert what he viewed as Danish sovereignty rights, based on the Norse settlements. Thus the Danes began a search for lost colonies, part of which involved the redrawing of maps from Norse sources, some of which are shown in this book (Maps 7, 8, and 9, pages 11 and 12).

After his third voyage, John Davis assisted mapmaker Emery Molyneaux in the drawing of a map and the construction of a globe incorporating the results of his discoveries. The map

Map 42.
Part of Rumold Mercator's new 1595 edition of his father Gerard's 1569 polar map (Map 10, page 13). Davis Strait and Frobisher's Strait have now been added. *A furious over fall* marks the entrance to Hudson Strait.

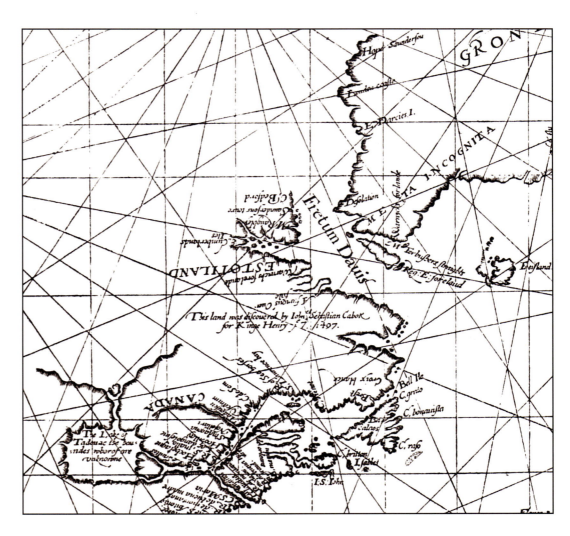

MAP 43.
"Humfray Gylbert knight his charte,"
a rather superbly bizarre polar map drawn by
John Dee for Gilbert in 1583. It shows a wonderful
Northwest Passage and, as if this were not enough, the
St. Lawrence flows clear through to California. Verrazano's
sea features prominently in the North American continent.
Maps like these were self-convincing; how could there *not* be
a Northwest Passage?

    Note Dee's plotting of Martin Frobisher's discoveries,
shown as the red-coloured two-pronged land at about 330° E
and 63° N, the same longitude at which Greenland is drawn.
Later maps (such as MAP 42) placed Frobisher's strait at the
southern tip of Greenland.

MAP 44 (*below, right*).
Part of the world map of 1599 by Edward Wright, based on a
1589 globe by Emery Molyneaux showing the discoveries of John
Davis in addition to those of Frobisher, all confused by information from the Zeno map of 1558. *A Furious Overfale* is marked,
upside down. The map uses the new Mercator projection,

Molyneaux drew is shown here (MAP 44). It is
confused by the Zeno map (MAP 12, page 14) in
that it shows *Estotiland* and *Frisland*, and
Forbushers Straights cut through the southern
tip of Greenland. But it does show *Fretum
Davis*—Davis Strait—and *Cumberlands Iles* at
the western end of an unnamed inlet, Frobisher
Bay, or Davis's Cumberland Sound. *A furious
Overfale* is marked in the position of Hudson
Strait, itself poorly delineated.

    Gerard Mercator had published his first
map of the Arctic as an inset to his great map of
the world of 1569 (MAP 10, page 13), and in 1595
his son Rumold published an updated version
which incorporated both Frobisher's and Davis's
discoveries (MAP 42). Unfortunately, the
younger Mercator was also influenced by the
troublesome Zeno map, and *Fretum Forbosshers*
(Frobisher's Strait) is again shown cutting
though the southern tip of Greenland.

Probing the Northern Seas

The great bay that bears the name of Henry Hudson may possibly have been known to European explorers before Hudson's time, although there is no evidence other than the existence of a bay shown on some older maps, such as the one by Cornelius Wytfliet, published in 1597, shown here (MAP 47). Portuguese navigators and others, notably Sebastian Cabot (see page 21), have at one time or another had the discovery of Hudson Bay attributed to them, but until Hudson no one documented any such discovery. And Hudson's voyage was almost not documented either.

Hudson was not the first to enter Hudson Strait; Frobisher had entered it in 1578, and in 1602 Englishman George Waymouth, also dispatched to find the way to the South Sea, had entered the strait but been forced back by a mutinous crew.

By 1610, when Hudson set out on his fourth and final voyage, he was already quite an experienced navigator. Under the aegis of the Muscovy Company, formed in England to trade with Russia, Hudson had undertaken two Arctic voyages in 1607 and 1608. The first was northwards, since the prevailing belief in an open

Arctic sea meant that Hudson should be able to sail right over the North Pole to China. Disillusioned of this in 1607, he tried again in 1608, this time sailing towards a supposed Northeast Passage (the north coast of Asia at this time almost universally being depicted too far south); he got as far as Novaya Zemlya, north of Russia, before being stopped by ice.

After this the Muscovy Company was understandably reluctant to finance another

MAP 45 (above).
Part of Abraham Ortelius's great world map of 1570. It shows a clear and unequivocal strait across the northern coast of the North American continent. A bay on this coast of North America is shown. Whether this is the result of some knowledge Ortelius had of Portuguese or other explorations to Hudson Bay, or simply cartographic licence based on lack of any information, is not resolved. The depiction of the Arctic follows Mercator's map of 1569 (MAP 10, page 13).

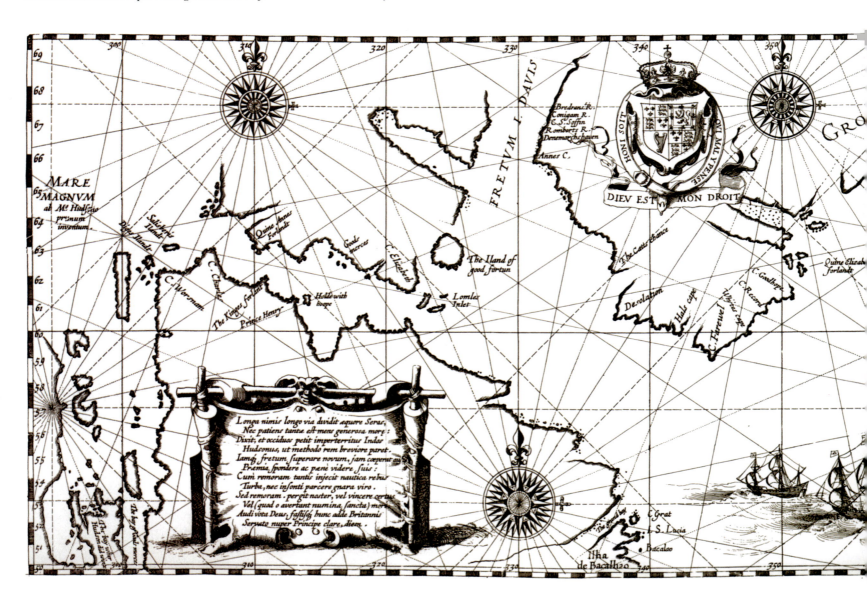

venture, but Hudson received an invitation from the Dutch East India Company to sail under its flag. The search for an open polar sea and a Northeast Passage received support from Peter Plancius, the official cartographer for the Dutch East India Company, and Hudson's contract was witnessed by Joducus Hondius, the great Dutch mapmaker, who also supported his ideas.

Sailing in April 1609, Hudson did not get as far as the previous year before being stopped by ice. Contrary winds and then, forebodingly, the dissensions of his part-Dutch, part-English crew, prevented him from proceeding. But sailing south again he had the idea to save face by sailing west and trying for a Northwest Passage, although this was not in his instructions. Hudson had noted in his log the previous year the notion of making a "trial of that place called Lumley's inlet and the furious over fall of Captain Davis" (see page 36), but had been unable to sail west due to the wind. So this was not a new idea for him.

But his crew, while agreeing to sail west, had had enough of the cold and insisted on a southward course once America was reached. Thus it was that Henry Hudson, probing the openings in the coastline north of the English settlement of Virginia, found the river now named after him and the site of today's New York City (see Map 422, page 272).

Late in 1609 Hudson returned, not to the Irish coast that he was aiming for, but to Dartmouth, England, and from there sent his report to the directors of the Dutch East India Company in Amsterdam. In his report he asked to be allowed to try again to the northwest the following year. But the directors would have none of it and ordered him to return to the Netherlands. The English government, hearing of the turn of events, forbade Hudson to leave the country.

With the consent of the English government, Hudson was persuaded to search for a passage to the northwest in 1610. Chronicler Samuel Purchas wrote that "Sir Thomas Smith, Sir Dudley Diggs and Master John Westenholm [Wolstenholme] . . . furnished out . . . Henry Hudson to try if, through any of the passages which Davis saw, any passage might be found to the other ocean called the South Sea."

Hudson sailed from London in April 1610 in his ship *Discovery*—the same ship used by Waymouth in 1602—and by August had sailed through Hudson Strait into "a spacious sea," the great bay that would later bear his name. But Hudson thought he had sailed through the Northwest Passage and out into the South Sea. One can imagine his disappointment several weeks later when, reaching the "bottom of the bay," he had to turn northwards.

Caught by the approaching winter, Hudson and his men were forced to overwinter. Lack of adequate provisions and other hardships led to dissension, and some of the crew died. By June, the ice appeared to have dissipated enough to allow an attempt to return to England, but it was not long before the ship was again surrounded by ice. It seems that Hudson ordered all the men's trunks broken open and any food hoarded redistributed to all. Whatever the immediate reason, open mutiny followed, and Hudson, men who were sick, and others who supported him were thrown into an open shallop and set adrift. They were never seen again.

Command was now assumed by Robert Bylot, a crew member who seems to not have had much to do with the mutiny. They barely made it back to England, but those who did had only their side of the story to tell, and although there was an initial move to hang them all for mutiny, lack of evidence allowed them to go free.

By sailing as an English expedition and by finding Hudson Bay and putting it clearly on the map—from actual exploration—Hudson established later English claims to the bay, and

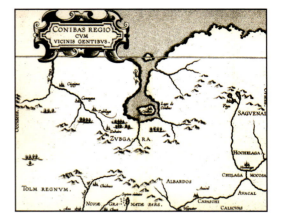

MAP 47.
The first regional map of Hudson Bay? A map by Cornelius Wytfliet published in an atlas of maps of the New World in 1597, the first atlas to cover only the Americas, designed to complement the Ptolemaic atlases then available which depicted only the Old World. Note the position of the bay relative to *Hochelaga* (Montréal); it is in more or less the correct place. Where did this information originally come from?

his discovery would underpin still later claims to its entire drainage basin.

If Hudson made a map of his voyage—and he surely did—it has been lost. It seems to have been sent to Peter Plancius in Amsterdam. Near the end of 1611 Dutch mapmaker Hessel Gerritz published an account of Hudson's voyage and included in it a map (Map 46) said to have been copied from Hudson's original. This map would serve as a model for mapmakers for fifty years. Samuel de Champlain was the first to incorporate it into his maps, the first in 1612 (see Map 70, page 52).

The popular rumour now was that Hudson had found a route to Cathay before the mutiny, and in 1612 a new company was formed called Company of the Merchants Discoverers of the North-West Passage, or Northwest Company. Welshman Thomas Button was selected to determine what had become of Hudson, and to complete "ye full and perfect discovery of the North-west Passage."

With two ships, *Resolution* and *Discovery* (the latter being the same ship used by Hudson), and taking Robert Bylot along, Button entered Hudson Bay in the summer of 1612 and sailed southwestwards, until he made a landfall on the west side of the bay, at a point he named *Hopes Checkt*, a logical enough name given his mandate. Button wintered to the south, at the mouth of the Nelson River, which he named after Robert Nelson, master of the *Resolution*, who died there. The whole coast Button named New Wales, after his homeland. The name would show up on many maps for a long time thereafter.

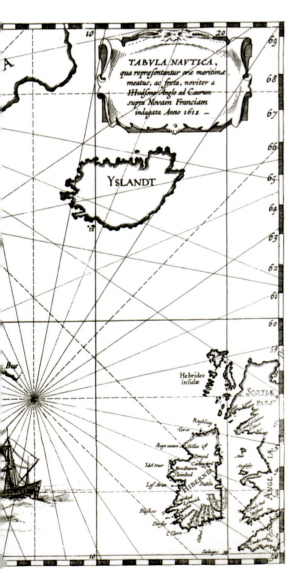

MAP 46.
Tabula Nautica, Hessel Gerritz's map of Henry Hudson's voyage. This is the 1612 edition. Starting with Hudson, the southern end of Hudson Bay was shown for a long time as two bays, with a fictional peninsula in between them. Even Thomas James, who explored the area in 1631, and after whom James Bay is named, showed it on his map as two bays (Map 57, page 44). Note the fictional islands of Frisland and Buss in the Atlantic, the latter said to have been discovered by one of Martin Frobisher's ships, *Emmanuel of Bridgewater*, a busse (a type of ship). Frobisher's "strait" is shown twice, once on the southeast coast of Greenland and once on the west side of Davis Strait; Davis had mistaken Frobisher's strait for a new inlet which he called Lumlie's Inlet.

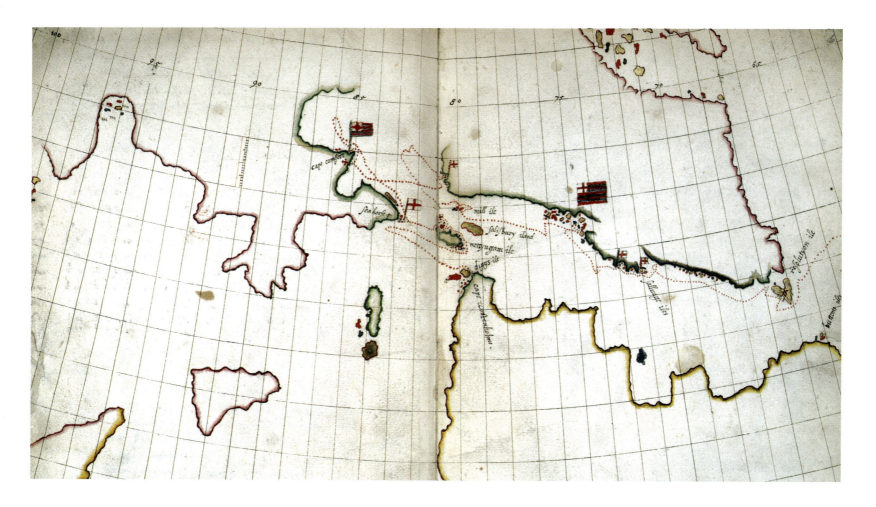

Many of Button's men died during the winter, but nevertheless the following spring he sailed northwards, until stopped at a channel later named Sir Thomas Roe's Welcome by Luke Foxe, which Button mistakenly took to be a bay. Having determined to his satisfaction that there was no passage leading out of Hudson Bay, at least in the right direction, in August 1613 Button abandoned his search and headed home.

None of Button's maps have survived, and his journal was impounded by the company when he arrived home. The first indication of his voyage was on a famous map, *The North Part of America,* by Henry Briggs, published in 1625 (MAP 48, above).

The following year the Northwest Company sent Button's cousin William Gibbons to continue the search through Hudson Strait, which they were convinced was the Northwest

Passage. Gibbons had been with Button in 1612–13. Gibbons got no farther than the Labrador coast, where ice forced him to spend ten weeks at a bay his crew called *Gibbons, His Hole.*

In 1615, the Northwest Company turned to William Baffin, perhaps the most proficient Arctic navigator of his day, adept at the mathematics of navigation. He had had previous experience in Greenland and Spitzbergen. He was always a pilot rather than a captain on these voyages. Under the command of Robert Bylot, one of the survivors of Hudson's voyage, Baffin sailed into Hudson Strait in Hudson's original ship *Discovery,* and he made one of the few surviving original charts of early Arctic exploration, shown here (MAP 49). Great attention was paid to measuring tides, which, it was thought, would indicate the direction of an opening at the western end of the Northwest Passage. But Baffin correctly concluded that Hudson Strait did not have a navigable western exit.

The next year, 1616, with the Northwest Company refusing to concede the non-existence of a passage, the search shifted northwards, and Bylot and Baffin were again sent in *Discovery* to probe for other openings westward. On this voyage, to today's Baffin Bay, they reached 77° 45′, a latitude that would stand as a "farthest north" for three and a half centuries, until 1852. Baffin mapped the whole coastline of the bay. One of the westward openings he mapped was *Sir James Lancaster's Sound,* named after one of the financial backers of the Northwest Company, but he did not recognize it for what it is, the true eastern entrance to the Northwest Passage. Given the prevailing mood of hysteria for a passage, the fact that Baffin's map did not show one consigned his map to oblivion. Chronicler Samuel Purchas wrote a marginal note in his account of the voyage: "This map of the author [Baffin], with the table of his journal and sayling, were somewhat troublesome and too costly to insert." Briggs's map (MAP 48) was used instead, which did not even show Baffin's northern explorations; but it did still suggest a possibility of a Northwest Passage. Reality had to conform to expectations!

So well was Baffin's work suppressed that by the beginning of the nineteenth-century searches for the Northwest Passage in 1818, many of his discoveries were doubted. One map published in 1818 showed "Baffin's Bay. According to the relation of W. Baffin in 1616 but not now believed." That year John Ross would finally vindicate Baffin by confirming his discoveries (see page 184).

Baffin himself continued to be convinced of the existence of a Northwest Passage, for in 1617 he went to the Pacific intending to search from the other direction. He never got anywhere near the Northwest Coast of America, however, and was killed in 1622 during an English siege of the Portuguese stronghold of Ormuz, in the

Gulf of Oman. He was attempting to find the range and height of the castle walls, using his mathematical skills to the last.

If a skilled navigator such as Baffin could not find a passage, would anyone be able to? English financiers had had enough, at least for a while. But in 1624 an effort was launched by a group of Danes. Up until this point, the Danes had been more interested in Greenland and Spitzbergen and the northeast, developing their whaling industry. But news of the exploits of the English navigators, and fear that they might very soon actually find a route to the riches of the Orient, prodded the Danish king into planning a voyage.

MAP 50.
A contemporary map of Robert Bylot and William Baffin's exploration of Baffin Bay, drawn in 1628 by Hessel Gerritz, cartographer to the Dutch East India Company. To the north is *Sir Thomas Smith's Sound,* today Smith Sound, where Greenland and Ellesmere Island approach each other. *Alderman Jones Sound* is shown, today Jones Sound, between Ellesmere Island and Devon Island, a nearly closed-end strait. Most important is the depiction of *Sir James Lancaster's Sound,* today Lancaster Sound, between Devon Island and Baffin Island, the true eastern entrance to the Northwest Passage. Baffin was the first European to locate this strait, and the first to show it on a map, but he did not recognize its significance. On 12 July 1616 Baffin simply noted in his journal: "On the 12th we were open of another sound lying in the latitude of 74° 20′, and we called it Sir James Lancaster's Sound. Here our hopes of a passage began to be less every day of another, for from this sound to the southward we had a wedge of ice between us and the shore, and but clear to the seaward."

MAP 52 (above).
Stretching the boundaries of the definition of a map is this map-illustration Jens Munk drew in his journal and reproduced as a woodcut, showing two scenes in one; he only had two ships. Here his men are hunting at the mouth of an unspecified river and, in the background, meeting with native peoples.

In 1629 Captain Luke Foxe, with the support of Henry Briggs and a new group of financiers, the London-based Company of Adventurers, petitioned the king for permission to send a ship to find the Northwest Passage. Charles I granted permission and lent the group a ship, the *Charles*. Hearing of this venture, a group of merchants in Bristol proposed to also send a ship. They were afraid that the London group would discover the Northwest Passage and then be granted a monopoly over trade through it, thus weakening their trading position.

King Charles also gave the Bristol group permission, and so, with no time to lose, they ap-

To lead this expedition he selected Jens Ericksen Munk, the most experienced officer in his navy. He had already sailed to Spitzbergen and Novaya Zemlya, so had some knowledge of Arctic conditions. But Munk and his men were hopelessly unprepared for the Canadian winter.

Munk sailed in 1619 with two ships and sixty-four men. When he arrived back in Denmark in late 1620, he had only one ship and two men. The rest had perished in the winter of 1619–20 on the western shore of Hudson Bay.

Munk took a long time to get to Hudson Bay; at one point he mistakenly sailed into Ungava Bay and couldn't get out for a while due to contrary winds. After a southwesterly traverse across Hudson Bay—the natural direction in which to head for India, his supposed destination—he ended up at the mouth of the Churchill River, where he was caught by the approach of winter. Despite having a good supply of medicines, no one knew how to use them, and by January 1620 his men started dying from scurvy. Munk's plan to continue his search for a passage the following spring had to be abandoned.

Munk's crude general map of his voyage (MAP 54) was nevertheless the first to show the whole of Hudson Bay. He also drew unusual illustrated maps which are half drawings, half maps.

MAP 51 (above).
Hudson Bay and Strait and the coast of Labrador are shown in this map by Dutch cartographer Hessel Gerritz. Drawn in 1628, it records only information from Hudson's and Baffin's voyages. It is part of a larger map including MAP 50 (previous page).

MAP 53 (below).
Munk's stylized map-illustration of his overwintering place at the mouth of the Churchill River, the first large-scale map of any part of Hudson Bay. Several times are shown in this composite. Wood is being cut for the winter, and one of Munk's men is being readied for burial, a victim of scurvy

MAP 54 (above).
Jens Munk's woodcut general map was published in 1624 to illustrate his account of his voyage. A little difficult to interpret, it is oriented with north towards the bottom left corner. Hudson Strait is now *Fretum Christiano*, after the Danish king, and Hudson Bay is shown as *Mare Christian*. Port Churchill is named *Munk[ene?]s Winterhaven*. Because Thomas Button's map was not published, this is the first published map of the west side of Hudson Bay.

pointed Captain Thomas James to command *Henrietta Maria*, named—since the London merchants had the king—after the queen. Justifiably concerned about mutiny, James, who had previous Arctic experience, selected only men who had none, thus making himself indispensable.

So sure were the backers of Foxe and James that the Northwest Passage would be discovered this time that both captains left England with letters from King Charles for the Emperor of Japan.

After crossing Hudson Bay to the western side, James explored southwards, looking for an opening. He passed and named Cape Henrietta

MAP 56 (below).
Luke Foxe's map, showing his track in 1631 around Hudson Bay and his attempts to sail to the northwest, where Foxe Channel and Foxe Basin are today named after him. Baffin's explorations are also shown. Foxe was from Yorkshire, hence his name *New Yorkshire* for what is today Manitoba.

Maria after his queen and his ship. With the weather beginning to be a problem, he decided he would "go to the bottom of Hudson Bay to see if [he] could find a way into the River of Canada [St. Lawrence]." In so doing he added *James his Baye* to the map, and it has been James Bay ever since. James ended up spending the winter on Charlton Island, temporarily sinking his ship to protect it from pounding by the surf and ice. The next year he tried to sail to the northwest, but was stopped by impenetrable ice. He returned to England in September 1632.

Luke Foxe, meanwhile, had sailed from England two days after James. He had first attempted to sail to the northwest and, in today's Foxe Channel, was stopped by the same ice. Foxe then sailed into Hudson Bay, meeting James at one point. Unlike James, however, Foxe did not overwinter, arriving back in England late in 1631.

After his voyage, Foxe concluded that if a passage existed it must be via *T[homas] Roe's Welcome*, at 65° N. Here on his map (below), where Briggs had *Ne ultra* (Go no farther) from Button's voyage, Foxe wrote *Ut ultra*—Go farther. Today it is Roes Welcome Sound, between Southampton Island and the mainland, leading, only with difficulty, back to Foxe Basin, and thus it is essentially a dead end.

MAP 55 (above).
"James his Baye" is marked on this enlarged inset map from Thomas James's manuscript map, the main part of which is shown overleaf (MAP 57). Charlton Island, where James wintered, is shown. James mapped his bay but left off the other fictitious one to the east that had been first shown on the Henry Hudson map (MAP 46, pages 38–39). James described his bay as "a shatttered, irregular thing with many shoal bays and guts . . . sprinkled with islands and sand-banks."

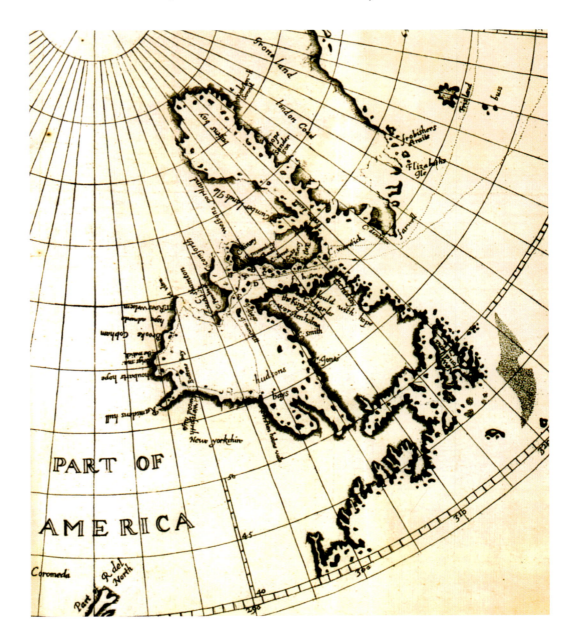

MAP 57 (*right*).

The manuscript version of Thomas James's map of his voyage. The engraved version was printed in 1633 in his book with the long but delightful title of *The Strange and Dangerous Voyage of Capitaine Thomas Iames, in his intended Discovery of the Northwest Passage into the South Sea Wherein The Miseries, Indured, Both Going, Wintering, Returning; & the Rarities observed, both Philosophicall and Mathematicall, are related in this Iournal of it.* The title of the map indicates the purpose of the voyage—for "the discoverye of a Passage into the South Sea." James was an accurate navigator, and many of his positions are correct. The name of James Bay derives from this map. Referring to the western end of Hudson Strait, James recognized that any Northwest Passage was likely to be often "most infinitely pestered with ice until August and in some years cannot be navigated even then." And he wrote, "There are certainly no commercial benefits to be obtained in any of the places I visited during this voyage." Yet in less than forty years the new Hudson's Bay Company would prove him wrong.

MAP 58 (*below*).

A summary map of English Arctic exploration from the 1698 *Atlas maritimus* of John Seller. Baffin's Bay is shown, based on the explorations of Baffin and Bylot in 1616, including *Sir James Lancaster's Sound,* the real eastern entrance to the Northwest Passage. *Forbisher Streight* (Frobisher Strait) is shown at the southern tip of Greenland, where it was misplaced for many years, the result of the inability to measure longitude accurately. Thomas Button's *Port Nelson* and *Hopes Checkt* are shown, and Seller has depicted Button's *New Wales* as *New North Wales* and *New South Wales.*

Early English Colonization Attempts

The first claim to Canada's lands by the English was the short-lived attempt in Newfoundland by Humfrey Gilbert in 1583 (see page 35).

By the beginning of the seventeenth century English, French, Portuguese, and Basque fishermen were making an annual voyage across the Atlantic to participate in the lucrative Newfoundland fishery. Some of these fishermen set up temporary "stages" on the shore to dry their fish, but there was no overwintering. In 1610, seeking first choice of beach space, the ability to start fishing earlier, and thus the opportunity to get their catch to market earlier, a group of Bristol merchants formed the Newfoundland Company to set up a "plantation." This, the first English colony in Newfoundland, was founded on the western shore of Conception Bay at Cupid's Cove (now Cupids) by its governor, John Guy, in 1610. Two years before, Guy had written "a Treatise to animate the English to plant there."

The settlers planted crops, and the root vegetables, at least, did well; the first winter was a relatively mild one; four men died, but this was considered a low mortality rate in those days. Compare this to the thirty-five that died at the first French settlement at Sainte Croix in 1604 (see page 50).

In 1612, late in the year (to avoid pirates who preyed on the fishing fleet during the summer), Guy led an exploratory expedition to find out more about the geography of Newfoundland, sailing "towards the pole Articke"—actually into Trinity Bay, the next major bay northwest of Conception Bay. It seems Guy hoped to find a passage into Placentia Bay, in fact cut off from Trinity Bay by the narrow isthmus that connects the Avalon Peninsula to the rest of Newfoundland, for his journal for 3 November says he "went Northwards towards a sound, which we weare in good hope woulde bring [us] to Placentia." They were likely at the northern end of Bull Arm, which is only about 8 km overland to Placentia Bay at Come By Chance. Guy probably thought he could reach Placentia Bay because of the indented coast-line and his likely familiarity with earlier maps that showed Newfoundland as an archipelago. The first English map to show Newfoundland as one island appears to have been that of Edward Wright, published in 1599 (Map 44, page 37).

In 1613, after a bad winter, Guy left for England and never returned. The Newfoundland Company appointed John Mason to succeed him. Mason, an experienced sea captain, was thought to be more able to deal with the piracy problem that plagued the early colonists.

More the explorer than John Guy, Mason spent the summers of 1616 and 1617 surveying the southern coastline of Newfoundland, perhaps reaching as far west as St. George's Bay. From this survey Mason drew a map of Newfoundland. It was the first map to be drawn as a result of actual exploration (Map 59, below).

In 1620 Mason published a promotional pamphlet entitled *Briefe Discourse of the New-found-land with the Situation, temperature, and commodities there-of inciting our Nation to goe*

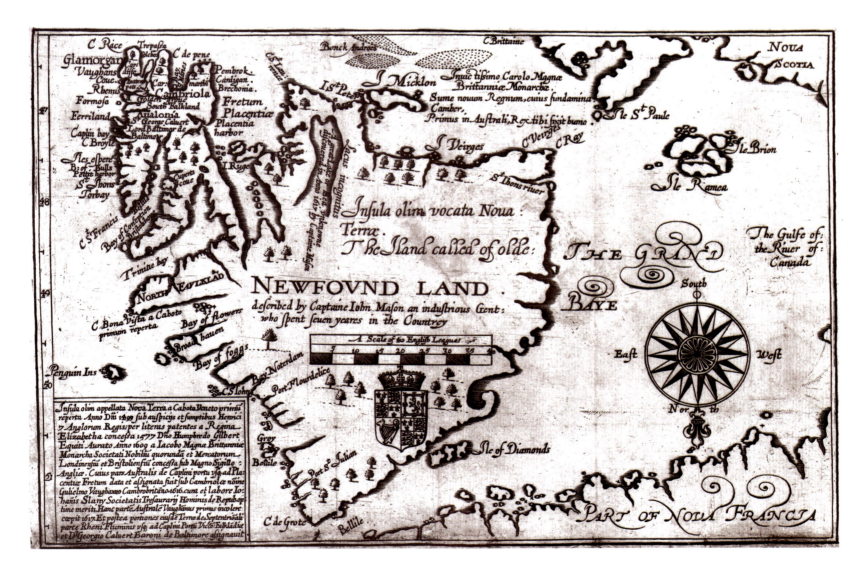

MAP 59.
John Mason's map of Newfoundland, from a book by William Vaughan published in 1625. Drawn principally from Mason's surveys in 1616 and 1617, this is the first map of Newfoundland drawn from exploration. South is at the top, and the Avalon Peninsula is at top left. Cupid's Cove is shown as *Cuperts Cove*. Nearby is *Bristol's Hope*. Baltimore's colony of Ferryland (*Ferriland*) is marked, as are Renews (*Rhenus*) and *Vaughan's Cove*. Both South and North Falkland are shown. Interestingly, *Placentia harbo[u]r*, labelled as such, also has the latin *Fretum Placentia*, Placentia *Strait*.

forward in that hopefull plantation begunne. It was published in Scotland and was designed to be read by, and attract investment from, a Scottish audience. In it, Mason expounded upon the virtues of Newfoundland, not least of which was that it was "the halfe of the way to Virginia," that other English colony founded in the Americas by this time.

John Mason gave up his governorship about 1621. The colony at Cupids lasted longer than that, but by 1630 it was down to just a few independent settlers subsisting by their own means.

Other attempts by the English to found colonies in Newfoundland included that of a group of merchants who formed the Bristol Society of Merchant Adventurers around 1616. This group included three "gentlemen proprietors": William Vaughan, a Welsh scholar; Sir Henry Cary, who would become Viscount Falkland and lord deputy of Ireland; and, perhaps most famously, Sir George Calvert, English secretary of state and later Baron Baltimore.

They received grants of land on the Avalon Peninsula from the company. The first Bristol settlement was at Harbour Grace in 1618, on land christened Bristol's Hope, again on the west side of Conception Bay. Its first (and only known) governor, one Robert Hayman, is remembered largely for his attempts to interest the king of England, Charles I, in colonization by proposing the founding of a new city in Newfoundland, to be named Carolinople in the king's honour.

William Vaughan, a man with some conscience for the well-being of tenant farmers in his native Wales, apparently became involved with colonization as a way of providing for the betterment of those less well off than himself. He received land at the southern tip of the Avalon Peninsula in 1616 and the following year sent his first settlers to the harbour at Aquafort. After one winter there, a newly appointed governor, Richard Whitbourne, moved the colony to a nearby harbour at Renews. But it was an

abortive effort; only six men were left to spend the winter there, and by the following year, 1619, they had all given up and headed home. Poor organization and poor support seem to have been the main causes for the colony's failure.

Whitbourne transferred his allegiances to Henry Cary, in 1621 Viscount Falkland. Cary acquired land both north of Trinity Bay, which he called North Falkland, and in a narrow strip westwards across the southern part of the Avalon Peninsula from Renews, dubbed South Falkland.

By 1622, Falkland was recruiting investors in Ireland for a Newfoundland colony, "Lords, Knightes & other gentlemen of that kingdome who shall freely and voluntarily offer themselves with their purses," as Whitbourne put it. In 1623 settlers were sent to South Falkland. Very little is known of the fortunes of this enterprise, but it evidently did not last very long.

Meanwhile, George Calvert had selected Ferryland, on the east coast of the Avalon Peninsula, as the site for his settlement, sending men

MAP 60.
William Alexander's map of Nova Scotia and the east coast of Canada, originally published in *An Encouragement to Colonies* in 1624. The map shown here was published in 1625. Alexander gave Nova Scotia its name—New Scotland. The name was originally applied to the region that is now the provinces of New Brunswick, Prince Edward Island, and Nova Scotia, plus part of Gaspé. Alexander also named some rivers after their counterparts in his homeland. The *Tweede* (Tweed) and the *Solway* separate New Scotland from New England, as their namesakes separate Scotland and England, information used many years later when the boundary between the United States and New Brunswick was being decided (see page 202). Note the name *Alexandria* for Alexander's land grant in Newfoundland, and also for the northern part of his *New Scotlande*.

there in 1621. The colony struggled, and in 1627, Calvert, now Lord Baltimore, came to Newfoundland to manage its affairs himself. Baltimore now considered his colony a place to "builde and sett and sowe," as he wrote. But even with his leadership, they found that the place they had built their settlement was too exposed, for "furious Windes and Icy Mountaynes doe play, and beate the greatest part of the year." Half the settlers became ill, and Baltimore, accustomed to a more genteel life, decided to move on. Leaving some of his flock to tough it out at Ferryland, he moved to the British colonies farther south.

By 1630 he was back in England to persuade the king to make him a further grant of land, but it was not until after his death in 1632 that his charter, that of Maryland, was finally approved. Today the American city of Baltimore, Maryland, immortalizes his name.

Baltimore's orphaned colony in Newfoundland lived on, though with a much reduced population. Most of the settlers found that to pursue fishing as their principal livelihood, they needed to be dispersed along the shore, a pattern that was to be followed thereafter. By 1660 only about 150 families remained in the scattered harbours of the Avalon Peninsula.

At about the same time that the English established their first colonies in Newfoundland, they also sent settlers to Nova Scotia. The man

promoting the colonization was the man who would give Nova Scotia its name, William Alexander, Earl of Stirling, a Scot who established himself as a favourite of both King James I and Charles I of England. (James I was also James IV of Scotland; in the period 1603–1707, kings and queens of England were also kings and queens of Scotland.)

Alexander was a poet, author, scholar, and courtier, a well-known literary figure in his time. He first obtained a grant of land in southwestern Newfoundland, which he called Alexandria, and it is marked as such on his map (MAP 60, below left). But Alexander had bigger ideas, and he persuaded King James that in order to get Scots to emigrate, he needed to create a new Scotland in the New World, in the same way as there was a New England and a New France. To do this, in 1621 Alexander was granted the entire region that is now Nova Scotia, New Brunswick, Prince Edward Island, and part of Gaspé. But this area had also been claimed by the French as Acadia, and in any case Alexander was unable to convince many of his countrymen to go to his new colony.

In 1622 he sent out a ship with colonists, but due to delays and the weather, they were left at St. John's, Newfoundland. The next year, a returning ship found only ten colonists still willing to continue. Although these potential colonists did land briefly in Nova Scotia, they did not stay.

In 1624 Alexander published a pamphlet entitled *An Encouragement to Colonies*, a promotional piece which included a map of his grant in Atlantic Canada, New Scotlande, which survives today as Nova Scotia. It is shown here (MAP 60).

Despite further efforts to recruit investors and the continuing support of a new king, Charles I, Alexander never got his project off the ground. In 1627 war broke out between England and France. Alexander's son, also named William, obtained a monopoly of trade in the St. Lawrence from the king, and it was under this commission that the Kirke family captured Québec and brought Champlain to England in 1629 (see page 55). Under this same commission Sir James Stewart established a colony at Baleine in Cape Breton. It lasted only two months before being attacked by the French.

The younger Alexander founded a colony at Port Royal in 1629 that he named Charlesfort. It was lost in 1632 as part of the treaty ending the war between England and France, the same treaty by which Champlain and the French were restored to Québec (see page 55). It would be 1711 before Nova Scotia was finally taken and held by the British (see page 73).

MAP 61.
Soon William Alexander's New Scotlande—in the Latin form Nova Scotia—was being incorporated into other maps. This map is from Robert Dudley's finely engraved sea atlas published in 1647, the first to use the new Mercator projection.

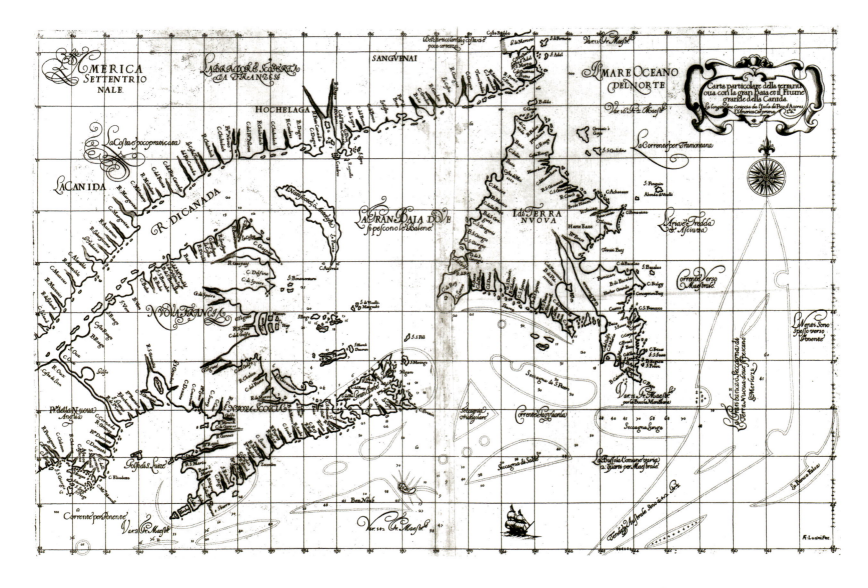

Map 62 (above).
Venetian mapmaker Vincenzo Coronelli's map of the Maritimes, 1695. This beautifully engraved map is as much a map of the fishing grounds of the Grand Banks as it is a map of the land. Numerous soundings are marked.

Map 63 (right).
This French map by Le Bocage-Boissaie was drawn in 1678 and would appear to be the first detailed map of the Grand Banks fishing grounds. Its many soundings were much copied.

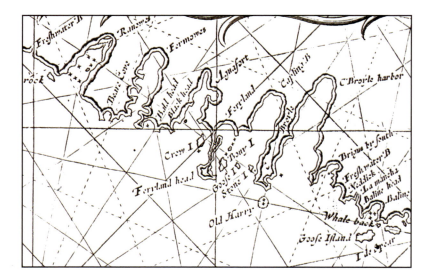

Map 64 (above).
Ferryland is shown on this map by Henry Southwood published in 1716 in his *English Pilot*, a navigational atlas.

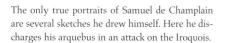

Samuel de Champlain—the Mapmaker Who Founded New France

The only true portraits of Samuel de Champlain are several sketches he drew himself. Here he discharges his arquebus in an attack on the Iroquois.

Samuel de Champlain was Canada's first major mapmaker. In 1612, he became the first to map the whole of eastern Canada, by linking Henry Hudson's map of northern Canada (MAP 46, pages 38–39) with his own. He also made extensive use of native reports gathered by himself and his men. As a result, by the time Champlain produced his last map in 1632, the country had been mapped west to Lake Superior.

Samuel de Champlain was born about 1570 at Brouge, in Saintonge Province, then an important seaport and centre of the salt industry on the west coast of France. In 1594 he fought side by side with an English contingent under Martin Frobisher (who was killed in the attack) to expel the Spanish from Brittany. By 1599 Champlain made his first crossing of the Atlantic as part of a trading voyage to the West Indies. After his return to France, he wrote and illustrated his first book, about this voyage.

At the turn of the sixteenth century, no European country had permanent colonies in North America. To bolster their claims to ownership against other European powers, the French encouraged permanent settlements by granting monopolies on the fishing and fur trade to private companies; the king had little money to spare for these activities, which were viewed as peripheral to waging wars and consolidating his position in France.

It was one of these monopolies which in 1603 gave Champlain the chance to sail to New France, in an expedition sent out by Aymar de Chaste under the command of François Pont-Gravé, destined to be Champlain's associate for nearly thirty years. They sailed from Honfleur, on the Seine below Paris, arriving at Tadoussac, halfway up the St. Lawrence at the mouth of the Saguenay River and then the centre of the fur trade, on 26 May. Here Champlain probably drew a draft of the first of many individual harbour charts he was to draw in the coming years.

While at Tadoussac, Champlain ventured some distance up the Saguenay to explore, and also gathered native information about the

course of this river for his maps. Some of this information was remarkably accurate. "These said savages from the north," he wrote, "say that they are in sight of a sea which is salt. I hold that, if this be so, it is some gulf of this our sea, which overflows in the north into the midst of the continent; and indeed it can be nothing else." This was the first knowledge Champlain had of Hudson Bay.

Champlain's ship carried in its hold a knocked-down smaller vessel , a pinnace. After its reassembly, on 18 June Champlain set off in it to sail farther up the St. Lawrence, also taking a longboat with him. He penetrated as far as Montréal before being stopped by the Lachine Rapids, which he named Sault Saint-Louis. Following in the footsteps of Jacques Cartier, he saw little Cartier had not previously documented; even less, in fact, for the native settlements of Stadaconé at Québec and Hochelaga at Montréal had completely disappeared by this time.

Again, however, he did learn more about the geography of the country from the natives. Champlain was told of the Ottawa River, leading north and then west, of the continuation of the St. Lawrence to Lake Ontario, of Niagara

Falls, Lake Erie, and even the Detroit River at the west end of Lake Erie. He received further information about brackish water, at the western ends of both Lake Ontario and Lake Erie. Misled by what may have been further references to Hudson Bay, Champlain stated that he believed Lake Erie was in fact the South Sea—the Pacific Ocean. In this, of course, he went too far.

Champlain returned to Tadoussac and sailed quickly back to France, arriving on 20 September 1603 at Le Havre , where they learned that their financial backer, de Chaste, had died.

But the expedition had been very profitable, and the next year the king of France reorganized the company, giving a monopoly on fur trading and colonization between 40° and 46° N, and granting control to Pierre du Gua, Sieur de Monts, who, like Champlain, was from Saintonge Province. In return, the company was to send out 100 settlers, including convicts.

In April 1604, three ships sailed from France; one was bound for Tadoussac, but two, one with de Monts and Champlain, the other with Pont-Gravé, sailed for Nova Scotia—Acadie—where, de Monts had been persuaded, a more favourable climate for colonization prevailed.

MAP 65.
The harbour at Tadoussac, at the mouth of the Saguenay River. This was Champlain's first port of call in Canada, though one he would subsequently pass through many times. The house of Pierre Chauvin, built in 1600, is shown. Chauvin had held the French king's fur trade and fishing monopoly before Aymar de Chaste, Champlain's sponsor. Champlain was in the habit of sprinkling his maps with letters and providing a key. These were partly, he wrote in his dedication to the king, to give "particular notice of the dangers into which one might run if they were not avoided." Here *B* is the harbour of Tadoussac; *D* is the place "where the savages encamp when they come to trade"; *G* is the Saguenay River; *M* is the anchorage where vessels wait for the wind and tide. Perhaps first drafted in 1603 when he arrived in Canada, this map was published in Champlain's book *Les Voyages du Sieur de Champlain* in 1613. Tadoussac is considered by many historians to be the oldest European occupation site in North America that has been continuously occupied.

Champlain reached Nova Scotia in early May. Then began a process of trying to find a suitable spot for a settlement. Champlain, in his first independent command, ranged along the coast and into the Bay of Fundy looking for harbours—and mapping them too. One that showed special promise was the Annapolis Basin, but for some reason this excellent site was not selected at this time. The harbour of Saint John, where the modern city now stands, was also inspected, but this site was not chosen either. Instead de Monts chose an island in the Sainte Croix River, which today is the boundary between Canada and the United States.

Probably chosen for defensive reasons, the island site was a disaster. It was unable to support the colony even in summer; as Champlain's map shows (MAP 66), gardens had to be planted on either side of the river. During the winter, which by all accounts seems to have been a particularly long and cold one, thirty-five of the seventy-nine men died of scurvy and other maladies. "Il y a six mois d'yuer en ce pays," wrote Champlain; "There are six months of winter in that country."

In September 1604, and again in June and July the following year, Champlain ranged south in the pinnace as far as Massachusetts, exploring and mapping harbours. But de Monts decided against any of these for his colony and moved instead to the Annapolis Basin, which Champlain had discovered the previous year. They dismantled most of the buildings they had erected on Isle de Sainte Croix and ferried them across the Bay of Fundy to their new site on the north side of the Annapolis Basin, which they named Port Royal. Champlain, of course, drew an excellent map (MAP 67, below).

Port Royal was much better than Sainte Croix, yet twelve more men died the following winter, 1605–06. After more explorations of the east coast south to Massachusetts in 1606 and 1607, Champlain sailed back to France, arriving in late September 1607.

Champlain drew a comprehensive map of the whole of southern Nova Scotia, the Bay of Fundy, and the American coast to Cape Cod (MAP 68, right). It was the first to take compass variation into account, and it set a new standard for maps of the east coast of Canada.

Champlain was not to visit Acadia again. A decision was made to abandon the Acadian enterprise and concentrate on the more likely profitable St. Lawrence, which would be nearer the source of furs. The French king was persuaded to renew de Monts' monopoly, and in the spring of 1608 three ships were sailed up the river to begin trading. Again a pinnace was assembled at Tadoussac, and Champlain sailed farther upriver to select a site for a fur-trading post. He soon found what he was looking for. At Québec, he wrote: "I looked for a place suitable for our settlement, but I could not find any more suitable or better situated than the point of Québec, so called by the natives, which was covered by nut trees. I at once employed a part of our work-

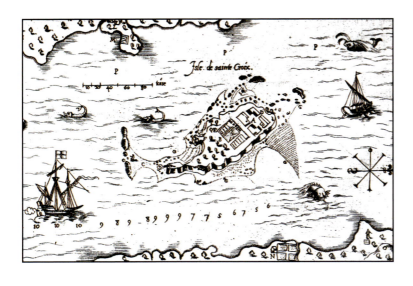

MAP 66 (*left*).
Champlain's map of *Isle de sainte Croix*, drawn during his first winter in North America, the hard winter of 1604–05. The island is now a part of the United States; the international boundary runs down this part of the Sainte Croix River. The Maine shore is at the top, that of New Brunswick at the bottom. *N* and *M* are gardens, as is *B* on the island. The buildings were at *A. G* is a "rocky shoal," and soundings in the river are shown.

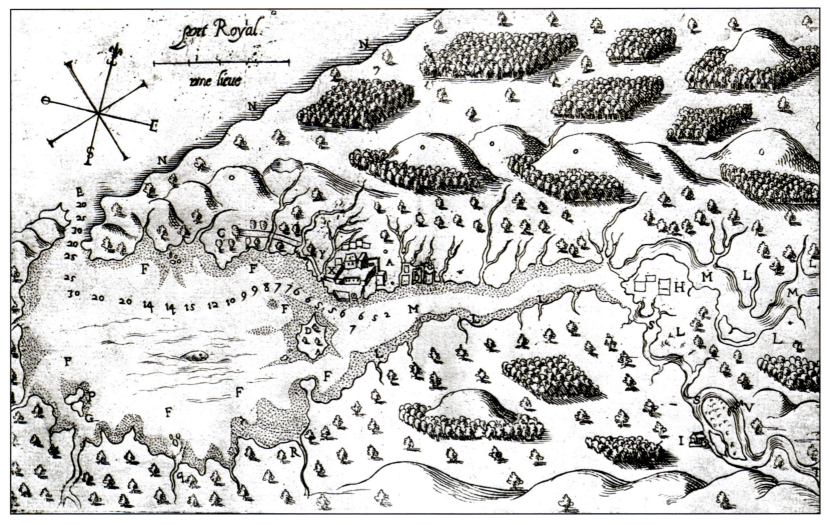

Map 68 (*above*).
Part of the summary map of Acadia and Norumbega (New England) drawn by Champlain in 1607. As far as is known, this is the only manuscript map of Champlain's that is still extant. *La baye françoise* was Champlain's name for the Bay of Fundy.

Map 69 (*right*).
Champlain's map of Saint John, New Brunswick, and the River St. John. The modern city covers most of the area shown on this map. Saint John Harbour is at centre. The famous reversing falls, which flow both ways depending on the state of the tide, are shown at *C*. Champlain noted the "waterfall between two lofty cliffs, where the water runs with such swiftness that if a piece of wood be thrown in, it sinks and is never seen again. But by waiting for high tide one can pass this place very easily."

Map 67 (*left*).
Champlain's map of the Annapolis Basin, Nova Scotia, his *Port Royal*. The settlement or *habitation* was at *A*, also shown in the photograph above and the picture plan at right. Gardens are at *B*, and *H* is a field for grains. *E* is the entrance to Port Royal, now called by the far less elegant name of Digby Gut; here the ferry from Saint John, New Brunswick, enters the basin to dock at Digby, on the extreme left of this map.

(*left*).
The 1939 reconstruction of the *habitation* on the site of Champlain's Port Royal.

(*right*).
Picture plan by Samuel de Champlain of the *habitation*, the buildings constructed at Port Royal. *D* is the house of Champlain and Pont-Gravé. *A* was for the workmen; *B* was a platform for cannon, *C* a storehouse, *E* a forge, *I* gardens, and *L* the harbour.

MAP 70 (*above*).

This map, published by Champlain in 1613, was drawn in 1612 after he had seen a copy of Henry Hudson's map of his discovery of Hudson Bay, which was published by Dutch cartographer Hessel Gerritz in 1612 (MAP 46, pages 38–39). Hudson had been trying to find a way to Cathay when he discovered the bay now named after him. Coupled with the piecemeal information he had already heard about a sea to the north, this map made perfect sense to Champlain, and he immediately set about combining the two to produce the first reasonably accurate map of eastern Canada in its entirety. Hudson is credited in the caption at the bottom of Hudson Bay, "the bay wher[e] Hudson did winte[r]." Champlain drew this map adjusted for local variation of the compass—to *son vray mondia,* the "true meridian" referred to in the title.

MAP 71 (*below*).
Part of a revision of MAP 70, probably published later in 1613, after Champlain's trip up the Ottawa River in May-June 1613. The cross he erected at Allumette Island is shown.

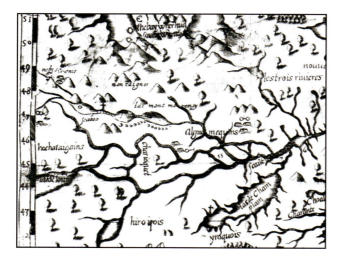

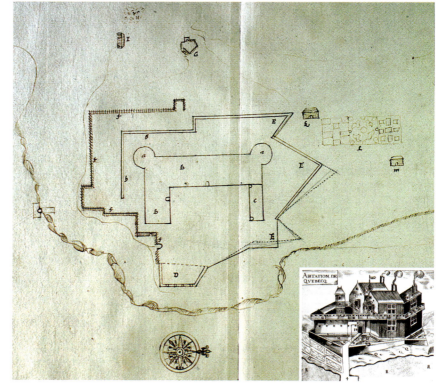

MAP 72.
Plan of the Québec *habitation,* constructed where the Lower Town of Québec now stands. It was drawn by French engineer and mapmaker Jean Bourdon. He arrived in Québec in August 1634, the year before Champlain's death. *a* are two towers; *b* is the armoury and workmen's quarters; *c* is Champlain's house; *D* is a platform for cannon. It is the earliest extant map only of Québec. Inset is a view, drawn by Champlain.

men in cutting them down to make a site for our settlement." It was 3 July 1608, the date which has generally been accepted as the birth of the city of Québec, the province of Québec, and for that matter Canada as a nation.

From that time on, Québec was also to be Champlain's home, for although he made many voyages back to France in the following years, he always came back to Québec, and would die there in 1635.

The first winter in Québec was terrible; only eight of Champlain's men survived, out of a total of twenty-four.

In June 1609 Champlain agreed to assist the Huron, Algonkin, and Montagnais in their ongoing war against the Iroquois, being promised assistance in exploration in return. Reinforcements came with Pont-Gravé on a ship from France that spring, and with the natives, Champlain ascended the Richelieu to a large lake, which he named after himself, Lake Champlain. There followed a pitched battle with the Iroquois in which the use of the arquebus, a firearm fired by a slow-burning match, made a critical difference in the balance of power, leading to an Iroquois defeat at Ticonderoga that would make them the bitter enemies of the French for many years.

It was during this excursion that Champlain first gave up the use of his heavy boat and started to use a native birchbark canoe. This canoe, with its tough flexibility and lightness for portaging, would provide Europeans with their most important transportation into the uncharted West for more than three centuries.

For many years Champlain returned to France each fall. Late in 1610, he married a young Hélène Boullé, after whom he would name Île Sainte-Hélène in Montréal, though she would not come to Canada until 1620, and then only for three years.

Gradually, by gathering information from natives, from some of his men, and from his own explorations, Champlain was able to build up a creditable view of the lands to the west.

In 1613, Champlain published a book, *Les Voyages du Sieur de Champlain*, in two volumes. Here for the first time the world saw his unfolding concepts of North American geography. All his individual harbour maps plus those of Québec and the Sault Saint-Louis, the Lachine Rapids at Montréal, were included in the book. There were two general maps. The first, *Carte geographique de la Nouvelle Franse* (MAP 75, page 54), was perhaps the first reasonably accurate map of the eastern coast and the St. Lawrence Valley. To the west, the map shows a recognizable Lake Ontario and part of Lake Huron, though no Lake Erie, which is surprising, considering he had written about it years before.

Also included in *Les Voyages* was a more hastily prepared smaller map, *Carte geographique de la Nouelle franse et son vray*

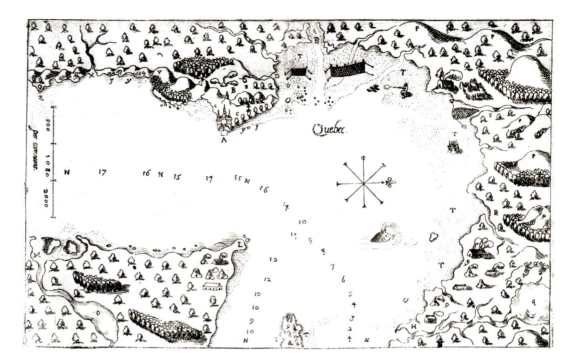

MAP 73 (*above*).
Champlain's map of the St. Lawrence at Québec. The *habitation* was built at a point (*A*) in the Lower Town approximately where the Church of Notre-Dame-des-Victoires now stands. *L* is Point Lévis; *I* (on island) is the Île d'Orléans; *H* is Montmorency Falls.

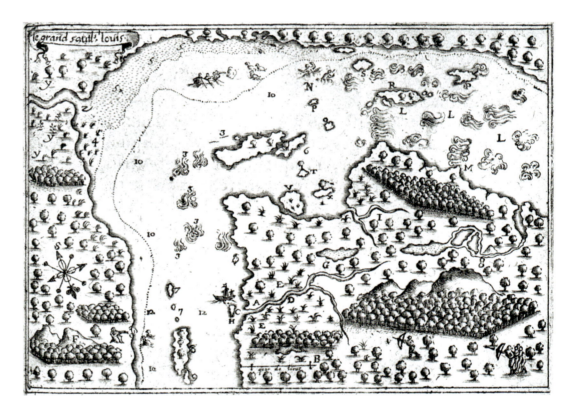

MAP 74.
Champlain's map of the St. Lawrence at Montréal. Le Grand Sault Saint-Louis (*L*) are the Lachine Rapids, long a barrier to further progress up the river. Referring to these rapids, Champlain wrote, "I assure you I never saw any torrent of water pour over with such force as this does, although it is not very high." *A* is a "little spot I had cleared," the site of Custom House Square in Montréal; *D* is the St. Pierre River, flowing from Lake St. Pierre. This lake also had an outlet upstream of the rapids. The lake and two streams follow the general route of the Lachine Canal, which opened in 1825. *H* is Mont Royal; *8* is Île Sainte-Hélène, named by Champlain after his wife. This seems to be the second map of Montréal, the first being the stylized Hochelaga drawn in 1556 (MAP 30, page 28).

mondia (MAP 70, left, top). While in Paris Champlain had seen a map by Hessel Gerritz that reproduced Henry Hudson's map of his voyage into the great bay (MAP 46, pages 38–39), and skilfully incorporated the information on this map into his own. The result was a massive extension northwards of the geographical area covered—and the immediate rendition of the first reasonably accurate map of the whole of eastern Canada.

Champlain revised this map shortly thereafter, incorporating the knowledge he had gained in 1613 from a foray up the Ottawa River. At that time Champlain only went as far north as Allumette Island (near Pembroke, Ontario), but he learned of the continuation of a route to the west via the Ottawa and Mattawa Rivers, Lake Nipissing and French River, to Georgian Bay, Lake Huron. MAP 71 (left, bottom) shows the revised map with this route marked.

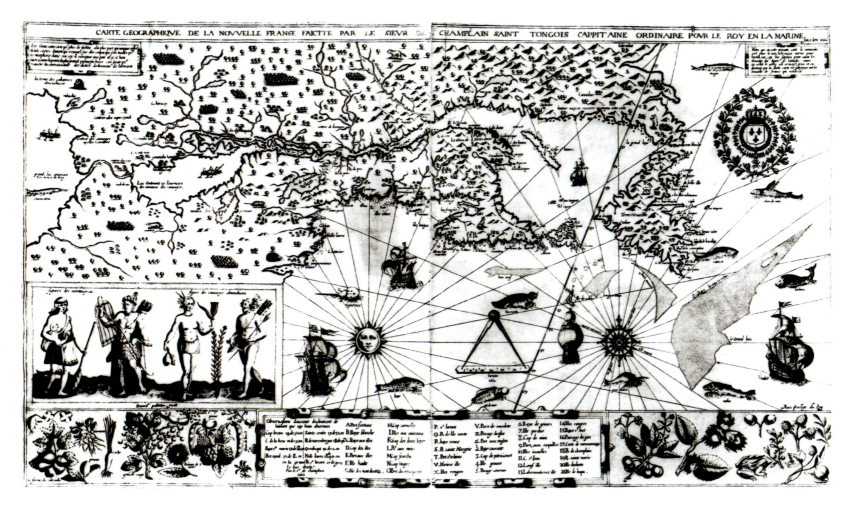

MAP 75.

The first of Champlain's published general maps of New France, drawn in 1612 and published in his *Voyages* of 1613. Unlike his other general map published at this time (MAP 70, page 52), this was drawn "according to the compass of France," that is, based on magnetic variation as measured in France at that time. Champlain wrote, "I have drawn the large map [this one] in this way, for the satisfaction of the majority of pilots and navigators to the coasts of New France, fearing lest, had I not made it so, they would have charged me with an error they would not have been able to explain." Montréal is first shown on this map. The map is laden with illustrations of the bounty of the country, all the better for Champlain to sell New France to his king.

In 1615, Champlain embarked on a second exploration, this time continuing much further west. He ascended the Ottawa and the Mattawa Rivers, arriving at Lake Nipissing where North Bay, Ontario, now stands, on 26 July. Continuing towards Lake Huron on the French River, he met Outaouais natives (from whom the name Ottawa is derived); at Champlain's request their chief drew a map with charcoal on a piece of bark. Reaching Georgian Bay, Champlain paddled south to the Midland Peninsula. He had heard about Lake Huron, which he called *La Mer Douce,* for so long; finally he had reached it.

The natives with Champlain were on the warpath, gathering men—now more than two hundred warriors—to fight against the Iroquois. Champlain went with them south to Lake Simcoe, then southeast along the route now followed by the Trent-Severn Waterway and into what is now New York State, at the eastern end of Lake Ontario. Here an unsuccessful battle was fought against Iroquois at their fort at Onondaga; Champlain was injured in the fracas. He lost face with the natives, for this battle proved that possession of firearms would not always win the day, and that the French were not invincible.

While recovering, Champlain spent the winter of 1615–16 with the Huron, gathering more geographical information about the Great Lakes, shown in the next map he drew (MAP 76).

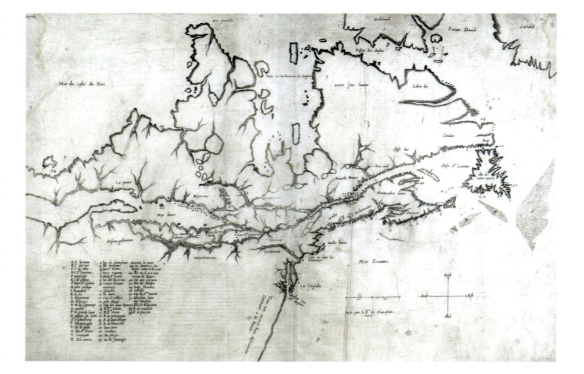

MAP 76.

Part of Champlain's 1616 map, perhaps printed in 1619. This was evidently a printer's proof of some kind, but the map was never published. This unique copy was found in an old atlas in a Paris antiquarian store in the 1950s. The whole extent of Lake Ontario, here called Lac St. Louis, is shown for the first time on this map, and it also shows the earliest representation of any part of Lake Huron: *Mer Douce* is Georgian Bay. The lake stretching westwards is also Lake Huron, with perhaps a suggestion of the native reports of other seas farther yet to the west—Lake Superior. The Ottawa-Mattawa river system link from Montréal to Lake Huron is also shown on this map for the first time, and reasonably accurately at that. This map shows Champlain's geographical knowledge of Canada in 1616, after his expedition of 1615– 16. Here 2 is Lake Champlain; 5 is Lachine Rapids; 7 is Lake Simcoe; 8 – 8 is Champlain's route up the Ottawa River. *Biferenis* is Huronia, and *Baye où ont hiverné les Anglois* (" Bay where the English winter") is Hudson Bay. The plate for this map appears to have been acquired by mapmaker Pierre du Val, who added information and used it for his own map (MAP 78, page 56).

MAP 77.
Champlain's final map, published in 1632. It shows all Champlain knew of Canadian geography up to about 1619. Here *Grand lac* is Lake Superior, which Champlain had heard about from Étienne Brûlé, one of his men who had penetrated farther west. *Lac St. Louis* is Lake Ontario, and *Mer douce* is Lake Huron; only what are perhaps suggestions of Lakes Erie and Michigan are present. The northern part of the continent is still derived from the information Champlain gained from Henry Hudson's map. *Nouvelle France*—New France—now covers the entire area north of the Great Lakes and the St. Lawrence, and also the area that is now Maine, New Brunswick, and Nova Scotia.

Shuttling now and then between Québec and France, Champlain for the remaining years of his life concentrated on building up the affairs of the company (ownership of which continued to change now and then). In Paris in early 1618 he addressed the chamber of commerce, trying to drum up support for the Canadian enterprise:

One may hope to find a short route to China by way of the River St. Lawrence; and . . . it is certain that we shall succeed in finding it without much difficulty; and the voyage could be made in six months; whence a notable profit may be gained such as the Portuguese and other nations derive, who go to the Indies.

As always, he got his backing, for Champlain was an excellent promoter.

"The Father of New France" encouraged the growth of the city of Québec that he had founded. But for most of the time that Champlain was in charge, the tenure of the French in Canada was far from certain. Thinking that conversion of natives was the best way to ensure survival, Champlain in 1615 had brought the Récollet missionaries to Canada, and in 1625 Jesuits arrived to assist. They would push yet more to the west and further map the unknown (see page 58).

In 1627 Cardinal Richelieu, the first minister of the king of France, created an organization called the Cent-Associés—the Hundred Associates—to promote French colonial and trade expansion overseas. Incorporated as La Compagnie de la Nouvelle France, it was granted vast monopolistic powers and planned to send out four thousand colonists in four years.

But such was not to be. Unknown to Champlain, England and France were at war, and the Scottish Kirke family was authorized to attack Québec. In three armed ships they blockaded the St. Lawrence in 1628, capturing or chasing off the ships of the Hundred Associates. Then they defeated a French relief fleet and demanded Québec's surrender.

Champlain refused to surrender, though the situation was desperate. Québec survived the winter of 1628–29, but with no relief ships from France, Champlain was forced to surrender his colony in the spring. He and many others were shipped to England, although later they were allowed to return to France. This was the first English capture of Québec.

The Treaty of Saint-Germain-en-Laye, signed on 29 March 1632, ended the war between England and France and provided for the return of Québec to the French. The French king, Louis XIII, agreed to pay a dowry for his sister Henrietta Maria; this had been promised when she married Charles I of England but had remained unpaid. Thus the French bought back Canada by paying a bad debt.

In 1632, during his enforced layover in France, Champlain published his last book, a large compendium of everything he had achieved to date. With it was printed a map (MAP 77, above), a beautifully engraved map which was a major summary of European knowledge of the north part of North America. Now *Mer douce* (Lake Huron) leads to *Grand lac*—Lake Superior. A very small Lake Erie is shown, and what is perhaps a suggestion of Lake Michigan projects southwards from the *Grand lac*. In thirty years Champlain had advanced geographical knowledge from the area adjacent to the coasts and the St. Lawrence to encompass a vast region west to Lake Superior.

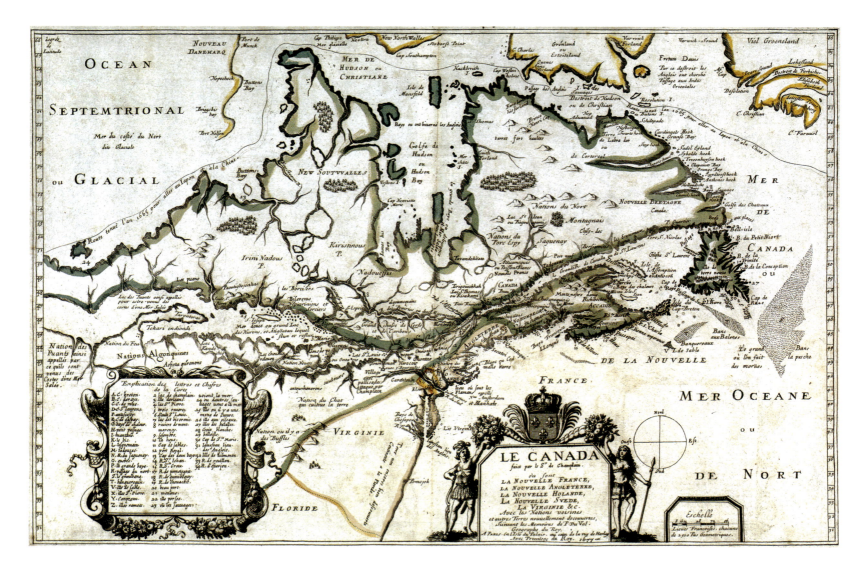

Map 78.

A map of New France (and New England, New Holland, and New Sweden too) by Pierre du Val, geographer to the French king. The map is based on Champlain's 1616 one (Map 76, page 54). This is a 1677 edition of a map originally produced by Du Val in 1653. At some point in the mid-seventeenth century Du Val acquired the finished plate of which Map 76 is a proof, and added geographical information to it. A "route taken in 1665 to go to Japan and China" is marked through Hudson Strait and into the *Ocean Septemtrional ou Glacial* ("Northern or Glacial Sea") beyond, shown in the region west of Hudson Bay. Champlain's suggestion of Lake Superior looks much like a strait. With two broad water channels leading westwards, it is hard to believe that this is *not* the way to Cathay. Note that *Accadie* is now marked in today's New Brunswick. Lake Ontario is shown (*Lac St. Louis*) and an *Erie Lac* is marked in what Champlain had shown as not much more than an unnamed widening of the river flowing into Lake Ontario.

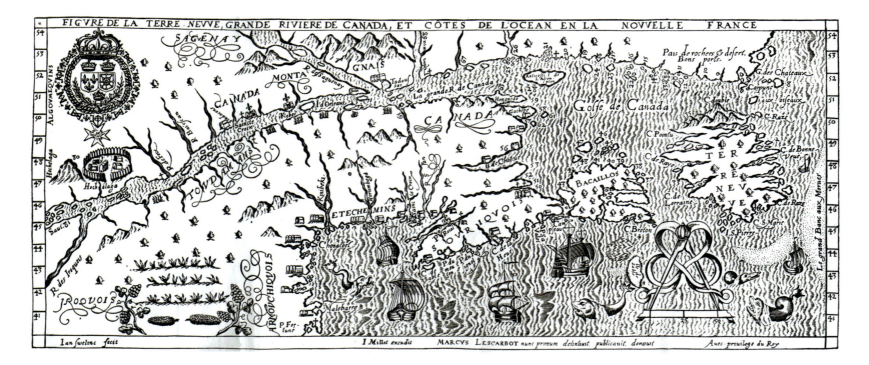

Map 79.

Marc Lescarbot's map of New France, published in 1609. Lescarbot, a Paris lawyer, had been with Champlain in Acadia, and on his return to France had prepared a book called *History of New France*. It covered not only Champlain's adventures to that date but also the previous efforts at exploration and colonization by Cartier and Roberval. This map was drawn to illustrate his book. It was soon to be superseded by Champlain's maps. Champlain and Lescarbot had a falling-out over the latter's book. Champlain felt Lescarbot was trying to pre-empt him; Champlain's style was more down-to-earth than Lescarbot's rather more flowery and literary style, which was nevertheless the style that was in vogue in seventeenth-century France.

The Founding of Montréal

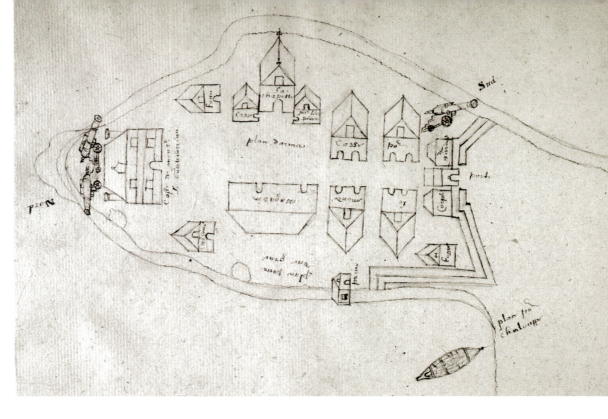

The site of Montréal had been occupied by native groups for a long time, and the map of the stockaded Huron village (MAP 30, page 28) visited by Jacques Cartier on the slopes of Mont Réal is, despite its likely inaccuracy, the first map of any part of the city.

The next map drawn of the site of Montréal was that of Samuel de Champlain in 1613 (MAP 74, page 53). It showed "a little spot" he had cleared, but there was no permanent settlement.

In 1640–41 a religious organization called the Société de Notre Dame de Montréal raised a large amount of money and obtained a grant of most of the island of Montréal with the purpose of founding a mission there for the conversion of natives to Catholicism. A party of some fifty devout colonists was recruited to take on the task. They were led by Paul de Chomedey, Sieur de Maisonneuve. The party arrived at Québec in late 1641 and, despite an upsurge in Iroquois attacks, pressed on to Montréal and founded their settlement on 17 May 1642 (some say it was 18 May) on the same spot Champlain had cleared, calling it Ville-Marie. They were lucky that the Iroquois were elsewhere at the time.

One of the colonists, Father Barthélemy Vimont, celebrated mass with the words "What you see is but a grain of mustard seed . . . I have no doubt that the seed will grow into a great tree, one day to achieve wonders." The location of Montréal was too advantageous and strategic for it to remain only a mission for long. Although an outpost of a colony hard-pressed by native attacks, Montréal soon became a centre for the fur trade, a function which was to continue into the nineteenth century.

MAP 80 (*above*).
Ville-Marie, founded by Maisonneuve in 1642. This little map was drawn by engineer and mapmaker Jean Bourdon five years later. The settlement was built on the St. Lawrence south of the Rivière St. Pierre, later the Lachine Canal. On the western (left) side is the governor's residence; to the north are the chapel and clergy's houses. At centre south is the king's store, and on the east side are smaller stores and the houses of the *habitants*. The site proved susceptible to flooding, and later development took place north of the Rivière St. Pierre. The original settlement site was rediscovered and is now preserved in the basement of the Pointe-à-Callière Museum.

MAP 81 (*below*).
A superb map of Montréal drawn in 1724 by French engineer Gaspard-Joseph Chaussegros de Léry.

Jesuits and the Fur Trade—French Exploration to 1700

Samuel de Champlain had thought that conversion of the natives was one way to assure permanency for his colony, and in 1615 he had been responsible for bringing from France a small group of Récollet friars. In 1625 these were replaced by Jesuits, who were more energetic proselytizers. They took up their mission to convert the Huron with zeal, becoming some of the earliest Europeans to push far inland from the St. Lawrence. These apparently fearless men believed that martyrdom was the way to heaven, and many achieved just that, undergoing horrible torture and death at the hands of the Iroquois, traditional foe of the Huron.

The Jesuits lived among the Huron, building missions in Huronia, the area east of Lake Huron and south of Georgian Bay. In 1634 they built St. Joseph mission at the tip of the Midland Peninsula, and others followed, notably the Ste. Marie mission, in 1639, near the mouth of the Wye River. Often referred to as "Sainte-Marie among the Hurons," this was an ambitious project, with a chapel, a hospital, residences, a mill, stables, and barns, around all of which was a log palisade with stone bastions. From this base, priests fanned out into the surrounding countryside to spread their message.

In 1634 Jean Nicollet de Belleborne, an agent of a French trading monopoly, Compagnie des Cent-Associés, voyaged to Lake Superior to establish trade with the Winnebago natives of that region. So sure was he that he would reach China that he took with him a splendid Chinese-style damask robe. He did not find China, but he doubtless impressed the Winnebagoes.

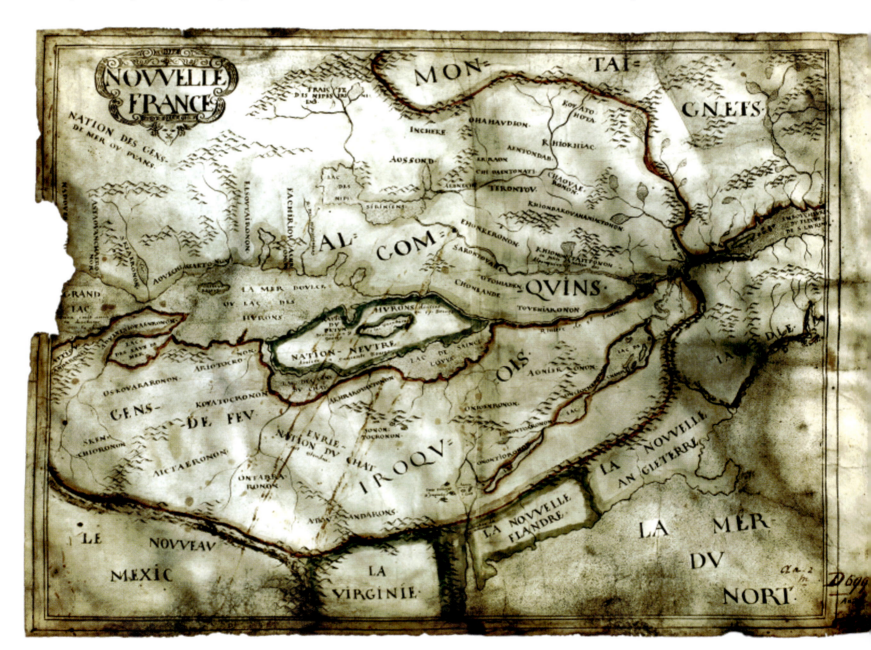

Map 82.

The Huron Map. This unique map, said to have been plundered from Québec in 1759, now resides in the United Kingdom Hydrographic Office, successor to the office of the Hydrographer of the British Royal Navy. Drawn about 1641, the map is unique because it is the only surviving map of Canada shown from the perspective of some of its original inhabitants. It is clearly a collaboration between a French mapmaker and Huron natives, for although many words are in French, others are Huron (Algonkin) words. The Huron pictured their world as an island, and on this map Huronia is shown as just that, right in the centre, surrounded by the Great Lakes and the Ottawa, Mattawa, and French Rivers. Many of the native groups are labelled with words ending in "onon," the Huron word for "people." South of Lakes Erie and Ontario (*Lac de Gens Du Chat* and *Lac de Sainct Louis,* respectively) is the land of the Huron's enemy the Iroquois, and beyond that, added by the French hand, the colonies of England and the Netherlands. *Grand Lac,* shown at left against the burned edge, is Lake Superior, which, says the caption, discharges itself towards China. The map is on an animal skin of some kind. The history of the map itself is far from certain. It seems that it was taken from the fallen Québec in 1759 by John Montressor, an officer in the British Royal Engineers who was known to have been in Québec at the time. The map was given to Joseph Frederick Wallet Des Barres (see page 120) sometime in the second half of the eighteenth century and Des Barres, being a naval officer, naturally lodged his maps with the Hydrographer of the Navy. The map is thought by many to be a uniquely Canadian treasure, and there were at one time calls for its repatriation to Canada, but it remains in Britain.

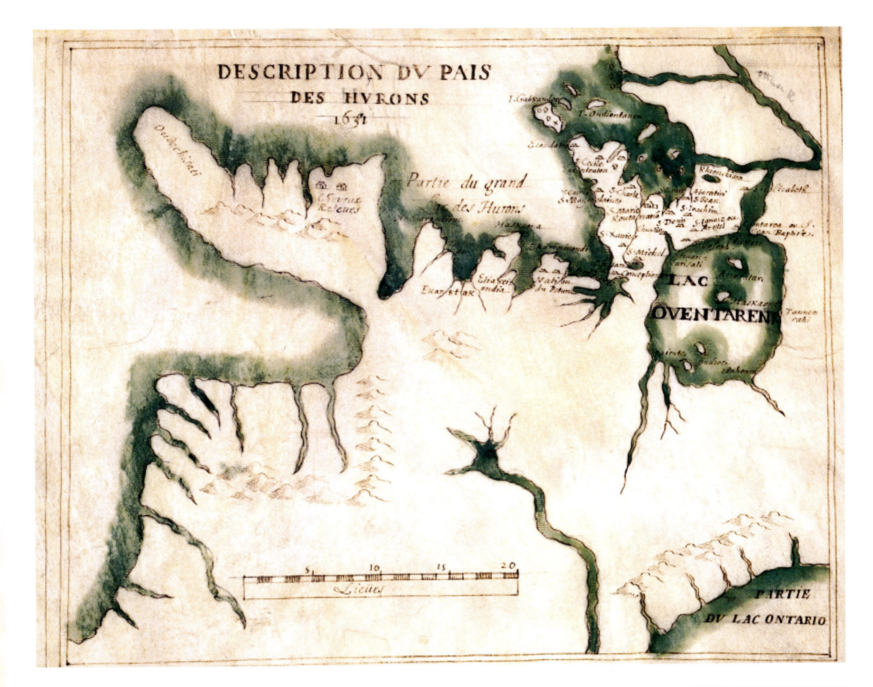

DESCRIPTION DV PAIS
DES HVRONS
1651

Partie du grand
... des Hurons

LAC
OUENTARENK

PARTIE
DV LAC ONTARIO

Lieues

Map 83 *(above)*.
This map was perhaps drawn by Jesuit Father Jean de Brébeuf sometime between 1639 and 1648. The lack of mission sites beyond those of the Huron area suggests a date no later than 1639, and the presence of Ste. Marie shows it could not have been drawn before that year. This may be a map known to have been drawn in 1639 by Brébeuf and other missionaries but subsequently lost. The change in date to 1651 may be due to small changes made at that date. The map was bequeathed to the Library of Congress by famous nineteenth-century map historian Henry Harrisse. Whatever its precise origin, the map is significant as the first to show the Jesuit missions in Huronia. *Lac Ouentaren* is Lake Simcoe; Lake Huron is to the north and west; Lake Ontario is in the southeast corner.

The Jesuits gained a first-hand knowledge of the geography of the Great Lakes, aided by native reports of what lay farther west and reports from the few more adventurous fur traders. "We are only at the entrance of a land which on the side of the west, as far as China, is full of Nations more populous than the Huron," wrote one Jesuit.

Several Jesuit maps have survived, and information from maps that did not was nevertheless incorporated into several contemporary maps made by other mapmakers.

Map 84.
Map of Huronia drawn by François Du Creux, a Jesuit missionary, and published in the *Relation* for 1660. The Jesuit *Relations* were a series of books published to inform the public about missionary works, attract donations, and encourage recruits. Together they form a rich source of contemporary information about early Canada. This map may well have been derived from Map 83, above. The area shown is that around today's Midland, Ontario. *S. Maria* is the Ste. Marie mission at the mouth of the Wye River; *Ins. Gahoedoë* is Christian Island; *Lacus Ouentaronius* is Lake Simcoe; and *Lacus Huronum* is Lake Huron. The names were written in Latin because the map was drawn to illustrate the text, which was in Latin.

MAP 85.
This map by Nicolas Sanson d'Abbeville, printed in 1656, was the first to show all five of the Great Lakes and the first to name Lake Superior and Lake Ontario. The westernmost lakes are shown open-ended. The northern boundary of New France is shown extending from the westernmost known point on the north shore of Lake Superior, illustrating the concept that if a region had been simply visited by French explorers, then it was *de facto* to be incorporated into the French domain.

During the 1630s, smallpox decimated the Huron population, and then, beginning in 1640, the Iroquois conducted a merciless campaign to rid themselves of their ancient enemies and fur trade competitors. In 1648 they attacked and destroyed the St. Joseph mission, and in 1649 the Jesuits reluctantly burned Ste. Marie to the ground—to prevent its desecration—and moved to St. Joseph Island in Georgian Bay, now called, appropriately enough, Christian Island. However, the island could not support the remaining Huron and over the winter, two-thirds of them died. The Huron dispersed, a once-proud nation annihilated.

But the Jesuits could only believe that this was part of God's grand design, for with the demise of the Huron, their priests would now have to voyage still farther west to work among more distant nations. And the French fur traders too now voyaged to the western Great Lakes in search of other native groups with whom to trade.

There had been some earlier attempts to penetrate farther west. In 1656 some thirty fur

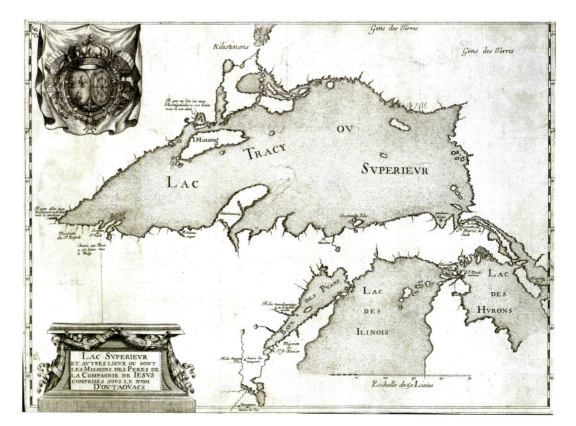

Jolliet was sent to join him the next year. Intendant Jean Talon had paid both men to search for a copper mine, but Peré, a merchant, was more interested in furs. They reached Lake Superior and did find copper, but the greater significance of Peré's journey was that he returned not via the established Ottawa-Mattawa Rivers route but by way of Lake Erie and Lake Ontario, thus opening up an alternative route to the west.

In 1672, a newly appointed governor general, Louis de Buade, Comte de Frontenac et de Palluau, recognizing the potential value of a year-round way into French territory, sent Louis Jolliet (Adrien's brother) to find the large river reported to flow to the south—the Mississippi. With Father Jacques Marquette, Jolliet went down the Mississippi to the Arkansas River, far enough to determine that the river had to empty into the Gulf of Mexico rather than the Pacific or Atlantic. René Robert Cavelier, Sieur de La Salle, was given permission to establish trading posts down the Mississippi, with the intention of claiming this area for France at little cost to the Crown. In 1682 La Salle reached the Gulf of Mexico.

During the period 1678–87 Daniel Greysolon, Sieur Du Lhut (also spelled Dulhut or Du Luth), a French officer, voyaged twice to the very end of Lake Superior and onwards to what is today the U.S. state of Minnesota and the headwaters of the Mississippi. In 1679 he was successful in negotiating a peace treaty between warring tribes that were interfering with French plans for extending the fur trade. He also sent three of his men westwards to discover the western ocean. They returned the following summer with salt given them by native guides, who said it came from a great lake twenty days' journey to the west. Du Lhut was convinced that this was the western ocean. It was more likely

MAP 86 (*far left*).
Map of the Great Lakes attributed to Jesuits Claude Dablon and Claude Allouez and published in the *Relation* for 1671. The outline of Lake Superior is notably accurate. In the *Relation* for 1666–67, Allouez's words were noted: "We entered Lake Superior, which will henceforth bear Monsieur de Tracy's name, in recognition of indebtedness to him on the part of the people of those regions." Alexandre de Prouville, Marquis de Tracy, had just defeated the Iroquois. Allouez was the most far-ranging of the Jesuits, second only perhaps to Jacques Marquette (explorer of the Mississippi). Dablon and Allouez journeyed around Lake Superior together in 1669, and they used the information they gathered to draw this map.

MAP 87 (*above left*).
The left-hand sheet of a rare map, engraved in 1657 from one drawn by the Jesuit Francesco Giuseppe Bressani, a superb achievement considering that Bressani had only one finger, the result of torture at the hands of the Iroquois. Only one copy of the complete map is known, held by the Bibliothèque nationale de France. The low survival rate of Bressani's map is probably because it was published separately from his book, in which he related the difficulties and horrors of missionary life in Canada. This half sheet is the only other copy of this map, and is held by the National Archives of Canada. Note the inset map of Huronia and the scene of native piety, which was included to balance a horrific scene on the other sheet depicting the martyrdom of Fathers Jean de Brébeuf and Gabriel Lalemant.

traders reached Lake Superior, among them Pierre Esprit Radisson and Médart Chouart de Groseilliers. These two would later defect to a group of English traders who in 1670 would become the Hudson's Bay Company (see page 77). To the English, they claimed to have reached Hudson Bay in 1660, and although this seems unlikely, they did know of the route to the bay from their native guides. It was this information with which they would interest the English after being rejected by the French.

Significantly, French traders by now had learned native methods of travel and survival and henceforth could be largely independent, excepting, of course, that they still needed natives to gather furs for them.

In 1665 Louis XIV's first minister, Jean-Baptiste Colbert, forbade *coureurs de bois* to leave the settled areas of the colony, fearing that France would overextend itself. But despite this edict, the economic imperative of the fur trade was too strong to resist. Beaver prices were fixed by ministerial decree, and this stimulated the westward drive for furs, as the normal laws of supply and demand did not come into play; the more furs that could be brought back, the more money could be made. The *Canadiens* in their attempts to bypass native middlemen pushed farther to the west, ever seeking new and abundant fur supplies.

The less-cautious Québec-based intendant, Jean Talon, began to send out exploration parties to the west and north of the St. Lawrence to look for minerals, to search for a route to the western ocean, and in the process to claim all the lands they passed through for France. But he also wanted to leapfrog over the Ottawa and establish trade with the Algonkin.

In 1668 Jean Peré was sent to look for copper "to the north of Lake Ontario," and Adrien

the Great Salt Lake in today's Utah. The American city of Duluth, at the western end of Lake Superior, is named after Du Lhut.

Du Lhut also established a trading post on Lake Nipigon to attempt to intercept natives going to Hudson Bay to trade with the new English Hudson's Bay Company. This is *Fort du Sr. Duluth* on Coronelli's map shown here (MAP 88).

In 1686, Jacques de Noyon found what would become a major route to the interior from Lake Superior, up the Pigeon River to Rainy Lake and Lake of the Woods. Until the loss of this route to the new United States in 1783, this would be the principal path to the interior, leading from the great fur trade interchange of Grand Portage on the shore of Lake Superior.

The fur trade grew. By 1680 there were perhaps 800 *coureurs de bois* (literally "wood runners") in the West. They changed the face of the land very little, with temporary campsites, few trading posts, and rivers for their transportation. But they changed the face of a nation by establishing French claims to a vast area.

Soon the whole area around the Great Lakes was regarded as French territory, at least by the French themselves. No doubt the natives would have disagreed.

The French also explored, and claimed, the regions north of the St. Lawrence and the Great Lakes, including Hudson Bay. Here they came into conflict with the English, who claimed the bay area by virtue of their prior exploration.

Ever since Champlain's incorporation of Henry Hudson's map into his own map of 1612–13 (MAP 70, page 52), the French had been aware of the great bay to the north. In 1647 the Jesuit Jean de Quen had ascended the Saguenay from Tadoussac as far as Lac Saint-Jean (a lake that from native information had appeared on maps a century earlier but had not been explorered by Europeans). But the first French expedition charged with getting to Hudson Bay was that of the Jesuit Charles Albanel, who had been with de Quen and also with Radisson and Groseilliers on their 1660 trading expedition to Lake Superior. In 1671, having heard of the English presence on Hudson Bay, Intendant Jean Talon dispatched Albanel with Paul Denis de Saint-Simon to reconnoitre the region and

MAP 88.

This superb map was engraved in 1685 and republished in 1688 by the Venetian Franciscan Vincenzo Coronelli, a prolific mapmaker who created over four hundred maps during his lifetime. "P.Coronelli" in the cartouche is Père (Father) Coronelli. He received manuscript maps from New France in his capacity as geographer to the French king. Drawn by Coronelli, this map was engraved and published in Paris by Jean Baptiste Nolin. Here the French claims in North America west of Montréal and south of Hudson Bay are laid out. Following the discoveries of Louis Jolliet, Marquette, and La Salle, the Mississippi is depicted flowing south from what is now Manitoba, with the Illinois River and the Ohio River flowing in from the east. In a matter of only forty years the French knowledge horizon has been pushed thousands of miles west and south. Du Lhut's post *Fort du Sr. Duluth* is shown beween Lake Superior and Hudson Bay.

Map 89 (*below*) and Map 90 (*right*).

Maps by master mapmaker Jean-Baptiste-Louis Franquelin, the king's hydrographer of New France during the period 1687 to 1697. Franquelin came to Canada in 1671 as a trader, but he had been given an art education when he was a boy in France, and obviously had a love of painting, for he started to draw and paint maps illustrated with animals and vegetation in the unexplored regions, of which, of course, there were many. His maps came to the attention of the governor; no wonder, for they were indeed beautiful. He was appointed to the position of hydrographer in 1687, beating out explorer of the Mississippi Louis Jolliet, who had much more field experience than Franquelin, but who drew maps that were crude by comparision. With this appointment, Franquelin became privy to much new geographical information. Almost all maps of New France passed through his office, and thus he was able to compile the most up-to-date maps available. These were then sent to the royal geographer, Vincenzo Coronelli (see Map 88, previous page) in France. Thus Coronelli and others tended to get the credit for work done by Franquelin. In fact, Franquelin never produced an engraved map.

Map 89 (*below*) was drawn in 1678. This beautifully illustrated pen-and-ink map shows the ignorance of the geography beyond the western end of Lake Superior at that time. The source of the new river discovered by Jolliet, the Mississippi, is shown near to an Arctic coast. The *Rivière des Outaouaks* is shown prominently; this is the Ottawa-Mattawa Rivers, the principal French pathway to the Great Lakes.

Map 90 (*right*) is a superb manuscript map drawn by Franquelin in 1688, the year after his appointment as the king's hydrographer was confirmed. A major addition as compared with his map of ten years before are the lakes to the west of Lake Superior. Geographical features often appeared on European maps some time before they were actually "discovered" by Europeans. This was due to native reports being incorporated into maps; what must surely be Lake Winnipeg on this map is an example of this. In 1688 no European was yet known to have reached the lake.

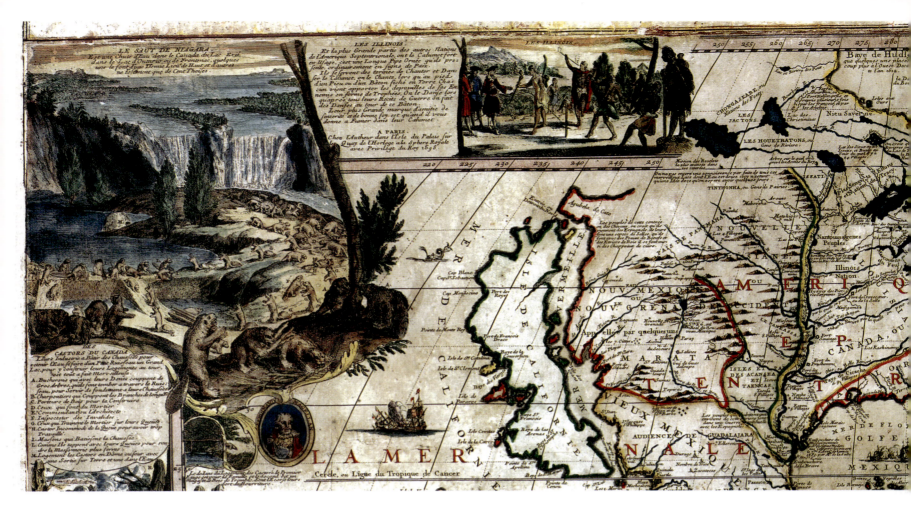

Map 91.

This stunning map (top part shown here) was drawn by Nicolas de Fer in 1698, and is known as the original "Beaver Map," from the illustration of beavers at work in the top left corner. In the background is a view of Niagara Falls derived from Louis Hennipin, one of the French explorers of the Mississippi. Clearly there was as yet no proper comprehension of what real beavers looked like in nature. The whole map covers all of North and South America. An interesting illustration of the Newfoundland cod fishery is at top right. On the map, North America is dominated by the recently discovered Mississippi, lakes west of the Great Lakes are shown from native information, and the West beyond that point is hidden conveniently behind another illustration.

determine if would be practicable to "make a storage from which ships might eventually be victualled if they should pass that way to discover the route between the two seas of the North and the South." It was not the fur trade but the lure of a Northwest Passage that motivated Talon.

Continuing north from the Saguenay and Lac Saint-Jean to Lac Mistassini, Albanel reached Hudson Bay, where he did see a ship flying an English flag, though he found the English post of Charles Fort abandoned. Nevertheless, Albanel claimed Hudson Bay for the king of France. In 1673 Albanel was again sent to the bay, but this time he was captured by the English and taken back to England. Some accounts say he was so exhausted that he asked to be taken with the English. He eventually returned to Québec via France.

Albanel had demonstrated the practicality of a route from New France to Hudson Bay. His route to the bay is shown on Alexis Hubert Jaillot's map of 1685 (Map 92, right).

Continuing concern about English activities on Hudson Bay led to the dispatch in 1679 of Louis Jolliet, now an explorer of some repute following his journey down the Mississippi in 1673–74. He was to assess the extent of English commerce with the native peoples. He followed essentially the same route as Albanel. Jolliet met Hudson's Bay Company traders; Governor Charles Bayly offered him "ten thousand frances down and a thousand livres a year" to join them,

but he declined. He returned to Québec convinced that Hudson Bay was the richest source of furs in the country and, presciently, that English control of the bay would make them masters of "all the trade of Canada."

In 1682, the Compagnie du Nord was formed by Canadian merchants to trade into Hudson Bay by sea, challenging the English for control of the bay. Pierre Esprit Radisson and Médart Chouart de Groseilliers, back with the French since leaving the Hudson's Bay Company in 1674, were sent by the Compagnie du Nord by sea to Hudson Bay.

In 1686 a force of ninety or a hundred men was sent to the bay under Pierre de Troyes, with instructions to seize the English forts. They ascended the Ottawa River, portaged to Lake Abitibi, and descended the Abitibi River to James Bay. There they overcame the surprised English at Moose Fort, Rupert House (Charles Fort), and Fort Albany, Hudson's Bay Company posts at the "bottom of the bay." Taking over the forts (and renaming the first and last Fort Monsoni and Fort Quichichouane), Troyes left one of his officers, Pierre Le Moyne d'Iberville, in charge, and sailed back to Québec in a captured English ship.

Ten years later, d'Iberville would be responsible for a series of raids along the Atlantic coast and the destruction of thirty-six English fishing settlements in Newfoundland (see Map 95, page 69).

D'Iberville was to have more involvement in the battle between the French and the Hudson's

Bay Company, notably in 1697, when, in command of the *Pélican*, he battled three English ships, two armed company ships and one, the *Hampshire*, a Royal Navy frigate, for control of York Fort, a trading post at the mouth of the Hayes River. Despite being outnumbered and outgunned, d'Iberville sank the *Hampshire* and captured one of the company ships.

The struggle for control of the rich fur region around Hudson Bay was to continue until 1713, when France surrendered all rights to the British by the Treaty of Utrecht. By this time the southern shores of Hudson Bay were well known to both the French and the British.

One other expedition of the late seventeenth century is of interest, that of Louis-Armand de Lom d'Arce, the third Baron La Hontan. The expedition, in 1688–89, is quite likely a fiction, but because of its impact on geographical perception, it is significant even if it never took place. Somewhere in today's Minnesota, La Hontan claimed to have reached a river flowing west, which he named the Long River. His account of this river was published in Europe in 1703 with a map (Map 94, page 68), and it was widely read and thus influential. Most explorers searching for a Western Sea after this time were aware of this work, and were searching for this river or one like it, notably the one often called the River of the West. Information from La Hontan's map was duly incorporated into the otherwise excellent general map of Guillaume de L'Isle (Map 93, page 68).

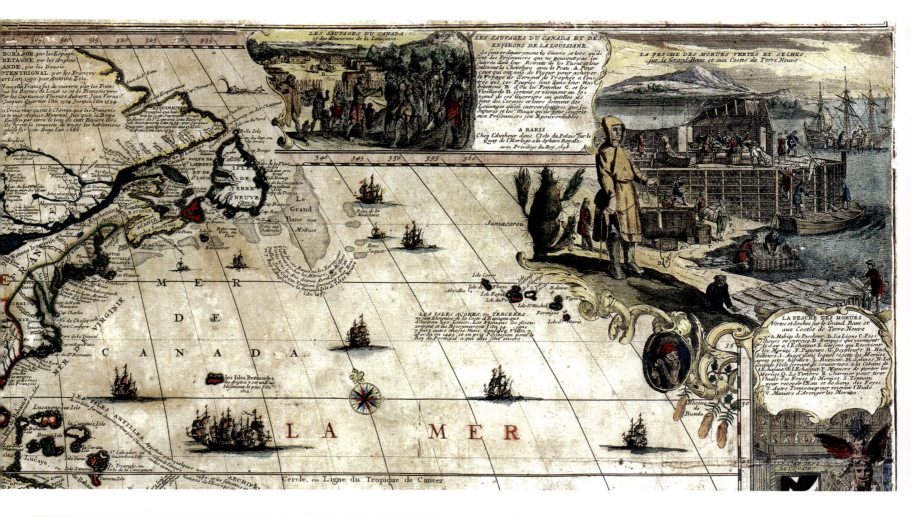

Map 92.
This map by Alexis Hubert Jaillot, published in 1685, shows the French approaches to Hudson Bay. Charles Albanel's route from Tadoussac is prominent. Here *Lac Timagaming* is Lac Mistassini, and *Anglois* on the east side of James Bay is Charles Fort, found empty by Albanel in 1671. The route which would be taken in 1686 by Pierre de Troyes from Montréal (shown) is also on this map: the Ottawa River (*Riviere des Outaouacs*), Lake Timiskaming (*Lac des Temiscaming*), Lake Abitibi (*Lac Tabitibis*), and the Abitibi River (*R. des Tabitibis*). English forts, marked *Anglois*, on the west side of James Bay are Moose Fort (bottom) and Fort Albany.

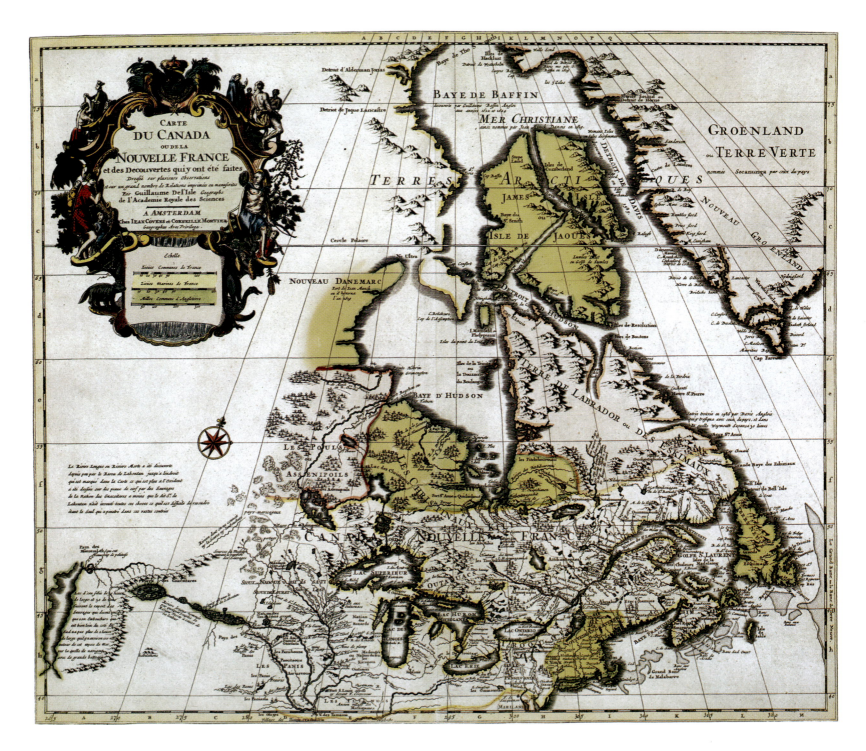

Map 93 (above).
The most accurate summary map of French Canada at the turn of the seventeenth century was this one by Guillaume de L'Isle.
Originally published in 1703, this 1730 version is exactly the same as the 1703 version geographically. Detroit is named on a map
for the first time. It was founded in 1701 by Antoine Laumet de Lamothe Cadillac (see page 72).

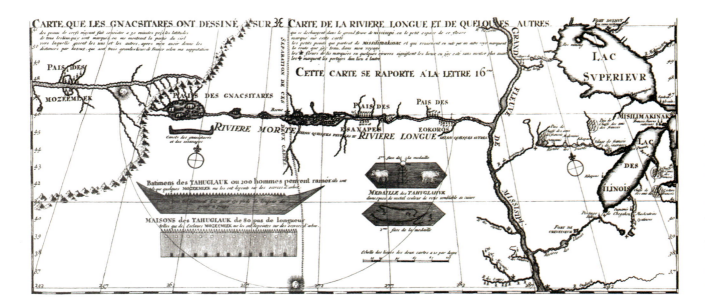

Map 94.
Baron La Hontan's influential
map of his "Long River," published in 1703. Illustrated with
native artifacts, it certainly made
it look as though La Hontan had
explored the river, especially as
it accompanied a two-volume
book. Yet most of the map was a
hoax, or at best a misconception.
It was, however, widely believed
at the time.

Map 95.

This rather beautiful combination of map and illustration refers to Pierre Le Moyne d'Iberville's depredations in Newfoundland in 1696 and 1697. Though seemingly in a battle, the French fleet is obscured by Newfoundland's omnipresent fog. In 1696, the French governor at Plaisance (Placentia), Jacques-François de Monbeton de Brouillan, with seven ships recently arrived from France, set off to raid English settlements; d'Iberville was to follow overland. But d'Iberville's men had no food, and by the time they had waited for a provision ship to arrive, Brouillon was back, without having succeeded in taking St. John's. The French fleet commander had had enough and left for France with six of the ships. Brouillon and d'Iberville then decided to carry out their plan anyway, despite now only having a single ship, which Brouillon used, again leaving d'Iberville to trek overland. On 28 November they were both at St. John's. A demand to the town to surrender was refused,

until an unfortunate English settler was scalped by some of the Abenaki natives who were with d'Iberville's force and sent to accompany another emissary demanding surrender. This so shocked the town's defenders that they immediately surrendered. The entire population of about four hundred was put on two captured ships and sent to England or France. Then the town was razed. Brouillon sailed back to Plaisance, but d'Iberville spent several months ransacking the countryside, capturing almost all the English settlements in Newfoundland, save Carbonear Island in Conception Bay. It was one of the less glorious episodes in the Anglo-French war of 1688–97. In May 1697, after d'Iberville had arrived back at Plaisance, five warships arrived, with one of d'Iberville's brothers, with instructions to launch another raid into Hudson Bay. One of the ships, and the one d'Iberville took command of, was the *Pélican* (see page 66).

The Defence of New France to 1713

Louis XIV's first minister, the exceptionally able Jean-Baptiste Colbert, had a grand design for France's colonies. They were to provide France with raw materials and markets for manufactured goods. New France was to supply furs, timber, and ship masts, and supply French Caribbean colonies with fish, wheat, and peas. In 1664 Colbert replaced the Compagnie des Cent-Associés with a new company, modelled on the Dutch and English East India Companies, called the Compagnie des Indes occidentales, with most of its capital provided by the Crown. Canada was now effectively a royal province governed by royal officials.

But first Colbert had to make the colony secure from the Iroquois, whose intermittent raiding was making trade very difficult. Four companies of regular troops were shipped to Québec, followed by eleven hundred men of the Carignan Salières regiment.

As part of a containment plan, forts were built at strategic points, such as at the confluence of the Richelieu River and the St. Lawrence. Here the Fort de Richelieu was constructed in 1665 at Sorel, just downstream from Montréal (MAP 96). Fort Saint-Louis was built the same year at a widening of the Richelieu River just east of Montréal, later Chambly (MAP 97).

In late 1666, the Carignan Salières regiment and four hundred militia under Alexandre de Prouville, Sieur de Tracy, pushed far into Mohawk territory and burned four villages with all their winter food supplies, but without en-

MAP 96 (above).
One of the first forts built by the Carignan Salières regiment was the Fort de Richelieu, constructed in 1665 to control the confluence of the Richelieu River, an Iroquois highway to New France, with the St. Lawrence. Built under the supervision of Captain Pierre de Saurel, the site of the fort (which no longer exists) is in the modern city of Sorel. This map was drawn by Intendant Jean Talon in 1665.

MAP 97 (right).
Fort Chambly, originally named Fort Saint-Louis, was built by Captain Jacques de Chambly of the Carignan Salières regiment in 1665 at a widening of the Richelieu River about 25 km east of Montréal. Destroyed by fire, it was rebuilt of stone in 1709–11 and was garrisoned until about 1850. This map was drawn in 1717 and shows the new stone fort. The photograph shows the fort as it is today, overlooking the Saint Louis Rapids on the Richelieu.

gaging the fleeing Mohawk. As a result, the following year the Five Nations of the Mohawks sued for peace.

The men of the Carignan Salières regiment were encouraged to remain in New France and some four hundred did so. Some officers accepted seigneuries along the Richelieu River, the men becoming their *censitaires* (see page 76). Thus a frontier settlement was established as a buffer against any future Iroquois attacks.

In 1672, Louis de Buade, Comte de Frontenac et de Palluau, became governor of New France. He was a more expansionist governor than those before him and, despite Colbert's edicts to the contrary, determined to promote the fur trade. To protect against Iroquois or English incursions, in 1673 he had a trading post named Fort Frontenac built at the eastern end of Lake Ontario, on the site of today's Kingston. Four hundred residents of Montréal were ordered to assist in its construction. The post proved expensive to run, however, and it was soon conceded as a seigneury to the Sieur de La Salle, who had to agree to garrison the fort at his own expense. For military purposes Fort Frontenac was poorly located, as it could easily be bypassed.

The Iroquois continued to menace New France for many years, encouraged by the English, who supplied them with muskets. In 1682 Iroquois attacked the Illinois, who had become allies of the French. What was supposed to be a punitive expedition by the French in 1684 ended with the Iroquois dictating peace terms. In 1687 a new governor, Jacques-René de Brisay de Denonville, led a punitive raid on the Seneca villages, and there were also attacks on the Onondaga. But this military action led to reprisals from the Iroquois; many French settlements were raided in 1689, including one particularly bloody attack at Lachine, where 1500 warriors fell on the settlements under cover of a hailstorm, killing twenty-four and capturing perhaps ninety more. As a result of the Lachine raid, and others, Fort Frontenac was abandoned and its garrison brought back to defend the colony.

In 1688, the French and the English were again at war with each other, and English incitement was involved in the Lachine and other raids. In 1689, privateers from Port Royal captured many New England fishing vessels, and Acadian natives, incited by the French, captured an English fort at Pemaquid, on what is now the coast of Maine, killing some two hundred settlers. In early 1690, Frontenac, returned to replace Denonville as governor, organized an attack on the English colonies. Canadiens and their native allies fell on Schenectady, and a massacre similar to that of Lachine ensued.

In May 1690, stepping up the attack on French colonies, a small New England fleet of seven ships under Sir William Phips appeared at Port Royal in Acadia and captured and plundered

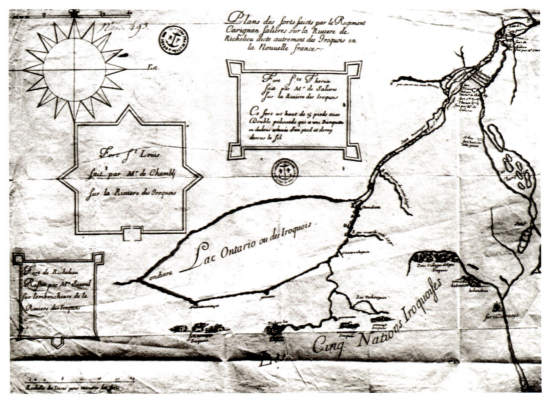

MAP 98 (*above*).
A map drawn about 1666 showing the forts built by the Carignan Salières regiment, with plans of some of the forts. The St. Lawrence flows from Lake Ontario, at centre, and the Richelieu River, shown at right, flows north from Lake Champlain to join the St. Lawrence at Sorel. These river valleys provided the Iroquois with easy attack routes to the French colonies around Québec; the forts were intended to control them.

MAP 99 (*below*).
The fort built by Frontenac in 1673 on the site of today's Kingston. Part of the west bastion—Bastion Saint-Michel—is all that survives today (*photo, right*), sitting on a traffic island guarding nothing but a fire hydrant. The shape of the bastion is still plainly visible. This is the top left bastion on the map.

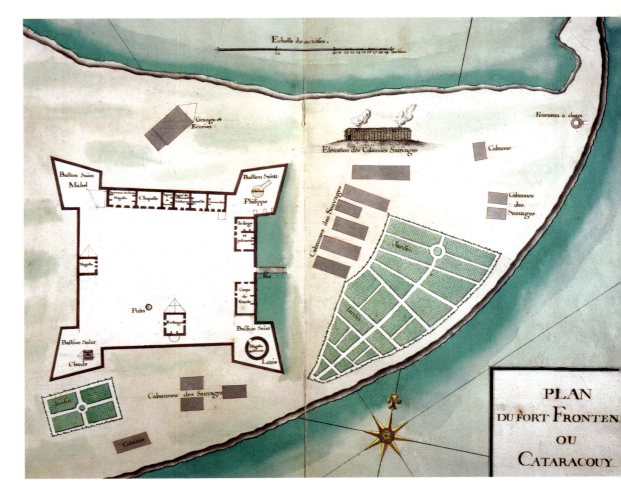

the French fort. English monarchs William and Mary later recognized the capture of Port Royal by uniting it with "The Province of the Massachusetts Bay," but no attempt was made to occupy Acadia.

Upon their return to Boston, the New Englanders found their venture to have been so profitable that a commercial company was founded to finance another attack, this time on Québec, which promised to yield such rich plunder as to give all the stockholders a good return on their investment.

An attack on Montréal was also planned, but due to bungled planning and the outbreak of smallpox, the raid was ineffective. Fifty *habitants* were killed in the area immediately south of Montréal, but more importantly from a military point of view, the French force sent to repel the raid was not kept at Montréal but was able to return to Québec in time to reinforce the town's garrison against Phips's attack.

Phips was again the commander of the fleet, which now had some thirty-four ships and 2,300 men. Sailing up the St. Lawrence, the fleet appeared before Québec on 16 October 1690, whereupon Phips demanded the surrender of the city. Frontenac's famous response was "I have no reply to make to your general other than from the mouths of my cannon and muskets." Phips disembarked more than 1,300 New England militiamen and prepared to do battle. But he soon found out what a superbly defensible site Québec was built upon. And the French force was well-positioned to defend Québec, with cannon lined up to cover all possible landing places. Phips's men were landed north of the Charles River but had to cross at low tide, the times of which, of course, were known to the French. After two days and nights of a mismanaged attack, harried by French fire and demoralized by an outbreak of smallpox, the New Englanders gave up. Phips realized that the season was getting late, decided he could not risk being trapped by ice in the St. Lawrence, and, on 25 October, sailed away.

In Québec's lower town a recently built chapel was named the church of Notre-Dame-de-la-Victoire.

In 1697, the war between France and England was ended by the Treaty of Ryswick, which called for the return of all captured territory; Port Royal was returned to the French, much angering the New England colonists, and most of the Hudson Bay posts, save three which remained in dispute, were returned to the English.

Not until 1701 were the Iroquois finally induced, with the help of 1,500 Troupes de la Marine sent from France, to accept a peace, known as the Great Peace of Montréal, agreeing to remain neutral in any wars between France and England.

And war there was. France and England again declared war in 1702, this time over the Spanish succession. Now there were two major French colonies in North America, for in 1701 Louis XIV ordered the creation of a new colony in the Mississippi Valley, to forestall the English—Louisiana.

In July 1701, Detroit was founded by Antoine Laumet de Lamothe Cadillac, who had sold the idea to Louis XIV to make France secure in its possession of the Great Lakes region.

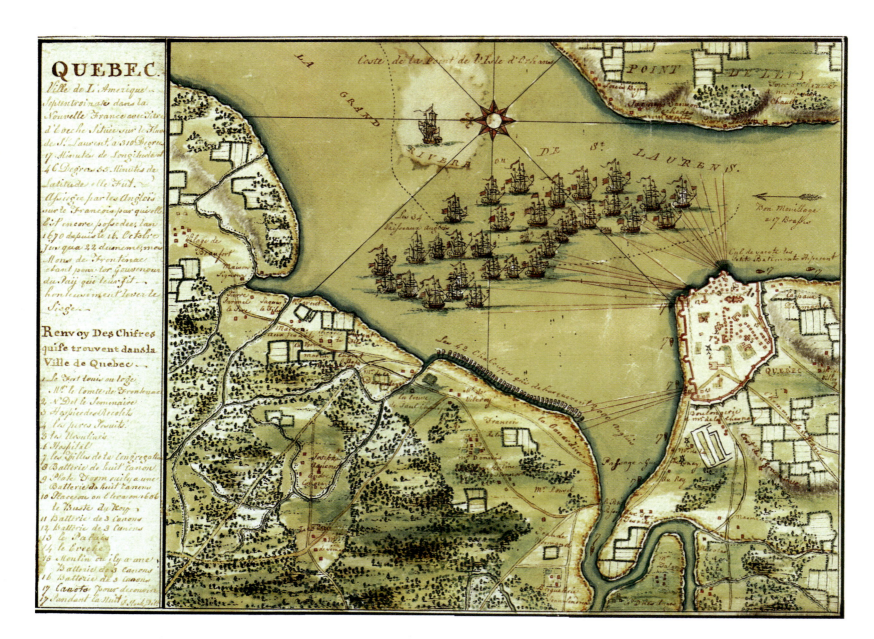

MAP 100.
This superb manuscript map by Nicolas de Fer, drawn about 1693, shows Sir William Phips's abortive four-day assault on Québec in 1690.
The wreckage of one of Phips's ships, *Elizabeth and Mary*, was found in 1994 off Baie Trinité, at the point the St. Lawrence begins to narrow.

Cadillac in fact simply wanted to monopolize the fur trade for his own profit.

A bloody raid by Canadiens and natives on the Massachusetts town of Deerfield in March 1704 led to a reprisal expedition against Acadia later that year, when a number of settlements were attacked.

In 1707 another attack of Port Royal was launched by a New England force. It failed, largely due to the efforts of a vigorous new governor, Daniel d'Auger de Subercase, who reputedly sold his silverware to finance repairs to the fort. But economic blockade was making life in French Acadia more tenous.

Promoted by an aggressive Scot named Samuel Vetch, who proposed nothing less than to drive both France and Spain from North America, plans were made by the English for a more massive attack on Acadia and New France, akin to the failed Phips expedition of 1690.

In October 1710 Port Royal was besieged by a combined British and New England fleet with 36 ships and 2,000 men, led by Francis Nicolson, a former governor of Virginia. Port Royal surrendered after only a week. Subercase, with only about 300 men, simply did not have the resources to combat such a large assault.

Port Royal was renamed Annapolis after the British Queen Anne, and Samuel Vetch became governor. This marked the turning point for the decline of the French Empire in America; from this time territory would only be lost. In a sense it was

MAP 101 (*above*).
This rather nicely drawn map shows the eastern seaboard of North America through English eyes in 1699. It is dedicated to the English king William, but the cartographer is unknown. It is one of the first maps to name the French *Baye Françoise* by its present name, the *Bay of Fundy*. In French territory, *Mont Royal* and *Quebeck* are shown. Lake Ontario is shown but not named; at its southwestern end, by the mouth of the Niagara River, stands *Fort Conty* (Fort Conti), the predecessor fort to Fort Niagara, established in 1679. The southern part of James Bay is depicted too far south. More emphasis is placed on the English colonies of Massachusetts and New York, which appear here as if extensively cultivated.

MAP 102 (*right*).
French plan of Fort du Port Royal in 1708, two years before it was taken by a British and New England force. The east bastion is truncated, having been eroded by the Annapolis River. A ravelin, or outpost bastion, faces downriver, towards the expected direction of attack. Compare this detail with the more general location map overleaf.

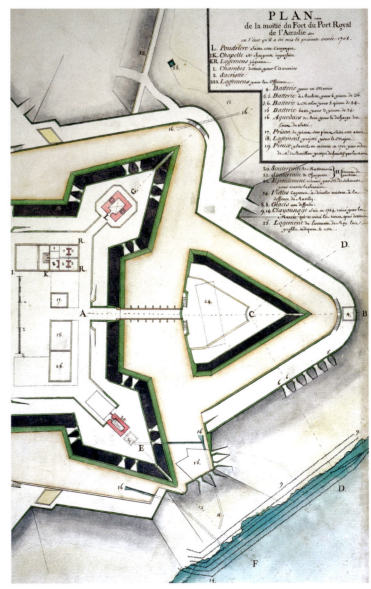

MAP 103.

Port Royal fort and the Annapolis River about 1708. The river is flowing from left to right; any attacking force would come towards the fort from the sea outlet towards the right on this map. There are several *marais* or marshlands noted along the river. These were tidal marshes diked and reclaimed by the Acadians. The tidal range in the Bay of Fundy is considerable, creating large exposed areas at low tide in some locations. Building the required dikes was likely as back-breaking as clearing land in the more conventional manner. However, the reclaimed land was very fertile. Today, at the narrow point of the river stands an electrical generating station that utilizes the tidal flows for power. The modern town of Annapolis Royal, so named by the British after they wrested the fort from the French in 1710, is located on the peninsula just to the west (left) of the fort. The fort acquired the name Fort Anne sometime in the 1720s, after an officer shortened "Annapolis" in his correspondence. At right is a view from Fort Anne today, looking downriver over the formidable earthworks. The forward ravelin is at the right.

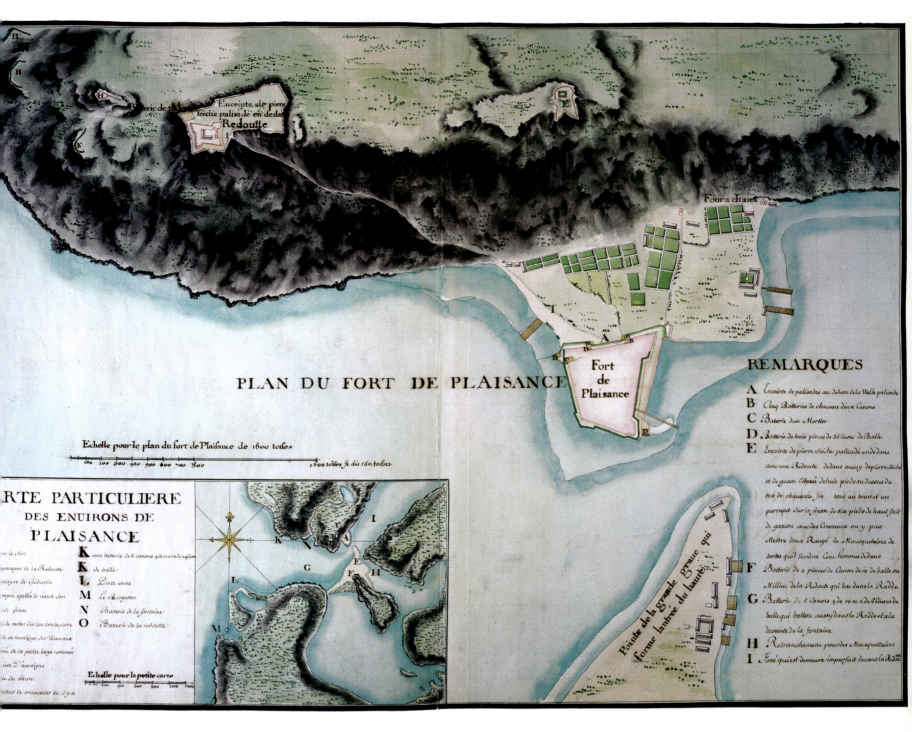

MAP 104.
The French fort at Plaisance, today's Placentia, Newfoundland. Plaisance became the first official French colony in Newfoundland after the island was claimed by France in 1624. It was a base from which to guard French fishing boats and, during the interminable wars with England, attack English settlements. The governor of Plaisance captured three forts in the British capital of St. John's in 1708. Plaisance remained the capital of French Newfoundland until the Treaty of Utrecht in 1713, when the whole island (except for some fishing rights) reverted to Britain. By royal order, the garrison and settlement were moved to L'Havre Anglais on Île Royale (Cape Breton Island) to found the new French fortified town of Louisbourg. Plaisance, renamed Placentia, was garrisoned by British troops until 1811.

perhaps inevitable, for the population of the British colonies in America had become so much larger than that of New France, that eventually it could be expected to overwhelm the French.

In 1711 came what was supposed to have been the grand finale, a combined overland and seaborne assault on Québec itself. A massive British fleet under Sir Hovenden Walker, with fifteen warships and forty transports carrying twelve thousand men, sailed from England, arriving in Boston in June, where it was joined by a New England contingent under Samuel Vetch. The fall of New France looked imminent.

But, in an amazing turn of events, Walker was to find out first-hand how difficult the St. Lawrence could be. On 2 September the fleet got lost in fog in the lower St. Lawrence near Anticosti Island. Walker was perhaps misled by a captured river pilot, but in any case exhibited appalling navigational skills, for the river is still 100 km wide at this point. During the night no less than eight ships were driven onto rocks, with the senseless loss of nearly a thousand lives. At this, Walker abandoned the idea of attacking Québec and sailed away.

The land force, commanded by Francis Nicholson, had progressed as far as the head of Lake Champlain when news was received of Walker's fate. Nicholson realized he would not succeed alone and also gave up.

Now the church of Notre-Dame-de-la-Victoire in Québec's lower town was renamed Notre-Dame-des-Victoires. It stands, with this name, to the present day.

When the Treaty of Utrecht was signed on 11 April 1713, France lost many of its claims in North America. Hudson Bay and Strait were "restored" to Britain, and a commission was established to define the boundary between French and British territory. Newfoundland was ceded to Britain, except that fishing rights were allowed to the French north of Cape Bonavista—the so-called French shore. An ambiguous "Nova Scotia or Acadia"—undefined at the time—was ceded to Britain, but the French were allowed to retain Cape Breton Island, which they called Île Royal. To guard the approaches to New France, here they would soon build the fortified town of Louisbourg (see page 88).

The Seigneurial System

Some British colonies used a pattern of squares to divide the land, but France devised a system for its colony in North America that would allow maximum access to first the rivers and later the few roads by ensuring a small frontage for everyone, with the bulk of the land in a thin strip at right angles to the line of communication.

Larger areas with this basic shape were granted to army officers, clergy, minor aristocrats, and others as seigneuries, with the caveat that they had to clear their grants and make them productive. A seigneur would subdivide his land and grant the portions to *censitaires,* who would clear and cultivate them, eventually paying the seigneur a small rent. But unlike the feudal system, duty to bear arms was still owed directly to the king rather than to the seigneur, and the seigneur also had duties and responsibilities to his *censitaires.*

Seigneuries were often granted to army officers, who would persuade their men to stay on as their *censitaires.* This way the frontier areas could be protected by a militia ready and trained to take up arms at a moment's notice to repel Iroquois or other threats to the colony. This is what happened in the Richelieu Valley in 1670–72, when men of the Carignan-Salières regiment were granted land (see page 71). Thus the infant colony of New France was populated and protected simultaneously.

After 1763, it was difficult for the British to adapt the pre-existing seigneurial system to their preferred system of landlords and tenants, and English settlers for that reason tended to migate to Québec's Eastern Townships, where land was not already subdivided.

Eventually the seigneurial system collapsed, largely due to lack of enforcement by the government, and in 1854 the system was abolished altogether. But to this day it has left an indelible mark on the political geography of much of Québec, where county and other boundaries still follow original seigneurial boundary lines.

MAP 105 (*right, top*).
The north shore of the St. Lawrence northeast of Québec was the first area to be subdivided into seigneuries, all fronting on the river. This map was drawn by Jean Bourdon in 1641. The Île d'Orléans is not yet settled.

MAP 106 (*right, centre*).
Part of a map of the St. Lawrence Valley in 1709, by Gédéon de Catalogne and Jean-Baptiste de Couagne, showing land divisions into seigneuries. Note the experiment in radial seigneuries near Quebec.

MAP 107 (*right, bottom*).
Drawn by Jean-Baptiste Larue in 1811, this map graphically depicts seigneurial land divisions on the north side of the St. Lawrence below Québec.

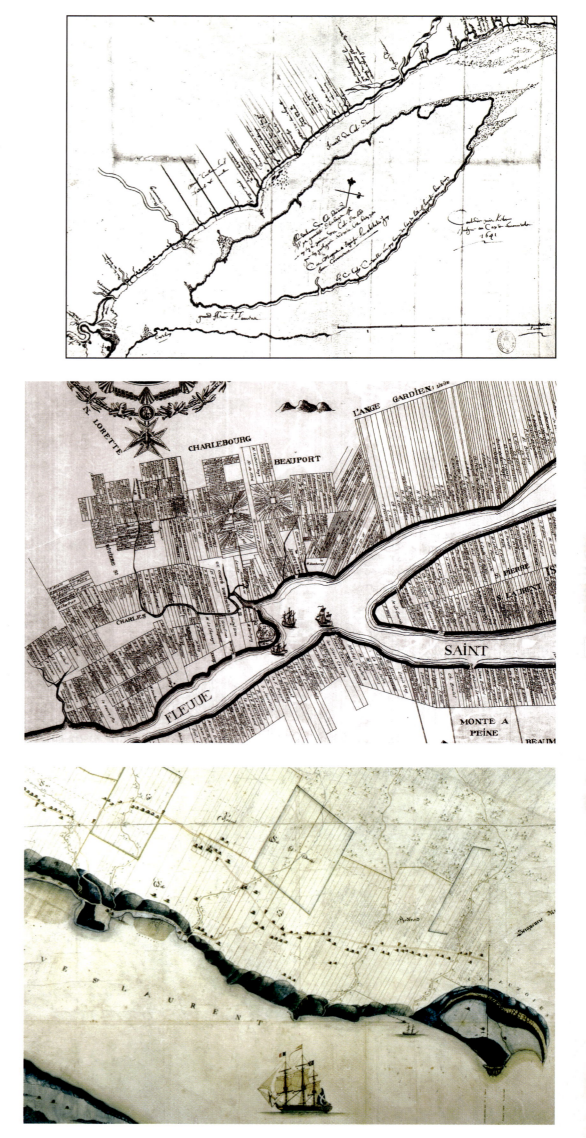

The Coming of the English—the Hudson's Bay Company

The French fur traders Pierre Esprit Radisson and Médart Chouart de Groseilliers, chafing at the trading restraints placed on them by the French government, arrived in London late in 1665 to seek new sponsorship. They could hardly have arrived at a worse time, for the bubonic plague was running amok, and when it abated much of London caught fire.

Nevertheless, their tale of easy riches was readily sold to willing investors, including the king of England, Charles II, and his cousin Prince Rupert. Radisson and Groseilliers claimed to have visited and gathered vast amounts of furs in Hudson Bay, although they probably had only heard of the bay from native sources. Still, investors were found, and a trial voyage to Hudson Bay was arranged, with two little ships, the *Eaglet* and the *Nonsuch*, sailing in June 1668.

MAP 108 (*right*).
Part of Jesuit François Du Creux's map of New France, *Tabula Novæ Franciæ*, drawn in 1660 and published in his book *Historiæ Canadensis* in Paris in 1664. Together with improved outlines of some of the Great Lakes, this map was the first to depict the river systems leading into James Bay. It showed the new route claimed to have been discovered in 1659 by Pierre Esprit Radisson and Médart Chouart de Groseilliers from Lake Nipigon to James Bay along the Albany River. They traded furs with the Cree—*Kilistones* on the map. Lake Nipigon is shown as *Lacus alimibeg8ecu*, just north of Lake Superior.

MAP 109 (*below*).
This wonderful map by John Thornton was drawn in 1673, just three years after the granting of a charter to the Hudson's Bay Company. It shows the extent of English knowledge of Hudson Bay at that time; information is particularly scanty on the western side of the bay. *Buttons bay*, visited by Thomas Button in 1612–13, is shown, as is *S[i]r Thomas Roe's welcome* (now Roes Welcome Sound), named for a financial backer by Luke Foxe in 1631.

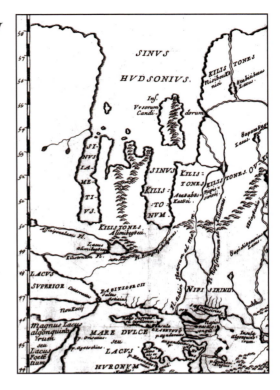

Map 110.

A map of Hudson Bay drawn in 1709 by Samuel Thornton. John Thornton and his son Samuel were among the foremost commercial mapmakers in England in the late seventeenth and early eighteenth century (see also MAP 109, previous page). This map would have been commissioned by the Hudson's Bay Company, probably for the use of captains of supply ships, although it may also have been a copy for reference in London. Other maps were produced for the Company by the Thorntons, but few have survived; this is the only one now in the Hudson's Bay Company Archives. The company posts are shown. Note *York Forte,* which had been built in 1684 where the Nelson River meets Hudson Bay. Churchill River is also shown, the mouth of which would later be the location for Prince of Wales Fort. The map shows in detail the area always known as the "bottom of the Bay," the most southerly part of James Bay. Thomas James's *Charlton* Island is shown, as are the *Ruperts, Moose,* and *Albany* Rivers, and *Albany Forte,* also built in 1684. Thornton also drew on this map a demarcation line between the territory of France and that of Britain, but it was his own concoction; it had no basis on the ground. In fact the whole region was disputed by the two countries until the Treaty of Utrecht in 1713, by which it was formally granted to Britain.

The *Eaglet* soon returned, having proved too small to brave Atlantic storms, but the *Nonsuch* continued on, overwintering successfully in James Bay and returning to England in October 1669 laden with furs.

The success of this first tentative venture led to the formation of a company to continue the trade. King Charles granted a charter to "The Governor and Adventurers of England tradeing into Hudson's Bay" and made Prince Rupert and his adventurer friends "Lordes and Proprietors" of all the land draining into the bay, a vast area of 3.9 million km² and including about 40 percent of the area of modern Canada. This was the region that for the next two hundred years would be known as Rupert's Land.

The first Bayside governor was a colourful character named Charles Bayly. An eccentric religious zealot who had once tried to convert the Pope to Protestantism, he had languished in the Tower of London for seven years before somehow being extricated and sent to Hudson Bay.

Once there, however, over a period of nine years he proved a competent manager, and it was he who set up the company's system of land-based forts instead of trading directly from ships. Forts on the edge of the bay were as far inland as the Company would get, with few exceptions, until a change of policy caused by competition with an upstart North West Company in the 1770s.

One of the exceptions was the journey of Henry Kelsey into the interior. He was selected because he had developed a reputation for being able to communicate well with the native population. One well-known Company letter notes that "Wee are informed hee is a very active Lad Delighting much in Indians Compa. being never better pleased then when hee is Travelling amongst them." Controversy surrounds his trek; his journal is unreliable and he drew no maps, so it is not known for certain how far west he got. An indisputable copy of his journal, partly in verse, was only found in the twentieth century (amongst the papers of Arthur Dobbs, a long-time company critic), which suggests that the company may not have received his journal at the time.

Kelsey was dispatched in 1690 not on exploration but to drum up business; he was to invite natives living in areas remote from the bay to bring their furs downriver to the Company's trading posts. He carried with him an array of trade goods with which to entice his potential customers. It seems he went about 1,000 km west of York Fort, perhaps to Cedar Lake, just west of Lake Winnipeg, and could have been the first European to see the Prairies. But Kelsey got little recognition for his trek, his journal was lost, and there was no follow-up.

Of serious concern to the Hudson's Bay Company was the constant hostility from French interests, and outright wars, in the period up to 1713. The battle with France in the late seventeenth century has already been described from the French side (page 66). The Treaty of Ryswick in 1697 provided for the return of forts seized by the Chevalier de Troyes and Pierre Le Moyne d'Iberville between 1686 and 1697. But France was at war with England again in 1702 and in the period to 1713 seized every Hudson's Bay Company fort save one, that at Albany. Only a masterful piece of lobbying by Company officials before the Treaty of Utrecht in 1713 managed to ensure that the restoration of all forts, and all of Rupert's Land, was included in the treaty. What might well have been a French empire on the bay resumed life as an English one.

A long-term governor, Sir Bibye Lake, who managed the Company's affairs from 1712 to 1743, was content to manage the Company conservatively and predictably to ensure dividends for shareholders; supplies were sent out, furs were sent back, and a healthy dividend paid. He saw no need for exploration or anything else that might cost money or disturb the flow of furs. This was the period in the Company's history when it famously "slept at the edge of a frozen sea." James Knight's abortive search for a Northwest Passage (Map 111, below) was the only exception to the status quo during Lake's tenure.

MAP 111.
This map, with north to the right, has been attributed to James Knight, Bayside governor, about 1719, with later additions. Knight was always searching for new resources that could be exploited and for perhaps a Northwest Passage which he felt must lie in the northwestern part of Hudson Bay. He collected information about the geography of the western and northwestern part of Hudson Bay from native sources. This map was his summary of this information, or may have been drawn later to illustrate his ideas. The map shows the many rivers flowing from the Canadian Shield into Hudson Bay and the Arctic Ocean; the whole coast is shown as a more or less straight line. Later additions to this map include Prince of Wales Fort, at the mouth of the Churchill River; the fort was named in August 1719. A later addition still is the drawing of the little ship with the notation "the furthest Capt Middelton went in the ship when on [a Voyage of?] Discovery." Christopher Middleton reached Repulse Bay in 1742 (see next page).

The British Attempt to Find the Northwest Passage in the Eighteenth Century

James Knight was appointed Bayside governor for the Hudson's Bay Company in 1713, just in time to receive York Fort from its French occupiers in 1714, under the terms of the Treaty of Utrecht. Over the next few years, Knight gathered information from natives about the geography of Hudson Bay, and he became enthused with the idea that there were sources of copper and gold to be located (the genesis of Samuel Hearne's later journey; see page 136) and that there was a Northwest Passage to a Western Sea to be found somewhere to the north of York Fort. A map he drew in 1719, or a later copy with his geographical ideas, is shown on page 79 (MAP 111).

In that year, Knight persuaded the Company to allow a voyage north to seek a passage. It was

a total disaster; Knight's two ships were wrecked on Marble Island, just to the south of Chesterfield Inlet, and Knight and all his men perished.

With Knight's demise, the Hudson's Bay Company was understandably cool about voyages of discovery for some time. It took considerable prodding before another voyage was approved. Arthur Dobbs, a wealthy Ulster landowner who had become convinced of the existence of a Northwest Passage and the commercial and imperial advantage its discovery would give Britain, wrote memoranda and lobbied both the Company and the British government. Even-

tually he managed to persuade Sir Charles Wager, First Lord of the Admiralty, to speak to King George II about it, and royal approval for another voyage was gained in 1740.

The following year, Christopher Middleton, an experienced Hudson's Bay Company captain whom Dobbs had interested in the concept of a a passage, was given a commission in the Royal Navy and put in charge of the expedition. Two ships were outfitted: *Furnace*, with Middleton, and *Discovery*, with another Company captain, William Moor. Britain was at war with Spain at this time, so manning the ships was

Map 112.
Map of Christopher Middleton's explorations in Hudson Bay, published by him in 1743. North is to the right. Cape Dobbs is shown at the entrance to *Wager River* (Wager Bay), which is (correctly) shown with two rivers at its western end. Middleton's discovery of Repulse Bay is correctly shown, with *C Hope* where the mainland trends west. Overall, it is an honest and reasonably accurate map.

MAP 113.
A manuscript copy of a map reputed to have been first drawn in 1742 for Arthur Dobbs on the floor of a London tavern by a disaffected *coureur de bois* named Joseph La France. The information about the West was gained by La France from native sources, who had told him of travels to a sea coast; this was probably Lake Winnipeg rather than the Pacific, but La France was unable to distinguish the two. Likely he was paid by Dobbs for information, and such information would have been more valuable if it showed Dobbs what he wanted to hear. The result was this rather interesting interpretation of the geography of western Canada. The map was engraved and published in a book by Dobbs in 1744.

difficult, and the Company was unenthusiastic, seeing the discovery of a passage as merely a ticket for interlopers to intrude on its monopoly. Nevertheless, the ships sailed in June 1741.

Middleton was not in Hudson Bay soon enough to attempt his northern probe in 1741, so he overwintered at Churchill, having had the foresight to insist on the Company's permission to do so. After a difficult winter, he sailed north on 1 July 1742.

Starting his search at 65° N, Middleton named Cape Dobbs and then, waiting for the ice to clear, found an inlet extending far westwards, which was explored in boats, and which he named Wager River (Bay). Middleton was convinced this was merely a bay and a river— he was right, of course—but controversy over this inlet was to follow. What was probably the sound of a waterfall was later asserted by Dobbs to be the tide. They passed a cape with land trending to the west, and Middleton wrote it gave him "great Joy and hopes of it's being the extream Part of America, on which Account I named it C. Hope." But, once again, he was to

be disappointed. It was a large bay, and despite careful examination of its shores, no passage could be found. A disillusioned Middleton named his discovery Repulse Bay.

Returning southwards, they found Rankin Inlet (named after John Rankin, one of Middleton's officers), but not Chesterfield Inlet, the entrance to which is screened by islands. William Moor recorded: "There is no Passage into the other Ocean between Churchill and the Latit^d 67° N."

Middleton investigated the source of the strong tides in Roes Welcome Sound, since they had been one of the reasons Dobbs felt a Northwest Passage must be near. He found they were coming from Frozen Strait, at the northern tip of Southampton Island.

Middleton arrived back in Britain in October 1742, not to a hero's welcome but to a diatribe from Dobbs, who, after first agreeing with Middleton's conclusions, seized on the fact that Wager Bay had not been explored to its western extremity to insist that this was in fact the Northwest Passage. Dobbs convinced some of Middleton's men, including Moor, that Middleton had

falsified his log and maps, and Middleton's clerk, John Wigate, later produced a rival map to Middleton's showing a possible passage through Wager "Strait" (MAP 115, overleaf).

Dobbs's continuing enthusiasm is hard to fathom, but he did gain hope from the map of Joseph La France (MAP 113, above) and the bogus account of a voyage through a passage from the so-called de Fonte letter (MAP 114, overleaf).

A petition to Parliament presented on Dobbs's behalf resulted in an Act of Parliament in May 1745 authorizing a reward of £10,000 for the finder of a Northwest Passage. In this way the government could be seen to lend support but not actually have to pay up unless the passage was found.

Amazingly, the tenacious Dobbs managed to find enough subscribers to a private fund to finance another voyage. One of the principal subscribers was the Earl of Chesterfield, who would subsequently be rewarded with his name on another inlet leading west from Hudson Bay.

Two ships were acquired; William Moor, who had been with Middleton, was captain of

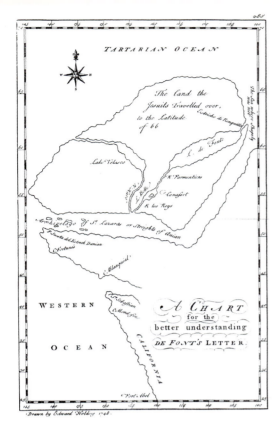

MAP 114 (above).
This map was published by T. S. Drage, the clerk of the *California*, in 1749. It was the result of an elaborate hoax, but this was not known at the time. The story of a Spanish admiral named Bartholemew de Fonte, who was said to have sailed from the Northwest Coast of America through a strait he discovered leading to Hudson Bay, was first published in 1708 in a short-lived magazine called *Memoirs for the Curious*. De Fonte's voyage was attributed to 1640, and the rediscovery of the story in the mid-eighteenth century was seized upon by Dobbs and others to demonstrate that a Northwest Passage really did exist. The geography of the de Fonte voyage found its way into some maps of the period, notably those of French geographers Joseph-Nicolas de L'Isle (MAP 184, page 133), Philippe Buache, and Robert de Vaugondy (MAP 183, page 132).

the *Dobbs Galley*, and Francis Smith, another Bay captain, master of the *California*, the name reflecting where they surely would end up. The ships sailed in May 1746, wintered near the Nelson River on the west side of Hudson Bay, and the following year sailed north, finding, of course, no passage. Explorations in ships' boats did yield one discovery, however, an inlet Smith named Bowden's Inlet but which became known as Chesterfield Inlet, the name given to it by Henry Ellis, Dobbs's agent with the expedition. On their return to Britain, Chesterfield Inlet was to assume greater significance than it had had on the voyage when Dobbs, by now grasping at straits like straws, fell upon this inlet as his missing Northwest Passage.

Wager Bay was explored farther west than Middleton had gone, and, as Henry Ellis wrote, they "had the Mortification to see clearly that our hitherto imagined Strait ended in two small unnavigable rivers."

Moor and Smith returned to Britain in October 1747. Dobbs turned his attention to discrediting the Hudson's Bay Company for not exploring inland, as well as not searching diligently enough for a Northwest Passage, but these allegations were in turn discredited by a parliamentary inquiry into the Company's monopoly in 1749. A bizarre map was prepared for submission to this inquiry to accompany the Company's evidence (MAP 116, right).

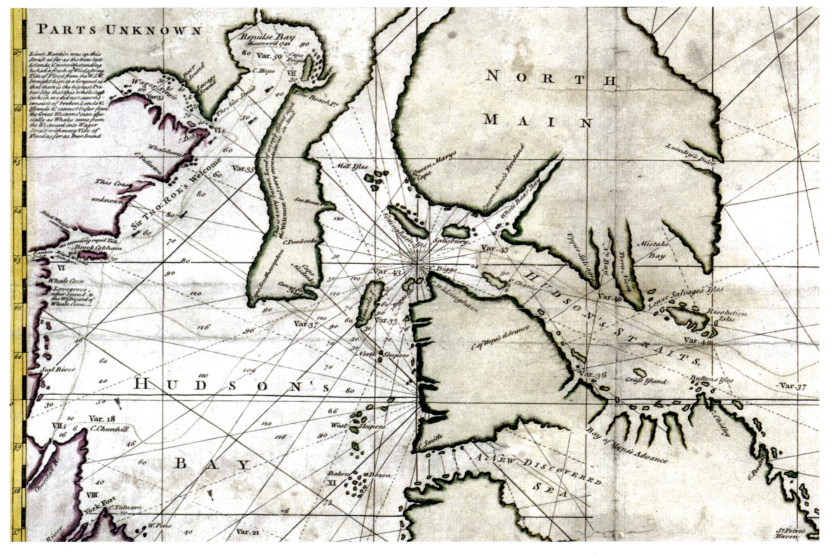

Map 116 (*above*).

Believe it or not, this map was commissioned by the Hudson's Bay Company for use in the parliamentary inquiry initiated by Arthur Dobbs against the Company in 1749. The Company was accused of failing to utilize its monopoly properly by not exploring inland and, of course, not searching for a Northwest Passage. The map was engraved by Richard Seale, a London mapmaker, but it is not clear whether it was drawn by Seale. Other maps by Seale suggest that he probably did not draw this map, but merely undertook the engraving work. Quite how this map could have been engraved without the Company's prior approval (engravings being done by copying a drawn map) is unclear. The Company was unable to use it for the inquiry, and only ten copies now exist; presumably the rest were destroyed on the Company's orders, so as not to tarnish its reputation as a conservative business.

Map 117 (*right*).

A map from an anonymous book entitled *An Account of a Voyage For the Discovery of a North-West Passage by Hudson's Streights. to the Western and Southern Ocean of America Performed in the Year 1746 and 1747, in the Ship* California, *Capt. Francis Smith, Commander.* By the Clerk of the *California.* The book was published in 1749, presumably by T. S. Drage, who was that clerk. Drage was one of the persons induced by Dobbs to rail against Middleton and the Hudson's Bay Company. The discovery of *Wager Water* is attributed solely to Moor and Smith, with no mention of Middleton, who was there first. *Mr Bowden's Inlet* is the name given here to Chesterfield Inlet, the end of which "was left undiscover'd," leaving Dobbs his straw to grasp.

Map 115 (*left*).

A rival map to Christopher Middleton's 1743 map was this one published by John Wigate in 1746. Wigate had been Middleton's clerk on board the *Furnace.* Wager River is not shown on this map but *Wager Strait.* Frozen Strait, at the tip of Southampton Island, is not shown, as water coming from this strait was Middleton's explanation for the strong tides experienced. Wigate instead chose to attribute the tides to the proximity to a Northwest Passage. Note yet another *New Discovered Sea* on the *eastern* coast of Hudson Bay. This was probably an exaggeration of the mouth of the Great Whale River (Grande Rivière de la Baleine), roughly mapped by Bay captain Thomas Mitchell in 1744. No doubt Wigate was disappointed it did not lead in the right direction!

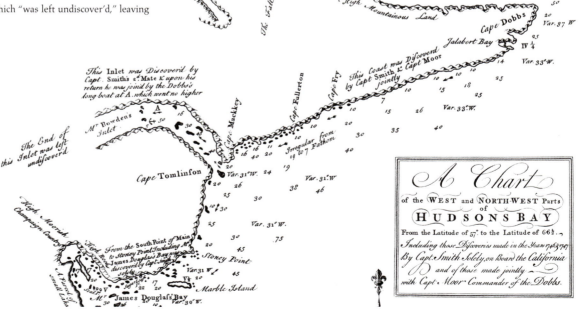

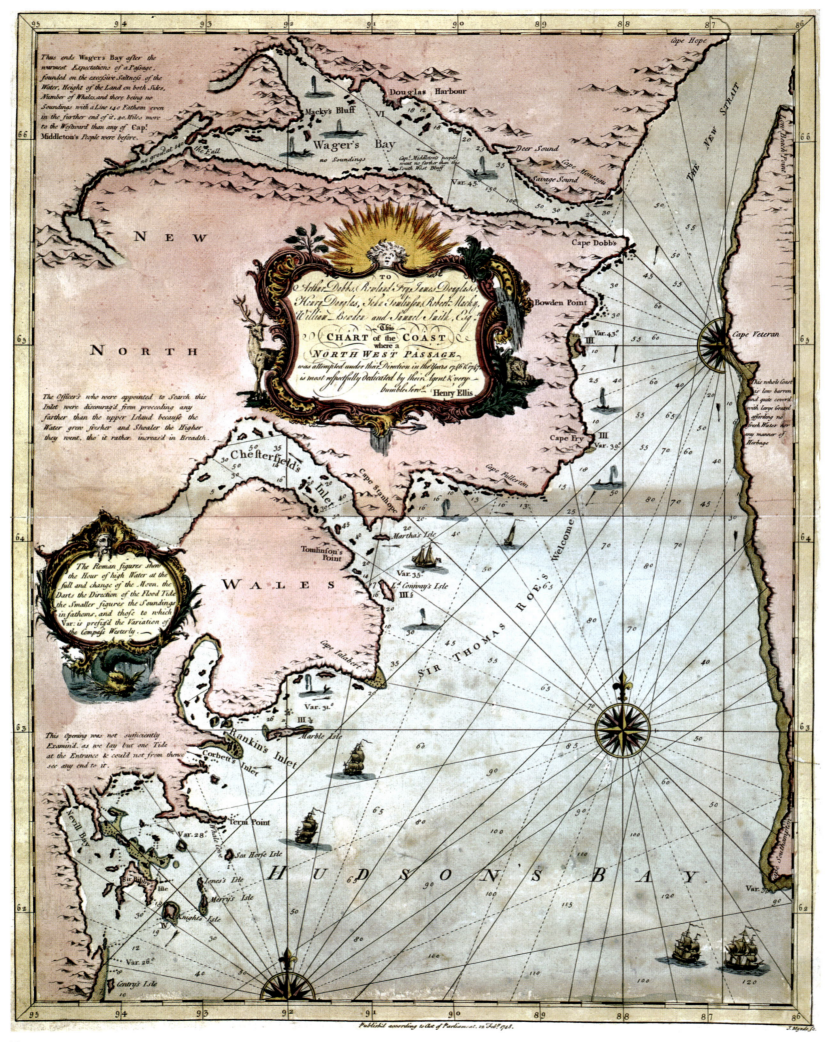

Map published by Henry Ellis in 1748 in his book *A Voyage to Hudson's-Bay by the* Dobbs Galley *and* California, *In the Years 1746 and 1747, For Discovering a North West Passage.* Ellis was Arthur Dobbs's agent (supercargo) on the voyage. The area shown is the northwest part of Hudson Bay, with *Sir Thomas Roe's Welcome* (now Roes Welcome Sound); Southampton Island is on the east side. In the northwest corner beside the western end of Wager's Bay is the notation "Thus ends Wagers Bay after the warmest Expectations of a Passage . . ." The northern part of Roes Welcome Sound, which leads to Middleton's Repulse Bay, is marked *The New Strait.* Chesterfield Inlet, which still had not been explored to its western extremity, is shown conveniently disappearing behind a cartouche. Unwilling to concede defeat, Dobbs seized on this as the "real" Northwest Passage.

The French Fur Trade Empire

French fur traders continued to push forward slowly during the first half of the eighteenth century but, with the notable exception of the La Vérendryes (see next page), they did not get much farther west than Lake Winnipeg. They were finding plenty of furs and so the economic impetus to expand was not great, and there was no encouragement from the French government. Most of the expansion in fact took place to the south, into what is now the American Midwest.

This map (MAP 119) is a remarkable record of the trading network they set up, and it was this network which would be inherited by the English and Scottish traders who replaced the French after 1763. Many of the French *coureurs de bois* adapted to the new conditions and stayed in the trade; adapting to their new masters, many became *voyageurs*, those paddling and portaging engines of the Canadian fur trade.

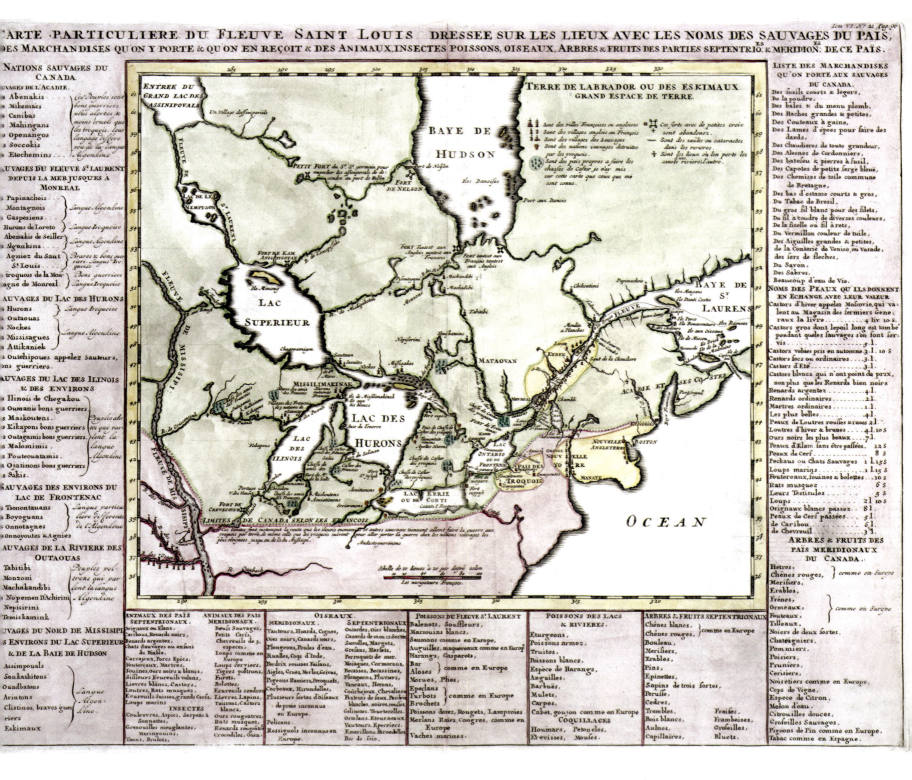

MAP 119.
This remarkable map shows the French network of fur trade routes and forts, and was drawn by Henri Chatelain in 1719. The Hudson's Bay Company's Fort Nelson is shown, while the posts at the bottom of the bay have the notation "sometimes English, sometimes French." The geography of the western part of the map is a little confused; a river flows from Lake Winnipeg at top left, through Lake Nipigon and into Lake Superior, while the Mississippi comes to within a stone's throw of the western end of Lake Superior. More correctly, the map shows *Kebek*, in the St. Lawrence Valley, as distinct from the rest of the French Empire, Fort Frontenac on Lake Ontario, Fort Niagara at the western end of that lake, and the Toronto carrying place through Lake Simcoe. Acadia is shown, though the depiction of the Bay of Fundy (*Baye Francoise*) is somewhat crude. Around the sides of the map are lists of native groups by region (at left), a list of trade goods and prices for the various types of furs (at right), and lists of animals, birds, fish, shellfish, trees, and fruits (at bottom). The map is a fine summary of French geographical knowledge of New France after the Treaty of Utrecht.

France Explores Westwards—the La Vérendryes

By the Treaty of Utrecht in 1713, France lost access to Hudson Bay, and in 1716 it was decided that fur traders should be encouraged to push westwards and establish forts, the *postes du nord*, in positions that would intercept natives taking furs to the English in Hudson Bay. In addition, a continued search for a Western Sea could be carried out at the same time, but, it was hoped, at no expense.

A post had been built on the shores of Lake Superior in 1713, at Kaministiquia, later Fort William and later still Thunder Bay. In 1717 the post was rebuilt as a strong fort. In 1718 a post was built on Rainy Lake but was not continuously occupied. By 1728 there were still only three forts in the west—Kaministiquia, and outposts at Nipigon and Michipicoten—when a new commandant was appointed with instructions to establish more forts and explore the West.

He was Pierre Gaultier de Varennes et de La Vérendrye, and together with his sons and a nephew, he was destined to vastly expand the region known to the French.

In 1731 La Vérendrye received a three-year monopoly on the fur trade with which he was supposed to finance his explorations and, specifically, find the Western Sea or at least the River of the West. La Vérendrye wrote that he would be "carrying the King's arms far afield, enlarging the colony, and extending its commerce."

He spent the next six years establishing new posts and collecting native information about the geography farther to the west. In 1731 Fort St. Pierre was established on Rainy Lake by his nephew and second-in-command, Christophe Dufrost de La Jemerais, and the following year Fort St. Charles was built at Lake of the Woods. In 1734, the first Fort Maurepas, named after the Minister of Marine, Jean-Frédéric Phélypeaux de Maurepas, was constructed on the lower Red River. But La Vérendrye found not a Western Sea, but a "sea of beaver."

He was hampered by the need to finance his own explorations through his fur-trading activities, but a sympathetic governor general, the Marquis de Beauharnois, allowed him at the end of his first monopoly term to subcontract his posts to others. Still La Vérendrye did not progress west fast enough for Maurepas.

In 1736 La Jemerais died of some disease, and La Vérendrye's oldest son, Jean-Baptiste, was killed along with a Jesuit, Father Jean-Pierre Alneau, and nineteen others by a Dakota war party at what is now named Massacre Island in Lake of the Woods. It seems that La Vérendrye, as part of his attempts to finance his explorations, also traded in Dakota slaves, thus incurring the wrath of that nation. La Vérendrye's attempts to find the River of the West slowed. In 1737, reporting back to Beauharnois in Québec, he had a map showing something which could be such a river, but he had not visited it himself.

Promising the governor he would speed up the pace of his explorations (as if opening the country to Lake Winnipeg was of no consequence), in 1738 he established Fort La Reine on the Assiniboine River, near today's Portage La Prairie, and set off on a journey to the southwest. By 1737 La Vérendyre had come to believe that the river he was seeking might flow not to the west but to the south, although still empty somehow into the Pacific Ocean.

La Vérendrye's exploration of 1738–39 is thought to have reached the Mandan villages of the upper Missouri. His travels are hard to follow because of the lack of references to identifiable landmarks, although this itself is indicative of the Prairies. In his journal he made the enigmatic statement that he had "discovered during this brief period a river that *runs to the west*," which could hardly be the Missouri. Certainly he came to realize that the upper Missouri was not the river that would lead him to the Western Sea. Ironically, the first American expedition to the Western Sea, that of Lewis and Clark some sixty-seven years later, would use the upper Missouri as its pathway, but *up*stream.

In 1741, after a sojourn in Québec, La Vérendrye was back at Fort La Reine to try again. Due to problems caused by native groups fighting one another, the new venture was delayed until the spring of 1742. During that winter, his son Pierre built Fort Dauphin on Lac des Prairies (now Lake Dauphin), and another fort, the first Fort Bourbon (in this region), was established at the point where Cedar Lake flows into Lake Winnipeg.

Finally, La Vérendrye decided to stay at Fort La Reine and instead sent two of his sons, Louis-Joseph and François (known as the Chevalier) to search for the River of the West and the elusive Western Sea.

With only two other men, they set off, again towards the southwest, in April 1742. Precisely how far they reached is not clear; they reported coming within sight of a range of mountains, and the probability is that these were the Big Horn Mountains, an outlying range of the Rockies, but they could also have been referring to the Black Hills, which are 150 km farther east. At any rate we know they reached the vicinity of what is now Pierre, South Dakota, for they buried a lead plate claiming possession of the land for Louis XV. This plate, which is generally accepted as being genuine, was found in 1913.

Louis-Joseph and the Chevalier returned to Fort La Reine in 1743. Minister Maurepas, when he heard of the latest travels of the La Vérendryes, was furious that they had not discovered at least a River of the West, and the elder La

Map 120.
Attributed to La Vérendrye or one of his family, this map shows what he knew, or presumed to know, about the geography west of Lake Superior in 1737. It was contained in a letter he sent to Governor Beauharnois in October of that year. North is approximately to the top left. The Saskatchewan River flows into *Lac 8inipegon* (Lake Winnipeg) from a small *Lac de la hauteur*, an assumed source. From there a River of the West flows to a *Mer Inconnue* (unknown sea). Fort St. Pierre and Fort St. Charles are shown. This is a copy of the original made in the mid-1850s.

The site of the La Vérendryes' Fort Rouge, established in 1738 at the point where the Assiniboine River (foreground) meets the Red River (at left). Today it is Winnipeg.

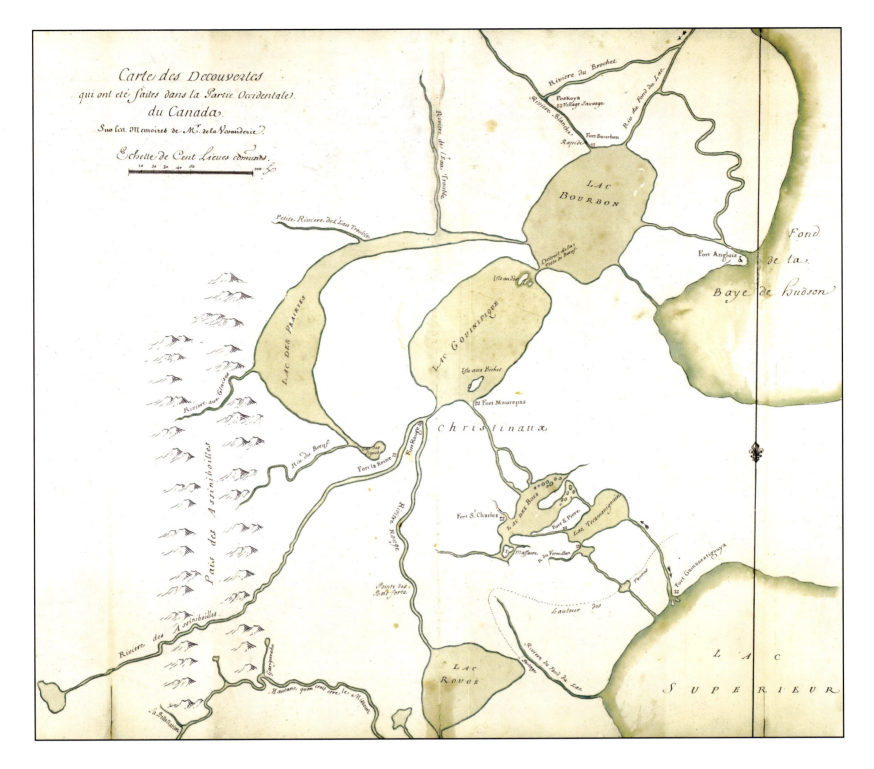

Map 121 .

A map of the discoveries of La Vérendrye and the network of forts he set up, drawn by Jacques-Nicolas Bellin in 1752. It is the fifth map in the Bellin manuscript atlas (see page 90), and is a copy of an anonymous map drawn about 1740. James Bay, the southern extension of Hudson Bay, is at top right, and Lake Superior at bottom right. From it rivers flow to—or is it from—Lake Winnipeg (*Lac Gouinipique*) via Rainy Lake (*Lac Tecamanigouin*) and Lake of the Woods (*Lac des Bois*). *Lac Bourbon* is the northern part of Lake Winnipeg, while the curving arc of *Lac des Prairies* is a combination of Lake Manitoba, Lake Winnipegosis, and probably Cedar Lake as well. *Lac Rouge* is Red Lake, Minnesota. The map has been drawn with north at the top, but the distances, especially from James Bay to the western lakes, are very compressed. All the forts established by La Vérendrye are shown, from Fort St. Pierre (*Ft S. Piere*) on Rainy Lake and *Fort St. Charles* on Lake of the Woods west to *Fort Bourbon*, where the Saskatchewan River is shown entering the northern part of Lake Winnipeg, *Lac Bourbon* (it actually enters Cedar Lake), and Fort Paskoya (*Poskoya*, at The Pas) and *Fort la Reine* (at Portage La Prairie). *Fort Maurepas* is shown at its second location, where the Winnipeg River enters Lake Winnipeg, and also shown is Fort Rouge, at the junction of the Red and Assiniboine Rivers, where Winnipeg now stands. Fort Kaministiquia (*Fort Gainanesfigouya*) is shown on the Lake Superior shore. This route to the west would be rediscovered by the North West Company after the Grand Portage route immediately south of it was denied to the company after the American Revolution. Fort Kaministiquia would become Fort William, and is now part of Thunder Bay, Ontario. This significant map shows the beginnings of the European understanding of the geography of western Canada.

Vérendrye lost his position as commandant of the *postes du nord*, but not before he established Fort Paskoya (or Paskoyac) on the Saskatchewan River near Cedar Lake in 1743. This is the modern city of The Pas, Manitoba. In 1746 he was reappointed, in tacit acknowledgement that he had not done such a bad job after all. He planned the exploration of the Saskatchewan River but died in 1749 before he could carry out further exploration of western Canada.

Despite some rather ambiguous explorations, over which there continues much debate as to the precise locations reached, the fact remains that La Vérendrye and his family were responsible for a vast extension of French influence and French geographical knowledge in a relatively short space of time. Had it not been for the policy of making La Vérendrye pay for everything himself, it is probable that the French would have pushed westwards to the Rockies by 1750.

As it was, the forts and trading network that La Vérendrye established would be essentially those taken over by the British after 1763 and used for a further push to the west that would culminate in the reaching of a Western Sea—the true Pacific—by Alexander Mackenzie in 1793, only fifty years after La Vérendrye's explorations ended.

The Fall of Louisbourg
in 1745

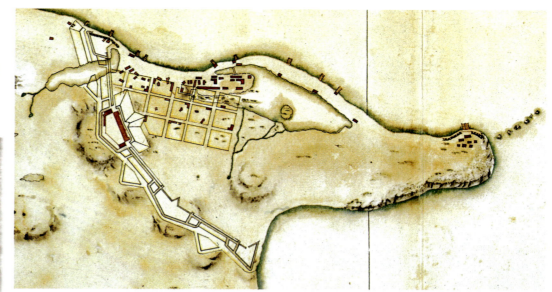

In the eighteenth century, both France and Britain were convinced that one of the keys to control of North America, and the key to control of the important cod-fishing industry, was control of Nova Scotia. This led the French to found Louisbourg, on the east coast of Cape Breton Island, soon after losing Newfoundland in the 1713 Treaty of Utrecht, which left them with Prince Edward Island (Île St. Jean) and Cape Breton Island (Île Royale).

Settlers had relocated from Placentia (Plaisance) in Newfoundland in 1713, attracted by the ice-free harbour. From 1719 onwards the French fortified Louisbourg to make it impregnable by sea. Unfortunately, they somehow overlooked the possibility of a land attack, and as it turned out, this was the way the fortress would be lost, not once, but twice, in 1745 and 1758.

In March 1744 France declared war on Britain; in North America this was known as King George's War. Harassment of merchant and fishing vessels followed, to the annoyance of New England merchants, and the governor of Massachusetts, William Shirley, pressed for an attack on the privateers' base, Louisbourg. He had a lot of persuading to do, for the American colonial legislatures initially saw little point in fighting in distant parts. But Shirley prevailed, promising, among other things, a British monopoly of the lucrative North Atlantic cod fishery.

Shirley's plan was to attack the French stronghold, not with British regular forces, but with New England militia, who would be joined by contingents from other American colonies. The attack was to be led by William Pepperrell, a colonel in the Maine militia and a successful merchant with much to gain from a British victory. Under his leadership, the endeavour gained widespread support.

The main contingent of 2,800 New England militia sailed on 4 April 1745 in fifty-one transport vessels. Others followed. Six armed colonial vessels had been dispatched in late March

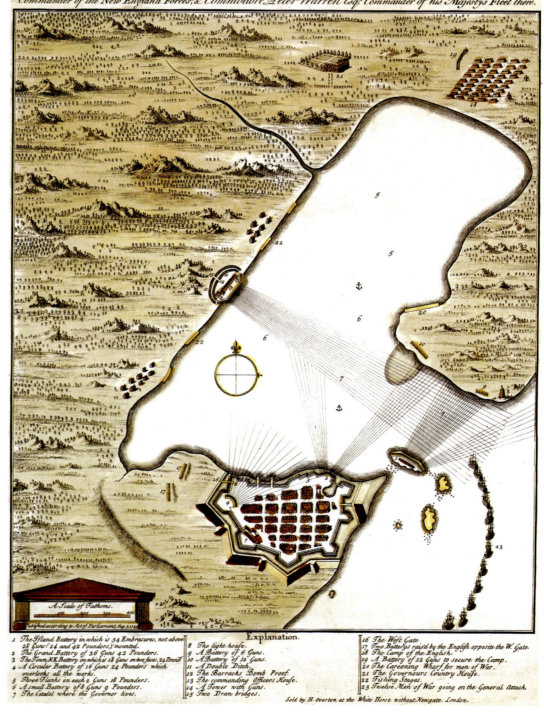

Map 123.

A broadsheet map published in England soon after the fall of Louisbourg in 1745. The key at the bottom gives this hastily coloured map the information British readers required. Warren's fleet sits outside the harbour.

MAP 122 *(left).*
A 1730 map of the town of Louisbourg. Not all the defences are complete at this date.

(far left).
The Dauphine Gate in the reconstructed Louisbourg

to begin a blockade of Louisbourg, and a supporting British fleet consisting of three warships under Commodore Peter Warren sailed from Antigua on 24 March. Two other British warships were to join them. All rendezvoused at Canso, at the northeast tip of mainland Nova Scotia.

On 11 May 1745 the attack began with the arrival of the combined fleet in Gabarus Bay, a very large bay to the south of Louisbourg, and the militia were landed at Kennington Cove.

The Grand or Royal Battery was taken first. This was a separate fortified cannon emplacement designed to face ships coming into Louisbourg Harbour, its intention being clearly shown in MAP 123. But, like Louisbourg itself, it was not designed to withstand an attack from the land. Hastily spiking the cannon, the French departed for the town. But in their haste they did not do a very good job, for the New Englanders soon began repairing the cannon, and then turned them on Louisbourg.

The governor of Île Royale, Louis Du Chambon, was no military genius; in fact he had little idea how to deal with the crisis that now confronted him. Louisbourg was now besieged and blockaded.

On 30 May the British blockade ships intercepted and captured a large French warship, the *Vigilant,* carrying over 500 men, 1,000 barrels of powder, 40 cannon, and a large amount of foodstuffs destined for Louisbourg. This may well have been the turning point of the siege, for it was both a material and psychological blow to the defenders of Louisbourg. A week later a New England force attacked the Island Battery (shown on all the maps here), but were repulsed. Though they were cheered by this, the end was near for the town's defenders.

On 23 June more British warships—which just happened to be passing, on their way to Annapolis Royal—joined Warren's force; he now had eleven warships at his command.

To the defenders it was beginning to look hopeless. Mercenaries deserted, bringing the intelligence that the French were running low on powder, whereupon Pepperrell gave his gunners orders to "Fire Smartly att ye Citty" until their cannon "ware So hott they could not fire any more." He was trying to get the defenders

to use up their remaining powder. Then the town's merchants put pressure on Du Chambon, fearing total loss of their wealth if Louisbourg were taken by force. This was the final straw. The prevaricating governor offered terms of surrender on 26 June. A deal was reached, and Louisbourg was in British hands on 28 June.

This rare example of co-operation between colonial American forces and regular British forces was not to last long. There was much bickering about who was responsible for Louisbourg's fall. The town remained in British hands for only three years, for in 1748, by the Treaty of Aix-la-Chapelle which ended the war, the British government restored Louisbourg to the French, much to the chagrin of New England. In this act lies one of the roots of the American Revolution. Not only that; the next time Britain went to war with France, in 1756, British forces would once again be faced with the job of taking Louisbourg, only this time it would be done with no American involvement (see page 96).

The New England forces remained at Louisbourg over the winter of 1745–46 and lost many more men to disease than had been lost during the siege; about 1,200 men died that winter on the barren shores of Cape Breton.

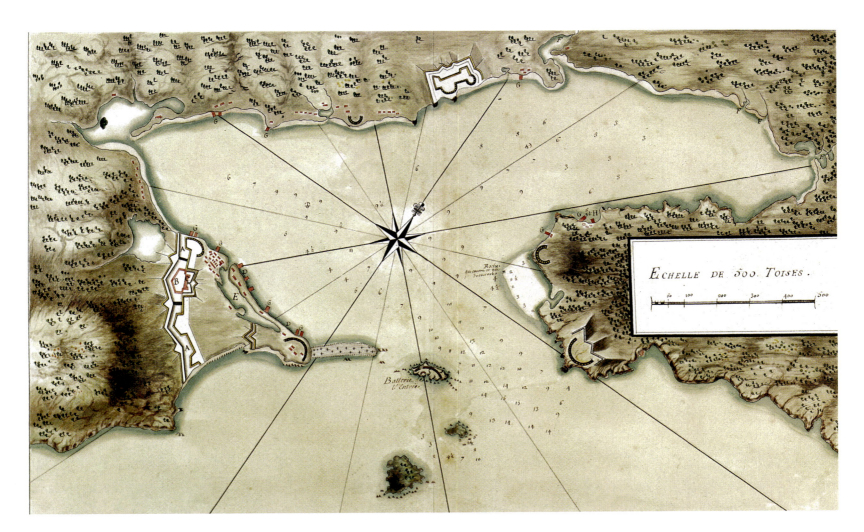

MAP 124.
This French map dated 1745 shows the salient features of Louisbourg's defences. Batteries are either side of the harbour entrance, and the Island Battery in the centre; the Royal or Grand Battery is on the shore at top centre. From the key to this map: *A* are the walls; *B* the King's Bastion; *C* the barracks; *D* the palisades; *E* the fish pond; *F* streams; *G* piers; and *H* careening wharves, where ships were taken out of the water for cleaning and repairs.

Jacques-Nicolas Bellin's Atlas

Jacques-Nicolas Bellin was a hydrographic engineer attached to the French office of marine maps and plans. In the middle period of the eighteenth century, he was responsible for some of the most beautiful and detailed general maps of French North America.

In 1752 Bellin produced a set of seven large maps. The maps were probably drawn as originals to send to be engraved at various times, for most also exist as engraved copies.

This manuscript atlas was presented to the Canadian government by the British government in 1967 as a Confederation centenary gift on the opening of a new archives building in Ottawa. It was obtained from a French source by some unknown hand, and contains the bookplates of two previous owners, one unidentified and one the fourth earl of Chesterfield, who died in 1773. The atlas now resides in the National Archives of Canada.

Four of the maps are reproduced here. The map of the St. Lawrence is the middle sheet of three, and the fifth map, showing the discoveries of the French explorer Pierre Gaultier de Varennes et de La Vérendrye, is shown as MAP 121 on page 87. Together these maps present a good overview of the state of French geographical knowledge of the northern part of North America in the mid-eighteenth century.

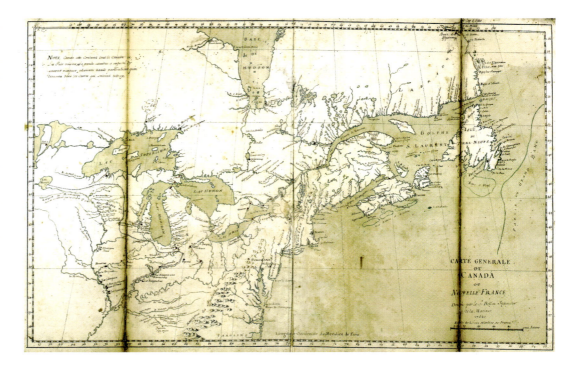

MAP 125 (*above*).
Bellin's general map of Canada in 1752. French forts are shown with red circles. This map is unfortunately perhaps the least well preserved in the Bellin manuscript atlas, but is still very clear for the most part. The route to the West, via Lake of the Woods to Lake Winnipeg from the western end of Lake Superior, is more or less correctly shown.

MAP 126 (*below*).
This is the middle sheet of a three-sheet map of the St. Lawrence River, navigational knowledge of which was so important for French ships sailing to supply Québec.

MAP 127 (*right, top*).
Bellin's map of the eastern coast of New France, the disputed territory of Acadia, British Nova Scotia, and the British territory of Newfoundland, conceded by the French in the 1713 Treaty of Utrecht.

MAP 128 (*right, bottom*).
Bellin's map of the Great Lakes. In 1752, when Bellin drew this map, New France extended well into what is now the American Midwest.

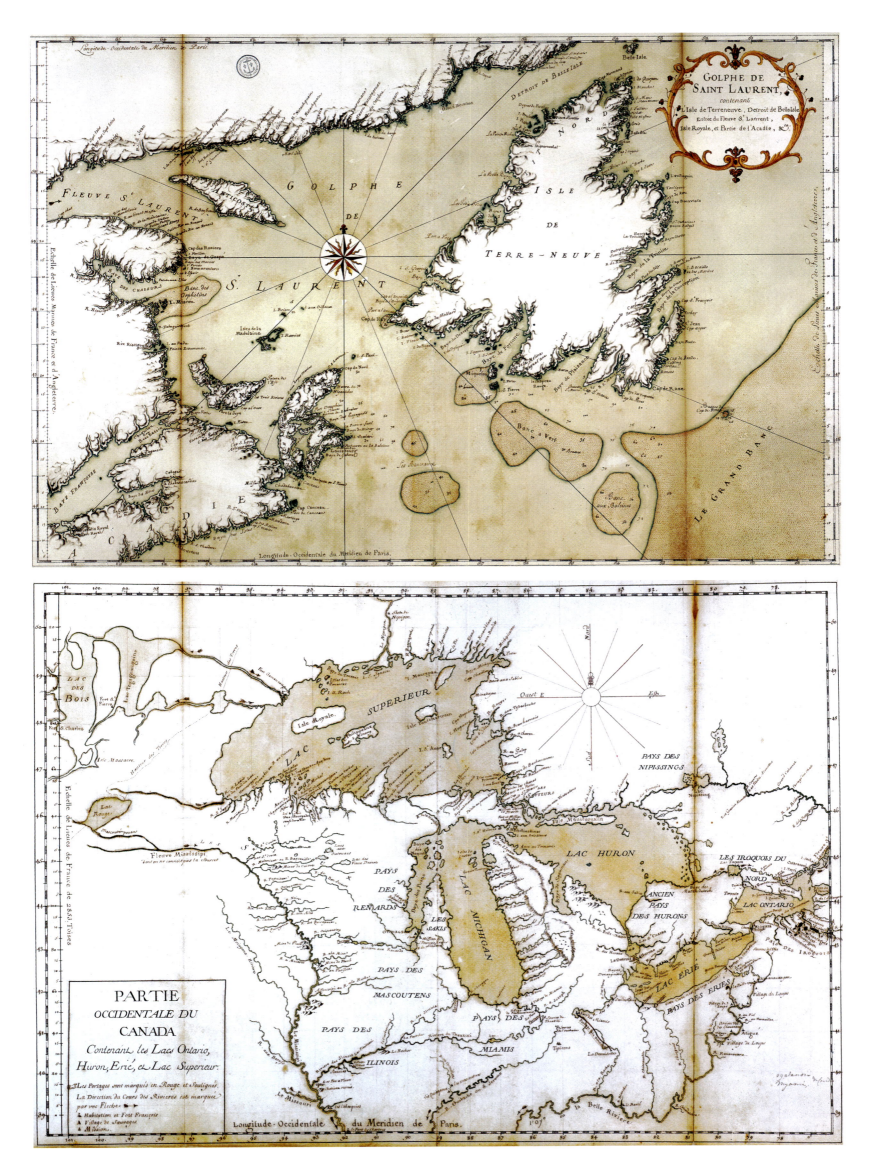

The Founding of Halifax

With the handing back of Louisbourg to the French by the Treaty of Aix-la-Chapelle in 1748, the British government decided to build their own base on the Nova Scotian coast, to guard the approaches to New England. They also wanted to counter what was seen as the Acadian threat, and exploit the cod fishery at the same time, by establishing what was the first British government–sponsored settlement scheme in North America.

The place they selected was a vast natural harbour 35 km long, in places over 3 km wide, called by the Mi'kmaq Kjipuktuk. When they had control of Acadia, the French had planned to fortify this harbour, which they called Chebucto, and in 1711 the military engineer Sieur De Labat had drawn up plans, but they had not been implemented.

In the summer of 1749, under Lieutenant Colonel Edward Cornwallis, who had been appointed governor, a dozen or so ships with about 2,600 settlers sailed into the harbour and began constructing a fortified town. We can, perhaps, be thankful that one George Dunk was also the Earl of Halifax, or the town might have received a different name.

Cornwallis had difficulty getting his settlers to help to build fortifications, for they were more intent on building their own houses. This problem was only solved by the arrival of troops transferred from Louisbourg, which had been handed back to the French that July.

Halifax was a superb location for a fortress, and as such it was almost bound to thrive. Time and again it would prove its worth as a British base, from the coming French and Indian War to the Second World War.

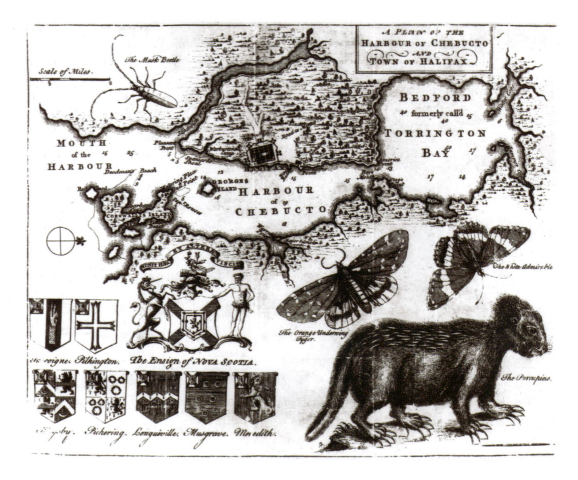

Map 129 (above).
A commercial map, published in *Gentleman's Magazine* in July 1750. Attributed to Moses Harris, an early resident, the map purports to illustrate the wildlife of the area; the map is popularly known as "the porcupine map."

Map 130 (left).
A spy map of Halifax drawn in 1755, attributed to François-Pierre de Rigaud de Vaudreuil, who was a prisoner at the time, having been captured in 1754 from a French ship that had strayed from a convoy. Vaudreuil attempted to smuggle out the map embedded in a cake of soap packed in an officer's trunk that was being returned to Louisbourg, following the gentlemanly conduct of the day. However, Vaudreuil was caught, for the map was sent to the Lords of the Admiralty in Britain. *1* to *5* are forts around the walls, and *12* is the artillery barracks.

Map 131 (right, top).
This stunning map published by British commercial mapmaker Thomas Jefferys in January 1750 is a composite, to show his readers all they needed to know about the new settlement. At top left is a general map of the Atlantic Coast, perhaps the first to show the position of Halifax; at top right is a plan of the town, just cut from the forest; at bottom right is a view of the town; and the main map shows Halifax Harbour. Incorporated into the elegant cartouche, the settlers build houses. Note that Jefferys advertises upcoming maps at the bottom of this one.

Map 132 (right, bottom).
A plan of proposed fortifications for the new town of Halifax, prepared by British military engineer John Brewse in 1749. Brewse's design proved too elaborate at the time and was not implemented.

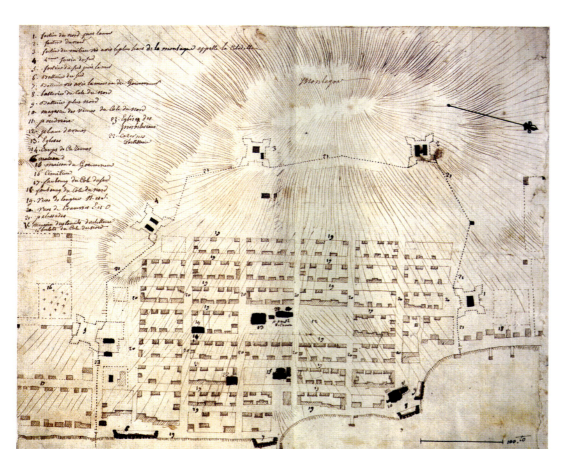

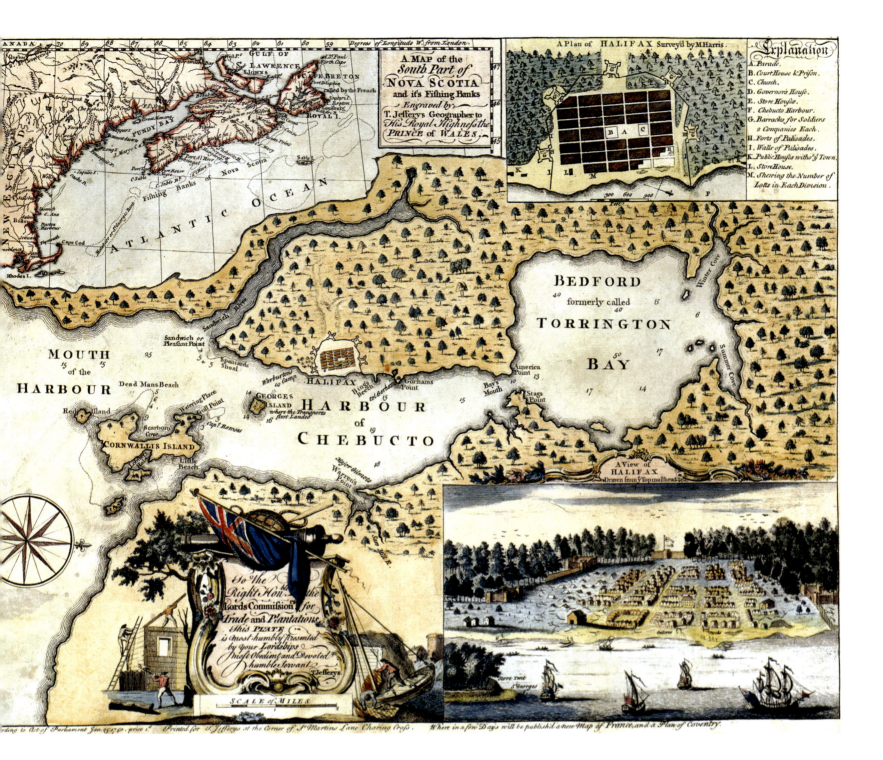

MAP 133. One of the first general maps to show the newly founded Halifax was this rather distorted but nevertheless fascinating map, drawn by Conrad Tobias Lotter and engraved by Matthias Seutter, published in Augsburg sometime after 1750. This may be a later edition, as versions of this map exist with only Lotter's name in the cartouche. The map has been included here, needless to say, for its artistic interest rather than for its accuracy. Lake Ontario is placed nearly in the Atlantic. The "squashed" appearance of the map has been referred to jokingly as the "Lotter projection."

The Acadian Deportation

Nova Scotia, or Acadia, had been ceded to Britain by France by the Treaty of Utrecht in 1713, but its boundaries, defined as its "former limits," were unclear. Thus France and England spent the next fifty years jostling for position, the final manoeuvrings of which were the war of 1744–48, with the British taking of Louisbourg, and the deportation of the Acadian population in 1755, followed by the war of 1756–63 and the fall of New France.

The area at the head of Chignecto Bay, being important for communications from Île Royale and the Saint John River Valley, was a flashpoint. In 1751, the British erected a fortification, Fort Lawrence, under the noses of French forces, whereupon the French countered by building Fort Beauséjour nearby (MAP 134).

A new offensive against the French was planned by Governor William Shirley of Massachusetts and Governor Charles Lawrence of Nova Scotia. Fort Beauséjour was taken by Robert Monckton in June 1755 after a short siege. The British forces managed to get their artillery so close that the French commander was sure his powder magazine would be hit, and thus surrendered.

Lawrence considered that for the continued security of the British in Nova Scotia, the existing French population should be removed. A decision to expel the French was made at a meeting on 28 July 1755 at which Vice Admiral Edward Boscawen, recently arrived from England, contributed and, it seems, encouraged. Lawrence obtained a legal opinion from his chief judge that seizure of Acadian lands was warranted because the people had refused to take an oath of allegiance and were thus "rebels."

In August 1755 Monckton ordered several hundred Acadians to assemble at Fort Cumberland (the renamed Beauséjour) and then arrested them as rebels, sending them to Fort Lawrence for deportation. For the next several months parties of British soldiers roamed the countryside as far south as Annapolis, rounding up the Acadians, declaring their lands forfeit, and burning their farms.

Between September and December 1755, 6,000 to 7,000 men, women, and children were deported from Acadia, and smaller numbers were deported over the next few years. The total that either were expelled or managed to escape probably was around 11,000 out of a total population of about 15,500. About 2,000 succeeded in reaching Canada, and a few went to France; but the majority were taken to the British American colonies where, it was hoped, their relatively small number would mean they could be easily assimilated. To this day, the United States has a small Acadian—Cajun—population.

MAP 134 (*right, top*). This beautiful plan of Fort Beauséjour was likely drawn in 1751, when the fort was built by the French engineer Louis Franquet at the head of Cumberland Basin. Franquet drew this plan. *Cazernes* are barracks; *Cazernes Projetées*, the gunroom; *Magazin des Vivres*, the store for provisions and supplies; *Poudriere,* the powder house; *Puit,* the well.

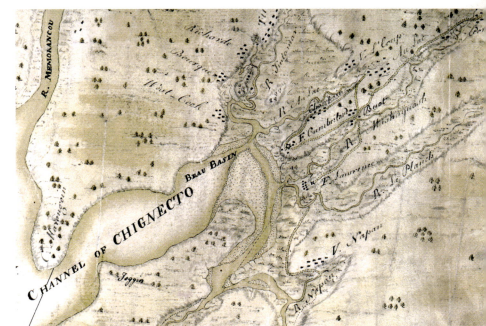

MAP 135 (*right, centre*). Part of a map of Nova Scotia drawn by Thomas Lewis in 1755. It shows both Fort Cumberland, the renamed Fort Beauséjour, captured from the French, and the British Fort Lawrence, which was erected close to Fort Beauséjour. The location is Cumberland Basin, at the head of the Chignecto Bay branch of the Bay of Fundy, on the border between New Brunswick and Nova Scotia.

MAP 136 (*below*). Annapolis Royal, with the fort, now British and renamed Fort Anne, in 1753. The map also shows Acadian farmlands, some of which had been reclaimed from the water by the construction of dikes. Many Acadians from the Annapolis Valley were among those expelled in 1755.

The Battle for a Continent—the French and Indian War

In 1756, the hostilities between France and Britain turned into a declared war, in Europe called the Seven Years War, but in North America, the French and Indian War.

In 1756 the French sent Louis-Joseph, Marquis de Montcalm, to command the French forces on the continent. The aggressive Montcalm took the initiative, and Fort Oswego, on the south side of Lake Ontario, fell to him in 1756, thus giving the French control of the lake (see MAP 139, overleaf). In the strategic Hudson River–Lake Champlain corridor, Fort William Henry fell in 1757, and Montcalm defeated the British Major General James Abercromby at Fort Carillon (Ticonderoga) in 1758.

To counter the French threat, Major General John Campbell, Earl of Loudon, was sent to command the British and colonial forces and, in early 1757, had devised the strategy that was ultimately to lead to the collapse of the French Empire in North America.

Loudon's plan was three-pronged: an attack up the Ohio Valley and Lake Ontario to Montréal from the west; another up Lake Champlain and the Richelieu River; and another by sea, first to take the French fortress of Louisbourg, and then to Québec, and finally also to Montréal.

A major factor in the success of the British effort was the rise to power in Britain of William Pitt, who became prime minister in July 1757. He was convinced that the future wealth and glory of Britain was in the possession of an empire, and he persuaded the king to allow a switch in emphasis and resources from the European war to North America, a change which the Hanoverian George II was at first reluctant to make.

And commitment of resources there was; a new military leader, Sir Jeffery Amherst, was appointed to execute this grand strategy, and in early 1758, Amherst sailed from England with Admiral Edward Boscawen and a fleet of 38 warships and 100 troop transports with 12,000 soldiers. They were to join others at Halifax. The first objective was Louisbourg.

The plan was to take Louisbourg and Québec in a single season, but as it turned out, the fortress was able to hold out long enough for this to become impractical. An able naval officer, the Chevalier Augustin de Drucourt, had assumed command at Louisbourg in 1754 and repaired its defences, damaged from the 1745 attack. A garrison of 3,500 professional soldiers manned the ramparts. Learning from history, Drucourt had installed entrenchments all along Gabarus Bay at likely landing places, with the help of the engineer Louis Franquet. But the size of the British force was overwhelming.

The fleet anchored in Gabarus Bay on 2 June 1758. Despite the entrenchments, the British forces made good a landing, largely because of an inexplicable temporary hole in the French defences at a redoubt near Cormorant Cove, where a retreating James Wolfe saw the weakness and ordered his men to immediately land; this turned out to be the decisive action of the siege, certainly noted by Amherst. Wolfe's battlefield decisiveness would lead to his appointment to lead the attack on Québec.

Having gained a foothold, the British force set up their cannon, dug emplacements, and commenced to pound Louisbourg unmercifully. So heavy was the bombardment that it was only a matter of time before the fortress surrendered, though it held out for seven agonizing weeks. At midnight on 26 July, a capitulation was signed.

It was now too late in the season to permit an assault on Québec, as had been planned; this would have to wait until the next year. In the meantime, Wolfe and James Murray were detailed to destroy the French supply sources; they set fire to farms and villages in the Gaspé and Miramichi, respectively, and St. Anne's (Fredericton) was burned by another officer, Moses Hazen.

That same summer, an American colonial officer, John Bradstreet, was sent to Lake Ontario with 3,000 men and instructions to take Fort Chouaguen (Oswego) and Fort Frontenac, destroy French ships, and thus regain control of the lake.

Bradstreet's men went down the Oneida River, finding Chouaguen in ruins. They continued to Fort Frontenac, approaching the fort in small craft: 123 bateaux and 95 whaleboats. When they arrived, on 25 August, Fort Frontenac was in no condition to withstand a siege; the French had not anticipated such an attack. Manoeuvring artillery within range under cover of darkness, the fort commandant, the

MAP 137.
This fine map of the British attack on Louisbourg in 1758 was drawn by military surveyor Samuel Holland. The British encampments are shown at left; part of Gabarus Bay, where the British landed, is at the extreme left. British batteries are shown surrounding Louisbourg.

A view of the restored King's Bastion at Louisbourg. The town and fortress were partially restored in the 1960s by the Canadian government, and today Louisbourg is perhaps the major tourist attraction on Cape Breton Island. During the summer, local people and students dress as townsfolk and soldiers, giving the town a very authentic appearance.

Sieur de Noyan, could see that the situation was hopeless, and quickly surrendered. French ships attempted to leave the harbour, but they were too late; they too were captured by Bradstreet's men.

A British military pincer was closing on New France. It would be the assault on Québec the next year that would finally make the French collapse inevitable.

MAP 138 (below).
This wonderful panoramic map depicting the assault on Louisbourg in 1758 was drawn and painted by a French admiral named Bockoune, about whom we know very little. He was likely an amateur painter who amused himself painting scenes with which he was familiar. Luckily his work has survived in this unique depiction of a seminal event in Canadian history. See also the title page for a detail of this map (MAP 1).

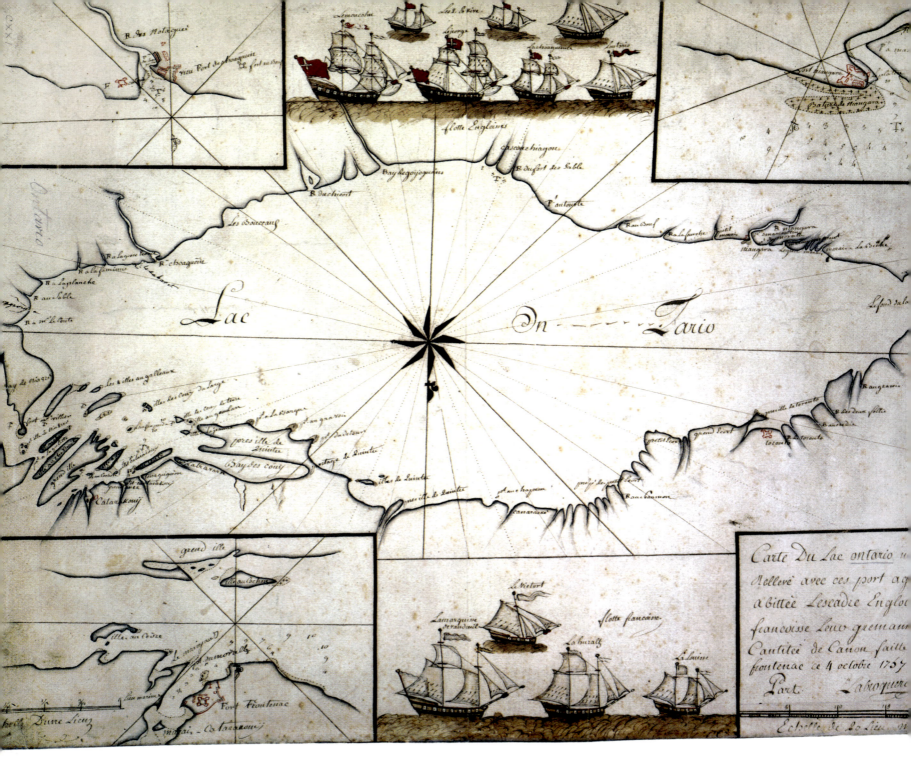

MAP 139 (above).
A rather beautiful French map of Lake
Ontario drawn in 1757, with a depiction of
the English fleet at the top and the French
fleet at the bottom. Note that south is at
the top; the St. Lawrence leaves the lake at
the left, where *Catarakouy* (Fort Frontenac,
and today Kingston) is marked. The inset
(bottom left) shows the fort. At top right
is the Niagara River, with Fort Niagara, the
French fort now on the American side. The
inset at top right shows the details. The fort
at Chouaguen (Oswego) is at top left, on
the main map and an inset. The French fort
at Toronto is also shown (in red, directly
above the word "Carte" in the title).

MAP 140 (right).
The defences of the city of Québec, 1750.
Up to 1745, there were few defences on the
landward side, but, spurred on by King
George's War, major new walls were built,
under the direction of the king's engineer
Gaspard-Joseph Chaussegros de Léry, and
completed in 1749. These are essentially the
walls the visitor to Québec sees today. In
addition, older batteries were improved and
new ones added. Thus when the war with
Britain began in 1756, the city had an extensive system of fortifications to complement its natural defences.

The Fall of Québec—and an Empire

The first English capture of Québec had been in 1629, by the Kirke family, but the Treaty of Saint-Germain-en-Laye of 1632 had returned the colony to the French. The second, unsuccessful, attempt to capture the city had been in 1690, by a fleet commanded by Sir William Phips. In a third attempt, in 1711, a large fleet under Sir Hovenden Walker sailed into the St. Lawrence, but it did not reach Québec largely due to poor navigation.

However, the fourth attempt, by a fleet commanded by Vice Admiral Charles Saunders

and a land force commanded by Major General James Wolfe in 1759, was not only to prove successful, but would irreversibly end French rule in Canada.

After the fall of Louisbourg the previous year, it was obvious to the French that an attack on Québec was coming. The French commander, Lieutenant General Louis-Joseph, Marquis de Montcalm, was convinced that the British would attack the Beauport shore, to the east of the city of Québec, where lower land would make a landing easier. Thus he set about building entrench-

ments and fortifications along the length of this shore. They can be seen on MAP 141, below, and on MAP 142, overleaf. And then he waited.

Saunders' massive British fleet sailed from Halifax and Louisbourg, a total of over 180 ships with thousands of soldiers and sailors. They navigated the treacherous St. Lawrence with help from James Cook (see page 106), the first transports arriving off the Île d'Orléans on 26 June, landing troops on the island and on the south shore, meeting little resistance. The first offensive was, however, Montcalm's.

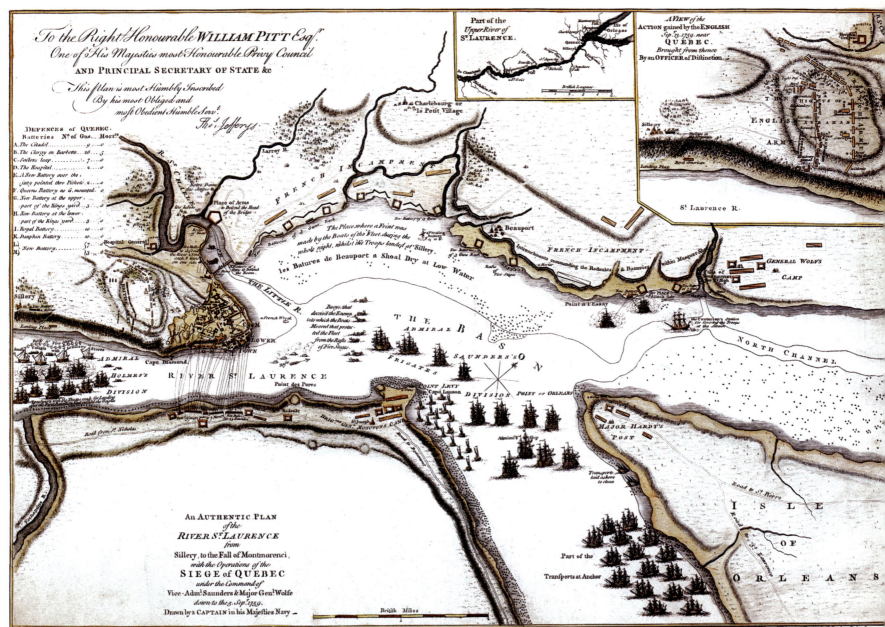

MAP 141.
The attack on Québec, 1759, as depicted in a map engraved by British mapmaker Thomas Jefferys. This fine map shows events which occurred at several times. Just off the lower town are shown the fire ships, the first French attack on the British fleet, on the night of 28–29 June. At right is the abortive British attack on the shore to the west of the Falls of Montmorency undertaken on 31 July; Jefferys' map has the wrong date, 30 July. The failure of this attack led Wolfe to decide to attack elsewhere. Shown in the river are transports anchored near the Île d'Orléans, Saunders' division, and Rear Admiral Charles Holmes's division, which assisted with the landing of the troops by longboat at the Anse-au-Foulon on 13 September. A feint attack the same night on the Beauport shore, designed to throw the French off-guard during the assault on the Plains of Abraham, is also shown.

ACCURATE PLAN
OF THE
ENVIRONS OF QUEBEC,
AND OF THE
BATTLE fought on the 13th. September, 1759:
Together with a particular Detail of
The FRENCH LINES and BATTERIES,
And also of the
ENCAMPMENTS, BATTERIES and ATTACKS of the
BRITISH ARMY,
And the Investiture of that City under the Command of
VICE ADMIRAL SAUNDERS,
MAJOR GENERAL WOLFE,
BRIGADIER GENERAL MONCKTON,
And BRIGADIER GENERAL TOWNSHEND.
Drawn from the ORIGINAL SURVEYS taken by the ENGINEERS of the Army.
Engraved by THOMAS JEFFERYS,
Geographer to His MAJESTY.

SCALES.

On the night of 28–29 June he had a number of fire ships, hulks filled with combustible material and set afire, made to drift downriver in an attempt to set the British fleet on fire. The British saw them coming and sent sailors in longboats to tow them to shore, and no damage was done to the fleet.

The siege of Québec now began. Cannon were moved near to Point Lévis, opposite Québec, and the city was bombarded. Through July and August Wolfe probed the French defences, trying to come up with a plan of attack, knowing that at the end of the season he would have to leave to avoid ice in the river.

On 31 July Wolfe put a plan he had hatched into operation. It involved a frontal assault on the French defences on the Beauport shore just west of the Montmorency waterfall. Grenadiers stormed ashore, covered by one of Saunders' largest warships, the *Centurion*. But the attack failed, partly because the troops got carried away and attacked the entrenchments on the cliffs instead of waiting for reinforcements on the lower part of the shore, and partly because a chance heavy thunderstorm made it impossible for troops to climb those cliffs. The attack is depicted on MAPS 141 (previous page), 142 (above), and 143 (overleaf). The failure of this assault, sometimes called the Battle of Montmorency, convinced Wolfe he could not succeed in an attack anywhere along this shore, and he began to search for alternatives.

In the meantime, Wolfe ordered that the villages and farms surrounding Québec be destroyed, to deprive the city of food. This rather dark side of the war was widely hated, but at the time it was seen as an essential part of the siege.

On 29 August Wolfe's three brigadier generals, Robert Monckton, Charles Townshend, and James Murray, presented him with a plan for an attack from above the town. Wolfe agreed this was the best alternative, but there remained the problem of finding a weak spot in the French defences, not to mention the city's natural defences. At Anse-au-Foulon, Wolfe found a small chink in the French armour, a narrow defile leading up the cliff face, and resolved to use it to get his troops onto the Plains of Abraham.

On the night of 12–13 September, troops were packed into longboats and rowed to the Anse. They were challenged by French sentries, but a quick-thinking captain replied in French. Since supply boats were expected at that time, it was assumed that the British boats were the French supplies. The British forces landed under cover of darkness, and many soldiers scaled the cliff directly, capturing a post at the top. In spite of difficulties, by early morning the British were firmly ensconced on the Plains of Abraham.

Initially they lined up with their backs to the cliff; Wolfe was evidently anticipating an early French attack. When none came, the troops were moved to face the walls of Québec. Wolfe now had 5,000 battle-ready men on the Plains.

Montcalm, camped across the St. Charles River in Beauport, was so sure that the cliffs were impossible for an army to scale that he refused at first to believe the messenger sent to tell him of the British landing. When he realized what had happened, he rushed all available men from Beauport to the Plains. By nine in the morning he had 4,500 men assembled in front of Québec. These were not all the men at Montcalm's disposal, for he had left 1,500 to guard the entrenchments at Beauport, still concerned that the real attack might take place there. And there were several thousand men in a division led by Colonel Louis-Antoine de Bougainville (later a noted explorer) camped farther west. Concerned that the British army,

MAP 142.
Another stunning map showing the attack on Québec in 1759, also engraved by Thomas Jefferys, then Geographer to the King. As with MAP 141 (page 99), Jefferys obtained his information from a number of different sources, combining it to create an informative map that would sell to a public anxious for news of the war. The procedure was no different for the myriad other maps produced by commercial mapmakers like Jefferys, for they had certainly not visited all the places they mapped. Like MAP 141, the events shown here took place over a span of time, which can lead to confusion if this is not appreciated.

MAP 143.
A depiction of the British assault on the French lines, 31 July 1759, the Battle of Montmorency. British forces took the Johnstone Redoubt (shown at *g*), only to find it already abandoned. A sudden thunderstorm prevented soldiers from ascending to the main entrenchments. Two British ships are shown grounded at *f*, as planned, on the mud flats, where they could cover the attack. HMS *Centurion*, a sixty-gun warship, is shown at *h*, firing on the redoubt. Wolfe's temporary encampment is on the east side of the Montmorency River and waterfall.

if given time, would be able to consolidate its position, and that yet more British soldiers would pour onto the field, at ten Montcalm made what would turn out to be his fatal mistake: he decided to attack immediately with the men he had. He evidently hoped Bougainville would hear the noise and rush to join the battle. This Bougainville did, but he arrived too late. For the battle was over by eleven, when Bougainville's forces arrived after a three-hour march from Cap Rouge, 15 km upriver. They found themselves completely outnumbered and would withdraw after a few shots.

The two armies closed for battle at about ten in the morning. This situation is depicted on the fine map of the environs of Québec on which the battle has been laid out (MAP 146, pages 104–05). The French advanced on the British lines too fast, firing an ineffective volley from too far away. Wolfe, however, had given orders for his men not to fire until the French were only 40 yards (36 m) away, and to charge their muskets with two balls instead of the usual one. The strategy worked; the French line was broken, and a rout began.

In the fighting, both Wolfe and Montcalm received fatal wounds. Wolfe died on the battlefield; Montcalm was carried into Québec, where he died early the next morning.

That night, many French militiamen deserted and went back to their homes. With the remaining forces, the Sieur de Ramezay, the senior officer who had now assumed command within the walls of Québec, felt that the city would fall to a renewed British attack, and wished to avoid the civilian casualties he thought inevitable in such a situation. On 17 September, De Ramezay agreed to the capitulation of Québec if

no help had arrived by eleven that night. None arrived, and so the next day, 18 September 1759, de Ramezay signed the surrender of the city.

The Chevalier de Lévis hastened from Montréal intending to gather the remaining French troops and save the city, but he was too late. By the time he arrived, the city had surrendered.

Montréal was now all that really remained of New France. There, at the beginning of 1760, the governor of New France, the Marquis de Vaudreuil, and François de Lévis, Chevalier de Lévis, now the commander of the French army, planned an attack on the British aimed at regaining Québec. They both knew their plan was dependent on help arriving from France. But France was too preoccupied with the war in Europe to spare money and men for what many viewed as a "few acres of snow."

Lévis called up all French militiamen, under pain of death if they did not report, and in April his army left Montréal in barges. They were low on powder and shot before they even left Montréal. A few days later, landing upriver from Québec, one of his men fell into the river and, on an ice flow, disappeared downriver. Lucky for him, he was rescued by the British as his ice flow passed Québec, but unfortunately for Lévis, the man then proceeded to give the British knowledge of the French troop movements.

Major General James Murray, in charge at Québec, thus was prepared when Lévis appeared, but, in a classic rewrite of history, made exactly the same mistake, with much the same rationale, that Montcalm had made the previous year. "I resolved to give the enemy battle before they could establish themselves," he wrote later. And he for this he suffered the same consequences

as Montcalm. This time the British lost the battle, and Murray hastily retreated to the safety of the city walls. This was called the Battle of Sainte-Foy, fought on 28 April 1760, although it was fought on almost exactly the same spot as the Battle of Québec (or Battle of the Plains of Abraham) in 1759. It is illustrated by MAP 144, right; MAP 145 (right, below) shows Lévis' battle plan, drawn up afterwards, as the battle had not been foreseen on that day by either side. Murray's troops all had trenching tools for building a defensive fortification.

Lévis now laid siege to Québec, opening fire on 11 May. But because of his lack of supplies, he had to ration his gunners to no more than twenty shots from each of four batteries daily. Hardly the way to win a war. Lévis intended to hold back for a final blow when French ships arrived. The critical factor was now which nation's ships would arrive first. If British ships arrived, Lévis could not sustain the siege, whereas if help arrived from France, it would be the British that would be in trouble.

It was, of course, British ships that arrived first. A single ship, the frigate HMS *Lowestoft*, appeared on 9 May, bearing supplies, including newspapers, which, in the politeness of the times, Murray sent over to Lévis in case he was bored. But the British newspapers bore no mention of the plight of Canada.

Still the French hoped their ships would appear, but on 15 May three more British warships appeared before Québec. Early the next morning, the French army retreated west towards Montréal.

On 6 September, the British Major General Jeffrey Amherst and his army, which had advanced northwards up the Richelieu Valley, arrived at Montréal, landing at Lachine with almost no opposition. Amherst demanded the surrender of Montréal. Vaudreuil overrode Lévis, who wanted to continue to fight; but knowing they had no chance, Vaudreuil was concerned about the safety of the population and agreed to the surrender.

On 8 September 1760 the articles of capitulation were signed by Vaudreuil and Amherst. With Vaudreuil's signature, the French Empire in North America came to an end, for not only Montréal, but all of Canada, Acadia, and the western posts, such as Detroit, and the Illinois country were surrendered.

The Treaty of Paris, signed in 1763, confirmed the surrender. Louisiana was lost to the Spanish. The French retained only some ill-defined fishing rights off Newfoundland and the islands of St. Pierre and Miquelon as a fishing base.

MAP 145 (*right*).
The French commander Chevalier de Lévis' plan for the Battle of Sainte-Foy, 28 April 1760. This must be a later copy of a rough plan, for Lévis, like Murray, had not anticipated a fight that day. After the battle, Lévis and Murray established a friendship that was to last a lifetime.

Map 144 (above).

The Battle of Sainte-Foy, 28 April 1760. Some 3,800 French troops fought with 3,866 British as part of an effort to retake Québec. The French won this battle and laid siege to the city, but had to withdraw when British ships arrived on 15 May. The map shows several different times during the battle. From the legend to this map, *A–A* is the initial formation of British troops; *B–B* is their position "soon after the action began in which position they nearly remained until they retreated which was a full three hours." *C* is an early position of ten companies of French grenadiers and three Canadian companies. *D–D* is the initial position of the French army "drawn up four deep"; *E–E* is a later position "in which they were favoured by the woods to conceal their movements"; *F* are French reserves. Numbers *1–5* are later British defences and gun emplacements; *a–f* are the bastions of the walls of Québec. Some letters are unexplained in the legend.

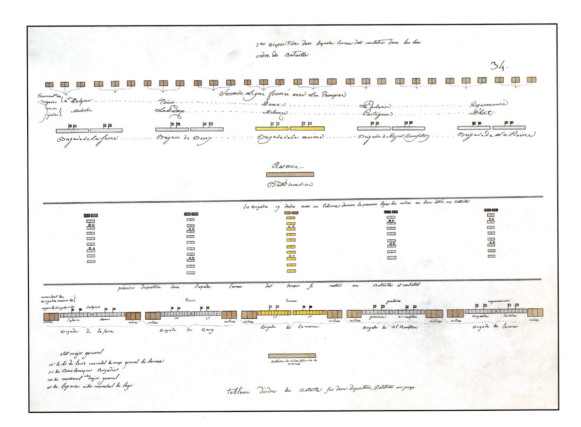

Map 146 (overleaf).

This superb map of the Battle of Québec shows Québec and the countryside around the city, and the battle, in considerable detail. It is a British map, drawn and painted in 1759 soon after the battle. Confusingly, however, it shows the situation at several times all on the same map.

The French battalions are shown in dark blue-grey, together with their names, and labelled *d–d*; they are advancing to the west. Iroquois, supporting the French, are on the flanks, all marked *e*.

The British battalions are shown in red, *b–b*, and are advancing to the east. The smaller red rectangles all marked *c* are various battalions deployed to cover the rear of the attacking force, and also the landing place, depicted at *a* by a gathering of small boats shown complete with oars.

The rectangles with divided colours are the positions of the British encampment after the 18 September capitulation of the city. The squares marked *h* are redoubts, or earthworks, raised to fortify the encampment.

The French encampment before the battle is shown by the divided white and blue-grey rectangles across the St. Charles River on the Beauport shore. The French entrenchments along the shoreline, anticipating a British attack at that location, are shown. Also shown is the bombardment of the city from cannon placed at Point Lévis (off the part of the map reproduced here), across the St. Lawrence from Québec. Note also the fortified approaches guarding the bridge across the St. Charles.

Today the Grand Allée, the main road into old Québec from the west, runs right through the site of the battle. It is a shame that the person who made this map is unknown, for it is such a beautiful map, illustrating an event of major significance in Canadian history.

Road from St. Fois

Road from Silley

HAUTEUR

Anse des M

River

St Charles

High water

TOWN of QUEBEC

D ABRAHAM

Colonies

Cap au Diamant

James Cook's Maps of Eastern Canada

The master navigator and mapmaker of many oceans, James Cook, began his career as a surveyor in Canada.

During the British assault on the fortress of Louisbourg in July 1758, Cook was the master of the *Pembroke,* one of the supporting ships of the Royal Navy. Shortly after the surrender, Cook met a surveyor in the British army, Samuel Holland, who was making a survey of the environs of the fort. Holland and Cook immediately liked one another, and Holland promised to instruct Cook on the use of the plane table. This chance meeting marks the beginnings of James Cook as perhaps the world's master mapmaker. Cook, who was interested in chart-making for navigational use, was introduced to what was, at the time, a much more exact science of land survey.

Following the decision not to attack Québec until the next year, the British fleet was engaged in the despicable task of destroying the settlements of the St. Lawrence so as to remove their ability to supply food to Québec. While this was going on, Cook put his newly learned skills to work carrying out a survey and making a map of Gaspé Bay (MAP 148). The chart was engraved and published in 1759, and it represents the formal initiation of Cook's illustrious career as a maker of maps.

For the final assault on Québec, the British navy faced the daunting task of safely sailing its fleet up the notoriously difficult St. Lawrence and, in particular, the channel just south and east of the Île d'Orléans known as the Traverse. To assist the navy to achieve this, Cook and Holland set to work to prepare a new chart.

Based at first on a compilation of previous British and captured French charts, it was modified "on the fly," for the *Pembroke* was one of the first ships up the river, one of four that sounded the Traverse under heavy guard prior to the arrival of the main fleet. The British fleet under Vice Admiral Charles Saunders ascended the river safely, using Cook and Holland's charts updated by soundings, along with captured French pilots on some of the ships, and the anchoring of ships' boats on either side of the more difficult channels to mark the route. Cook produced a final version of his chart in 1761, with all the updates required for safe navigation by British supply ships. Part of this massive chart is shown below. It is in Cook's own hand, except for two sets of remarks, and is signed by him. It is one of the treasures of the National Archives of Canada.

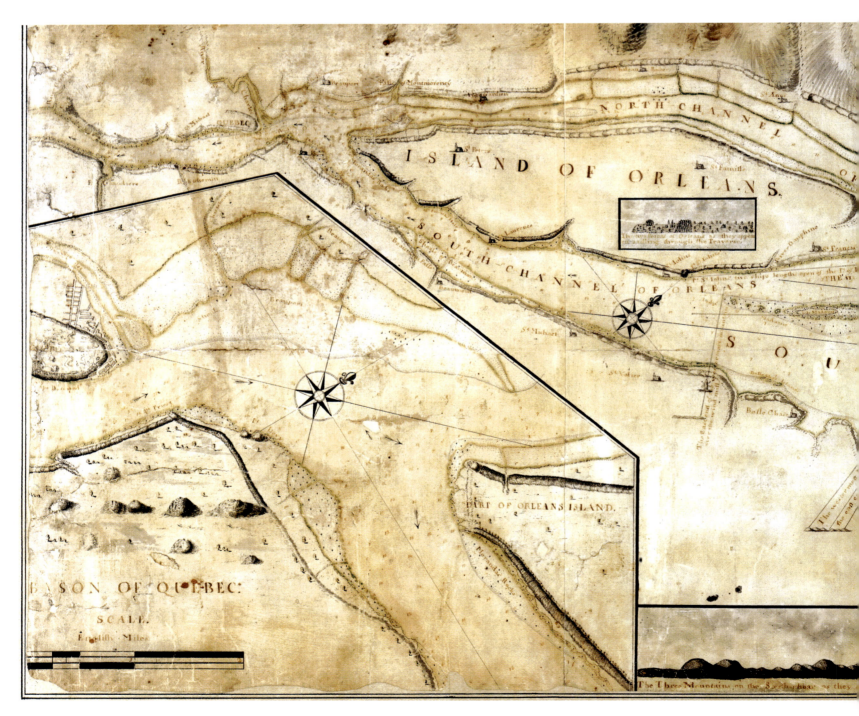

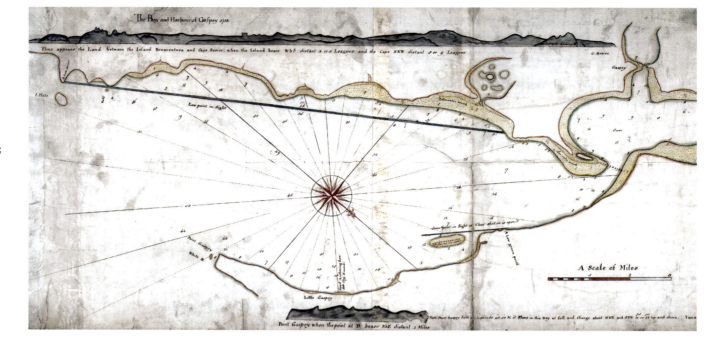

MAP 148 (*right*).
Probably the first map
James Cook ever made is
this 1758 map of the Baie
de Gaspé. This is the
original manuscript map;
it was engraved and
published the next year.
The map was made using
a plane table, a flat surface
with a ruler with a sighting
device, allowing angles for
triangulation to be transferred directly onto paper.

MAP 147 (*below*).
The western part of James Cook's magnificent map of the St. Lawrence, incorporating the information used by the British fleet in the taking of Québec in 1759. In a real sense, this is a map that changed
the course of Canadian history. The Traverse, the narrow shifting channel that was the graveyard of so many ships, is that part of the river south of the eastern end of the Île d'Orléans.

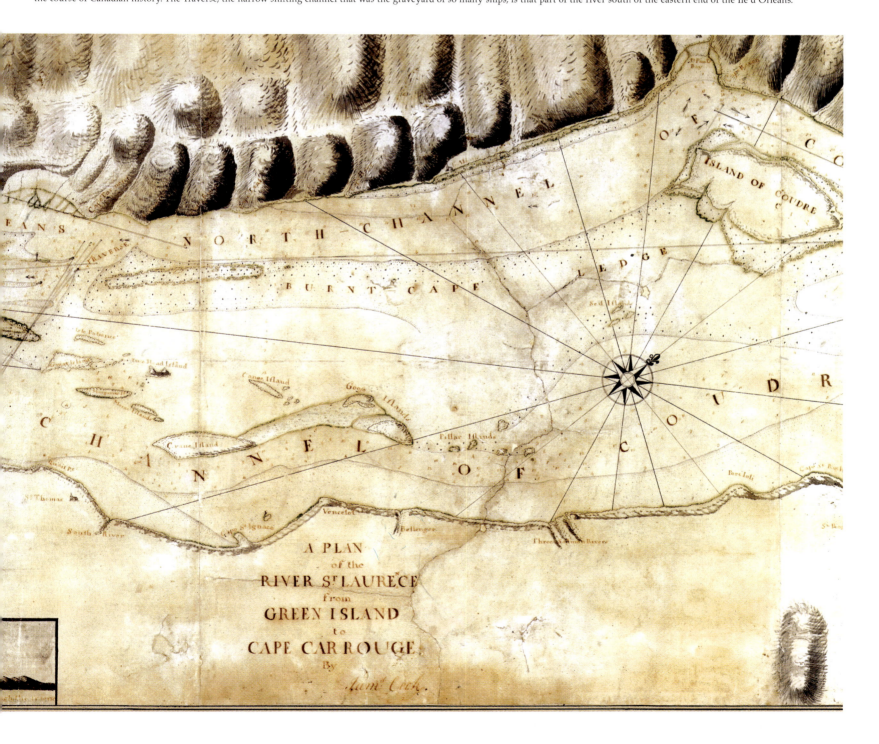

Map 149.

This stunning map is one of the detailed surveys of the Newfoundland and Labrador coasts that Cook produced in the years 1763 to 1767; this one was done in 1763. York Harbour is at the northern entrance to the Strait of Belle Isle, and one of the first available places of refuge for a ship crossing the Atlantic, heading for the strait and thence to Québec. The location is marked on the smaller-scale map overleaf (Map 150, page 110). Without a map, this rock-studded bay would likely have proven more of a hazard than a help. Clearly Cook liked his work; there are hundreds of soundings that have been taken, each carefully recorded, and the artwork is well beyond what the navy would have expected. But it was maps like this one that marked Cook as being a suitable candidate for the voyage of exploration to the Southern Continent to which he was assigned in 1767, what was to be the first of three vastly significant circumnavigations for which he is justly famous today.

A VIEW OF THE COAST OF LABRADORE; WHEN CASTLE ISLAND BORE NE½E DISTANCE 3 or 4 LEAGUES.

…hour, which lyeth Nth.⅙W 8½ Leagues from Cape de Grat in Newfoundland, and NWb4 W 5 Leagues from the SW end of Bell Isle, may
… known by two very remarkable Rocks on Castle and Henley Islands which are flat at tops and has something the resemblance of
… and likewise by five or Six small Islands to the Eastward, nothing appearing to the Westward but an even Bold shoar,
… into it, keep point Grenville either open or shut with the West point of Henley Island, giving the Stag Rocks a proper birth
… into the Harbour between the shoal in the entrance and the black rock off the point of Henley Island, keeping within half a Cables
… of the rock; this passage is recommended only to those who are unacquainted because the black rock is a good mark to sail in by
… the two points before mentioned cannot be easily distinguished by strangers, they had best leave one third of the Bay on the
… side, untill Seal Island is brought behind Henley Island, then edge over towards Esquimaux Island and observe the foregoing
… There is exceeding good anchoring ground in all the different branches of this Harbour particularly in Pitts Harbour which
… recommended as the best for King's Ships, as having the most room and being the most convenient for wooding and watering.
… men would certainly find their account in settling this place as Cod and Seals are here in great plenty, and Temple
… Pitts Harbour will afford Timber for Building such as Fir, Spruce, Juniper and Birch, Henley Harbour seems to be
… convenient place for cureing of Fish, and Seal Islands for catching of Seals where there appears to have been a
considerable Seal Fishery.

REFERENCES.

O. Rocks above Water.

+. Rocks under Water.

The Figures denote the depth of Water in Fathoms at low Water.

Note. The Tides flows full and Change East and West, and rises and falls upon a perpendicular four feet.

BAD BAY

PT. SANDWICH

SANDWICH BAY

FOX ISLAND

SANDWICH ISLES

Latitude 52..01 N.

Var. 25 30′W

B 188

Shelf Ah 4

Only two other copies exist, both in Britain. This map was engraved and printed and published by Thomas Jefferys; it was used for navigation on the St. Lawrence for fifty years.

Cook was transferred to the *Northumberland,* which, after being involved in the relief of the British garrison at Québec in 1760 (see page 99), spent a considerable time in Halifax Harbour. Cook then took part in the retaking of St. John's in 1762; the city had been captured by the French earlier that year.

By the end of the war with France in 1763, Cook's achievements were becoming well known, and in 1763 Cook was assigned to chart the coasts of Newfoundland and Labrador for the new governor of Newfoundland, Thomas Graves. The French had been awarded some fishing rights around the Newfoundland coast, and accurate maps were required. As his first task, Cook charted the islands of St. Pierre and Miquelon before they were handed over to the French, who had been given them under the terms of the Treaty of Paris.

Now Cook was given his first command, a small schooner named, after the British prime minister, *Grenville,* and so began five years of painstaking survey.

He was in particular to "take a compleat survey" of all possible harbours, and one of the first he charted, in 1763, was York Harbour on the coast of Labrador, producing a stunning map that is just as much a work of art as it is a practical guide to navigation (MAP 149). Using the system that by now he had perfected, Cook drew large-scale maps of the coast that were to stand for a long time. His system involved the accurate determination of points and baselines from which a constantly rechecked triangulation was used to fix the positions of everything else. Governor Graves was impressed with Cook's work; his "pains and attention are beyond my description," he wrote to the Admiralty. During a sojourn in England to complete his maps, such was Cook's work noticed that he was even summoned to a meeting with the First Lord of the Admiralty, Lord Egmont. It was virtually unheard of for a mere ship's master to meet with the First Lord.

The next year, 1764, Cook was back to continue his survey, this time for Hugh Palliser, who succeeded Graves as governor of Newfoundland. Palliser had been Cook's captain and an early supporter of his career.

After another season's survey, *Grenville* was back in England, where she was, at Cook's suggestion, refitted as a brig, the sail arrangement of which allowed for considerably more manoeuvrability in tight situations. The following year, 1765, she was back in Newfoundland waters again. Now on the southeast coast, Cook surveyed the intricate coastline, previously uncharted in any detail, with unprecedented accuracy.

A
SKETCH
OF THE
ISLAND OF NEWFOUNDLAND
Done from the latest Observations.
By James Cook. 1763.

SCALE OF LEAGUES 20 to a Degree

EXPLANATION
English Fisheries for many years.
English Fisheries of late years.
Where the French are allowed to fish.
Doubtfully described.

Map 150.

Although not exhibiting the fine detail of his larger-scale maps, this summary map was the most detailed and most accurate map of Newfoundland when it was drawn in 1763, the year Cook began his intricate surveys of the island. The grey band drawn inland from the coast on the northern part of the island shows where the French were allowed to fish after the 1763 treaty. The yellow coastlines are the "doubtfully described" ones that Cook was about to remedy. Note the location of York Harbour, on the Labrador coast at the entrance to the Strait of Belle Isle, shown in detail on Map 149 on the previous page.

During the winter of 1765–66, as his methods evolved, Cook persuaded the Admiralty to provide a tent for land-based fixing of his position astronomically. The next season, 1766, Cook surveyed the southwest coast of Newfoundland. Typical Cook Newfoundland surveys are huge rolls, three to four metres long, kept at the United Kingdom Hydrographic Office, the successor to the Office of the Hydrographer of the Navy. They are beginning to crack from age, and these historically highly significant unique maps are in desperate need of conservation, for which reason we have been unable to reproduce them here.

In August 1766 Cook observed on his own initiative an eclipse of the sun on one of the Burgeo Islands near Cape Ray, at the southwestern tip of Newfoundland, deducing the island's

MAP 151 (*above*).

When Cook sailed off on his famous three voyages around the world, he gave his Newfoundland surveys to Thomas Jefferys, geographer to the king and perhaps the foremost commercial mapmaker. It was a peculiarity of the times that naval personnel appointed to a surveying task by the Admiralty, and paid by it, still had to pay for any commercial engraving and printing themselves, which could be a major problem for the impecunious. Jefferys combined the survey work of Cook with that of his successor, Michael Lane, and published a set of charts of the Newfoundland coast which remained the definitive maps for many years. Part of the published map of the entire island is shown here—the Avalon Peninsula, Placentia Bay, and the southwestern part of the Newfoundland coast. Compare the detail with that on MAP 150, drawn by Cook before his detailed surveys began. Even this map is somewhat generalized; individual section sheets are yet more detailed.

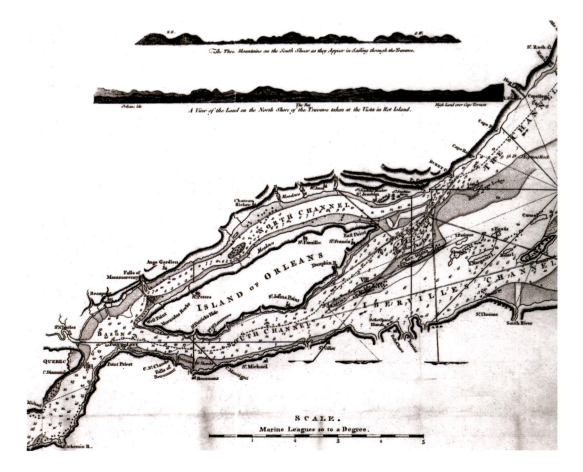

longitude from the event. This information was given to a member of the Royal Society when Cook returned to England, who in turn presented it to the whole society the following year, bringing Cook to the attention of that learned body. This recognition would be a major factor in his selection to lead an expedition to the Pacific.

Cook spent one more year working on his Newfoundland survey, the 1767 season, but he was not allowed to finish it because of his selection for the first of the three voyages which were to make him famous. Taking into account his astronomical work and the maps Cook produced in Newfoundland, it is not hard to see why he was selected for a voyage to the Pacific in 1768, to observe from Tahiti the transit of Venus and to search for the Southern Continent. After 1767, Cook would not see the country that is now Canada again until he reached Nootka Sound on Vancouver Island in 1778, on his third voyage (see page 158).

MAP 152 (*left*).

Part of the map of the St. Lawrence, surveyed by Cook in 1759–61 and engraved and published by Thomas Jefferys in 1775. Clearly shown are the shoals and sandbanks that made this part of the river so treacherous for sailing vessels. Jefferys revised this map based on later information from other surveys; the shoals and sandbars are forever on the move. *The Old Traverse* is marked, as is a newer navigation channel, marked *The New Traverse*. Note the views, coastal profiles drawn to assist ships in visually determining the location of channels.

James Murray's Map

James Murray had been one of James Wolfe's three brigadier generals at the fall of Québec and the commander of the British troops at the Battle of Sainte-Foy the next year.

In the period between the French surrender at Montréal in 1760 and the formal peace treaty of 1763, Murray was the military governor of Québec.

In 1760 Murray decided to put his surveyors to work to create a definitive map of the country now under his command. He appointed Captain Samuel Holland, James Cook's mentor, to survey the areas around Québec and Montréal, and several others assisted in other regions. The area south of Montréal, to Lachine, was surveyed by Lieutenant John Montressor, another military engineer and surveyor.

The maps produced as a result of these surveys were by far the best existing at the time, and, as can be seen from the examples here, they were very beautiful maps too. They were mounted on forty-four linen sheets and stand as a superb record of "the settled part of the Province of Québec"—the overall title of the maps—at the end of the French regime.

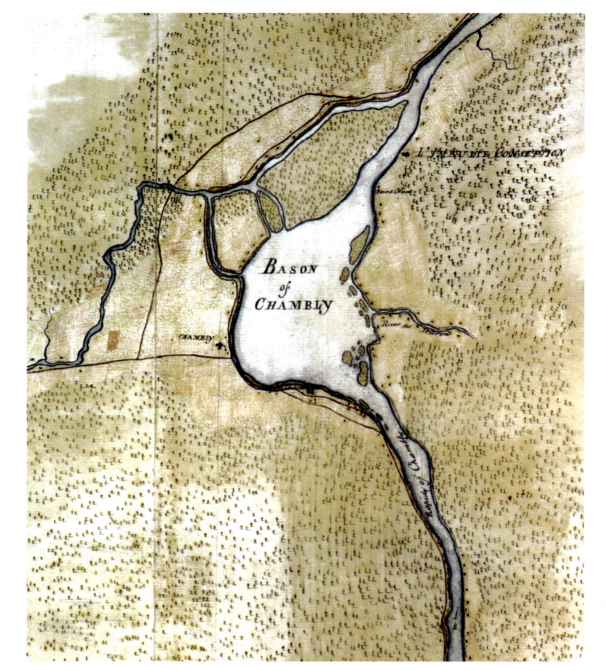

MAP 153 (*above*); MAP 154 (*left*); MAP 155 (*right*). Three sections of the map produced for General James Murray over a three-year period immediately after the French surrender in 1760. The map was intended as a British military assessment of the populated parts of Québec province.

MAP 153 (*above*), of the area around Chambly, on the Richelieu River just east of Montréal, notes (not reproduced here) that there are 201 families in the area and 299 "Men able to bear Arms." Fort Chambly, with rare poor cartography, is almost obscured by the roads. The north-south road was one from near Sorel to Saint-Jean, one of the first Canadian roads away from the St. Lawrence (although it was not until 1763 that Montréal and Québec were connected by road). The road leading in from the west (left) was a connecting road from La Prairie, opposite Montréal, begun in 1739 to connect the fort to Montréal and open up the countryside. This map and MAP 155 (*right*), of the Montréal area, are fine examples of the work of the able Samuel Holland, who had taught James Cook to survey in the Gaspé in 1758, after the fall of Louisbourg. Holland was assisted in his work by his ability to speak French; this skill also had other benefits, for in 1762 he eloped with the daughter of a French landowner.

MAP 154 (*left*), of the Lachine area, was the work of John Montressor. It shows the point at which the later Lachine Canal, built in the 1820s to circumvent rapids on the St. Lawrence, left the river. The work of Murray's surveyors was combined into one multi-sheet map; this is now in the National Archives of Canada.

LAWRENCE

LONGUEIL

Montreal

St. PAUL

References of Montre...

a. Cathedrale and Semina...
b. Recollets Convent
c. Irwin's Cottage
d. General Hospital
e. Hotel Dieu
f. Sisters of the Congregation
g. Governors House
h. Intendants House
i. Chappel
k. Battery
l. Kings Store

French Works on the Island
Helions made during the Sieg...

Québec under the British

With the signing of the Treaty of Paris in 1763, Canada passed officially into British hands, together with Île Royale, renamed Cape Breton Island. A new region called the Province of Québec was defined to refer to the St. Lawrence heartland, home of the majority of the French population. Thus were the British first to extend the use of the name Québec from the city to a wider area. They probably chose to do this to distinguish it from the vast former French Empire that, apart from Louisiana, was now under British control. The boundaries of the new province are shown on MAP 156, at right. Significantly, although the French population could not hold office, they were guaranteed property rights and limited religious freedom, a major concession for a British king whose oath demanded all his subjects be Protestant. Yet it was thought essential by the British in order to govern their new possession.

A Royal Proclamation in 1763 defined the legal basis for government of the newly conquered territories, in Canada and elsewhere. A large area outside the Province of Québec was defined as an Indian reserve and allowed negotiation of treaties with aboriginal peoples. This continues today; the Constitution Act of 1982 allows no diminution of native rights from those in the Royal Proclamation.

The restrictive boundaries divided French from English-speaking areas and also, it was hoped, meant that Britain would only lose the St. Lawrence Valley should there be a reversion to France at any time in the future.

In August 1763 James Murray received a commission as Captain-General and Governor-in-Chief of Québec. But despite the title he was to be a civil governor, not a military one, and he was unhappy to lose his military command. He protested, but to no avail. The British government's policy was to rule its colonies with civil governors and keep the military under the command of an officer appointed from Britain, just in case the governor tried to exceed his powers.

In 1774 the Québec Act was passed. It was mainly the idea of Sir Guy Carleton, later Baron Dorchester, the second British governor of Québec, who had taken over from James Murray in 1768. Carleton had been James Wolfe's quartermaster general at the fall of Québec.

The Québec Act extended the boundaries of the province to include Labrador, the Île d'Anticosti, and the Îles de la Madeleine; as well as the Indian territory south of the Great Lakes, between the Mississippi and the Ohio Rivers. This recognized the fact that the 1763 Royal Proclamation had left large tracts of land with no laws. The Act was to have far-reaching consequences.

Britain's American colonies were outraged over what they saw as a pre-emption of the land into which they wished to expand, and denounced it as an "intolerable act"—one attributed as one of the roots of the American Revolution.

Québec was to be governed by the governor and seventeen to twenty-three appointed councillors. The Act allowed an oath of office without reference to religion, and thus the largely Roman Catholic French could now hold

office. British criminal law but French civil law were established. Thus the seigneurial system of land holdings (see page 76) was continued.

The Québec Act was eventually replaced by the Constitutional Act of 1791, which abolished the Province of Québec as such, substituting in its place the province of Lower Canada, with Upper Canada (Ontario) as a new province to accommodate the influx of Loyalists after the American Revolution (see page 126).

Map 156.
Jonathan Carver's map of the new Province of Québec, with the original 1763 boundaries. These boundaries would be extended in 1774 to include much of what is today the United States. The extension was one of the many causes of the American Revolution, and resulted in the loss of much territory to the new country in 1783 (see page 124).

The American Attack on Québec

When the opening shots of the American Revolution were fired, Québec was viewed by the incipient Americans as just another British colony that would likely want to join the revolution. In October 1774 the Continental Congress at Philadelphia published an address to the people of Québec denouncing the Québec Act as a violation of human rights and inviting Québec to send representatives to Philadelphia. It was widely disseminated by the newpapers of the province.

There was certainly some interest shown, particularly in Montréal. But Québec was much more dependent on its colonial status for trade than were the American colonies, and there was no more general upwelling of support.

On 20 May 1775, Governor Guy Carleton learned that the Americans were invading Québec via the Lake Champlain route. Carleton called out the militia but was disappointed to find that not all answered his summons. Luckily for him, the American incursion, which was not sanctioned by the provisional government, was not very well organized.

Earlier in May, American revolutionaries Benedict Arnold and Ethan Allen had captured forts at Ticonderoga and Crown Point, about 180 km south of Montréal, and by 19 May had also captured British ships on Lake Champlain. There they paused; Congress had decided to sponsor a "real" invasion, and for this, preparations took time. Arnold was replaced as commander by Richard Montgomery, an Irish general and one-time fellow officer of Carleton's. Ethan Allen was sent to Montréal to recruit Canadians for the Revolutionary cause but, in late September, succeeded only in getting himself captured by a force led by Carleton himself.

Montgomery's forces advanced up the Richelieu River and took Fort Chambly, capturing its food supplies and gunpowder, and a fort at Saint-Jean fell on 2 November. At this, Carleton decided Montréal was indefensible, retreated to Québec, and prepared for a siege. The Americans, unopposed, occupied Montréal on 13–14 November.

In the meantime, Benedict Arnold, not to be outdone by Montgomery, had organized a Massachusetts force and advanced on Québec via another route, that of the Kennebec and Chaudière Rivers; the latter enters the St. Lawrence just upstream from Québec. This was a tortuous, not very practical route (MAP 157) completely unsuited to the movement of an army, but somehow Arnold and seven hundred men made it to Québec, arriving in mid-November. They actually arrived a few days before the returning Carleton, but retired upstream to await the arrival of Montgomery's force.

On the night of 31 December 1775, in a blizzard, Montgomery attempted to take Québec. He landed in the Lower Town (the place is marked on MAP 158), hoping by taking that part of the city to force the surrender of the rest. Fighting in the narrow streets of the Lower Town followed, with scenes of great confusion. Montgomery was killed, Arnold was injured, and the assault failed.

The siege, however, continued through the winter. In April 1776 gun batteries were set up opposite the city, in the same spot that Robert Monckton, one of James Wolfe's brigadier generals, had set up cannon in 1759. Cannon were also set up across the St. Charles River. The locations are shown on MAP 158.

In the same month the American Congress sent representatives, including Benjamin Franklin, to Québec to discuss terms of union. They were wasting their time; they got nowhere, and soon left.

MAP 157.
The route Benedict Arnold took with seven hundred Massachusetts troops to attack Québec in November 1775. The route follows the Kennebec River, the Dead River, and the Chaudière River. The route was unsuitable for an army, but Arnold made it to Québec anyway, being helped at one point by a native map drawn on birchbark (see page 152).

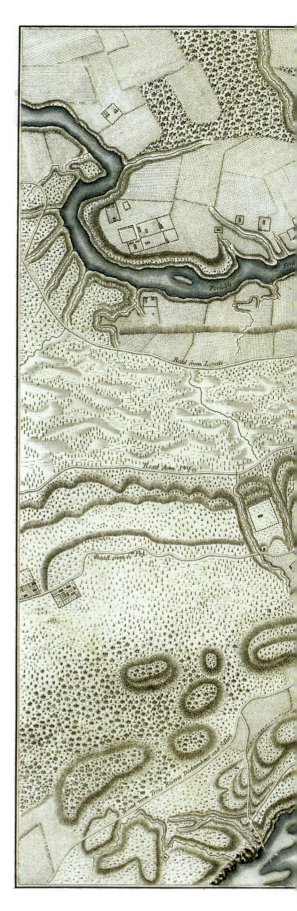

Now, following a pattern that may seem somewhat familiar by this time, British reinforcements arrived; on 6 May the warship *Surprise* anchored before Québec, from the American point of view living up to its name, for it was the first of a fleet carrying ten thousand troops.

The Americans hastily withdrew to Sorel, where the Richelieu enters the St. Lawrence. American forces in Montréal abandoned the city on 9 May. Then, anticipating their own reinforcements, the Americans advanced once again

Map 158.

This beautifully engraved map was prepared by William Faden, the king's geographer after Thomas Jefferys, maker of a long line of informational maps similar to this one. The map was a commercial venture published in London in September 1776 to feed the appetite of a public voracious for news of the war. As is normal for this type of map, it depicts events that actually occurred at different times. The gun emplacements of April 1776 are shown, and the notation on that across the St. Lawrence from Québec states that it was the same place Robert Monckton set up his guns in 1759. Another battery of mortars is shown on the Plains of Abraham. Guns set up in December 1775 on the Plains are also shown. In the Lower Town, where the assault of 31 December 1775 took place, *L* is where Montgomery landed "between 4 and 5 in the morning," and *M* marks the location of Arnold's attack and where he was wounded. The walls of Québec and the layout of the city are very clearly shown.

as far as Trois Rivières. Here they found themselves opposed by a much larger British force than they had anticipated, and so, once again, they retreated, quickly and in disarray, but now they continued south to Lake Champlain.

That was the end of the first American invasion of Canada. Carleton was knighted for defending Québec but chastized for letting the American forces retreat without intervening. Thus when it came time for a British force to invade what is now American territory, Carleton was not in charge, but General John Burgoyne.

It was perhaps just as well for Carleton. Due to a lack of boats, it was a year before Burgoyne could advance down Lake Champlain. He ended up on 17 October 1777 at Saratoga, where he was forced to surrender his entire army to an American one that included Benedict Arnold; it was one of the more celebrated American victories of the Revolutionary War.

Prince Edward Island

After the loss of Acadia to the British by the Treaty of Utrecht in 1713, the French government hoped that the inhabitants of that region would relocate to Île St. Jean (Prince Edward Island) or Île Royale (Cape Breton Island). But, reluctant to abandon established farms, they did not move in any number.

After the fall of Louisbourg in 1744 (see page 88), a British detachment was sent to Île St. Jean, landing at and occupying Port La Joie. But the Treaty of Aix-la-Chapelle in 1748 returned the island (and Louisbourg) to the French, and with the founding of Halifax in 1749, French settlers from Acadia flooded to Île St. Jean. The population swelled from only 650 to about 4,500.

There was no respite from turmoil; in 1758 Louisbourg fell again, and British troops descended on Île St. Jean and began to expel the French settlers, as had happened in Acadia three years before. And this time, with the Treaty of Paris in 1763, the island remained British; renamed the Island of St. John, it was added to Nova Scotia.

Demand for land on the fertile island was high, and the government decided to essentially give it away. With a variation on earlier colonization schemes, they gave it not to a single company but to sixty-seven proprietors, chosen in 1767 by lottery. They were supposed to settle "foreign Protestants" on their lands, to avoid a drain on Britain's population. But such settlers were difficult to find, and absentee landlords—who often did not pay their taxes—and lack of freehold lands meant there was only slow population growth thereafter.

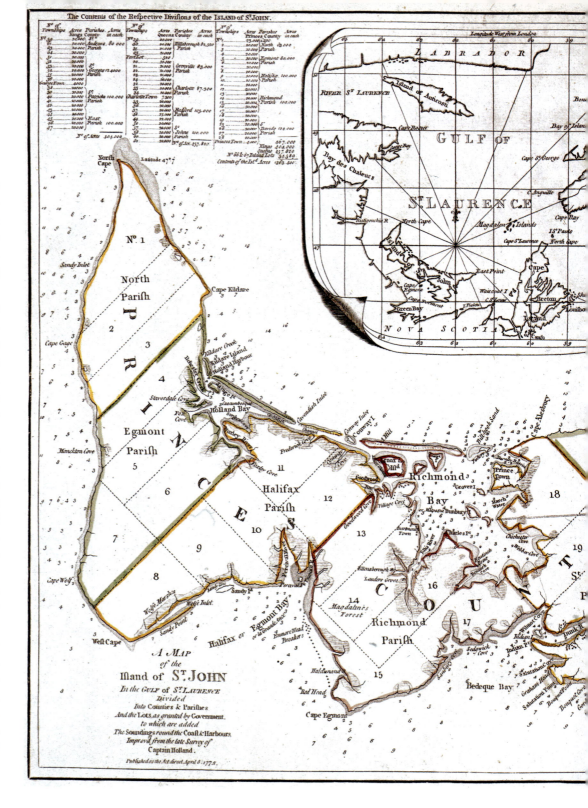

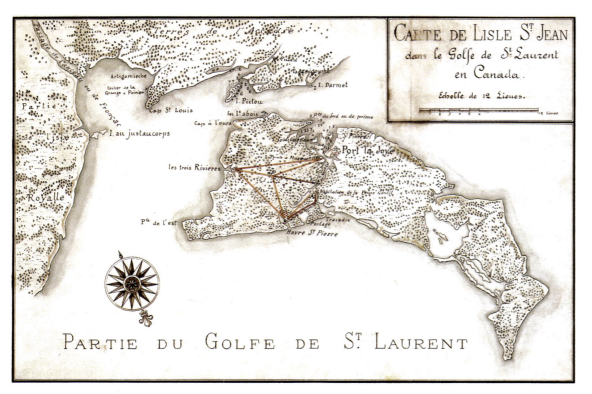

MAP 159 (left).
A French map of Île St. Jean, 1751, drawn by French engineer Louis Franquet. South is at the top. *Port La Joye* (Port La Joie) was the capital. It is on the site of the ruins of the British Fort Amherst, across the harbour from today's Charlottetown,

MAP 160 (above).
One of the surveyors of the Island of St. John was Samuel Holland. The British king, George III, interested in surveying his newly acquired realm, instructed Governor James Murray of Québec to survey the island in 1764, and Murray sent his surveyor general, Samuel Holland, to do the job. Holland was responsible for the subdivision of the island into sixty-seven lots; these were given away by lottery in 1767. In this, he received Lot 28, and he was one of the few to bring in settlers. This map, engraved and published in 1775, clearly shows the "Lots as granted by Government . . . Improved from the late Survey of Captain Holland." The new site of Charlottetown is shown. The townsite was laid out in 1768 by Charles Morris, the chief surveyor of Nova Scotia, of which the island was part until 1769, when it was made a separate colony. Morris selected a site across the harbour from the French Port La Joie. The town was named after Queen Charlotte, the wife of George III.

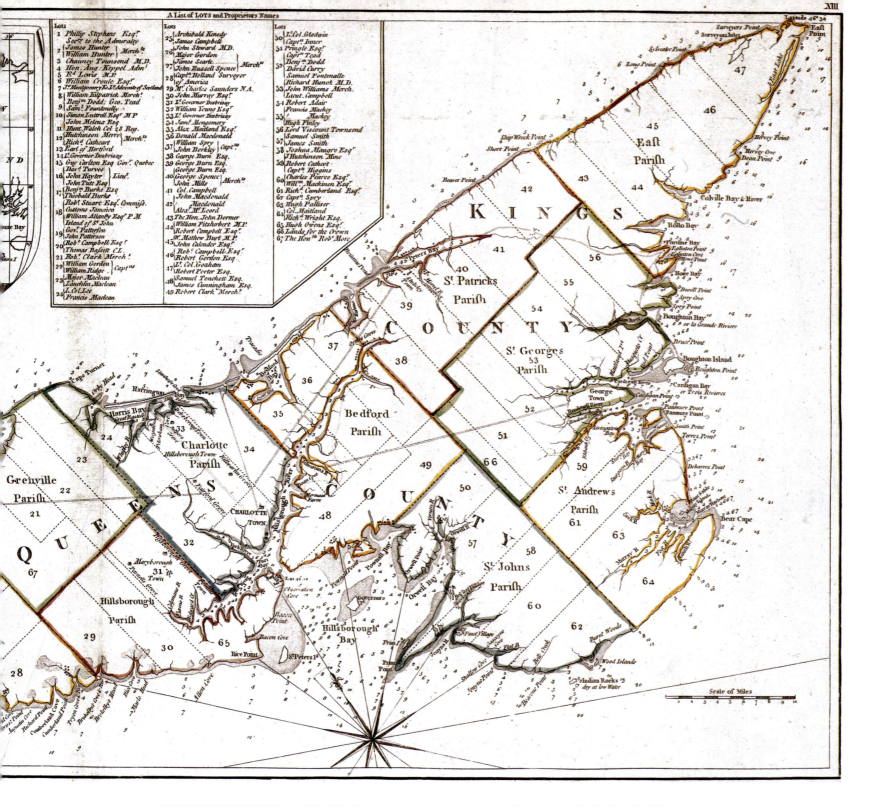

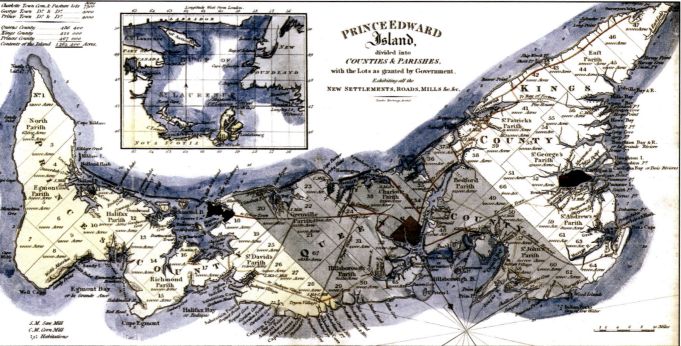

Map 161 (*right*). A map by H. Ashby, 1798. In 1799 Île St. Jean was renamed Prince Edward Island, after a son of George III stationed at the time in Halifax. Prince Edward was later the father of Queen Victoria. The decision to rename the island was obviously made by 1798, for this map, the first to use the new name, predates the official implementation of the name in 1799.

The Coastal Surveys of Des Barres

As we have seen, after the fall of Québec the British wanted to survey their newly acquired realm. James Cook covered Labrador and Newfoundland, Samuel Holland and others the Province of Québec and Prince Edward Island.

A Swiss-born military surveyor, Joseph Frédéric Wallet Des Barres, who, like Holland and Cook, had been with James Wolfe at Québec, was appointed by the Admiralty to survey the coasts of Nova Scotia and Cape Breton Island. Des Barres' efforts were destined to consume more time than those of his compatriots. He worked from 1764 to 1774 surveying, followed by another ten years preparing, publishing, and revising his charts.

It was not until 1777 that Des Barres was able to publish the first edition of the work he is famous for, his navigational atlas called the *Atlantic Neptune*. The atlas is a masterpiece of precise surveying and is also artistically presented. Des Barres was professionally trained in landscape drawing and typically added views to

assist map users in recognizing navigational features, as in MAP 163, above.

In later life, for his achievements he was appointed governor of the new colony of Cape Breton Island in 1784, and in 1785 he laid out the settlement that would become Sydney. From 1804 to 1812 he was governor of Prince Edward Island.

When he died in 1824 his obituary in a Halifax newspaper stated: "The charts he prepared from his own surveys of this province will give his memory claims of gratitude upon the nautical world and could only have been performed by a man of surprising perseverance."

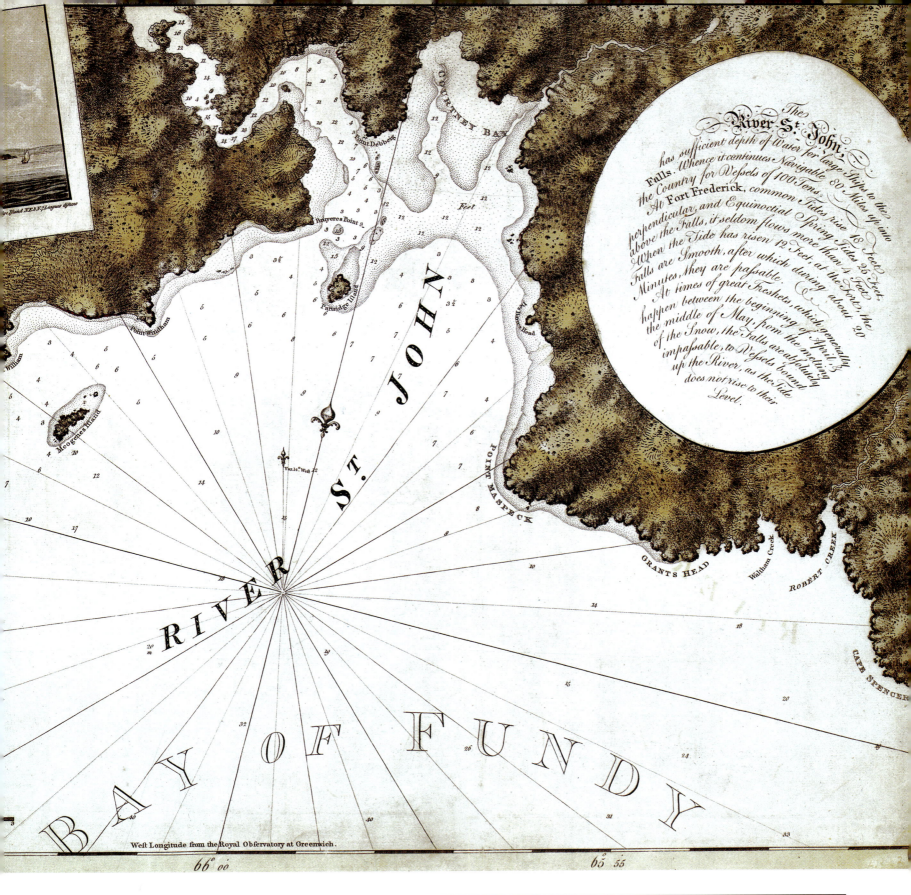

MAP 162 (*left*).
Des Barres' chart of Halifax in 1777.

MAP 163 (*above*).
This map of the entrance to the harbour at Saint John is typical of the quality of Des Barres' surveys. It is from the 1780 edition of his *Atlantic Neptune,* an atlas of navigational charts originally prepared for the British navy, but also sold commercially. The design and engraving are of a very high standard; even the writing in the cartouche is beautifully executed.

MAP 164 (*right*).
Part of the summary map of the eastern coast of Canada, again from the 1780 edition of the *Atlantic Neptune.* Although at small scale, it gives a good idea of the amount of surveying work that must have gone into Des Barres' maps.

The Demise of the Beothuk

The Beothuk of Newfoundland are thought to be the original "Red Indians," so-called from the ochre with which they painted their faces. They are a vanished people. Life was always a struggle on the island due to the rugged nature of the land. When European settlers arrived, the Beothuk shunned contact with them and retreated into the interior, where life was even harder. The Beothuk were at one time often hunted down by settlers intent on preventing theft, for the Beothuk acquired the iron and other goods they wanted not by trade but by theft.

Lieutenant John Cartwright spent the years 1766–70 in Newfoundland as a magistrate. He became aware of the plight of the Beothuk and set out to document their condition. In 1768 he was sent by Governor Hugh Palliser to one of the remaining areas of Beothuk concentration, along the Exploits River, which flows from Red Indian Lake—called Lieutenant's Lake by Cartwright—in central Newfoundland northwest to the Atlantic past the modern town of Grand Falls–Windsor. The map he drew (MAP 167), complete with illustrations of artifacts, is one of the few records of Beothuk life that survive.

In 1810, realizing Beothuk numbers were dwindling, the British government belatedly issued a proclamation protecting them and began attempting to contact them. But after centuries of conflict, the communication efforts often backfired. Settlers at Twillingate were still shooting Beothuk on sight in 1810, when an expedition led by Lieutenant David Buchan finally made contact. To gain their trust, Buchan de-

MAP 165.
John Cartwright drew this map of Newfoundland in 1773, after a five-year stay on the island. The *River Exploits* (Exploits River), the main area of the Beothuk at the time, is clearly marked. *Lieutenant's Lake* (Red Indian Lake) is incorrectly joined to *Lake Mickmac* (Grand Lake). The map was submitted to Governor Palliser with Cartwright's report, which also included MAP 167 (*right*).

tailed two of his men to stay overnight at the Beothuk camp while two Beothuk warriors slept with his party. In the morning, his Beothuk departed suddenly. Later, Buchan found the bodies of his two men, beheaded and mutilated, ending the mission. Buchan went on to become an Arctic explorer (see page 184).

In the winter of 1818–19, after Beothuk had stolen a boat belonging to a local landowner, a group of settlers went up the River Exploits to attempt to recover it. The governor of Newfoundland commissioned them to capture some Beothuk. With nineteenth-century logic, the idea was to use the captives as a means of establishing friendly relations with these elusive people. They captured one native woman, Demasduit, later named Mary March by her captors. This was a patently absurd way to attempt to improve relations with the Beothuk; the settlers shot Demasduit's husband when he tried to prevent them from taking her away. As it was, Demasduit contracted tuberculosis and died soon after reaching a coastal settlement.

In 1823, after another clash, Beothuk numbers were reduced to very few, and one native woman, Shanawdithit, Demasduit's niece, allowed herself to be captured, along with her mother and sister, who both died from tuberculosis soon after their capture. For five years Shanawdithit lived at the house of a wealthy landowner as a servant. In 1828 she was sent to the Beothuk Institution, founded by William Epps Cormack in 1827 with the goal of "opening a communication with and promoting the civilization of the Red Indians of Newfoundland." Cormack had gained fame in 1822 by walking across Newfoundland .

Cormack's motives were good, and he looked after Shanawdithit well, but she also contracted the dreaded tuberculosis. She died in June 1829.

In the few months that she was with Cormack, Shanawdithit learned to communicate with him, and when he provided her with pencils, she drew a series of maps and pictures that provide the bulk of the information we have about the Beothuk today.

Shanawdithit drew maps that recorded both the Buchan and Mary March episodes, one of which is shown here (MAP 166).

It seems likely that Shanawdithit was the last Beothuk alive, for no more people of her race were ever found.

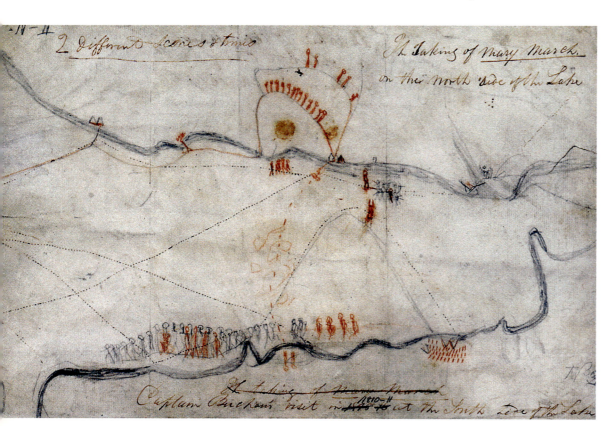

MAP 166 (*left*).
Shanawdithit's map of the 1819 "Taking of Mary March" incident *and* Captain Buchan's visit in 1810. The map was drawn for William Cormack in 1828 or 1829. It depicts scenes from both the Mary March and Buchan incidents; someone has written "2 different scenes and times" on the map. The red figures are the Beothuk—the "Red Indians." The activity shown on the southern shore of Red Indian Lake records the visit of David Buchan in 1810; a line of marines and four natives is shown going along the shore of the lake towards the Exploits River. On the north shore the kidnapping of Demasduit (Mary March) is shown. Beothuk wigwams are shown on the shore, and one is red, perhaps indicating it was covered with the sail from the stolen boat. The two semicircles with figures are the rest of the Beothuk hiding in the woods, including, presumably, a young Shanawdithit. The settlers are shown standing on the ice in fainter outline. The red figure in front of them is Nonosgawut, Demasduit's husband, protesting the kipnapping, while the figure lying on the ice is Nonosgawut after being shot by the settlers.

Map 167.

The map drawn by John Cartwright to illustrate his report of the condition of the Beothuk, submitted to Governor Palliser in 1773. It illustrates his expedition to the Exploits River in north central Newfoundland in 1768. The map contains some of the only evidence of the Beothuk way of life that survives. The locations of Beothuk wigwams and square dwellings are marked, lining the riverbanks. The reddish ink has faded somewhat. The map also contains drawings of Beothuk artifacts. At bottom left is a view of a Beothuk conical wigwam built around a framework of saplings and covered with sheets of birchbark. Also illustrated are a Beothuk canoe and paddle, a bow and arrow, quivers, an axe, and containers. The map is oriented with southeast at the top.

Defining Canada, 1783

As the American Revolutionary War drew to a close, the British came to realize that, since they had held on to Canada, a new boundary would need to be defined separating their remaining territories from those of the new nation.

Treaty discussions opened in Paris in 1780. Initial American demands were for the concession of all of Canada. Benjamin Franklin, one of the American representatives, suggested Britain should be willing to make a "voluntary offer of Canada" as a reconciliatory measure. Richard Oswald, the British negotiator in Paris, was inclined to agree, contending the "government of Canada" was "worth nothing."

Later, American demands were based on the restricted boundaries of the Province of Québec according to the Royal Proclamation of 1763. This boundary was actually agreed to by the British government in August 1782, so great was the desire for peace at any price. The British were concerned at the time over the possibility of Franco-Spanish co-operation in the war, and a Spanish attack on Gibraltar was imminent.

Had the treaty been completed in the next month, the United States probably would have gained all the territory up to the line running east-southeast from Lake Nipissing (see MAP 156, pages 114–15), which includes most of the the territory of modern Ontario. Oswald followed his government's instructions and drafted a treaty during September and early October which conceded this not inconsiderable territory to the United States.

However, by the end of September sentiment in Britain had changed; Gibraltar had withstood the Spanish onslaught and the British government now wanted a boundary line which did not interfere with the fur trade out of Montréal, now run by largely Scottish interests. A boundary along rivers and lakes was now negotiated, which was considered easier to define. John Mitchell's great 1755 map of America, 1775 edition, was used, and on it the proposed boundary line was drawn (MAP 168, right). The problem was that unbeknownst to the negotiators on both sides, the map had a number of inaccuracies which would later lead to considerable problems defining the boundary in the field.

The map showed the Mississippi River rising in Canada, so when the negotiators reached Lake of the Woods and ran out of known territory to the west, they simply drew a line due west to the Mississippi, an impossible situation. MAP 169 shows an interpretation of the treaty with the Mississippi in the wrong location, while the map by Robert Sayer (MAP 170) acknowledges the problem with two boundary lines that do not meet. Again, in the east, the disagree-

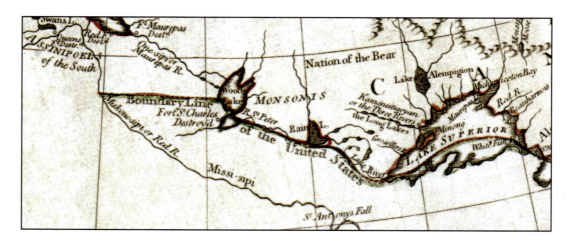

MAP 169.
This anonymous map dated 1785 shows the boundary between the United States and British territory exactly as described in the 1783 Treaty of Paris. The boundary is drawn due west from Lake of the Woods (here *Woods Lake*) to the Mississippi. The problem was that in reality the Mississippi was further south.

MAP 168 (*above*).
John Mitchell's map of the eastern part of North America has been called the most important and the most famous map in American history. It is arguably just as important for Canadian history, for this 1775 edition of the map was used by Treaty of Paris negotiators to agree on a boundary between the United States and what would become Canada. This is part of the eastern half of this very large map, thought to be the one actually used by the negotiators. A red line defining the agreed-upon boundary has been drawn by British representative Richard Oswald in 1782, and because of this it is popularly known in the British Library, where it is kept, as "the red-lined map." British interpretations of boundaries from the Treaty of Utrecht in 1713 have also been drawn on the map. John Mitchell was a Virginia-born physician and botanist living in England when he turned his hand to cartography with the intent of illustrating the French threat to the British colonies. The map took him five years to complete and the first edition was published in 1755. It is large (197 x 140 cm) and comprehensive in scope. Further editions were published, confusingly all still with the 1755 date, of which the last was the 1775 edition, published seven years after Mitchell's death.

ment of the terminology of the treaty with geography left 31 000 km^2 in dispute. Most of the problems of border definition were not solved until 1842 (see page 202).

A preliminary new Treaty of Paris was signed on 30 November 1782; it was ratified by the United States on 15 April 1783, and by Britain on 6 August. With it, the modern boundaries of the eastern half of Canada were defined, subject only to the resolution of discrepancies caused by inadequate maps and imperfect geographical knowledge.

MAP 170.
Part of a 1786 map by British mapmaker Robert Sayer. The map is now more accurate; Sayer places the Mississippi nearer to its correct position, but in the process two boundary lines are created that do not meet. The dangers of drawing a boundary when your maps are wrong is graphically illustrated!

The Coming of the Loyalists

After the end of the French regime in 1763 the English-speaking population of Canada did not grow very much for a dozen years. But after 1775, and particularly after 1783, the English-speaking population grew rapidly, and the new province of Upper Canada, now Ontario, and the new colony of New Brunswick were created.

The reason for this sudden increase in population was the migration of Loyalist set-tlers from the area which became the United States of America, offically recognized by Brit-ain in 1783. The American Revolution caused a massive redistribution of population within North America and, in the process, kick-started the growth of Canada.

During the years 1783 and 1784, 50,000 Loyalists flooded into the territory that is now Canada. In the summer of 1783 some 32,000 Loyalists left New York City for Nova Scotia, and another 1,300 left for Québec. Measures had to be taken to accommodate this influx.

In Nova Scotia, most good land had already been transferred into private hands by the British, who were trying to encourage settlement. The expulsion of the Acadians had left a lot of land vacant. After the fall of Louisbourg, the French threat had been removed, and Governor Charles

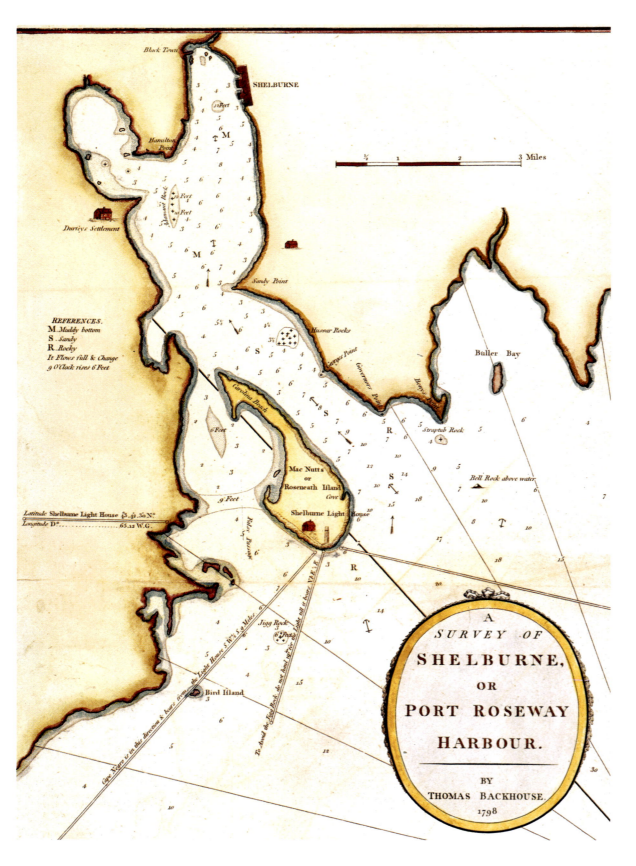

MAP 171.
Alexander McNutt, a land promoter, acquired a great deal of land in Nova Scotia from the land grants of the 1760s. One of his promotions was Port Roseway, on the coast south of Halifax, on what appeared to be a good harbour. It did not prosper until, in 1783, returned to the government by escheat, it attracted 3,000 Loyalist settlers, with many more to follow. By the end of the year the population was probably 12,000, larger than that of Halifax. Renamed Shelburne, it seemed set for a bright future. But the harbour was found to be too shallow for merchant ships, and agricultural potential proved to be limited on the infertile and rocky land. Shelburne quickly shrank as settlers moved to other areas. This beautiful map was prepared in 1798 by Thomas Backhouse.

Above is a view of modern Shelburne. The village centre has been reconstructed as authentically as possible. This is the market square.

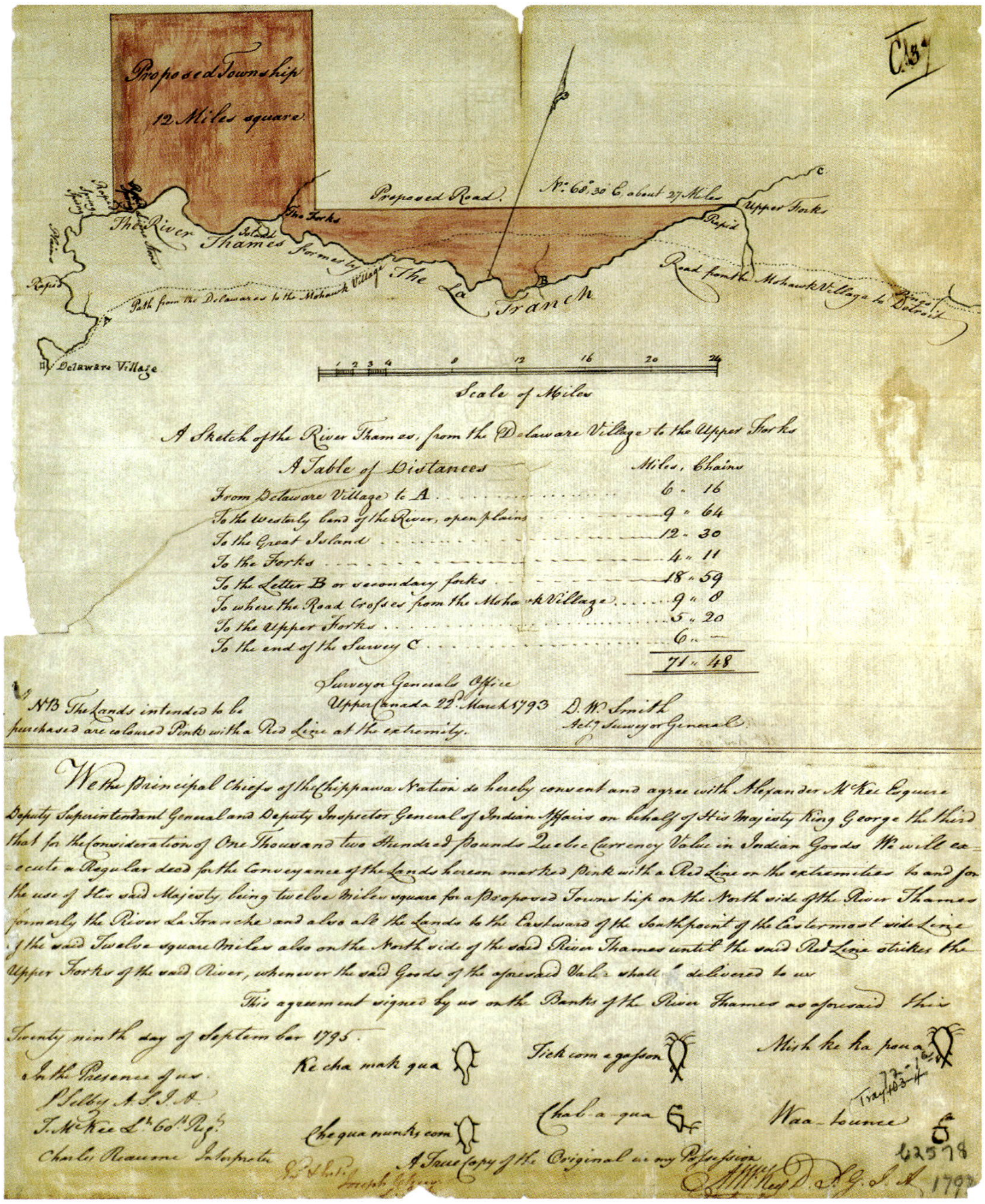

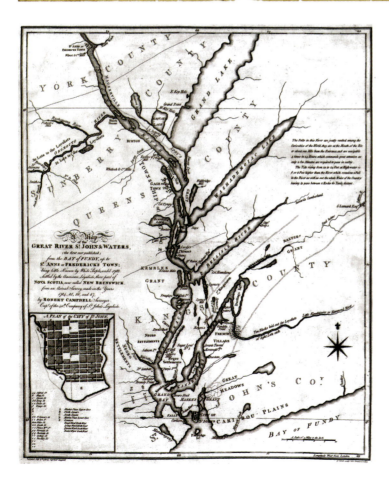

Lawrence had offered "vacated lands" in Nova Scotia to prospective settlers. Three million acres had been granted in 1765 alone. By 1764 the Nova Scotia population had reached almost 13,000, including about 2,600 Acadians who had managed to escape deportation. Nevertheless, vast amounts of land granted to absentee landowners had not been settled but held as a speculation.

These land grants were cancelled by a process called escheat and made available for Loyalists. Charles Morris, the surveyor general, was appointed by Governor John Parr to both survey and allocate lands. The first wave of Loyalists arrived at Port Roseway, on the east coast, in May 1783. Soon a quick survey and townsite layout were made, and buildings constructed. Rapidly becoming larger than Halifax, Port Roseway was renamed Shelburne after Parr's patron, the Earl of Shelburne. But this town was not to prosper; by 1787 it had shrunk to a small village, for in the haste, the harbour had not been properly assessed, and it turned out to be too shallow to accommodate larger ships.

Other groups of Loyalists settled on the Saint John River, north across the Bay of Fundy, the remotest part of Nova Scotia at the time. Fertile land suitable for farming was the attraction here, and Saint John itself was situated on a fine harbour. Some of the last British soldiers to leave New York arrived after the best lands near Saint John had been allocated and so moved farther upriver, laying out a town at St. Anne, which became Fredericton, named after a son of George III.

The new settlers lobbied for independence from far-off Halifax, and in June 1784, the colony of New Brunswick was created by the British government.

In Québec, most of the 10,000 Loyalists were soldiers already in the province, having successfully defended against American incursion attempts. About 800 Loyalists remained in Québec, taking up seigneurial lots, and a few went to Cape Breton Island, which, in anticipation of an influx, was made a separate colony in 1784. But the majority settled in what is today southern Ontario.

The governor of Québec, Frederick Haldimand, who had succeeded Guy Carleton in 1778, was aware of the potential of lands along the St. Lawrence and the shores of the Great Lakes, and this is where he decided to locate his disbanded Loyalist troops.

After the peace in 1783, Haldimand at first considered this "upper country" to be a good place to settle native groups who had sided with the British in the war, and in 1784 Six Nations native people led by Mohawk chief Joseph Brant were granted a large tract of land centred on the Grand River, around today's Brantford, Ontario.

Since 1763, the British had recognized native land ownership in southern Ontario, and

MAP 172 (above).
A deed with a map showing the purchase of land in the Thames River Valley from the Chippewa in 1795 and the proposed Loyalist township, at the location of today's city of London, Ontario. The map was drawn by D. W. Smith, the acting surveyor general, and is signed by six native chiefs. The document carries the notation "A True copy of the Original in my Possession," with the signature of Alexander McKee, the deputy superintendent general of Indian affairs for Upper Canada.

MAP 173 (left).
This map of the Saint John River was drawn by Robert Campbell, who in August 1783 led 190 civilian Loyalists to what he called "this remote part of Nova Scotia," which the following year would become the separate colony of New Brunswick. Locations where lots have been reserved for Loyalists are marked, as is the newly expanded settlement of *St Anns or Fredrick's Town*, today Fredericton.

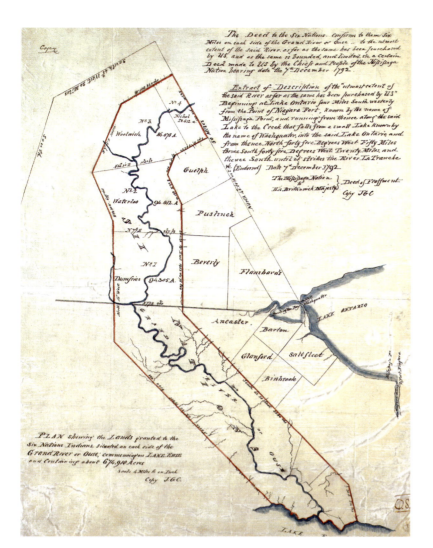

The Deed to the Six Nations conform to them Six Miles on each side of the Grand River or Ouse ... to the utmost extent of the said River, as far as the same has been purchased by US, and as the same is Bounded, and limited, in a Certain Deed made to US by the Chiefs and People of the Missisaga Nation bearing date the 7th December 1792.

Extract of Description of the utmost extent of the said River as far as the same has been purchased by US. Beginning at Lake Ontario four Miles South westerly from the Point of Niagara Fort, Known by the name of Missisaga Point, and running from thence along the said Lake to the Creek that falls from a small Lake Known by the name of Waslegnaten, into the said Lake Ontario and from thence North forty five Degrees West Fifty Miles thence South forty five Degrees West Twenty Miles, and thence South until it strikes the River La Tranche
&c (Endorsed)   Date 7 December 1792.

The Missisaga Nation to
His Britannick Majesty   Deed of Proffment
                              Copy JGC

PLAN showing the Lands granted to the Six Nations Indians, situated on each side of the GRAND River or Ouse, commencing on LAKE ERIE and containing about 674,910 Acres.
Scale 4 Miles to an Inch
Copy JGC

so along the St. Lawrence and Lake Ontario, surrenders of land were negotiated with the Algonkian Mississauga. This provided a legal basis for the granting of lands to Loyalists. The surrenders were often defined as the land a day's march back from the river- or lakefront.

Since land tenure was still officially that of seigneuries, Haldimand worked out a way around this. Seigneuries would have created tenancies, and the Loyalists had been promised ownership. Technically the Crown was to be the landlord. Haldimand then ordered his surveyors, led by his surveyor general Samuel Holland, with deputy John Collins, to begin the process of laying out land holdings, which included townsites as well as agricultural lots. He also arranged for the supply of equipment and food for an interim period while the Loyalists cleared the land for farming.

In 1784, with surveying and allocation continuing apace, thousands of Loyalists left Montréal and made their way upriver. They were followed by many more over the next few years, such that by 1791 there were probably 30,000 people living in the "upper country." In that year the region became Upper Canada—today's province of Ontario—thus creating a largely English-speaking counterbalance to the rest of what had been Québec, which was now to be called Lower Canada. By 1811, nearly 90,000 people had settled in Upper Canada.

MAP 174 (left).
The land grant made to Joseph Brant and the Six Nations in 1792. The grant was made at the suggestion of Frederick Haldimand, the governor of Québec. The land granted was the area six miles in each direction from the Grand River. This map is a copy of the one attached to the deed of land. Today Brantford, Ontario, in the centre of this land grant, bears Chief Joseph Brant's name.

MAP 175 (below).
Plan of the township of Johnstown, signed by deputy surveyor William Chewett and dated 7 February 1792. Names of settlers are included in a faint list in pencil on the right-hand side. Johnstown did not grow and prosper, for the harbour was found to be unsuitable for ships of any size. Located just off the Trans-Canada Highway at its junction with the road to Ottawa, Johnstown is today barely a small village.

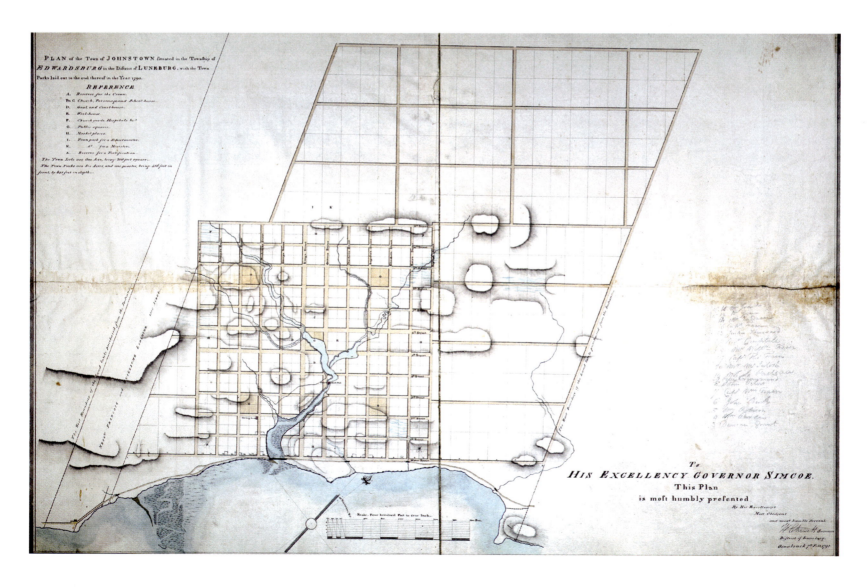

PLAN of the Town of JOHNSTOWN situated in the Township of EDWARDSBURG in the District of LUNEBURG, with the Town Parks laid out to the end thereof in the Year 1790.

To
HIS EXCELLENCY GOVERNOR SIMCOE.
This Plan
is most humbly presented

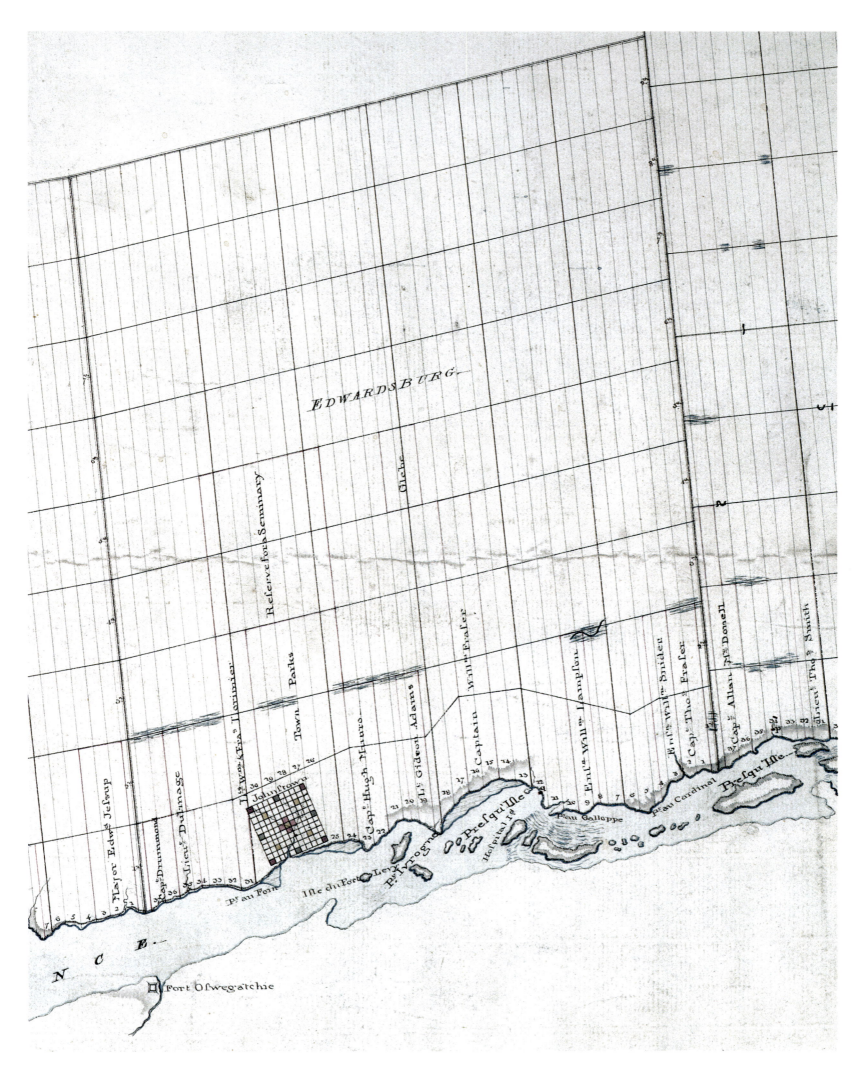

EDWARDSBURG

Glebe

Reserve for a Seminary

Major Edwd Jessup

Capt Drummond

Lieut Dulmage

Wentk Fras Torimier

Town Parks

Johnstown

Capt Hugh Munro

Lieut Gideon Adams

Capt Willm Fraser

Captain

Ent Willm Hampton

Ent Willm Snider

Capt Thos Fraser

Capt Allan McDonell

Lieut Thos Smith

Presqu'Isle

Presqu'Ile

Hospital Id

Peau Gallope

Peau Cardinal

Pt au Foin

Isle du Fort

Leut Drogno

Pt Is Drogno

N C E

Fort Oswegatchie

MAP 176.

Part of a large map drawn by William Chewett and dated 7 February 1792 showing lots and the townsite of Johnstown on the St. Lawrence east of Kingston, with the names of the officers to whom the lots have been granted. Most of the lots were strips back from the river frontage. Prominent Loyalist commander Sir John Johnson, who had been a major landowner in New York prior to the Revolution, acquired land here. The other townsite on this large map (not shown) was Cornwall, today a city of fifty thousand; but Johnstown, hampered by a shallow harbour, did not grow. The name of Luneburg District was changed to Eastern District in 1791.

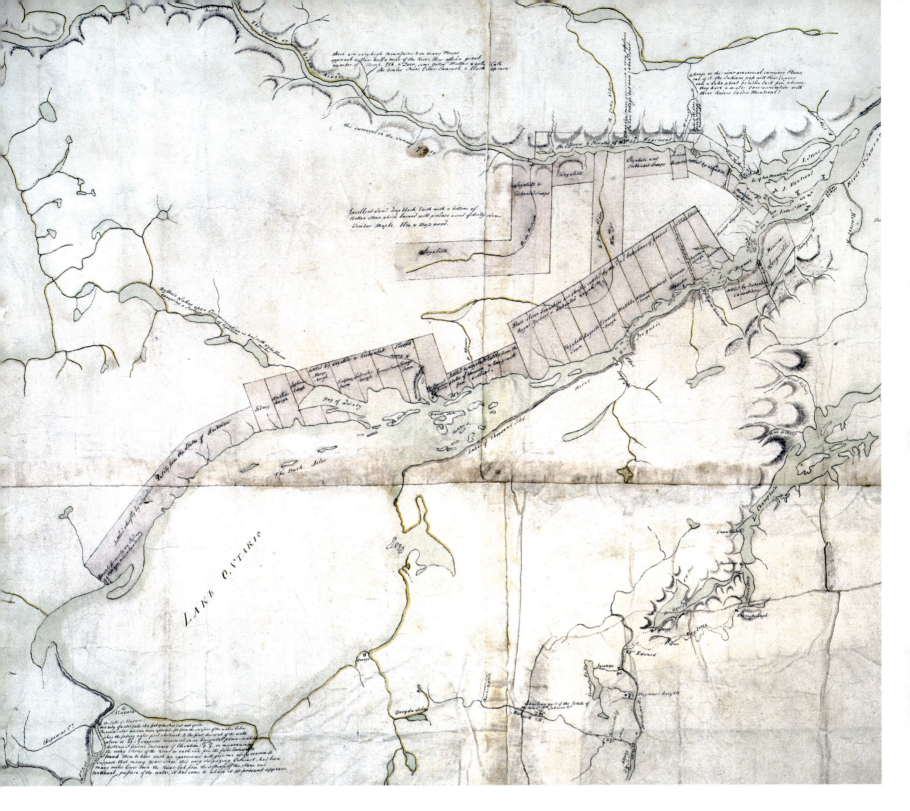

MAP 177 (*above*).
Part of a map drawn about 1790 by an unknown mapmaker showing Loyalist land grants along the north shore of Lake Ontario, the north bank of the St. Lawrence, and in the Ottawa Valley.

MAP 178 (*below*).
This map by surveyor Patrick McNiff shows Loyalist settlements along the north shore of Lake Erie. It was drawn in 1791.

MAP 179 (*right, top*).
A summary map of the new province of Upper Canada, drawn by William Chewett in 1792 and engraved and published by William Faden in 1800. This map was the first printed map of Upper Canada and incorporates the growth from Loyalist settlement in the previous twenty years. The new lieutenant-governor, John Graves Simcoe, continued to try to attract new settlers, and to this end began building a system of both military and concession roads to allow communication with the newly developed lands. Two of the major ones, Yonge Street and Dundas Street, are shown on this map.

MAP 180 (*right, bottom*).
This 1771 map by British mapmaker Thomas Jefferys shows Nova Scotia with its original extent, covering the territory which is now New Brunswick (created as a new colony in 1784); Isle St. John (created as a separate colony in 1769), which became Prince Edward Island in 1799; and the present province of Nova Scotia. Cape Breton Island was made a separate colony in 1784, but was reunited with Nova Scotia in 1820.

MAP 181 (*far right, bottom*).
The new colony of New Brunswick, created out of Nova Scotia in 1784, largely as a result of the influx of Loyalists to the Saint John Valley. This map is dated 1817.

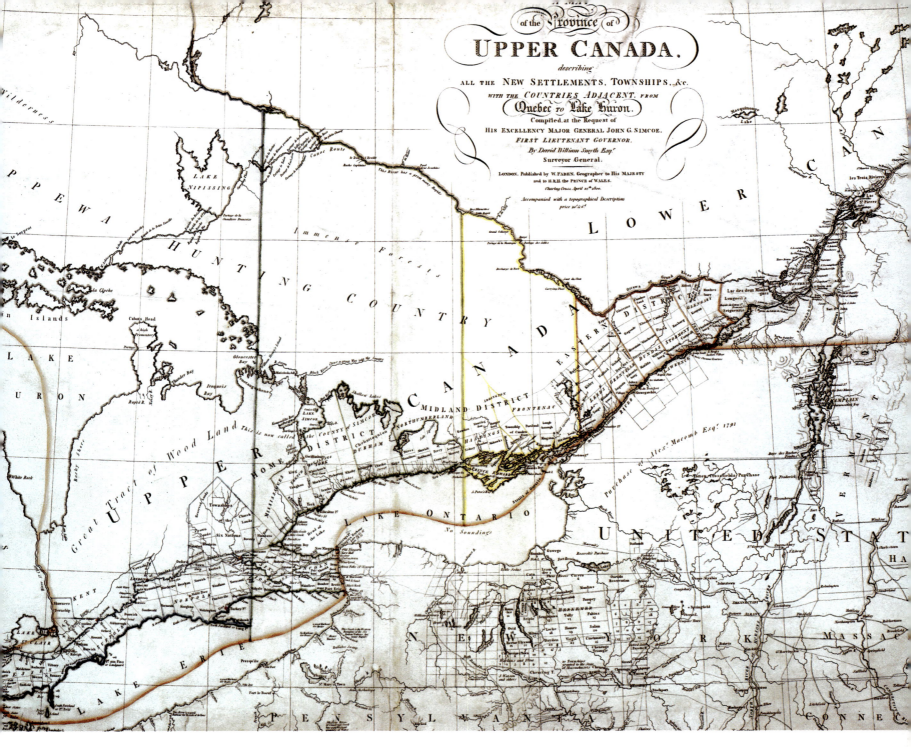

of the Province of

UPPER CANADA.

describing

ALL THE NEW SETTLEMENTS, TOWNSHIPS, &c.

WITH THE COUNTRIES ADJACENT, FROM

Quebec to *Lake Huron*,

Compiled, at the Request of

HIS EXCELLENCY MAJOR GENERAL JOHN G. SIMCOE.

FIRST LIEUTENANT GOVERNOR.

By David William Smyth Esq.

Surveyor General.

LONDON, Published by W. FADEN, Geographer to His MAJESTY
and to H.R.H. the PRINCE of WALES.
Charing Cross, April 12th 1800.

*Accompanied with a topographical Description
price 10s.6d.*

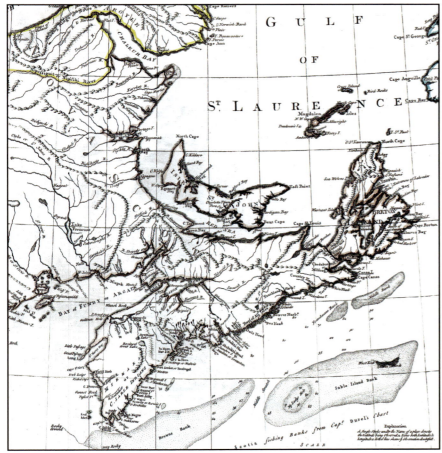

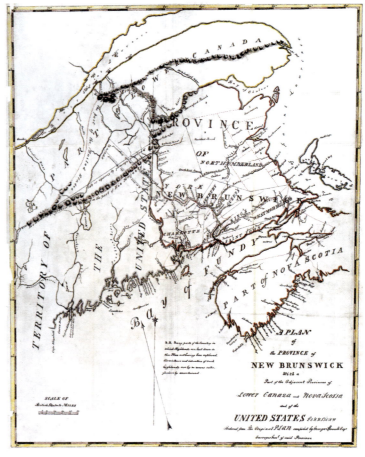

A PLAN of the PROVINCE of NEW BRUNSWICK With a Part of the Adjacent Provinces of Lower Canada — Nova Scotia and of the UNITED STATES Territory

Perceptions of the West

Several long-lived myths about the geography of western Canada persisted from the time of early French settlement until the end of the eighteenth century.

The first was the Sea of the West, sometimes referred to as the Western Sea. The myth likely originated in native stories told to early fur traders, referring in fact to large lakes which were interpreted literally as seas. It was perhaps a matter of early explorers hearing what they wanted to hear; many were convinced that the South Sea, or at least a passage to it, was over the next mountain. This is shown as early as 1616, on Samuel de Champlain's map (Map 76, page 54). And myths, once established, are hard to suppress; as exploration progressed westwards, so the location of the Sea of the West migrated west also. At first it was the Great Lakes, but later Lake Winnipeg and other Manitoba lakes took over the role. Explorers and fur traders, convinced of the existence of a Western Sea but not finding it, simply assumed it to be over the *next* horizon. As late as the 1780s bizarre maps were still being published showing a huge Sea of the West, such as that in Map 182, above. They live on to amuse us.

The second persistent myth was that of the River of the West. This was the long-sought overland passage to Cathay, the westward-flowing river that was thought necessary to "balance" the St. Lawrence in the east. In a way, this was a less outrageous myth than some of the others, for there *was* a long westward-flowing river, the Columbia, but, of course, it ran only from the Rocky Mountains, not clear across the continent as is shown in some maps. The myth would persist until the Americans Meriwether Lewis and William Clark reached the mouth of the Columbia in 1805, after a difficult traverse of the Rocky Mountains, and even beyond, in the search for a mysterious "Buenaventura River" farther south. The attraction of an easy highway west—and remember that virtually all overland travel was by canoe—was not easily forsaken.

The third myth was that of an ice-free Northwest Passage, a role that was taken up in the mid-1700s by the so-called Fonte myth. As we have seen (pages 34, 38, and 77), the search for a Northwest Passage to Cathay had long driven explorers on abortive missions west. In 1708, a magazine article was published reporting a supposed voyage in 1640 by a Spanish admiral named Bartholemew de Fonte, who was reported to have sailed from the Northwest Coast of America through a strait he found leading to Hudson Bay. This hoax was revived by Arthur Dobbs, a promoter of the Northwest Passage concept, in the 1740s (see Map 114, page 82).

Map 182 *(left)*.
Part of a world map published by commercial mapmakers Jean Covens and Corneille Mortier about 1780. It shows a particularly clear Northwest Passage leading from Hudson Bay through Manitoba, Alberta, and British Columbia to a magnificent Sea of the West stretching from Vancouver Island to Nebraska. At least they were clear about their concept. By 1780, they should have known better; their map was certainly different from others on sale at the time. But Covens and Mortier were producing the map to sell, and perhaps hoped no one would use it for navigation. Even today, it is something different and unusual that sells, and it was no different in the eighteenth century.

Map 183.
This map produced by the French mapmaker Didier Robert de Vaugondy in 1755 shows perhaps the most complex system of seas, lakes, straits, rivers, islands, and passages of any map ever produced. The passage of "Amiral de Fonte" is shown, as is a magnificently huge Sea of the West.

The Fonte strait was copied by many mapmakers in the mid-eighteenth century, and even James Cook's explorations of the Northwest Coast in 1778 did not destroy the myth, for he left a large part of the coastline undefined (see MAPS 226 and 227, page 158). Not until George Vancouver's meticulous survey of 1792–94 did mapmakers realize once and for all that no such strait could exist.

A further myth that permeated the maps of North America until Alexander Mackenzie's explorations (page 143) was the idea that the continent was much narrower than it is in reality. There are seventeenth-century English maps

of Virginia that show the Pacific—the South Sea—ten days' march from the headwaters of the rivers flowing into the Atlantic. This narrow-continent concept was for centuries bound up with

MAP 184.
This is a particularly bizarre example of one mapmaker's ideas of what lay in western Canada. The northwest quadrant of the continent is in stark contrast to the reasonably accurate other three quadrants. The map was published in 1752 by a normally quite sane French cartographer, Joseph-Nicolas De L'Isle. Here an enormous Sea of the West inhabits the whole of western North America, with an outlet at the Strait of Juan de Fuca. At this time the strait said to have been discovered by de Fuca in 1592 was entirely unproven—another myth, in fact. When Charles Barkley found the real strait in 1787, he assumed he had rediscovered it and named it after its presumed original discoverer, de Fuca. On the northwestern coast, de L'Isle's map shows an archipelago, and indeed there is one, the Alexander Archipelago of the Alaska panhandle, but it is nothing like the shape shown here. Beyond that, even vestiges of reality disappear, as a series of rivers, straits, and lakes conveys the idea, though it is not drawn clearly, of a passage from the Pacific to Hudson Bay. Could it be that de L'Isle wasn't quite sure of his information?

the idea that the Sea or River of the West was just at hand. But even after 1778, when Cook fixed the longitude of the West Coast accurately— and his book was published, and therefore widely

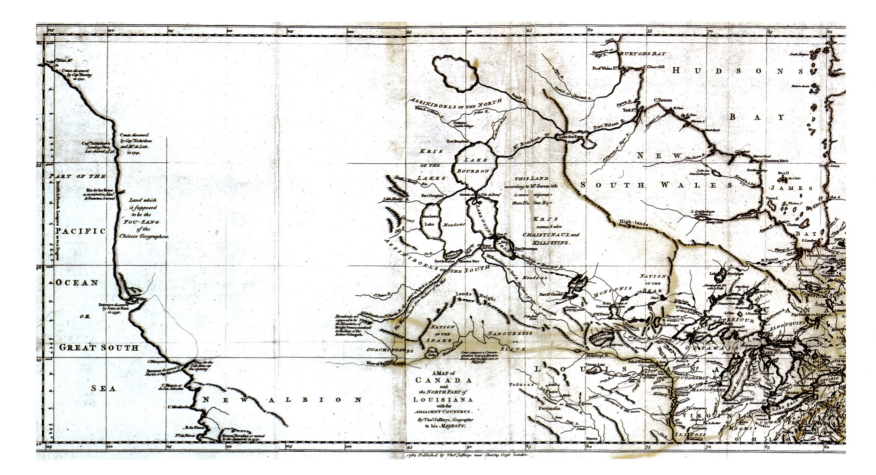

Map 185 (above).
This map by Thomas Jefferys, published in 1764, is reasonably accurate until real geographical information is exhausted just west of Lake Winnipeg. Even then, Jefferys leaves the unknown area completely blank. British Columbia is depicted as *Land which is supposed to be the Fou-Sang of the Chinese Geographers*, a coast where Chinese fishermen were said to have been wrecked after currents had carried them clear across the North Pacific Ocean. The West Coast is shown about 6° (about 425 km) too far east.

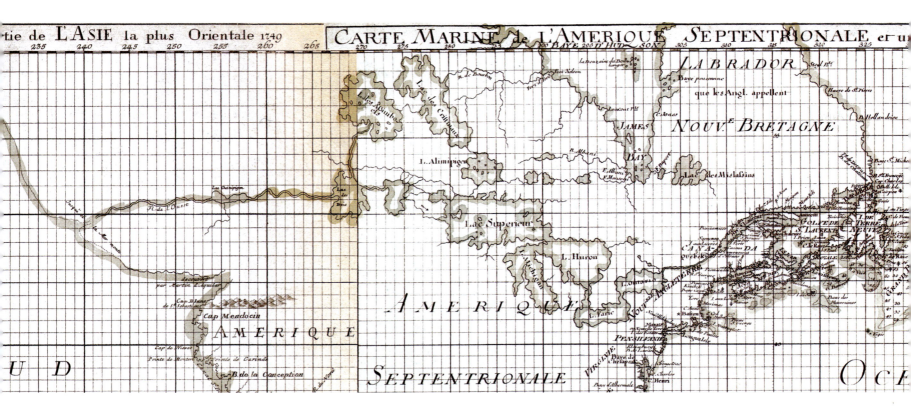

available, in 1784—all that happened for a while was that the interior river and lake systems, well known to the fur traders, were shown on maps as too near to the coast. This was mainly due to an inability to measure longitude accurately until the end of the eighteenth century. The longitudinal squeezing of geographical features is classically shown in the maps of the trader Peter Pond (pages 140–42).

These myths had largely died by the turn of the nineteenth century, but maps showing them remain to document their bizarre splendour.

MAP 187 (*above*).
The River of the West is the major feature of this 1749 map by Isaac Brouckner. Longitudinally, it is one of the more accurate maps for its time. Certainly Brouckner paid attention to the positions of features, as is evidenced by the tight grid, unusual for a map of this time. The western side of Lake of the Woods (*Lac de Bois*) is shown at 267° E, or 93° W; the correct longitude is 95° W. The mouth of the River of the West is shown at about 240° E, or 120° W; the longitude of the mouth of the Columbia is 124° W. Thus Brouckner, despite the appearance of this map, was only 2° out. If the River of the West had really flowed westwards from Lake of the Woods, it would have been a remarkably accurate map.

MAP 188 (*below*)
An honest attempt to show only that which was known. This is a map by French mapmaker Jacques-Nicolas Bellin, published in 1758. Some points of reference are given. Coasts discovered by the Dane Vitus Bering in 1728 and 1741 are shown (in Alaska; in fact he did not seen the coast of the American continent in 1728 but sailed into Bering Strait), as is the supposed Strait of Juan de Fuca (*Entrée de Juan de Fuca en 1592*). A Sea of the West (*Mer de l'Ouest*) is shown, but completely undefined. Again the Northwest is not known to be land or sea, and much of the West is also unknown; *Tout ceci est inconnu* ("All this is unknown").

MAP 186 (*left*).
This map of North America by John Roque, "Topographer to the King," was published in 1762, just before the Treaty of Paris handed Canada to the British. The discoveries of La Vérendrye are noted; Lake Winnipeg and the other large Manitoba lakes are depicted, together with some trade posts such as Queen's Fort (Fort La Reine; Portage La Prairie). But most of the West is "intirely unknown." Confused by stories of a Sea of the West, Roque has marked *The West Sea* but not defined it; elsewhere he has written: *It is very uncertain whither this part is Sea or Land*. The Strait of Juan de Fuca is shown as *A Strait entered by John de Fuca 1592*. Farther north, the 1741 American landfall of Vitus Bering is marked. The notation *If a North West Passage Exists it must be through one of these Bays* is written along the west coast of Hudson Bay, reflecting the British and other attempts to probe the various inlets in the seventeenth and eighteenth centuries. Interestingly, the position of the the west coast of Canada is shown here too far *west*, a reversal from the cartographic norm at this time. This map is an excellent summary of the state of geographic knowledge in 1762.

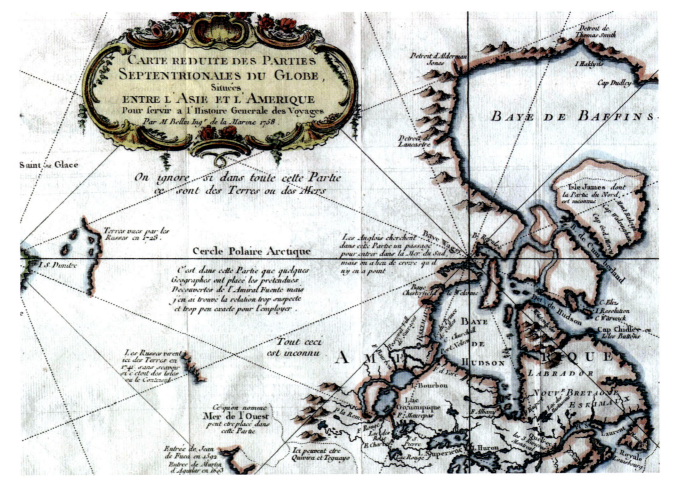

An Inland Journey

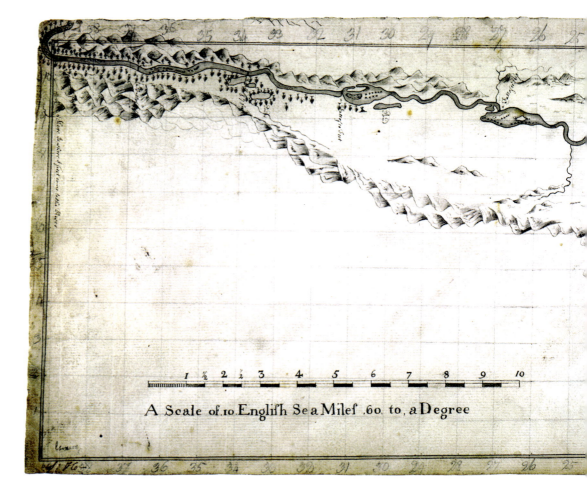

Although the Hudson's Bay Company had from time to time been pressed to explore west, principally to search for a Northwest Passage, not until the middle of the eighteenth century did the company begin to reverse its policy of establishing forts on the shores of Hudson Bay and waiting for natives to bring furs to them to trade. An era of exploration into the interior thus began, with the aim of finding new customers. Eventually, after 1774, and in response to competition, the Company would begin to build inland trading posts as well.

James Isham, chief of York Fort, was the first to encourage inland exploration. In 1754 he sent Anthony Henday on an extensive reconnaisance in which he may have reached the vicinity of Red Deer, Alberta. There is considerable doubt as to his actual route, as Henday left no maps, and four copies of his journal differ in details. Henday was instructed to look for the Sea of the West. No follow-up to his journey was undertaken by the Company.

The next major foray inland did not occur for another sixteen years. In 1769 Moses Norton, governor of Prince of Wales Fort and a collector of geographical information from native sources (see MAP 221, page 155), sent Samuel Hearne into the interior to search for copper—and the Northwest Passage. After two false starts in 1769 and 1770, Hearne finally set off in December 1770, accompanied by Chipewyan chief Matonabbee and an entourage that grew to two hundred natives.

On 13 July 1771 Hearne arrived at the Coppermine River, which flows into the Arctic Ocean in Coronation Gulf. After helplessly watching a horrific attack by the Chipewyan on an Inuit encampment, he arrived at the Arctic shore on 17 July. "I am certain of it being the sea or some branch of it," he wrote, "by the quantity of whalebone and seal-skins which the Esquimaux had at their tents, and also by the number of seals which I saw on the ice."

Hearne was correct, but he incorrectly calculated his latitude; he thought he was at 71° 54′ N, and this is shown on his map, but he was actually only at 67° 49′ N. He was 450 km south of where he thought he was. This proved that there could be no Northwest Passage south of the mouth of the Coppermine, but since Hearne's book on his travels was not published until 1795—the Hudson's Bay Company not thinking it important—this information was not widely disseminated.

Hearne was the first European explorer to reach the Arctic Ocean coast of today's Canada, and the first to map any part of it. His map of the Coppermine River is shown as MAP 189.

MAP 189.
Samuel Hearne's map of the Coppermine River, 1771. Hearne was the first European to reach the shores of the Arctic Ocean. The map is oriented with west at the top, with the Arctic Ocean on the right. Bloody Falls, the location of the battle between the Chipewyan and the Inuit, is shown with the notation: *Fall of 16 Feet is where the Northern Ind[ia]ns killd the Eskamaux.*

MAP 190 (*below*).
A plan of York Fort drawn by James Isham about 1740. This fort was on the north bank of the Hayes River, on the shores of Hudson Bay, downstream from the present site. A group of canoes are arriving to trade, and native tents are pitched in front of the fort. For security, the ground around the palisade is cleared, and cannon line the wharf.

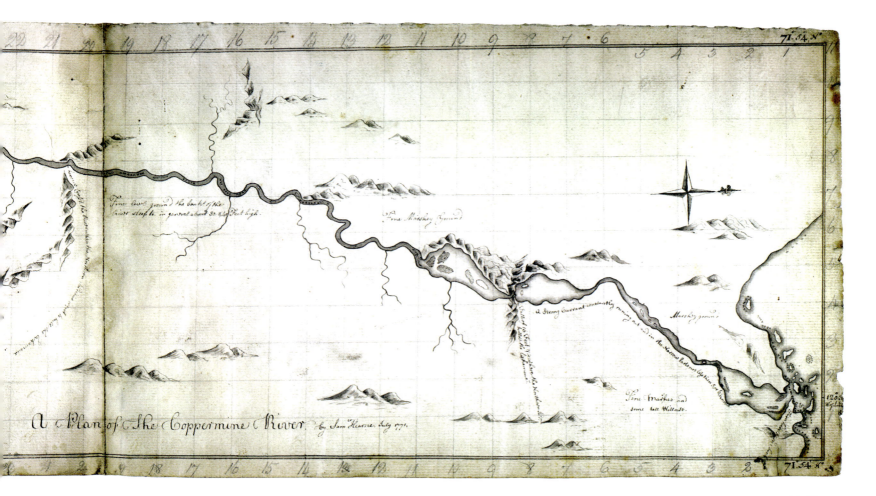

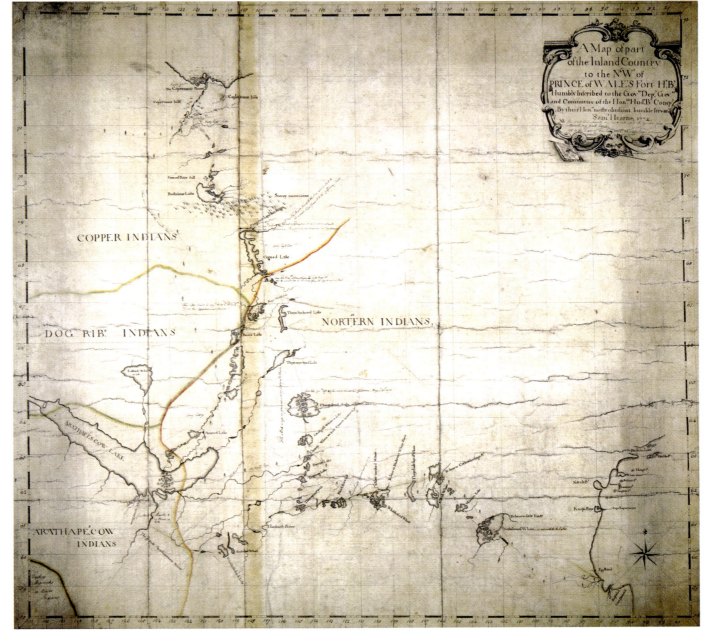

Map 191.
Samuel Hearne's map of his journey from Prince of Wales Fort to the mouth of the Coppermine River on the shores of the Arctic Ocean in 1770–72. *Arathapescow Lake* is Great Slave Lake, and its western end shows an outlet which proved to be the Mackenzie River. Hearne derived this information from native reports. The line shown with little trees is the treeline; Hearne's map seems to have been the earliest depiction of this feature. By limiting the map principally to only the rivers and lakes that he travelled, Hearne simplified what is in reality a huge maze of inter-linked water covering most of the area west of Hudson Bay. Without the aid of native guides it is unlikely Hearne would have been able to find his way to the Arctic Ocean.

Alexander Henry's Great Map of the West

After the fall of Québec, the fur trade based in Montréal was largely taken over by Scottish, English, and American traders, who employed the French *voyageurs* to paddle the canoes. To the chagrin of the Hudson's Bay Company, which had thought that the British victory would consolidate its monopoly, the fur trade was now open to vigorous new competition despite it. A number of partnerships grew up in Montréal. In the winter of 1783–84, after a number of temporary arrangements, the partnerships amalgamated into the North West Company, to better handle the financial and geographical challenges of a fur trade reaching ever farther west.

A partner in one of the preliminary partnerships was an American trader, Alexander Henry, called "the elder" to distinguish him from his nephew (Alexander Henry "the younger"). In the mid-1770s, Henry was pushing westwards into new fur hinterlands, outpacing the Hudson's Bay Company men.

In June 1776 Henry may have reached as far west as Lac Île-à-la-Crosse, on the Churchill River system. Then on 1 July 1776, back at his fort on Amisk Lake (which he called Beaver Lake), Henry met a large delegation of Chipewyan natives from the Lake Athabasca area. From them, Henry learned some more about the geography of the Arctic- and Pacific-draining rivers beyond Lake Athabasca. In his journal he wrote:

They [the Chipewyans] informed us, that there was, at the further end of that lake, a river, called Peace River, which descended from the Stony or Rocky Mountains, and from which mountains the distance to the salt lake, meaning the Pacific Ocean, was not great; that the lake emptied itself by a river, which ran to the northward, which they called Kiratchinini Sibi or Slave River [the Slave River still today], and which flows into another lake, called by the same name [Great Slave Lake]; but whether this lake was or was not the sea, or whether it emptied itself or not into the sea, they were unable to say. They also made war with the Indians who live at the bottom of the river, where the water is salt. They also made war on the people beyond the mountains, toward the Pacific Ocean, to which their warriors had frequently been near enough to see it.

Henry traded a huge number of furs, by his own count 12,000 beaver as well as otter and marten. The quantity and quality of these furs from the Athabasca country would encourage traders to pool their trade goods and send one of their number, Peter Pond, into the region, and

MAP 192.
Alexander Henry the elder's great map of the Canadian West, drawn late in 1776, as the Montréal-based fur traders were poised to enter the Arctic drainage basin. The map was presented to the governor of Québec, Guy Carleton, likely to impress him with their exploratory prowess; the Montréal fur traders wanted to persuade the British government to grant them a monopoly over the fur trade in regions not within the Hudson's Bay Company charter. The Arctic watershed which they were about to enter was technically outside of Rupert's Land, the area draining into Hudson Bay. Although this map is hand-drawn, all the names and other information have been printed. This was probably done only because it was to be presented to Governor Carleton, and thus needed to look as authoritative as Henry and his associates could make it.

Cumberland House (here *Fort Cumberland*), founded by Samuel Hearne in 1774, is shown at the confluence of the *Posquyaw* (Saskatchewan) River and *Sturgeon Lake* (Cumberland Lake). *Beaver Lake* is Amisk Lake, *Beaver River* and *Bad River* are the Sturgeon-weir River, and *Missinabie River* is a compressed composite of the Churchill River with a series of lakes and rivers, including Lac La Ronge, Pinehouse Lake, Lac Île-à-la-Crosse, Peter Pond Lake, the Loche River, the Methye Portage, the Clearwater River, and the Athabasca River, all allowing a route to *Orabuscow Lake*—Lake Athabasca. Methye Portage was the portage into the Arctic drainage system crossed by Peter Pond in 1778. The *Kiutchinini* River could be the Peace, Slave, or even Mackenzie River; it is impossible to say for sure.

All information west of Lac Île-à-la-Crosse was derived from native reports, which often did not distinguish direction in the way generally understood today (see, for example, MAP 111, page 79). Thus the Churchill River–Lake Athabasca route is shown as a more or less straight line, even though in reality the Athabasca River runs north. The map shows very clearly the route the fur traders took from Lake Superior to Lake Winnipeg (*Lake Winepegon*) through Rainy Lake (*Rain Lake*) and Lake of the Woods (*Wood Lake*), via Grand Portage, shown as the *Great Carrying Place*. This was the first and most strenuous portage around the rapids of the Pigeon River. South of Lake Winnipeg the Red River is shown, with its tributary the Assiniboine (*Ousiniboin River*) and the post built by La Vérendrye in 1738, Fort La Reine (*Queens Ft*), near modern Portage la Prairie (see page 86).

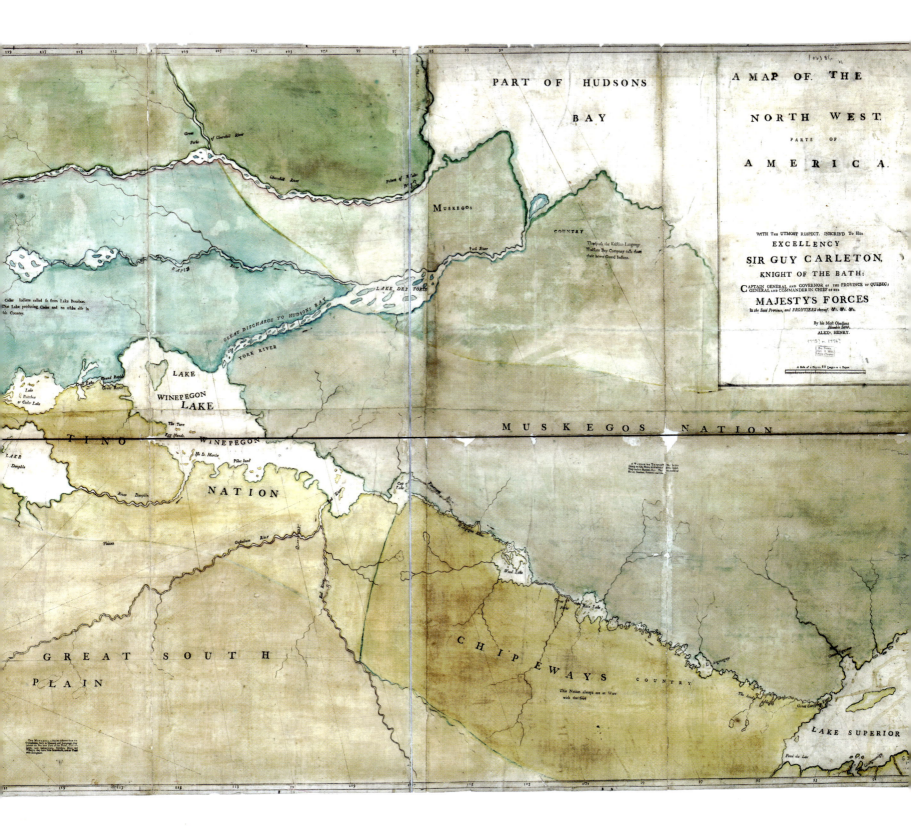

Various map labels visible:

PART OF HUDSONS BAY

A MAP OF THE NORTH WEST PARTS OF AMERICA

WITH THE UTMOST RESPECT, INSCRIBED TO HIS EXCELLENCY SIR GUY CARLETON, KNIGHT OF THE BATH: CAPTAIN GENERAL AND GOVERNOR OF THE PROVINCE OF QUEBEC; GENERAL AND COMMANDER IN CHIEF OF HIS MAJESTYS FORCES In the Said Province, and FRONTIERS thereof, &c. &c. &c.

By his Most Obedient Humble Serv.t ALEX.r HENRY.

MUSKEGOS COUNTRY

MUSKEGOS NATION

LAKE WINEPEGON

WINEPEGON NATION

GREAT SOUTH PLAIN

CHIPEWAYS COUNTRY

LAKE SUPERIOR

---

thus push the fur-trading frontiers farther west. The end result would be the formation of the North West Company to deal with the increasing logistical problems of distance.

In 1776, Henry summarized all the new geographical information he had gathered and drew the very large map—it is 2.15 m wide—shown here (MAP 192). It was the most advanced map of the West at the time it was drawn, and is a significant compilation of information from actual exploration together with information from native reports. It would be Peter Pond, one of the traders who had been as far as Lac Île-à-la-Crosse with Henry in 1776, who would cross into the Athabasca River drainage system, which flows into the Arctic Ocean, becoming the first European to do so. This would prove to be the richest fur region of all, for a colder climate breeds thicker furs.

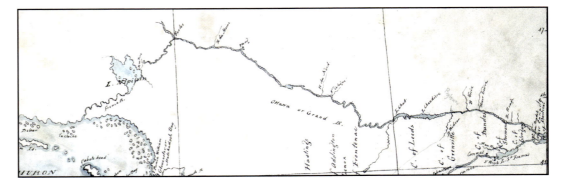

MAP 193.
Part of a map drawn about 1793 by Elizabeth Simcoe, wife of John Graves Simcoe, the lieutenant governor of Upper Canada. It shows the route taken from Montréal by North West Company men to the Great Lakes: up the Ottawa River, west up the Mattawa River and over a short portage to Lake Nipissing, and then via the French River to Lake Huron. They would then paddle close to the shores of Lakes Huron and Superior to reach Grand Portage, at the western end of Lake Superior and the transshipment point for the interior. After Grand Portage was lost to the United States, the North West Company set up a new post a little farther north, Fort William. A later hand has added "Bytown" (later Ottawa) in pencil, and an extension of the Rideau River southwards. It seems that someone had realized the strategic importance of what would become the Rideau Canal (see page 181).

The Maps of Peter Pond

In August 1775, when Alexander Henry was on Lake Winnipeg, he noted in his journal that he had been joined by fellow independent fur trader Peter Pond, "a trader of some celebrity in the northwest." Pond was by all accounts a colourful character, a Connecticut Yankee with a quick temper that had already resulted in a duelling death. His semi-literate journal noted, "We met the Next Morning Eairley & Discharged Pistels in which the Pore Fellowe was unfortenat."

But Pond had one characteristic that made him valuable to his fur trade companions: he had an ability to communicate with natives in a way that always resulted in a bountiful supply of furs. The traders noted that furs being brought by natives from the Lake Athabasca area were particularly plentiful and of high quality. Thus it was natural enough that when a group of them wanted to exploit the area west of Lac La Loche, over the Methye Portage, it was Pond that they sent.

Pond crossed into the Arctic watershed in 1778, and over the next ten years his trading flourished. Pond's communication skills enabled him to gather myriad details of the geography of the Northwest from natives, and, also drawing from his own experiences, he developed an excellent idea of the river and lake system in the region.

In the winter of 1783–84 the loose partnership of groups of independent fur traders finally coalesced into the North West Company, and Pond was a partner. The new company would remain a thorn in the side of the rival Hudson's Bay Company until they merged in 1821. For now, the North West Company knew more about the Northwest than their rivals and intended to exploit this fully.

By 1785, the area to the Rocky Mountains was relatively well known to Pond, and he took to drawing maps—beautifully detailed maps that, while their distances and proportions left something to be desired, were nevertheless by far the best maps of the Northwest at the time. Pond became the geographical expert all consulted.

The first map Pond drew, or at least the earliest that has survived, was one he presented to the Congress of the new United States in 1785, designed to illustrate the ease with which Americans could move into the Northwest (MAP 195). The river system goes no farther west than the Rocky Mountains, although it does show a river flowing north to the Arctic Ocean. Derived from native information, this was the Mackenzie River, and Pond's was the first map to show it entering the northern ocean.

Sometime in 1785, Pond seems to have acquired information about James Cook's 1778 voyage to the Northwest Coast, likely the un-authorized account by John Ledyard, one of Cook's officers who was American. It contained a map showing the location of King George's Sound—now Nootka Sound—on the west coast of Vancouver Island, with Cook's fixing of the longitude of that place, done accurately for the first time with a chronometer as well as careful astronomical observations. This revolutionized Pond's thinking, for he had been unable to accurately plot his own position and thought he was much farther west than he really was. When Cook's accurate coastal position and coastal trend were combined with Pond's inaccurate positions of interior features, the result was a map that made it look like it was just a hop, skip, and a jump to the Pacific. MAP 196, overleaf, illustrates Pond's excitement. This map was presented to the lieutenant-governor of Québec in 1785 as part of the North West Company's efforts to persuade the government to give them a fur trade monopoly in the new regions they had opened up.

When James Cook explored what is now Cook Inlet, in the vicinity of Anchorage, Alaska, in 1778, he had not pursued his surveying to the very end of the inlet, and as a result showed it on his maps as Cook's River. Pond seized on this, for at some time during the next two years, further questioning of native sources had led Pond to conclude that there was a major river flowing west out of Great Slave Lake. This must be, he reasoned, Cook's River, and it would provide an easy route to the Pacific—after all, the lake and the coast were so close! He wasn't quite sure enough at this point to draw in the connection, but his map (MAP 194) strongly suggested it.

It was a map like this that Pond showed his 1787–88 wintering partner, a young Alexander Mackenzie, sent by the partners of the North West Company to take over the Athabasca trade from Pond, whose volatility had led him to involvement in the death of another fur trader; despite his skills, Pond was becoming too much of a liability. In 1788, Pond left the Northwest forever, leaving the field to Mackenzie, but not before he had imparted to the young man his view of the geography of the Northwest. MAP 194 is called the "Empress of Russia map," because Pond gave it to Mackenzie to present to Catherine, Empress of Russia, when, the following year, Mackenzie was to make his way down this river Pond knew led to the Pacific and Russian possessions in Alaska.

In 1790, a London magazine published a map that had been sent to them by a Québec court clerk, Isaac Ogden, with whom Pond had discussed his ideas on his way back to Connecticut. It shows what might be considered Pond's

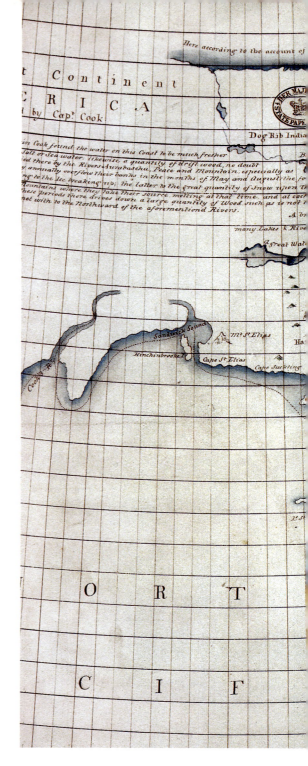

MAP 194.
This is a contemporary copy of the map drawn by Peter Pond in 1787 and given to Alexander Mackenzie for presentation to Catherine, Empress of Russia, who, Pond felt, Mackenzie would surely meet if he proceeded down the river leading out of Great Slave Lake to Russian forts on the coast of what is now Alaska. In fact, as Mackenzie would find, the river, the Mackenzie, led only to the Arctic Ocean. The main problem with this map is neither the coastline, which is reasonably accurately positioned, nor the river and lake system of the Northwest that Pond knew so well, but their juxtaposition far too close to each other. Despite its distortions, Pond's map was a monumental achievement for its time, and one for which he should be recognized. Considering the instrumentation available to him—a compass and not much else—he did remarkably well to draw such a map of this huge and complex region.

final concept of western geography, and now, at last, the connection is made: Cook's River leads out of Great Slave Lake to Cook Inlet and Prince William Sound. The map is significant, for it demonstrates clearly the notions that Alexander Mackenzie must have had in his head as he set out on his voyage down the Mackenzie River in 1789.

Map 195 (right).
Copy of a Map presented to the Congress by Peter Pond, a native of Milford in the State of Connecticut. This is a 1785 copy of a 1784 map originally drawn by Peter Pond. The legend under the title states:

This extraordinary man has resided 17 years in these countries & from his own Discoveries as well as the reports of Indians, he assures himself of having at last Discovered a passage to the N.O. [Nord Ouest] Sea, he is gone again to ascertain some important observations. New York 1st March 1785. The original Map being incumbered with great deal of writing I have thought it best to transcribe it separately with the references marked, by ye numbers. Copied by St. John de Crèvecoeur for his Grace of La Rochefoucauld.

This is the first of Peter Pond's surviving map copies, presented to the United States Congress, then sitting in New York, in 1785. It was copied by J. Hector St. John de Crèvecoeur. There are several versions of this map still extant; this is the one from the British Library. The transcript referred to giving the meaning of numbers on the map has been lost, but it seems likely many of them were "forts," in the sense of camping or stopping places. Flowing from the west into the Slave River, between Pond's *Arabasca Lake* (Lake Athabasca) and Great Slave Lake, is *Great Cave R.* This is the Peace River, the river Mackenzie eventually would take to the Pacific.

MAP 196 (*above*).
Peter Pond's map of 1785, sent to the lieutenant-governor of Québec, Henry Hamilton, as part of a North West Company memoir asking for a monopoly of the fur trade over the newly-opened-up areas. Here for the first time Pond inserts the sea coast as derived from the maps of James Cook, published in 1784. The position and trend of the coast are reasonably accurate; the river and lake system of the interior is detailed, and again reasonably accurate except north of Great Slave Lake, beyond which Pond had not been. But it is the relative positioning of the two that is the map's major error. Pond was unable to measure longitude and thus placed his rivers and lakes too far west, giving the impression that it was only a small distance to the Pacific.

MAP 197 (*right*).
The culmination of Pond's ideas is shown in this map published in *Gentleman's Magazine*, in London, in 1790. It was the only Pond map to be published. The map was derived from one Pond had shown Isaac Ogden in Québec, who had enclosed it in a letter to his father in London. Referring to the river flowing out of Great Slave Lake, Ogden wrote, "You will readily conjecture what River [it] is known by, when it empties into the Ocean. To save you much trouble I will tell you it is Cook's River."

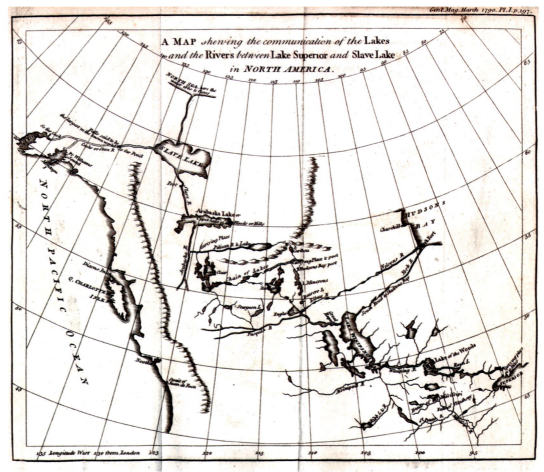

Alexander Mackenzie Crosses the Continent

Alexander Mackenzie spent the winter of 1787–88 with Peter Pond at his post on the Athabasca River, being fascinated, no doubt, by Pond's geographical ideas. Mackenzie, a North West Company partner, had been sent to take over from Pond, who left the Northwest for good in May 1788.

Mackenzie resolved that winter to attempt to journey to the Pacific. The North West Company wanted to find a route for shipping furs via a Pacific port and thus save having to carry them the immense distance back to Montréal. This would make it more competitive with the Hudson's Bay Company.

On 3 June 1789 Mackenzie set out for the Pacific from Fort Chipewyan, a new post he had built on Lake Athabaska. He followed the Slave River north to Great Slave Lake, circled the lake's perimeter, and paddled down the Mackenzie River. For three days the river flowed in a northwesterly direction, the direction he wanted to go, but then, at a great bend in the river known as Camsell Bend, it changed direction to the north.

Rivers change direction locally all the time, so this did not concern Mackenzie at first, but he came to realize that it was no longer flowing towards the Pacific. On reaching the beginning of the Mackenzie Delta, he confided to his journal: "I am much at a loss here how to act being certain that my going further in this Direction will not answer the Purpose of which the Voyage was intended, as it is evident that these Waters must empty themselves into the Northern Ocean."

And indeed they did. On 12 July Mackenzie entered the Arctic Ocean, although at the time it seems he thought it might be a large lake. Later the same day he landed on Garry Island, which he named "Whale Island" on account of having seen these animals. For many years hence,

MAP 199.
"Chart called Mackenzie's Map." This is a direct copy of the map Mackenzie made of his 1789 expedition down the river that now bears his name. It was found in British Colonial Office files early in the twentieth century.

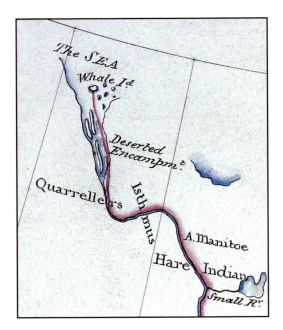

An aerial view of Mackenzie's "Whale Island," Garry Island, in the Arctic Ocean just north of the Mackenzie Delta. Mackenzie's first camp was on the beach on the right of this photograph. The view is to the southeast. Note the snow visible even in July.

MAP 198 (left).
Part of a manuscript map of Mackenzie's route (MAP 201, overleaf), showing the Mackenzie Delta and his "Whale Island," actually Garry Island, above.

maps of the Arctic would show Whale Island; the confusion was only resolved in the 1930s, with the beginning of air survey.

Mackenzie returned to Fort Chipewyan in September, although the journey back took much longer, as it was all upstream. He spent the next three years figuring out what had gone wrong, and planning his next attempt. He even went to London in order to learn how to more accurately fix his position and to buy instruments and books.

In the fall of 1792 he was ready to try again. He left Fort Chipewyan on 10 October, this time taking a sharp left turn, instead of going north down the Slave River, and entered the Peace River, which he now considered his best bet to reach the Pacific. He reached as far as the confluence of the Peace and Smoky Rivers that season, and wintered at a location close by he called Fort Fork.

With one canoe, ten men, and a dog, Mackenzie pushed off from Fort Fork on 9 May 1793. It was an easy paddle until they came to the Peace River Canyon, just west of today's Hudson Hope, British Columbia. This obstacle was surmounted only with much portaging and near tragedy when a tow line broke. Eventually they reached the confluence of the Parsnip River, flowing from the south, and the Finlay River, from the north, and took the "southern branch" based on native advice Mackenzie had been given at Fort Fork.

The going then became very tough indeed, for although the Peace River route uniquely traverses the main ridge of the Rocky Mountains, the Parsnip leads only to a difficult ridge farther west, and this now had to be crossed. A few years later, in 1806, another North West Company man, Simon Fraser, would find an easier route by taking a tributary of the Parsnip, the Pack River, and this would become the commercial route for the company. But now Mackenzie and his men were in for a rough ride, taking a wet week to find their way down the Bad River, or James Creek. But they had crossed the watershed, and henceforth the waters did indeed flow to the Pacific.

However, it was not as easy as that, for Mackenzie was now on the Fraser River system, and the Fraser only flowed to the sea by a circuitous and nearly impassable route through the Fraser Canyon. Taking native advice, Mackenzie struck out overland, up the valley of the West Road River, which flows into the Fraser between Prince George and Quesnel. He followed a well-established native trade trail, a so-called grease trail, named for the oolichan grease traded by coastal natives with those inland.

On 20 July 1793, at today's village of Bella Coola, Mackenzie finally was able to record, "We got out of the river, which discharges itself by various channels into an arm of the sea," a remarkably restrained comment for the attainment of an objective after five years. The arm of the sea was North Bentinck Arm; it was salt water, and it was the Pacific Ocean.

Borrowing a Nuxalk sea-going canoe, Mackenzie and his men made it to a rock in Dean Channel, about 60 km from Bella Coola. This is "Mackenzie Rock," where his left his famous inscription: "Alexander Mackenzie, from Canada, by land, the twenty-second of July, one thousand seven hundred and ninety-three." But here he was pursued by unfriendly Heiltsuk natives and so cut short his stay, and, apart from a stop to fix his position, paddled hard back to Bella Coola.

The return journey was achieved in a remarkably fast time; he knew the way now. In thirty-two days he was back at Fort Fork, returning to Fort Chipewyan later in the season.

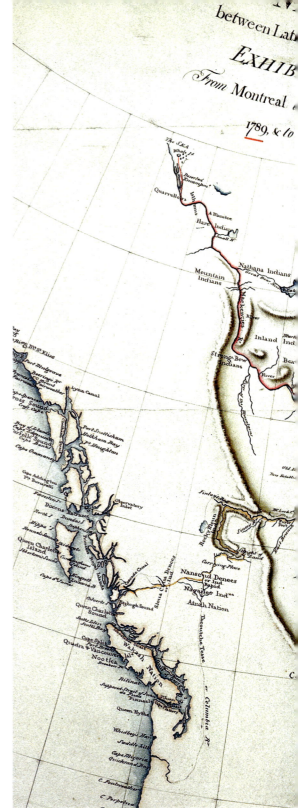

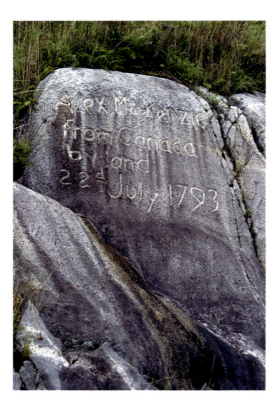

A recreation of Mackenzie's inscription at Mackenzie Rock, on Dean Channel, near Bella Coola, British Columbia.

AMERICA

...th and Longitudes 45° & 180° West

...MACKENZIE'S TRACK

...yan *from thence to the* North Sea *in*

...ific Ocean *in* 1795.

Map 200 (*left*).
The earliest surviving cartographic record of Alexander Mackenzie's achievement is this map by London mapmaker Aaron Arrowsmith. This printed map was published in 1798 or 1799, and on this, his own copy of the map, Arrowsmith has written updating notes for his next edition, something he did all the time. The positions of three points on Mackenzie's route have been marked in red ink, including the one on the coast.

Map 201 (*above*).
This magnificent map is much the same as the one Arrowsmith engraved for Mackenzie's book, published in 1801. It might have been drawn for the engraver, though this copy, from British Colonial Office files, was likely given to the government as "pre-release" information. The "B.O." stamp is that of the Board of Ordnance.

Map 202 (*right*).
This is a detail of the map above, showing the route Mackenzie took from Fort Chipewyan to the Pacific. *East Branch* is the Smoky River, near Fort Fork. The *Tacoutche T*[esse] is marked; this is the Fraser River, flowing south. Mackenzie thought this river was the Columbia, not the Fraser. The *Cascade Canal*, shown at the western extremity of Mackenzie's route, was named by George Vancouver the same year that Mackenzie reached the coast. In fact, the two missed each other by only fifty days.

The Hudson's Bay Company Moves Inland

As early as 1754, the Hudson's Bay Company had realized that more information about the geography of the interior was required. During the period from 1754 to 1778, when Philip Turnor arrived at York Fort, the Company sent a series of fur-trading men to the west to explore and later to determine where to best site trading posts. The problem was that none had training in surveying or mapmaking, and hence many of the maps were inaccurate. Perhaps the most notable of these was Anthony Henday, sent in 1754 on a grand tour (see page 136). Samuel Hearne did much better in 1770–71 on his "inland journey" (see page 136), but misjudged his latitude and longitude.

In June 1772 Andrew Graham, in charge of York Fort, sent his second-in-command, Matthew Cocking, west to, once again, contact native groups and encourage them to come down to Hudson Bay to trade. Cocking was away until June the following year, during which time he reached almost as far west as the current Saskatchewan-Alberta boundary, southwest of the Eagle Hills. On his travels Cocking met many "pedlars," the independent fur traders from Montréal that were taking business away from the Hudson's Bay Company. They would soon coalesce into a fully fledged rival, the North West Company. Graham drew a map, dated 1774, that incorporates the new geographical information gained by Cocking (MAP 204).

Cocking, like most Bay men, was not skilled at handling a compass, so his log contains many errors, but he was a good writer and observer.

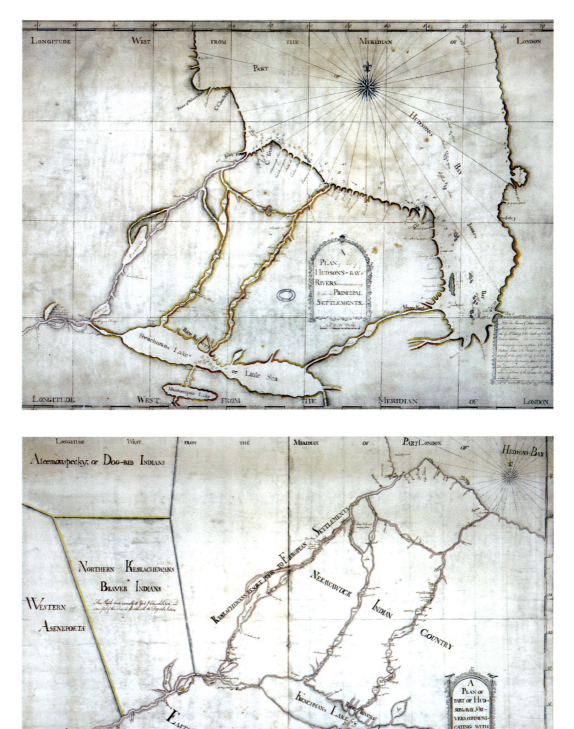

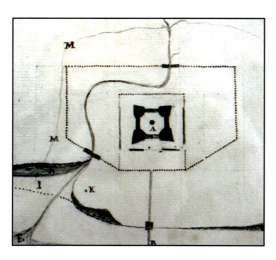

MAP 203 (above, top).
This map was drawn in 1772, probably by Andrew Graham, who was instrumental in plotting the Company strategy to set up posts inland from Hudson Bay. It shows the state of Company knowledge of the interior before the explorations of Samuel Hearne and Matthew Cocking. The map shows the main routes from the bay to Lake Winnipeg and the Saskatchewan River. The lake is here called *Frenchman's Lake or Little Sea*. The map does reflect the inland journeys of Bay man William Tomison in 1767–68 and 1769–70.

MAP 204 (above).
When Graham drew this map two years later, in 1774, Company knowledge had extended westwards to encompass a section of the Saskatchewan River as far west as the South Saskatchewan River in the vicinity of today's Saskatoon, reflecting Matthew Cocking's travels in 1772–73. Also shown are the lands of the native groups that came to the Bay posts to trade, the first map to show these ethnographic divisions. Graham was scientifically minded; as well as writing about natives, he described 111 species of birds.

MAP 205 (left).
A plan of York Fort by Joseph Colen, drawn in 1786–87 to show proposed improvements.

The Hudson's Bay Company's Great Surveyors—Philip Turnor and Peter Fidler

During the 1770s, the Hudson's Bay Company committee, stung by the increasing trade loss to the independents, came to realize that they needed a properly constructed general map of the country west of Hudson Bay into which they could fit traders' reports, and which could be used to plan Company strategy.

They therefore resolved to hire a proper surveyor. Finding "a Person skilled in Mathematics," twenty-seven-year-old Philip Turnor, the company appointed him "their surveyor for settling the Latitudes, Longitudes, Courses and distances of the different Settlements Inland."

Turnor arrived at York Fort by the 1778 supply ship and almost immediately began his work, setting off for Cumberland House, on the Saskatchewan River near the modern Manitoba-Saskatchewan boundary. He spent the winter there before pushing on to Hudson House, near present-day Prince Albert, Saskatchewan. The map that resulted from this first foray west is MAP 206, drawn in 1778–79.

For ten years Turnor criss-crossed the river and lake systems of the Canadian interior. In 1788 he went back to London for two years, and then he was sent out again, this time specifically to survey the Athabasca country, which the company realized was yielding large numbers of excellent furs to their competitor, now the North West Company. He likely had with him a copy of Samuel Hearne's map (MAP 191, page 137), still unpublished, its accuracy questioned by prominent geographer Alexander Dalrymple, hydrographer of the East India Company.

On 7 October 1789 Turnor arrived at Cumberland House, where he spent the winter instructing a young David Thompson in the art of surveying. Thompson would have accompanied Turnor to Athabasca but was recuperating from an injury to his leg. Turnor therefore instructed Peter Fidler, who had arrived at Cumberland in June 1790, and it was he who accompanied Turnor to Lake Athabasca and Great Slave Lake.

Wintering at Île-à-la-Crosse and on Lake Athabasca, Turnor and Fidler spent 1790 to 1792 in the Athabasca country, three times meeting Alexander Mackenzie of the North West Company (see page 143); Turnor is credited with having persuaded Mackenzie to acquire more surveying skills and instruments before his expedition to the Pacific. It was Turnor who finally fixed the position of Lake Athabasca, establishing its location relative to the Pacific and to Chesterfield Inlet; the latter was hoped by some in the Hudson's Bay Company to offer an easier route to Athabasca.

Turnor returned to England in late 1792 and began the task of collating the information he had gathered into a map. MAP 207 is one of the

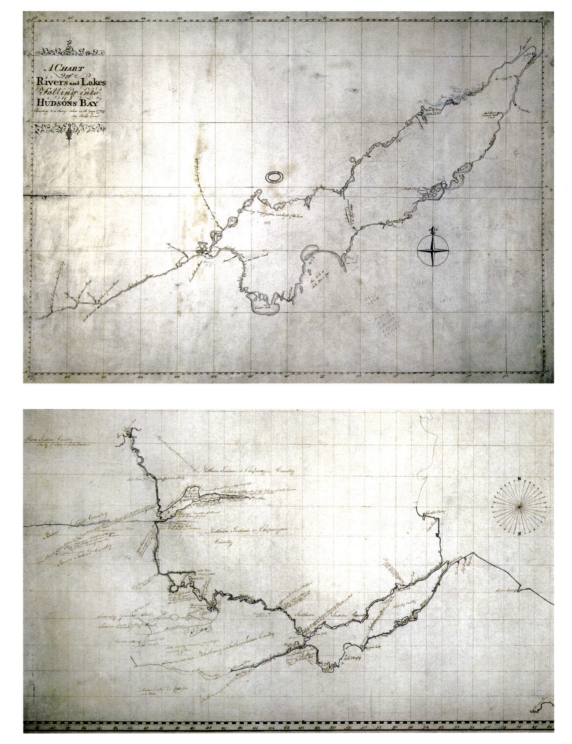

MAP 206 (*above, top*).
One of the first maps drawn by Philip Turnor for the Hudson's Bay Company was this one, drawn in 1778–79, showing the connections of the Nelson and Hayes river systems with Lake Winnipeg (*Sea Lake or Lake Win-e-peg*, shown at centre bottom, with only the northern part defined). It also shows routes to the Saskatchewan River and the west. *York Factory* (previously York Fort) is shown, on Hudson Bay.

MAP 207 (*above*).
This was the first map Turnor drew when he was back in London in 1792. Now the Hudson's Bay Company had a map of the route to the rich fur territories around Lake Athabasca, information they would exploit in the coming years.

preliminary maps, drawn in late 1792; but Turnor's masterpiece was not ready for another two years (MAP 208, overleaf). This huge map, 2.6 m wide, plotted not only Turnor's own information but every snippet of detail from others that he could lay his hands on. The result was a superb map of the Canadian West.

At the beginning of the following year, 1795, the London mapmaker Aaron Arrow-smith published his first map of North America, *A Map Exhibiting all the New Discoveries in the Interior Parts of North America*, largely based on Turnor's information. "The Public stands indebted," Arrowsmith wrote, "for the many positions so accurately settled by Mr. Philip Turnor . . . which has laid the permanent Foundation for the Geography of that part of the Globe."

Map 209 (right).
Aaron Arrowsmith's map of North America, first published in 1795, used Turnor's mapped information for most of the interior detail. Arrowsmith was the only mapmaker privy to Hudson's Bay Company information at this time. This is Arrowsmith's own copy of the 1796 edition of the map, and he has used it for updates to be added to the next edition. In red ink is an extension of the Rocky Mountains and the positions of Alexander Mackenzie's route to the Pacific (also Map 200, page 144). Before Turnor fixed the position of Lake Athabasca, some thought that Chesterfield Inlet would lead to it or connect with it, a supposition that does not seem unreasonable looking at this Arrowsmith map, particularly when one realizes that the latitude of the lake was unknown. Turnor was the first to accurately show the relationship of the lakes and rivers in the Arctic watershed to those in the Hudson Bay watershed; Peter Pond had shown the connection but, lacking instruments and surveying skills, had not shown the rivers in the correct positions (see Map 194, pages 140-41).

At left, Tammy Hannibal, map archivist at the Hudson's Bay Company Archives, holds the partially open map, and below is the ornate cartouche from the map, dedicating it, of course, to Turnor's Hudson's Bay Company masters and commissioners. Overleaf (Map 214, page 151) is another section of the Turnor map, showing Peter Fidler's explorations towards the Rockies in 1792–93.

Map 208 (all on this page).
Philip Turnor's 1794 summary map. The only known copy of this map is at the Hudson's Bay Company Archives in Winnipeg. It is very large, 2.59 x 1.59 m, and is currently kept rolled up. It is due for restoration work; it has a nasty tendency to crack if unrolled too far. Hence the only photography possible at the moment is in small sections, two of which, overlapped, are shown here. The area from the Athabasca River (*Athapiscow River*) to (Great) *Slave Lake* is shown, first mapped from actual survey by Turnor and his assistant, Peter Fidler, in 1791–92. Turnor shows only those rivers and shorelines he actually surveyed; no speculative mapping here! Thus only the northern shore of Great Slave Lake is mapped, reflecting the route taken. But there is information from all manner of other sources deemed reliable, including some from the rival North West Company. Because Turnor was in England, the map reflects information only to 1792–93; the Peace River, trailing off at left from Athabasca (*Athapiscow*) Lake, is the route Alexander Mackenzie finally took when he achieved his goal of reaching the Pacific Ocean, in 1793. Turnor does not yet have this information from the rival company. The map is Turnor's last surviving work, executed while he was in England on Company pay of one guinea a week.

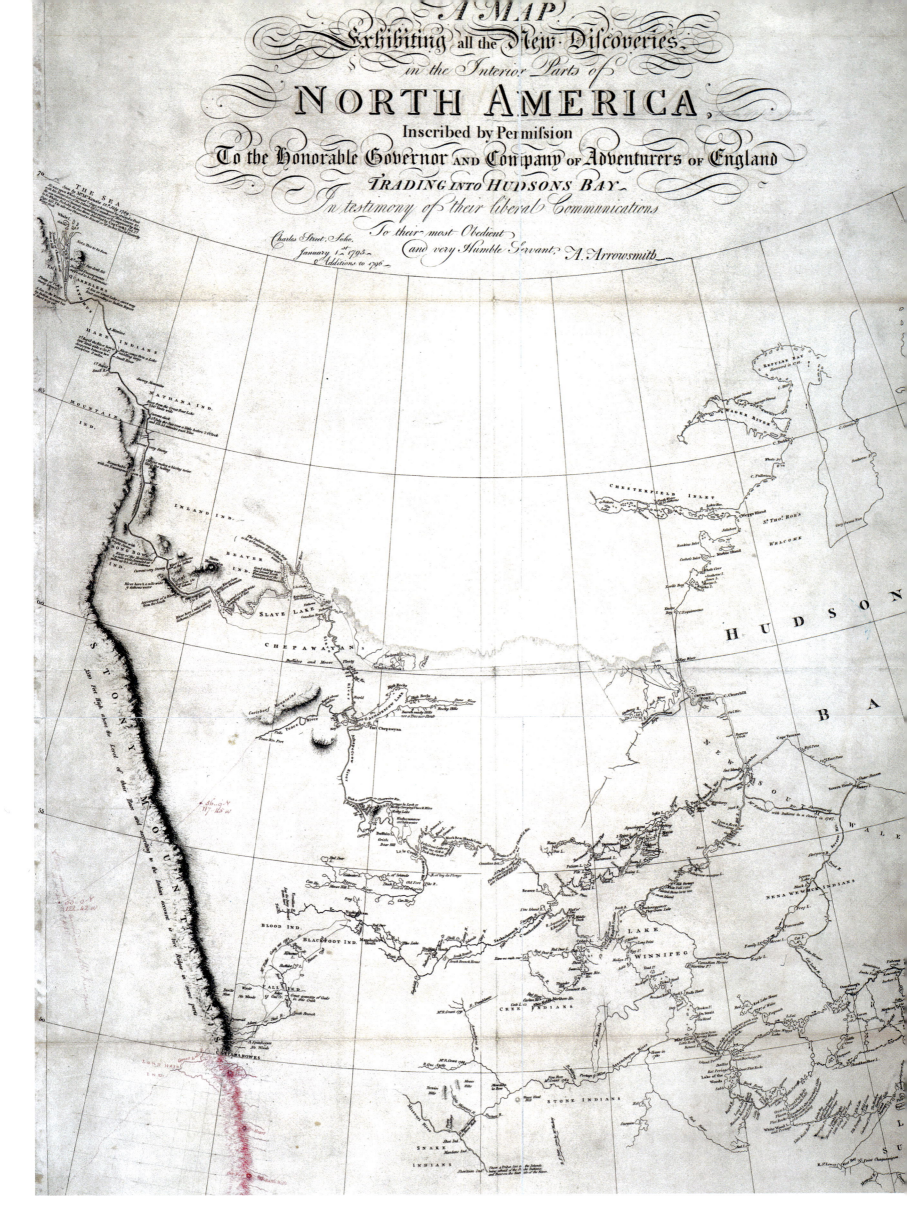

A MAP
Exhibiting all the New Discoveries
in the Interior Parts of
NORTH AMERICA,
Inscribed by Permission
To the Honorable Governor and Company of Adventurers of England
TRADING INTO HUDSONS BAY.
In testimony of their liberal Communications
To their most Obedient
and very Humble Servant, A. Arrowsmith

Charles Street, Soho.
January 1st 1795
Additions to 1796

Philip Turnor's surveying assistant, Peter Fidler, took over the job of surveyor to the Hudson's Bay Company when Turnor left Canada for good at the end of 1792. By this time, taught by Turnor but with a clear talent for the art, Fidler was well-suited for the task.

Peter Fidler had been hired by the Company in 1788 as a labourer. But his skills soon became apparent; as one writer put it, "the call of adventure rather than the nudge of necessity" must have prompted him to join up. He was soon made a clerk and was selected to be Turnor's assistant after David Thompson could not accompany Turnor to the Athabasca because of a broken leg.

Perhaps initially from Turnor's instructions, Fidler acquired the habit of making ongoing sketch maps of the route he was travelling, something Turnor never did. As a result, Fidler's journals and notebooks are full of little maps. During the winter of 1791–92, while Turnor was on Lake Athabasca, Fidler took it upon himself to spend the time with the Chipewyan, in order to learn the language. Fidler seems to have been a bit of a linguist, for in the course of his long career he collected more maps from native sources than anyone else ever did. Many of these are shown on pages 152–55.

On 4 September 1791, Fidler's journal records, "In the afternoon I embarked with 4 Canoes of Jepewyans, in order to remain the whole Winter with them, & acquire their Language." This was an amazing undertaking; Fidler was twenty-two; he had no provisions, no tent, little clothing, and not much ammunition, yet off he went into a country with poor resources and a very cold winter climate. But he succeeded, arriving back at Lake Athabasca on 10 April 1792, "having acquired a sufficiency of their Language to transact any business with them." And, wrote Fidler, "On the whole this has been rather an agreeable winter than otherwise."

Fidler took meticulous details of his courses when on the move. A typically dense passage from his journal, with almost no punctuation, is this, from 23 September 1791:

At 8 AM got underway (being very early with the Jepewyans) Went NW 1/4 WNW&NWbN 1/3 WSW S&SW 1/2 SSW&SSE 1/4 WSW&SSW 1/3 SWbW 1/3 SSW&SWbW 1/4, WNW&SbW 1/2 SWbS 1/4 WbS1/4 SW 1/4 WNW 1/4 NNW&ENE 1/3 NWbN 1/3 W 1/4 NbE 1/4 WbN 1/4 N 1/2 NWbN 1/3 . . .

Not exactly easy reading!

During the seven months he was with the Chipewyans, Fidler made fifty-six sets of observations, determining the latitudes of thirty-two locations, each resulting in a page of calculations in his notebook, similar to the ones shown here.

With Turnor back in England, Fidler took over the duties of company surveyor. In November 1792 he set off to spend another winter with a native group, this time the Piegans of the Blackfoot Nation of southern Alberta. This time he found another person, John Ward, to go with him. They set off on horseback accompanied by a band of natives who were returning to their wintering grounds around what it today High River.

On 20 November Fidler crossed the Red Deer River and recorded, "Here I first got sight of the Rocky Mountain," about 150 km away. He wrote that they looked "awfully grand, stretching from ssw to wbs [west by south] by Compass, very much similar to dark rain like clouds rising up above the Horizon in a fine summers evening." Fidler, naturally, was recording his position all the time, and now he became the first to correctly locate the Rocky Mountains on

MAPS 210 (*above, top*) and 211 (*above*).
Maps from Peter Fidler's notebook drawn while with Philip Turnor in Athabasca in 1791.

MAP 210 (*top*) shows the southern shore of Lake Athabasca and the position of the North West Company post Fort Chipewyan (at its original location on Old Fort Point on the south shore); it here is given another name as well, "Athapescow House." Fidler was here fulfilling his mandate to plot the positions of the trading posts of the rival company. This was Alexander Mackenzie's starting point for his expeditions both to the Arctic Ocean in 1789 and the Pacific Ocean in 1793.

MAP 211 shows the western end of Lake Athabasca, and it is shown upside down from its position in the notebook, depicting the lake more conventionally, with north at the top. A comparison with the modern topographic map of the area shows that the outline of the lake as mapped by Fidler has changed quite considerably. Fidler's outline coincides with the marshy area to the north and west of modern Fort Chipewyan, on the north side of the lake, and reveals two hundred years of silting up where the Rivière des Rochers leaves the lake. This short river connects with the Peace River before, as the Slave River, it flows north into Great Slave Lake.

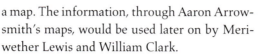

Map 213 (right).
Sketch map from Fidler's notebook for 1792 showing the positions on the Saskatchewan River of the original Cumberland House, built by Samuel Hearne in 1774, and a new one, built in 1790.

a map. The information, through Aaron Arrowsmith's maps, would be used later on by Meriwether Lewis and William Clark.

Fidler was the first European to cross the Battle, Red Deer, Bow, and Highwood Rivers, again placing them on his maps. He documented the vast herds of buffalo on which the natives depended, and described buffalo jumps and pounds. He was the first to discover coal on the prairie, in February 1793 at Kneehills Creek, which much later was mined as the Drumheller Coalfield. Fidler also wrote the first description of the prairie cactus, opuntia.

Fidler's route in 1792–93 was shown on the great map that Philip Turnor prepared in London in 1794, shown in Map 214, though the track is hardly visible. His route, and in particular the location of the Rockies, was shown on Arrowsmith's maps of North America, such as Map 209.

In 1800 Fidler built Chesterfield House at the confluence of the Red Deer River and the South Saskatchewan, and while there he gathered a number of maps from native chiefs which expanded his knowledge to distant regions that he had never visited. We are indebted to Fidler for preserving these maps, for he redrew them

on paper after being shown them on the ground or on bark (see pages 152–55).

In 1802 Fidler was sent back to Lake Athabasca to trade furs in competition with the North West Company. There he he built Nottingham House, at the west end of the lake. He spent many years, in fact, as a trader rather than a surveyor, which was perhaps a shame, given his obvious skills. But the period was a difficult one for the Hudson's Bay Company, and trading wars on more than one occasion led to violence.

Fidler's maps were used by Lord Selkirk to select the site of his Red River Settlement, and it was Fidler who delivered the Pemmican Proclamation to the Nor'Westers, banning the export of pemmican from the colony (see page 178). Fidler was also involved in surveying lots for the settlement, and a number of his maps survive (see Map 274, page 179).

Fidler has tended to be overshadowed by the feats of his contemporary, David Thompson. Fidler's large summary maps, unlike those of Thompson, have not survived, except insofar as they were used by Arrowsmith. Yet there is no doubt that Fidler made a major contribution to the mapping of the West.

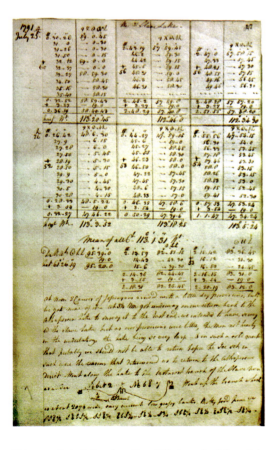

Map 212.
A typical page of Peter Fidler's journal while he was on the move. This covers the period from 24 to 26 August 1791, when he and Turnor were surveying the shores of Lake Athabasca. The journal is full of these "on the run" sketch maps, with observations for latitudes. By contrast, Turnor's journal for the same period contains only text.

This page of calculations from Peter Fidler's notebook for 25 July 1791 illustrates the immense amount of work required to take astronomical observations and calculate a longitudinal position. Fidler and Turnor were on Great Slave Lake at the time.

Map 214.
Peter Fidler's track towards the Rocky Mountains in 1792–93 is shown here on the 1794 map compiled by Philip Turnor in London. Fidler was the first to accurately fix the position of the Rockies. His route is also shown on Aaron Arrowsmith's map of North America, with 1796 updates (Map 209, page 149).

Native Maps

Natives, just like European explorers and fur traders, sometimes needed to record geographical information, perhaps about the location of a food source or a route taken, and a map was the easiest way of passing on the information.

Unfortunately for historians, many native maps were ephemeral in nature, having been drawn in dust on the ground or with charcoal on a piece of birchbark. As a result, there are few extant native maps on original media. Luckily, however, a number of fur traders and explorers copied these maps onto paper, and it is in this way that most have survived.

Native maps are mainly maps drawn from memory. They generally show a good understanding of the geography of the country in which their creators lived or through which they travelled. They do not necessarily have any particular regard for the Western concepts of exact direction, distance, proportion, or scale. In many ways native maps are little different from those drawn by early fur trade travellers, who, lacking a means of fixing their positions, also drew often disproportionate yet essentially accurate maps of the rivers and lakes that were the lifeline of their trade. The maps of Peter Pond (page 140) are a good case in point. But native maps often added an element that was not present in European maps, that of the cosmological. The blending of the geographical with the spiritual was common, and naturally enough this makes them difficult to comprehend unless one is also aware of native cosmological concepts.

One of the obvious practical uses natives had for maps was that of leaving messages for those who followed as to a route taken. Typically, these would be etched on birchbark, or perhaps written with charcoal, and placed in a split at the top of a stick. A tree might be blazed to draw attention to the message. MAP 215, below, seems to be the oldest surviving North American map on birchbark. It was found by a military surveying party in 1841, somewhere on the portage from the Mattawa–Ottawa River system to Lake Nipissing–Lake Huron. The map likely only survived because it was found by surveyor Captain Bainbrigge, who, taking a liking to it, took it home with him. He then added a drawn explanation of what the map showed, since the incisions on the bark were hard to see, and framed it for protection.

Benedict Arnold found a birchbark map such as this one when he was marching to attack Québec in 1775; it was said to have assisted him.

Such message maps are few. By far the largest group of maps are those drawn by natives at the request of Europeans, to extend knowledge beyond the area known to the fur traders or explorers. The Hudson's Bay Company, in particular, was always keen to gather information about other native groups who might be induced to trade with it, and from quite an early date, various traders gathered and drew these maps. The map drawn by, or from information obtained by, James Knight in 1719 is one of the earliest to use native information (MAP 111, page 79).

Moses Norton, who became the governor at Prince of Wales Fort, was very keen on gathering native information, and in particular about rumoured copper mines—he would send Samuel Hearne to look for them in 1770—and he made it his business to collect native maps. One of these was drawn in 1767 by Matonabbee and Idotlyazee, two Chipewyan natives he had sent inland in 1762 (MAP 221, page 155). It gives a very reasonable account of the geography as far west as Great Slave Lake.

The most prolific collector of native maps was Peter Fidler, who filled his notebook with the maps of Blackfoot natives while he was at Chesterfield House, on the Prairies, in 1800–1802.

MAP 215 (*below*).
An army surveyor, intent on teaching young army recruits a lesson in mapmaking, preserved this very rare example of a native map, still visible, incised on a piece of birchbark. It is the oldest surviving native birchbark map in North America. It shows a route across the Ottawa–Lake Huron watershed portage, about 1841.

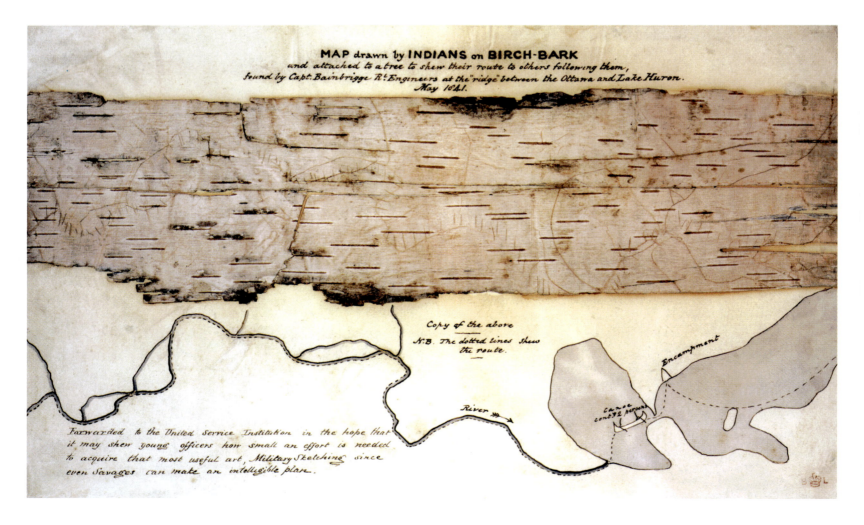

MAP drawn by INDIANS on BIRCH-BARK
and attached to a tree to shew their route to others following them,
found by Capt. Bainbrigge R.¹ Engineers at the "ridge" between the Ottawa and Lake Huron.
May 1841.

Copy of the above
N.B. The dotted lines shew the route.

River

Encampment

Forwarded to the United Service Institution in the hope that it may shew young officers how small an effort is needed to acquire that most useful art, Military Sketching since even Savages can make an intelligible plan.

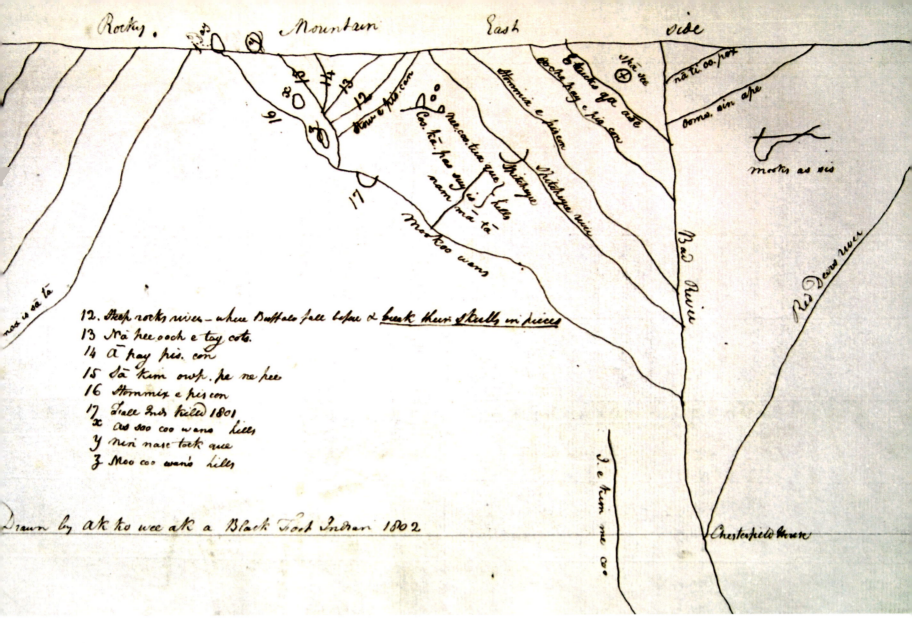

Map 216 (*above*).
Peter Fidler's redrawing of a map by Ak ko wee a ka, "a Black Foot Indian," 1802, showing a large area of western Canada as far west as the Rocky Mountains. North is to the right. The Bad River is the South Saskatchewan and the Hudson's Bay Company's Chesterfield House is shown. Ak ko wee a ka's map is not as detailed as that of Ac ko mok ki's (*below*), but still shows an extensive knowledge of all the major streams flowing from the mountains.

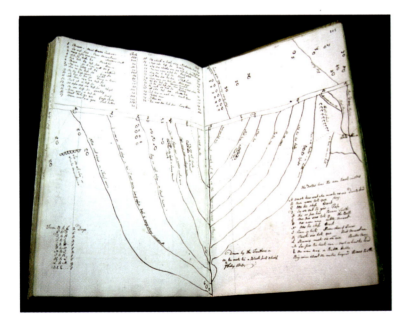

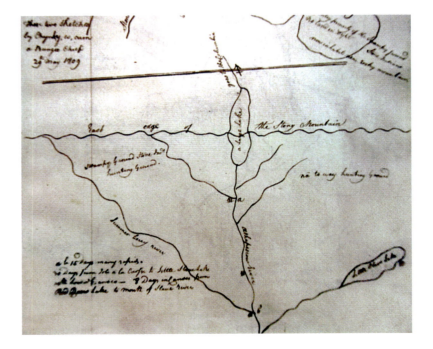

Map 217.
Ac ko mok ki's famous map of western Canada and the western United States, drawn in February 1801. The river system in the centre is that of the Missouri, and the smaller one to the right is the Saskatchewan. North is to the right, and the sea coast is represented by the top edge of the pages. Beyond the Rocky Mountains are two rivers which have variously been interpreted as the Columbia, Snake, or Fraser Rivers. At right, about halfway down, Chesterfield House is shown, at the junction of the Red Deer River and South Saskatchewan. This was Fidler's base from 1800 to 1802, on the frontiers of the Hudson's Bay Company territories. Thus around him there was a good deal of land unknown to Europeans, and this was the reason Fidler tried to collect as much information as he could from the natives of the region. As this map amply demonstrates, they knew quite a lot.

Map 218.
Map of the Athabasca River flowing from the Rocky Mountains (the wavy line labelled *The Stony Mountain*), drawn by Peter Fidler from a map by Chynk y es cum, a "Bungee" Chief, dated 29 May 1809. The lake on the right is Lesser Slave Lake, but no lake seems to correspond to the lake shown at the line of mountains.

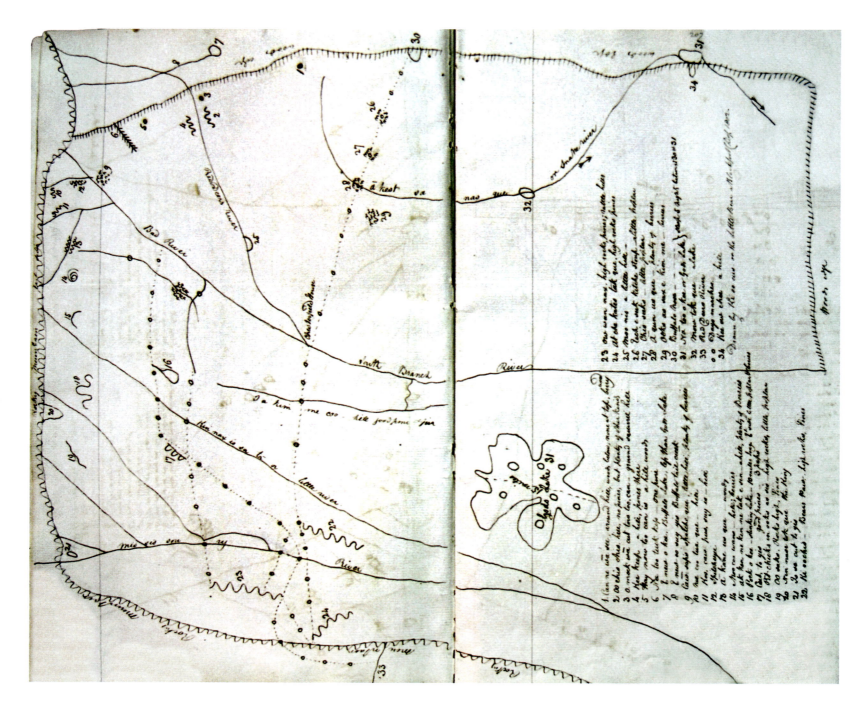

The handwritten map labels include: Bad River, South Branch, River, Chesterfield House, and various native-language notations along with numbered lists (1–34) at the right side.

Lake into the one which runs to the Sea is not long and that
River which he calls the Esquimay River and says it is a
bold deep _____ River without any falls in it but rather strong
current and no woods growing about it the under is his description of it

The river Mackenzie went down

The Indian pointed out the course N b C or about N 37 C b[y]
true Compass but am doubtfull and even hope he only meant

Map 219 (*above*).

Peter Fidler recorded this map originally drawn by Ki oo cus,
or Little Bear, a Blackfoot chief, in 1802. Here it has been
oriented with north at the top. The *Bad River* and *South
Branch River* are the South Saskatchewan, and Chesterfield
House is again shown at the junction of the Red Deer River.
Tracks across the prairie are shown as dashed lines, with each
circle representing a "sleep"; thus the number of circles indicates the number of days' travel. In addition to rivers and lakes,
this map shows the *woods edge*, extending along the eastern
and northern edges of the map. This was the boundary of the
open grasslands with the more wooded regions. Another map
that shows biogeographic information is that of Samuel Hearne,
drawn in 1772 (MAP 191, page 137), which shows the treeline,
derived from native sources.

Map 220 (*left*).

A map drawn by a Chipewyan native man, Shew ditha da, and
copied by Philip Turnor into his journal in 1791. It depicts the
area from Great Slave Lake, on the left, to a river or inlet flowing
into Hudson Bay, perhaps Chesterfield Inlet, on the right. The
vast area of the Barren Lands between Great Slave Lake and
Hudson Bay has been shown as a single lake, surrounded by *no
woods*. It could also be a depiction of Dubawnt Lake, the largest
lake in the region. It is separated from Great Slave by a carrying
place around a high falls. A small lake to the southeast of Great
Slave Lake is labelled *Lake they kill Deer at*. At the west end of
Great Slave Lake Turnor has added the information *The river
Mackenzie went down*, referring to Alexander Mackenzie's
descent of the Mackenzie River in 1789.

Map 221 (*right*).
Perhaps the most famous Canadian native map is this, Matonabbee and Idotlyazee's map of the rivers and lakes inland from Hudson Bay, about 1767. This map was drawn by Moses Norton, the governor at Prince of Wales Fort, from information provided by the two Chipewyan natives. Norton had commissioned the two five years earlier to "go & trace to ye mouth of ye Largest River to ye Northward," after he had heard rumours of copper mines to the north. Later Samuel Hearne would be sent on the same mission (see page 136). The red dots (at top) are *copper mines*, in reality probably simply places copper had been found on the ground, as Hearne was to discover in 1771. The map shows the eastern coast of Hudson Bay from the Churchill River (at the bottom) to the Coppermine River (at the top). The latter river is on the northern coast of Canada, and the straight coastline shown on this map is a generalization of the coast running south-north and that west-east, without any indication of the change of direction. Just to complicate matters further, the map was originally drawn the other way up from the way it is shown here; it has been oriented in a more familiar way here to facilitate its understanding. The scale from west to east is compressed. The large lake is Great Slave Lake, quite recognizable in shape, complete with the Mackenzie River flowing from its western end. The river is here called the *Kis-Ca-Che-Wan*, a Cree name. Since the map was drawn by Chipewyans, they would likely have considered Great Slave Lake as their mental starting point for this map, and from there the rivers radiate out in various directions.

One of the maps he redrew from an ephemeral native map was one that showed the entire upper Missouri drainage basin and part of the Saskatchewan; this information was used by Aaron Arrowsmith in compiling his maps of North America. The map (Map 217) was originally drawn by Ac ko mok ki, a Blackfoot chief with an extensive basic knowledge of the geography of vast areas of the West. A feature of interest on this map is the population statistics; the map contains a list of tribes by numbers of tents.

The history of Canada, as being mainly a progressive encroachment onto previously occupied native lands, contains many examples of maps that include native information. Such information was often used to extend knowledge beyond the area known to European explorers.

In the Arctic, it seems that the mapmaking skills of the Inuit were particularly well developed, perhaps due to a sensitivity to the presence of water as a place for hunting. The map obtained by Edward Parry in 1822 (Map 290, page 188) was partly drawn by Parry and extended by the Inuit Iligliuk. John Ross did much the same in 1829–30 (Map 294, page 191).

Alexander Henry (Map 192, page 138) and Peter Pond (pages 140–42) both used native input to extend their maps beyond their own knowledge, and Alexander Mackenzie probably would not have found his overland route to the Pacific had it not been for native drawn maps.

Symbolism is used in making all maps; they cannot depict features to exact scale, and this is no different with native drawn maps. It is just that the symbols used are often different, and may have meanings unknown to persons of other cultures who view them. Communication of geographical ideas, like any other, requires that those communicating first understand each other's language.

The First Map of the West Coast

In 1773, the Northwest Coast of North America remained unmapped even in general trend, a major gap in the map of the world; only the polar regions were similarly unmapped. Lack of motivation was the reason for this state of affairs; no European power, up to that point, was really interested. There were no reports of gold to lure men northwards to these often unpleasantly chilly coasts, there were vast distances to cover in any case, and the currents and winds made sailing northwards along the coast very difficult. Without motivation, no one tried.

The Russian advance eastwards from Kamchatka to the Aleutian Islands changed all that. The Spanish had long regarded the Pacific Ocean as their own, and wanted to ensure that no other nation encroached on their territory. So in 1773 the Spanish viceroy in New Spain—Mexico—instructed one of his senior naval captains, Juan Josef Pérez Hernández (usually known simply as Juan Pérez), to draw up plans for a voyage to the north to determine if Russian traders were encroaching on the coast.

Pérez sailed from the Mexican port of San Blas in January 1774 in the *Santiago*, with a complement of about eighty-six men including,

as second-in-command, Estéban José Martínez, and pilot Josef de Cañizarez.

The viceroy had instructed Pérez to sail to 60° N. He was, on his southward return, to follow the coast, "never losing sight of it." Not only that, Pérez was to carry tropical spices such as cinnamon and nutmeg to show any natives he might encounter what the Spanish were looking for; it seems that they had little concept of the real nature of the Northwest Coast.

Pérez sailed from Monterey, at the time the most northerly outpost of Spanish power, on 6 June. Then, sailing offshore, he set a course to the northwest, changing to north at 50° N. On 18 July they sighted land off the northernmost point of the Queen Charlotte Islands, and the following day, near Langara Island (named *Santa Margarita* by Pérez) in Dixon Entrance, they met Haida in canoes, with whom they bartered. But, fearing treachery, they did not venture ashore.

Although he remained in the area for four days, Pérez was never able to anchor, and his latitudes are confused. He maintained that he was at 55° 24′ N when he saw and named a cape he called *Santa Maria Magdalena*; it is marked

on MAP 224 (right) as *Pᵗᵃ de Sᵗᵃ Maria Magdalena*. This has been identified as Cape Muzon, the southern tip of Dall Island, at almost exactly 54° 40′ N.

Not coincidentally, this is also the southern tip of the Alaska panhandle, the northernmost coast of British Columbia. When the United States inherited the territorial claims of Spain in 1819 they claimed the coast up to 54° 40′ N and in fact threatened to go to war with Britain in 1845–46 if they didn't get it. As it happened, of course, they settled for 49° N instead. But 54° 40′ N was accepted as the southern limit of Russian claims, so that when the United States purchased Alaska from the

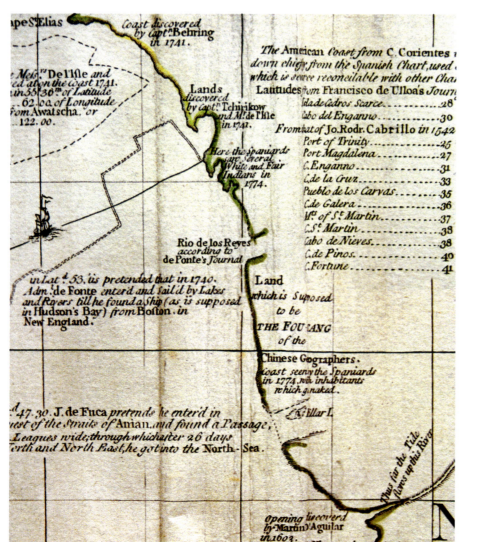

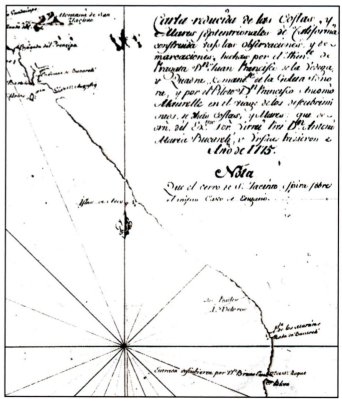

MAP 222 (*below, left*).
A map from British mapmaker Thomas Jefferys' *American Atlas* of 1775. At about 55° N is the note *Here the Spaniards saw several White and Fair Indians in 1774*, and at about 50° N, presumably from Pérez's encounter at Nootka Sound, the map is marked *Coast seen by the Spaniards in 1774 with inhabitants which go naked*. How the British obtained this information so quickly is a mystery. The British Columbia coast is the *Land which is supposed to be the Fousang of the Chinese geographers*. This idea comes from ancient Chinese tales of voyages across the Pacific. There are many recorded instances of disabled junks drifting across the Pacific and becoming shipwrecked on the shores of the Northwest Coast. For example, in 1833 three Japanese sailors were rescued by Hudson's Bay Company men from a shipwrecked junk near the entrance to the Strait of Juan de Fuca.

MAP 223 (*below*).
The west coast of North America from a map drawn in 1775, from a follow-up voyage by Juan Francisco de la Bodega y Quadra. He did not see British Columbia, and so joined with a faint line the coasts he had seen. The map bears a considerable resemblance to the one James Cook would draw three years later (MAPS 226 and 227, overleaf), believing it to be the first map of the Northwest Coast.

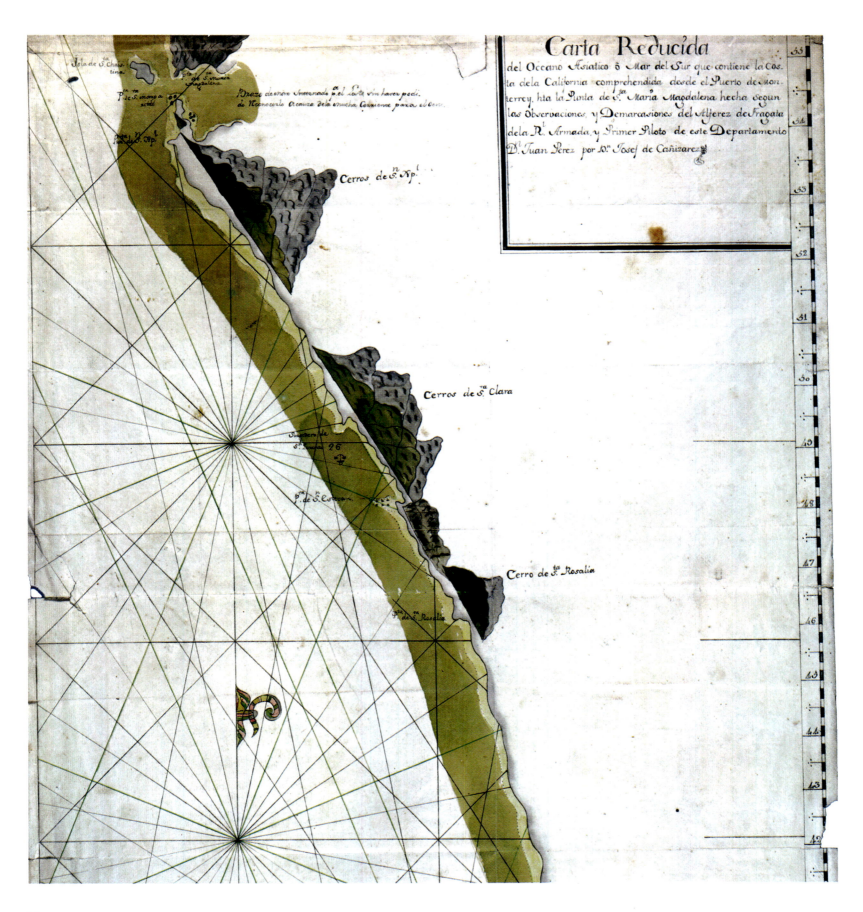

Carta Reducida
del Oceano Asiatico ô Mar del Sur que contiene la Costa dela California comprehendida desde el Puerto de Monterrey, hta la Punta de S.ta Maria Magdalena hecha segun
las Observaciones, y Demarcasiones del Alferez de Fragata
dela R.l Armada, y Primer Piloto de este Departamento
D.n Juan Perez por D.n Josef de Cañizarez

MAP 224.

Part of the map drawn by Josef de Cañizarez of Juan Pérez's voyage in 1774. It is the first map of the coast of British Columbia drawn from exploration, fully four years before James Cook would arrive on the Northwest Coast. This map remained forgotten until 1989, when it was rediscovered in the United States National Archives. How it arrived there is unknown, but one possible explanation is that it was acquired by the American government to build a case for boundary negotiators, perhaps for the boundary settlement of 1846, when the government did acquire numbers of old maps. Perhaps this one was not useful for that purpose and was stuffed in a drawer somewhere and forgotten.

Russians in 1867, this latitude became the boundary between British—now Canadian—territories to the south and American territories to the north.

Pérez gave up at this latitude; although he had been instructed to sail to 60° N, he had seen no evidence of Russian encroachment. He tried to keep the coast in view as he returned south-

wards, without much success until he reached Vancouver Island. There he chanced on the entrance to Nootka Sound, which he named *Surgidero de San Lorenzo*. Unable to make it into the sound itself, he anchored outside on 7 August and again traded with natives.

The voyage farther south was uneventful and speedy; they arrived back at Monterey on

28 August. Juan Pérez's voyage did not fulfil his instructions, but it was the first Spanish voyage north, and a number of other Spanish voyages would follow.

MAP 224 was drawn by Josef de Cañizarez, Pérez's pilot, and is the first map of what is now the coast of British Columbia drawn from actual exploration rather than from conjecture.

James Cook—Defining the Width of Canada

James Cook mapped much more of Canada's eastern coastline than of the West Coast (see page 106), but his mapping of the latter was at the time of considerably greater significance. Not only did Cook determine the general trend of the whole Northwest Coast, but for the first time he accurately calculated its longitude. In this he was aided by the new and experimental chronometers he carried with him. And with the fixing of the position of the West Coast, for the first time the width of North America, and thus Canada, was accurately determined.

The consequences were enormous. Now cross-country explorers would know how far it was to their goal of the Pacific Ocean. This, plus Cook's incomplete mapping of the inlet on which Anchorage, Alaska, now stands, would soon excite Peter Pond to draw his maps (see page 140) and ultimately drove Alexander Mackenzie to the Arctic and the Pacific searching for this apparently easy and short route to the western ocean (see page 143).

After taking almost a month to work his way northwards from his appropriately named initial landfall at Cape Foulweather in Oregon, James Cook arrived on the coast of British Columbia on 29 March 1778, staying four weeks in Nootka Sound, which he called King George's Sound. Cook was searching for a western entrance to a Northwest Passage, and his instructions, reflecting this purpose, stated: "[Take] care not to lose any time in exploring Rivers or Inlets . . . until you get into the . . . latitude of 65°." As a result, Cook did not map the coast of today's British

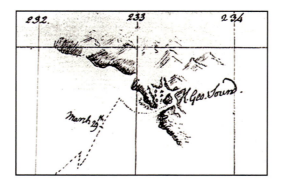

Columbia in any detail, except at Nootka. Instead, his maps show much of the coast south of Alaska only as a tentative trend line. In fact, the most important results of Cook's 1778 third voyage were in Alaska, where he finally correctly mapped the true relationship of the Asian and American continents.

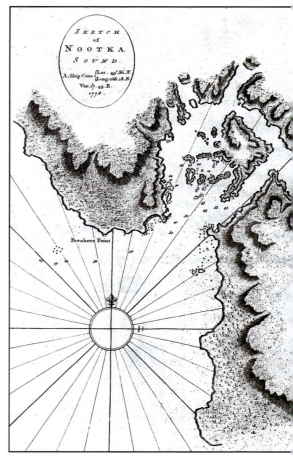

MAP 225 (above, middle).
Detail of Cook's arrival at Nootka Sound, from the journal of one of his officers, James Burney.

MAP 226 (below) and MAP 227 (below, inset).
James Cook's general chart of the Northwest Coast of America. MAP 226 is the map published in 1784, while MAP 227 (here inset) is the original manuscript map Cook enclosed in a letter sent via the Russians to Philip Stephens, Secretary of the Admiralty, on 20 October 1778, and received in London on 6 March 1779. Both show the coast of British Columbia as a trend line, except for the details at Nootka Sound.

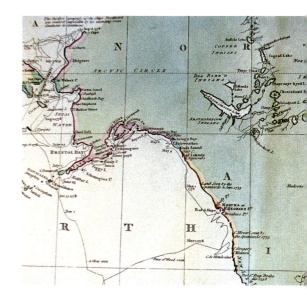

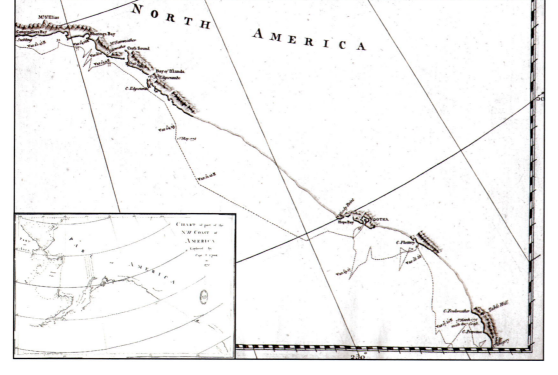

MAP 228 (above, top).
An engraved map of Nootka Sound, from Cook's book, published in 1784. Cook named the inlet King George's Sound, but by the time the book was published, the Admiralty had changed the name to Nootka, probably to avoid confusion with a similarly named place in Australia. Note Cook's calculated position in the cartouche. His longitude, of Ship Cove, now Resolution Cove, on the east side of Bligh Island (marked *A* on the map), is 233° 18′ E (126° 42′ W). This compares well with the true longitude (126° 31′ W).

MAP 229 (above).
One of Cook's senior officers, Henry Roberts, was charged with the job of summarizing all of Cook's discoveries on a map of the world. In 1784 Roberts published a map of the world updated to include all of Cook's discoveries, in Australia, New Zealand, Hawaii, and on the West Coast of North America, from all of his three voyages. Roberts somehow got hold of Samuel Hearne's as yet unpublished map showing the rivers and lakes of the interior Northwest (see page 136), and added to the coastline determined by Cook. The result was that the interior features were placed far too close to the coast. But it was Hearne, not Cook, who positioned his rivers and lakes incorrectly. Cook's calculations of longitude were almost exactly right.

West Coast Exploration and Trade

Not to be outdone by Britain's James Cook, the French planned a major scientific circumnavigation of their own, designed to recoup the prestige of France judged to have been lost to Cook. A respected naval officer, Jean-François Galaup, Comte de La Pérouse, was selected to lead the expedition, and it arrived on the Northwest Coast, near Mount St. Elias in Alaska, in July 1786.

Realizing the difficulty of sailing northwards, La Pérouse sailed southwards along the coast, surveying, mapping, collecting information, and searching for a Northwest Passage, pausing principally at Lituya Bay, in Alaska. He had been given only three months to survey the entire coast, a task which would later take George Vancouver three years, so it is not surprising that La Pérouse soon came to realize the impossibility of the task.

Nevertheless, he managed to produce the best general map of the coast at the time, a map reasonably accurate except for its gaps. Although this map (MAP 231) was drawn in 1786, it was not engraved and published until 1797, long after La Pérouse's demise on a reef in the South Pacific in 1788. Thus his achievement did not get the recognition it deserved.

After Cook's visit to the West Coast in 1778, and particularly after the publication of his book in 1784, the revelation that there was indeed money to be made in this heretofore neglected part of the world led to a flurry of activity from British and American fur traders searching for the exquisite fur of the sea otter.

Thus many maps of parts of the British Columbia coast came to be drawn, for although the traders were there for commercial purposes, maps were still required so that lucrative fur trade locations could be remembered and shipwreck avoided. One trader was James Colnett, who from 1787 to 1790 compiled the highly detailed map of the British Columbia coast shown here (MAP 232, right).

MAP 230 (below).
Not all fur traders were scrupulous in their mapping. One, John Meares, published this map in 1790, purporting to show a voyage from the Strait of Juan de Fuca to north of the Queen Charlottes, creating a sort of mega–Vancouver Island.

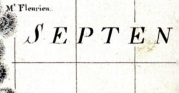

MAP 231.
Part of an original pen-and-ink map of the west coast of North America, showing the British Columbia coast, with the track of the La Pérouse expedition in 1786. It was drawn by two of the expedition's scientific staff, Gérault-Sébastien Bernizet, the surveyor, and Joseph Lapaute Dagelet, the senior astronomer. This survey was superior to Cook's or to Spanish maps at the time, but since it was not published until 1797, it was overshadowed by the British effort in the same way the Spanish maps were; the latter were not published until 1802 (see page 162).

MAP 232 (below).
Fur trader James Colnett's map of the coast of British Columbia, drawn in 1787 to 1790. The intricate details illustrate the level of knowledge of the coast just before the arrival of George Vancouver. Details were limited, however, to those areas of interest for fur trading; Vancouver Island is still shown as part of the mainland. The Strait of Georgia held lesser numbers of sea otters than the harbours and bays of the outer coast, and thus did not attract the attention of the fur seekers. The southern tip of the Queen Charlotte Islands is shown at top left, and the entrance to the Strait of Juan de Fuca, rediscovered in 1787 by another fur trader, Charles Barkley, is shown at bottom right.

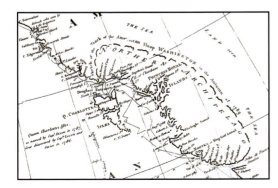

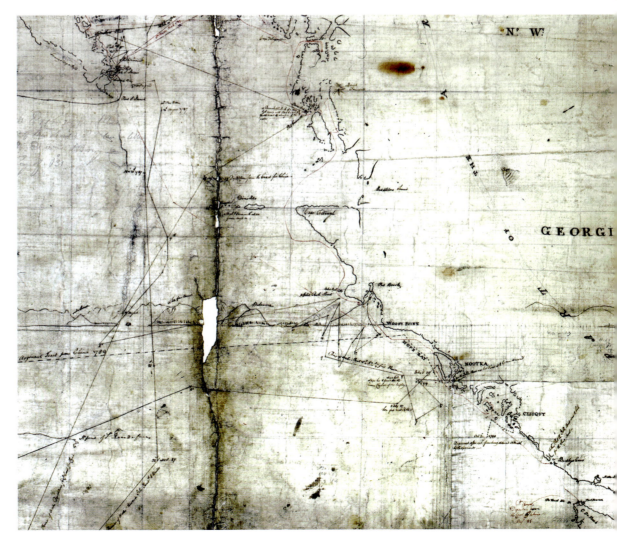

Spanish Explorations of the West Coast

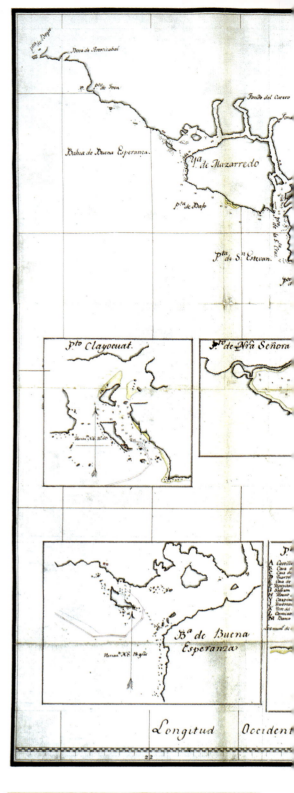

Continued Spanish concerns about a Russian advance into their territory farther south led to the establishment of a fort at Friendly Cove (Yuquot) in Nootka Sound in 1789. Although temporarily abandoned later that year, it was reoccupied soon after, and it remained until 1795; it was the only Spanish settlement in today's Canada (MAP 233, below).

In 1790, from his base at Friendly Cove, Spanish commander Francisco de Eliza dispatched two expeditions, one to Alaska to check on the Russians, and one into the Strait of Juan de Fuca, under Manuel Quimper. This latter expedition mapped the southern coast of Vancouver Island but did not turn northwards into the Strait of Georgia.

The following year, after trying without success to sail north from Nootka, Eliza himself led another expedition into the Strait of Juan de Fuca, and this time he sent José María Nárvaez, with pilot Juan Carrasco in a small schooner, the *Santa Saturnina*, and José Verdía in a longboat to explore northwards through the channels of the San Juan Islands and into the Strait of Georgia. They explored both sides of the southern part of the Strait of Georgia to a point just north of Texada Island and were the first Europeans to map any part of what is today the City of Vancouver.

Towards the end of 1791, Eliza had a summary map prepared showing the knowledge gained from his expedition that year, along with that from Manuel Quimper the year before (MAP 235). This map is a superb summary of the state of Spanish knowledge of the southwestern part of British Columbia prior to the arrival of the master surveyor George Vancouver in 1792.

The year 1792 marked the culmination of Spanish exploration of the Northwest Coast. Juan Francisco Bodega y Quadra was sent to Friendly Cove to meet with George Vancouver and comply with the terms of the Nootka Convention, signed by Britain and Spain in 1790, in which Spain was to evacuate its posts north of the Strait of Juan de Fuca and recognize the principle of sovereignty by occupation rather than first discovery. Bodega y Quadra, who had first sailed to Alaska in 1775 in a nine-metre boat (see MAP 223, page 156), was an adept mapmaker and in particular was able to combine the maps of others to draw significant summary maps of the entire western coast of North America. The British Columbia portions of three of these maps are shown overleaf (MAPS 238, 239, and 240).

Jacinto Caamaño was sent north to explore a gap in the mapped coastline which was still considered a possible Northwest Passage, Clarence Strait. His map of the Queen Charlotte Islands and Clarence Strait (copied by the English) is shown here (MAP 234).

Dionisio Alcalá Galiano and Cayetano Valdes were dispatched in two ships, the *Sutil* and the *Mexicana*, with instructions to determine if the Northwest Passage was hidden somewhere inside the Strait of Juan de Fuca.

After calling at Nootka, Galiano and Valdes entered the Strait of Juan de Fuca in June 1792 and turned north into the Strait of Georgia, where they met William Broughton, who was with *Chatham* assisting George Vancouver. On 14 June Galiano and Valdes found and entered the North Arm of the Fraser River, anchoring there for the night. They were the first Europeans to find and enter the river.

Galiano finally met Vancouver near today's City of Vancouver, and maps were exchanged. The local name of Spanish Banks commemorates this meeting. Galiano and Valdes sailed in company with Vancouver and Broughton northwards for some distance. After separating, both commanders found their way through the myriad channels and islands that lie between Vancouver Island and the mainland. Finding themselves in the Pacific, they returned southwards to Nootka.

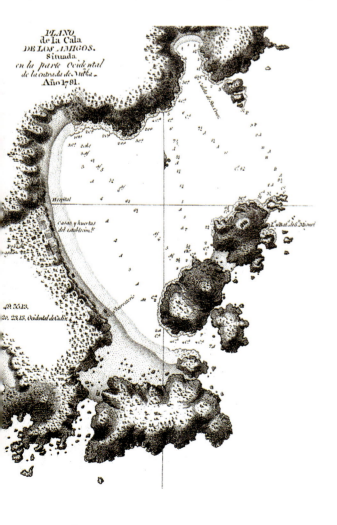

MAP 233 (*left*).
The Spanish map of Friendly Cove in 1791, engraved and published in 1802 in the *Relación*, a book that belatedly tried to show the world that the Spanish had explored the Northwest Coast long before the British.

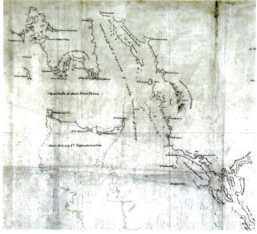

MAP 234 (*above*).
When Caamaño sailed into Nootka, George Vancouver had arrived, and was allowed to copy his maps. This copy, shown here, led to the retention of a number of Spanish place names by Vancouver, many of which are still on the map today. *Estrecho dl Aimirante Fuentes y Entrada d. N^{stra} S^{tra} Carmen*, Admiral de Fonte's Strait, however, is not. Vancouver named it Clarence Strait. This was, the Spanish thought, the last possible location for the elusive western entrance to the Northwest Passage, but Caamaño followed it only to 55° 30′ N, where bad weather forced him to return.

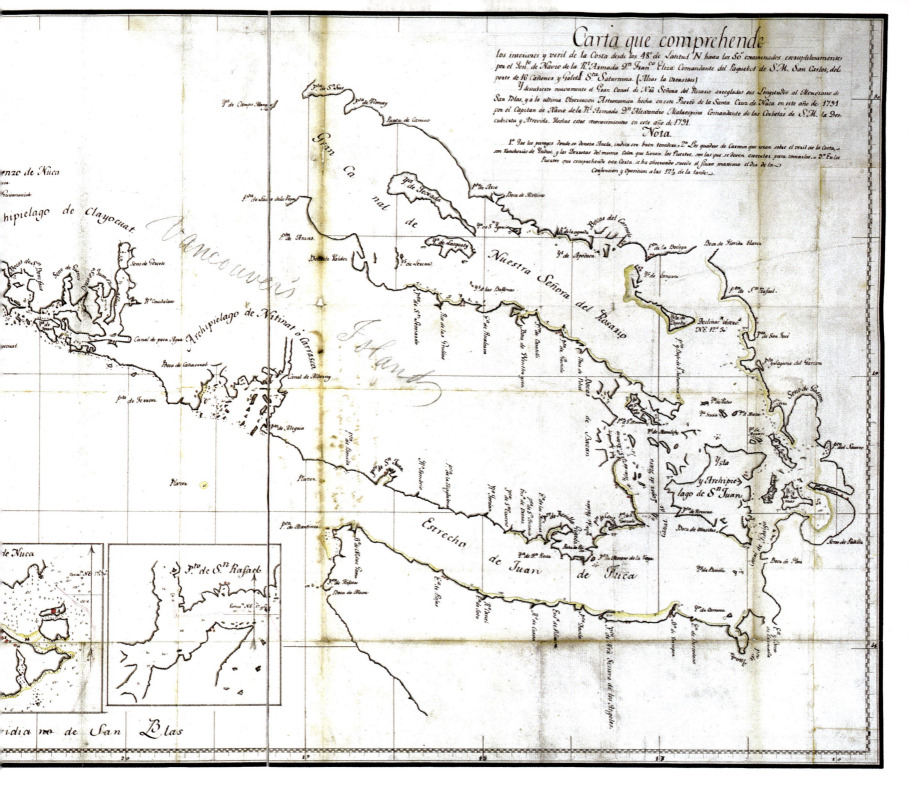

Carta que comprehende

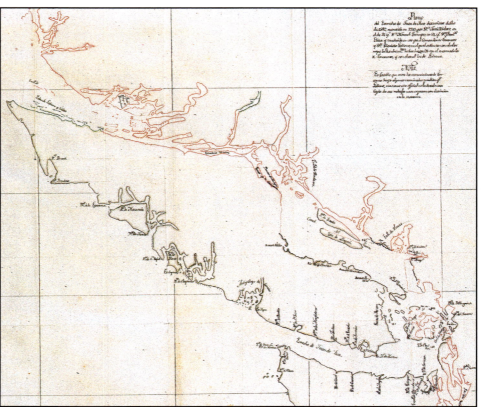

Map 235 (above).
Perhaps the single most significant Spanish map of the British Columbia coast, this is the *Carta que comprehende*, a "map of all that is known." It summarizes Spanish knowledge of Vancouver Island and southwestern British Columbia at the end of 1791, just before the arrival of George Vancouver. It reflects the longboat exploration of José María Nárvaez with Juan Carrasco in *Santa Saturnina* as far north in the Strait of Georgia as Texada Island, and maps the shores, with considerable omissions, of today's City of Vancouver. *Ys[la] de Langara* is Point Grey, and *Ysla de Zepeda* is Point Roberts. *P[un]ta de la Bodega* is Point Atkinson, and *Bocas del Carmelo* is Howe Sound. *Boca de Florida Blanca* is the inner part of Burrard Inlet. *P[uer]to de Cordova* is Victoria Harbour. There are several inset maps of various harbours. From top left they are *P[uer]to Claycuot* (Clayoquot Sound); *P[uer]to de Nu[estr]a Señora de los Angeles* (Port Angeles, Washington); *B[ahi]a de Bueno Esperanza* (Esperanza Inlet, at the north end of Nootka Island); *P[uer]to de la Santa Cruz de Nuca* (Friendly Cove and Yuquot, Nootka Island); and *P[uer]to de S[a]n Rafael* (at the north side of Flores Island). *Vancouver's Island* is written in pencil down the length of Vancouver Island. This map, now in the Library of Congress, was transferred from the War Department in 1929; it may perhaps have been used during the negotiations for the Canada-U.S. boundary in 1846, and annotated at that time. A detail of this map is shown as Map 377, page 236.

Map 236 (right).
This 1792 map by Spanish commander Juan Francisco de la Bodega y Quadra recognizes the co-operation of Dionisio Galiano with George Vancouver. The brown-black lines are those mapped by the Spanish, while the red lines are those mapped by Vancouver. Compare this map with the corresponding one drawn by Vancouver (Map 244, page 164).

Because Galiano had gone to Nootka first while Vancouver had entered the Strait of Juan de Fuca immediately, the Spanish ships became the first to circumnavigate Vancouver Island, even though Vancouver preceded Galiano to Nootka by a few days.

The considerable co-operation between the Spanish and the British is well documented in the maps both produced (MAP 236, and MAP 244, page 164), and Vancouver's published maps also acknowledged this, so it is a sad footnote to history to record that Galiano met his death in 1805 while fighting the British fleet under Horatio Nelson at the Battle of Trafalgar.

Galiano's maps were not published until 1802, and his fine map of what is now southwestern British Columbia is shown here (MAP 237, right).

MAP 237 (right).
The work of Dionisio Galiano and Cayetano Valdes was not published until 1802, and then only as part of a general survey of Spanish exploration on the Northwest Coast designed as a foil to the recently published works of George Vancouver. The survey of Spanish exploration, the *Relación*, attempted to right the perception that the British had more valid claims to the region by showing that Spanish exploration dated back another two hundred years. It had been Spanish policy to keep every discovery secret, even to the extent of sometimes not giving an expedition the previous one's maps.

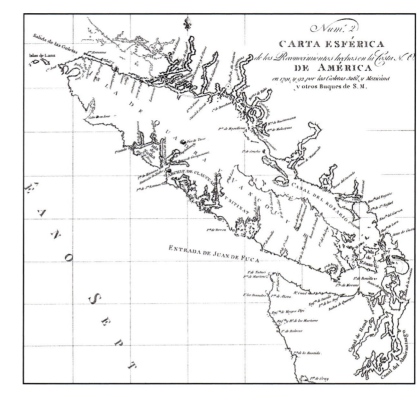

MAP 238 (*top right*); MAP 239 (*centre*); MAP 240 (*bottom left*).
This sequence of maps of the British Columbia coast was drawn by Juan Francisco de la Bodega y Quadra. They show the increasing Spanish knowledge of the intricacies of the coastline between the beginning of 1791 and the end of 1792, and represent the situation at the end of 1790, 1791, and 1792, respectively. They progress from top right to bottom left by date.
MAP 238, dated 1791, shows the Strait of Juan de Fuca as a closed-end basin, after Manuel Quimper's explorations of 1790, and a tentative coastline on the mainland behind the Queen Charlotte Islands. The middle map, MAP 239, was drawn at the beginning of 1792 and shows the southern end of Vancouver Island now defined by the explorations of José María Nárvaez and Juan Carrasco under the command of Francisco de Eliza in 1791. The northern coast, as before, has a tentative part. MAP 240 was drawn at the end of the exploration season of 1792. Now Vancouver Island—named Quadra and Vancouver's Island by George Vancouver in honour of the Spanish and British co-operation—is shown for the first time as an island, following Dionisio Galiano and Cayetano Valdes (and George Vancouver) in the summer of 1792. Farther north, much of the coastline has been defined following the voyage of Jacinto Caamaño that year, although what is now Clarence Strait in the Inland Passage of Alaska is still left tantalizingly open-ended, for Caamaño was prevented by bad weather from sailing far enough north to determine that it was a strait, not a last possible location for the western entrance to a Northwest Passage. It would be George Vancouver's exhaustive surveys, lasting until the end of 1794, that would finally show that no such passage existed.

George Vancouver Surveys the West Coast

George Vancouver had been a midshipman—a trainee officer—with James Cook on his second and third voyages. He had thus previously visited the Northwest Coast in 1778, and, indeed, there exists a map of Alaska he drew at the time.

Rising through the ranks, Vancouver was a natural choice to command another British expedition to the coast, although he was actually a second choice, as Henry Roberts, Cook's mapmaker (see Map 229, page 158), withdrew due to ill health.

Vancouver arrived back on the Northwest Coast in April 1792 and sailed north to begin his comprehensive survey. He had two ships, *Discovery* and *Chatham*; he would spend one and a half seasons surveying the British Columbia coast alone, and an equal time on the coast of Alaska.

Vancouver had been instructed to look for a Northwest Passage, and in so doing, he explored every nook and cranny of the intricate

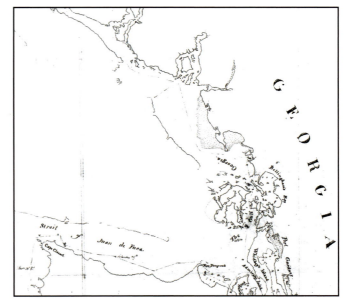

Map 241 (*right*).
George Vancouver's preliminary map of the mainland coast and the Strait of Georgia, sent to London in his dispatches, 1792.

Map 242 (*below, middle*).
James Johnstone's first survey of Johnstone Strait, which established the insularity of Vancouver Island and a way northwards back to the Pacific in July 1792.

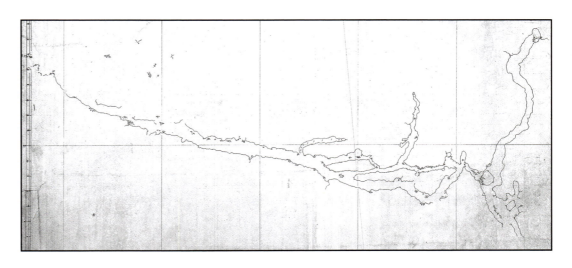

Map 243 (*below*).
Vancouver's preliminary chart of *Johnstone's Passage* between the mainland, to the north, and Vancouver Island, to the south. It is now Johnstone Strait. The map was drawn in July and August 1792 and sent to London in dispatches.

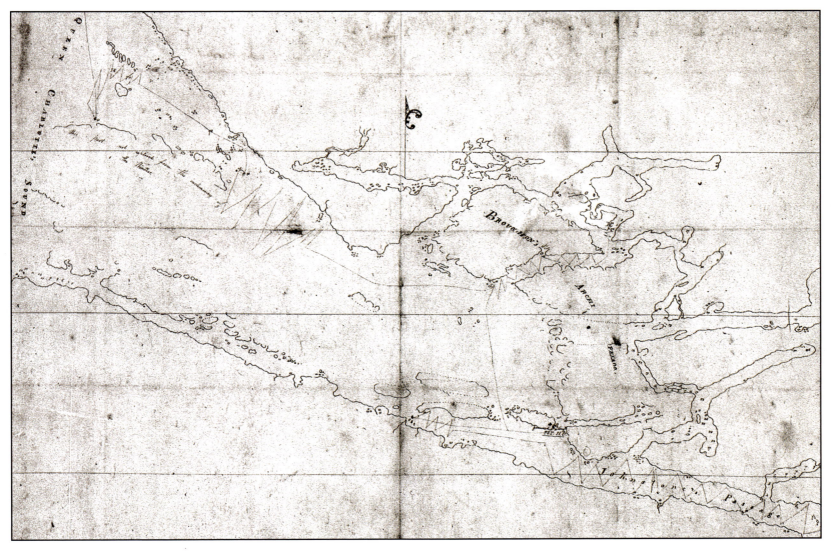

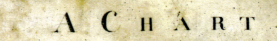

MAP 244.
This was the first of George Vancouver's maps to incorporate information given to him by the Spanish, which information is shown in red. Compare this map with MAP 236, page 161; the equivalent Spanish map shows the British information in red. This map was sent to England with Lieutenant William Broughton at the end of 1792. Vancouver sent Broughton from Monterey to England after obtaining permission from Bodega y Quadra for Broughton to cross New Spain; Broughton then found a ship able to take him to England. As Vancouver's ranking subordinate officer, Broughton was sent so he could explain any details regarding the lack of agreement over the transfer of lands from the Spanish to the British under the Nootka Convention. Vancouver also required new instructions given the impasse that had been reached; he never received any. Peter Puget took over as captain of *Chatham*. Broughton did not arrive back on the Northwest Coast until 1796, after Vancouver had left, and then carried out a survey of the northeast coast of Asia, a survey that bears little resemblance to Vancouver's monumental effort, and demonstrates that it was Vancouver who was personally responsible for the high standard of his survey.

MAP 245.
This is the British Columbia part of George Vancouver's summary map of the West Coast entitled *A Chart shewing part of the N.W. Coast of North America with the Tracks of His Majesty's Sloop Discovery and Armed Tender* Chatham. It is from the atlas accompanying Vancouver's book *A Voyage of Discovery to the North Pacific Ocean and Around the World*, published posthumously in 1798.

coastline of what he termed the "continental shore" to ensure that he had covered everywhere that such a passage could possibly begin. This is why his maps do not pay much attention to Vancouver Island or any other islands, for they were not potential harbourers of a passage. Instead, he obtained much information from the Spanish and the Russians.

Due to the nature of the coast, much of Vancouver's survey was done in small boats, and it was gruelling and time-consuming work. Vancouver first surveyed Puget Sound, and then, while anchored in Birch Bay (now in Washington State), his second-in-command William Broughton met with Dionisio Galiano and Cayetano Valdes, the Spanish captains surveying the coast at the same time; mutual assistance was offered.

Later, as we have seen, Vancouver himself met with Galiano and Valdes and was shown the Spanish maps, including the *Carta que comprehende* (MAP 235, pages 160–61). At this time Vancouver confided to his journal: "I cannot avoid acknowledging that on this occasion I experienced no small degree of mortification in finding the external shores of the gulf had been visited, and already examined." However, a short distance north of the meeting place, Spanish geographical knowledge ran out. Vancouver would end up surveying the entire coast in minute detail, something the Spanish had not done.

Galiano and Valdes accompanied Vancouver northwards for a while, although they carried out their surveys independently.

On one boat excursion, James Johnstone, the master of *Chatham*, discovered a passage through the maze of islands that led back to the Pacific. His original survey is shown in MAP 242, page 163. This was Johnstone Strait, and it finally established the insularity of Vancouver Island.

Vancouver found his way through the newly discovered passage and sailed to Nootka, where he met with Juan Francisco Bodega y Quadra. He was instructed to take back the area from the Spanish, as Britain and Spain had agreed in 1790 under the Nootka Convention. But Bodega y Quadra and Vancouver could not

find an interpretation of the convention that both could agree to, so, as gentlemen, they agreed to disagree and await later instructions from their governments. Bodega y Quadra paid Vancouver a compliment by naming the large island that both he and Galiano had just proven to be an island "Quadra and Vancouver's Island." Vancouver showed it as such on his maps, including the published ones, but over the years, as the Spanish empire retreated and the name became too much of a mouthful, the name became just Vancouver's Island. Later still the "s" was also dropped.

During the 1792 season, Vancouver had surveyed as far north as today's Bella Coola, to Point Menzies in North Bentinck Arm. The former was named after his naturalist, Archibald Menzies, whose most enduring memorial is the Douglas fir, with the Latin name *Pseudotsuga menziesii*.

At the beginning of the 1793 season, Vancouver began at the point he left off the previous season. In a historical "near miss," he thus came close to meeting with overland traveller Alexander Mackenzie, who arrived only fifty days after Vancouver left the area (see page 143).

That year, Vancouver surveyed farther north, to a point in the Alaska panhandle; the following year he sailed directly to Cook Inlet (which he renamed after exploring to its termination what had been called Cook's River), and surveyed east and south, to meet his 1793 survey at a place he named, appropriately enough, Point Conclusion.

The significance of Vancouver's survey—and why it stands out from all others—was its comprehensiveness, accuracy, and integrity. The only errors of consequence were where he had relied upon Russian or Spanish maps, and these were in locations that did not affect his survey of the "continental shore." Vancouver finally proved beyond a shadow of a doubt that there was no western entrance to a Northwest Passage anywhere on the coast.

This was a magnificent achievement considering the intricately indented nature of the coastline. Yet Vancouver has not received due recognition; the bicentennial of his visit to the British Columbia coast in 1992 was deliberately disregarded by officials from governments at all levels, and even Canada Post refused to issue a commemorative stamp, as they have done for many less worthy individuals.

Yet Vancouver's maps live on as his memorial. In many places, they were not surpassed for a hundred years. Pacific scholar J. C. Beaglehole noted that the Northwest Coast is "so remarkably complicated that Vancouver's systematic and painstaking survey ranks with the most distinguished work of the kind ever done."

Defining the West—David Thompson

David Thompson sailed into Hudson Bay as a new employee of the Hudson's Bay Company in 1784, at the age of fourteen. From that point on, he travelled more than 120 000 km of Canada and the northwestern United States, as a trainee fur trader, surveyor, and explorer. The maps he would produce were the first comprehensive maps of the western half of Canada.

The turning point in Thompson's career came in December 1788, when he broke a leg falling down a riverbank. The leg's failure to heal quickly led to him spending the next winter at Cumberland House, on the Saskatchewan River, where he met an overwintering Philip Turnor, who taught him the elements of surveying and mapmaking. Thompson liked the work and took to it easily, being methodical and patient while at the same time adventurous.

Thompson did some surveying for the Hudson's Bay Company, which certainly recognized his talents, presenting him with instruments and giving him a large pay increase, such that in 1796 his salary was larger than that of his supervisor, Malcolm Ross. Nevertheless, in 1797 he was lured away by the North West Company, which promised him more money and more independence to explore and survey. The move seems to have been premeditated, for Thompson had not sent his surveys to London for two years before. Thompson much later wrote that he had received a letter from Joseph Colen, the Bay governor at York Fort, telling

him that he "could not sanction any further surveys," but this letter has never been found, and Thompson's reporting of it may have been later justification for his actions. At any rate, Thompson "determined to seek that employment from the Company of Merchants of Canada, carrying on the Furr Trade, under the name of the North West Company."

Thompson's new employer was at this time, better off than the Hudson's Bay Company. Its posts were distributed over a wider area, and it made more profit. Thompson did not have to work as a trader, but could devote himself to surveying, producing maps of the routes between the far-flung posts. As one writer put it, the extent of Thompson's surveys is a testament to the wealth, as well as the vision, of the North West Company.

In 1799 Thompson was given additional duties as a trader, and in 1804 he was made a partner in the company. In 1801 he made an unsuccessful attempt to cross the Rocky Mountains, as the North West Company tried to find a practical trade route to the Pacific, spurred on by the idea of a cheaper and faster way to ship out its furs. Another partner, Simon Fraser, would explore the Fraser River in 1808 as part of this same effort.

By 1806 Thompson had mapped most of the area east of the Rocky Mountains. That year the partners decided he should again attempt to cross the Rockies, and in 1807 Thompson found

Howse Pass and crossed into the headwaters of the Columbia, which he called the Kootenae River. Over the next four years he found the routes and sites for posts that would add a Columbia Department to the regions of the North West Company.

In 1810 Thompson was "going down on rotation"—heading east to a well-earned furlough—and reached Rainy Lake, where he heard of John Jacob Astor's rival Pacific Fur Company's attempts to establish a post at the mouth of the Columbia. He turned around and headed back to the Rockies. To avoid natives who did not want him to supply their enemies, Thompson crossed the mountains during the winter of 1810–11 at the Athabasca Pass, site of today's Jasper, Alberta.

MAP 246.

In 1813 David Thompson completed a huge map of the West based on his own explorations and the information he was able to collect from others. It was based on his meticulous observations, fixing the position of thousands of points all over the West. The result was by far the most accurate map of the West at the time, and it remained so for perhaps another fifty years. The map was delivered to the North West Company and was hung on the wall at Fort William, the company post and transshipment point at the western end of Lake Superior. That map, regretfully, was lost, but Thompson made another very similar map the following year, on which he made a few corrections, such as the elimination of a phantom river, the Caledonia, he had plotted (from information he had been given) flowing to Puget Sound just south of the Fraser. As he drifted into poverty in the 1840s, the map was sold by one of Thompson's sons. It was this map that ended up in the hands of the government of the province of Ontario. So good was the map that it was used as late as 1857 by Thomas Devine, the surveyor general of Canada West, to draw a new map designed for settlers pushing into the West.

Thompson's 1814 map, shown here, can be justly described as one of the cartographic treasures of Canada. Regretfully, it is not as well preserved as might be hoped, not so much because it hasn't been looked after but because the materials with which it is made have deteriorated over time. Thompson used an ink rendered from growths on apple trees called apple galls, as was common at that time, and this has turned brown with age, blending into the paper, which has also browned, spreading, as one writer put it, "a web of sepia across the linen continent." In addition, Thompson glued together some twenty-five separate sheets in order to make a map so large—it is 5 m wide and 3 m high. The glue overlaps have lightened over time, blurring the outlines of the map in many places. There is no doubt the map would benefit, and be stabilized by, some extensive restoration, unfortunately expensive. The map is currently on display in a unique fashion near the entrance to the Archives of Ontario in Toronto. As can be seen from the photograph at left *(Archives of Ontario)*, it is in a large temperature- and humidity-controlled glass case, protected by a dark curtain. Pressing a button turns lights on and the curtain slides back to reveal the map for perhaps one minute before closing again.

The map contains all sorts of interesting details. At the mouth of the Fraser River is the notation *Mr Fraser and Party returnedfrom the Sortie of the River* and, just north of Hope, in what is now British Columbia, there is written *To this Place the White Men have come from the Sea,* referring to a tantalizing tidbit of information given to Simon Fraser by the natives; it has never been determined what "white men" the natives might have been referring to. At what is now Prince George, is the notation *NW Co*[mpan]*y. The Place of Mr Simon Fraser and Party's departure.* In fact, this map can be regarded as the earliest surviving cartographic record of Simon Fraser's expedition in 1808 to the mouth of the river that now bears his name, for Fraser's own maps have been lost. But no doubt Thompson saw them. It was Thompson who named the Fraser River after his friend; Fraser returned the compliment by naming its major tributary the Thompson.

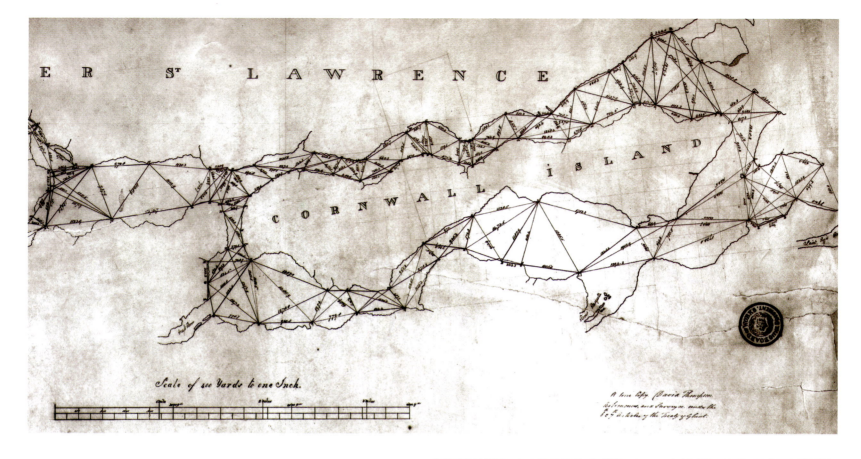

MAP 247 (above).
A survey of part of the Canada–United States boundary line along the St. Lawrence, carried out by David Thompson in 1820. The boundary had been described in the 1783 Treaty of Paris, which ended the War of American Independence (see page 124), but not surveyed. The triangulation method, the geometric technique still in use today, was used to fix points precisely. If the length of a baseline and the angles at either end are known, then the position of the point sighted by the two angles can be fixed precisely, and hence the distances of the other two sides of the triangle also become known. This system of triangles can be extended to construct a map.

After many delays, he reached the mouth of the Columbia on 15 July 1811, only to find the American fort, Astoria, already built. He had beaten an American overland party, led by Wilson Price Hunt, but not Astor's ship, which had sailed around the Horn. Nevertheless, Thompson had discovered what the North West Company had been looking for since the days of Alexander Mackenzie—a *practical* route across the Rocky Mountains to the Pacific.

Thompson had, all this time, been making observations by laborious astronomical techniques to fix the position of hundreds of points throughout the West. Added to the thousands he already had, Thompson now had the means to construct an accurate map of the entire West, and when he retired from the fur trade in 1812, he began work on a monumental general map. It was completed in 1813 and presented to the North West Company; it was hung in the great hall at Fort William. A revised edition drawn the next year has survived, and is illustrated on the previous page (MAP 246). The map was the most accurate map of the West for fifty years.

Thompson's maps were often copied, usually without acknowledgement. Aaron Arrowsmith's general map illustrating Alexander Mackenzie's book *Voyages from Montreal*, published in 1801, was a Thompson copy. This map is shown in the endpapers; it is an engraved copy of MAP 201, pages 144–45.

Having left the North West Company, Thompson began a long career as an independent surveyor and mapmaker. His work was held in such high regard that he was accepted by both the Americans and the British to survey the newly-agreed-upon boundary in 1820. MAP 247, above, is part of the boundary line Thomp-

son surveyed along the St. Lawrence and shows the triangulation method he used. MAP 248 is another of the many maps drawn by Thompson during the boundary survey; this one is of the contentious Lake of the Woods area.

David Thompson died in 1857, poverty-stricken after poor business dealings. Before he died he wrote his *Narrative*, an account of his travels and work in the Northwest, and this, together with his superb maps, are his legacy to Canada.

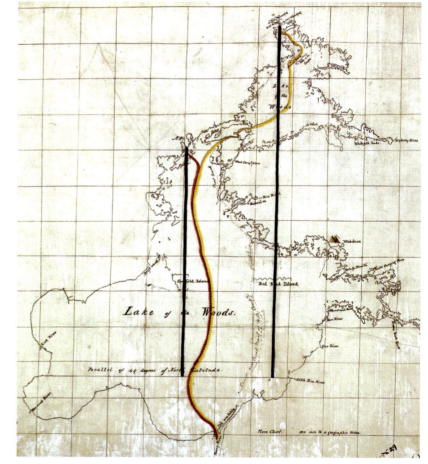

MAP 248.
This map of Lake of the Woods was surveyed by David Thompson in the summer of 1823 and later used by Anthony Barclay, one of the British boundary commissioners. On it has been marked (the red line) the recommended international boundary, from Angle Inlet, marked *NW*, to Rainy River. The yellow line was another boundary that was considered, from Rat Portage (at the top of the lake), but it was decided by an astronomer, Johann Tiarks, that the "most northwest point" of the lake, referred to in the treaty of 1783, was at the head of Angle Inlet rather than at Rat Portage. It was a case of making the facts match the theory, for in 1783 no one knew what they were referring to when they used the term in the treaty.

Early Toronto

The site of the future city of Toronto was at the southern end of a native portage from Lake Ontario to Lake Simcoe. The name *tkaronto* refers to fish weirs in the river near present-day Orillia, Ontario. The name, with various modifications, was applied to Lake Simcoe and later to a native village on the shores of Lake Ontario. MAP 249 (right, top) shows Lake Simcoe as *Lac de Taranto* and the native village as *Teyeyagon*.

The French soon learned of the shortcut from their native allies, and Étienne Brûlé, one of Champlain's explorers, is considered to have used the carrying place as early as 1615.

After building a small storehouse near the site of present-day downtown Toronto, the French constructed a fortified post in 1750–51. It lasted until 1759, when it was burned by its garrison before being abandoned in the face of advancing British troops. The ruins of the fort are shown on the map by military engineer Gother Mann, drawn in 1788 (MAP 251).

With the loss of the territory south of the lakes to the Americans in 1783, the Toronto portage assumed greater importance, and the British decided to locate a settlement there, as

MAP 249 (right, top).
The earliest map showing the word "Taranto," applied to Lake Simcoe. This is a French map dated about 1675.

MAP 250 (right, middle).
The proposed location for Toronto by surveyor Alexander Aitken, drawn in 1788. It was not used, for John Graves Simcoe, the lieutenant-governor of the new province of Upper Canada, created in 1791, established York at the mouth of the Don River. The original carrying place is shown as a straight line from the mouth of the Toronto River, and is labelled *Carrying place to Lake le Clay* [Lake Simcoe] *about 30 miles*. The word "York" has been added by a later hand.

MAP 251 (right, bottom).
Another proposed plan, by military engineer Gother Mann, also dated 1788, and also not used. The ruins of the French Fort Rouillé are shown.

MAP 252 (below).
The Toronto carrying place is shown on this map by the lieutenant-governor's wife, Elizabeth Simcoe, drawn about 1793. It shows the location of the new capital of Upper Canada, York.

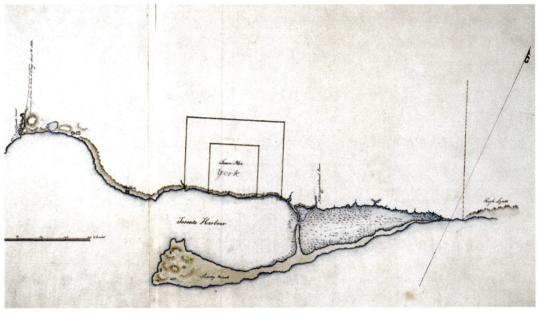

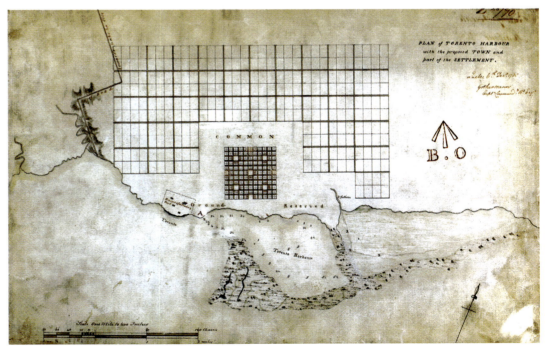

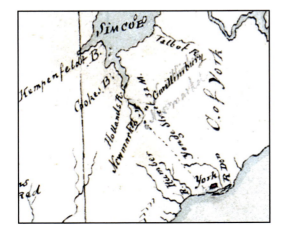

North 68 degrees East 14 Miles.

North 22 degrees West 24 Miles and 45°

South 22 degrees East 28 Miles

Carrying Place.

Maple Tree blazed on 4 Sides.

R. Etobicoke

5 Miles 8¼

South Outlet

R. Credit

Toronto.

Toronto Bay.

The Peninsula.

LAKE ONTARIO.

The descriptive plan of the Toronto purchase made 23d September and compleated on the 1st day of August 1805.

W. Claus Deputy Supd. Genl. on Behalf of the Crown

Witnesses present

Jos. Williams Capt. d. Regt.

Jno. Brackenbury Ens. 49th Regt.

D. Cowie

J. B. Rousseaux

Chechalk

Quenepenon

Wabukanyne

Okemapenesse

Wabenasa

Kineboneucana

Osenego

Achston

MAP 254.
Detail of an anonymous map drawn about 1790 showing *Toronto formerly an Indian village now abandoned.* A larger part of this map is shown as MAP 177, page 130.

MAP 253.
The "Toronto Purchase" map. The original agreement to sell the land on which the City of Toronto now sits was made on 23 September 1787, on the Bay of Quinte, between Mississauga chiefs and John Collins, the deputy surveyor general. The exact limits of the land to be conveyed were not defined. The price was £1,700 in cash and goods such as flour and cloth. The stores were delivered to the Mississauga the following year, at Toronto. The boundaries of the land purchased, plus some amendments from the original contract, were incorporated into another agreement signed in 1805 at the River Credit. The map is signed *William Chewett, Senior Surveyor.* The inset shows the signatures; they are on the reverse side of the map. The document was signed for the government by William Claus, deputy superintendent general of Indian affairs for Upper Canada, and by Chechalk and others for the Mississauga Nation.

Map 255 (*above*).
A beautifully drawn map of the townsite of York, surveyed in 1818, but not drawn by military surveyor George Phillpotts until 1823. The townsite chosen by John Graves Simcoe, ignoring the plans of Aitken and Mann, was just to the west of the River Don; this is the area with somewhat more houses than the rest of the town. At this stage, York would have had perhaps a thousand inhabitants. The fort guards the entrance to the harbour at left.

part of the ongoing plans to settle Loyalists along the lakeshore. An agreement to purchase the land was made with the Mississauga in 1787. A proper definition of the land purchased, with adjustments, was shown in a deed made in 1805. The map attached to the document, signed by Mississauga chiefs, is shown here (Map 253).

Since the site of Toronto was both centrally and strategically located, the new lieutenant-governor, John Graves Simcoe, decided to create a settlement there and make it the capital of Upper Canada, created in 1791. In 1793 a town was laid out, and renamed York. Simcoe and his wife Elizabeth arrived in July 1793; Mrs. Simcoe wrote in her diary that she had "walked through a grove of fine Oaks where the Town is intended to be built." The lieutenant-governor chose to ignore the earlier plans for a townsite (Maps 250 and 251), and had the town laid out nearer to the Don River.

Buildings for a parliament were erected, and in 1796 the legislature of Upper Canada moved away from its original site at Newark (Niagara-on-the-Lake), on the Niagara Frontier, which was considered too vulnerable to American attack.

Roads were constructed; bridging the original carrying place, in 1796 Yonge Street was opened northwards to the Holland River, giving access to Lake Simcoe and Georgian Bay. This was not a road in the sense it is known today, but merely a rough track hacked through the forest with the help of Loyalist settlers along the way.

By 1812, York had about seven hundred residents, for merchants and others were required to service the garrison and the legislature. With the onset of the War of 1812, the little town was sacked twice, both times in 1813 (see page 172).

By 1834, now with over 9,000 inhabitants, York was renamed Toronto, and incorporated as a city. Its first mayor was William Lyon Mackenzie (see page 200).

(An account of the later growth of Toronto is continued on page 242.)

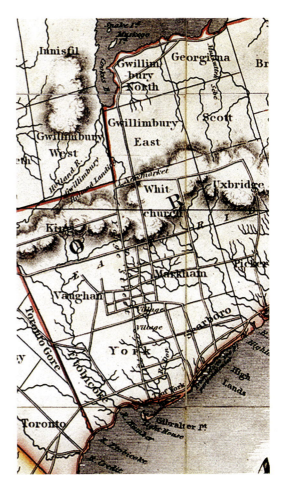

Map 256.
This part of a map by James Chewett dated 1825 shows the portage from Lake Ontario to Lake Simcoe provided by the Etobicoke and Holland Rivers. T[own] *of York* is marked. A larger part of this map is shown as Map 281, pages 182–83.

A Mere Matter of Marching—the War of 1812

With the end of the War of American Independence in 1783 came a ten-year period of peace until 1793, when Revolutionary France declared war on Britain. Since the United States and France had been allied during the previous war, it seemed probable that Canada might be attacked by the Americans again.

In 1794 a rumour that an American attack on Québec was to be accompanied by the French fleet sailing up the St. Lawrence caused great alarm, but the threat did not materialize.

In 1795 there was another rumour, that a French fleet was about to attack Halifax, prompting strengthening of fortifications in a hurry, and in 1801, there was yet another rumour, of an invasion from Vermont.

A peace accord was signed by the British and the French in 1802, but it lasted only a year before war was declared again, for this was the era of Napoleon's empire building in Europe.

In October 1805 the French were soundly defeated by Horatio Nelson at the Battle of Trafalgar, and from that point on the British navy ruled the seas. In June 1807, after refusing to submit to a search for deserters, the American ship *Chesapeake* was attacked at sea by the British warship *Leopard*. American deaths and injuries, plus the removal of four alleged deserters, united American public opinion in a demand for war on Britain.

But the British government quickly disavowed the action and the American Congress was not in session, so war was averted by President Thomas Jefferson. The British then decided that all neutral ships carrying supplies to Napoleon's Europe would be regarded as enemies. The response to this from the Americans was a total embargo on trade.

But minor skirmishes continued, and in particular, impressment of sailors from American ships into the British navy. The idea of attacking British Canada grew out of the notion that this might be a good way to retaliate, and to satisfy some American thirst for new territory in the process. New American president James Madison formally declared war on Britain on 19 June 1812.

The main theatre of war was Upper Canada, seen as exposed and "ripe for the plucking." The Maritime colonies were not a target because they were protected by superior British sea power and the buffer of the New England states, which opposed the war. Québec had its fortress, and American forces had not taken it in 1775. But taking Upper Canada was seen, in Thomas Jefferson's famous words, as "a mere matter of marching." How wrong he proved to be.

Map 258 (*right*).
Although some British defences had been strengthened, particularly at strategically important Halifax and Québec, defences generally were in need of repair. This is York Redoubt, one of the fortifications at the entrance to Halifax Harbour, in 1800. Gun emplacements are on the left; the guardhouse is the square building on the extreme right; and the circular building, with a drawbridge, is a Martello tower, a fortification popular in England during the Napoleonic Wars. Others were built on the Plains of Abraham in Québec.

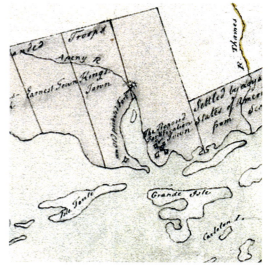

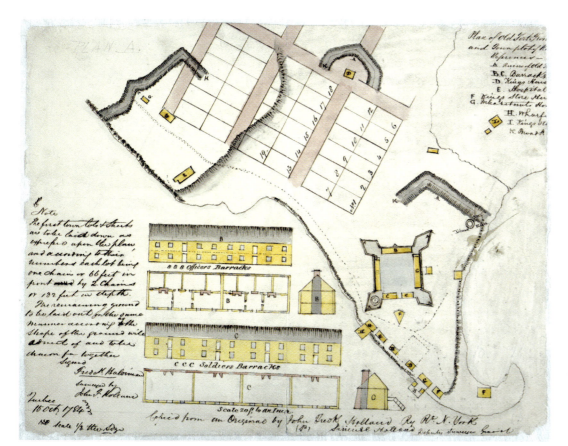

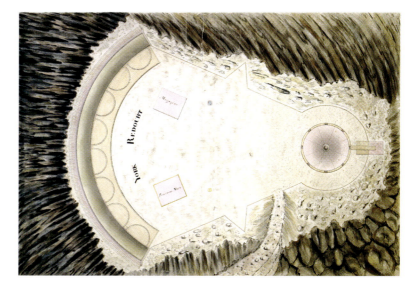

Map 257 (*left*).
Kingston township, originally termed Cataraqui Number One, was granted in 1784 to a group of New York Loyalists, and more than two hundred town lots were granted around Fort Cataraqui, a garrison post on the site of the original French fort (see Map 99, page 71). Kingston was the first major military establishment in Upper Canada.

Map 259 (*above*).
Part of a map drawn about 1790 showing the proposed fort for Kingston. This was Fort Henry, built during the War of 1812.

Map 260.

Part of a survey of Lower Canada authorized by Guy Carleton, Lord Dorchester, in 1794–95. The map was drawn by Samuel Gale and Thomas Duberger, and is a superb record of Canada at that time. Accurate maps are a vital component of defence. This map showed the main possible invasion routes to the St. Lawrence Valley: the Chaudière River, to Québec, and, on the part illustrated here, the Richelieu River. Also shown is the Châteauguay River (bottom left), which was used by American commander Major General Wade Hampton in 1813 after he had found his intended invasion route, down the Richelieu, more heavily defended. He was defeated by a Canadian army under Lieutenant Colonel Charles-Michel d'Irumberry de Salaberry at the Battle of Châteauguay (see page 177, and Map 267, page 176).

The first action of the war was a surprise attack by British forces from Fort St. Joseph, near today's Sault Ste. Marie, on the American fort at nearby Michilimackinac. This was calculated by the British commander, Major General Isaac Brock, to bring natives to the British side, and it did.

General William Hull led an American western army across the Detroit River from Fort Detroit on 12 July 1812, the first invasion of Canadian territory. Hull expected the population, which contained many Americans, to join his side, and he issued a proclamation offering freedom "from tyranny and oppression," but most people, not feeling oppressed, did not rush to join him.

Brock hurried to the scene, arriving on 14 August via British-controlled Lake Erie. But by this time the invasion had collapsed, with Hull worried about his supply lines and the possibility of native attack. The next day, taking advantage of the situation, Brock crossed the river with a small British force accompanied by natives led by their chief, Tecumseh. Fearful of a native massacre, threats of which were carefully fed to him by Brock, Hull surrendered Fort Detroit without a shot being fired. The effect was a major morale booster for the British side.

Brock then rushed back to the Niagara Peninsula—then termed the Niagara Frontier—where the next invasion threat was expected. American troops had massed on the east bank of the Niagara River, and on 13 October they crossed at Queenston. Brock was killed as he tried to retake Queenston Heights without waiting for all his men to arrive from Fort George. Roger Hale Sheaffe, Brock's second-in-command, took over and did retake the heights, taking a thousand American prisoners.

Both sides recognized the need for control of the lakes, and throughout the war an arms race of sorts went on, as each side upped the ante by building bigger and better ships. In October 1812, the American commander, Isaac Chauncey, arrived at his base at Sackets Harbor, at the eastern end of Lale Ontario, and began preparing the small American fleet for action. On 10 November his squadron chased the British ship *Royal George* into Kingston Harbour, fighting a pitched battle with the shore defences.

On 22 April 1813 an army of 1,700 men under General Henry Dearborn embarked on Chauncey's fleet at Sackets Harbor, and on 27 April they arrived off York. A field force under Brigadier General Zebulon Pike—of western American exploration fame—was landed west of the settlement and fort. After difficult fighting, the British, under Roger Sheaffe, retreated east, marching to Kingston. As they left, they blew up the powder magazine, and there were many American casualties, including Pike.

The retreating British force destroyed a ship nearing completion on the stocks, and the Americans captured only one ship—and that so rotten it could only be used as an ammunition tender. The

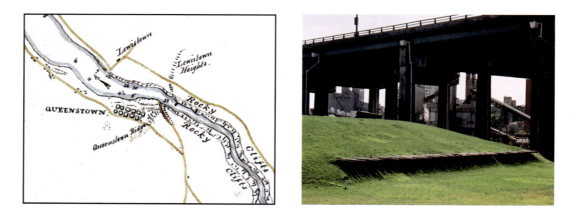

MAP 261 (*above, top*).
Part of a British map drawn in 1811, the year before the war, showing the Detroit River, the American Fort Detroit, and Amherstburg, with Fort Malden.

MAP 262 (*above, middle*).
A military map of the provincial capital of York—now Toronto—and environs in 1814, the year after the American raids. It was drawn by military surveyor George Williams. The key refers to military sites, and in particular includes the number of men at each location, thus giving a commanding officer a useful immediate reference to the disposition of his forces. Note the fort at the harbour entrance and the blockhouse on Gibraltar Point opposite it. There is also a guardhouse on the spit, to guard a portage across it—a shortcut for friend and foe alike.

MAP 263 (*above, bottom left*).
This part of an 1817 map shows the battlefield at Queenston Heights. American troops crossed the Niagara River from Lewiston to Queenston and took the British positions on the heights above the village. Isaac Brock was killed leading an assault on the heights, trying to retake this strategic military position.

The photograph shows Fort York as it looks today—Toronto's past overshadowed by the Gardiner Expressway.

By December, the American position on the Niagara Peninsula had become so tenuous that Fort George was abandoned and troops were withdrawn across the Niagara River, but not before burning the town of Newark—now Niagara-on-the-Lake—and turning its inhabitants out into the frigid night. Later that month the British in turn stormed across the Niagara River and took Fort Niagara, the old French fort and then American stronghold at the eastern entrance to the river.

At the other end of Lake Ontario, the British attacked the American base at Sackets Harbor in May while Chauncey's fleet was away, doing a lot of damage but nothing permanent. The raid was led by newly arrived Commodore James Lucas Yeo; he and a contingent of Royal Navy men and officers had been sent to replace some of the men of the Provincial Marines who had previously operated the British ships, a change to professional sailors that was to make a big difference to the effort on Lake Ontario.

On Lake Erie, the balance of naval power was swinging towards the Americans. At Presqu'Ile—today Erie, Pennsylvania—Captain Oliver Hazard Perry was building ships during much of 1813. The British commander, Captain Robert Barclay, engaged Perry's fleet on 10 September at Put-in-Bay, in the tiny Bass Islands,

MAP 264.
This British military map was prepared in 1810. It shows the British Fort George, with Navy Hall, the first legislative assembly building for Upper Canada, and the Town of Niagara, for a time called Newark and now the pretty village of Niagara-on-the-Lake. Across the Niagara River, on a strategic point at the river's mouth, is the American Fort Niagara. This was the original French fort, founded in 1678 and rebuilt in stone in 1726. Lake Ontario is at top.

MAP 265.
This map, published in 1826 by American mapmaker John Melish, shows the battlefields of the Niagara Frontier.

loosely disciplined American troops burned the parliament buildings and raised havoc in the town for several days before their commanders got them under control again.

Chauncey then transported the army to Niagara, where the American army took Fort George, the British fort at the mouth of the river, on 27 May. The British commander, Brigadier General John Vincent, withdrew his men west,

pursued by the Americans. The same day Fort Erie was abandoned by the British garrison.

On the night of 5–6 June, Vincent turned on his pursuers at Stoney Creek, and, although outnumbered, claimed a decisive victory which abruptly halted the American advance into Upper Canada. On 24 June, a small native force defeated and captured six hundred American soldiers at Beaver Dams, a little east of Stoney Creek.

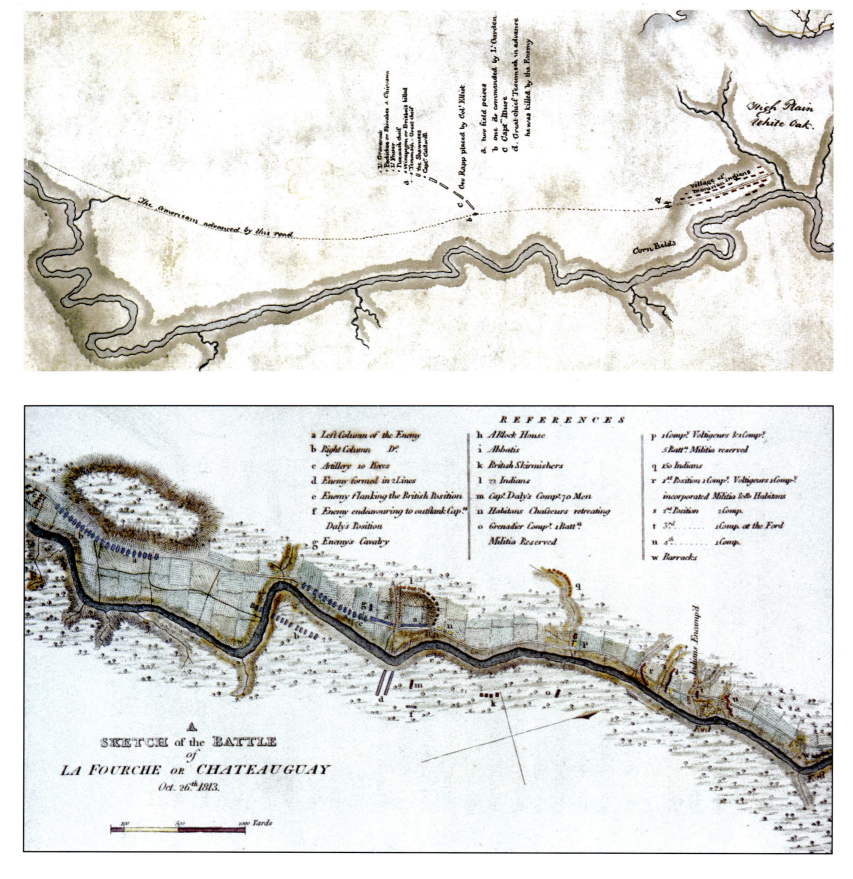

A SKETCH of the BATTLE of LA FOURCHE or CHATEAUGUAY Oct. 26.th 1813.

REFERENCES

a *Left Column of the Enemy*
b *Right Column Do.*
c *Artillery 10 Pieces*
d *Enemy formed in 2 Lines*
e *Enemy flanking the British Position*
f *Enemy endeavouring to outflank Capt. Daly's Position*
g *Enemy's Cavalry*

h *A Block House*
i *Abbatis*
k *British Skirmishers*
l *22 Indians*
m *Capt. Daly's Compy. 70 Men*
n *Habitans Chasseurs retreating*
o *Grenadier Compy. 1 Batt.n Militia Reserved*

p *1 Compy. Voltigeurs & 1 Compy. 5 Batt.n Militia reserved*
q *150 Indians*
r *1st Position 1 Compy. Voltigeurs 1 Compy. incorporated Militia & 8o Habitans*
s *2d Position 2 Comp.*
t *3d 1 Comp. at the Ford*
u *4th 1 Comp.*
w *Barracks*

MAP 266 (*above, top*).
Plan of the Battle of Moraviantown, 5 October 1813. The river is the Thames. Note the inscription *Great chief Tecumseh in advance he was killed by the Enemy.*

MAP 267 (*above*).
The Battle of Châteauguay, fought on 26 October 1813. The map has been drawn to illustrate Salaberry's strategy. The Canadian victory stopped the American advance on Montréal.

MAP 268 (*right*).
This map of the Niagara River where it enters Lake Ontario shows the positions of Fort George and Newark (Niagara-on-the-Lake). Also shown is the American Fort Niagara, and the British Fort Mississauga, built between 1814 and 1816. The latter fort was intended to replace Fort George, which had proved too vulnerable to bombardment from Fort Niagara. Thus Fort Mississauga was constructed with more massive earthworks, which still survive today; a golf course has been built around it. The fort was hardly used, for the War of 1812 ended before it was finished.

just south of what is now Canada's southernmost point, on Pelee Island. Barclay's inferior fleet had been kept so short of supplies that he outfitted a nearly finished ship, the *Detroit*, with cannon borrowed from Fort Malden at Amherstburg. Nevertheless he put up a courageous fight, destroying the American flagship *Lawrence* and forcing Perry to transfer his colours to another ship. The entire British fleet was captured or destroyed, and with this defeat, control of Lake Erie passed to the Americans.

As a result, the British land force in southwestern Ontario, led by Colonel Henry Proctor and supported by native warriors led by Tecumseh, began to fall back towards Niagara. They were pursued by the American army, now led by Brigadier General William Harrison, the governor of Indiana Territory. Proctor retreated up the

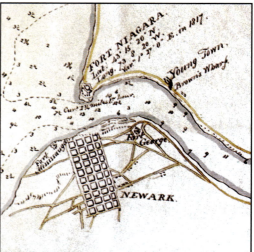

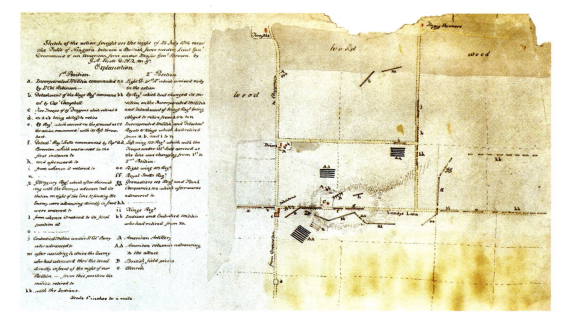

MAP 270 (*above*).
Another view of the Battle of Lundy's Lane, drawn in 1814. Today the location of the battle is urban, a rather sad area of cheaper motels and bars close to the tourist attraction of Niagara Falls.

MAP 269 (*above*).
A detailed sketch of the Battle of Lundy's Lane, fought 25–26 July 1814. This pivotal battle finally ended American designs on Upper Canada.

MAP 271 (*left*).
When the British reoccupied Fort Erie it was in a sorry state, having been blown up by the retreating American army.

The photograph shows the American flag raised above Fort Erie during a re-enactment of the American occupation.

Thames Valley, only to be caught by Harrison near Thamesville on 5 October. The much larger American force soundly defeated the British, and Tecumseh was killed. This was the Battle of Moraviantown (MAP 266). Harrison now could have pressed farther into Upper Canada, but chose instead to withdraw.

The third prong of the American offensive of 1813 was towards Montréal, thought easier to take than heavily defended Kingston. There were two American armies. One, led by Major General James Wilkinson, was to advance on Montréal down the St. Lawrence from Sackets Harbor. The other, led by Major General Wade Hampton, was to advance up that tried-and-true invasion route, Lake Champlain and the Richelieu River.

From Plattsburgh, on the western side of Lake Champlain, Hampton first advanced north along the Richelieu, invading Canada on 20 September 1813. His force was turned back at the Lacolle River by unexpected resistance, and they then marched west to the Châteauguay River, which flows northwards to the St. Lawrence just upstream from Montréal. There, at a location near Ormstown, Quebec, on 26 October, they were met by a native and Canadian force commanded by Lieutenant Colonel Charles-Michel d'Irumberry de Salaberry. He was a French Canadian officer who had formed the Voltigeurs, a light infantry, almost guerrilla corps. At Châteauguay he was to use their skills well, for the American army was again stopped by Salaberry's force, despite the fact that they were vastly outnumbered. Hampton scuttled back to American soil. MAP 267 shows the plan of the battle, as noted by Salaberry shortly afterwards.

In the meantime, Wilkinson's army had been moving down the St. Lawrence. They were engaged on 11 November at John Crysler's farm. a battle site now submerged beneath the waters of the St. Lawrence Seaway. Although the Americans were defeated, the way to Montréal was still clear, but they heard the news of Châteauguay and decided to retreat. Montréal was safe.

Although the American government intended that Kingston should be the main objective in 1814, this plan was not made clear to a new commander, General Jacob Brown. Instead, American attention was again focussed on the Niagara Frontier.

At the beginning of July 1814, an American force led by Brigadier General Winfield Scott crossed the Niagara and took Fort Erie. British troops advancing from Fort George were defeated by the Americans at Chippewa on 5 July. The American plan was now to push on to York, but planned naval support from Chauncey did not arrive, and this delay allowed the British to regroup. General Gordon Drummond hurried from York to take direction of a now reinforced British army.

There followed the hardest-fought battle of the war at Lundy's Lane, almost within earshot of Niagara Falls, on 25–26 July. The attack began in the late afternoon and continued into the night. There were heavy casualties and Scott, Brown, and Drummond were badly wounded. By midnight, the Americans were too exhausted to attack again, and fell back; the British, in turn, were too exhausted to pursue them. There were to be no more American offensives that year. In November the Americans abandoned Fort Erie and crossed the river, having lost their taste for invasions.

There was more fighting, however. The British attacked the American capital in August, setting the White House afire and forcing President James Madison to flee. And in September came the famous but futile British bombardment of Fort McHenry, near Baltimore, scene of the "rockets' red glare" that found its way into the American national anthem. Also in September, George Prevost led a large invasion force to Plattsburgh, but withdrew after a naval defeat on Lake Champlain. At this the British lost their taste for invasions as well.

The fight had gone from both sides. On Christmas Eve 1814 the Treaty of Ghent was signed , ending the war and restoring the boundaries between Canada and the United States as they were before the hostilities.

In April 1817, Richard Rush, for the United States, and Charles Bagot, for Britain, signed an agreement limiting any future arms race on the Great Lakes, which, it was thought, would make it impossible for either side to gain a military advantage. This agreement has been hailed as the birth of the "undefended border," although years of defensive building would ensue before this would become a reality. The final agreement resulting from the War of 1812 was the Convention of 1818, which further defined the boundary between the two countries (see page 180).

The Selkirk Grant and the Red River Settlement

Thomas Douglas, Earl of Selkirk, was a Scottish philanthropist who was concerned about the plight of dispossessed tenant farmers in Scotland and Ireland. In 1803 he settled some eight hundred Scottish Highlanders on Prince Edward Island. By 1808, he had decided that another good place for settlement would be on the Red River in today's Manitoba, and since this was in the Hudson's Bay Company territory of Rupert's Land, he set about persuading the Company to grant him settlement rights. In an unlikely alliance with former explorer Alexander Mackenzie, he began buying up the stock of the company. Mackenzie had simply wanted to gain control in order to obtain concessions for his North West Company, and as soon as he realized Selkirk's motives, he withdrew. Nevertheless, Selkirk was able to gain enough influence to enable him to persuade the Company, for the princely sum of ten shillings, to grant him 300 000 km² of land, the area shown on the deed map (MAP 272). The agreement was signed on 12 June 1811, and with a stroke of a pen a massive area of today's Canada belonged to one man.

The land stood in the path of the North West Company's supply routes to Athabasca and the West, and was bound to cause problems. The company had lobbied hard in London to prevent the grant, but to no avail.

Selkirk wasted no time, and the following month he appointed a governor, Miles Macdonell, who with 115 men arrived on 24 September 1811 at York Fort, where, because it was now too late to proceed inland, they overwintered. It was 29 August 1812 before they finally arrived at Red River, landing at a place they called Point Douglas, about 3 km from the confluence of the Red and Assiniboine Rivers, where the North West Company's Fort Gibraltar was located.

Macdonell's party was joined by an Irish group in October. The first winter was bad, and the group only survived because of assistance from the North West Company traders. The next winter, Macdonell had had enough. Fed up with seeing Fort Gibraltar ship off pemmican—dried buffalo strips perhaps mixed with berries—to their posts farther west, while his own settlers were near starvation, he issued the so-called Pemmican Proclamation. This edict, issued on 8 January 1814, forbade the export from the colony of any food supplies, principally pemmican. He followed this up by seizing a shipment of pemmican on its way west. The Nor'Westers were incensed.

It was 1815 before they could retaliate, for the War of 1812 had disrupted their supply lines, but they obtained a warrant for the arrest of

MAP 272 (*above*).
When the Hudson's Bay Company granted Assiniboia to the Earl of Selkirk, this map was attached to the signed deed. Selkirk's signature can be seen at top right. Signed on 12 June 1811, the map was likely drawn by Aaron Arrowsmith, though certainly with information from Peter Fidler. The deed granted 300 000 km² and covered land in today's Manitoba, North Dakota, and Minnesota.

MAP 273 (*right*).
It was some time before an agreement was reached with the native peoples to cede land in the Red and Assiniboine River valleys. It was finally signed on 18 July 1817. The chiefs' signatures are the animal figures. Peter Fidler probably sketched the map for the treaty, for he was present at the ceremony, as was Lord Selkirk.

Macdonell under a law that placed the West under the same laws as the rest of the Canadas. Macdonell soon found himself a prisoner, charged with the theft of pemmican, and was taken to Montréal. The Nor'Westers, led by Duncan Cameron, a British officer from Fort Mackinac and also a Nor'Wester, persuaded many of the colony's settlers to move elsewhere, transporting them to Lake Winnipeg, from whence they could go to Upper Canada or back to Hudson Bay. There were few left when the settlement was burned to the ground.

On his way east, Macdonell met Colin Robertson at Lake of the Woods. Robertson had been employed by the Hudson's Bay Company to mount an expedition to the Athabasca country and was bringing supplies to Selkirk's colony. When Robertson arrived at Red River he quickly retrieved the settlers from Lake Winnipeg, rebuilt the houses, and in September, harvested the grain still growing in the fields. The next month his regrouped settlers were joined by ninety more, including Robert Semple, appointed by the Hudson's Bay Company to be the new governor not only of Assiniboia, but of all its western territory.

Semple set about establishing his authority. In the spring of 1816 he sent Robertson to Fort Gibraltar to arrest Duncan Cameron on a charge of burning the settlement the previous year and to tear down the fort. This was achieved, and Robertson left for Hudson Bay with his prisoner, to take him for trial in London.

In the meantime, Selkirk, fed up with trying to control the situation from Britain, came to Montréal late in 1815. He was unable to achieve much in that North West Company town, although he did secure the freedom of Macdonell.

In 1816 the North West Company sent Archibald Macleod to Red River, armed with a commission as a magistrate; the idea was to allow him to "legally" arrest and send his opposition to Montréal for trial. But things got out of

hand. The mixed-blood Métis, led by Cuthbert Grant, were becoming upset about the intrusion of settlers onto their buffalo-hunting grounds and, aided and abetted by the Nor'Westers, set off on a marauding spree. On 19 June 1816, across the river from Fort Douglas, the settlement's fort at Point Douglas, seventy Métis and Nor'Westers attacked a party of thirty settlers led by Semple, killing him and twenty-two of his men. This was the incident that has come to be called the Seven Oaks Massacre. Grant's men then followed up by destroying Fort Douglas.

But Selkirk was on his way now with a force of soldiers discharged after the War of 1812, mainly men of the Swiss De Meuron Regiment. Unable to persuade any magistrates to go with him, Selkirk took the law into his own hands. With his now superior force he seized the North West Company fort at the western end of Lake Superior, Fort William, arresting luminaries Simon Fraser, John McLoughlin, and William McGillivray. Among McGillivray's papers Selkirk found some of his own letters, clear proof of their illegal interception.

Selkirk overwintered at Fort William and in the spring of 1817 reached Red River, where he found the culprits of the atrocities long gone. He quickly established control, settled his Swiss soldiers on his land, and rebuilt. It was at this time that Selkirk signed a treaty with the Salteaux chief, Peguis, that gave the settlers right of access to the Red and Assiniboine Rivers (MAP 273).

The year 1817, and in particular Selkirk's capture of Fort William, marked a watershed for the North West Company. Never again would it prevail. In 1821, a merger of the company with the Hudson's Bay Company was arranged, and with another stroke of a pen the Hudson's Bay Company became master of the fur trade to the Pacific and the Arctic, achieving the goals it had striven for, against increasingly violent opposition, for the previous fifty years.

In 1836 Selkirk's heirs sold Assiniboia back to the Hudson's Bay Company, taking payment in Company shares. But not all of the original land grant was returned, for in 1818 nearly half had become part of the United States (see page 180).

MAP 274.
Peter Fidler's map of the Red River Colony in 1819. The map is oriented with south at the top. From 1812 to 1819 Fidler was a trader at Brandon House, a Hudson's Bay Company post on the Assiniboine River; it is shown on the map. Site of today's Brandon, Manitoba, it was named after the Duke of Brandon, an ancestor of Selkirk's. The Company post at Fort Douglas, now Winnipeg, is also marked. Lots are shown along the river in that location, though not accurately at this scale; it is only a sketch map. *Coal* is noted on the Pembina Hills.

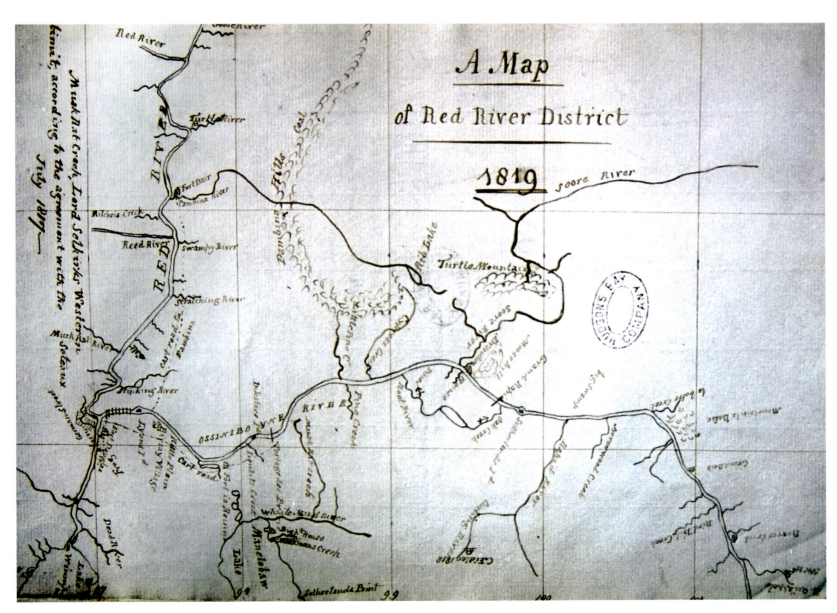

Fixing the Forty-ninth Parallel Boundary Line

The Treaty of Ghent, signed in 1814, ended the War of 1812 and attempted to redefine the boundary line between the United States and the Canadas and British territory. The idea was to restore the status quo from before the war.

But the division of territory west of Lake of the Woods had never been properly decided, for the Treaty of Paris of 1783 had described an impossible boundary—due west from the lake to the Mississippi, which is actually farther south.

In 1818, a convention was held in London between the United States and Britain to decide the issue. The American negotiators were Albert Gallatin, American minister in Paris, and Richard Rush, American minister in London. The British nominated Henry Goulburn, who had been one of the commissioners at the Treaty of Ghent, and Frederick Robinson, president of the Board of Trade.

The convention agreed on a new definition for 1 372 km of boundary. The boundary west of Lake of the Woods would be from "the North Western Point of the Lake of the Woods, along the forty Ninth Parallel of North Latitude."

If the northwestern point of the lake was not on the forty-ninth parallel, then a line was to be drawn north or south to intersect it. This, once the area was surveyed, first by David Thompson and then by Johann Tiarks and Anthony Barclay, led to the creation of an isolated spur of American territory, the so-called Northwest Angle.

Farther west, the agreed upon division line stopped at the Rocky Mountains. Beyond that was the Oregon Country, stretching north from 42° N (the present Oregon-California boundary) to 54° 40′ N and including all the territory of today's Oregon, Washington, and British Columbia (see Map 319, page 204). Unable to agree here, the commissioners determined on "joint occupancy" for a period of ten years.

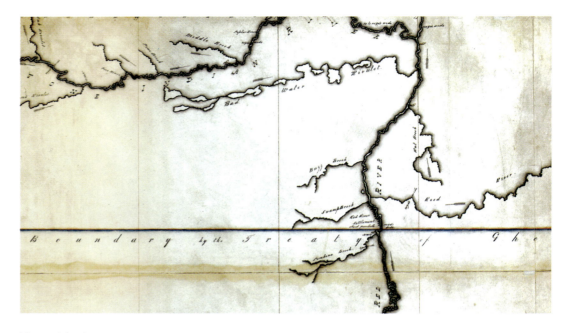

Map 275 (*above*).
Part of a map drawn by David Thompson in 1840 as a result of his work surveying and defining the 49th parallel. The part shown is the Red River and the Red River Settlement. The boundary line went right through Pembina, all but one house being now in the United States, but most of its inhabitants elected to remain there "under the protection of the United States government."

Map 276 (*below, middle*).
Part of an American map dated 1817. A boundary is tentatively delineated, and labelled *U.S. division line not yet ascertained*.

Map 277 (*below, bottom*).
Another version of a boundary line prior to 1818. This map was published in that year, and *the American Map published in Philadelphia 1816* referred to on the map was one by John Melish. Melish's map attempted to define the watershed encompassing the Louisiana Purchase. The map shown here also shows the boundaries of the Selkirk grant (see page 178).

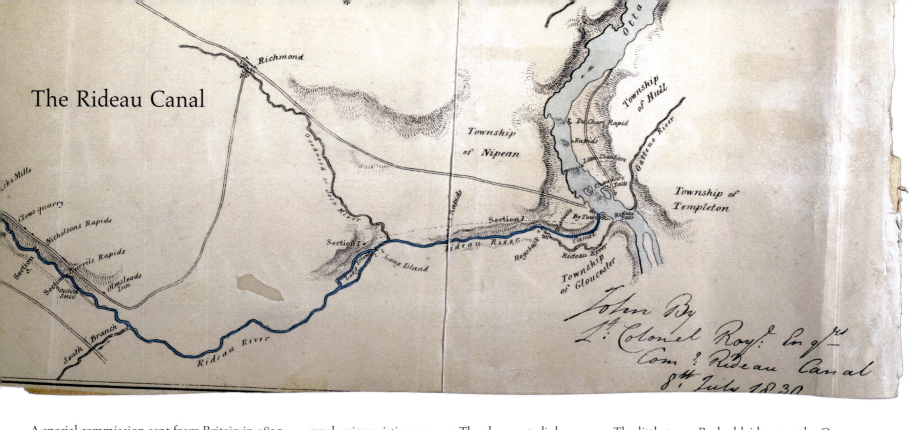

The Rideau Canal

A special commission sent from Britain in 1825 determined that an alternative route to Kingston from Montréal was required, because the international boundary along the St. Lawrence was open to attack in wartime.

An officer of the Royal Engineers, Lieutenant Colonel John By, was selected to plan and supervise the work. He arrived in 1826, passing on his way canal works already under way on the Ottawa River at today's Hawkesbury, Ontario. Reaching the site of the modern capital of Canada, By selected a natural gully leading south from the Ottawa River, today beside the Parliament Buildings. He spent the winter of 1826–27 planning the canal, using existing surveys. The plan was to link the Rideau River and the Cataraqui River via the Rideau Lakes. The specifications for the canal were enlarged by By, who could see that steamboats would soon take over. The canal was built by Montréal contractors, employing thousands of French Canadians augmented by Irish immigrants. When the canal was completed in May 1832, By was the first through the system—in a steamboat.

By should have received honours for his achievement, one of the great engineering feats of the nineteenth century; instead he was subjected to an enquiry into canal finances and he died only four years later.

The little town By had laid out at the Ottawa River end of his canal became known as Bytown, renamed Ottawa in 1855. In 1857 it was chosen as the capital of the United Province of Canada (see page 238).

MAP 278 (*above*).
Captain Thomas Burrowes was an army engineer working on the canal project. He stayed on to maintain it until 1846. He drew this beautiful little map of part of the Rideau Canal in 1830. Burrowes painted over a hundred scenes of the canal—and this map.

MAP 279 (*below*).
Map and cross-section of the Rideau Canal, complete with a table of estimated versus actual costs. The map was signed by Lieutenant Colonel John By in February 1829.

The Canada Company

The Canada Company was a land and colonization company set up in 1824 and chartered in 1825, designed to promote the settlement of lands hitherto unoccupied by Europeans.

The company was the idea of John Galt, a Scotsman. He had been hired by Loyalists attempting to gain redress for damages they suffered during the War of 1812. Unable to persuade the British government to pay directly, the creation of the Canada Company was a compromise, using instead the available resource— land. Investors were to provide money, land was to be purchased and subdivided, and settlers were to be attracted. The company would lay out townships and build roads, thus increasing the value of the land. The company would "open access to the settlement of the lands by a steady and industrious population."

The land-granting system that had been set up to accommodate the influx of Loyalists after 1783 (see page 126) was discontinued in 1826, being replaced with an open market for land. It was into this new environment that the Canada Company stepped.

At a cost of three shillings and sixpence per acre (about $7.40 per ha) plus some annual payments that went towards the governmental expenses of Upper Canada, the company acquired a little over a million hectares of land, including 400 000 ha in an area of western Upper Canada that became known as the Huron Tract. MAP 280 (below) shows this land. The rest of the company's land was more scattered. MAP 281, drawn in 1825 or 1826 and beautifully engraved, was the general map compiled for the Canada Company soon after its land purchase. The "blank" on the map in the western part of Upper Canada, a space so conveniently filled with a sample township plan, is the area that became the Huron Tract. Galt's company was responsible for laying out the towns of Goderich and Guelph. The former was named after Viscount Goderich, briefly the British prime minister in 1824–25. The town of Galt was named in honour of John Galt; it is now part of the city of Cambridge.

MAP 280 (*below*).
The Canada Company's Huron Tract as it was in 1832. The districts were mostly named after investors in the company, not settlers.

MAP 281 (*right*).
A large general map produced for the Canada Company in 1825 or 1826, following the purchase of the lands in Upper Canada which it intended to develop, but before anything except planning had been done. The map, drawn by James Chewett under the supervision of the surveyor general of Upper Canada, Thomas Ridout, stands as a superb documentation of the geography and development of Canada at that date. It incorporated a map of Lake Huron surveyed and drawn by Lieutenant Henry Wolsey Bayfield, who had carried out hydrographic surveys of the lake at the British Admiralty's behest between 1816 and 1825, producing the most accurate maps at that time. Lake Erie is also based on an Admiralty chart. These charts were not published until 1828, and the Canada Company was only allowed to use the information after agreeing to leave it unattributed. This map was the most comprehensive and detailed map of Upper Canada for several decades.

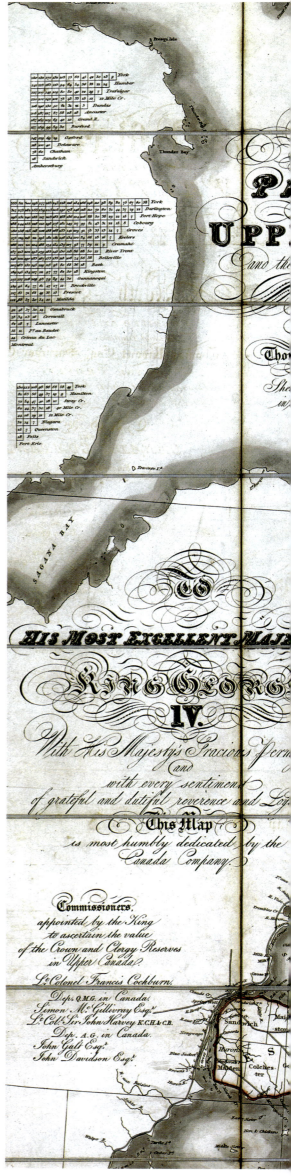

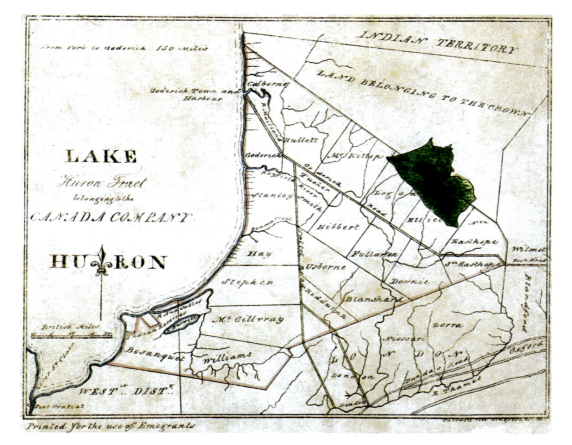

Arctic Exploration
1818–1859

In the early nineteenth century, no more was known about the Canadian Arctic north of Hudson Bay than was known at the end of the sixteenth century, after the voyages of John Davis into the strait that bears his name (see page 36).

Then, in 1818, a string of exploratory voyages began, a new round of searching for the elusive Northwest Passage across the top of the American continent. With the end of the Napoleonic Wars in Europe in 1815, the British navy suddenly found itself with a surfeit of men and ships, as Britain entered a century that would bring no major wars save for the Crimean War (1853–56). What better way to utilize this overcapacity, and in the process hopefully bring glory to the country, than to embark on heroic exploration? And heroic it was, some of it, as we shall see.

The guiding light behind the revival of interest in the Arctic was John Barrow, second secretary (the top civil servant) to the Admiralty. In 1817 he published a theory of an open Polar Sea and an explanation of the presence of south-flowing icebergs in Davis Strait, which he thought were caused by an ocean current from Bering Strait (MAP 283, right). At the time, the more or less closed northern end of Baffin Bay was doubted, despite William Baffin's maps (see page 41), and Baffin himself was in some disrepute. In addition, a whaler, William Scoresby, noted a lack of ice north of 74° N.

The resulting British naval expeditions of the next forty years were to transform the Canadian Arctic from a blank on the map and reveal a labyrinth of islands and channels.

In 1818, the Admiralty fitted out and dispatched two expeditions consisting of four ships. HMS *Dorothea* and *Trent*, under David Buchan (see page 122) and John Franklin, sailed north, east of Greenland, with the intention of testing the open Polar Sea theory. At the same time, HMS *Isabella* and *Alexander*, under John Ross and William Edward Parry, sailed into Baffin Bay to seek the fabled Northwest Passage.

Neither of these expeditions got very far. The best that can be said for the *Dorothea* and *Trent* voyage was that it gave John Franklin his first experience of the Arctic, reaching 80° N before turning back. Ross and Parry's voyage had much more far-reaching consequences, however, not due to the voyage itself, but from a follow-up voyage undertaken by Parry the year after. Poor John Ross has been much maligned for his order to turn back from what was to prove to be the real eastern entrance to the Northwest Passage, Lancaster Sound. His map (MAP 284), published in 1819, shows a line of mountains that he named Croker's Mountains after the first secretary of the Board of Admiralty.

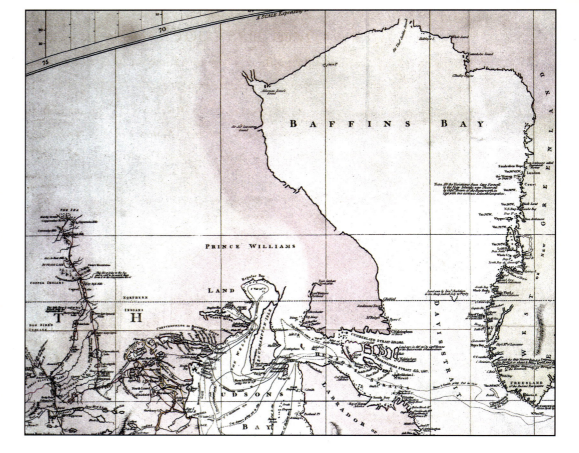

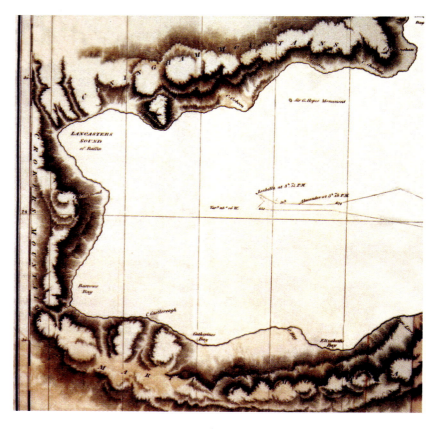

MAP 282 (*above*).
Part of the world map of Aaron Arrowsmith, 1794. This shows the knowledge of the eastern Arctic prior to the British naval expeditions starting in 1818.

MAP 283 (*right, centre*).
The map published by John Barrow in 1817, illustrating his ideas of an open Polar Sea and the current from Bering Strait to Davis Strait.

MAP 284 (*right*).
A map of one of the more famous mistakes in the history of exploration. This is John Ross's map of the eastern entrance to Lancaster Sound, the gateway to the real Northwest Passage, published in 1819. But Ross shows it as just another bay, having somehow been tricked into believing that mountains blocked his path. He made the additional mistake of not soliciting the opinions of his officers, so the error in judgement became his alone. Ross's second-in-command, William Edward Parry, who expressed doubts, was sent the following year to determine who was right.

Arriving at Lancaster Sound at the end of August 1818, Parry wrote:

If we may venture to question the authority of that navigator [William Baffin] respecting his having seen the bottom of this inlet, or, as he calls it, I suspect gratuitously, sound, it certainly has more the appearance of the wished-for straits than any place we have yet seen. In the first place, the sea is perfectly clear of ice; and secondly, the water is warmer than we have found it since the 7th instant, being 36° [F] at the surface, and 31° at the bottom. The swell of the sea, the breadth of the opening, and the depth of the water, are all flattering appearances, independently of which we are not at a great distance from where the sea was seen by Mr. Hearne, at the mouth of the Coppermine River.

Edward Parry's voyage of 1819 was approved after the Admiralty had read words such as these and realized that Ross might have made a mistake. Parry was given command of HMS *Hecla*, and Matthew Liddon was appointed captain of HMS *Griper*. Parry was instructed:

To proceed in the first instance to that part of the coast [Lancaster Sound] and use your best endeavours to explore the bottom of that Sound; or, in the event of its proving a strait opening to the westward, you are to use all possible means, consistently with the safety of the two ships, to pass through it, and ascertain its direction and communications; and if it should be found to connect itself with the northern sea, you are to make the best of your way to Behring's Strait.

Aware of the possible significance of Lancaster Sound, Parry noted on 1 August 1819, "We were now about to enter and explore that great sound or inlet which has obtained a degree of celebrity beyond what it might otherwise have been considered to possess, from the very opposite opinions which have been held with regard to it."

Although, to be fair to Ross, it should be acknowledged that ice conditions change from year to year in the Arctic, Parry was able to sail straight through Ross's "mountains" and discovered a long wide channel westwards—Lancaster Sound, Barrow Strait, Viscount Melville Sound, and McClure Strait, now all together also named Parry Channel.

He did have one dead end. Running into ice at a point near the northeast tip of Somerset Island, Parry found "a broad and open channel" to the south. He followed this "with the intention of seeking, in a lower latitude, a clearer passage to the westward than that which we had just been obliged to abandon." This was Prince Regent Inlet. But it led nowhere. "With the increasing width of the inlet," Parry wrote, "we had flattered our-

selves with increasing hopes; but we soon experienced the mortification of disappointment."

Finally unable to penetrate farther west, Parry arrived at what he named Winter Harbour, on Melville Island, on 24 September 1819 (MAP 285). He nearly didn't make it into a safe haven; as it was his men had to cut a channel in the ice to get the ships into the harbour.

After a pioneer overwintering, during which the ships were converted into covered shelters, they were finally able to leave when the ice released them on 1 August 1820, more than ten months after their arrival.

Parry then attempted to follow his instructions and sail westward towards the Pacific. But his luck had run out. The ice would allow no further passage west or south. *Hecla* and *Griper* reached 113° 48′ 22.5″ (actually 113° 46′ 43.5″), which Parry was careful to point out was the "westernmost meridian hitherto reached in the Polar Sea," at a point about 80 km west of Winter Harbour. "The situation the ships were now placed," Parry wrote in a studied understatement, "when viewed in combination with the shortness of the remaining part of the season, and the period to which our resources of every kind could be extended, was such as to require a more than ordinary consideration." After consulting with all his officers they decided not to risk another winter trapped in the ice, and sailed for home on 23 August.

Parry had penetrated more than 1 000 km west from "the opening into Sir James Lancaster's Sound" and discovered half of the real Northwest Passage. It was a stunning and major addition to the map of the Arctic.

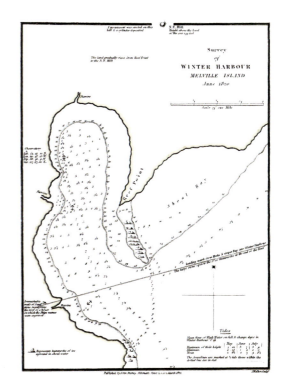

MAP 285 (*above*).
Winter Harbour, Melville Island. *Hecla* and *Griper* spent over ten months, from 24 September 1819 to 1 August 1820, iced in at this location, on the south shore of Melville Island. How could Parry name it anything else but Winter Harbour? Parry's overwintering at Winter Harbour was the first overwintering using ships, suitably covered, as housing. The lessons learned would be useful for the many expeditions that followed. From Winter Harbour, in the spring Parry explored Melville Island. Keen to have as long a season as the climate would allow, attempts were made to leave the ice-choked bay in late July, without success. On 1 August 1820, while equipment was being transferred from the beach (where it had spent the long winter, in order to provide more space on board), Parry sounded the entrance to the harbour to complete the survey for this map. Due to the ice he had not been able to do this previously. On that day they were finally free!

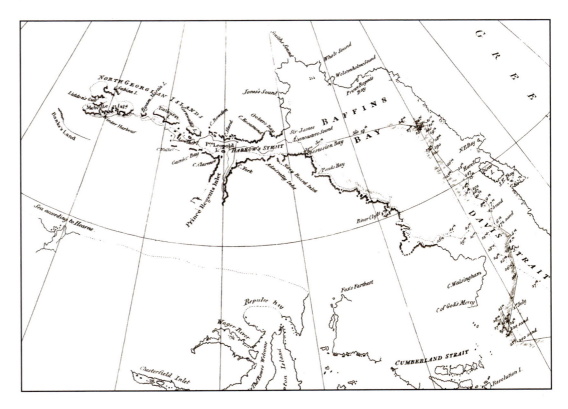

MAP 286.
This general map from Edward Parry's book about his voyage of 1819–20 shows the major swath of coastline he put on the map. Samuel Hearne's Coppermine River is shown, but the knowledge of the area to the north of Hudson Bay is much as it was seventy years before. The name of Parry's *North Georgian Islands* was changed to Parry Islands in 1834, and the whole body of water he first placed on the map, from Lancaster Sound in the east to M'Clure Strait in the west, was designated Parry Channel in 1959.

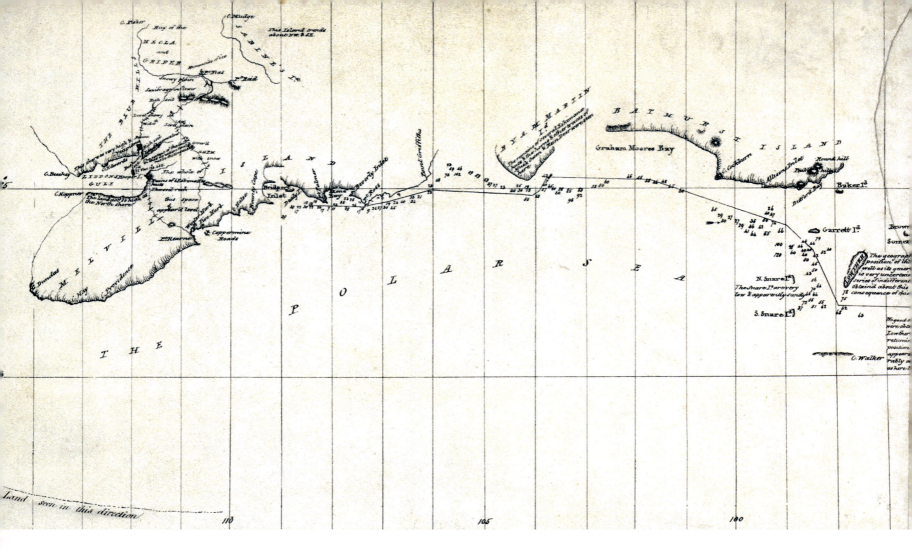

In 1819 the British government dispatched an expedition by land north from known territories "to determine the latitudes and longitudes of the Northern Coast of North America" and to "amend the very defective geography of the northern part of North America." The expedition was led by naval lieutenant John Franklin, back from his Arctic foray with the *Trent*.

Franklin, accompanied by twenty men including John Richardson and midshipmen George Back and Robert Hood, arrived at York Fort on Hudson Bay and made their way to the north via the river systems known to the fur traders. North of Great Slave Lake they built a cabin at Winter Lake, naming it Fort Enterprise. Here they overwintered in 1820–21. Leaving here on 14 June 1821, Franklin descended the Coppermine River and reached the Arctic Ocean on 18 July, at precisely the same location as Samuel Hearne fifty years before.

Following his instructions, Franklin then surveyed the coast eastwards to the Kent Peninsula at a place he named, appropriately enough, Point Turnagain.

So far, so good; but from here, however, things went distinctly downhill. Supply problems, due in large part to the feud between the Hudson's Bay Company and the North West Company just prior to their merger in 1821, meant Franklin was now desperately short of food. In the resulting struggle to return to his base at Fort Providence, on Great Slave Lake, ten of his *voyageurs* died of starvation and Hood, who had become incapacitated, was murdered by one of natives, named Michel. Fearing for their own lives, Richardson had at the first opportunity killed Michel.

MAP 287 (*above*).
Patched together from two sheets of paper, this is the map drawn by Edward Parry in 1819 during his historic first penetration of the Northwest Passage, from Baffin Bay, through Lancaster Sound, to his winter quarters at Winter Harbour on Melville Island, exploring Prince Regent Inlet to the south on his way. Everything west of Lancaster Sound was here first placed on a map by Parry. It was the most spectacular addition to the map of the world since James Cook's mapping of the coastlines of the Pacific Ocean. In place of John Ross's Croker's Mountains, the land that supposedly barred his way west, Parry has diplomatically converted them to *Croker's Bay*; the notoriously unpleasant John Wilson Croker was too significant a man to Parry's career—he was first secretary of the navy—to risk offending him. Ross's Barrows Bay is now an extended *Barrow's Strait*. Parry's track is shown, almost all the way to Winter Harbour on Melville Island, where he wintered in 1819–20, including his abortive attempt to sail south down the inlet he named after the Prince Regent. Also shown are the results of the overland expedition on Melville Island in June 1820. The *Land seen in this direction* is Banks Island, named by Parry after Sir Joseph Banks, and named *Bank's Land* on Parry's published map (see MAP 286, previous page).

MAP 288 (*below*).
Aaron Arrowsmith's 1824 published map of North America, onto which has been pasted the additional new coastline east and west of the Mackenzie Delta mapped by John Franklin's two land expeditions. This map belonged to the Hudson's Bay Company, and Company officials pasted on the new information. Eventually incorporated into Arrowsmith's printed maps, this unique map graphically demonstrates the considerable additions to geographical knowledge—and Canada's northern coastline—made by Franklin.

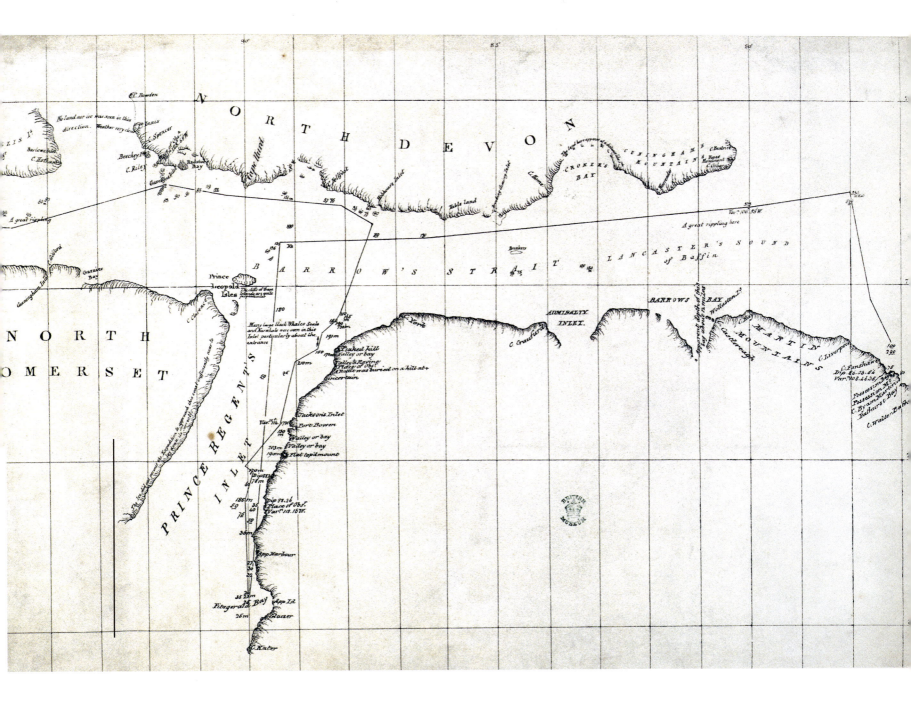

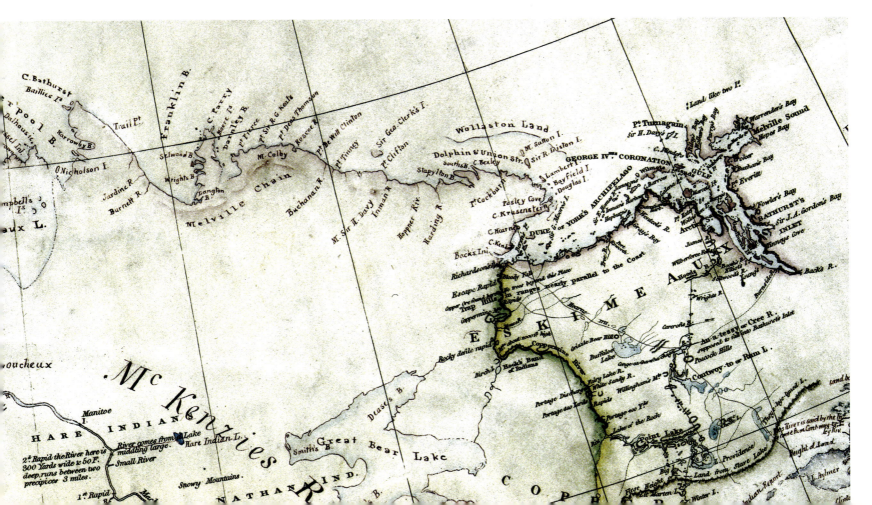

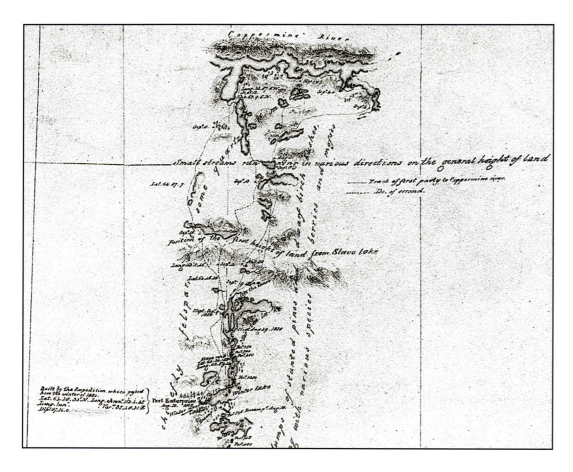

ond voyage in command had not been anywhere near as successful as his first, but nevertheless did add a substantial length of hitherto unmapped coastline to the charts.

In his explorations Parry was aided by Inuit people, who were persuaded to draw maps for him—maps that made sense. MAP 290, below, shows one of these, as reproduced in Parry's book.

In 1824, the British Admiralty organized no less than four concurrent expeditions, hoping to finally define the Northwest Passage. John Franklin was to descend the Mackenzie River and survey east and west along the Arctic shore, to his previous survey at the Coppermine River to the east, and westward to link with ships commanded by Frederick Beechey, sent through Bering Strait and then to the east. Parry, now on his third voyage, was to follow Prince Regent Inlet southwards and find any westward-leading straits. Finally, George Lyon was to sail into Repulse Bay and strike out overland until he reached Franklin's Point Turnagain.

All of these endeavours except Franklin's proved hopelessly optimistic. Lyon ran into bad weather in shallow seas and nearly lost his ship; he returned to Britain the same year. Beechey did survey part of the northern coastline of Alaska (then Russian America), but failed to meet Franklin. Parry sailed again with *Fury* and

During this ordeal, the men ate whatever they could find that was at all edible, and Franklin achieved renown as "the man who ate his shoes." They arrived at Fort Providence, and their salvation, on 11 December 1821. The Gothic tale of hardships told in Franklin's book published in 1824 was devoured by the British public. Franklin did achieve the geographical aims of the expedition, mapping well over 300 km of Arctic coastline, putting, as one historian aptly noted, a roof on the map of Canada.

In 1821, fresh from his wildly successful first (independent) voyage, Edward Parry was sent out again, to locate what was thought to be an alternate and more southern path to the Northwest Passage, the route favoured by many of the earlier seekers in previous centuries, from Foxe Basin, north of Hudson Bay. Parry himself had thought his discoveries in 1819–20 "served also to point out the most probable means of [the] accomplishment [of a Northwest Passage], by a route farther away from the permanent ice pack."

In April 1821 Parry sailed in HMS *Fury*, with George Lyon in HMS *Hecla*. His instructions stated that "finding a passage from the Atlantic to the Pacific is the main object of the Expedition, and . . . the ascertaining of the Northern boundary of the North American Continent is the next." Interestingly enough, he was also ordered to take John Franklin on board, should he meet him. Parry, like George Vancouver, was to survey by following the "continental shore" and thus delineate the northern coast of North America to meet with that of Franklin.

But Vancouver was not hampered by ice; Parry was. He surveyed the eastern coast of the Melville Peninsula, overwintering once at Win-

ter Island, at the entrance to Lyon Inlet, and just 100 km east of Repulse Bay; and once at Igloolik Island, at the peninsula's northern end. He did find a passage to the west, which he named the *Strait of Fury and Hecla*, after his ships. This is the strait between the Melville Peninsula to the south and Baffin Island to the north, but it was clogged with ice and impenetrable to Parry's ships. In any case it in fact only led to the Gulf of Boothia, essentially a dead end. Parry's sec-

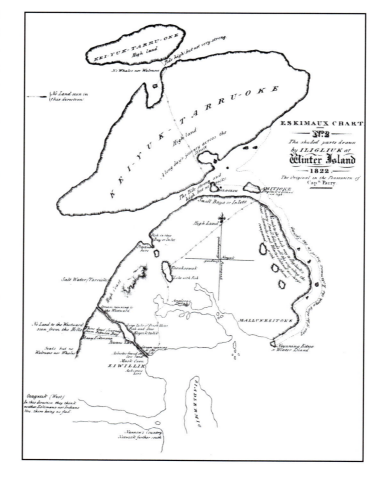

Hecla, but met with horrendous ice conditions in Prince Regent Inlet. In August 1825 *Fury* was driven ashore at what became Fury Beach, on the eastern side of Somerset Island, and had to be abandoned; Parry and his men limped back home crowded into his remaining ship. *Fury*'s supplies had been unloaded on the beach; they became a source of survival later for John Ross (see page 191), and the remains of the stores are still on the beach today.

John Franklin, on his second overland expedition, as on his first, travelled by the rivers and lakes of the Canadian Northwest, this time descending the Mackenzie River to the Arctic Ocean. With him again were John Richardson and George Back, and midshipman Edward Kendall was to draw the maps.

After wintering on Great Bear Lake at a place they named Fort Franklin (now Déline), on 22 June 1826 they set out, splitting up at Point Separation, where the Mackenzie Delta begins, with Franklin and Back going west and Richardson and Kendall east.

Franklin and Back, with two four-metre boats they named *Lion* and *Reliance*, were hampered by hostile natives, poor weather, and poor ice conditions, but they nevertheless surveyed the coast as far west as a place they called Return Reef at 148° 52´ W, just west of today's Prudhoe Bay, Alaska. They were only 250 km east of a boat sent from Beechey's expedition to pick them up. Franklin and Back retraced their steps and were back at Fort Franklin on 21 September.

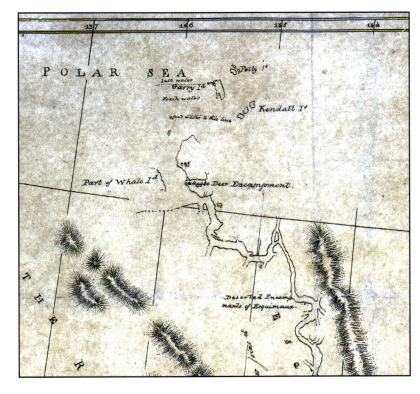

Meanwhile, Richardson and Kendall, with two boats named *Dolphin* and *Union*, surveyed the coast eastwards. They mapped and named Liverpool Bay, just east of Tuktoyaktuk; Franklin and Darnley Bays, separated by the Parry Peninsula; and part of Victoria Island, which they named Wollaston Land (now the Wollaston Peninsula), across Dolphin and Union Strait (named after their boats), connecting with their previous survey at the mouth of the Coppermine River. They then made their way back to Fort Franklin, arriving on 1 September 1826; all were back in Britain a year later.

Map 288, pages 186–87, shows the extensive coastline Franklin and Richardson added to the map of northern Canada.

Map 291 (*above*). Edward Parry's map of the *Strait of Fury and Hecla*, now Fury and Hecla Strait, between the Melville Peninsula (the south shore) and Baffin Island (called *Cockburn Island*, after another lord of the Admiralty, on his map). Parry's wintering place in 1822–23, Igloolik Island, is shown at bottom right; this is at the northwestern end of Foxe Basin, north of Hudson Bay.

Map 292 (*left*). Part of the original map drawn by Edward Kendall during John Franklin's second land expedition, 1825–27. It shows the Mackenzie River delta area and the *Polar Sea* (Arctic Ocean). Alexander Mackenzie's *Whale I*[slan]*d* is shown, while the island Mackenzie actually named has been renamed *Garry I*[slan]*d* by Franklin.

MAP 293.

A superb summary map of explorations to 1823, published by mapmaker John Thomson in 1827. The discoveries of William Edward Parry in 1819–20 and 1821–23 are shown: the water channel west of Lancaster Sound as far as Melville Island, including the northern part of Prince Regent Inlet, were mapped by Parry during his 1819–20 voyage; the Melville Peninsula and Fury and Hecla Strait during his 1821–23 expedition. Non-existent *Cockburn Island* north of the strait is actually part of Baffin Island, whose eastern shore had been remapped by John Ross in 1818. Also shown is the coast mapped by John Franklin during his first land expedition, to the mouth of the Coppermine River and beyond in 1819–22, also shown in the inset. The geographical puzzle is beginning to be filled in. Note the *Estuary of the Coppermine River according to Hearne in 1771*; Samuel Hearne, the first European to reach the Arctic Ocean, was unable to properly fix his position, and had shown the shore of the Arctic Ocean too far north (see page 136).

Thus by 1827, Parry had defined the main spine of the Canadian Arctic, Lancaster Sound and Parry Channel, and Franklin had defined much of the northern coast of North America; thus the general pattern of land and sea had been revealed. The problem now was to find a way of achieving that southward jog which would be required to link the two together. The difficulty was not to find a channel per se—sufficient probing would find that—but to find one that was navigable and not clogged with ice.

We now know that the thicker, multi-season ice tends to drift eastwards and southwards from the Arctic Ocean pack through Parry Channel and south through M'Clintock Channel. It was this stream that halted in turn Parry in 1819–20, and would halt Franklin in 1845–46, and Robert M'Clure in 1856 and again in 1857, all in completely different locations. It was Francis Leopold M'Clintock in 1859 who finally defined the route a ship would have to take to achieve a Northwest Passage—east of King William Island—avoiding the multi-year ice, a route that was not actually taken until Roald Amundsen's first passage in the tiny *Gjøa* in 1903–06 (see page 248).

A notable attempt on the Northwest Passage was made in 1829–33 by none other than John Ross, discredited since his failure to sail through the opening to Lancaster Sound in 1818. Ross advocated the use of a steam vessel for Arctic navigation, but was unable to persuade the Admiralty to let him try again. He therefore obtained private financing from a friend, Felix Booth, who had made his fortune selling gin. Thus it was that the name of a well-known brand of gin ended up gracing various geographical features of the Canadian Arctic.

Ross outfitted the *Victory*, a steam paddle-wheeler previously engaged in transporting the mail to the Isle of Man. Convinced the Northwest Passage could be found at the southern end of Prince Regent Inlet, *Victory* steamed south. But the southern end of the inlet was clogged with ice. In October 1829 Ross was stuck fast in the ice at a place he named Felix Harbour, after his sponsor. The entire peninsula was named Boothia Felix (now the Boothia Peninsula) and the water (or ice) body the Gulf of Boothia.

Ross was stuck in the ice not for one winter but three; after the first winter the ship got only 6 km; after the second only another 16 km. During the first winter, the steam engine was dismantled and left on the beach at Felix Harbour, where parts of it remain to this day.

During the winter of 1829–30, Ross was visited by Inuit people, some of whom proved once again able to draw maps. They showed the southern end of the Gulf of Boothia to be a dead end, with the only hope of a westward-leading channel on the other side of the Boothia Peninsula.

Several crossings of the Boothia Peninsula were made in the spring of 1830. Ross's nephew,

Two Inuit, Ikmalick and Apelaglu, are shown in John Ross's cabin on board the *Victory* drawing maps. The illustration is from Ross's book; Ross called the Inuit people "Boothians." It was a prime example of Euro-centricity: name the country you have discovered after your patron's gin, and then name its inhabitants after it as well.

Map 294 (*right*).
One of the maps drawn by the Inuit at John Ross's request in the winter of 1829–30, and illustrated in his 1835 book. From this Ross learned that the southern end of the Gulf of Boothia was no passage but a dead end. It was Committee Bay, surveyed and mapped by John Rae in 1847 (Map 299, page 194). The Inuit map also hints at another body of water to the west of the Boothia Peninsula. James Clark Ross was to explore the western side of *Boothia Felix* in an attempt to discover a westward-leading channel.

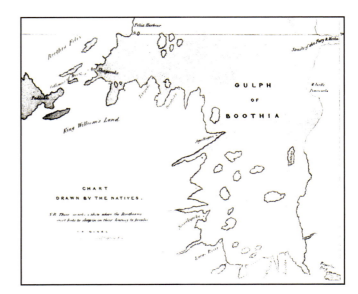

James Clark Ross, led one expedition in which he discovered King William Island (although he thought it part of the mainland) and came within 350 km of Franklin's Point Turnagain. On the west coast of King William Island, Ross made a number of comments about the impassability of the ice, which were prescient in view of the fact that John Franklin's final expedition would later become stuck in the ice in this area. One wonders if Franklin ever read Ross's book, yet presumably he must have.

The following spring, after another winter with *Victory* stuck fast in the ice, James Clark Ross made another sledge journey across the peninsula and then, turning northwards along the western shore, he located the North Magnetic Pole.

In the spring of 1832, John Ross realized it was unlikely *Victory* would ever be released from the ice, and so the decision was made to abandon her. The crew made their way north to Fury Beach, where they built a wood and canvas structure they called Somerset House. Attempting to leave in the summer of 1832, their

boats were turned back by bad weather and ice, and they returned to Fury Beach, where they spent a fourth winter in the Arctic. Placing ice blocks iglu-style around the canvas of Somerset House, they were well supplied with food and other supplies left by Parry, unloaded from *Fury* in 1825.

Finally, in the summer of 1833, their boats made it to the entrance of Lancaster Sound, where they were rescued by whalers; the ship that picked them up was none other than Ross's old ship *Isabella*. In Britain, they had been given up as lost.

In February 1833 George Back had left Britain on a rescue attempt, planning to descend the Great Fish River (now the Back River) to Chantrey Inlet, just south of King William Island. While at Great Slave Lake the following winter, he received news of Ross's rescue, but still descended the river, with the intention of striking out along the coast and connecting with Franklin's Point Turnagain. But the mouth of the Back River is well over 500 km from Franklin's farthest east, and Chantrey Inlet was

blocked by ice, so he did not get far. But he did detect a strait between King William Island and the mainland, suggesting that the former was indeed an island, and that "Poctes's Bay," shown by dotted lines at the bottom of Ross's map (Map 295, below), was non-existent.

In 1836 George Back led another effort to map the coastline east from Franklin's Point Turnagain. The plan was to sail into Repulse Bay and then drag boats across the Melville Peninsula. But his ship, HMS *Terror*, was caught in ice before reaching Repulse Bay and had to overwinter; Back only just made it home the following year, beaching his crushed and leaking vessel in Ireland.

Map 295.
A beautiful map from John Ross's book showing the southern part of the Gulf of Boothia, the Boothia Peninsula (*Boothia Felix*), and *King William Land,* a merging of what is now King William Island with the mainland of northern North America. James Clark Ross's discovery of the North Magnetic Pole is also shown. *Somerset House Fury left here* is marked on Prince Regent Inlet; this today called Fury Beach

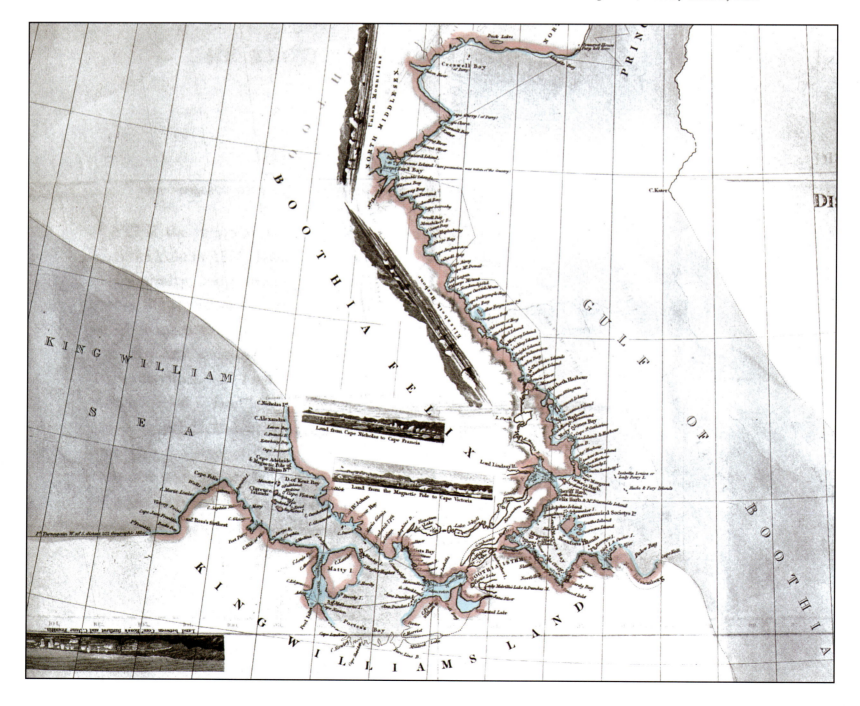

This part of the coast was finally mapped by two Hudson's Bay Company traders, Peter Warren Dease and Thomas Simpson, as part of a plan by the Company to complete the mapping of the northern coast and thus enhance its chances of a renewal in 1842 of its licence to trade exclusively in Rupert's Land. The coast of Alaska, linking Beechey's survey with Franklin's, was surveyed in 1837. In 1838 and 1839 Dease and Simpson completed a survey from the mouth of the Coppermine River to a point on the western coast of the south part of the Boothia Peninsula, noting Victoria Land (Victoria Island) and the strait south of King William Island on the way. The northern coastline of Canada was now almost completely defined.

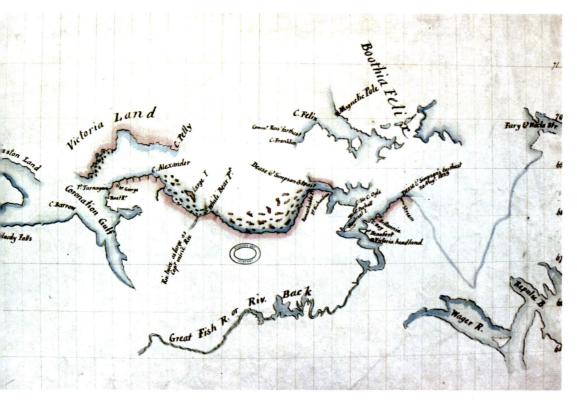

Map 296 (above).
This map, drawn in 1858, shows the extent of geographical knowledge at the time John Franklin set out on his final and fatal voyage in 1845. The map was said to be a copy of one of those given to Franklin on his departure.

Map 297 (left).
A Hudson's Bay Company map of the explorations of Thomas Simpson and Peter Warren Dease in 1838 and 1839, when they "filled in the gap" between Franklin's Point Turnagain and the maps of James Clark Ross of King William Land (Island) and the Boothia Peninsula. King William Island is separated from the mainland to the south, but is not yet shown to be an island.

It was at this stage of geographical knowledge that what was to be the final voyage of John Franklin was planned. The British Admiralty thought that all Franklin had to do was find a new route south from the defined northern channel originally found by Parry to the now defined southern channel, following the shore of northern North America.

But they had forgotten the fickle ice of the Arctic. Sir John Franklin in HMS Erebus and Francis Crozier in HMS Terror, taking the cream of experienced Arctic officers and men with them, sailed from Britain in 1845, passed some whalers in Baffin Bay—and were never seen again.

Unable initially to turn south due to ice, Franklin explored Wellington Channel to the north (a secondary possible route in his instructions), wintered at Beechey Island, at the southwest tip of Devon Island, then in 1846 sailed south into Peel Strait—a channel, but not a clear one. North of King William Island they met the multi-year ice seen and described by James Clark

Ross and stuck fast, never to be released. Franklin himself died in June 1847, and the remaining crews, led by Francis Crozier, abandoned the ships and made their way south, heading for the Back River. It was a disaster. The last of the men died at Starvation Cove on the Adelaide Peninsula, just south of King William Island.

In terms of new geographical knowledge, the Franklin expedition contributed nothing, but the extensive searches for the missing ships, which would consume the Admiralty and the British public for the next fifteen years, contributed so much that by the time the fate of Franklin had finally been determined, the basic map of the southern part of the Canadian Arctic had largely been drawn.

The search for Franklin involved scores of ships and thousands of men, and at times became logistically quite complex. There were so many individual expeditions—forty in all—that geographically they are best studied using maps, a number of which were produced by most of

the mapmakers of the day. Map 301 (overleaf) shows the discoveries and explorations of expeditions up to 1854, and a good final summary is shown on the Canadian government map on page 196 (Map 302), after Canada took formal possession of the Arctic islands from Britain in 1880.

Franklin's expedition had supplies for several years, so it was not until 1847 that the first concern was felt. The search methods employed marked a considerable change from exploration methods commonly employed up to that time. Now ships would remain in one place, acting as bases, while sledge parties would fan out from the ships to search. In this way much more ground was covered and, incidentally, much more ground mapped.

In 1848, a three-pronged search was mounted. Firstly, James Clark Ross, with HMS Enterprise and HMS Investigator, approaching from the east, was to follow Franklin's instructed route, but the ice was unco-operative, and he only got as far as the northeastern tip of Somerset Island, although sledge parties did search Barrow Strait and Prince Regent Inlet.

Secondly, Thomas Moore in HMS Plover and Henry Kellett in HMS Herald, the latter diverted from surveying duties in the Pacific, were to search through Bering Strait as far as the Mackenzie Delta. William Pullen and William Hooper actually carried out the search, using boats, in 1849. The following year they went even farther eastwards, reaching Bathurst Inlet.

MAP 298 (*above*).
Map of Robert M'Clure's completion of the Northwest Passage, by ship and sledge, in 1853, drawn by William Fawckner, acting lieutenant of HMS *Breadalbane*, a transport ship that sank near Beechey Island in 1853 after being nipped in the ice. M'Clure's ship HMS *Investigator* was iced in at Mercy Bay, on the north shore of Banks (Baring) Island. Found by Bedford Pim of HMS *Resolute*, stationed at Dealy Island, M'Clure returned with Pim, who thus became the first to make that connecting link from west to east, appropriately enough on a sledge named *John Barrow*, named after the Second Secretary to the Admiralty (to 1845), Sir John Barrow, the man who had started the nineteenth-century search for the Northwest Passage. The track of *Investigator* and the sledge is marked. In 1850, iced in at Princess Royal Islands halfway up Prince of Wales Strait, M'Clure had sledged to Russell Point, at the northeast tip of Banks Island, where he had been able to see Melville Island and thus recognized that he had connected the last link in a Northwest Passage. But he was preparing to abandon his ship and make for the mainland to the south when found by Pim. Although M'Clure found a Northwest Passage, it turned out not to be a practical one, due to the multi-year ice. The practical passage, first suggested by Francis M'Clintock in 1859, first traversed by Roald Amundsen in *Gjøa* in 1903–06, was south down Peel Inlet and along the east coast of King William Island (Land). One of M'Clure's officers, Lieutenant Samuel Gurney Cresswell, returned to England in 1853 in HMS *Phoenix* (its track is marked on the map), thus becoming the first person to completely travel through the Northwest Passage.

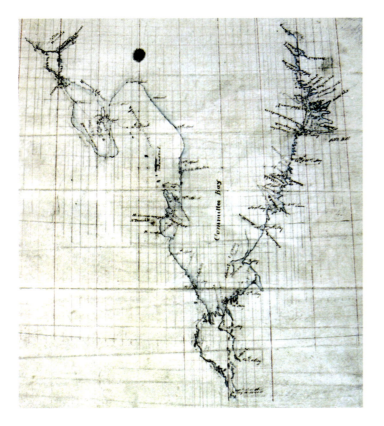

MAP 299 (*left*).
Hudson's Bay Company explorer John Rae finally defined the southern limit of the long arm of the sea that is Prince Regent Inlet and the Gulf of Boothia, a Northwest Passage dead end that had misled several Arctic explorers, including Parry and Ross. This is Committee Bay, mapped by Rae in 1847. It was Rae who, in 1854 while mapping the west coast of the Boothia Peninsula from Thomas Simpson's survey north, discovered the first evidence of Franklin's demise.

MAP 300 (*right*).
John Arrowsmith's map from Francis Leopold M'Clintock's book, 1859. The location at which the Franklin expedition's boats and skeletons were found is marked on the west coast of King William Island.

Finally, a land expedition, led by Franklin's old friend John Richardson, accompanied by John Rae, was sent to search the coast between the Mackenzie and Coppermine Rivers. This was achieved, and in 1850–51 Rae continued the search, this time exploring the southern coast of Victoria Island.

In 1850 a massive effort was launched. Four ships were sent to search from the east. Horatio Austin in HMS *Resolute*, Erasmus Ommanney in HMS *Assistance*, John Bertie Cator in HMS *Intrepid*, and Sherard Osborn in HMS *Pioneer*. In addition that year they were joined by John Ross in a privately financed venture, with *Felix* and *Mary*; and, financed by Lady Jane Franklin, Charles Forsyth in *Prince Albert*. Two others, sponsored by the British government, also joined the effort: William Penny in HMS *Lady Franklin* and Alexander Stewart in HMS *Sophia*. The same year the first American expedition to assist was mounted by Edwin De Haven, sponsored by philanthropist Henry Grinnell. Despite this huge concentration of resources, a lot of coastline was mapped but no sign of Franklin found. Their searches can be followed on MAP 301, above right, and MAP 302, overleaf.

Also in 1850, the Admiralty sent Richard Collinson in HMS *Enterprise* and Robert M'Clure in HMS *Investigator* to search through Bering Strait and then eastwards. Collinson's voyage was to last until 1855, during which he sailed his ship as far east as Cambridge Bay on Victoria Island, a tremendous feat. But it is Robert M'Clure who became famous, for in the five

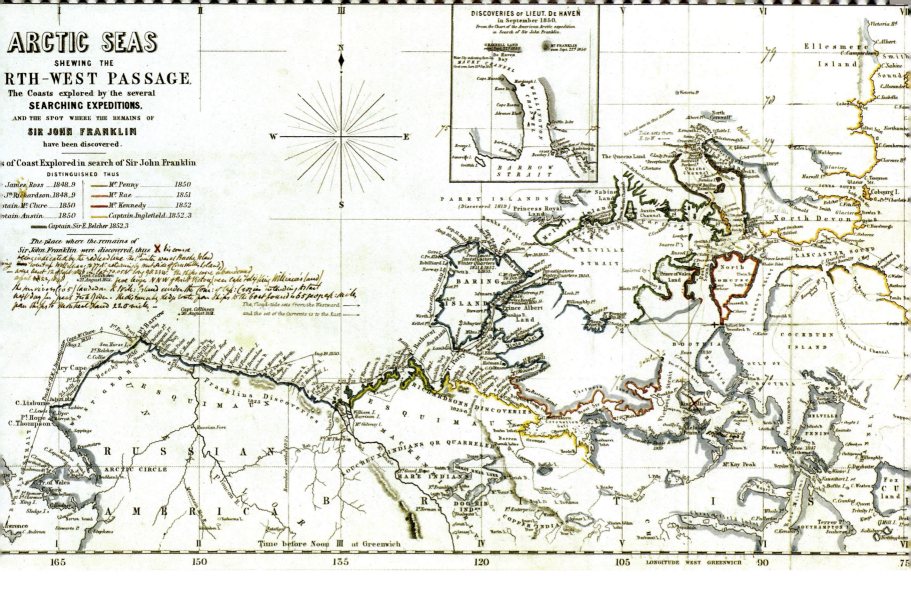

ARCTIC SEAS
SHEWING THE
RTH-WEST PASSAGE,
The Coasts explored by the several
SEARCHING EXPEDITIONS.
AND THE SPOT WHERE THE REMAINS OF
SIR JOHN FRANKLIN
have been discovered.

s of Coast Explored in search of Sir John Franklin
DISTINGUISHED THUS

James Ross ___ 1848.9
Jn. Richardson 1848.9
tain McClure 1850
tain Austin 1850
Mr. Penny 1850
Mr. Rae 1851
Mr. Kennedy 1852
Captain Inglefield 1852.3
Captain Sir E. Belcher 1852.3

The place where the remains of
Sir John Franklin were discovered, thus ✗ his course

years from 1850 to 1855, he managed to, after a fashion, become the first to connect east and west through the Northwest Passage, although only by abandoning his ship in Mercy Bay, on the north coast of Banks Island, and sledging to other search ships iced in at Dealy Island, just east of Parry's Winter Harbour on the south coast of Melville Island. A map of M'Clure's feat is shown here (MAP 298). One of M'Clure's officers, Samuel

Gurney Cresswell, went back to England in 1853 on HMS *Phoenix* (the rest of the crew followed the next year), thus becoming the first to traverse the entire Northwest Passage.

A final massive effort to find Franklin was made in 1852, under the general command of the inept Edward Belcher. Belcher in HMS *Assistance*, Sherard Osborn in HMS *Pioneer*, Henry Kellett in HMS *Resolute*, Francis M'Clintock in HMS *Intrepid*, and William Pullen in HMS *North Star*, the latter used as a base at Beechey Island, again mounted a huge sledge search. It was during this venture that Bedford Pim, a lieutenant on *Resolute*, located Robert M'Clure in Mercy Bay, allowing M'Clure to sledge to the other ships and thus claim the first traverse of the Northwest Passage, which he would not have been able to do independently.

Although Belcher's expedition searched a large area, when four of the ships became iced in, Belcher prematurely ordered their abandonment and arrived back in Britain in 1854 having found nothing but lost four of his five ships.

At this point the British government gave up, reasoning that if Franklin could not be found with such a massive infusion of resources, he was probably never to be found, and was certainly not likely to be alive anyway.

John Rae of the Hudson's Bay Company finally found the first evidence of Franklin's demise, while on a survey to complete the map of the mainland coast on the western side of the southern part of the Boothia Peninsula in

MAP 301 (*above*).
This detailed summary of Arctic exploration carried out as the result of the search for John Franklin was published by the Edinburgh-based commercial map company W. & A. K. Johnston in 1854. Maps such as this were printed in black only, and then coloured by hand-painting all the coasts explored by the various expeditions. The result is an attractive and highly informative map. A notation about the location of Franklin's demise has been written in, probably as the map was published and this information became available in late 1854. The red X on *King William Land* (Island) indicates the presumed location of the Franklin tragedy. There is also additional written detail, added well after publication—it mentions the Franklin expedition boat found by M'Clintock— together with a red line (now faint orange, having faded), drawn to indicate Franklin's probable route.

1854. He purchased from Inuit a silver plate engraved with Franklin's name.

Essentially the final expedition of the Franklin saga was the voyage of Francis M'Clintock, in *Fox*, from 1857 to 1859. His was a private venture financed by Lady Franklin and public subscription. From the eastern end of Bellot Strait, in April to June 1859, M'Clintock made a sledge journey right around King William Island. He found a boat abandoned by Franklin's men and also the only written evidence of the fate of the expedition.

To this day people continue to search for Franklin relics, fascinated by the tale of hardship. In 1993 a scientific expedition found the remains of another boat as well as bones, which when subjected to laboratory tests showed high levels of lead, supporting the idea that Franklin's demise may have been partly due to by lead poisoning from tin cans. They also found evidence of cannibalism.

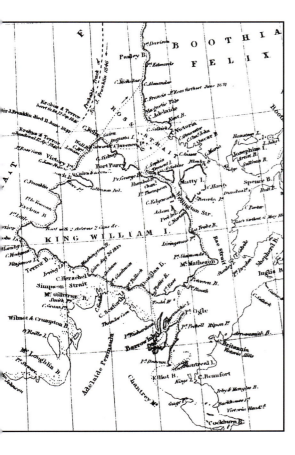

Map 302.
Canadian government map published in 1904, summarizing explorations and discoveries in the Canadian Arctic. The two colour keys have been moved from their original positions on this map.

Westward Expansion of the Fur Trade

With the amalgamation of the North West Company with the Hudson's Bay Company in 1821, the latter inherited all the trading posts west of the Rockies, an area in which it had never traded on its own account.

A vigorous, and a bit tyrannical, new governor, George Simpson, was appointed to oversee the Company's business in North America. Simpson was determined to extract higher profits from the trade, and he set about a program of expansion into new areas that would, it was hoped, provide increased fur production. On his instructions a number of new probes were undertaken into territory hitherto unknown to Europeans.

In 1823, John McLeod was sent on a reconnaisance of the South Nahanni River, which flows into the Liard River west of Fort Simpson, on the Mackenzie. He was to establish trading relations with the natives of the area. He found Virginia Falls, a waterfall on the river that is higher than Niagara. McLeod found few natives, and fewer furs, but did put the Nahanni on the map. He returned briefly in 1824. His expedition was recorded by the Company on their map (Map 304, overleaf).

Murdoch McPherson was the clerk in charge of Fort Liard, which had been established by the North West Company in 1800. In 1824 he was sent to explore the Liard River and its tributary the Beaver; this time the river was found to be rich in furs. McPherson's map is shown here.

In 1821, Samuel Black, a Nor'Wester who had gained a reputation for ruthlessness aimed at the Hudson's Bay Company, was not rehired by the merged company. But by 1823, concerned that he might become an independent rival, Simpson rehired him and sent him on a expedition to explore the Finlay branch of the Peace River. This was the river Alexander Mackenzie had chosen not to pursue in 1793, ascending the Parsnip instead on his way to the Pacific Ocean. Black had read Mackenzie's book, and those of other explorers, and desperately wanted to join that illustrious group. So he jumped at the chance to explore a river as yet unknown to Europeans. George Simpson thought that north of the Finlay there would be another river, this time on the west side of the Rockies, paralleling the Mackenzie and flowing into the Arctic Ocean; Black was instructed to find it.

Wintering at Rocky Mountain Portage on the Peace River, Black heard from native sources that north of the Finlay, there was a river flowing into the Pacific rather than the Arctic. Black set off in the spring of 1824 and located the source of the Finlay, Peace, and Mackenzie Rivers at Thutade Lake. The distance from the lake to the sea is 3 800 km.

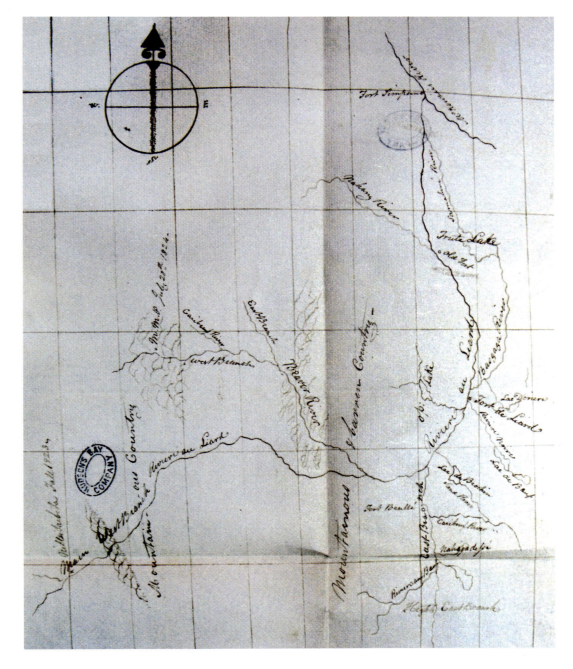

Map 303.
Murdoch McPherson's map of his exploration of the Liard and Beaver Rivers, 1824. His starting point was Fort Simpson, named after new Hudson's Bay Company governor George Simpson, at the confluence of the Liard and the Mackenzie (at top left).

Black then struck north on foot through the mountains, where he found a westward-flowing river that he called the Schadzue. It was the Stikine, and would have been a very useful find for the Hudson's Bay Company had Black followed it to the sea. Although it emerges in what was then the territory of the Russian-American Company in the Alaska panhandle, the Hudson's Bay Company could have controlled the interior part of the river, intercepting the flow of furs to its rival. But Black had very strict orders from Simpson to search for a northward-flowing river, so he did not follow the Stikine.

Black continued north, and on 17 August found a large eastward-flowing river which, he was forced to acknowledge, was likely a tributary of the Liard. It was. Black named it Turnagain River, for this was where he gave up; it is still called by this name, and it is a tributary of the Kechika, a feeder of the Liard. Black's discoveries are very well shown on the Company map overleaf (Map 304).

In 1831, John McLeod was sent to explore the headwaters of the Liard River itself, a tall order due to the incredible ferocity with which the river flows over rapids and waterfalls, and through canyons. McLeod thought he had reached the source of the river at a lake he named Simpson's Lake, on the Frances River (which he thought was the main stream of the Liard) just north of the modern community of Watson Lake, on the British Columbia–Yukon boundary. On the return journey his canoe was dashed to pieces and several of his men drowned.

Map 304.
This is part of the 1824 Aaron Arrowsmith map of North America that belonged to the Hudson's Bay Company. The printed map probably contained information up to about 1822. The explorations of Company men have been added on patches of paper stuck onto the map, and the new information drawn. At the time, this would therefore have been the most up-to-date map of the region in existence, and it now provides a unique record of the Company's new geographical knowledge between 1822 and 1825. John McLeod's 1822 exploration of the South Nahanni is indicated, but the major addition is that of Samuel Black's exploration up the Finlay River (*Finlay's Branch*) in 1824. His Turnagain River (*River Turn again*), a tributary of the Kechika, itself a tributary of the Liard, is shown, as is his "Schadzue," shown here as the *Shehadzue*—it is the Stikine. Thutade Lake (*Tutade L.*), found by Black and the ultimate source of the entire Mackenzie River system, is also shown. The map in addition shows Fort Kilmaurs (*Kilmaurs Ft. or Babine Ft.*), established by the Company on Babine Lake in 1822, and *Simpson's R.*, flowing out of Babine Lake and by a dashed line to Observatory Inlet. This is the Skeena River, confused for many years with the Nass (which actually flows to Observatory Inlet). "Simpson's River" was even legally the northern limit of the new colony of British Columbia for some time after its establishment in 1858 (see Map 322, page 206). *Fort St. James* and *Fraser's Lake Ft* are shown. They were founded by Simon Fraser for the North West Company in 1806. Farther south, the initial exploration of the lower Fraser Valley by James McMillan in 1824 is recorded on this map; three years later, McMillan would be sent to found Fort Langley on the lower Fraser.

In 1834 McLeod ascended another tributary of the Liard, the Dease, which flowed in from the southwest. He found Dease Lake, then westward-flowing waters that turned out to be the Stikine. This time the Company realized their significance. In 1838 Robert Campbell was sent to open a communication between the Mackenzie District and the Hudson's Bay Company posts on the coast. Led by natives, Campbell attended a great native trading rendezvous at the junction of the Stikine and Tahltan Rivers.

Two years later, ascending the Liard, Robert Campbell made his way beyond McLeod's Simpson Lake on the Frances River, discovering Frances Lake (which he named after Simpson's wife) and a short river, the Finlayson, that runs into it. Following this river he arrived at a short portage to a west-flowing river, the Pelly. Though he did not realize it at the time, the Pelly is part of the Yukon River system. Map 307 was drawn by Campbell to illustrate his find.

To the north, John Bell had explored the Peel River in 1839 and in 1840 had opened Peel

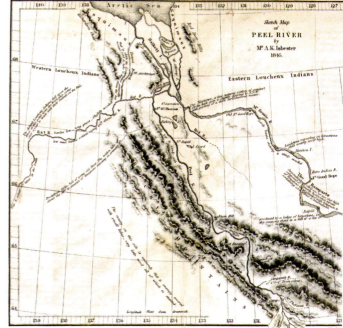

Map 305 (right).
Alexander Kennedy Isbister's map of Fort McPherson (Peel River Post) and area. The Rat River is shown flowing in from the west; at one point this river actually mingles with the Bell, even though they flow to different oceans. The place was discovered by Isbister in 1841, but the significance of the find was not realized at the time. Isbister was a Métis clerk under John Bell. His original map has not survived, but this engraved copy was published by the Royal Geographical Society in 1845. Isbister left the Hudson's Bay Company in 1842 and became a lawyer. Clearly a man of many talents, he also wrote a treatise on the geology of the Arctic.

River Post, later Fort McPherson. The following year, his clerk, Alexander Isbister, found a connection between two small rivers, the Rat and the Bell, which flows to the Porcupine and then to the Yukon. Due to ice and snow, he did not realize they were separate rivers; both are shown as the Rat on his map (Map 305).

Bell, however, looking for a way over the mountains, did find a river in 1842 he called the Little Bell, and in 1844 he followed it to the Bell, the Porcupine, and then to a larger, westward-flowing river. This was the Yukon. His route and the rivers are shown on the northern part of Map 306. In 1847, senior clerk Alexander Murray founded Fort Yukon where the Porcupine met the Yukon; it would later prove to be in American territory and have to be abandoned.

Perceptions of river courses in this region were confused by the widespread feeling that Bell's Yukon and Campbell's Pelly were another river called the Colville, the Arctic Ocean mouth of which had been discovered in 1837 by Thomas Simpson and Peter Warren Dease. In fact the Colville is a short and relatively insignificant river.

Impressed with the trade possibilities of the Pelly River, Robert Campbell established Fort Selkirk in 1848, where that river meets the Yukon River. In 1852 it would be sacked by Chilkat natives and have to be abandoned.

The part of the Yukon above Fort Selkirk is sometimes referred to as the Lewes River, and it is shown as this on Map 306.

Campbell set off in June 1851 from Fort Selkirk on a final exploration of the Yukon River and soon after came to Murray's Fort Yukon at the mouth of the Porcupine. Thus Campbell proved that his Pelly River and the river John Bell had discovered in 1844 were one and the same. The puzzle of the river pattern in the northwestern corner of the American continent had been solved.

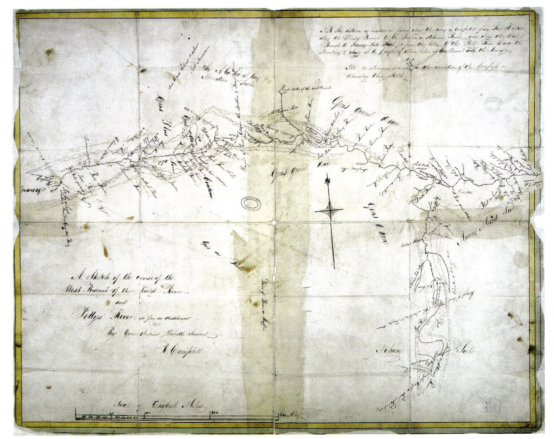

The Rebellions of 1837 and the United Province of Canada

In the 1830s, bad weather and insect infestations worked with poor farming practices to bring Lower Canada to the point of starvation. With rampant cholera and increased immigration from Britain, the embers of incipient French-Canadian nationalism were fanned into flames. The nationalists were led by Louis-Joseph Papineau and his Parti Patriote. After failed attempts in the legislature to withhold monies for government, the Patriotes held protest rallies and prepared for an armed insurrection.

The British government, however, had seen the rebellion coming, and had dispatched troops to hold Lower Canada. On 16 November, the government tried to arrest Patriote leaders, but they escaped. On 23 November British troops were defeated at Saint-Denis-sur-Richelieu, northwest of Montréal, but two days later the Patriotes were defeated at nearby Saint-Charles. On 14 December the British captured Saint-Eustache, a short distance east of Montréal, after a fierce battle, and the rebellion collapsed, to much looting and burning by British volunteers. Papineau fled to the United States. Other attempts at armed rebellion during 1838 were quickly defeated, mainly by volunteers.

In Upper Canada, rebels took advantage of the fact that British regulars had been sent to quell the rebellion in Lower Canada. Initially, a Reform Party under William Lyon Mackenzie had only intended to pressure the government, but on

Map 308.
After the defeat of the Upper Canada rebels by Loyalist forces, the rebel leader William Lyon Mackenzie escaped to Navy Island, in the Niagara River, and there proclaimed a Republic of Upper Canada. The new "republic" collapsed on 14 January 1838, after volunteers burned the rebel supply ship *Caroline*. Americans supporting the rebellion continued sorties into Canada during 1838, notably at Pelee Island, at the southern end of Lake Erie, in February; across the Niagara into the Short Hills in June; and at Prescott, on the St. Lawrence northeast of Kingston, in November, at the so-called Battle of the Windmill. In each case the invaders were repelled by British forces and volunteers.

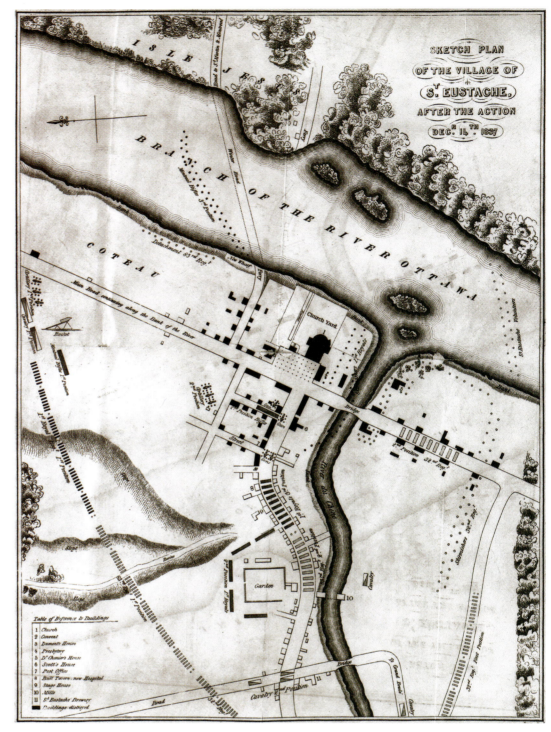

Map 309 (*above*).
A plan of the final major battle of the rebellion in Lower Canada, that at Saint-Eustache, fought on 14 December 1837. Despite resisting fiercely, the Patriotes were crushed.

16 November 1837 it issued a draft constitution for Upper Canada based on that of the United States. On 5 December a force of perhaps 700 rebels marched down Yonge Street in Toronto but were dispersed by a Loyalist group of 250 volunteers, and on 8 December a Loyalist force of over 1,000 marched to Montgomery's Tavern, about 3 km north of Toronto, and routed the rebels.

The rebellions led to the appointment of Lord Durham as governor general, and the famous Durham Report recommended that the Canadas be united and that responsible government be introduced. The Act of Union was passed by the British Parliament in 1840 and the United Province of Canada—divided into Canada East and Canada West—was born the following year. The first capital was Kingston.

Map 310 (*below*).
An 1841 plan of Kingston showing proposed improvements. Kingston was chosen as the capital of the new United Province of Canada. This "plan to regulate [Kingston's] extension" was submitted by Robert Gourlay, a reformer and man of many causes. He urged the people of Kingston to recognize that their city would grow by virtue of its status as a capital city.

Linking the Lakes

The Welland Canal, the vital link in the St. Lawrence and Great Lakes system that bypasses Niagara Falls, grew as an extension of a plan by WilliamHamilton Merritt, a sawmill owner, to feed water to his mills on Twelve Mile Creek, which emptied into Lake Ontario at Port Weller, near St. Catharines. The Welland was promoted as a foil to the American Erie Canal, construction of which started in 1817. The Erie, opened in 1825, allowed ships to travel from Buffalo to Albany and thence down the Hudson to New York, completely bypassing Montréal.

After delay caused by the concern that the proposed canal was too near the American border, the first Welland Canal was begun in 1824 and completed in 1829. It connected the Welland River with Twelve Mile Creek, which emptied into Lake Ontario.

The Welland Canal Company was taken over by the government in 1841 and a more direct route cut through to Port Colbourne on Lake Erie. In addition, locks were enlarged to accommodate the new steamships then coming into use. The improved canal opened in 1845.

Since then, there have been two further major new canals dug, opening in 1887 and 1932. Today a 100-m lift is gained with just eight locks, compared to the original canal's forty.

MAP 311.
Proposals for various routes for the first Welland Canal are shown in this 1826 map, drawn before the first canal was completed.

MAP 312 (right).
The general line proposed for the second canal, which allowed ships to continue south into Lake Erie rather than take the diversion via the Welland River, which flows into the Niagara. The part of the Welland River used for the first canal leads east (right) from Port Robinson, about halfway down the map.

MAP 313 (below).
Details of the proposed improvements and realignments for the second canal, completed in 1845. North is oriented to the bottom right, and the line of new locks forms the *Line proposed for steamboat navigation* visible on MAP 312, between the villages of St. Catharines and Thorold. The first canal is shown in blue, the new second canal in yellow; the water supply arrangement is shown in red. This map, and MAP 312, were drawn for or by Lieutenant Colonel George Phillpotts of the British army for a report on the inland navigation of the Canadas.

Drawing the Line—
the Webster-Ashburton Treaty

The boundary between the new United States and British territories after the American War of Independence had been described in the Treaty of Paris of 1783, but, as we have seen (page 124), because of incomplete geographical knowledge, reflected in the maps used, the line as described in the treaty was in places at best ambiguous and at worst, impossible. And the Treaty of Ghent, which ended the War of 1812, had simply returned the boundary to where it was before the war.

One particularly ambiguous area had always been the Maine–Québec–New Brunswick boundary. One part of this boundary had been settled in 1796–98, along the St. Croix River; although referred to in the 1783 treaty, there was at that time no river clearly of that name, and it had been decided that the Chiputneticook River was meant. This is the river today called the St. Croix.

In 1830, Britain and the United States had agreed to submit their respective claims to an arbitrator, the king of the Netherlands, for a decision, but his award, handed down in 1831, adopted a compromise between the two claims. This the Americans considered beyond his mandate and, pressured by Maine, they rejected it.

In 1842, the parties agreed again to negotiate a settlement of the boundary. The American commissioner was Daniel Webster, the secretary of state, and the British commissioner was Alexander Baring, Baron Ashburton, a famous British banker.

After a series of meetings they hammered out an agreement in which the northern boundary of Maine was taken as that proposed by the king of the Netherlands, but the northwest Maine-Québec boundary was adjusted in favour of Britain to be some distance from the St. Lawrence. Even so, there was a storm in Britain over the "lost" territory; one newspaper said Ashburton had been "bullied, or bamboozled, or both."

The 1842 treaty also described for the first time the boundary from Lake Huron to Lake of the Woods. Now the international boundary was settled from the Atlantic to the Rocky Mountains.

Map 314 (*left*).
This British map, drawn in 1814 and published in 1817, shows one British interpretation of the boundary line between Maine and Québec and New Brunswick. Naturally enough, British territory dominates.

Map 315 (*right*).
A detail of Joseph Bouchette's map of the Canadas, 1831. The thin yellow line near the top of the map shows the boundary claimed by the United States; that claimed by Britain is the red and green line farther south.

Map 316 (*below*).
Published in 1842 by London mapmaker James Wyld to illustrate the Webster-Ashburton agreement, this map shows the boundary claimed by the United States (thin red line at top), the boundary claimed by Britain (thin red line in the middle of the map), and the 1831 award of the king of Holland (who, when he started on the arbitration, was king of the Netherlands, but lost the Belgian half of his kingdom to a revolt in October 1830). This is the orange and green boundary on its northern part only. The balance of the northwestern boundary, also in orange and green, is the final adjustment, away from the strategic St. Lawrence, negotiated by Ashburton and Webster.

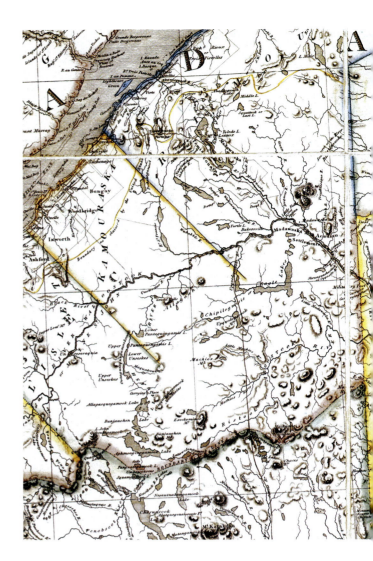

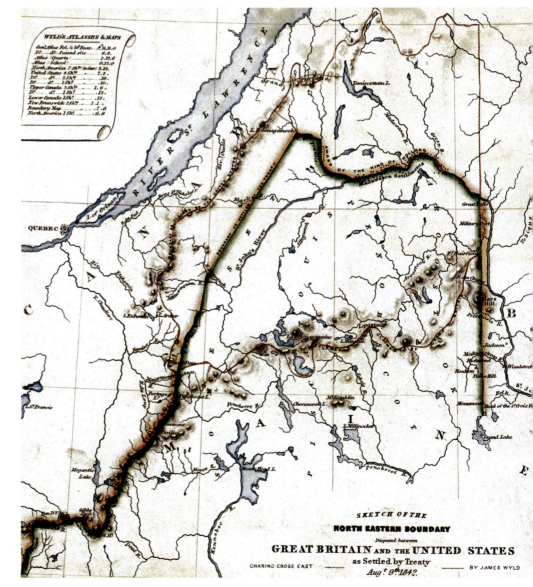

The Founding of Fort Victoria and the Colony of Vancouver Island

The Hudson's Bay Company inherited the fur territories of the North West Company west of the Rocky Mountains when the two merged in 1821. In 1824–25, the Company established its regional headquarters at Fort Vancouver on the lower Columbia River, and in 1827 the trading post of Fort Langley on the lower Fraser.

Fort Vancouver had never been considered very healthy due to its low-lying situation next to the wide Columbia, and from time to time other possible locations had been considered. In 1837, Chief Factor John McLoughlin sent Captain William McNeill in the company steamer *Beaver* to examine harbours farther north. He selected Victoria Harbour as the most promising location. McLoughlin and James Douglas, his senior trader, visited the site later that year, but McLoughlin preferred Fort Vancouver, so no action was taken.

However, the governor of the Hudson's Bay Company, George Simpson, could see the writing on the wall; American settlers were pouring into Oregon, and he felt it was only a matter of time before the joint occupancy of the Oregon Country would end and the British would lose the Columbia. He was, of course, correct. If the Company had to retreat northwards, then the best location for their new headquarters, it was reasoned, would be on Vancouver Island, because it could be more easily defended.

Simpson sent James Douglas, accompanied by Adolphus Lee Lewes as surveyor, to Vancouver Island to determine a specific site for a new Company post. Douglas selected Camosack, or Camosun Inlet, now Victoria Harbour, as the site. "The place appears a perfect Eden, in the midst of the dreary wilderness," wrote Douglas. With Lewes he drew a map showing their recommended site, really a land-use map, for it shows the distribution of meadow and forest lands around the site (MAP 317).

Douglas's recommendation was accepted, and on 13 March 1843 Douglas arrived back in Victoria Harbour with fifteen men to begin building the new Fort Victoria.

In 1849, after the drawing of the forty-ninth parallel boundary, the Company officially moved its Columbia Department headquarters to Fort Victoria. The whole of Vancouver Island was created a new British colony, and ceded to the Hudson's Bay Company for a rent of seven shillings a year, on condition that the Company establish settlements within five years.

Initial settlement was very slow, for the Company did not really want settlement, although they did want Vancouver Island. It would take a gold rush in 1858 (see page 206) to jump-start real population growth.

MAP 317 (*above*).
The first map of Victoria, British Columbia. Drawn in 1842 by James Douglas and Adolphus Lee Lewes, it was included with their report recommending the site of Fort Victoria, shown as a red square. Forests are dark green, "plains" light green, marshy areas yellow.

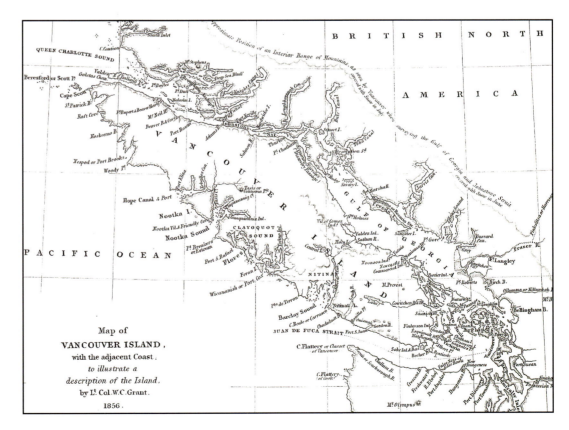

MAP 318.
A map of the Colony of Vancouver Island, drawn for Walter Colquhoun Grant, the island's first settler, who was also the Hudson Bay Company's first land surveyor. With eight others, Grant established himself at Sooke, southwest of Fort Victoria. Although he personally did not stay, this marked the beginning of the European population of today's British Columbia.

The Forty-ninth Parallel Extends to the Sea

In 1818, unable to determine the boundary between American and British territory west of the Rocky Mountains, the Convention of that year had left the Oregon Country, from 42° N to 54´ 40° N, as an area of "joint occupancy" for ten years (see page 180).

Although renewed at the end of the ten years, the joint-occupancy agreement was an ongoing problem for the Hudson's Bay Company, which saw an increasing number of American settlers pour across the Rockies. In 1843, seeing the writing on the wall, the Company relocated its Columbia Department headquarters to Fort Victoria.

In 1841 a visit by an American expedition led by Charles Wilkes led the American government to realize that they needed Puget Sound, as it was the only good harbour north of San Francisco. In 1845, James Polk, an expansionist, became president and pressed for the cession of the whole Oregon Country to the United States. A slogan of his election platform had been the famous "Fifty-four forty or fight!"

There were many proposals for a compromise boundary. The British wanted the Columbia River, then fell back to a proposal that would have given the Americans the Olympic Peninsula but not Puget Sound. But Puget Sound was the desired prize. The Americans seemed ready to fight; in fact, this is just what they were about to do farther south, taking California from the Mexicans.

The British Foreign Secretary, Lord Aberdeen, was not very strong-willed, and the British government at that time was engrossed in domestic problems and did not want a foreign war. So, when the Americans proposed a simple extension of the forty-ninth parallel to the Pacific, right through Vancouver Island (it is marked on MAP 319, right), he was amenable, provided Vancouver Island, with its new Hudson's Bay Company fort, was left as British. This was the

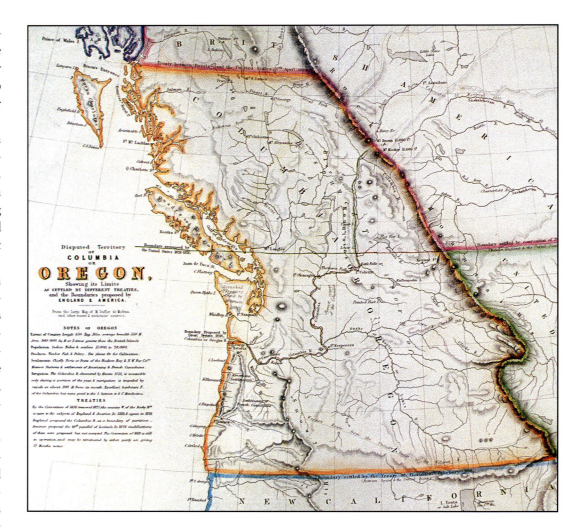

compromise agreed upon, and, except for a dispute over the definition of the boundary through the San Juan Islands (which was settled in 1872), the present-day boundary was defined. The Oregon Treaty, called by the Americans the Treaty of Washington, was signed on 15 June 1846. The boundary was surveyed between 1857 and 1862.

During a resurvey in 1901–07, it was found that the boundary had been marked not at 49° N, but a few hundred metres north of that line. On 11 April 1908 a new treaty was signed, accepting the boundary as surveyed, rather than as defined in the 1846 treaty.

MAP 319 (above).
The Oregon Country—today's British Columbia and the states of Washington and Oregon—is shown on this map published in January 1846. The American proposal of a forty-ninth parallel boundary right through Vancouver Island is marked.

MAP 320 (below).
This 1858 map by James Wyld does not yet depict British Columbia, but *British Territory*. It shows the boundary at 49° N but the British interpretation of the 1846 treaty, with the San Juan Islands included as British. After some sabre-rattling during the so-called Pig War, when an American settler shot a Hudson's Bay Company pig, joint occupation of San Juan Island was agreed to, and between 1860 and 1872 there were both British and American military camps on the island. Finally, an arbitration award by the German kaiser in 1872 gave the islands to the Americans.

A Pioneer Road Map of Canada

It is often not fully appreciated how difficult it was to move around the country before the coming of the railway. Rivers and lakes remained vital components of communication until the aviation era. Early roads tended to be no more than tracks, where the vegetation was removed but little else was done. Well into the twentieth century automobiles habitually got stuck in the mud.

Nevertheless, there were some good roads, and by the middle of the nineteenth century some—but very few—had even been "macadamized." This was a process invented in Britain by John McAdam in 1815 where layers of successively smaller stones were laid on top of one another to yield a tolerable surface. This should not be confused with "tarmacadamizing," which

created the hard surface we know today—the "tarmac." Many macadamized Canadian roads made do with much less stone than McAdam had intended.

Other roads had been planked, forming a wooden road, which was a reasonable surface but one that did not last long. Others were made of unsawn logs, creating a bone-jarring corrugated surface for horses or people.

About 1850, the British army authorized the mapping of all the roads in Upper Canada, and the task fell to Major Baron de Rottenburg, the assistant quartermaster general. He collected information from just about every local map he could find and created an enormous (5.88 x 3.72 m) twelve-section map. Not only did he classify the

roads by type, but he also added the accommodation possibilites, noting the number of men and horses that could be billeted in each location—information that was of importance to the military. Rottenburg's map was probably the first true road map of any major part of Canada.

MAP 321.
Part of one sheet of Baron de Rottenburg's road map of Upper Canada, drawn about 1850, showing the Niagara Peninsula. The beige-coloured areas are cleared land. Macadamized roads are black; planked roads, "country and concession roads," and "principally travelled roads other than Plank or McAdamized ones," are shown in red, now difficult to distinguish from each other; and "obscure roads" are uncoloured. Notes indicate the condition of some roads. Railways are also shown (with cross-marks). The numbers in circles are distances between the two nearest marked places, a convention seen on modern road maps. The pairs of numbers at settlements are the number of men (first figure) and horses (second figure) that could be billeted there.

British Columbia Discovers Gold and Becomes a Colony

In 1858, gold was discovered in sandbars of the canyons of the Fraser and Thompson Rivers, and before the year was out, over 25,000 gold seekers had streamed into what is now mainland British Columbia, then termed New Caledonia.

This sudden influx of American "adventurers" was of considerable concern to James Douglas, governor of Vancouver Island. Douglas had seen how American settlers flooding into the Oregon Country in the 1840s had led to the loss of territory, and he decided to use his initiative to prevent this happening again. As Douglas exercised control, most assumed he had the legal authority to do so, and a firm British hand was kept on the mainland territory.

In the meantime, a new British Colonial Secretary, Edward Bulwer Lytton—an erstwhile novelist who once began a book with the legendary words "It was a dark and stormy night"—had persuaded his cabinet colleagues that the time was right to create a new colony west of the Rocky Mountains, to counterbalance the influence of the Americans to the south.

The bill to create a new colony, New Caledonia, was proposed to the British Parliament on 1 July 1858. The bill was passed on 2 August, but not before Queen Victoria had intervened to change the name of the new colony to British Columbia. Douglas was appointed the governor; he was sworn in at Fort Langley on 19 November 1858.

A detachment of Royal Engineers was sent to British Columbia to lay out towns and build roads. The new capital of New Westminster was selected by the Royal Engineers' commanding officer, Richard Clement Moody. It was considered a more defensible site than Derby, the first proposed site, near Fort Langley on the south side of the Fraser River. MAP 322 shows the plan for

the city as laid out by the Royal Engineers; it was originally called Albert City (MAP 323) until, once again, the name was changed by Queen Victoria.

The colonies of British Columbia, the mainland territory, and Vancouver Island were separate until 1866, when they amalgamated to form one colony, which took the mainland name, British Columbia. In 1871, the colony became the Province of British Columbia on joining Canada.

MAP 322 (below).
The plan for the new capital of British Columbia, New Westminster, laid out by the Royal Engineers in 1861.

MAP 323 (below, inset).
New Westminster's original name of Albert City shown on an 1858 map, before Queen Victoria changed the name.

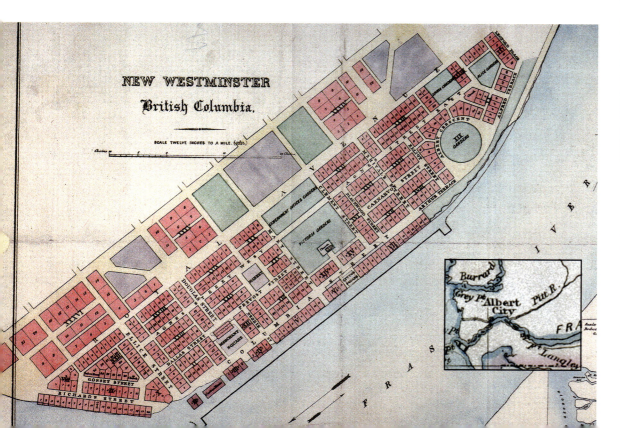

MAP 324 (above, top).
Published on 29 August 1858, only twenty-seven days after the official creation of British Columbia, this map was probably the first to show the new colony. The northern boundary is shown at the non-existent *Simpson's River*.

MAP 325 (above).
This map, drawn about 1860 by Lieutenant Richard Charles Mayne, a Royal Engineer, shows the gold-mining activities on the various sandbars in the Fraser Canyon.

Henry Hind's Expeditions

Scientific explorations were in vogue from the middle of the nineteenth century, in Canada as elsewhere. With increasing pressure on the Hudson's Bay Company to relinquish Rupert's Land, the Canadian and British governments were interested in assessing the land for its agricultural, and thus settlement, potential. Three expeditions were organized, one led by John Palliser (see overleaf) and two by Henry Youle Hind, a university professor of geology and chemistry from Toronto.

Hind's first expedition explored the country between Lake Superior and the Red River "with a view to determine the best route for opening a communication" for settlers. It was officially led by George Gladman, a retired Hudson's Bay Company man, and Hind was the principal scientist.

In 1857, the Canadian Red River Exploring Expedition, as it was known, explored the West as far as the Red River, and Hind was able to recommend a route for settlers that would take only twenty-two days from Liverpool to the Red River Settlement. His report also considered the agricultural potential of the Red and Assiniboine River valleys, and one of his conclusions was that the lack of a market due to the difficulty of transportation was hindering the growth of the population.

The following year, Hind was asked by the Canadian government to explore farther west. He was to study the geology, natural history, topography, meteorology, and potential river navigation, and the forest and soil resources, all with a view to assessing agricultural potential. This

The Hind expedition camped on the banks of the Red River in 1857. Birchbark north canoes such as this one were often used by fur traders and explorers alike as shelter for the night. *(Photo: National Archives of Canada)*

"Assinniboine [*sic*] and Saskatchewan Exploring Expedition" took place during 1858.

Unlike John Palliser, Hind wrote a two-volume book about his two expeditions, which did much to promote settlement in the Northwest, although immigration on a massive scale would have to await the coming of the Canadian Pacific Railway (see page 218). Hind's book was a veritable cornucopia of information on the resources of the region.

MAP 326 (*right*).
A map from Henry Hind's 1860 book showing the "fertile belt"—the yellow-coloured area—stretching in a great arc from the Red River to the foothills of the Rocky Mountains. Information west of the forks of the Saskatchewan was taken from Palliser's paper, which the British government published in the same year. Hind subscribed to the view that the land farther south was too arid for agriculture, being an extension of the "Great American Desert." A major conclusion of Hind's was that this fertile belt could be settled and cultivated from just west of Lake of the Woods to the Rockies, and that any future "line of communication" should traverse it; the first line surveyed for the Canadian Pacific Railway followed this northern route. Hind utilized David Thompson's 1814 map (MAP 246, pages 166–67), recently acquired by the government of Canada West (Ontario).

MAP 327 (*below*).
Henry Hind's own map—covered with copious notes—showing the route from Lake Superior to the Red River Settlement, from the 1857 expedition.

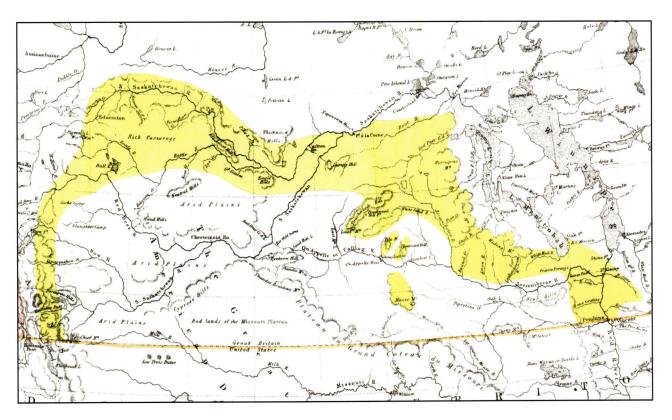

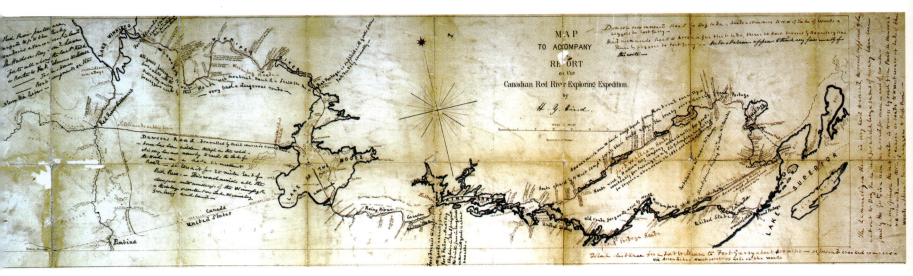

The Palliser Expedition

John Palliser liked adventure. In 1847–48 he spent eleven months hunting buffalo and other animals in the American Great Plains. By 1857 his wanderlust had again gotten the better of him. Though an Irish landowner, Palliser didn't have a lot of money to indulge his passion for exploration, so he submitted a plan to Britain's Royal Geographical Society; the plan called for him to explore west from the Red River Settlement to the Rocky Mountains, along the as yet unsurveyed forty-ninth parallel international boundary.

The society expanded the original plan into a full-scale scientific expedition and asked the British government to support it. Since both the Canadian and British governments were wondering at this time what to do about the Hudson's Bay Company's trading monopoly over Rupert's Land, the timing of the request was propitious. The request for support was granted, and additional scientists were added to the party. Geologist James Hector, French botanist Eugène Bourgeau, astronomical observer James Sullivan, and magnetic observer and Royal Artillery officer Thomas Blakiston became members, and suddenly Palliser found himself in charge of a sizable government-backed scientific expedition.

For the next three years, Palliser and his colleagues criss-crossed the Prairies. Although the expedition had initially only been intended, like Hind's, to take a single year, Palliser had not completed his work and twice obtained an extension of time and funding. In 1858 and 1859 they crossed the Rocky Mountains, mapping no less than six passes, including the little-known Kananaskis Pass, named by Palliser after a native guide.

James Hector did a lot of exploring on his own, and it was he who found Kicking Horse Pass, so-named by Hector after being injured by his horse. Today it is the route taken by the Canadian Pacific Railway and the Trans-Canada Highway. In 1859 Hector, searching for more passes, found Howse Pass, originally discovered by Hudson's Bay Company trader Joseph Howse in 1810.

As a result of the work of Palliser, Hector, and the others, the southern part of the Canadian Rockies was mapped accurately for the first time, with all its major passes. The map of the Prairies and the Rockies was "hung" on fourteen locations that Palliser—or, rather, Sullivan—had fixed astronomically. Everything else was mapped in relation to these fixed points. When Palliser

got back to London, all the data was handed over to the veteran Arrowsmith firm of mapmakers, where John Arrowsmith spent long hours putting it all together. He took so long, in fact, that the Colonial Office became impatient and took the work away from him, sending it to his rival Edward Stanford, so that the final map, published in 1865, has the attribution "Stanford's Geographical Estab^t," ignoring Arrowsmith's contribution. As can be seen from the small portion of this map reproduced here (MAP 328, below), this now famous map was very comprehensive and detailed. It was considered so good a map that all surveys in the Northwest for a long time afterwards used the Palliser map as their base.

Palliser's expedition was undoubtedly itself the most comprehensive that had yet been attempted. As one Hudson's Bay Company man said, "They did not let a flower or a fly or an insect escape their spectacles and their nets." Bourgeau, the botanist, collected 10,000 dried specimens of 819 species belonging to 349 genera for the collection at the Royal Botanical Gardens at Kew. Hector made observations of mammals, reptiles, and insects as well as geology. He collected mountains of fossils and geological

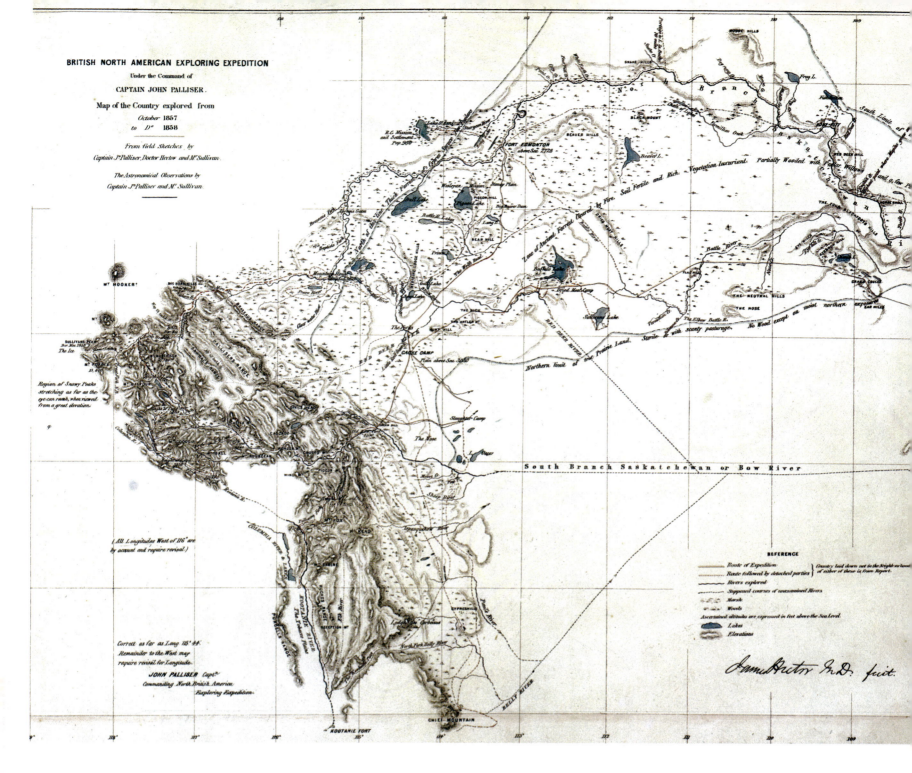

BRITISH NORTH AMERICAN EXPLORING EXPEDITION

Under the Command of

CAPTAIN JOHN PALLISER.

Map of the Country explored from

October 1857

to D° 1858

From field Sketches by

Captain J.ᵗ Palliser, Doctor Hector and M.ᵗ Sullivan.

The Astronomical Observations by

Captain J.ᵗ Palliser and M.ᵗ Sullivan.

MAP 328 (*left*).
Part of the large map of western Canada published in the last of John Palliser's reports, in 1865. The data collected by his expedition had been collated and mapped by John Arrowsmith and Edward Stanford, the two commercial map titans of their day. The area shown is that around the Hudson's Bay Company post of Fort Edmonton, on the North Saskatchewan River. Note the plethora of comments regarding the nature of the soil, vegetation, topography, and more. The development of the lithographic printing process had made it comparatively easy to add comments like these to a map—which was perhaps just as well for Palliser.

MAP 329 (*above*).
Part of the map James Hector drew in 1858 as he recorded the myriad of scientific details he observed. This portion is of southern Alberta and the Rocky Mountains. The map is signed *James Hector M. D. facit* ("James Hector made it"). The dashed red line shows Hector's routes through the Rockies. At the left of the map, near the *Region of Snowy Peaks*, is Hector's route through the pass he named after the cause of his accident there—*Kicking Horse Pass*. Today it is the main route through the southern Rockies, through which pass both the Trans-Canada Highway and the main Canadian Pacific rail line. The map has biogeographical details such as *North of this line Thick Forrest* that were transferred also to the published summary map of the expedition (MAP 328, left). *Mountain House* is Rocky Mountain House; *Fort Edmonton* (Edmonton) is marked, but not Calgary, which was not founded until 1875 (see page 230).

specimens, and drew fifty-one geological sections. His geological map was considered "the first really trust-worthy general geological map of the interior portions of British North America."

But Palliser is really remembered today for his delineation of what has come to be known as "Palliser's Triangle," the triangular-shaped zone south of the so-called fertile belt that Palliser considered to be an arid or semi-arid desert, destined, as his report put it, to "forever be comparatively worthless" for agriculture, except for a few exceptions. It was thought to be a northward extension of the "Great American Desert," an inaccurate concept in vogue at the time. The term "desert" was used more loosely then than now, and just about any thirsty-looking region could be labelled a desert by European explorers accustomed to the lush green fields of their homes; Palliser, of course, came from Ireland. Hector wrestled with the problem; he thought there was enough moisture to support more vegetation than existed, but finally attributed the aridity to the "excess of evaporation over rainfall."

Palliser's arid triangle was one reason why the original line for the Canadian Pacific Railway followed a northerly course, only reverting to a southern route at the urgings of botanist John Macoun (see page 219). Palliser was wrong, but not completely wrong. As settlement progressed westwards, it was first attracted to the "fertile belt" north of Palliser's Triangle. And during the low-rainfall years of the 1920s, it was the dry areas within Palliser's Triangle that lost the most population. Today irrigation alleviates the worst problems of drought, and the region has become some of the finest wheat-growing land in the world.

The work of the Palliser expedition was a vital forerunner to the European settlement of the Prairies, providing volumes of information on the resources of this vast region. Palliser's comprehensive map is a valuable record of the geography of the Prairies before any substantial European settlement.

The Coming of the Railway

Samson, Canada's oldest surviving railway locomotive, is preserved at the Museum of Industry in Stellarton, Nova Scotia. Although the locomotive was controlled from the rear, the firebox was stoked from the front, a dangerous and uncomfortable process.

Most of Canada's first railways were portage railways, designed to meet river traffic and ferry it past rapids. The very first was a portage intended to shorten the distance to Montréal, from boats coming north on the Richelieu River. Instead of making the longer trip by water via Sorel, where the Richelieu meets the St. Lawrence, passengers met a train at Saint-Jean and were transported to La Prairie, opposite Montréal, where another boat ferried them across the river to the city. This was the Champlain and St. Lawrence Railroad, opened on 21 July 1836.

The second railway in Canada, in Nova Scotia, opened in 1838 to transport coal from Albion Mines (now Stellarton) to Pictou Harbour. *Samson* (pictured above) ran on this railway and was the first on the continent to burn coal and run on all-steel rails. It is now the oldest surviving Canadian locomotive.

Canada's third railway was not opened until 19 November 1847, then promptly shut

down again for the winter. This was the Montréal and Lachine Railroad, which paralleled the Lachine Canal; both were built to circumvent the St. Louis Rapids on the St. Lawrence.

Other short portage railways followed, but by the 1850s there was more interest in long-distance lines. The world's first international railway, from Longueuil, across the river from Montréal, to Portland, Maine, an ice-free harbour on the Atlantic coast, was inaugurated on 18 July 1853. Thus travel to Montréal from Europe was freed from the restrictions of the ice-bound St. Lawrence in winter. In January 1855 the Great Western Railway line between Niagara Falls and Windsor was opened, and later that year, the Ontario, Simcoe and Huron Rail-

way line was completed from Toronto to Lake Huron. By the 1860s, the Great Western Railway had a considerable network of lines in the western part of Ontario.

The Grand Trunk Railway, which had been planned as a continuous line from the Atlantic

MAP 330 (*left*).
The short pioneer line, opened in 1838, on which *Samson* ran is shown on this part of an 1849 geological map; the black-coloured area represents coal formations. Coal was carried from Albion Mines, now Stellarton, to Pictou Harbour.

MAP 331 (*above*).
Detail of a map dated 1851 showing the terminus of the Champlain and St. Lawrence Railroad at La Prairie, opposite Montréal. This railway was Canada's first, opening in 1836.

MAP 332 (*below*).
Another part of the same map, this time showing Canada's third railway, the Montréal and Lachine Railroad; it opened in 1847. The line followed the route of the Lachine Canal, completed in 1825, and for the same purpose—to avoid the rapids on the St. Lawrence. For many years it connected with steamers at Lachine. The rail line at bottom right, continuing onto a wharf on the river, is an extension of the Champlain and St. Lawrence to St. Lambert, completed in 1852.

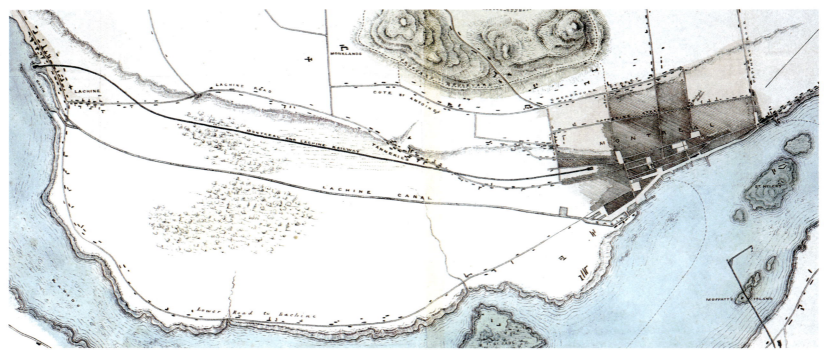

to the American Midwest through the Canadas, began service between Toronto and Montréal on 27 October 1856. By the end of that year, the rail line was already the longest in the world. The line was formed by the amalgamation of a number of shorter railway charters, and later expanded by taking over other lines. The Grand Trunk Railway lasted until 1923, when it became part of Canadian National Railways.

Canada would soon also have two country-uniting railways, the Intercolonial Railway, considered on the next page, and the Canadian Pacific Railway, discussed on page 218.

MAP 333 (*right, top*).
An unknown hand has drawn proposals for rail lines in this 1843 map. The railways are the double lines with dots between them; plank roads are shown with a double line only. It is clear from this map how Toronto was alarmed at the prospect of losing its position to Hamilton. There are two basic ideas here: first, use rail as a portage, a shortcut from Lake Huron to Lake Ontario; and second, connect with the American rail network at Detroit. The Grand Trunk Railway would eventually stretch from Montréal to Windsor, allowing immigrants to the American Midwest to travel through Canada.

MAP 334 (*right*).
Railways often drastically changed the face of the cities they served. This map of Kingston in 1858 shows the line to be followed by the Grand Trunk Railway, with a previous proposal. The area of water between the rail line and the coast is to be filled in. The line narrowly misses the site of the old French Fort Frontenac (see MAP 99, page 71).

MAP 335 (*below*)
An 1866 map showing railways and macadamized and plank roads (as red lines) in southern Ontario. The ideas shown in MAP 333 (*above*) have largely been implemented, although the rail line from Montréal to Toronto is not shown.

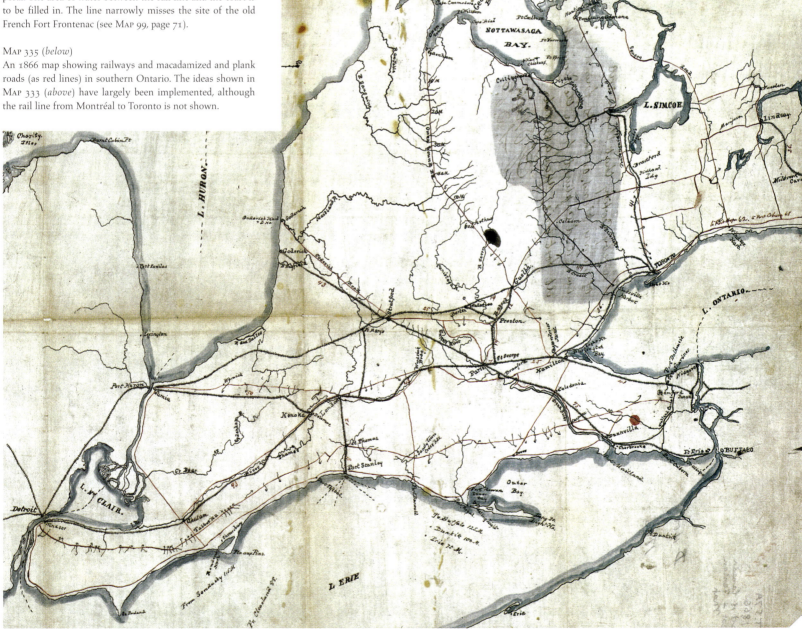

Confederation and the Intercolonial Railway

In 1864, the Maritime colonies were timidly considering the idea of a conference to discuss a possible union. The Province of Canada asked to attend, and the conference was arranged for 1 September, at Charlottetown.

Here a union of all the British colonies in North America was discussed and agreed upon in principle. Another conference was held in Québec the following month, with representatives of Newfoundland also attending. The composition of a parliament, the division of powers between federal and provincial authorities, and the financial arrangements were all discussed, producing seventy-two resolutions which were to form the basis of Confederation.

Under the auspices of the British government, a further conference was held in London from December 1866 to February 1867, and the resolutions were translated into laws. The British North America Act was signed into law by Queen Victoria on 29 March 1867 and proclaimed on 1 July. The colonies of Nova Scotia and New Brunswick joined with the Province of Canada, now split into two, Ontario and Québec, to form the Dominion of Canada, with its capital at Ottawa. Prince Edward Island demurred, but would join Confederation six years later. Newfoundland, however, would remain as an independent colony until 1949. Sir John A. Macdonald, who was largely responsible for the federal constitution, became the Dominion's first prime minister.

MAP 336 (*above*).
The proposal for the Intercolonial Railway, from an 1864 report by Sandford Fleming, who had been appointed to survey the potential routes for the rail line and recommend the one to be followed. In less than a year, Fleming had surveyed the entire route. Note the *Air Line* (a straight line) and the modified *Military Air Line*. Strategic concerns kept the shortest military route away from the American boundary.

One of the conditions of the British North America Act was the construction of a railway linking the new provinces. "It shall be the Duty of . . . Canada to provide for the commencement within Six Months after the Union, of a railway connecting the River St. Lawrence with the City of Halifax," states the Act.

The Intercolonial Railway, as its name implies, was proposed before the union, having been recommended by Lord Durham as early as 1839. Parts of the line were built, but its completion became an essential element of Confederation after 1867. One of the first acts of the new Dominion Parliament was to approve the raising of a loan of $4 million to finance the railway.

Sandford Fleming, who had surveyed the route in 1864–65, recommended the route the rail line eventually took, the so-called northern route, as far from American territory as was possible. He was appointed chief engineer to oversee the railway's construction. He demanded a high standard of construction; only three bridges were not made of steel.

By 1 July 1876 the railheads at both ends, Rivière du Loup and Truro, were finally connected; the Intercolonial Railway was a reality.

MAP 337.
This map, from an 1876 atlas, shows the Intercolonial Railway under construction. The line from Halifax is shown reaching as far west as Dalhousie, and the western section stops at Rimouski. By the end of 1875 the line had reached Saint Flavie (now Mont Joli), just northeast of Rimouski, and Campbellton, just west of Dalhousie, and the remaining section was completed six months later. On 1 July 1876 Sandford Fleming declared the Intercolonial Railway ready for traffic.

The Riel Rebellion of 1869

In December 1867, not long after the opening of a new session of Parliament following Confederation, a resolution was introduced requesting the British government to arrange the transfer of the Northwest to Canada. This previously intended step was now thought imperative following the Russian sale of Alaska to the Americans, the agreement for which had been signed on 30 March 1867, the day after Queen Victoria had signed the British North America Act.

To John A. Macdonald's government, it seemed like the Americans were attempting an end run around the West it now saw as its own; something needed to be done quickly to stem the American advance.

Negotiations with the Hudson's Bay Company moved slowly, however, and were not completed until 19 November 1869, when the Company signed the transfer agreement in return for £300,000 and several million acres of farmland. The transfer was set for 1 December.

In its haste to take over Rupert's Land and the Northwest, the government had already authorized surveying to begin in the Red River Valley, so as to lay out lots ready for the expected influx of new settlers. But no one had bothered to inform the people of Red River what was going on. Thus when surveyors suddenly appeared on their land, running lines without regard to long-established Métis land holdings, there was bound to be resentment.

On 12 October 1869, a group of Métis stopped the surveyors. The point at which they were stopped is clearly indicated on the surveyor's map, shown here (MAP 338).

The Métis were led by Louis Riel, son of one of the leaders of a minor rebellion against the Hudson's Bay Company monopoly in 1849. Educated and fired with a religious zeal, Riel was determined to force the Canadian government to listen to the needs of the French-speaking Métis.

On 31 October the Métis blocked the trail to Pembina and halted the newly appointed lieutenant-governor of the North-West Territories, William McDougall. He had been on his way to take up the reins of government on 1 December. Two days later the Hudson's Bay Company's Fort Garry was seized without a fight.

William McDougall tried to organize an attack on Riel's force. It failed, and many of his men were captured. Riel then proclaimed a provisional government and drew up a bill of rights as a basis for negotiation with the Canadian government. This would be used the following year to formulate the terms of the Manitoba Act (see overleaf). The Canadian government agreed

to recognize Riel's provisional government provided the men held captive were released. But as he was about to release them, Riel and his men were attacked by another group intent on freeing the first. The attack failed. Riel released his original captives but now held new ones, including one Thomas Scott, who Riel later shot after a summary trial for "insubordination and striking the guards." At this, public opinion in English-speaking Canada was incensed. A battalion of British regular troops, led by Colonel Garnet Wolseley, was sent to Red River, and, on 24 August 1870, Riel was forced to flee from the advancing troops. The Red River Rebellion, as it is sometimes called, was over.

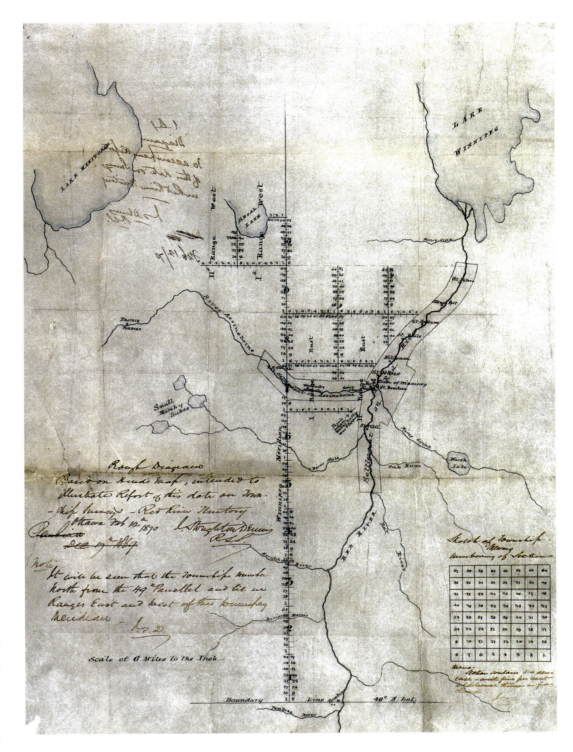

MAP 338.
The map that started it all. This is Lieutenant Colonel John Stoughton Dennis's map of the lots laid out at the Red River Settlement—surveyed *before* the transfer of the Northwest to Canada. It shows the place, just southwest of the forks of the Red and Assiniboine Rivers, where Major A.C. Webb's surveying party was stopped by Louis Riel's Métis on 12 October 1869. The surveyors were on the "hay privilege" lands at the rear of the long and narrow riverfront lots. There was no violence; all Riel's men did was stand on the surveyors' chains. Webb saw that it was hopeless to try to continue in the face of such determined opposition and withdrew. This was the first overt resistance of the Riel Rebellion. The township plans being laid out are shown by the example at bottom right. The township is divided into sixty-four sections of 800 acres (323 ha) each. The delay in surveying caused by Riel allowed the adoption of the American system of a six-mile-square township divided into thirty-six sections of 640 acres (259 ha) each.

Manitoba Becomes the Fifth Province

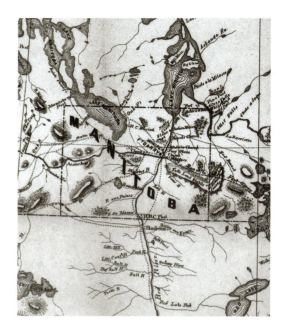

In the winter of 1869–70 the Canadian government, searching for a way out of the impasse, sent for Alexandre-Antonin Taché, bishop of St.-Boniface, who happened to be at that moment visiting Rome. He hurried back, arriving four days after the execution of Thomas Scott, carrying with him an amnesty. Taché persuaded Riel to release all his prisoners and send delegates to Ottawa to negotiate terms that would be acceptable to all.

Using their bill of rights, the Riel representatives negotiated with the federal government. The result was the Manitoba Act, passed on 12 May 1870, becoming effective 15 July. French and English rights were protected, and the Métis were granted some 566 580 ha of land.

Nevertheless, the federal government retained control of resources and in particular all unallocated lands, which were intended to be sold to support the building of a Pacific railway and encourage immigration. The new province was small (Map 339); Manitoba did not achieve its current boundaries until 1912 (see page 252). French language rights were eliminated by a provincial act in 1890, but the rights of both languages were restored in 1984.

Map 339 (below).
In contrast with Map 340, this map was much better. It is the first *official* map of the new Province of Manitoba, drawn in 1871 by Alexander Lord Russell, who had worked on the 1869 survey. He was assistant to Lindsay Russell (see Map 348, page 220). The grid showed suggested township layouts, but they had not yet been laid out on the ground. The map is still not entirely accurate, because it was compiled from a number of other maps.

Map 340 (above).
Published in 1870, this was the first map to show the new Province of Manitoba. The map was actually prepared without the province being shown, and the name and boundaries were hastily added and the map rushed into print. It is inaccurate.

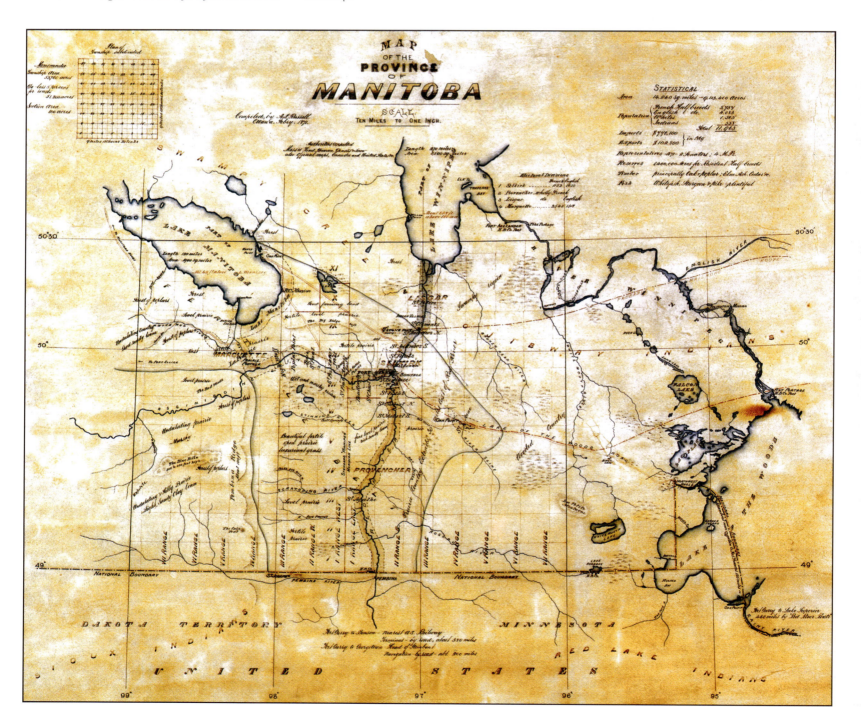

British Columbia Joins Confederation

Meanwhile, in the late 1860s, a groundswell for confederation with Canada had been growing in Britain's Pacific colony, British Columbia. On 12 March 1870 the colony's legislature agreed to send a delegation to Ottawa to negotiate a union. They wanted full representative government, the assumption of the colonial debt of over a million dollars, a program of public works, a wagon road to Canada, and, more than anything else, a railway to connect the Pacific with Ontario. Construction of the railway was to begin within three years of the union.

A delegation that included Anthony Musgrave, the governor of British Columbia, and Joseph Trutch, creator of the map shown below, left for Ottawa by the most practical route, which was through the United States—by steamer to San Francisco, thence by the newly completed Central and Union Pacific Railroads. They left Victoria on 10 May 1870 and arrived in Ottawa on 3 June—a lengthy trip, but much shorter than what would have been required just a few years before.

The Canadian government was being led temporarily by George-Étienne Cartier, as John A. Macdonald was ill. Cartier quickly revealed the Canadian government's resolve to build the railway to the Pacific, to the delight of the British Columbia delegation, and an agreement was speedily negotiated.

According to the terms agreed upon, a railway was to be begun within only two years—and completed within ten. "Sir George Cartier says they will do that or 'burst,'" wrote Musgrave. British Columbia ratified the agreement on 18 January 1871. Cartier had more trouble with his Parliament, however, due to concerns about the cost. But the bill passed and British Columbia formally became Canada's sixth province on 20 July 1871.

MAP 341.
This map of the southern part of the new Province of British Columbia was drawn by James Launders. He had been a map draftsman with the Royal Engineers, and had arrived in the new colony in 1858–59. He decided to stay when the detachment disbanded. The map was drawn under the direction of Joseph Trutch, the colonial surveyor general, and the map is popularly known as "the Trutch Map." When British Columbia joined Canada in 1871, Trutch was appointed the first lieutenant-governor.

This famous map, the first to be drawn of the new province, is an excellent and very detailed summary of the state of geographical knowledge of the region in 1871. It incorporates information from John Palliser (page 208) and the many different surveys carried out by British Royal Engineers, sent to the new mainland colony in 1858. The Cariboo goldfields are shown. Hydrographic details come from British naval surveys at the same time, and in particular the work of Captain George Henry Richards, who surveyed the southern coast in 1858 and 1859 in anticipation of an increase in shipping traffic. The result was an accurate, detailed map that would stand as the finest map of the mountainous province for many years.

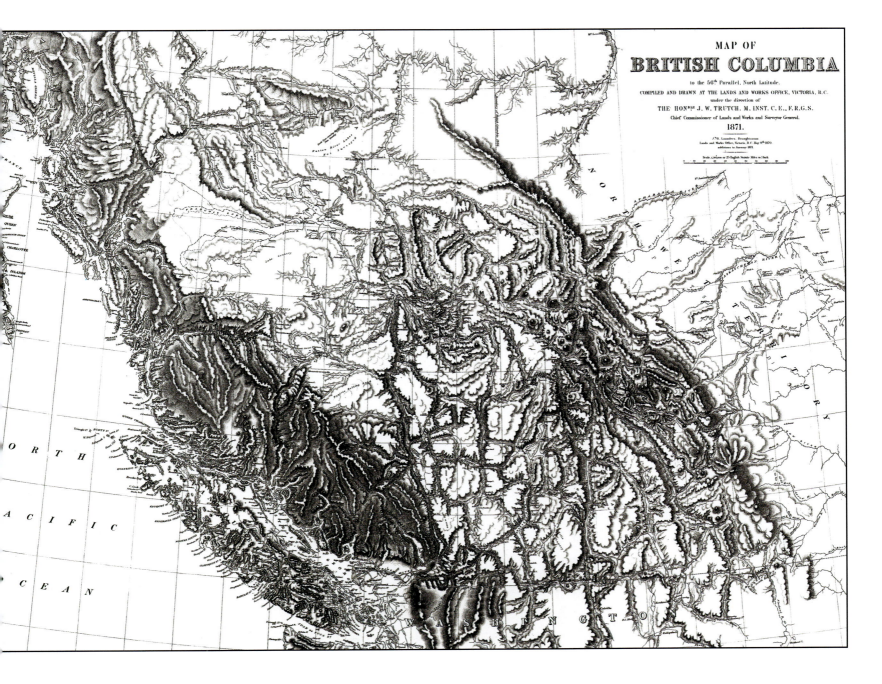

The North-West Rebellion, 1885

By the 1880s, the rapidly diminishing numbers of buffalo had reduced many of the natives of the Prairies to near starvation. Métis and even European settlers were exasperated by perceived mishandling of the allocation of land by the federal government. The North-West Territories had no representation in the Parliament in Ottawa. The Métis, in particular, wanted a return to the river lot pattern of land division instead of the square townships of the Dominion Lands Survey. To agitate to improve their situation, as had been successful in Manitoba, the Métis organized a resistance movement. They invited Louis Riel, at that time living in Montana, back to lead it.

Riel had by this time developed his religious zeal to the point where he considered himself to be a prophet and God's instrument for a resurgence of the Métis. Riel arrived at Batoche, on the South Saskatchewan 75 km downriver from modern Saskatoon, in July 1884, accompanied by Métis leader Gabriel Dumont. He spoke in Prince Albert, advocating free title to land, more land for homesteading, representation in Parliament, and no violence. For this he gained the support of the non-native population.

A petition was sent to Ottawa, where it was duly ignored. So Dumont and Riel hatched a plan to seize Fort Carlton, a Hudson's Bay Company post with a North-West Mounted Police garrison. They hoped thereby to precipitate action by the federal government to address their grievances; the ploy had worked at Red River, so why not now? But the threat of violence lost Riel the support of the non-native population. And Prime Minister Sir John A.

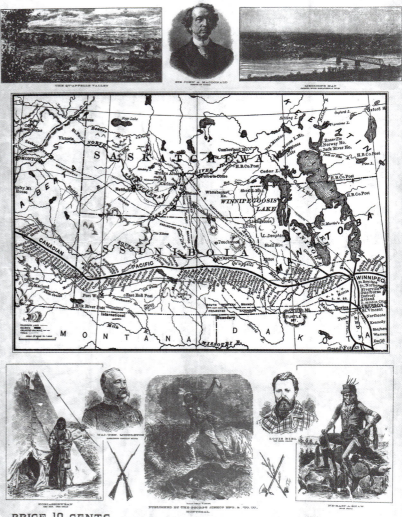

BISHOP'S NORTH-WEST WAR MAP.

PRICE, 10 CENTS.

MAP 342.
A broadsheet published in 1885 to inform the public about the rebellion. Unfortunately, the map is not very useful, having been made before the rebellion. It was likely the only available map the publisher could lay hands on in a hurry. It is a copy of a Canadian Pacific Railway map, so the best information is that along the track. A number of action locations, such as Fish Creek and Cut Knife Hill, are not even marked. But it was the illustrations that sold the map. The picture of a native scalping a dead soldier was sure to arouse public anger.

MAP 343 (below).
Another map for public information, published on 2 April 1885, with trails in red, and mileages noted. The location of the 26 March action at Duck Lake has been hastily added.

Macdonald was determined not to be intimidated again. On 23 March 1885 Major General Frederick Middleton was ordered west with an army of militia several thousand strong. This time Riel had miscalculated and could not succeed; not only could the government muster 8,000 militia drawn now from the Maritimes as well as central Canada, but it had the means to deliver them quickly to the scene of the insurrection—the Canadian Pacific Railway. Although the railway still had unfinished sections, these could be overcome. Within two weeks Middleton had enough troops at Qu'Appelle to venture north to meet Riel and Dumont.

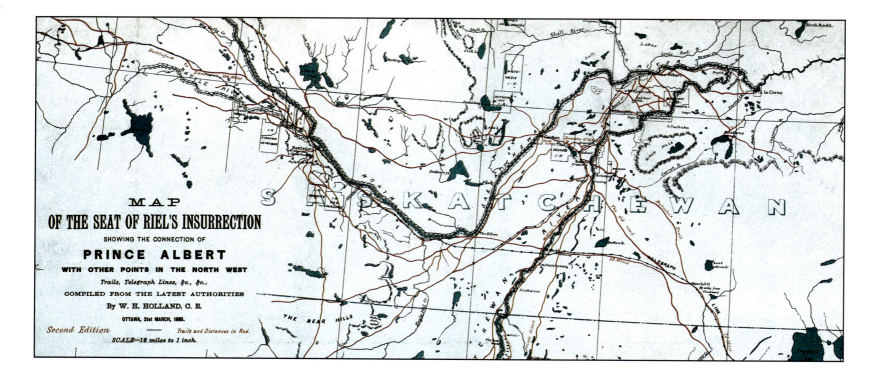

MAP
OF THE SEAT OF RIEL'S INSURRECTION
SHOWING THE CONNECTION OF
PRINCE ALBERT
WITH OTHER POINTS IN THE NORTH WEST
Trails, Telegraph Lines, &c., &c.,
COMPILED FROM THE LATEST AUTHORITIES
By W. H. HOLLAND, C. E.
OTTAWA, 31st MARCH, 1885.
Second Edition — Trails and Distances in Red.
SCALE—12 miles to 1 inch.

Riel declared a provisional government on 19 March 1885, cut the telegraph lines from Prince Albert to Regina, and seized a few officials. On 21 March Riel demanded the surrender of Fort Carlton, which was refused. But on 26 March, unwisely not waiting for reinforcements, the police garrison from the fort, together with volunteers, ventured out to obtain provisions at a store at Duck Lake, where they were routed by the Métis.

At this a native force joined the fray, pillaging Battleford. Fort Carlton was evacuated, as was Fort Pitt, commanded by Francis Dickens, the son of noted author Charles Dickens.

Middleton then arrived on the scene. He was ambushed by Dumont at Fish Creek. But Middleton's superior numbers were bound to win the day. Although one of his commanders, Lieutenant Colonel William Otter, was defeated by a Cree force under their chief, Poundmaker, at Cut Knife Hill, Middleton eventually caught up with Riel and Dumont at Batoche on 9 May. The battle lasted three days, so well were the Métis entrenched, and despite the fact that Middleton had the new Gatling gun, that early machine gun as nearly symbolic of late-Victorian British imperialism as the gunboat. The Métis ran out of ammunition and many were reduced to firing nails. The breakthough for the militia finally came as Middleton was having his lunch!

Dumont got away, fleeing to Montana, but Riel gave himself up on 15 May. At Battleford, on 26 May, Poundmaker surrendered to Middleton, and the final surrender was that of another Cree chief, Big Bear, on 2 July.

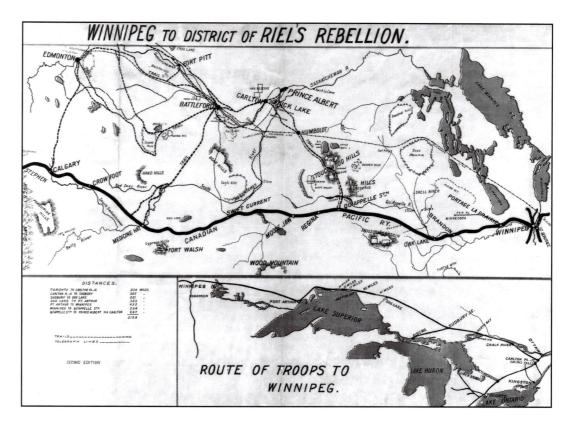

Map 344 (above).
One of the most accurate maps to be published in 1885 to inform the public about the rebellion. The inset shows the incomplete sections of the Canadian Pacific Railway north of Lake Superior, with their distances. Over these gaps the troops had to unload their equipment and haul it in sleighs. The map is simplified; in fact there were sixteen gaps in the track. The troop transport proved once and for all the value of the continental railway for a government trying to paste together a country in which distances were so immense.

Macdonald insisted that Riel be tried in the North-West Territories, not in Winnipeg, where he could insist on a twelve-man, half French-speaking, jury. So Riel was taken to Regina, where he was charged with treason. Riel's lawyers insisted he was insane; Riel protested that he was not. On fine legal points Riel was found guilty and hanged, an action that was met with outrage in French Canada. The federal cabinet could have commuted Riel's sentence, but chose not to, for purely political reasons. The debate over the legitimacy of Riel's execution continues to provoke heated debate even today, especially in Manitoba and Québec.

Map 345 (right).
Part of a map of the action at Batoche, 9–12 May 1885, drawn by George Cole, a quartermaster with the North West Field Force. He attached certificates of authenticity and accuracy from officers present. The map shows places where officers were killed—"Fraser shot" or "Phillips shot." The house where Riel's papers were found after the action is marked at right. The river is the South Saskatchewan. The map was a stand-alone commercial information sheet, and was surrounded by advertising.

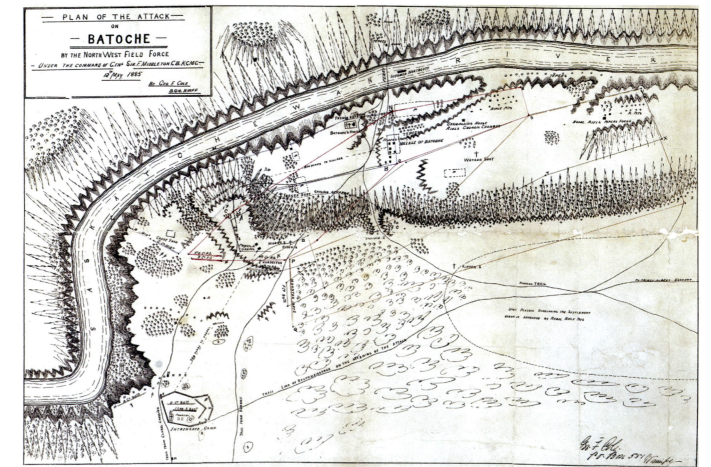

The Canadian Pacific Railway—the Settlement of the Prairies and the Linking of a Nation

The story of the Canadian Pacific Railway has been told many times, for in a real sense it is the story of the link that facilitated the final coalescence of the nation, ensuring that much of the West did not become part of the United States instead.

By the 1860s much of the good land in the Province of Canada (Canada West and Canada East) had been taken up, with the result that in that decade population was lost to the American Midwest. This led to the absorption of Rupert's Land, owned by the Hudson's Bay Company, into the new Dominion of Canada in 1870. What better than a railway to connect the vast potential agricultural region to the rest of Canada? Yet between the settled area of Canada and the prairie West was a huge area of the

Canadian Shield north of Lake Superior which would not only be unproductive in terms of railway traffic, but was also full of difficult country for a railway to traverse.

John Palliser (see page 208) had been pessimistic about the possibility of building a railway within Canada, feeling that the route north to Winnipeg (then Fort Garry) from the United States was much more practicable, and from a purely engineering viewpoint, it was. Henry Hind's expedition, sent by the Canadian government (page 207), was an attempt to determine if a viable route existed to the West within Canadian (British) territory. An 1862 pamphlet published by Hind contained an appendix written by a visionary Sandford Fleming that maintained that it did. The following year Fleming

was placed in charge of locationary surveys for the Intercolonial Railway (see page 212), and in 1872 he was made engineer-in-chief of the Pacific railway surveys.

For the government of John A. Macdonald had determined to build a railway to the Pacific, not only to connect with the Prairies, but also because in 1871 such a line had become one of the conditions for the entry of British Columbia into the Canadian Confederation. In addition, the government had become aware of American intentions to build a railroad close to the international boundary and perhaps entice the West into union with the United States. The tendency of geography to favour north-south traffic had to be subverted by an east-west line of good communication, and the only practical possibility was a railway.

Government railway surveys were authorized in March 1871 and began on 20 July, coincidentally the same day the union of British Columbia became effective. At their peak, the surveys, under Sandford Fleming, employed some eight hundred men. But such industry was uncharacteristic of the speed at which things would move for the next decade. Although a Canadian Pacific Railway was incorporated in 1873 by Sir Hugh Allan, a shipping magnate, it was largely a front for American investors and American control. After allegations surfaced that money had been improperly contributed to Macdonald's re-election in return for concessions for the railway—the so-called Pacific Scandal—Macdonald resigned in November 1873.

His successor as prime minister was Alexander Mackenzie, whose Liberals were not so keen on the idea of a Pacific railway and even less keen on its associated cost. Mackenzie had an economic depression to deal with, and his government still had another uncompleted railway project on their hands (the Intercolonial Railway, not finished until 1876).

Map 346.

Sandford Fleming's surveys of possible routes across the Rocky Mountains to Pacific tidewater, contained in a report on progress published in 1874. Fleming had completed his survey work for the Intercolonial Railway in 1869. The surveys started from a location near North Bay (now Bonfield, Ontario), the place designated temporarily as the "official" terminus, as it was equidistant from Montréal and Toronto, both of which wanted the terminus for themselves. Fleming faced a daunting 4 000 km of survey to the Pacific, not counting the alternative routes that would also have to be surveyed. He finally recommended a route through the Yellowhead Pass, a route that would later be declined, resulting in the necessity of re-surveying thousands of kilometres.

(top)
In what is arguably Canada's most famous photograph, Donald Smith drives the last spike in Eagle Pass on 7 November 1885, completing the Pacific railway. (Photo: CPR Archives)

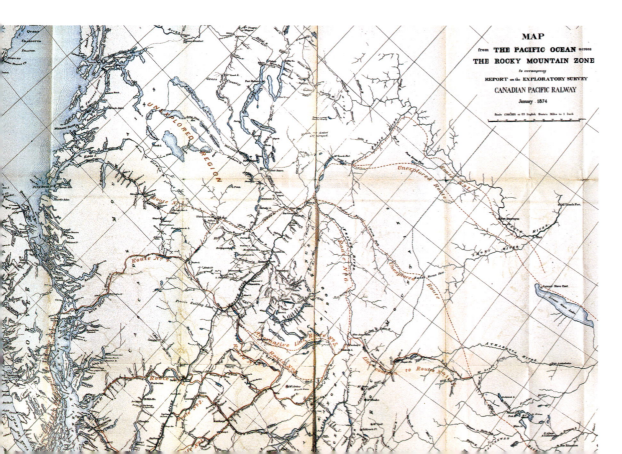

MAP
from THE PACIFIC OCEAN across
THE ROCKY MOUNTAIN ZONE
to accompany
REPORT on the EXPLORATORY SURVEY
CANADIAN PACIFIC RAILWAY
January 1874

The Canadian Pacific Railway Act of 1874 was promulgated in the hope that private enterprise could be tempted to build the railway, but despite offered subsidies of $12,000 and 20,000 acres of land per mile (5 030 ha/km), there were no takers.

In October 1878, John A. Macdonald was returned to office and soon began searching for ways to proceed with the Pacific railway. He found a group of savvy railway financiers and builders led by George Stephen and Donald A. Smith.

Donald Smith had been appointed chief commissioner for the Hudson's Bay Company in Canada in 1871, following the surrender of Rupert's Land to Canada in 1870. He was not opposed to settlement in the West the way his predecessors had been; he felt that the Company's prime asset was the seven million acres (2 833 000 ha) it had received under the terms of the surrender. In 1872 he became involved with James J. Hill, a Canadian-born American railroad builder, in promoting a railway to link Manitoba with American territory to the south. Although this project did not materialize, it did get Smith's cousin George Stephen interested in railways. Stephen would in due course become the virtual founder and first president of the Canadian Pacific Railway.

Stephen had been a director of the Bank of Montreal since 1871 and in 1876 became its president. He was to prove a dedicated and skilled railway financier over the next decade, without whom the CPR would not have been built.

In 1878, Stephen, Hill, Smith, and Norman Kittson, an operator of steamboats and barges on the Red River, gained control of a bankrupt American railroad, which they extended northwards to Winnipeg, and the first train from St. Paul steamed into Winnipeg on 2 December 1878. All the entrepreneurs made money on this venture. Land sales in Manitoba took off.

It was Stephen, Smith, and Hill whom Macdonald found in 1880. Hill was interested primarily because he thought it would be impossible for the CPR to traverse the muskeg and rock north of Lake Superior, and thus his American lines would benefit from the CPR as a vast western feeder line; he resigned from the syndicate when he found he was wrong. But Stephen and Smith would prove to be the driving forces behind the building of an all-Canadian transcontinental railway.

For a while, the government attempted to move the project forward themselves. Sir Charles Tupper, Macdonald's minister responsible for the railway, made the decision to route the railway through Winnipeg instead of through Selkirk, and then to Portage La Prairie, south of Lake Manitoba, but although Fleming's route through Yellowhead Pass was questioned, it was still considered to be the best route through the Rockies. A contract was awarded for the first hundred miles (160 km) west of Winnipeg in August 1879, and later that year

the contract for the first part of the railway in British Columbia, the section from the head of navigation on the Fraser River at Yale to Kamloops Lake, was given to Andrew Onderdonk, an experienced American engineer. Construction started in May 1880.

At Tupper's initiative, the government decided to offer a cash subsidy of $20 million and 30 million acres (12 million ha) of land to get the Pacific railway built. After much negotiation with several potential groups, George Stephen submitted an offer to build the railway for a cash subsidy of $25 million and a land grant of 25 million acres (10 million ha), which was accepted by the government. A formal contract was signed on 21 October 1880.

The railway was defined as a line extending from "the terminus of the Canada Central Railway near Lake Nipissing ... to Port Moody." The government agreed to complete and hand over 710 miles (1 142 km) of track already begun or under contract. Stephen's group agreed to complete the rest of the line to the Pacific, some 1,900 miles (3 060 km). Land grants were to be tax-free for twenty years or until sold. The bill confirming the contract received royal assent on 15 February 1881, and the Canadian Pacific Railway was incorporated the following day. Sandford Fleming thought the railway should be built by the government, so he resigned.

Principally with the idea of forestalling possible incursions by American railroads, a decision was now made to route the rail line on a more southerly path than that envisaged by Fleming's surveys, and with the adoption of the Kicking Horse Pass route through the Rockies in preference to the Yellowhead Pass recommended by Fleming, much of the early survey work was rendered useless. The government permitted Kicking Horse Pass, surveyed by Major Albert B. Rogers, to be used as the route through the Rockies because it was more than a hundred miles (160 km) from the American boundary line. The avoidance of Palliser's Triangle (see page 209) as being too arid was questioned by a noted exploring botanist, John Macoun. He met with the railway directors in May 1881 and convinced them that a southern route would be through land well suited for agriculture. Time has proven him correct, although significant irrigation schemes in the region have helped.

During the first season of construction of the main line to the Pacific, only about 165 km of track was laid, a rate which obviously was not going to work; the company would bankrupt itself before traffic could build. So in October 1881 James Hill recruited William Cornelius Van Horne, an American railroad builder of considerable experience and reputation. He took over on 2 January 1882. This was an event of

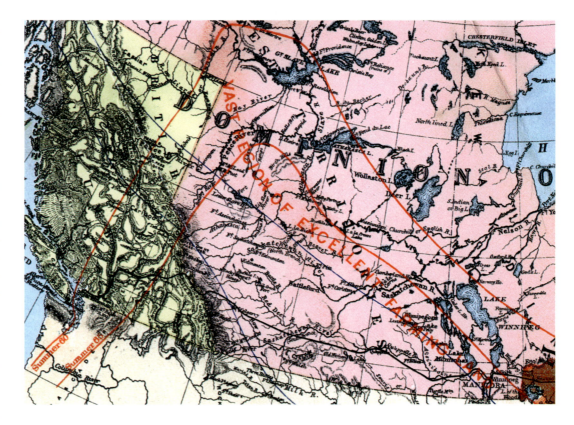

Map 347.

Map by John Macoun showing a *vast region of excellent farming land*. It was published in his book in 1882 and illustrates the advice he gave to the Canadian Pacific Railway that influenced the decision to reroute the line farther south than that surveyed by Sandford Fleming. The farthest north red line is the summer 60°F (15.5°C) isotherm, and the other red line is the summer 65°F (18.3°C) isotherm. The northernmost blue line is the winter 15°F (−9.4°C) isotherm, and the other blue line the 20°F (−6.7°C) isotherm. These isotherms were probably intended to represent average temperatures over a period; daily minima and maxima are in fact more critical for agriculture. Macoun met with the directors of the Canadian Pacific Railway in May 1881 and persuaded them that a southern route for the railway would not mean that it was traversing arid lands unsuitable for agriculture. He argued that rain could not penetrate a baked crust on the surface of the soil but would if this crust were broken. "Thus," he wrote, "the apparent aridity vanishes before the first efforts of husbandry."

MAP 348 (above).

This impressive map is a superb summary of western Canada in 1882, the year it was drawn by Lindsay Russell, surveyor general of Canada. The red flags are North-West Mounted Police posts. The green area represents land surveyed and subdivided according to the Dominion Lands Survey (see page 226); the uncoloured squares are preliminary surveys only. The large black rectangles are coal districts. Provincial and provisional district boundaries, the latter being administrative areas within the North-West Territories, are shown outlined in red.

MAP 349 (right, top).

Part of a map drawn by botanist John Macoun in 1880, while he was exploring the Prairies and assessing their agricultural potential. This part covers an area from the South Saskatchewan River south to the United States boundary. The Red Deer River is at left; the point at which it joins the Saskatchewan is today close to the Alberta-Saskatchewan boundary near Empress, Alberta. The South Saskatchewan at Elbow is now flooded to form Lake Diefenbaker. South of this river is a smaller river named *Strong Current River*. Today the city of Swift Current stands on its banks. Macoun confined his observations to the narrow band of land he had actually travelled, and the map thus lacks the details of John Palliser's map of 1857–60 (MAP 328, page 208).

MAP 350 (right).

This map of a newly surveyed Regina gives the impression that a vast city already exists, when in fact it shows merely the surveyed lots, few of which contained houses. The map was drawn by the Canadian Pacific Railway Lands Department in 1882. The blocks outlined in blue may represent lots already sold.

considerable significance, for Van Horne would prove remarkably adept at pushing the railway construction forward. He hired Thomas Shaughnessy as his purchasing agent; he was to prove invaluable at making sure the right supplies were in the right place when they were needed. Railway contractors Langdon and Shepard were awarded the contract to lay the track as far as Calgary.

The building of the line took off. Despite a slow start due to flooding of the Red River, by the end of 1882 some 420 miles (675 km) of main line track had been laid. Track extended beyond Swift Current, about 925 km west of Winnipeg. Since October trains had been operating to the new settlement of Regina, a North West Mounted Police fort which would soon become the capital of the North-West Territories (MAP 350).

The CPR was now burning through money at an extraordinary rate, $22 million in 1882 alone. It was just as well that George Stephen was good at raising money. He persuaded a new contractor, the North American Railway Contracting Company, to take on the task of completing the line; they were to be paid partly in CPR shares. Although improving finances in 1883 led the CPR to complete the line itself, Stephen's move instilled confidence that the line would in fact be completed. Stephen also sold more shares in New York, raising yet more money.

In May 1883 the government-built line from Winnipeg to Thunder Bay was handed over to the CPR, and on 8 July the first train from Winnipeg arrived at Port Arthur.

Track-laying across the prairie continued apace. Medicine Hat (MAP 355, page 223) was reached by 1 June, and at Lathom (near Bassano, Alberta) a record 6 miles (9.7 km) of track was laid in one day. The NWMP fort of Calgary was reached in mid-August, and Van Horne showed his appreciation for his contractors by naming the last two sidings before Calgary "Langdon" and "Shepard." A place called "Twenty-ninth Siding"—later renamed "Banff"—was reached on 27 October as the rails edged up the Bow River Valley into the Rocky Mountains. At the end of the 1883 season the rails were only just shy of the Continental Divide, and British Columbia, in Kicking Horse Pass.

Now came the perhaps more exciting but infinitely slower task of laying track down the steep western slopes of the Rockies and across the Selkirk Mountains. The entire 1884 season would see the rails laid only 120 km farther westward.

The track now had to descend the tortuous Kicking Horse River Valley. Major Rogers had surveyed a line on the upper canyon section from Wapta Lake to Field keeping to the mandated 2.2 percent maximum grade, but the line had to traverse unstable steep slopes on the valley sides, and a 425-m tunnel would also be required. Van Horne could not contemplate the

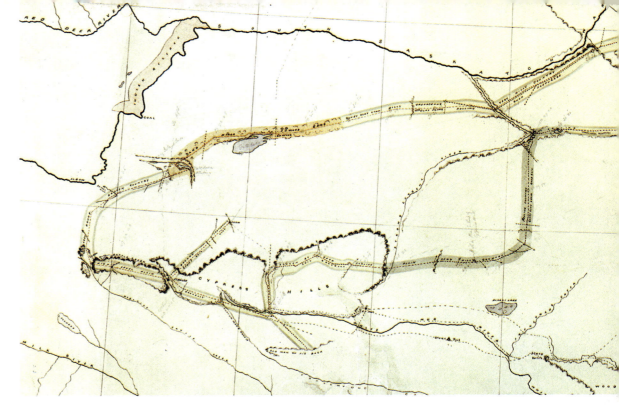

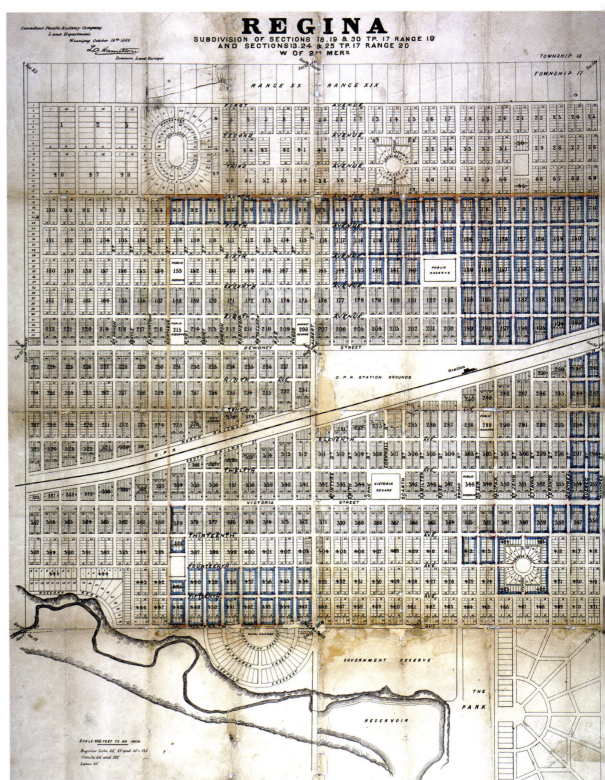

Map 351 (above).
This map, from John Macoun's book, published in 1882, shows the railway ending at Moose Jaw Creek, which was the status of the line as of early September 1882.

time this would take to build, and so a temporary solution was allowed. For 7.25 km, the track was laid at a 4.4 percent grade, twice the normal maximum. This was the infamous "Big Hill." It required an array of helper locomotives to be on hand at all times, and the track had three runaway spurs to contain trains that might lose control on the way down. Although intended to be temporary, the Big Hill lasted until 1909, when the innovative, Swiss-inspired Spiral Tunnels were built. By extending the length of the track with loops within the tunnels, the grade was reduced.

The lower canyon of the Kicking Horse was difficult too, prompting construction superintendent James Ross to send a telegram to Van Horne once they were finally out of it: "Tracks on Columbia thank God." By the end of the 1884 season the track had reached Beaver, on the Columbia at its confluence with the Beaver River.

Meanwhile, George Stephen had been fighting financial fires. CPR stock had declined, which was a serious matter for financing that used stock as security. In September there had been a severe early frost on the Prairies, and it had done a lot of damage. The western land boom, which the building of the CPR had touched off, collapsed, and there were attacks on the CPR in the press. By March 1885 Stephen felt that the end was near for the railway, but help arrived at the last minute. Macdonald's government was too tightly identified with the Pacific railway to let it flounder at this stage, a fact they came to realize at the eleventh hour. And public sentiment suddenly changed with the outbreak of Louis Riel's North-West Rebellion (see page 216). The relatively speedy transport of troops, despite problems at the gaps in the track and sections of unballasted track north of Lake Superior, graphically demonstrated the value of the Pacific railway, making it much easier for Macdonald to gain passage of a bill to provide further assistance to the CPR. As it was, it did not receive royal assent until 20 July.

Track had slowly been laid through the difficult territory along the north shore of Lakes Huron and Superior from the Canada Central Railway line up the Ottawa Valley. By the end of 1882, the line reached only as far west as

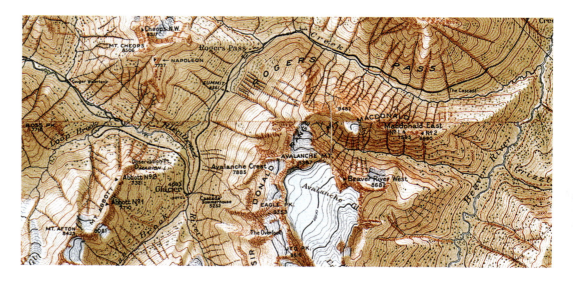

Map 352.
The first tariff, for freight only, was issued by the new Canadian Pacific Railway in June 1881 and carried a map showing a line completed west to Portage La Prairie and a total route mileage of 272 miles (437 km). The western line was rerouted farther to the south a few months later, to provide a more direct route.

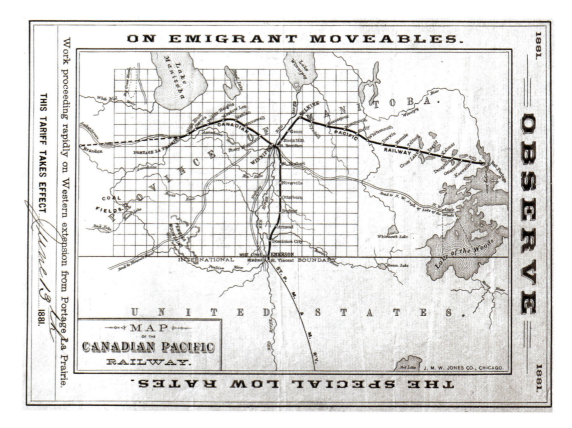

Map 353.
This 1902 map shows some of the engineering required for the section of the line in Rogers Pass, in the Selkirk Mountains. The multiple hairpin-type loops at the confluence of the Illecillewaet River and the appropriately named Loop Brook are clearly visible. They were bypassed in 1916 with the building of the Connaught Tunnel, and another tunnel was completed in 1988 to give a track in each direction. This is the Macdonald Tunnel, at 9 km the longest tunnel in the western hemisphere.

the north shore of Lake Nipissing; but by the end of 1884 only a few particularly difficult sections on the north shore of Lake Superior remained unfinished. Due to the North-West

Rebellion, which had publicly demonstrated the value of the railway, the honour of driving the last spike in the entire Montréal to Winnipeg part of the line was given to the troops'

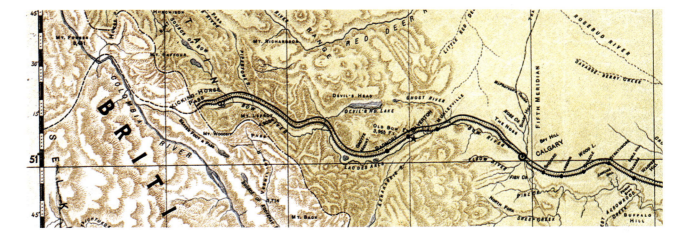

MAP 354 (*right*).
The Canadian Pacific Railway (tracked line) and the railway telegraph (solid line) halt at the base of the Rocky Mountains in this 1883 map. The dashed line shows the projected route.

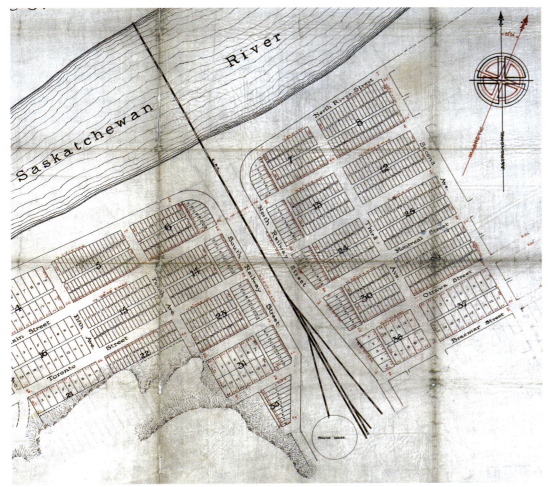

MAP 355 (*left*).
Medicine Hat, as mapped by the CPR Lands Department surveyors in 1883; it has written additions that date from 1888. The map is signed by Lauchlan A. Hamilton, who would later survey much of the railway's land in Vancouver. The townsite lots, as always, focus on the railway station. Note the roundhouse, a shed for locomotives, with a turntable so that a shed housing perhaps a dozen locomotives could be serviced by a single rail line.

MAP 356 (*below*).
The Canadian government granted vast tracts of land to the Canadian Pacific Railway as its contribution to the costs of building the expensive line. Much of the financing of the CPR was dependent on land grants, which the railway could sell after making them infinitely more valuable with the presence of the rail line. This map is dated 1886. "The Company's Lands in Part Consist of the Odd-Numbered Sections within the Belt Coloured Green," the legend on this map explains, "the Remaining Sections being Government Homestead Lands."

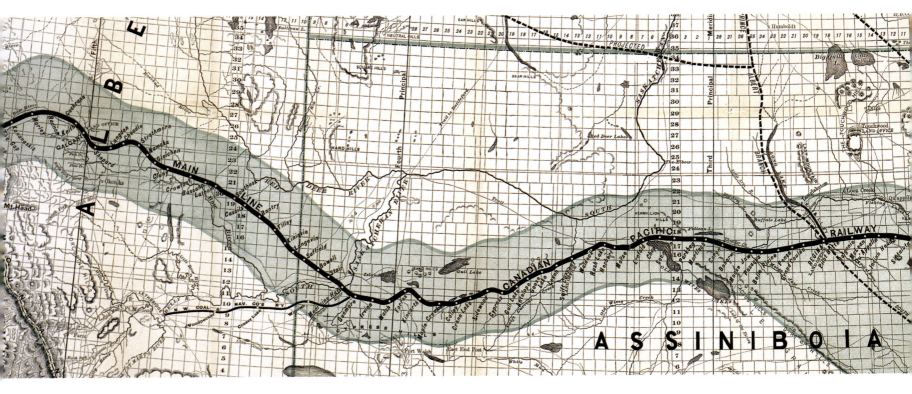

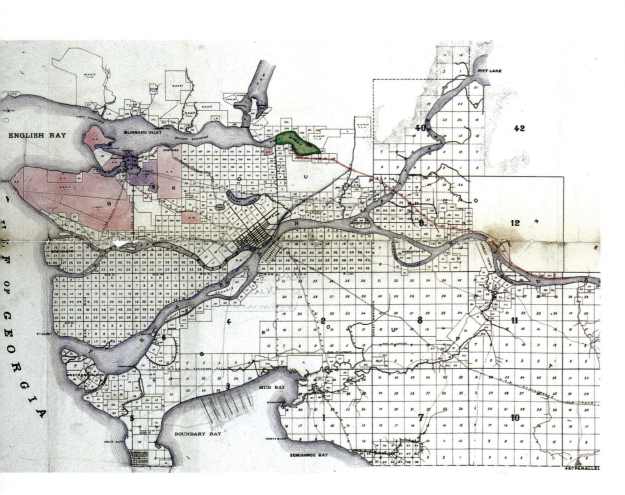

Map 357 (above).
This map, prepared in 1874, shows the planned location of the Pacific tidewater terminus at Port Moody. This was simply the nearest tidewater on this route, but once the line had been built, it would take the CPR less than a year to extend it to a more commercially viable site on Burrard Inlet at the site of today's downtown Vancouver. The isolated section of line is shown petering out in the Fraser Valley; this was clearly a map drawn to consider the location of the western terminus only, at this early stage of planning, by the Canadian government rather than a commercial Canadian Pacific Railway. This map has interesting suggestions sketched in pencil. Someone was obviously thinking of extension to English Bay, shown as one pencil line, and to possible wharves and docks on Boundary Bay, shown in rather scribbled fashion, again with a pencil line indicating the possible line of track. The idea was to place docking facilities as near to incoming ships from the Strait of Juan de Fuca as possible, as potential American competition was always a possibility. The map was given to the commercially chartered Canadian Pacific Railway by the government, probably in 1880 or 1881, as the map is now in the railway company's archives.

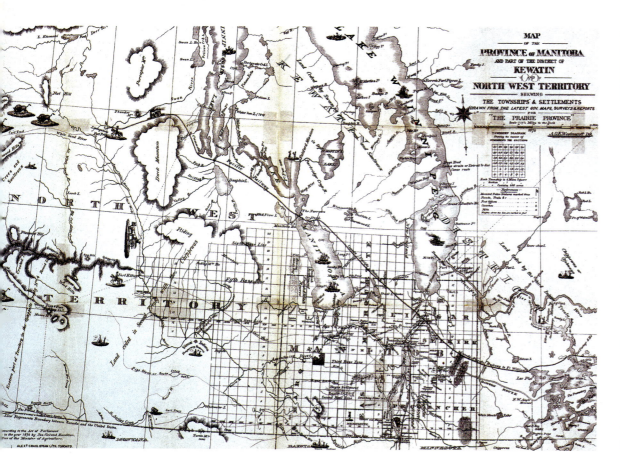

Map 358 (left).
This rather whimsically illustrated map of the Prairies in 1876 shows quite well the extent of coverage of the Dominion Lands Survey at that time. Not until the coming of the railway did land survey proceed westwards at a faster pace. Note the original northern alignment of the proposed railway along the route surveyed by Sandford Fleming.

commanding officer, Lieutenant Colonel W. R. Oswald, who drove the spike at Jack Fish Bay on 18 May 1885.

In the west, Andrew Onderdonk had completed the government-contracted Yale to Port Moody section in January 1884 and reached Savona, just west of Kamloops, by the end of 1884. By the summer of 1885, now under contract directly to the CPR, his construction team was driving hard eastwards until, on 26 September, they ran out of rails at the western end of

Map 359.

The selling of the Canadian Pacific Railway. Not chancing a "Build it, and they will come" philosophy, the cpr set about a massive advertising campaign to lure settlers to the land grants around the line. These settlers, it was hoped, would grow the wheat that would help to make the line profitable. This superb and certainly comprehensive advertisement was an independently printed sheet published about 1883–85. The railway line is shown through to tidewater at Port Moody, but was not in operation at the time the map was printed.

Eagle Pass in the Monashee Mountains. Now all depended on James Ross's team. From Beaver, the end of the track in 1885, a route up the Beaver River Valley was followed into Rogers Pass, discovered in 1882 by Major Rogers but surveyed by him only in 1884. Progress was slow. The summit of the Selkirks was attained on 17 August, and the difficult gorge of the Illecillewaet River, east of Revelstoke, was next; it was only navigated by the construction of many loops, totalling a dizzying 2,500 degrees.

Finally, with the season running out, they approached the Onderdonk track, where, at a point named Craigellachie, the last spike on the entire Pacific railway was driven by Donald Smith on 7 November 1885. Although many, many improvements, repairs, and ballasting of yet unballasted track would still be necessary for commercial operation, Canada's rail line to the Pacific was a reality. That season, a demonstration freight shipment of forty drums of oil was arranged, from the naval storekeeper in Halifax to his counterpart in Esquimalt on Vancouver Island. Held at Québec pending completion of the line, it took seven days to arrive at Pacific tidewater, and was delivered in Esquimalt two days later. The first passenger train had to await the following year; the line was abandoned for the winter. The first transcontinental passenger train arrived at Port Moody on 4 July 1886.

The first train from the east arrives in Port Moody, 4 July 1886.

At the end of 1886 George Stephen estimated that the total cost of building the Pacific railway had been $164 million, a gargantuan amount in those days. And Stephen himself had been responsible for raising a large part of it.

Although settlers had begun to pour into Manitoba with the connection of Winnipeg to American lines in 1878, it was the coming of the Canadian Pacific Railway that made settlement of the Prairies in any numbers possible.

From the moment Rupert's Land was acquired from the Hudson's Bay Company, it was the government's intention to facilitate settlement as quickly as possible, mainly to pre-empt possible American incursion into the region. To curb the depredations of American whiskey traders on the native population, the North-West Mounted Police were formed in 1873.

The Dominion Lands Survey was devised to allow for quick settlement by European immigrants. It was a system that subdivided land into uniform squares with sides of 6 miles (9.65 km); each township contained 36 sections of 1 square mile, which were subdivided again into quarter sections of 160 acres (65 ha) each. Most detailed maps of Prairie settlements to this day show this characteristic checkerboard pattern. Free grants of quarter sections, and provisions for pre-emption of additional quarter sections, were used as incentives to encourage settlement. Later, land could also be purchased from the CPR, and later still from other railways, which had been granted alternate sections extending back from the rail line. In addition, lands had been granted to the Hudson's Bay Company as part of the Rupert's Land surrender agreement.

In order to be able to legally sell lands, the government concluded a number of treaties with First Nations, covering areas which chronologically fan out west and north from Manitoba, preceding European settlement. Treaties 1 and 2, signed in 1871, and Treaty 3, signed in 1873, covered present-day southern Manitoba and adjacent areas. Northern Manitoba was covered with Treaty 5, in 1875 (with later additions in 1908–09); Treaty 6, signed in 1876, covered a large region of present-day central Saskatchewan and central Alberta. Treaty 7, the "Blackfoot Treaty," ceded most of southern Alberta in 1876. It was not until 1899 that Treaty 8 was signed, for the northern areas of today's Saskatchewan, Alberta, and British Columbia. Other treaties followed for land farther north, but the main regions of potential settlement were now covered by these treaties, with the notable exception of southern and central British Columbia.

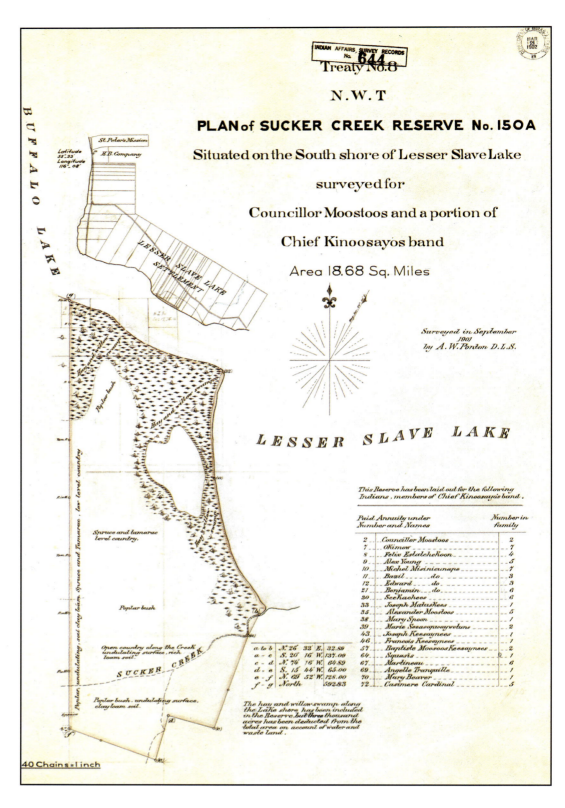

MAP 360 (*above*).
This survey map of the Sucker Creek Reserve, today Grouard, Alberta, was the first survey and allocation of reserve land under Treaty Number 8, concluded in 1899. Chief Keenooshayoo (spelled *Kinoosayos* on the map) had been one of the negotiators for the treaty, which may account for his reserve having been surveyed first. The allocation of land was done on the basis of a quarter section, one-quarter square mile or 160 acres (65 ha) per family of five, and otherwise pro-rated. Thus the map contains a list of the residents of the reserve together with the family sizes.

MAP 361 (*right*).
Part of a land sales map of 1900, showing the Dominion Lands Survey. The principal meridian, north of Winnipeg, is shown. Each square is a section of one square mile.

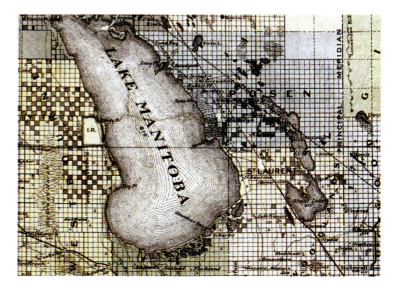

Winnipeg— Gateway to the West

Lord Selkirk's Red River Colony (page 178) spread out along the banks of the Red and Assiniboine Rivers. The City of Winnipeg, incorporated in 1873, developed around a store built at the corner of what is now Portage and Main in 1862, rather than around the Hudson's Bay Company's Fort Garry near the confluence of the Red and the Assiniboine.

The name "Winnipeg," applied to the settlement rather than the lake to the north, was first used by a newpaper editor as the header for a local newspaper, the *Nor'Wester*, on 24 February 1866.

The creation of the Province of Manitoba jump-started growth; Winnipeg grew from only about a hundred persons in 1870 to well over three thousand in 1874, the date of the two maps shown here. The confirmation in 1881 that Winnipeg would be on the route of the transcontinental railway set off a land boom. Winnipeg was promoted as the "Gateway to the West." During the boom, some land prices were higher than those in Chicago. By 1884 (Map 372, page 233) the population had grown to 17,000.

In 1886 the board of trade negotiated a 15 percent discount on goods shipped by the Canadian Pacific Railway west from Winnipeg. The same discount on goods shipped to Winnipeg from the east was granted in 1890. This favourable treatment promoted the growth of Winnipeg over all other settlements on the Prairies, and led many eastern companies to open branches in the city, further encouraging growth. Winnipeg also became the centre of the grain trade of the West.

The city quickly became the largest urban centre in western Canada. Immigrants flooded to the Prairies, and many stayed in Winnipeg. By 1911 Winnipeg was the third largest city in Canada, a ranking it held until the 1920s, when it lost it to Vancouver. Today Winnipeg is Canada's eighth largest city.

Map 362 (*right, top*) and Map 363 (*right, bottom*).
Two maps of Winnipeg in 1873–74. Winnipeg was incorporated as a city in November 1873, and these maps were drawn shortly thereafter. The population was about 3,400 at the time. Map 363 (*bottom*), drawn for the new city government, gives a misleading picture of the amount of development; the majority of the surveyed lots shown were in fact undeveloped. Map 362 (*top*) gives a fairer view. At this time (the survey was November 1873) the built-up area of Winnipeg reached only from Fort Garry, shown on both maps, northwards to the bend in the Red River upstream of Point Douglas. The latter place (the most pointed peninsula on the map) was the original landing place of Selkirk's settlers in August 1812. The coming of the railway and the land boom it touched off in 1881–82 changed the face of the city forever. Bird's-eye maps (Map 372, page 233, and Map 375, page 234) show the difference in development between 1880 and 1884, although once again the tendency to overstate is evident on both of these maps. Note the filled-in oxbow lake on Map 362, a former meander of the Red River.

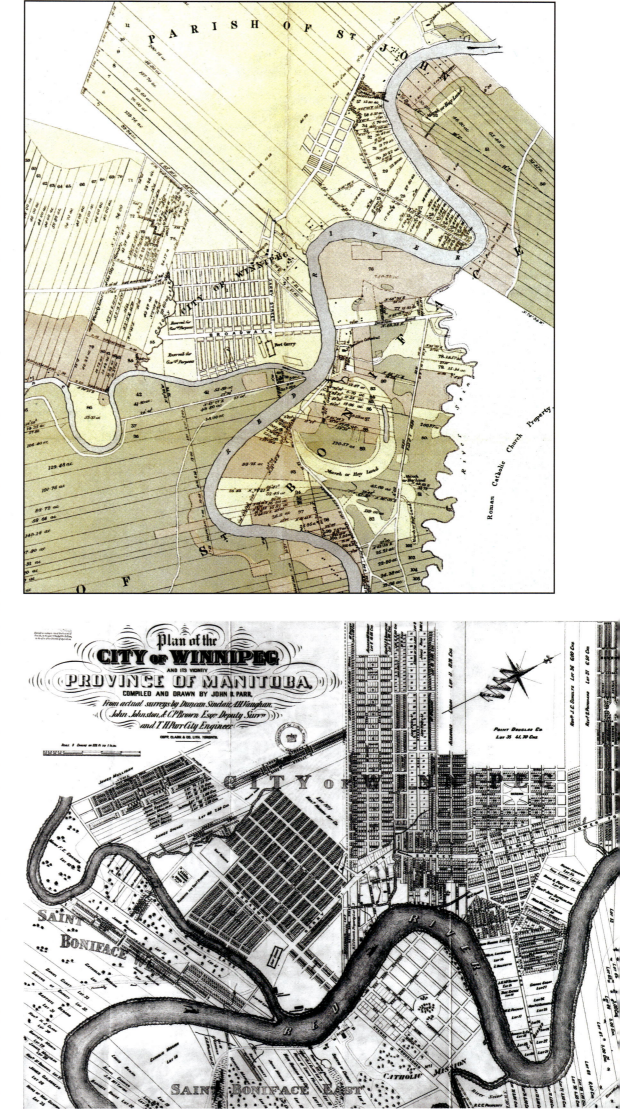

Edmonton— Gateway to the North

The Hudson's Bay Company's Fort Edmonton was first established as Edmonton House just downriver of Fort Saskatchewan in 1795. Because of flooding or running out of wood to cut in the immediate vicinity, its location was moved many times between then and 1832. That year the Company finally got fed up with the flooding and moved to a high location on a bluff well above the river, and here the fort would endure (Map 364, below).

Until 1905, settlement was slow. In 1861 Father Albert Lacombe established an Oblate mission at St. Albert, and some settlement occurred around the fort. In 1874 the North-West Mounted Police established a post as part of the Hudson's Bay Company fort; the Company traders were glad to have them. By the end of 1879 the telegraph finally reached Edmonton (Map 366, below right).

The superb map shown here (Map 365) was surveyed for the Dominion Lands Survey in 1882. The growth of the region was not helped by the decision of the Canadian Pacific Railway to lay its line through Calgary instead of the northern route through Edmonton. The settlement did get its own railway in 1891, a branch line from Calgary terminating south of the river. This allowed the growth of South Edmonton, later renamed Strathcona. Edmonton itself had grown large enough to be incorporated as a town in 1892.

The years 1904 and 1905 were signal ones for Edmonton. In 1904 Edmonton was incorporated as a city, and the following year the Canadian Northern Railway, a transcontinental railway in its own right, reached Edmonton. Also in 1905, Alberta was increased in size and

Map 364 (below).
A plan of Fort Edmonton, surveyed in 1846 by Mervin Vavasour, an officer in the British army. He was on a grand tour of the West to assess British and American defences in case the two countries came to war over arguments about the location of the boundary west of the Rocky Mountains. In this role, Vavasour drew maps of many western settlements, including Fort Victoria and Fort Vancouver (on the Columbia River). The boundary location was settled peacefully in that year (see page 204).

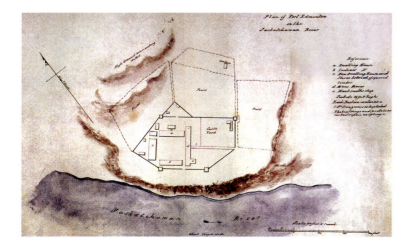

Map 365 (above).
A superb survey map of Edmonton in 1882, showing settlers' lands. Later land transfers are indicated in red ink. The lots are mainly river lots, long and narrow and fronting the river. Later subdivision would revert to the square-shaped lots of the Dominion Lands Survey, as in the map of Calgary, overleaf, drawn in the same style. The 3,000 acre (1 214 ha) land reserve of the Hudson's Bay Company is the major feature of this map, and Fort Edmonton, the Company post first located here in 1832, is also shown. In 1882 it also contained a garrison of the North-West Mounted Police. The Alberta legislature building is today about 100 m immediately north of the fort's location. Due south of the fort, across the river, is the land (Lot 9) of John Walter (here misspelled *Water*). He was an Orkney boatman who had worked for the Hudson's Bay Company since 1870. In 1876 he built a house in this location and soon obtained title to the land. The surveyor would have taken account of the locations of houses and the areas of clearing or cultivation for each settler before laying out the lot boundaries, thus allowing each a legal lot instead of the simple land appropriation by individual settlers before this survey. Some of the lot lines shown here are traceable today as the lines of some of Edmonton's streets.

PLAN
OF
EDMONTON
SETTLEMENT
N. W. T.

Scale 20 Chains to 1 Inch.

Department of the Interior
Dominion Lands Office
Ottawa, 25th May, 1883.

Approved and Confirmed

A. Russell

For the Surveyor General.

EXPLANATION of COLORS:

Woods:............ Green.   Scrub, or Prairie and Woods: Dotted green.   Water............ Blue.
Marshes: Yellow with small strokes of black.   Hills or Slopes: Etching or Grey Shade.
Brulé (Burnt Woods)............ Brown.   Settler's Improvements:............ Pink.

transformed into a province of Canada; Edmonton was chosen as its capital. As a provincial capital, the city's stability was assured, though growth still relied on agricultural activity in the surrounding area. In 1912 the cities of Edmonton and Strathcona amalgamated, setting a pattern of geographic expansion that continues to the present.

During World War II the Alaska Highway was built, and Edmonton became the "Gateway to the North." After the war oil was discovered in volume at nearby Leduc, and the foundations of Edmonton and Alberta's modern growth were laid.

Map 366 (right). Part of a map dated 1880 showing the extension of the first telegraph line into Edmonton. The line became operational on 1 January 1880. Before that the telegraph had ended at Hay Lakes, 32 km from Edmonton.

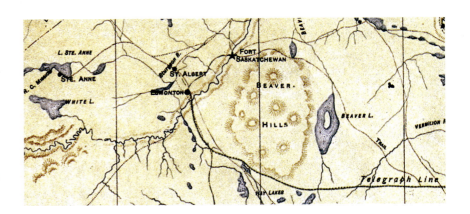

Calgary—from Police Post to Oil Capital

In the 1860s, American traders moved north into southern Alberta, creating a network of fortified posts from which they traded often adulterated whiskey to native peoples for buffalo pelts. The most notorious of these posts was Fort Whoop-up, established at today's Lethbridge in 1869, but another was set up within the city limits of what is now Calgary. It was the presence of these illicit traders that determined the Canadian government to send a force to police its newly-acquired territory—the North-West Mounted Police, the forerunners of the Royal Canadian Mounted Police.

One of the forts the police established, in 1875, was at the confluence of the Bow River with the smaller Elbow River. It was named Fort Brisebois, after the police inspector in charge, but the following year the name was changed to Calgary. Lieutenant Colonel James Macleod had proposed changing the name to Fort Calgary, after a village in Scotland, and the name was accepted but shortened.

In the 1870s the buffalo disappeared from the prairie, but this opened the way for open-range cattle farming, and in 1880 the government started to allow leasing of large tracts of land for this purpose. This drew settlers to southern Alberta and to Calgary.

The police post, two trading posts, and a number of surrounding dwellings existed when, in mid-August 1883, the Canadian Pacific Railway reached Calgary. This was the situation when the area was surveyed by the Dominion Lands Survey, producing the beautiful map shown here (MAP 369, far right).

Soon, of course, surveyors working for the railway moved in and laid out a town around the station, so lots could be sold. This happened in the latter half of 1883, and MAP 368 (below) was the result. As with most of the Canadian Pacific Railway town plans, it represented hopes rather than actual development; the map tends to give the impression that a large urban area already exists, when in reality there were but stakes on a prairie.

But the coming of the railway assured a future for Calgary. It was incorporated as a town in 1884, and as a city in 1893. Calgary became a centre for the livestock industry as well as a transportation centre, then a centre for the growing settlement and farming of the southern prairie with an influx of immigrants.

In 1914, Calgary's development was given a boost by the discovery of oil in the nearby Turner Valley (see overleaf), and to this day Calgary is the head office city for the majority of oil companies, despite the later more significant finds of oil near Edmonton. Reflecting this dominance, and its role as a transportation centre, today Calgary ranks second only to Toronto in numbers of company head offices.

MAP 369 (*right*).
This superb map is a Dominion Lands Survey of the township that is now Calgary, dated 8 March 1884 but reflecting survey work done the previous summer. Detailed enough to show individual settlers' houses, barns, and lots, it is also an elementary land-use map, with marshy areas coloured yellow and wooded areas green. The new Canadian Pacific Railway has just reached Calgary and ends on this map, the situation in mid-August 1883. The station, not yet built, and the surrounding subdivision shown in MAP 368, below, is in township 15. The North-West Mounted Police fort is shown just to the west of the confluence of the Elbow River and the Bow; the Hudson's Bay Company post is just to the east, marked *H B*.

MAP 367 (*right*).
Calgary shown on an 1886 map of the posts of the North-West Mounted Police. The red flag denotes a police post. The new Canadian Pacific Railway is shown, with the last two stations before the contract of railway builders Langdon and Shepard ran out at Calgary (see page 221).

MAP 368 (*below*).
A map drawn by the Lands Department of the Canadian Pacific Railway in Winnipeg, dated 1 January 1884. It is signed by Dominion Lands Surveyor Archibald McVittie. Lots surround the railway station. The map was perhaps used for lot sales.

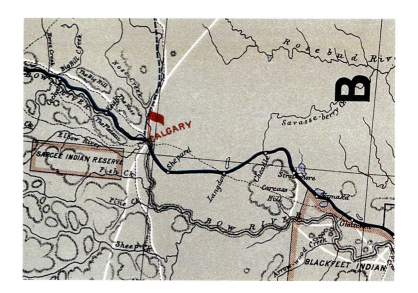

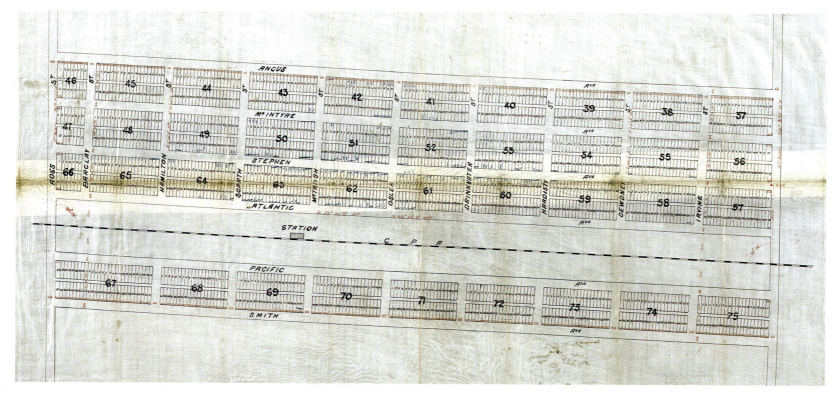

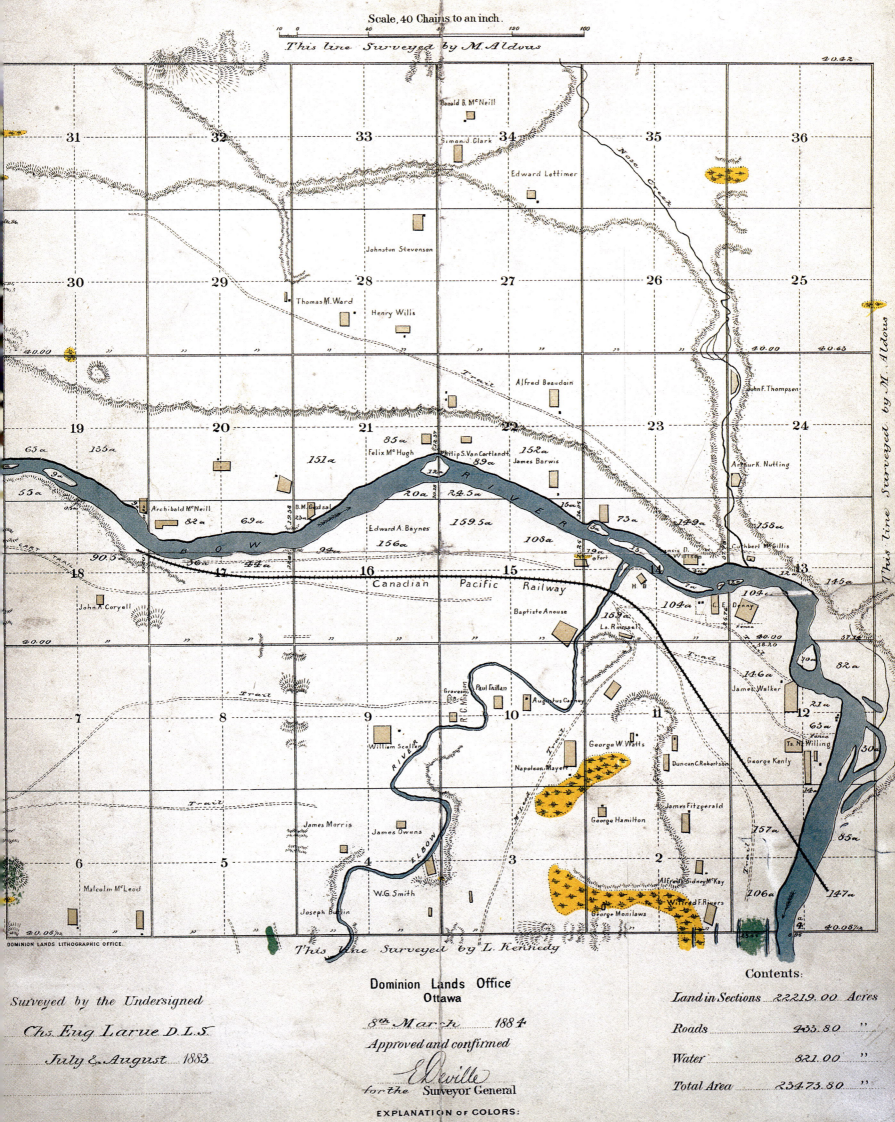

PLAN OF
TOWNSHIP № 24
RANGE 1 WEST OF FIFTH MERIDIAN

Scale, 40 Chains to an inch.

This line Surveyed by M. Aldous

This line Surveyed by L. Kennedy

DOMINION LANDS LITHOGRAPHIC OFFICE.

Surveyed by the Undersigned

Chs. Eng. Larue D.L.S.

July & August 1883

Dominion Lands Office
Ottawa

8th March 1884

Approved and confirmed

E. Deville

for the Surveyor General

Contents:

Land in Sections	22219.00	Acres
Roads	433.80	"
Water	821.00	"
Total Area	23473.80	"

EXPLANATION OF COLORS:

Woods............Green.   Scrub, or Prairie and Woods: Dotted green.   Water............Blue.

Marshes: Yellow with small strokes of black.   Hills or Slopes: Etching or Grey Shade.

The Discovery of Oil

In the fall of 1913, at the same time a real estate boom in Calgary was ending, oil was struck in the Turner Valley nearby, setting off another round of mania, this time for land, oil leases, and shares in "oil companies" that sprang up in the city overnight. The intense staking of claims is reflected in Map 371, below.

In 1911, a farmer, William Herron, noticed leaking petroleum gas on his property. He bought land and mineral rights, and persuaded Archibald Dingman, of the Calgary Natural Gas Company, to drill. On 6 October 1913 they struck oil—or at least what they thought was oil. In fact it was naptha; oil in any quantity would not be extracted until after 1920, but nevertheless, Alberta's oil industry was born.

The Turner Valley oil strike was small by today's standards. The birth of the modern oil industry in Alberta would have to wait until 3 February 1947, when oil erupted from a well drilled by Imperial Oil at Leduc, near Edmonton.

MAP 370 (*right*).
Ink-drawn wells, drill sites, processing plants, and pipelines are all in evidence on this 1915 map of the Turner Valley.

MAP 371 (*below*).
A complex 1914 map of oil leases by a stunning number of oil companies all trying to get in on the action in the Turner Valley. The creator of this map, Theodore Seyler, found the best way to depict the activity was in a circle, and his system seems to work well.

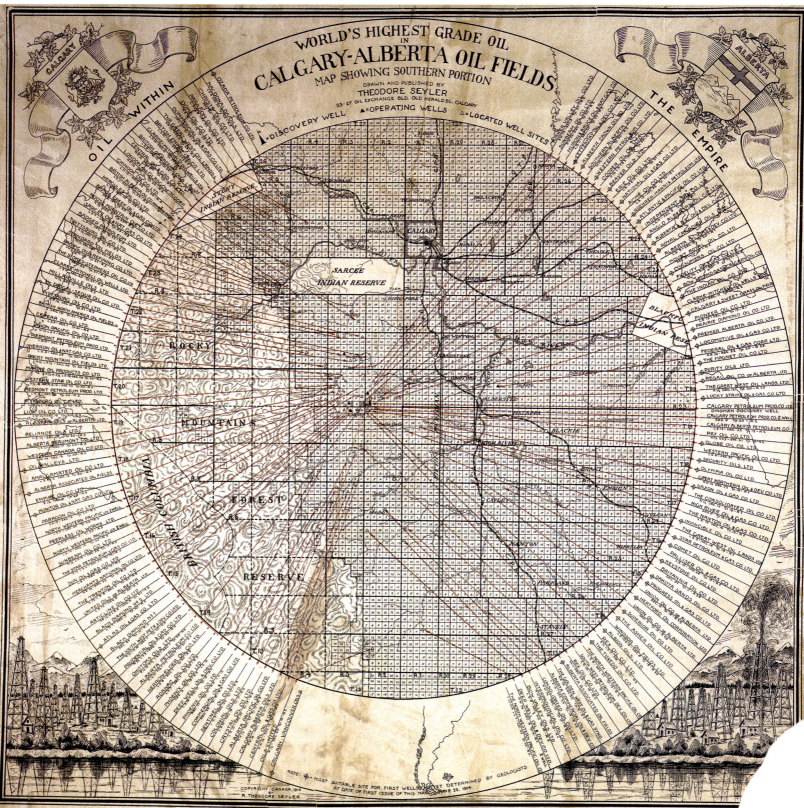

The Art of the Bird's-Eye

Bird's-eyes or panoramic maps of urban areas were common in the second half of the nineteenth century, aided by advances in printing processes that had reduced the cost of producing them. Most were published as separate maps, sold commercially to promote settlement in the city, often by real estate agents.

Bird's-eye maps typically show an overdone amount of commercial activity in order to give the impression of a bustling and vital city. Preparing the maps required a great deal of painstaking work. After drawing a perspective grid for the streets, the artist had to sketch buildings

Map 372 (*right*).
A bird's-eye map of Winnipeg in 1880, drawn by Thaddeus Fowler, who produced similar views of well over four hundred North American cities and whose career lasted fifty-four years.

Map 373 (*below*).
Detail of a magnificent bird's-eye map of Chatham, Ontario, published about 1880. The artist was not credited.

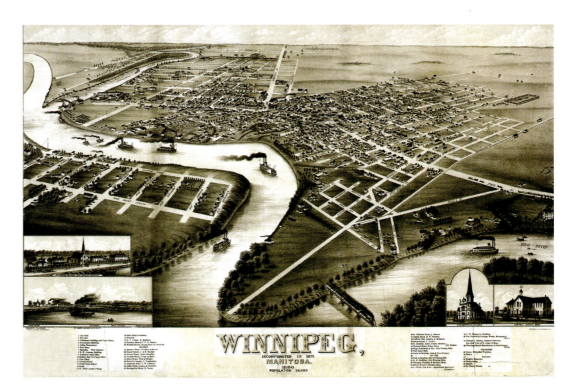

individually and then place them on the grid such that they appeared to be viewed from a height. This was, of course, long before aerial photography. The result was an often stunning map, purchased, then as now, for display. Today these maps provide an invaluable and detailed historical record of many North American cities.

A representative sample of these maps is shown here; others are to be found throughout this atlas. (See *Bird's-eye maps* in the index for a complete list.)

Map 374 (*right*).
This magnificent bird's-eye map of Halifax in 1890 truly lives up to the term "panoramic." The amount of work that went into such a map must have been prodigious, for every building had to be sketched on the ground and transposed to be viewed at the same—and for the artist, imaginary—vertical angle.

Map 375 (*below*).
A classic bird's-eye map, of Winnipeg in 1884. Compare this with the 1880 map of the same area on the previous page, prior to the railway-induced land boom of 1881–82. The map below is less correct in its perspective, though perhaps more maplike, since the angle of view is more vertical. Pictures of public buildings, plus the commercial premises and houses of those prepared to pay for the privilege, adorn the perimeter.

Map 376 (*right, bottom*).
A bird's-eye map of London, Ontario, in 1878. This map is less a view and more a map, due to the yellow street colour. Every detail is shown, down to people and horse-drawn carriages on the streets.

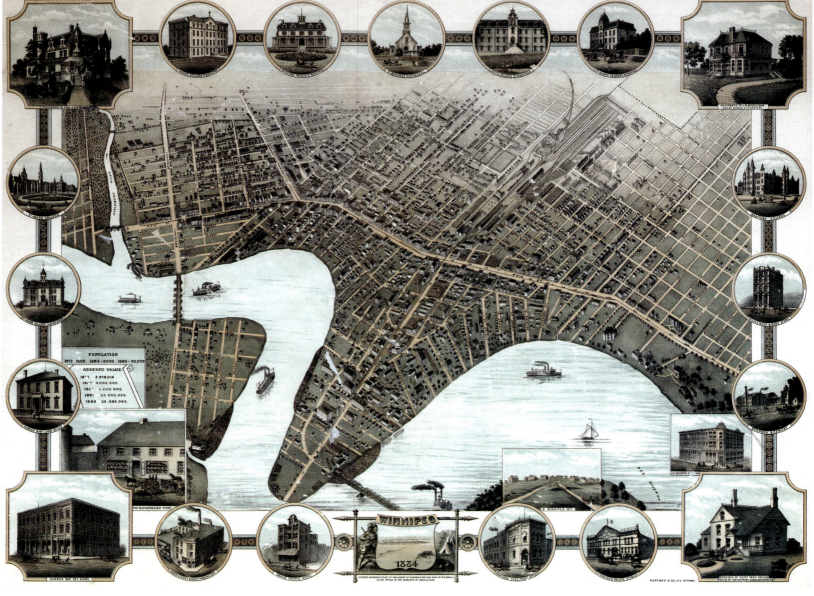

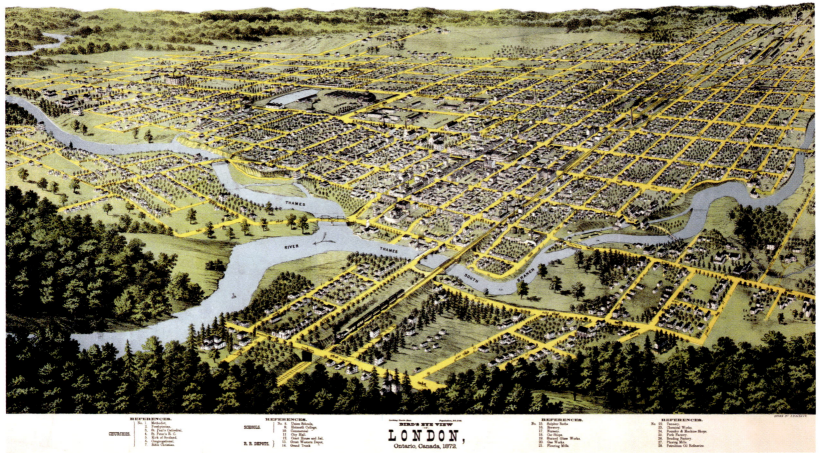

CHURCHES.	No. 1. Methodist.
	2. Presbyterian.
	3. St. Paul's Cathedral.
	4. St. Peter's R. C.
	5. Kirk of Scotland.
	6. Congregational.
	7. Bible Christian.

SCHOOLS.	No. 8. Union Schools.
	9. Hellmuth College.
	10. Ornamental
	11. City Hall.
	12. Court House and Jail.
R. R. DEPOTS.	13. Great Western Depot.
	14. Grand Trunk

REFERENCES.	No. 15. Sulphur Baths.
	16. Brewery.
	17. Nursery.
	18. Gas Houses.
	19. Barrel Glass Works.
	20. Gas Works.
	21. Flouring Mills.

REFERENCES.	No. 22. Tannery.
	23. Chemical Works.
	24. Foundry & Machine Shops.
	25. Pork Factory.
	26. Bending Factory.
	27. Planing Mills.
	28. Petroleum Oil Refineries.

BIRD'S EYE VIEW

LONDON,

Ontario, Canada, 1872.

Vancouver—
Pacific Terminus

The naturally advantageous site of today's Vancouver had been used by natives for generations. The first map of the area, however, was that of the Spanish explorers in 1791. The whole map is shown on pages 160-61 (Map 235) and an enlarged portion is shown here (Map 377). Dionisio Galiano seems to have been the first European to find the mouth of the Fraser, and he anchored in the North Arm on 14 June 1792. George Vancouver entered Burrard Inlet the same year, giving it its name. In 1808, when Simon Fraser descended the Fraser River, he found an extensive Musqueam village on the North Arm of the delta.

In 1827 the Hudson's Bay Company established Fort Langley as a trading post in the Fraser Valley. Following the formation of the mainland Colony of British Columbia in 1858, New Westminster was laid out by the Royal Engineers.

In 1862, three entrepreneurs, noting reports of coal at what is now Coal Harbour and thinking that clay was likely present also, preempted land on Burrard Inlet and established a brickworks. The three, John Morton, Samuel

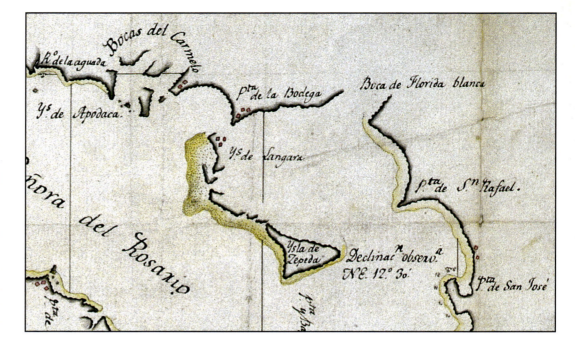

Map 377 (*above*).
Part of the Spanish *Carta que comprehende* ("map of all that is known") drawn in 1791, showing the Vancouver area. This is the first map of Vancouver. The information about what is now Vancouver came from the longboat exploration of José María Nárvaez with Juan Carrasco in *Santa Saturnina* as far north as Texada Island. Clearly many of the features were mapped by sighting from a distance, for *Ysla de Zepeda*, Point Roberts, is shown as an island, and the peninsula of the City of Vancouver had only its western tip shown, as *Ys[la] de Langara*, Point Grey. *Boca de Florida blanca* is the inner part of Burrard Inlet (Vancouver Harbour). Thinking this the entrance to a possible Northwest Passage, and using this map, Dionisio Galiano tried unsuccessfully the following year to penetrate north from Boundary Bay, south of Vancouver, only to find low land. He later did not bother to explore Burrard Inlet, a more likely passage, because he met George Vancouver, whose survey had shown it only as an arm of the sea. *P[un]ta de la Bodega* is Point Atkinson, *Bocas del Carmelo* is Howe Sound, and *P[un]ta de S[a]n Rafael* is Kwomais Point, the southwestern tip of South Surrey at Ocean Park. The Strait of Georgia is *Gran Canal de Nuestra Señora del Rosario* (the name only partially seen on this detail). In 1792, George Vancouver was shown this map when he met Galiano, and expressed "mortification" that the coast had already been surveyed. The whole map is shown as Map 235, pages 160-61.

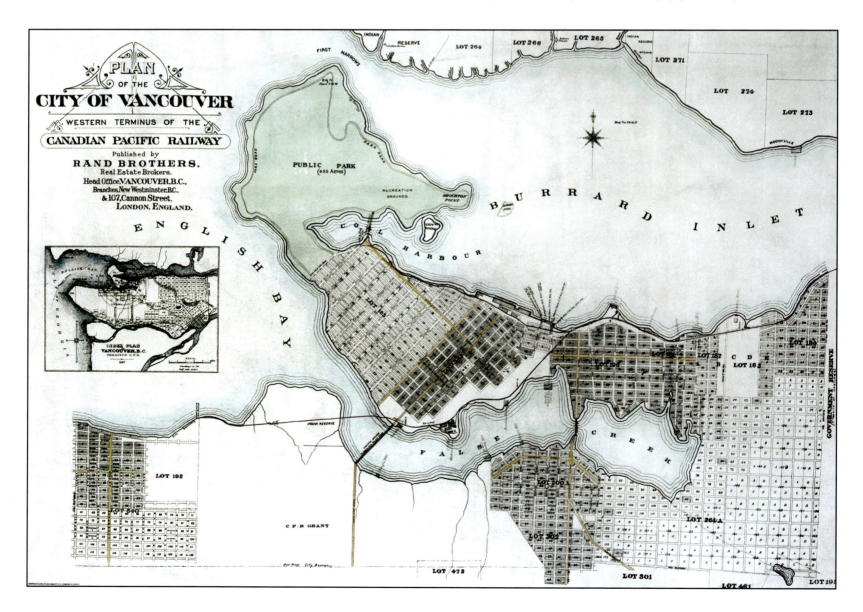

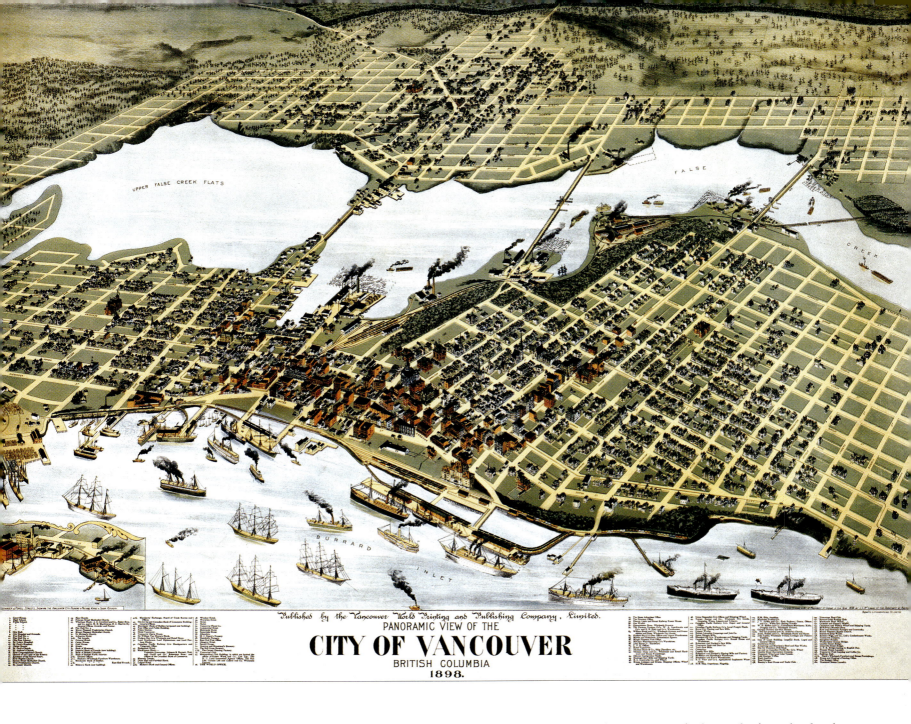

Published by the Vancouver World Printing and Publishing Company, Limited.

PANORAMIC VIEW OF THE

CITY OF VANCOUVER

BRITISH COLUMBIA
1898.

Map 378 (*left*).
A map of Vancouver published in 1887, the year the first Canadian Pacific Railway train reached the City of Vancouver. As was usual for railway maps, the impression of a city already in existence is given by the large number of subdivided lots shown. Even by 1898 (Map 379, *above*), the lots were by no means all built upon. The index map shows the large land grant extending south and covering much of the central part of today's City of Vancouver. A single line runs west to the shores of English Bay, ending at a point in today's Kitsilano marked 2909¼ miles from Montreal. False Creek extends considerably farther eastwards than it does today. It was not until 1914 that the eastern section was filled in to make room for the station and yards of the Canadian Northern Railway, which could not otherwise find land close to Vancouver not already owned by its rival, the Canadian Pacific Railway.

Map 379 (*above*).
A superb bird's-eye map of the City of Vancouver in 1898, with the usual hectic commercial activity depicting the city as a bustling port. A small inset at bottom left is a continuation of the shoreline eastwards; it shows a foundry and a sugar refinery, the cartographer being unwilling to leave out any significant economic activity. The large white steamship just approaching the dock, above the word "Vancouver" in the title, is the Canadian Pacific Railway's ship *Empress of India*. As in Map 378, False Creek extends far to the east.

Brighouse, and William Hailstone, were the so-called three greenhorns. In anticipation of the arrival of the railway, and hoping to make their fortunes, they later had a townsite surveyed;

the plan, drawn in 1882, was for a city to be called Liverpool.

In the 1860s and 1870s, sawmills were established around Burrard Inlet, so that by the time the Canadian Pacific Railway was casting its eyes towards English Bay, there were three little settlements: Moodyville, on the North Shore; Hastings, by the Second Narrows; and Granville, colloquially known as Gastown, after a colourful and talkative hotel owner named John "Gassy Jack" Deighton. It was this latter settlement that would grow into the City of Vancouver.

There was also a small settlement at the head of the inlet, Port Moody, and it was at this closest tidewater that the Canadian Pacific Railway first terminated in 1885 (see page 225).

In order to persuade the CPR to extend its line from Port Moody to Burrard Inlet, the province granted the railway a great deal of land; the agreement was reached in February 1885. A long waterfront area was made available for docks and terminals, 480 acres (194 ha) of land on what is now the downtown peninsula; 39 lots were granted in the townsite of Granville, as was a large amount of land on False Creek for marshalling yards, a roundhouse for locomotives,

and maintenance facilities. The far-sighted William Cornelius Van Horne also acquired another 5,800 acres (2 350 ha) south of English Bay and False Creek, for residential use. Thus the railway came to own and develop, among others, the area now known as Shaughnessy, named after the railway purchasing agent Thomas Shaughnessy, who went on to become president of the railway.

It was Van Horne, however, who had suggested the name "Vancouver" for the new city. It was incorporated under this name on 6 April 1886. Two months later, on 13 June, a fire almost completely destroyed the wooden city. But with the railway coming, nothing was going to stop Vancouver now, and rebuilding commenced immediately. The first transcontinental train steamed into the new city on 23 May 1887.

The City of Vancouver expanded in 1911 to include Hastings Townsite, and in 1929 amalgamated with the municipalities of South Vancouver (incorporated in 1892) and Point Grey (incorporated in 1908). Today the urban area has expanded to the North Shore mountains, the American border, and eastwards up the Fraser Valley, and Vancouver is Canada's third largest city.

Ottawa—the Nation's Capital

There had been scattered European settlement in the Ottawa Valley from about the 1790s, and by 1825, Wrightsville, later Hull, on the north bank of the river, had perhaps a thousand inhabitants. The Ottawa Valley itself had been an important route west for the fur trade since the beginnings of European settlement; Samuel de Champlain had passed by in 1615 (see page 54).

Then, in 1826, work began on the Rideau Canal, designed for strategic reasons to avoid the St. Lawrence. Lieutenant Colonel John By was appointed to supervise the construction (see page 181). By established a construction camp close to the flight of locks at the north end of the canal, leading down to the Ottawa River. He made it his headquarters, forsaking the more comfortable Kingston, at the other end of the

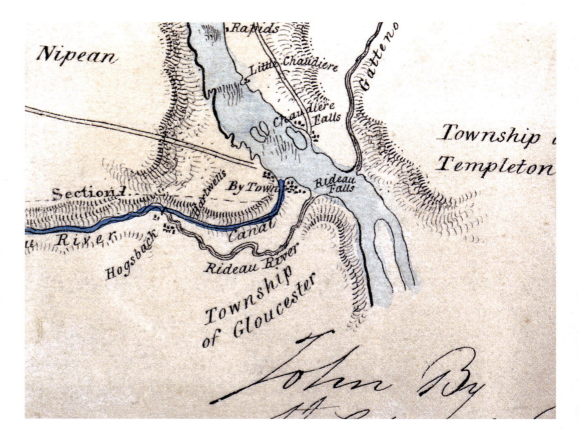

Map 380 (*right*).
Detail of an 1830 map, drawn by Captain Thomas Burrowes and signed by John By, showing the eastern end of his Rideau Canal and the location of Bytown.

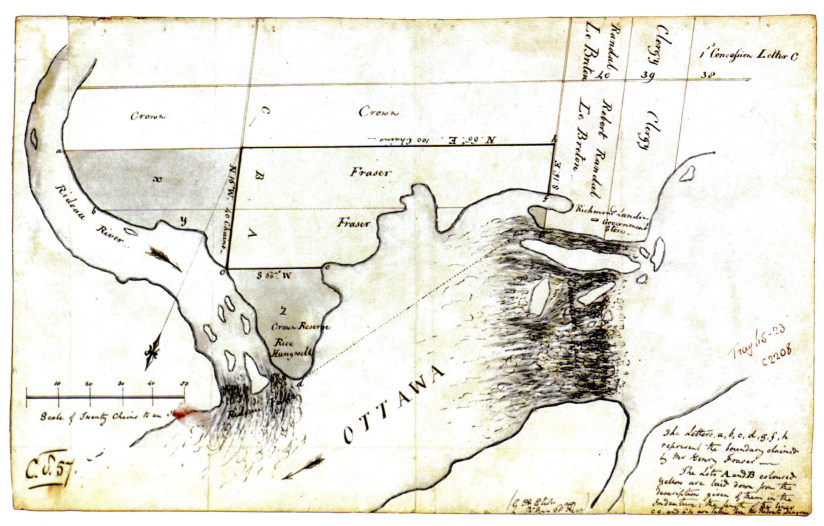

Map 381.
This map, one of the earliest of the Ottawa area, was attached to a deed transferring land from Hugh Fraser to the Crown, "for public use." It is dated 18 June 1823. Part of the land transferred eventually became the site for Canada's Parliament Buildings, on which construction was begun in 1859 and completed in 1865, after Ottawa had been chosen as the new capital for the united Province of Canada in 1857. The entrance to the Rideau Canal was constructed in the first bay south of the point where the Rideau River enters the Ottawa River, originally called Sleigh Bay and renamed by John By Entrance Bay. North is to the bottom of the map.

CITY OF OTTAWA, CANADA.

WITH VIEWS OF PRINCIPAL BUSINESS BUILDINGS.

Map 382.

This magnificent bird's-eye map of Ottawa, published in 1895, is an archetypical example of this map genre. It has views of individual business buildings around the edges, no doubt those businesses who subscribed to the map as an advertising promotion. This particular example is in the Library of Congress, and has a faint red stamp in the lower right: *War Dept. Military Information Division, Map Section*. It seems that in 1895 knowledge of the streets of Ottawa was of strategic interest to the American government, which as late as 1903 was threatening Canada with military action, if not war, over the Alaska boundary (see page 252).

canal. The site attracted others and by 1827 a little town flourished, which quickly became known as Bytown.

There were two settlements, Lower Bytown, to the east of the canal, and Upper Bytown, to the west. The town overtook Wrightsville as the principal centre of the lumber industry, and in the 1850s the Chaudière and Rideau Falls were utilized for power to saw timber, which was barged down the Ottawa River to American markets.

In 1850 Bytown was chartered as a town, and in 1855 it was incorporated as a city and renamed Ottawa. In 1841 Upper and Lower

Canada had united, and after a succession of capitals, Queen Victoria chose Ottawa as the capital in 1857. Not only was the city right on the boundary between the two Canadas, but it was also a safe distance from a potentially aggressive United States.

Parliament buildings were built on government reserve land between the original Upper and Lower Bytown. In 1867 the city was selected as the capital for the new Dominion of Canada. The growth due to government was dramatic, with the city tripling its population between 1851 and 1871.

In the 1890s the hydroelectric potential of the falls was tapped, providing power for a pulp and paper industry in addition to the lumber industry. By 1895, the date of Map 382, the spectacular bird's-eye map above, the population was about fifty thousand.

Since the 1920s, many new parks and federal buildings have been constructed, and, during World War II, the federal government became the largest employer, adding some thirty thousand people in that period. After 1945, rail lines and yards were removed or relocated and the Rideau Canal preserved. With a greenbelt formed from federally reserved land, the result has been the creation of a well-planned urban area with a great deal of open space—a beautiful city fit to be Canada's capital.

Toronto in the Nineteenth Century

(For early Toronto, see page 169.)

York was a growing town of 9,250 people when in 1834 it was incorporated as a city—Toronto. Its new mayor, William Lyon Mackenzie, would lead a rebellion in 1837 (see page 200).

During the 1840s the city added many stone and brick buildings, and many streets were serviced with sewers and gas. A tide of immigrants from Britain, and especially from Ireland following the 1845–49 potato famine, swelled the city population. But the advent of the railway contributed most to Toronto's growth, starting in 1851, when the first line was opened, reaching Lake Huron in 1855. In the same year the Great Western Railway extended its line into Toronto from Hamilton. In 1856 the Grand Trunk connected Toronto with Montréal. It completed its link on to Sarnia, with American connections, in 1859. The railways drew vastly more resources into Toronto's purview, extending its hinterland and commercially subjugating rival cities such as Hamilton and Kingston. By 1871, Toronto had 56,000 inhabitants.

Toronto quickly became the preferred location of new industries and new businesses. Retail icon Timothy Eaton opened his store in 1869, and Robert Simpson in 1872. Major banks, vital for the financing of growth, were founded, challenging the pre-eminence of the country's then largest, the Bank of Montreal. The Bank of Toronto opened its doors in 1855, the Bank of Commerce in 1867, the Dominion in 1869, and the Imperial in 1873; after mergers, they would form the major Canadian financial institutions of today. And the Toronto Stock Exchange had been founded in 1852, catering to the city's grain dealers and wholesalers.

Finance and industry grew hand in hand. A series of amalgamations led to the geographical expansion of the city in the 1880s, and, as can be seen from Map 386, created in 1893, Toronto was a huge urban agglomeration well before the turn of the twentieth century.

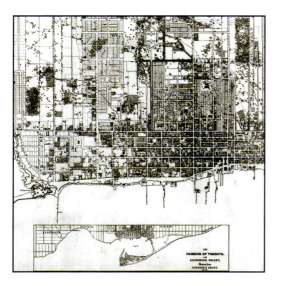

Map 383 *(below, left)*.
Toronto in 1851, the year the first railway out of the city began construction. This was the Ontario, Simcoe and Huron. It reached Lake Huron in 1855. After 1858 the line became the Northern, and the creator of this map, Sandford Fleming, its chief engineer. The map is thus that of Toronto on the verge of the railway age, an era during which it would grow enormously.

Map 384 *(above)*.
Part of a military map dated 1851, showing the old Fort York and the new fort (*New Barracks*) and other features, including the *Lunatic Asylum*. At the time these were on the western edge of the growing city. The military road connecting the two forts is today almost exactly under the Gardiner Expressway.

Map 385 *(right, top)*.
This splendid bird's-eye map of Toronto was published in 1876. With mind-boggling details both on the map itself and in the pictures around the edges, it must have taken a very long time to compile. The businesses around the sides would have subscribed to the map's publication. The railway lines of the Great Western and Grand Trunk usurp much of the waterfront. Fort Toronto is visible at bottom left.

Map 386 *(right)*.
This magnificent bird's-eye view of Toronto was created in 1893. The original is huge (1.1 m x 1.95 m), dominating a wall at the Toronto Public Library when it is on display. The two bird's-eye maps on this page together display perhaps the apex of the panoramic map artist's work; both are wonderfully detailed results of an age of commercial boosterism, when it was commercially feasible for an artist to spend months composing maps such as these. For more on bird's-eye maps, see page 233.

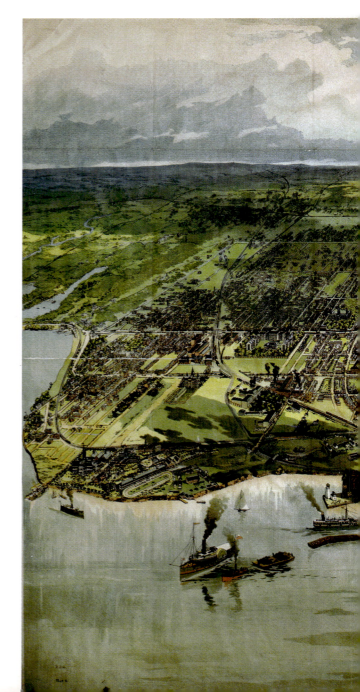

Montréal after the Fall of New France

(See also The Founding of Montréal, *page 57.)*

On 8 September 1760 the governor of New France, Pierre de Rigaud de Vaudreuil, wrote to General Jeffrey Amherst, "I have remitted to the commander the articles of capitulation which I signed." With this, Montréal, and New France, surrendered to the British forces.

There followed three years of military government, until the signing of the Treaty of Paris in 1763. In 1761, a report on the size of the population of Montréal tallied 24,957 persons.

Late in 1775, an American invading force briefly occupied Montréal, largely expecting the population to convert to their cause. The Americans were driven from the city when British forces regrouped after the defence of Québec.

Montréal under the French regime had become the centre for the western fur trade, and it was no different under the British. A coalition of partnerships formed in 1785 produced the North West Company, headquartered in Montréal, and until 1821 this concern was the princi-

pal competition to the Hudson's Bay Company. Forward-thinking traders such as Alexander Mackenzie were responsible for an enormous growth in the industry. It is no surprise that Mackenzie's own book of his explorations was entitled *Voyages from Montreal.*

It had long been recognized that the Rivière St. Pierre might be used as the basis of a canal to bypass the St. Louis Rapids, and an attempt to dig such a canal had been made as early as 1689. In 1825 the Lachine Canal became a reality and fostered the growth of an industrial area around it. The canal was closed to navigation in 1970, a victim of the St. Lawrence Seaway.

Montréal was growing, and in 1832 received a charter as a city. As the commercial centre of the Canadas, Montréal was capital of the united province during the period 1843 to 1849, losing the distinction when the parliament building was burned down in a riot. A painting

of Queen Victoria was saved on this occasion by a Scot named Sandford Fleming.

In the 1850s, dredging of the St. Lawrence below Montréal was begun, with the result that larger vessels could now reach the city. This was critical if Montréal was to maintain its premier commercial position.

After the construction of the Grand Trunk Railway, Montréal was for a time an important railway hub, and after the completion of the Canadian Pacific Railway in 1886, Montréal again had significant connections with the West, for the rail line ran directly to that city rather than to Toronto. Reflecting this, the head offices of the Canadian Pacific Railway were established in Montréal. For a long time, much of the wheat from the West was shipped through Montréal. A number of grain elevators are evident in the bird's-eye map of 1889 shown here (MAP 388).

By 1911, the population of greater Montréal was over half a million people, and the city

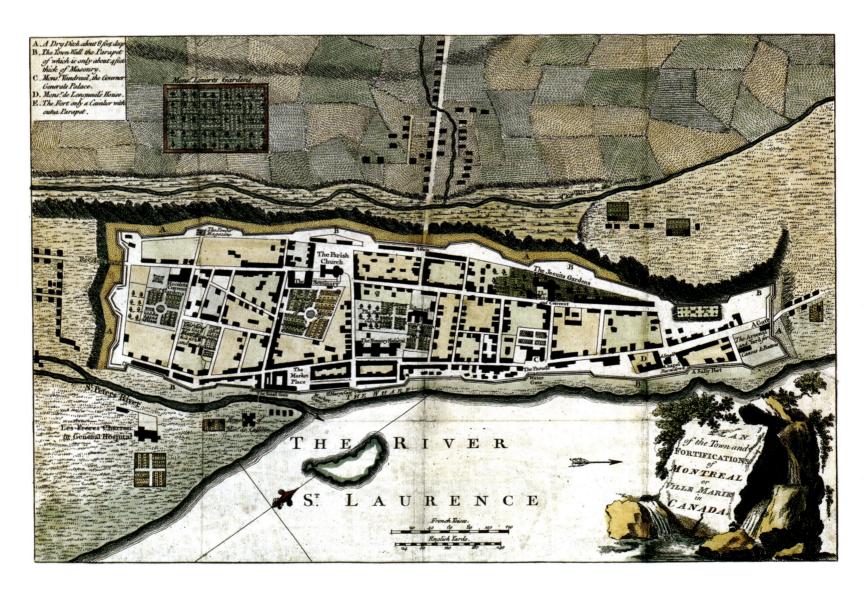

MAP 387.
Montréal surrendered on 8 September 1760, completing the capitulation of French Canada. This map of Montréal was published in English in 1759. It was copied from French sources. In 1716 the French decided to replace the wooden stockade around the city with a stone wall, though this was not completed until 1746; it is shown in this map.

was the foremost commercial centre in Canada. It was only later in the twentieth century that this position was lost to its long-time rival, Toronto.

Today Montréal is arguably Canada's most cosmopolitan city, and with well over three million inhabitants in the metropolitan area, is second only to Toronto in size.

MAP 388 (*above*).
A bird's-eye panoramic map of Montréal in 1889. A grain elevator appears to stand on what is now the Point-à-Callière Museum, the site of the original settlement of Ville-Marie. Behind it is the Lachine Canal. Mont-Royal dominates the city skyline. In the foreground is the Victoria Bridge, opened in 1860 as a single-track covered bridge (as shown here); it was later expanded and converted to carry road traffic, and remains one of the city's important bridges. As is usual in this type of map, an inordinate amount of commercial activity is evident.

MAP 389 (*below*).
A military map of the environs of Montréal printed in 1863, but from an 1839 survey. It was printed by the British War Office during the American Civil War, when there was concern that Canada might again be attacked. The Lachine Canal is clearly visible, and the line of the Champlain and St. Lawrence Railroad, opened in 1836, is marked, terminating at La Prairie, across the St. Lawrence from Montréal (see page 210). A planked road runs northwest to Longueuil, at which point a ferry crosses the river. A number of winter roads are shown, roads passable only when the mud had frozen. At Kahnawake (*Gauchnawaga*), a ferry ride from Lachine, are *Indian Hunting Lands*.

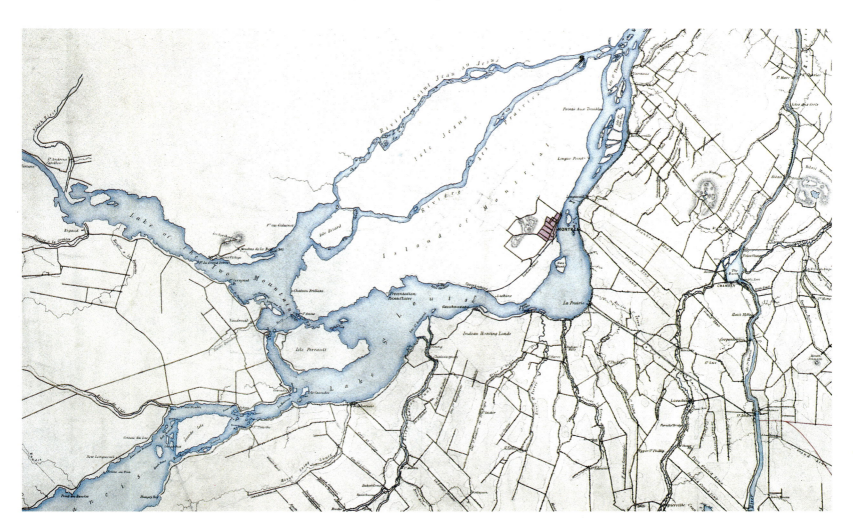

Gold in the Klondike

In August 1896 an American, George Washington Carmack, and two natives, Skookum Jim and Tagish Charlie, found gold on Rabbit Creek, a small tributary of the Trondec or Klondike River, itself a tributary of the Yukon. It was soon renamed Bonanza Creek, and the discovery of gold set off a human surge that was to change the history of the North.

Over two hundred claims were staked immediately, but the gold rush proper only started in the summer of 1897, when the first group of gold finders reached the outside world, arriving in San Francisco on 15 July and Seattle on 17 July. In the next few years, something like 100,000 hopefuls set out for the Yukon, although perhaps only 40,000 actually made it that far.

The Canadian government, mindful of what could happen when Americans came in great numbers, beefed up the North-West Mounted Police, only allowing in those who could prove they had enough supplies to survive, and regulating navigation on the Yukon River. Countless lives were saved, and the reputation of the North-West Mounted Police assured. The mandating of 520 kg of solid food for each person, together with other equipment, meant numerous back-and-forth trips up the mountain passes and added considerable distance that was conveniently forgotten on the maps showing the routes to the goldfields.

The North-West Territories government attempted to assert its authority and began collecting fees for the importation of liquor, which was a usurpation of federal jurisdiction. As a direct result of this the federal government passed the Yukon Territory Act, which separated the Yukon District from the North-West Territories, as of 13 June 1898.

A railway, the White Pass and Yukon, was hastily built between Skagway and Lake

Map 390 (right, top).
A commercial map of the Klondike goldfields and the Canadian routes to them, published in 1897 with various backings, from paper to canvas, depending on the use intended. American maps tended to emphasize American routes, while Canadian maps emphasized Canadian routes. There was for a time considerable rivalry between Seattle, Vancouver, and Victoria, as merchants in those cities wanted the miners to equip themselves at their emporiums. As with many gold rushes, the real money was made by suppliers. In a not-so-subliminal message, the principal colours of this map are yellows and golds. The interpretation of the international boundary in the Alaska panhandle follows Canadian claims, though the boundary claimed by the United States is also shown.

Map 391 (right, bottom).
A bird's-eye view of Dawson. Like most bird's-eye views, this was intended to promote the city commercially. It was published in 1903, after the gold rush had faded, as an attempt to revive the city's sagging fortunes. Even on this promotional map the houses are scattered. The Yukon River is in the foreground, and the Klondike River flows in at right.

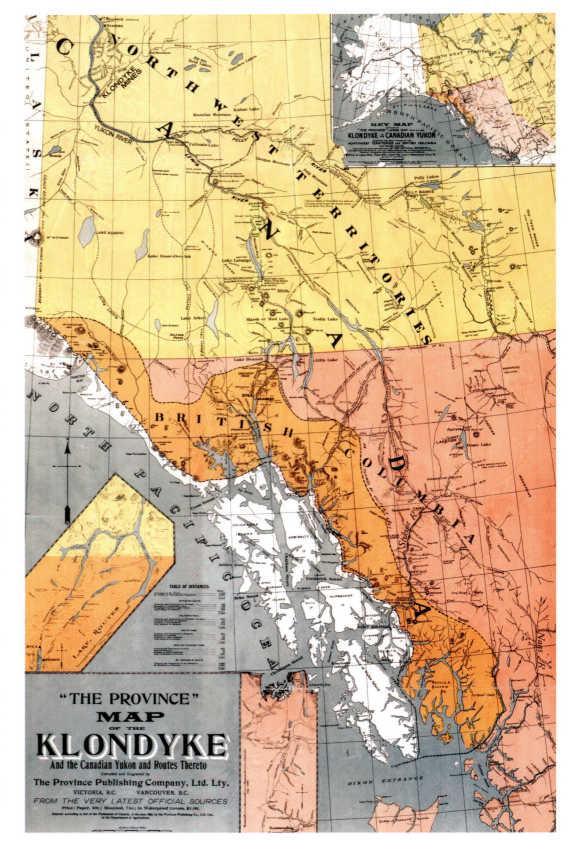

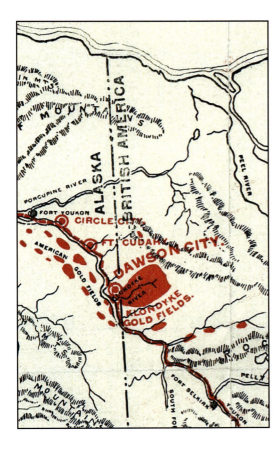

Map 392 (above).
This hastily printed American map is at pains to emphasize the *American* goldfields. The boundary between American and British territory has been moved eastwards so that part of the Klondike River, and even Dawson City itself, is shown as being on American soil, when in reality it is more than 70 km from the boundary. (Map 393, at right, provides an easy comparison with the correct situation.) But then the map, printed in Pittsburgh in 1897, was aimed at American miners, so all the better to show the gold in the United States.

Map 393 (right).
Part of an American promotional map, published in 1897, showing the goldfields and the various routes to the Klondike. The international boundary in the Alaska panhandle follows American claims, with no consideration of those of Canada. But at least Dawson and the Klondike are in Canada.

Bennett, completed in July 1899, although by this time the bulk of the influx of miners had already passed. The following year the line was extended as far as Whitehorse, a new town which had sprung up at the head of navigation on the Yukon River. And in 1901 the telegraph finally made it to this farthest outpost of Canadian territory, thus enhancing the ability of the federal government to control the region.

The gold-yielding area was limited to the few creeks around the original find, so the gold rush did not last very long. It has been estimated that only four thousand people actually found gold, and only three hundred of them found enough to be considered rich; of those, only fifty managed to retain their new-found wealth.

Map 394 (right, inset).
Vancouver and Victoria competed with each other, and with Seattle and San Francisco, to be the supply base for the would-be gold miners, no doubt recognizing that there was as much money to be made supplying the miners as in mining the gold. This is an advertisement for Vancouver printed in 1897, with just about *every* route to the Klondike leading from the Vancouver waterfront.

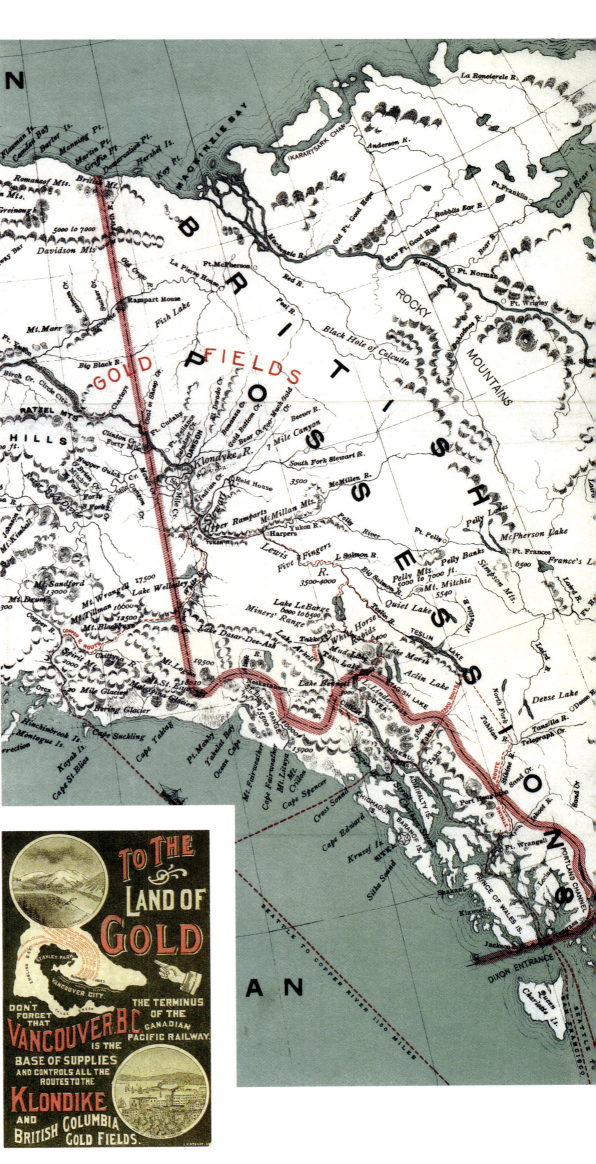

The British Dominion

This colourful map was published in 1902, as a stand-alone information sheet. Such publications were a common way of obtaining information in the days before radio and television. It promoted the idea of Canada as part of the British Empire, complete with a map of the British Isles. Certainly the word "British" is deliberately predominant here.

And there is no denying that Canada was very British in 1902. A census held the previous year showed a total population of 5,371,315, although it must be noted that the Aboriginal and Asian populations were likely underenumerated. Nevertheless, the figures from the census are a good guide. Of the total, 57 percent declared Britain as their country of origin. Twenty-three percent were from England, the rest being from Scotland, Wales, and Ireland, the whole of the latter country being at that time part of Britain.

Those of French origin formed 30.7 percent of the total population, while 8.5 percent were from countries in Europe other than Britain or France. People of Asian origin were enumerated at only 0.4 percent, the Aboriginal population at 2.4 percent.

These stated countries of origin did not mean that all were born in those countries, merely descended from original immigrants from them. In the 1901 census, 13 percent of the population was foreign-born.

Today, Canada's population has more diverse origins, and many more people come from Asian countries, but still nearly three-quarters of the total has British or French origins.

MAP 395.
Map of Canada as part of the British Empire, published in 1902. Canada is shown surrounded by other countries of the Empire, all, of course, coloured red. Britain is shown to a scale 233 percent larger than the map of Canada. Canada's Arctic still has parts of its coasts not mapped, although the configuration of islands is generally correct. In the Dominion of Canada, Ontario, Québec, New Brunswick, Nova Scotia, Manitoba, Prince Edward Island, and British Columbia are provinces; Newfoundland is a separate British colony. Yukon is a separate territory, formed in 1898 in response to the Klondike gold rush (see page 244). All the other political divisions are provisional districts of the North-West Territories, including that of Franklin, covering the Arctic islands and created in 1895 (see page 253). The international boundary with Alaska is shown as per the British claim; the American claim is shown with a thinner line. The compromise boundary would be determined the following year, 1903 (see page 252). The provinces of Saskatchewan and Alberta do not exist; the smaller areas with those names are still provisional districts of the North-West Territories. The new provinces would be created in 1905. The northern boundaries of Ontario and Québec are considerably farther south than they are today, and Manitoba, while larger than its original size, is still relatively small. These boundaries would change in 1912 to those that exist today, except for the boundary of Québec with Labrador, which would not be settled until 1927 (see page 256).

246

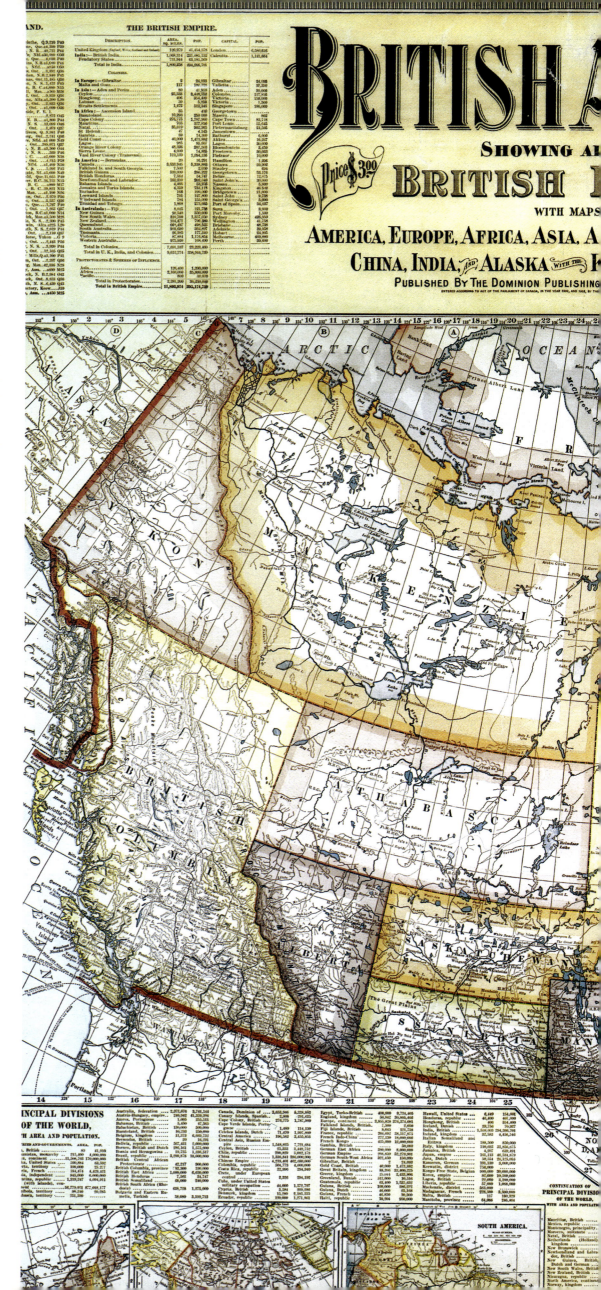

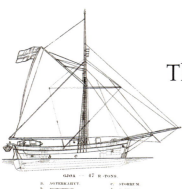

Amundsen's ship *Gjøa*.

The Canadian Arctic and the Northwest Passage Achieved

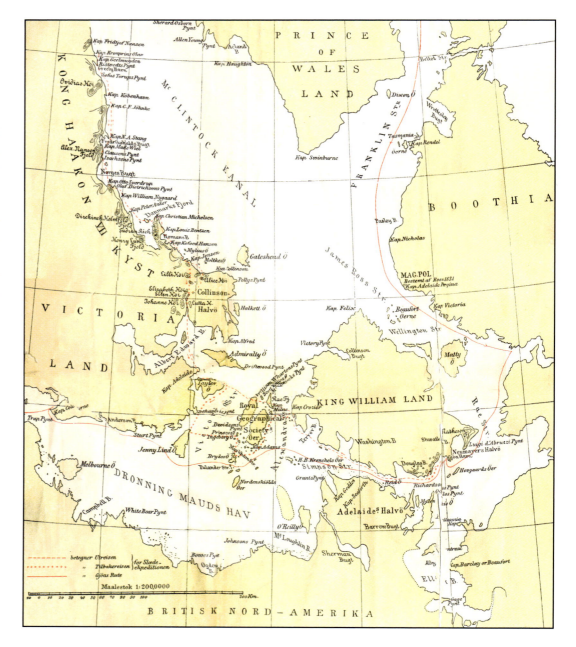

On 9 October 1880, Britain transferred to Canada its claims to the Arctic islands north of the North American mainland. It had been prompted by two requests for land grants near Cumberland Sound in 1874. One request was by an American naval officer. Britain did not want to assume government of the region, but did not want to lose it to the United States either. Thus the British asked Canada to take over claims to sovereignty. Such were the machinations of government that it took six more years for the transfer to occur.

Even then, legal ambiguities meant that sovereignty was in doubt, until on 2 October 1895 they were resolved by the issuance of a Canadian order-in-council establishing the provisional districts, within the North-West Teritiries, of Ungava, Franklin, Mackenzie, and Yukon.

In the meantime, there had been some continuing exploration. In 1871–73 an American expedition led by Charles Hall had failed in an attempt to reach the North Pole through Smith Sound, between Ellesmere Island and Greenland. In 1875–76 a British expedition under George Nares, also attempting to reach the North Pole, explored the coast of Ellesmere Island, and the American Frederick Schwatka was in the King William Island area in 1878–80, searching for evidence of Franklin's demise.

Although a Canadian expedition under William Wakeham had proclaimed sovereignty on Baffin Island in 1897, these efforts were entirely overshadowed by the Arctic efforts of other countries' explorers, especially the American Robert E. Peary, whose reconnaisances on Ellesmere Island in 1898 would lead to a series of efforts culminating with his still-debated attainment of the North Pole in 1909.

Otto Sverdrup, a Swede who had been the captain of Fridtjof Nansen's ship *Fram* during its celebrated drift in the polar ice in 1893–96, explored the islands now called the Sverdrup Islands in 1898–1902. He spent four winters in the Arctic, using *Fram* as a base. Exploring by sledge, he located and mapped 2 800 km of new coastline over an area of 250 000 km², including Axel Heiberg, Ellef Ringnes, and Amund Ringnes Islands and the northern coast of Devon Island (MAP 397), publishing his findings in a book called, appropriately enough, *New Land*. Expecting a claim to the land, he submitted his findings to the Swedish—and after 1905, the Norwegian—government (Norway having separated from Swe-

MAP 396 (*above*).
Amundsen's routes, from his 1908 book, in Norwegian. The solid red line is the track of *Gjøa*, the dashed red line the route of the outbound sledge expedition, and the dashed red line with cross-marks is the returning sledge route.

MAP 397 (*below*).
Otto Sverdrup's map of his newly discovered islands, named after sponsors. The group is now the Sverdrup Islands.

den in 1905), but, perhaps luckily for Canada, neither was interested in pursuing such claims. The Norwegian claim was outstanding until 1930, when it was abandoned, with Canada paying the expedition's costs—and acquiring its maps.

It was a private expedition—just like the first voyages—that finally achieved a transit of the Northwest Passage. This was the 1903–06 voyage of Roald Amundsen in his little ship *Gjøa*. A Swede when he set out, he was a Norwegian when he completed his famous voyage.

Just as pursuing creditors threatened to forestall his expedition, Amundsen slipped away from Kristiana (now Oslo) on 16 June 1903. He had a crew of six, and *Gjøa* was piled to the gunnels with enough provisions for four years. After making magnetic observations on Beechey

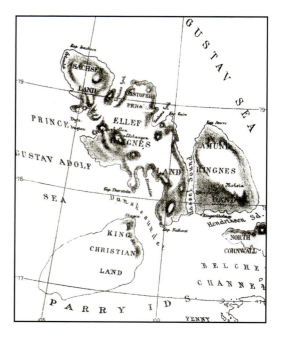

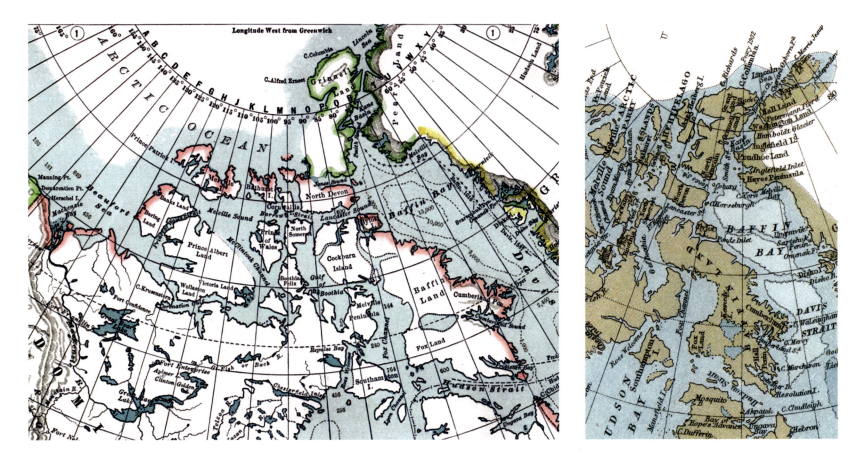

MAP 398 (*left*) and MAP 399 (*right*).
This pair of atlas maps, dated 1897 and 1905, show the change in knowledge due to the expedition of Otto Sverdrup in 1898–1902. On the 1897 map (*left*), only the hint of an island is shown north of those whose south coasts were found by Parry in 1819–20 (see MAP 287, pages 186–87); whereas in the 1905 map (*right*), Axel Heiberg Island is shown and named, and Ellef Ringnes and Amund Ringnes Island are shown (but not named), as is the east coast of Ellesmere Island. These are small-scale atlas maps, which by their nature are not accurate in their detail.

Island in August, he pushed south, intending with his small ship to keep close to the continental shore. After surviving storms and groundings, on 12 September *Gjøa* anchored in a small harbour on the southeast of King William Island, which was promptly christened Gjøa Havn (later Gjoa Haven; MAP 400). This was to be home to the seven men for the next two winters.

While at Gjøa Havn, Amundsen created a network of magnetic observing stations and located (but did not achieve, due to miscalculations) the magnetic pole, which had migrated about 65 km since it was first found by James Clark Ross in 1831 (see page 192). A series of sledge expedi-

tions was organized each spring, and Amundsen found and named the Royal Geographical Society Islands in Victoria Strait, named, as of old, after one of the expedition's sponsors.

In 1905 they sailed westwards, creeping carefully through the ice, through the passage now known as Amundsen Gulf, and got as far as King Point, about halfway between the Mackenzie Delta and Herschel Island, before becoming beset in the ice. Here Amundsen wintered once more, near the American whaling fleet. That winter, he made a five-month trek to Eagle City, Alaska, the end of the telegraph, to send out his story to the British *Times* newspaper, which had promised to pay him for an exclusive story. Unfortunately for Amundsen, the telegraph was not a private communication; others printed the story and the *Times* refused to pay.

Amundsen sailed out through Bering Strait on 30 August 1906 and reached San Francisco in October, becoming the first to traverse the long-sought Northwest Passage.

Canada rather slowly made attempts to ensure that the Arctic remained Canadian. Albert Peter Low of the Geological Survey sailed to Baffin and Ellesmere Islands in 1904, taking formal possession for Canada.

Then in 1906, Joseph-Elzéar Bernier began a series of three voyages at the behest of the

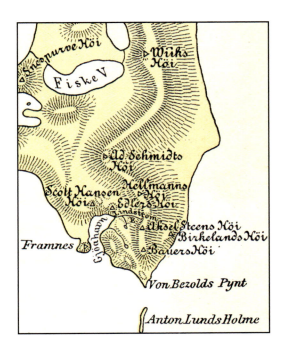

MAP 400 (*left*).
The tiny harbour at the southeastern tip of King William Land (King William Island) in which Amundsen spent two winters, 1903–05. He called it "the finest little harbour in the world." The map is from Amundsen's book.

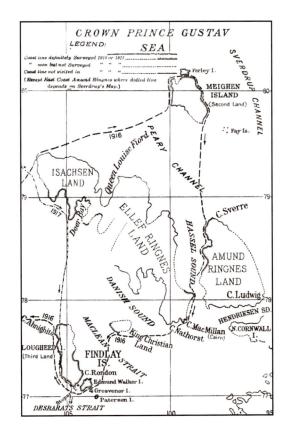

MAP 401.
Vilhjalmur Stefansson's map of his discovery in 1916 of Meighen Island, just to the north of Sverdrup's Ellef Ringnes and Amund Ringnes Islands. Here he corrected Sverdrup's map (MAP 397, previous page). Meighen Island, until 1948 the most recently discovered new land in Canada, may have been discovered by Frederick Cook in 1909, but his accounts were at variance with two Inuit that accompanied him, and Cook denied having seen the island. Meighen Island was named after Arthur Meighen, solicitor general in Robert Borden's government at the time of its discovery. Meighen became prime minister in 1920.

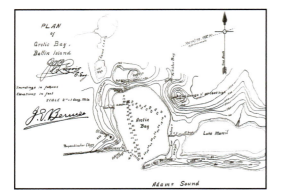

MAP 402 (above).
Bernier's map of Arctic Bay on Baffin Island, signed by him. Arctic Bay and Adams Sound are also marked on MAP 403. They are on the east side of Admiralty Inlet near the north end. Bernier wintered here in 1910–11. The bay is named not for Bernier's ship *Arctic*, but for a whaler with the same name that visited in 1872; the whaler's captain was W. Adams.

MAP 403 (right).
Brodeur and Borden Peninsulas at the north end of Baffin Island, as surveyed by Joseph-Elzéar Bernier in 1910–11; the dates he was in each location are marked. At the top is Lancaster Sound. Baffin Island is still called *Cockburn Land*. Nobody had paid much attention to the northern part of Baffin Island before, because it didn't lead, or even potentially lead, to a Northwest Passage. The southern part, by contrast, was the location of one of the first Arctic voyages, that by Martin Frobisher in 1576 (see page 34).

Canadian government (1906–07, 1908–09, and 1910–11), which now wished to "avoid encirclement by the United States." Bernier formally established Canadian possession at a number of points around the Arctic islands. On Dominion Day, 1 July 1909, he unveiled a tablet affixed to a cairn at Winter Harbour, Melville Island— Edward Parry's original wintering place (see page 184). The tablet announced possession of the entire Arctic Archipelago for Canada, sovereignty which has not seriously been challenged since.

In 1913–18, Vilhjalmur Stefansson, on behalf of the Canadian government, carried out a series of land and sea expeditions called the Canadian Arctic Expedition, considerably improving knowledge of the Arctic. Stefansson discovered more islands for Canada: Lougheed, Borden, Brock, and Meighen Islands (MAP 401, previous page), and travelled some 32 000 km, including some distance while drifting on ice floes. Stefansson advanced the idea that the Arctic was not a barren wasteland but a habitable region which should be developed; he published a book called *The Friendly Arctic* in 1921. In that year Stefansson created an international diplomatic incident when he claimed Russia's Wrangell Island for Canada.

MAP 404 (right).
Vilhjalmur Stefansson's map of his explorations in 1916, when he discovered Lougheed, Borden, Brock, and Meighen Islands and reached his "farthest north," all marked on this map. *Findlay Island* is a phantom from older charts, recognized as such by Stefansson, and his *Borden Island*, which he named after Robert Borden, the prime minister, is in fact two islands, Borden (the northern part), and Mackenzie King Island (the southern part). The fact that there are two islands here, not one, was only determined in 1947, from aerial survey.

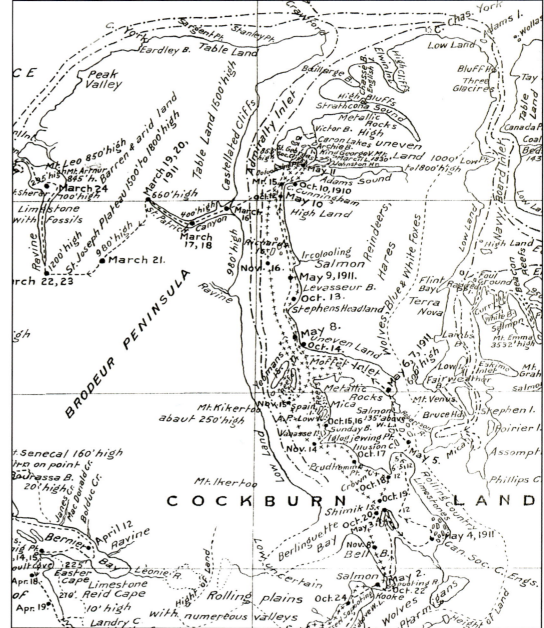

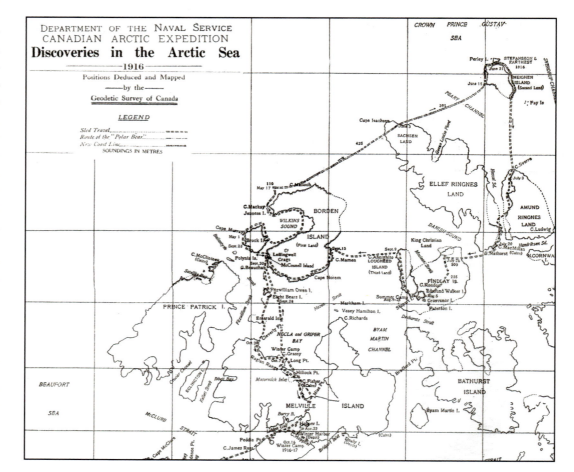

Fire Insurance Maps

For almost a hundred years from the middle of the nineteenth century, large-scale maps of many North American cities were produced for and by fire insurance companies to help them assess the risk they were insuring. Constantly updated and containing all manner of information, much of which is available from no other source, these maps now form a valuable historical record.

Although the first fire insurance map seems to have been created in the United States as far back as 1788, the growth of urban areas in the latter half of the nineteenth century created a strong demand for them, particularly as the principal building material was usually wood. The introduction of lithography about 1840 meant that these maps could be printed quickly and cheaply.

To satisfy the demand for detailed information about risk, a number of specialized firms sprang up, employing their own surveyors and cartographers. In Canada, one of the most important was the Charles E. Goad Company, the company that produced MAP 405. It is quite typical of plans of larger industrial concerns such as warehouses, canneries, mills, or, as in the case shown here, breweries. Other maps were published by the Sanborn Map and Publishing Company, the Dakin Company, and others. Maps of whole communities were often published.

Anything that might affect the assessment of fire risk was included on many of these maps, including the type of construction, the number of storeys, the use of the building, and even the location of any occupants of Oriental or East Indian extraction, as these individuals were considered more likely to use open flames when cooking. Hence the maps are often full of annotated information.

Fire insurance plans continue to be used today, although in a much more circumscribed fashion than during the nineteenth century. But the historical record remains. The National Achives of Canada holds about 30,000 sheets covering more than 1,000 communities across the country, and fire insurance maps were made for about 1,300 areas in total; the wide coverage of these maps makes them an even more invaluable resource for historical research.

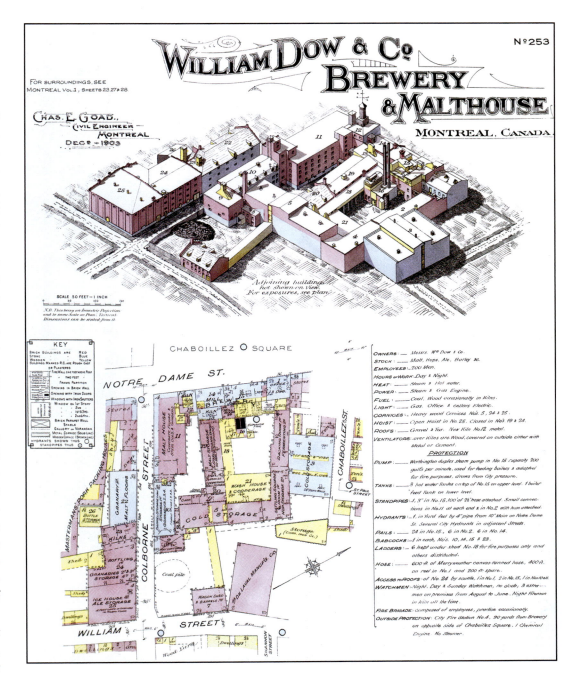

MAP 405 (*above*).
A fire insurance map by the Charles E. Goad Company of a brewery complex in Montréal, dated December 1903. Note the colour-coding on both the plan and the isometric three-dimensional view. Red-pink denotes brick buildings, stone structures are light blue, and yellow ones are wood.

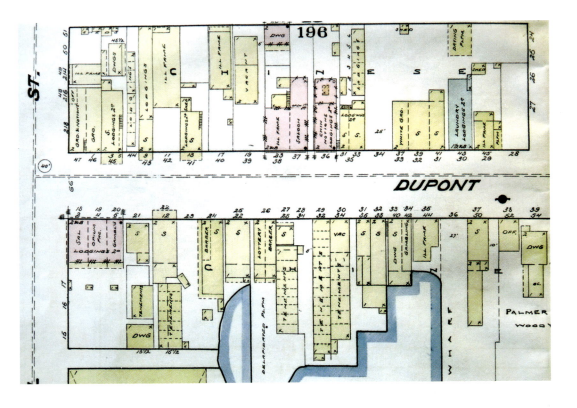

MAP 406.
A fire insurance map of part of Vancouver in 1889, three years after a fire had virtually destroyed the entire city. This map was by the Dakin Company of San Francisco and is rare because all this company's records were lost in the earthquake of 1906. The area shown is on the north side of False Creek, at the end of a shallow arm then extending to Dupont Street, now Pender Street. Carrall Street is at left; Columbia at right. Most of the buildings are wood frame (yellow and green); a few are brick (red). Note the uses of the buildings: one is an opium factory, and many are noted as *ill fame*.

The Boundary with Alaska

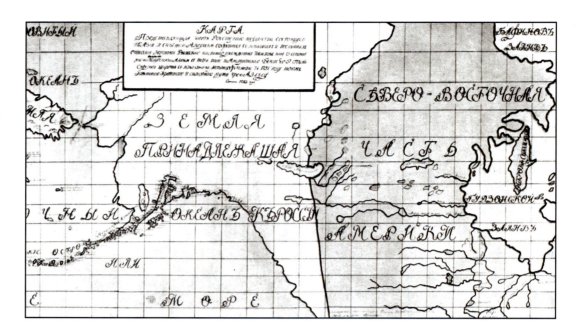

Russian fur traders had expanded their territory from Siberia to the North American continent by the late eighteenth century, and with no other European country to contend with, happily claimed vast tracts of the new land as their own. Map 407 shows one such interpretation.

After 1821, the Hudson's Bay Company became interested in the territory west to the Pacific Ocean, and in 1825 the British and Russian governments reached an agreement as to the limits of each other's territory. But due to the lack of accurate maps, the boundary was not clearly defined, and when the United States purchased Alaska from the Russians in 1867, this ambiguity was also transferred.

In this relatively remote area this was not really a problem until, in 1897, the discovery of gold in the Klondike brought hordes of American miners into Canadian territory. Britain and the United States had nearly fought each other over a boundary dispute between British Guiana and Venezuela in 1895–96; President Grover Cleveland had espoused the idea that it was "unnatural and inexpedient" for a country in America to belong to a European country. The Alaska dispute quickly escalated, with threats of military action if it was not settled, and so in 1903 the United States and Canada agreed to a six-person tribunal to decide the issue.

A host of old maps was gathered, and many redrawn ones produced, with each country trying to find boundary lines that supported their

MAP 407 (*above*).
This map drawn by Russian trader Grigorii Shelikov in 1796 shows much of what is now northwest Canada claimed for Russia.

MAP 408 (*right*).
This map was prepared for Prime Minister Sir John A. Macdonald in 1886 to illustrate the claims of the Americans in relation to those of the Canadian government. The blue lines are boundaries taken from American maps, the red from British.

MAP 409 (*left, bottom*).
This Canadian Pacific Railway map, published in 1898, clearly shows the disputed area between the boundaries claimed by Canada and the United States. The map was intended to show the steamer connection from Vancouver to the goldfields, traversing as little American territory as possible. Had the boundary been settled as the Canadian government wanted, the heads of the inlets in the Alaska panhandle would have been in Canadian territory, and hence an all-Canadian route to the interior would have been possible.

own position drawn by the other on its own maps, or, of course, by Russians on Russian maps.

The main question was whether the boundary line should be drawn to include or exclude the heads of the numerous inlets which lined the coast—important because if it included them, it would allow Canadian water access to the interior.

Since the tribunal, which met in London, was made up of three legal experts from each

side, it was expected to end in a stalemate. However, one of the experts, a British judge, sided with the Americans, and thus a boundary was agreed upon. Although the decision appeared to draw a line approximately down the centre of the two claims, it had the effect of excluding the heads of the inlets from Canadian territory. Although accepted by the government, the decision was met with public outrage in Canada.

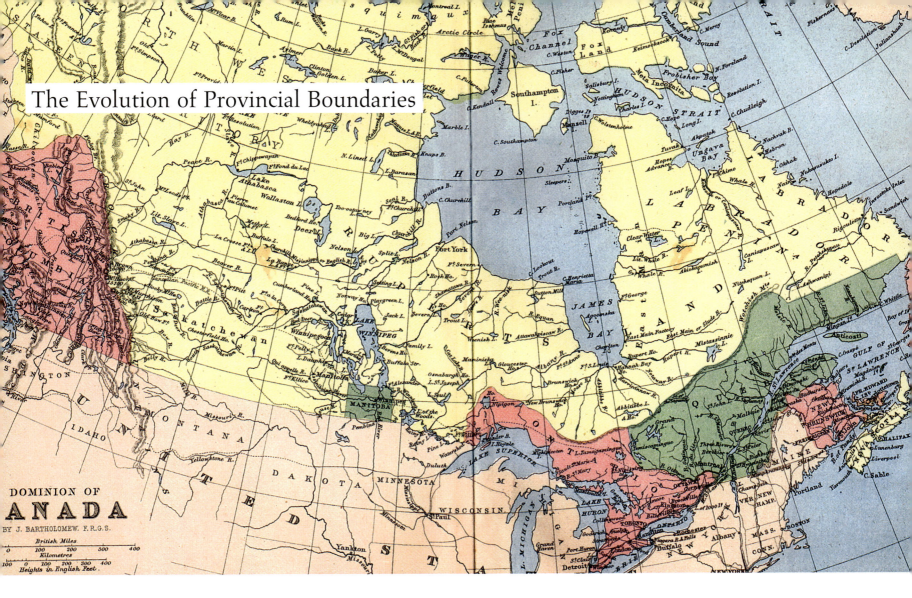

The Evolution of Provincial Boundaries

DOMINION OF
ANADA
BY J. BARTHOLOMEW. F.R.G.S.

British Miles
0   100   200   300   400
Kilometres
100   0   100   200   300   400
Heights in English Feet.

At Confederation in 1867, the new Dominion of Canada consisted of four provinces: Ontario, Québec, New Brunswick, and Nova Scotia. The territorial growth of the country since that time has been documented in atlas maps, some of which are presented here. A caution is in order, however; the date of the maps does not necessarily mean the geographical situation shown is correct as of that date. Atlases were, and still are, a commercial venture, and the use of maps that were out-of-date, but cheaper, was not uncommon.

In 1870 the Hudson's Bay Company relinquished Rupert's Land, which, together with the North-Western Territory in the far west, became the North-West Territories of Canada. Manitoba was the fifth province, created out of a patch of

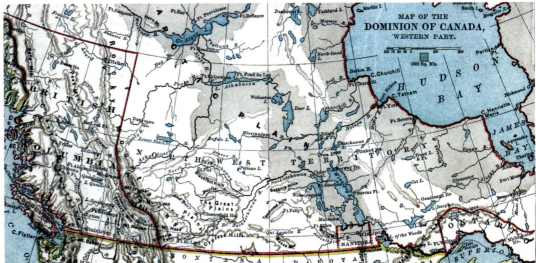

MAP 410 (top).
This map was not up-to-date when it was published, probably about 1875. The Dominion of Canada includes a small Manitoba (1870), British Columbia (1871), Prince Edward Island (1873), and the Hudson's Bay Company's Rupert's Land and the North-Western Territory, which have become the North-West Territories (1870). However, the northern boundary of British Columbia is shown as it was from 1862 to 1866, extending to *Simpson's River*, which was interpreted here to mean the Nass (*Nasse*) River. The extension of British Columbia's boundary to 60° N occurred in 1866. The Stickeen Territory (here labelled *Stakeen*) lasted only from 1862 to 1866, having been created to deal with a gold rush that never really materialized.

MAP 411 (right, centre).
An atlas map dated 1878, but which shows western Canada as it was from 1871 to 1881, when the boundaries of Manitoba were extended. In 1871 British Columbia had entered Confederation, and in 1876 new provisional boundaries of northern and western Ontario were defined, but these have been ignored on this map.

MAP 412 (above).
In 1881, the boundaries of Manitoba were extended as shown here. The eastward extension was contested by Ontario, and that boundary lasted only until 1889. North of Manitoba is a new provisional district of the North-West Territories, Keewatin.

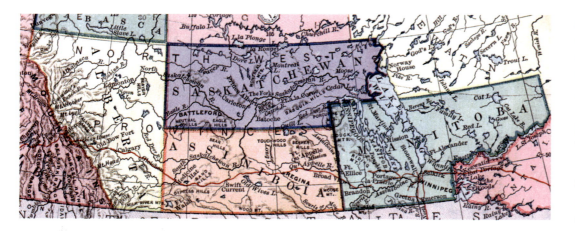

this territory the same year, in response to the Riel Rebellion (see page 213). British Columbia, lured by the promise of a railway, joined Confederation in 1871 (see page 215), and Prince Edward Island joined Confederation in 1873.

Starting in 1876 with the creation of Keewatin, Canada started to divide the North-West Territories for administrative purposes.

In 1880, Canada extended its jurisdiction northwards to include the islands of the Arctic (see page 248), but it was not until the creation of the provisional district of Franklin in 1895

MAP 413 (left, top).
This 1882 map shows the province of Manitoba inaccurately extended eastwards in 1881—in fact it was to the shore of Lake Superior—but this was disputed by Ontario; one interpretation of the Ontario claim is shown here. The new provisional districts of the North-West Territories, created in 1882, are also shown. They are Assiniboia, Saskatchewan, Alberta, and Athabasca.

MAP 414 (left, centre).
The boundaries of the provinces were not the same originally as they are today. Ontario and Québec's northern boundaries (excluding the Labrador boundary of Québec) were defined in 1912. Québec's northern boundary, the height of land separating it from Rupert's Land, is shown here in an 1868 map. Boundaries were often ill defined; the easternmost boundary of Québec certainly extended farther along the north shore of the St. Lawrence than is shown here, and this was at the time, of course, an *international* boundary.

MAP 415 (below).
This map of western Canada published in 1905 reflects the situation as it was between 1898 and 1905. The North-West Territories are divided into provisional districts: Assiniboia, Saskatchewan, Alberta, Yukon, Mackenzie, and Keewatin. In 1905 new provinces would be created on the Prairies. The provisional districts were created as purely administrative areas, but were still under the control of the federal government.

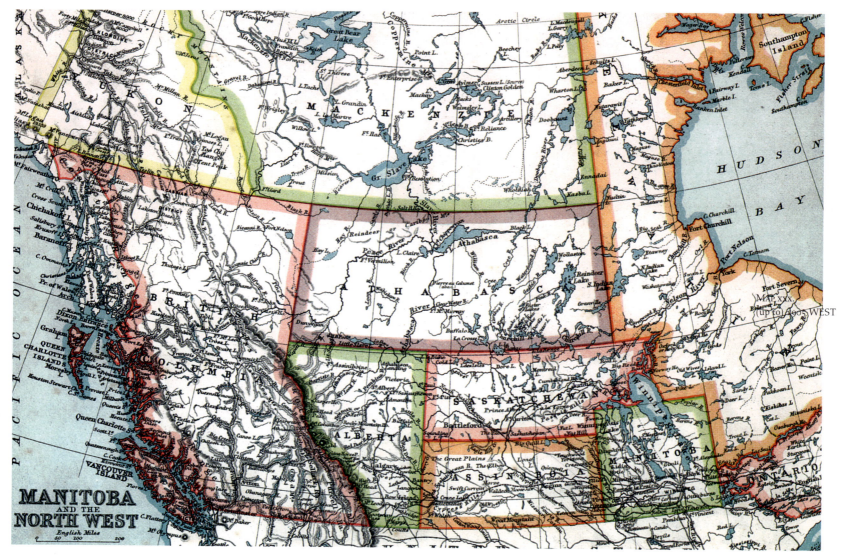

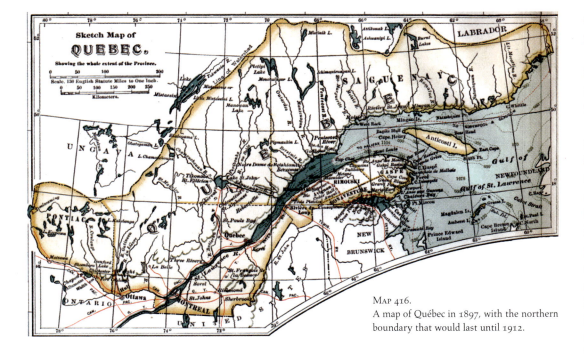

MAP 416.
A map of Québec in 1897, with the northern
boundary that would last until 1912.

side of Lake of the Woods, where the southern
part of the Manitoba-Ontario boundary is today.

In 1898, in response to the gold rush in the
Klondike (see page 244), Yukon was created as a
territory, separate from the North-West Territories and under the direct control of Ottawa.

Then, in 1905, after considerable debate as to
their proper geographical configuration, the provinces of Saskatchewan and Alberta were created
from the four districts then existing. The debate
as to their preferred boundaries centred around
the desire to create provinces with enough population and agricultural potential to be able to support their own governments. There was considerable support for just one province, an idea first
advanced by John Palliser (see page 208), although
his single colony would have included the Red
River Settlement, which by now was within Manitoba. Another proposal called for two provinces,
but divided along a line of latitude, an idea liked
by Calgarians, who aspired to provincial capital-
hood; other proposals were for three or four provinces, variously divided. In the end it was the prime
minister, Wilfrid Laurier, who, despite opposition,
decided in favour of the two provinces, the Alberta
and Saskatchewan of today. There were now nine
provinces and two territories. Manitoba remained
small, and the northern boundaries of Québec and
Ontario were unchanged.

MAP 417 (below).
From the same atlas as MAP 415 comes this map of eastern
Canada in 1905. Both Ontario and Québec have northern
boundaries considerably more circumscribed than their current boundaries, which date from 1912. North of Ontario is
the North-West Territories' provisional district of Keewatin,
while north of Québec most of the Labrador Peninsula is the
Ungava district. Labrador itself, which was a dependency of
Newfoundland, then a separate colony, is a narrow strip of
land along the coast; it would remain so until 1927, when the
extent of Labrador would be considerably enlarged, much to
the chagrin of Québec, which never recognized the new boundaries (see MAP 419, overleaf).

that the inclusion of the region was legally
acknowledged.

The boundaries of the original "postage
stamp" Manitoba were extended in 1881 to the
west, north, and east, but their extension to the
east, where an outlet to Lake Superior was provided for, brought conflict with Ontario (MAP 412
and MAP 413). This dispute was resolved in 1889,
when the eastern boundary was set at the west

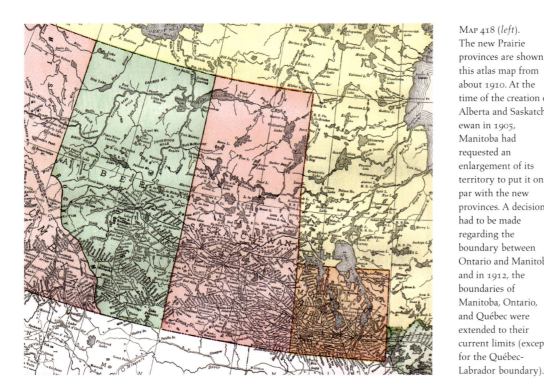

Map 418 (left). The new Prairie provinces are shown in this atlas map from about 1910. At the time of the creation of Alberta and Saskatchewan in 1905, Manitoba had requested an enlargement of its territory to put it on a par with the new provinces. A decision had to be made regarding the boundary between Ontario and Manitoba, and in 1912, the boundaries of Manitoba, Ontario, and Québec were extended to their current limits (except for the Québec-Labrador boundary).

Map 419.
This 1947 atlas map shows how the area of Labrador was increased by the decision of the British Privy Council in 1927, a change Québec never accepted. Compare this map with Labrador in Map 417, previous page. The original coastal strip was intended to provide shore bases for the fishing industry. It was attached to Newfoundland in 1763 by the Royal Proclamation, transferred to Québec in 1774, and back to Newfoundland in 1809. At the time, the boundary shown was international.

In 1912, Manitoba was enlarged, achieving access to Hudson Bay, and the northern boundary of Ontario was extended to its present-day position. The northern boundary of Québec was also changed, to include all of the previous provisional district of Ungava, almost doubling its area. The boundary with Labrador remained undetermined; this would finally be settled in 1927 by a decision of the British Privy Council (Map 419). Since it removed a large area from Québec as then defined, the province refused to acknowledge this change.

In 1925 the Canadian government officially laid claim to the entire area up to the North Pole based on an extension of lines of longitude northwards. This "sector principle" has been applied elsewhere, both in the Arctic and in the Antarctic.

The last major addition to the territory of Canada was the addition of Newfoundland in 1949, after prolonged and often bitter debate in the colony. The British Colony of Newfoundland had become bankrupt in 1934 and had been governed by a British-appointed commission from that year onward. The forces for Confederation, led by Joseph Smallwood, who became the Province of Newfoundland's first premier, won out in 1948 after two referendums, close polls in which the rural and outport areas were generally for joining Canada, while the urban area of St. John's was against. The final result totalled only 52.3 percent in favour of Confederation. In 2001, the province's name was officially changed to Newfoundland and Labrador, to better reflect the territory it encompasses.

In 1993, the Northwest Territories was divided into two, the western half with the same name and with its capital at Yellowknife, and the new territory of Nunavut, with its capital at Iqaluit, previously called Frobisher Bay. The bay itself, however, remains named after the intrepid explorer who sailed into it in 1576, thinking it a strait on the way to Cathay.

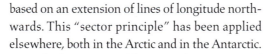

Map 420.
Canada in 1897. The North-West Territories were divided again in 1895 to create the districts of Mackenzie and Franklin. The latter was the final legal recognition that the Arctic islands had been incorporated into Canada after being transferred from Britain in 1880. Then in 1897, with the influx of gold miners to the Klondike, the Provisional District of Yukon was created, to better allow for the administration of this region remote from Ottawa. In 1897 there were still considerable tracts of little known or improperly mapped lands, particularly in the Arctic, shown here by a profusion of tentative coastlines. Much of the interiors of these islands would have to await the advent of aerial photography to be properly mapped. As late as 1948, whole islands were still being discovered. The most recently discovered land in Canada is Prince Charles Island, Air Force Island, and Foley Island, islands of not inconsiderable size on the eastern side of Baffin Island, in Foxe Basin. They were discovered in 1948 by air, from a Lancaster of the Royal Canadian Air Force 408 Photo Squadron.

Map Catalogue

Map titles, creators,
dates, and sources

Abbreviations

AGI   Archivo General de Indias, Sevilla, Spain
AN   Archives nationales, Paris
ANQ   Archives nationales du Québec, Québec
AO   Archives of Ontario, Toronto
AOA   Archives d'Outre-Mer,
    Aix-en-Provence, France
BAV   Biblioteca Apostolica Vaticana,
    Vatican City
BCA   British Columbia Archives, Victoria
BEM   Biblioteca Estense, Modena, Italy
Beinecke
    Beinecke Rare Book and Manuscript
    Library, Yale University, New Haven, CT
BL   British Library, London
BNF   Bibliothèque nationale de France, Paris
BNQ   Bibliothèque national de Québec, Québec
BSB   Bayerische Staatsbibliothek,
    Munich, Germany
CPRA   Canadian Pacific Railway Archives,
    Montréal
CVA   City of Vancouver Archives, Vancouver
DKB   Det Kongelige Bibliotek,
    Copenhagen, Denmark
FLP   Free Library of Philadelphia, Philadelphia
Glenbow
    Glenbow Museum Library, Calgary
Hatfield House
    Hatfield House, Hertfordshire, U.K.
HBCA   Hudson's Bay Company Archives,
    Winnipeg
Huntington
    Huntington Library, San Marino, California
JCBL   John Carter Brown Library at Brown
    University, Providence, RI
JFBL   James Ford Bell Library,
    University of Minnesota, Milwaukee
LC   Geography and Map Division,
    Library of Congress, Washington, DC
McGill
    Rare Books and Special Collections Division,
    McGill University Library, Montréal
MMPH
    Maritiem Museum Prins Hendrik,
    Rotterdam, Netherlands
MTL   Metropolitan Toronto Library,
    Special Collections
Museo Naval
    Museo Naval, Madrid, Spain
NARA
    United States National Archives and
    Records Administration, Washington, DC
Newberry
    Newberry Library, Chicago
NM   Newfoundland Museum, St. John's
NMC   National Map Collection,
    National Archives of Canada, Ottawa
NMM   National Maritime Museum,
    Greenwich, U.K.
NYPL   New York Public Library, New York
OHS   Oregon Historical Society,
    Portland, OR
PANS   Public Archives of Nova Scotia, Halifax
PRO   Public Record Office, London
SHM   Service historique de la Marine,
    Vincennes, France
SLB   Sächsische Landesbibliothek,
    Dresden, Germany
SMM   Stewart Museum at the Fort, Montréal
SQ   Musée de la civilization, fonds d'archives
    du Séminaire de Québec, Québec
UA   Map Library, University of Alberta,
    Edmonton
UBC   Special Collections, University of British
    Columbia, Vancouver
UKHO
    United Kingdom Hydrographic Office,
    Taunton, U.K.

Uncredited maps are from the author's or other
private collections.

MAP 1 (TITLE PAGE)
*Plan du Cap Breton dit Louisbourg avec les
environs pries par L'Amiralle Bockoune Le 26
Jullet 1758*
[?] Bockoune, 1758
LC: G3424 .L6 S26 1758 .B6 vault

MAP 2 (COPYRIGHT PAGE)
[Globe gores called the Ambassadors' Map]
Anon., possibly George Hartman, c1530
(issued c1550)
Nordenskiöld, 1889

MAP 3 (PAGES 6–7)
[North America, from a world map]
Nicolas Desliens, 1541
SLB

MAP 4 (PAGE 8)
*Nova Totius Terrarum Orbis Ivxta Neotericorum
Traditiones Descriptio*
Abraham Ortelius, 1564
BL: Maps.C.2.a.6

MAP 5 (PAGE 9)
[Part of a map of the world]
Giovanni Contarini (Engraved by Francesco
Rosselli), 1506
BL: Maps.C.2.cc.4

MAP 6 (PAGE 10)
Vinland Map
1440 (claimed)
Beinecke

MAP 7 (PAGE 11)
*Siurdi Stephanii terrarum hyperborearu
delineatio Ano 1570*
Sigurdur Stefánsson, 1670, copy of a 1590 map
DKB: gl. kgl. saml. 2881 4° (10v)

MAP 8 (PAGE 11)
Gronlandia Iona Gudmundi Islandi
Jón Gudmonson, c1640
DKB: gl. kgl. saml. 2881 4° (11R)

MAP 9 (PAGE 12)
[Map of the North Atlantic]
Hans Poulsen Resen, 1605
DKB: 1977-108/1

MAP 10 (PAGE 13)
[Arctic regions]
Inset in: *Nova et Aucta Orbis Terrae Descriptio
ad Usum Navigantium emendate accomodata*
Gerard Mercator, 1569

MAP 11 (PAGE 14)
*Illustri Viro, Domino Philippo Sidnaes Michael
Lok Civis Londinensis Hanc Chartam
Dedicabat: 1582*
Michael Lok, 1582
From: *Divers Voyages touching the Discoverie of
America*, Richard Hakluyt, London, 1582

MAP 12 (PAGE 14)
*Carta da Navigar di Nicolo et Antonio Zeni
Furono In Tramontana Lano MCCCLXXX*
From: Niccolò Zeno, the younger (compiler),
*Dello scoprimento dell' Isole Frislanda, Eslanda,
Engrouelanda, Estotilanda & Icaria*, 1558.
Nordenskiöld, 1889

MAP 13 (PAGE 14)
Estotilandia et Laboratoris Terra
Cornelius Wytfliet, 1597
From: *Descriptionis Ptolemaicæ Augmentum*
NMC 6169

MAP 14 (PAGE 15)
*Orbis Typus Universalis Iuxta Hydrographorum
Traditionem*
Martin Waldseemüller, 1513
Nordenskiöld, 1889

MAP 15 (PAGE 15)
Tierra Nueva
Giacomo Gastaldi, 1548
From: *Cosmographia*
LC: G1005 1548

MAP 16 (PAGE 16)
[Part of a map of the world]
Giovanni Contarini (Engraved by Francesco
Rosselli), 1506
BL: Maps.C.2.cc.4

MAP 17 (PAGE 17)
*Universalior Cogniti Orbis Tabula Ex
Recentibus Confecta Observationibus*
Johann Ruysch, c1507
NMC 19268

MAP 18 (PAGE 17)
[Part of an unsigned, hand-drawn map of the world]
Francesco Rosselli, 1508
NMM: 47 MS9928/p.27.f.1; C 4568/B

MAP 19 (PAGE 18)
[Northeastern coastal detail of world map]
Juan de la Cosa, c1500
Museo Naval

MAP 20 (PAGES 18–19)
[Western half of world map]
Juan de la Cosa, c1500
Museo Naval

MAP 21 (PAGE 20)
[Part of a world map known as the
King-Hamy map]
Anon., c1502
Huntington

MAP 22 (PAGE 21)
[Part of a world map known as the
Cantino planisphere]
Anon., 1502
BEM
(*Su concessione de Ministero per i Beni e le
Attività Culturali*)

MAP 23 (PAGE 22)
[Part of the "Map of the Atlantic"]
Pedro Reinel, 1504
BSB

MAP 24 (PAGE 23)
[Part of a world map]
Diogo Ribiero, 1529
BAV

MAP 25 (PAGE 23)
Septentrio Orbis Universalis Descriptio
Robert Thorne, 1527
Nordenskiöld, 1889

MAP 26 (PAGE 24)
[Part of a world map]
Girolamo Verrazano, 1529
BAV

MAP 27 (PAGE 25)
[Part of a map of North America and the
Caribbean]
From: *Boke of Idrography*, Jean Rotz,
1534 or 1535
BL: Royal 20.E.IX, ff. 23 verso

MAP 28 (PAGE 26)
[Part of a world map known as the "Harleian"]
Anon., c1542–44
BL: Add MS 5413

MAP 29 (PAGE 27)
[Part of a world map]
Nicolas Desliens, 1541
SLB

MAP 30 (PAGE 28)
La Terra de Hochelaga Nella Nova Francia
Giacomo Gastaldi, 1556
NMC 116744

MAP 31 (PAGE 29)
[World map]
*Faicte A Arques par Pierres Desceliers PBRE:
L AN 1550*
Pierre Desceliers, 1550
BL: Add MS 24065

MAP 32 (PAGE 30)
[Part of a world map]
Gerard Mercator, 1569
MMPH

MAP 33 (PAGE 31)
[Untitled engraved world map]
Paolo Forlani, 1560
NMC 97953

MAP 34 (PAGE 31)
*Universale Descrittione di tutta la terra
conosciuta fin qui*
Paolo Forlani, 1565
LC: G3200 1565 .F6 vault

MAP 35 (PAGE 32)
[World map]
Sebastian Cabot, 1544
BNF: RES Ge AA 582 Rc C 2486

MAP 36 (PAGE 32)
[Map of the Gulf of St. Lawrence]
Jean Alfonce, c1544
From: *La Cosmographie*
BNF: MS français No. 676

MAP 37 (PAGE 33)
Detail of MAP 38

MAP 38 (PAGES 32–33)
[Map of part of eastern North America,
known as the Vallard map]
Anon., for or by Nicolas Vallard, 1547
Huntington

MAP 39 (PAGE 34)
[Part of map of North Atlantic]
William Borough, 1575 or 1576, with additions
by Martin Frobisher of his discoveries, 1576
Hatfield House, *Courtesy The Marquess of
Salisbury*

MAP 40 (PAGE 35)
[Map of the North Atlantic and the
Northwest Passage]
James Beare, 1578
From: *A True Discourse of the Late Voyages . . .
of Martin Frobisher*, George Best, London, 1578

MAP 41 (PAGE 35)
[Part of a world map]
George Best, 1578
From: *A True Discourse of the Late Voyages . . .
of Martin Frobisher*, London, 1578

MAP 42 (PAGE 36)
*Septentrionalium Terrarum descriptio Per
Gerardum Mercatorem Cum Privilegio*
Gerard Mercator, 1595
From: *Atlas Sive Cosmographiæ, Dulsburgi*, 1595
BL: Maps C.3.c.4

MAP 43 (PAGE 37)
Humfray Gylbert knight his charte
John Dee, 1583
FLP

MAP 44 (PAGE 37)
[Part of a world map]
Edward Wright, 1599, based on Emery
Molyneaux, 1589 (see note 37, page 264)
From: *The principall navigations, voiages, and
discoveries of the English nations*, Richard
Hakluyt (ed.), 1599 edition; copy from
Nordenskiöld, 1889

MAP 45 (PAGE 38)
Typus Orbis Terrarum
Abraham Ortelius, 1570
From: *Theatrum Orbis Terrarum*
LC: G1006 .T5 1570b Vault

MAP 46 (PAGES 38–39)
*Tabula Nautica, qua repræsentâtur oræmaritimæ
meatus ac freta, noviter a H Hudsono Anglo ad
Caurum supra Novum Franciam indagata Anno
1612*
Hessel Gerritz, 1612
From: *Descriptio ac delineatio Geographica
Detectionis Freti*, Hessel Gerritz (Henry
Hudson?), 1612

MAP 47 (PAGE 39)
Conibas Regio Cum Vicinis Gentibus
Cornelius Wytfliet, 1597
From: *Descriptionis Ptolemaicæ Augmentum*

MAP 48 (PAGE 40)
The North Part of America
Henry Briggs, 1625
NMC 6582

MAP 49 (PAGE 40)
[Chart of Hudson Strait]
William Baffin, 1615
BL: Add MS 12206, folio 6

MAP 50 (PAGE 41)
[Part of] *Carte naurique de bords de Mer du
Nort, et Noruest, mis en longitude latitude et en
leur route selon les rins de vent par Hessel
Gerritsz*
Hessel Gerritz, 1628
BNF

MAP 51 (PAGE 42)
Another part of MAP 50

MAP 52 (PAGE 42)
[Map-illustration of the shores of Hudson Bay]
Jens Munk, 1624
From: *Danish Arctic Voyages*,
Hakluyt Society, London, 1896

MAP 53 (PAGE 42)
[Map-illustration of the mouth of the
Churchill River]
Jens Munk, 1624
From: *Danish Arctic Voyages*,
Hakluyt Society, London, 1896

MAP 54 (PAGE 43)
[Map of Hudson Bay and Strait, called the "Stockholm Chart"]
Jens Munk, 1624
From: Danish Arctic Voyages,
Hakluyt Society, London, 1896

MAP 55 (PAGE 43)
[Untitled inset map in:] The Platt of Sailing for the di'coverye of a Passage into the South Sea 1631 1632
Thomas James, 1631–32
BL: Add MS 5415, G.1

MAP 56 (PAGE 43)
[Map of the North Polar region]
Luke Foxe, 1635
From: North-west Fox or, Fox from the North-west Passage, B. Alsop and Tho. Fawcet, London, 1635
BCA: 1-61569

MAP 57 (PAGE 44)
The Platt of Sailing for the di'coverye of a Passage into the South Sea 1631 1632
Thomas James, 1631–32
BL: Add MS 5415, G.1

MAP 58 (PAGE 44)
A Chart of the North Part of America
John Seller, 1698
From: Atlas maritimus, John Seller, 1698

MAP 59 (PAGE 45)
[Newfoundland]
John Mason, 1616–17 (1625)
From: Cambrensium Caroleia, William Vaughan, 1625
NMC 21046

MAP 60 (PAGE 46)
["New Scotlande" and eastern Canada]
William Alexander, 1625
SMM

MAP 61 (PAGE 47)
Carta particolare della terra nuova con la gran Baia et il Fiume grande della Canida
Robert Dudley, 1647 (1661)
From: Dell' Arcano de Mare, Florence, 1661 edition
NMC 21048

MAP 62 (PAGE 48)
Canada Orientale nell' America Settentrional
Vincenzo Coronelli, 1695
NMC 17219

MAP 63 (PAGE 48)
Partie de TerreNeuve
Le Bocage Boissaie, 1678
BNF/NMC 136201

MAP 64 (PAGE 48)
The Coast of New=Found=Land From Cape Raze to Cape St. Francis Described by Henry Southwood
Henry Southwood, 1716
From: The English Pilot, Henry Southwood, 1716

MAP 65 (PAGE 49)
[Tadoussac, Saguenay River, and St. Lawrence]
Samuel de Champlain, 1608
From: Les Voyages du Sieur de Champlain, Samuel de Champlain, 1613

MAP 66 (PAGE 50)
[Isle de sainte Croix]
Samuel de Champlain, 1604–05
From: Les Voyages du Sieur de Champlain, Samuel de Champlain, 1613

MAP 67 (PAGE 50)
[Annapolis Basin]
Samuel de Champlain, 1605–07
From: Les Voyages du Sieur de Champlain, Samuel de Champlain, 1613

MAP 68 (PAGE 51)
[Southern Nova Scotia, southern New Brunswick, and the Bay of Fundy]
Samuel de Champlain, 1607
LC: G3321 .P5 1607 .C4

MAP 69 (PAGE 51)
[Harbour of Saint John, New Brunswick]
Samuel de Champlain, c1606
From: Les Voyages du Sieur de Champlain, Samuel de Champlain, 1613

MAP 70 (PAGE 52)
Carte geographique de la Nouelle franse en son vray mondia
Samuel de Champlain, 1612
From: Les Voyages du Sieur de Champlain, Samuel de Champlain, 1613

MAP 71 (PAGE 52)
Carte geographique de la Nouelle franse en son vray meridiein
Samuel de Champlain, 1613
From: Les Voyages du Sieur de Champlain (later printed copies only), Samuel de Champlain, 1613
NMC 6329

MAP 72 (PAGE 52)
Plan de labitation [habitation] faicte par le Sr Bourdon
Jean Bourdon, 1634 or 1635
McGill

MAP 73 (PAGE 53)
[The St. Lawrence River at Québec]
Samuel de Champlain, 1608–12
From: Les Voyages du Sieur de Champlain, Samuel de Champlain, 1613

MAP 74 (PAGE 53)
[The St. Lawrence River at Montréal]
Samuel de Champlain, 1610–12
From: Les Voyages du Sieur de Champlain, Samuel de Champlain, 1613

MAP 75 (PAGE 54)
Carte geographique de la Nouvelle Franse faicte par le Sieur de Champlain Saint Tongois Cappitaine Ordinaire pour le Roy en la Marine
Samuel de Champlain, 1612
From: Les Voyages du Sieur de Champlain, Samuel de Champlain, 1613
NMC 6327

MAP 76 (PAGE 54)
[Untitled proof map of New France]
Samuel de Champlain, 1616 (printed 1619?)
JCBL

MAP 77 (PAGE 55)
Carte de la nouvelle france
Samuel de Champlain, 1632
From: Samuel de Champlain, Les Voyages de la Nouvelle France occidentale dicte Canada faits par le Sr de Champlain, Paris, 1632
NMC 51970

MAP 78 (PAGE 56)
Le Canada faict par le Sr de Champlain
Pierre du Val, 1677
NMC 14080

MAP 79 (PAGE 56)
Figure de la Terre Neuve, Grande Riviere de Canada, et Côtes de l'Ocean en la Nouvelle France
Marc Lescarbot, 1609
From: Histoire de la Nouvelle France, Marc Lescarbot, 1609

MAP 80 (PAGE 57)
[Plan of first settlement at Ville-Marie or Montréal]
Jean Bourdon, c1642–45
McGill

MAP 81 (PAGE 57)
Plan de la Ville de Montréal
Joseph Gaspard Chaussegros de Léry, 1724
Newberry: Ayer MS Map 30, sheet 107

MAP 82 (PAGE 58)
Nouvelle France ["The Huron Map"]
Anon., c1641
UKHO/NMC 44351

MAP 83 (PAGE 59)
Description Du Pais des Hurons
Jean de Brebéuf [?], 1639–48
LC: G3460 1651 .D4

MAP 84 (PAGE 59)
Pars Chorographia regionis Huronum
François Du Creux, 1661
Inset in: Tabula nova franciae
From: Historiæ Canadensis seu Novæ-Franciæ, 1664

MAP 85 (PAGE 60)
Le Canada ou Nouvelle France
Nicolas Sanson d'Abbeville, 1656
NMC 21100

MAP 86 (PAGE 60)
Lac Superieur et Autre Lieux ou sont les Missions des Peres de la Compagnie de Jesus comprises sous le Nom d'Outaovacs
Claude Dablon and Claude Allouez, 1671
From: Jesuit Relation, 1671
NMC 10296

MAP 87 (PAGE 61)
Novæ Franciæ Accurata Delineatio 1657
Francesco Giuseppe Bressani, 1657
(Left-hand sheet only)
NMC 6338

MAP 88 (PAGES 62–63)
Partie Occidentale du Canada ou de la Nouvelle France
Vincenzo Coronelli, 1688
NMC 6411

MAP 89 (PAGE 64)
Carte Gnlle De La France Septentrionalle, contentant la découverte du pays de Ilinois
Jean-Baptiste-Louis Franquelin, 1678
SHM: 4040B, No. 11

MAP 90 (PAGES 64–65)
Carte de Amerique Septentrionale
Jean-Baptiste-Louis Franquelin, 1688
ANQ: NC-89-11-64

MAP 91 (PAGES 66–67)
L'Amerique divisee selon 'entendue de ses principales parties
Nicolas de Fer, 1698
NMC 26825(1) and 26825(2)

MAP 92 (PAGE 67)
Partie de la Nouvelle France
Alexis Hubert Jaillot, 1685
NMC 6348

MAP 93 (PAGE 68)
Carte du Canada ou de la Nouvelle France
Guillaume De L'Isle, 1730
NMC 8462

MAP 94 (PAGE 68)
Carte que les Gnacsitares/Carte de la Riviere Longue
Louis-Armand de Lom d'Arce, Baron La Hontan, 1703
From: Nouveaux Voyages de Mr. le Baron de Lahontan dans L'Amérique Septentrionale, 1703

MAP 95 (PAGE 69)
Cartouche [?] carte du combat d'Iberville a Terre-Neuve 1696
Pierre Le Moyne d'Iberville [?], 1696
ANQ: NC 89-11-56 (BNF)

MAP 96 (PAGE 70)
[Plan of the location of the Richelieu fort]
Inset: Plan du fort de Richelieu
Jean Talon, 1665
AOA: Dépôt des fortifications des colonies, Amérique septentrionale, 492 c.

MAP 97 (PAGE 70)
Idée de la Situation du Fort de Chambly
Anon., c1717
Newberry: Ayer MS Map 30, sheet 109

MAP 98 (PAGE 71)
Plans des forts faicts par le Regiment Carignan Salieres sur la Riviere de Richelieu dicte autrement des Iroquois en la Nouvelle France
Anon., c1666
SHM

MAP 99 (PAGE 71)
Plan du Fort Frontenac ou Cataracouy
Anon., c1720
Newberry: Ayer MS Map 30, sheet 108

MAP 100 (PAGE 72)
Quebec Ville de L'Amerique Septentroinale [sic] dans la Nouvelle France
Nicolas de Fer, c1693
NMC 2711

MAP 101 (PAGE 73)
A Map of the English Possessions in North America and Newfoundland as it was presented and Dedicated to his most Sacred Majesty King William 1699
Anon., 1699
LC: G3300 1699 .M vault

MAP 102 (PAGE 73)
Plan de la moitié du Fort du Port Royal de l'Accadie en l'état qu'i; a été mis la presente année 1708
Anon., 1708
Newberry: Ayer MS Map 30, sheet 92

MAP 103 (PAGE 74)
Plan de la banlieue du Fort Royal a Lacadie et de ses environs
Anon., 1708
Newberry: Ayer MS Map 30, sheet 91

MAP 104 (PAGE 75)
Plan du Fort de Plaisance
Anon., c1715
Newberry: Ayer MS Map 30, sheet 98

MAP 105 (PAGE 76)
[Québec and environs, showing seigneuries]
Jean Bourdon, 1641
BNF

MAP 106 (PAGE 76)
[Québec and environs, showing seigneuries]
Gédéon de Catalogne, 1709
BNQ (copy)

MAP 107 (PAGE 76)
Plan Figuratif de la Seigneuries des Eboulements dite De Sales situee du cote Nord du Fleuve St Laurent dans le comte de Northumberland dans le District de Quebec commence le 6 aout et fini le 20 novembre
Jean-Baptiste Larue, 1811
ANQ

MAP 108 (PAGE 77)
Tabula nova franciae
François Du Creux, 1661
From: Historiæ Canadensis seu Novæ-Franciæ, 1664

MAP 109 (PAGE 77)
A New Mapp of the north part of America from Hudson Straights commonly call'd the Norwest Passage
John Thornton, 1673
NMC 14045

MAP 110 (PAGE 78)
[Hudson Bay and Strait] Made by Saml: Thornton at the Signe of the Platte in the Minories London Anno: 1709
Samuel Thornton, 1709
HBCA: G2/2

MAP 111 (PAGE 79)
[Map of the coast and rivers flowing into the western side of Hudson Bay and the Arctic Ocean]
James Knight, 1719 [?], with later additions
HBCA: G1/19

MAP 112 (PAGE 80)
Chart of Hudson's Bay and Straits
Christopher Middleton, 1743
NMC 27782

MAP 113 (PAGE 81)
A New Map of North America
Joseph La France/Arthur Dobbs, c1744
MS map bound into volume of Account of Hudson's Bay, Arthur Dobbs, 1744
BL: MS map in 213 c.11

MAP 114 (PAGE 82)
A Chart for the Better Understanding of De Font's Letter
[T. S. Drage?]
From: An Account of a Voyage For the Discovery of a North-West Passage by Hudson's Streights. to the Western and Southern Ocean of America Performed in the Year 1746 and 1747, in the Ship California, Capt. Francis Smith, Commander. 1749

MAP 115 (PAGE 82)
Chart of the Seas, Straits, &c. thro' which his Majesty's Sloop Furnace pass'd for discovering a Passage from Hudsons Bay, to the South Sea
John Wigate, 1746
BL: Maps 70095.(7)

MAP 116 (PAGES 82–83)
North America with Hudson's Bay and Straights Anno 1748
Richard Seale (engraver), 1748
HBCA G4/20b

MAP 117 (PAGE 83)
A Chart of the West and North-West Parts of Hudsons Bay
T. S. Drage[?], 1749
From: An Account of a Voyage For the Discovery of a North-West Passage by Hudson's Streights . . . . , 1749

MAP 118 (PAGE 84)
Chart of the Coast where a North West Passage was attempted
Henry Ellis, 1748
NMC 21058

258

MAP 119 (PAGE 85)
Carte Particuliere du Fleuve Saint Louis Dressee sur les lieux avec les noms des sauvages du pais
Henri Chatelain, 1719
AO 2419

MAP 120 (PAGE 86)
Carte contenant les nouvelles decouvertes de l'ouest en Canada Rivieres Lacs etc nations qui y habittant en l'annee 1737
One of the La Vérendrye family [?], 1737
SQ: Q-15 (copy)

MAP 121 (PAGE 87)
Carte des Decouvertes qui ont eté faites dans la Partie Occidentale du Canada
Jacques-Nicolas Bellin, 1752
Manuscript atlas, map #7
NMC 85136

MAP 122 (PAGE 88)
Plan de Louisbourg
Anon., 1730
NMC 492

MAP 123 (PAGE 88)
A Plan of Louisbourg on the Island of Cape Breton in North America
Anon., 1745
NMC 500

MAP 124 (PAGE 89)
Plan de la Rade, Ville et Forts de Louisbourg
Anon., c1744
NMC 117622

MAP 125 (PAGE 90)
Carte Generale du Canada
Jacques-Nicolas Bellin, 1752
Manuscript atlas, map #1
NMC 85135

MAP 126 (PAGE 90)
Cours du Fleuve St Laurent
Jacques-Nicolas Bellin, 1752
Manuscript atlas, map #4 (middle sheet, 2/3)
NMC 17780(2)

MAP 127 (PAGE 91)
Golfe de Saint Laurent
Jacques-Nicolas Bellin, 1752
Manuscript atlas, map #6
NMC 15012

MAP 128 (PAGE 91)
Partie Occidentale du Canada
Jacques-Nicolas Bellin, 1752
Manuscript atlas, map #2
NMC 88134

MAP 129 (PAGE 92)
A Plan of the Harbour of Chebucto and Town of Halifax ["The Porcupine Map"]
Moses Harris (attrib.), 1750
From: *Gentleman's Magazine*, July 1750
NMC 814

MAP 130 (PAGE 92)
[Map of Halifax]
Francois-Pierre de Rigaud de Vaudreuil (attrib.), 1755
PRO: State Papers, Naval, SP 42/38, p. 224

MAP 131 (PAGE 93)
[Map of Halifax Harbour]
with inset maps:
A Map of the South Part of Nova Scotia and it's Fishing Banks and
A Plan of Halifax Survey'd by M. Harris
Thomas Jefferys, 1750
NMC 1012

MAP 132 (PAGE 93)
Project for Fortifying the Town of Hallifax in Nova Scotia 1749 Jn⁰ Brewse
John Brewse, 1749
NMC 812

MAP 133 (PAGE 94)
Partie Orientale de la Nouvelle France ou de Canada
Conrad Tobias Lotter; Matthias Seutter (engraver), after 1750
NMC 24732

MAP 134 (PAGE 95)
[Plan of Fort Beauséjour]
Louis Franquet, 1751
NMC 709

MAP 135 (PAGE 95)
A Map of a Part of Nova Scotia or Acadie
Thomas Lewis, 1755
PANS: V7/205-1755

MAP 136 (PAGE 95)
A general Plan of Annapolis Royal as Surveyed by Captⁿ. Hamilton
[?] Hamilton, 1753
LC: G3424 .A45 1753 .H3 vault

MAP 137 (PAGE 97)
Plan of Louisbourg, the Harbour, Part of the Coast with the French Retrenchments along the Same And The Attack by the British Troops under the Command of Major General Amherst
Samuel Holland, 1758
NMC 109811

MAP 138 (PAGES 96–97)
Plan du Cap Breton dit Louisbourg avec les environs pries par L'Amiralle Bockoune Le 26 Jullet 1758
[?] Bockoune, 1758
LC: G3424 .L6 S26 1758 .B6 vault

MAP 139 (PAGE 98)
Carte Du Lac ontario nouvellement relleve avec ces port a grand poid
[?] La Broquerie, 1757
BL: Maps K.Top.121.14

MAP 140 (PAGE 98)
Plan de la Ville de Quebec
Anon., 1750
LC: G3454 .Q4 1750 .P5 vault

MAP 141 (PAGE 99)
An Authentic Plan of the River St. Laurence from Sillery, to the Fall of Montmorenci, with the Operations of the Siege of Quebec
With inset maps:
Part of the Upper River of St. Laurence
and
A View of the Action gained by the English Sepᵗ 13 1759 near Quebec Brought from thence By an Officer of Distinction
Thomas Jefferys, 1759–60
NMC 97970

MAP 142 (PAGES 100–101)
A Correct Plan of the Environs of Quebec and of the Battle fought on the 13th September, 1759
Thomas Jefferys, 1759–60
NMC 54105

MAP 143 (PAGE 102)
[Map with the operations of the Battle of Montmorency, part of MAP 146]
Anon., 1759–60
NMC 21345-2

MAP 144 (PAGE 103)
Plan of the Battle fought on the 28th of April 1760 upon the Heights of Abraham near Quebec, between the Brittish Troops Garrison'd in that place and the French Army that came to beseige it [Battle of Sainte-Foy]
Signed Patᵗ McKellar, Major Ch. Engʳ, 1760
NMC 14081

MAP 145 (PAGE 103)
Tableau d'ordre de Bataille sur deux disposi-tions, Relatives au Pays. Québec, 28 Avril 1760
François-Gaston Lévis, 1760
NMC 1921

MAP 146 (PAGES 104–05)
Plan of the Town of Quebec the Capital of Canada in North America with the Bason and a part of the adjacent Country, shewing the principal Encampments and Works of the British Army, commanded by Major General Wolfe, and those of the French Army, commanded by Lieut. General the Marquis of Montcalm, during the Siege of that Place in 1759.
Anon., 1759
NMC 21345-1

MAP 147 (PAGES 106–07)
A Plan of the River St. Laurence from Green Island to Cape Carrouge by Jams. Cook
James Cook, 1759-61
NMC 21353

MAP 148 (PAGE 107)
The Bay and Harbour of Gaspey 1758
James Cook (attrib.), 1758
UKHO: A306 Ah1
Reproduced from the original by permission of the Controller of Her Majesty's Stationery Office and the UK Hydrographic Office.

MAP 149 (PAGES 108–09)
A Plan of York Harbour on the Coast of Labradore; Surveyed by Thos. Graves Esqr. Governor of Newfoundland &c. &c. &c. By James Cook 1763
James Cook, 1763
UKHO: B188 Drawer 1
Reproduced from the original by permission of the Controller of Her Majesty's Stationery Office and the UK Hydrographic Office.

MAP 150 (PAGE 110)
A Sketch of the Island of Newfoundland Done from the Latest Observations By James Cook 1763
James Cook, 1763
UKHO: Vv2
Reproduced from the original by permission of the Controller of Her Majesty's Stationery Office and the UK Hydrographic Office.

MAP 151 (PAGE 111)
A General Chart of the Island of Newfoundland
James Cook, 1759–61; Thomas Jefferys, 1775
UBC: G3435 1775 .J4

MAP 152 (PAGE 111)
A New Chart of the River St. Lawrence
James Cook, 1759–61; Thomas Jefferys, 1775
NMC 54110

MAP 153 (PAGE 112)
Plan of the Settled Part of the Province of Quebec
Sheet 11, Chambly
[Samuel Holland], 1760–63
NMC 135045

MAP 154 (PAGE 112)
Plan of the Settled Part of the Province of Quebec
Sheet 8, Montréal (left-hand side, Lachine)
[John Montressor], 1760–63
NMC 135042

MAP 155 (PAGE 113)
Plan of the Settled Part of the Province of Quebec
Sheet 8, Montréal
[Samuel Holland], 1760–63
NMC 135042

MAP 156 (PAGES 114–15)
A New Map of the Province of Quebec according to the Royal Proclamation, of the 7ᵗʰ of October 1763
With four inset maps:
A Particular Survey of the Isles of Montreal
Plan of Montreal or VilleMarie
The City of Quebec
Course of the River St. Laurence from la Valterie to Quebec
Jonathan Carver, 1776
NMC 21404

MAP 157 (PAGE 116)
A View of the Rivers Kenebec and Chaudiere, with Colonel Arnold's Route to Quebec
R. Baldwin, 1776
NMC 6696

MAP 158 (PAGES 116–17)
Plan of the City and Environs of Quebec, with its Siege and Blockade by the Americans from the 8ᵗʰ of December 1775 to the 13ᵗʰ. of May 1776
William Faden, 1776
NMC 55019

MAP 159 (PAGE 118)
Carte de Lisle Sᵗ Jean dans le Golfe de Sᵗ Laurent en Canada
[Louis Franquet, 1751]
NMC 197

MAP 160 (PAGES 118–19)
A Map of the Island of Sᵗ John In the Gulf of Sᵗ Lawrence Divided into Counties & Parishes And the Lots as Granted by Government
Samuel Holland, 1775
NMC 1852

MAP 161 (PAGE 119)
Prince Edward Island divided into Counties & Parishes, with the Lots as granted by the Government.
H. Ashby, 1798
NMC 206

MAP 162 (PAGE 120)
The Harbour of Halifax
Joseph Frédéric Wallet Des Barres, 1777
From: *The Atlantic Neptune* Vol. 2, Part 1, No. 48
NMC 18358

MAP 163 (PAGES 120–21)
The River St John.
Joseph Frédéric Wallet Des Barres, 1780
From: *The Atlantic Neptune* Part 2, No. 16, 1780
NMC 27970

MAP 164 (PAGE 121)
The Coast of Nova Scotia, New England, New York, Jersey, the Gulph and River of St. Lawrence, the Islands of Newfoundland, Cape Breton, St. John, Anticosty, Sable etc.
Joseph Frédéric Wallet Des Barres, 1780
From: *The Atlantic Neptune*, 1780

MAP 165 (PAGE 122)
A Map of the Island of Newfoundland
John Cartwright, 1773
NMC 14033

MAP 166 (PAGE 122)
The Taking of Mary March on the north side of the Lake/ Captain Buchan's visit in 1875-76 1810–11 at the South side of the Lake
Shanawdithit, 1828–29, with title and notes added later by an unknown hand; with wrong date crossed out
NM

MAP 167 (PAGE 123)
A Sketch of The River Exploits and The East End of Lieutenant's Lake in Newfoundland
John Cartwright, 1773
NMC 27

MAP 168 (PAGES 124–25)
A Map of the British Colonies in North America ["The red-lined map"]
John Mitchell, 1755; 1775 edition [?], with MS additions by Richard Oswald, 1782
BL: Maps K.Top.118.49.b

MAP 169 (PAGE 124)
British Colonies in North America
Anon., 1785
NMC 6961

MAP 170 (PAGE 125)
A new map of the whole continent of America
Robert Sayer, 1786

MAP 171 (PAGE 126)
A Survey of Shelburne, or Port Roseway Harbour
Thomas Backhouse, 1798
NMC 19085

MAP 172 (PAGE 127)
A Sketch of the River Thames [showing the lands surrendered by the Chippewa Nation] from the Delaware Village to the Upper Forks.
D.W. Smith. Countersigned A. McKee
D. W. Smith, 1795
NMC 4113
From: Ontario Ministry of Natural Resources
© Queens Printer for Ontario, 2002

MAP 173 (PAGE 127)
A map of the great River St. John & waters
Robert Campbell, 1788
NMC 254

MAP 174 (PAGE 128)
Plan shewing the lands granted to the Six Nations Indians
Anon., 1792
NMC 4800

MAP 175 (PAGE 128)
Plan of the Town of Johnstown
William Chewett, 1792
AO 1364

MAP 176 (PAGE 129)
General Plan of the District of Luneburg
William Chewett, 1792
AO 1316

MAP 177 (PAGE 130)
[Map of Loyalist settlements]
Anon., c1790
AO 1363

MAP 178 (PAGE 130)
Plan of Lake Erie
Patrick McNiff, 1791
AO 496

MAP 179 (PAGE 131)
A Map of the Province of Upper Canada describing all the New Settlements, Townships, etc.
William Chewett, 1792; William Faden, 1800
NMC 15289

MAP 180 (PAGE 131)
A New Map of Nova Scotia and Cape Breton Island with the adjacent parts of New England and Canada
Thomas Jefferys, 1771
From: *American Atlas*, Sayer and Bennett, 1776
LC: G 3420 1775 .J4 vault

MAP 181 (PAGE 131)
[New Brunswick]
Anon., 1817
NMC 11686

MAP 182 (PAGE 132)
Mappe Monde ou Globe Terrestre en deux Plans Hemispheres. Dressee sur les observations de Mrss de L'Academie Royal Des Sciences
Jean Covens and Corneille Mortier, c1780
NYPL

MAP 183 (PAGE 132)
Carte Generale Des Decouvertes de l'Amiral de Fonte et autres navigateurs Espagnols Anglois et Russes pour la recherche du passage a la Mer du Sud. pas M. De L'Isle de l'Academie des Sciences etc.
Didier Robert de Vaugondy, 1752
From: *Encyclopédie, ou Dictionaire Raisonne des Sciences, des Arts et des Metiers*, Denis Diderot, 1755

MAP 184 (PAGE 133)
Carte des Nouvelles Découvertes Au Nord de la Mer du Sud
Joseph-Nicolas de L'Isle, 1752
NMC 21056

MAP 185 (PAGE 134)
A Map of Canada and the North Part of Louisiana with the Adjacent Countrys
Thomas Jefferys, 1764
NMC 13264

MAP 186 (PAGE 134)
A General Map of North America/ Cartes Generales de L'Amerique Septentrionale
John Roque, 1762
NMC 116793

MAP 187 (PAGE 135)
Carte Marine entre Californie et une Partie de l'Asie la plus Orientale (left part of map shown)
and
Carte Marine de Amerique Septentrionale Partie de la Bᵉ d'Hudson (right part of map shown)
Isaac Brouckner, 1749
NMC 14044 and 14043

MAP 188 (PAGE 135)
Carte Reduite des Parties Septentrionales du Globe Situées Entre L'Asie et L'Amerique
Jacques-Nicolas Bellin, 1758
Beach Maps, Toronto

MAP 189 (PAGES 136–37)
A Plan of the Coppermine River by Samᵉˡ Hearne, July 1771
Samuel Hearne, 1771
JFBL

MAP 190 (PAGE 136)
[Plan of York Fort]
James Isham, c1740
HBCA: G2/5

MAP 191 (PAGE 137)
A Map of Part of the Inland Country to the Nʰ Wˢ of Prince of Wales Fort Hˢ, Bᵃ, Humbly Inscribed to the Govᵉʳ Depʸ, Govᵉʳ and Committee of the Honᵇˡᵉ Hudᵐˢ Bʸ Compʸ By their Honᵉˢ, moste obedient humble servant. Samˡ Hearne; 1772.
Samuel Hearne, 1772
HBCA: G2/10

MAP 192 (PAGES 138–39)
A Map of the North West Parts of America, with the Utmost Respect, Inscrib'd to His Excellency, Sir Guy Carleton, Knight of the Bath: Captain General and Governor of the Province of Quebec: General and Commander in Chief of His Majesty's Forces in the Said Province, and Frontiers thereof. &c. &c. &c., By his Most Obedient Humble Servt. Alexʳ Henry.
Alexander Henry, 1776
LC: G3470 1776 .H4 vault

MAP 193 (PAGE 139)
[Sketch map of Upper Canada]
Elizabeth Simcoe, c1793
AO 1352

MAP 194 (PAGES 140–41)
[Copy of a map of western Canada and the North Pacific Ocean thought to have been prepared by Peter Pond for presentation by Alexander Mackenzie to the Empress of Russia]
Copied from the original signed P. Pond Araubaska 6th December 1787 (marginal notation)
Anon. (Peter Pond), 1787
PRO: CO 700 America North and South 49

MAP 195 (PAGE 141)
Copy of a Map presented to the Congress by Peter Pond, a native of Milford in the State of Connecticut
Anon. (Peter Pond, 1784), 1785
BL: Add. MS 15332c

MAP 196 (PAGE 142)
[Map of western Canada presented to the lieutenant-governor of Québec, Henry Hamilton]
Anon. (Peter Pond), 1785
PRO: MPG 425

MAP 197 (PAGE 142)
A Map shewing the communication of the Lakes and the Rivers between Lake Superior and Slave Lake in North America
From: *Gentleman's Magazine*, March 1790

MAP 198 (PAGE 143)
[Mackenzie Delta]
Detail of MAP 201

MAP 199 (PAGE 143)
"Chart called Mackenzie's Map, illustrative of his tract from Athabasca Lake down Mackenzie River to the North Sea"
Anon. (Alexander Mackenzie), c1789
PRO: CO 700 America North and South 54

MAP 200 (PAGE 144)
A Map Exhibiting all the New Discoveries in the Interior Parts of North America Inscribed by Permission To the Honorable Governor and Company of Adventurers of England Trading into Hudsons Bay In testimony of their liberal Communications To their most Obedient and very Humble Servant, A. Arrowsmith Charles Street, Soho, January 1st 1795 ~ Additions to 1796
Aaron Arrowsmith, 1798 or 1799, with MS additions from *Information Given me by Mr [Joseph] Colen [of the Hudson's Bay Company]*
BL: Maps 69917.(70)

MAP 201 (PAGES 144–45)
A Map of America between Latitudes 40° & 70° North and Longitudes 40° & 180° West Exhibiting Mackenzie's Track From Montreal to Fort Chipewyan & from thence to the North Sea in 1789, & to the North Pacific Ocean in 1793.
Anon. (Aaron Arrowsmith[?]/David Thompson/ Alexander Mackenzie), c1800
PRO: CO 700 Canada 59A

MAP 202 (PAGE 145)
[Mackenzie's route from Fort Fork to the Pacific]
Detail of MAP 201

MAP 203 (PAGE 146)
A Plan of Part of Hudson's-Bay & Rivers communicating With the Principal Settlements
Andrew Graham (attrib.), 1772
HBCA: G2/15

MAP 204 (PAGE 146)
A Plan of Part of Hudson's-Bay, & Rivers, Communicating with York Fort & Severn
Andrew Graham (attrib.), 1774
HBCA: G2/17

MAP 205 (PAGE 146)
[Plan of York Fort to show proposed improvements]
Joseph Colen, 1786–87
HBCA: G1/111

MAP 206 (PAGE 147)
A Chart of Rivers and Lakes Falling into Hudsons Bay According to a Survey taken in the years 1778 & 9 By Philip Turnor
Philip Turnor, 1779
HBCA: G1/22

MAP 207 (PAGE 147)
Chart of Lakes and Rivers in North America by Philip Turnor those Shaded are from Actual Survey's the others from Canadian and Indian information
Philip Turnor, 1792
HBCA: G2/13

MAP 208 (PAGE 148)
To the Honourable the Governor, Deputy Governor, And Committee of the Hudson's Bay Company This Map of Hudson's Bay and the Rivers and Lakes Between the Atlantick and Pacifick Oceans Is most humbly Inscribed By their most obedient & dutiful Servant, Philip Turnor
Philip Turnor, 1794
HBCA: G2/32

MAP 209 (PAGE 149)
A Map Exhibiting all the New Discoveries in the Interior Parts of North America
[As MAP 200]
Aaron Arrowsmith, 1798 or 1799; MS additions
BL: Maps 69917.(70)

MAP 210 (PAGE 150)
[Southern shore of Lake Athabasca showing position of Fort Chipewyan]
Peter Fidler, 1791
HBCA: E3/1, folio 10 verso

MAP 211 (PAGE 150)
[Western end of Lake Athabasca]
Peter Fidler, 1791
HBCA: E3/1, folio 11

MAP 212 (PAGE 151)
[Page from Peter Fidler's journal showing sketch maps of the shores of Lake Athabasca]
Peter Fidler, 1791
HBCA: E3/1, folio 23

MAP 213 (PAGE 151)
[Cumberland House]
Peter Fidler, 1792
HBCA: E3/1, folio 86 verso

MAP 214 (PAGE 151)
Detail of MAP 208, showing Peter Fidler's track in 1792–93 towards the Rocky Mountains

MAP 215 (PAGE 152)
[Birchbark map of Ottawa–Lake Huron watershed route]
Anon., found by P. J. [?] Bainbrigge, 1841
BL: Maps.C.18.c.21

MAP 216 (PAGE 153)
[Part of western Canada with the rivers draining from the Rocky Mountains]
Drawn by ak ko wee ak a Black Foot Indian 1802
Copied by Peter Fidler, 1802
HBCA: E3/2, folio 103 verso

MAP 217 (PAGE 153)
[Map of western Canada and the United States, showing the rivers draining from the Rocky Mountains]
Drawn by the Feathers or ac ko mok ki a Blackfoot chief 7 Febᵞ 1801
Copied by Peter Fidler, 1801
HBCA: E3/2 folios 106 verso - 107

MAP 218 (PAGE 153)
[Map of rivers draining from the Rocky Mountains in Alberta]
These two sketches by Chynk,y,es,cum a Bungee Chief 29ᵗʰ May 1809 [bottom map only]
Copied by Peter Fidler, 1809
HBCA: E3/4, folio 15

MAP 219 (PAGE 154)
[South Saskatchewan River drainage basin]
Drawn by Ki oo cus - or the Little Bear a Blackfoot Chief 1802
Copied by Peter Fidler, 1802
HBCA: E3/2, folios 85 verso - 86

MAP 220 (PAGE 154)
[Great Slave Lake to Hudson Bay]
Shew ditha da, copied by Philip Turnor, 1791
HBCA: B9/a/3, page 83

MAP 221 (PAGE 155)
[Matonabbee and Idotlyazee's map of the region between Hudson Bay and Great Slave Lake]
Captain Mea'to'na'bee & I'dot'ly'a'zees Draught.
Moses Norton, 1767–68
HBCA: G2/27

MAP 222 (PAGE 156)
A chart containing the coasts of California, New Albion, and Russian Discoveries to the North with the Peninsula of Kamschatka, Asia, opposite thereto And Islands dispersed over the Pacific Ocean to the North of the line
Thomas Jefferys, 1775
From: *An American Atlas*, 1775
BCA: NW 912.7 J45am (1)

MAP 223 (PAGE 156)
Carta reducida de las costas, y mares septentrionales de California construida bajo las observaciones, y demarcaciones hechas por . . . de Fragata Don Juan Francisco de la Vodega y Quadra commandante de la goleta Sonora y por el piloto Don Francisco Antonio Maurelle
Juan Francisco de la Bodega y Quadra, 1775
AGI: MP, Mexico 581

MAP 224 (PAGE 157)
Carta Reducida del Oceano Asiatico õ Mar del Sur que contiene la Costa de la California comprehendida desde el Puerto de Monterrey. hta la Punta de Sᵗᵃ. Maria Magdalena hecha segun las observaciones y Demarcaciones del Aljerez de Fragata de la Rˡ. Armada y Primer Piloto de este Departamento Dⁿ. Juan Perez por Dⁿ. Josef de Cañizarez.
Josef de Cañizarez, 1774
NARA: RG 77; "Spanish maps (of unknown origin)" No. 67

MAP 225 (PAGE 158)
Track from first making the Continent, March 7th, to Anchoring in King George's Sound.
From: Journal of James Burney, 1778
PRO: ADM 51/4528

MAP 226 (PAGE 158)
Chart of the NW Coast of America and the NE Coast of Asia explored in the years 1778 and 1779 The unshaded parts of the coast of Asia are taken from a MS chart received from the Russians.
James Cook, 1784
From: *Voyage to the Pacific Ocean*, James Cook, 1784

MAP 227 (PAGE 158)
Chart of part of the N W Coast of America Explored by Capt. J. Cook in 1778
[Map enclosed with Cook's letter to Philip Stephens, Secretary of the Admiralty, from Unalaska, sent 20 October 1778 (21 October in Cook's journal), received in London 6 March 1780.]
PRO: MPI 83 (removed from ADM 1/1621)

MAP 228 (PAGE 158)
Sketch of Nootka Sound A. Ship Cove 1778
James Cook, 1784 (1778)
From: *Voyage to the Pacific Ocean*, James Cook, 1784

MAP 229 (PAGE 158)
General Chart exhibiting the discoveries made by Capt. James Cook in this and his preceding two voyages, with the tracks of the ships under his command.
Wm. Faden
Henry Roberts, published by William Faden, 1784
BCA: CM B1189

MAP 230 (PAGE 159)
Chart of the N.W. Coast of America and the N.E. Coast of Asia, explored in the Years 1778 and 1779 by Capt Cook and further explored, in 1788, and 1789.
John Meares, 1790
From: *Voyages made in the years 1788 and 1789 from China to the North West Coast of America*, John Meares, 1790

MAP 231 (PAGE 159)
Carte de la Côte Ouest de l'Amérique du Nord, de Mt. St. Elias à Monterey, avec la trajectoire l'expédition de La Pérouse et la table des données de longitude compilées par Bernizet et Dagelet
Joseph Dagelet and Gérault-Sébastien Bernizet, 1786
AN: 6 JJ1: 34B

MAP 232 (PAGE 159)
N. W. America Drawn by J.C. from his own Information & what could be collected from the Sloop Pr Royal & Boats in the Years 1787 1788
James Colnett, 1788
UKHO p24 on 87

MAP 233 (PAGE 160)
Plano de la Cala De Los Amigos situada en la parte occidental de la entrada de Nutka. Ano 1791.
From: *Relación, atlas*, 1802
VPL: SPA 970P E77r2

MAP 234 (PAGE 160)
Chart of the West Coast of North America with The Isles adjacent . . . copied from one constructed principally, and laid down, from The Observations, of & by Dⁿ Caamãno, a Lieuténant in the Spanish Navy, in yᵉ year 1792, & shewing the Straits said to be discovered by De Fonte in yᵉ year 1640.
Anon., 1792
UKHO: 355/3 on Ac 1

MAP 235 (PAGES 160–61)
Carta que comprehende los interiers y veril de la costa desde los 48° de Latitud N hasta los 50°.
1791
José María Nárvaez [?], 1791
LC: G3351.P5 1799.C vault, Map 12

MAP 236 (PAGE 161)
Plano del estrecho de Juan de Fuca descuvierto el ano 1592, reconocido en 1789 por Dⁿ Jose Narvaez en el de 90 . . . Dⁿ Manuel Quimper, en 91 . . . Dⁿ Fran^{co} Eliza y concluido en . . . el Comandame Vancouver y Dionisio Galiano en el qual sedenetan con el color negro los descubrim los hechos . . . con el ecarnado los Vancouver y con elazul los de Galiano
Juan Francisco de la Bodega y Quadra, 1792
OHS: Neg #097867

MAP 237 (PAGE 162)
Num. 2 Carta Esferica de los Reconocimientos hechos en la Costa N.O. De America en 1791 y 92 por las Goletas Sutil y Mexicana y otres Bruques de S.M.
Dionisio Galiano, 1792
From: *Relación*, atlas, 1802

MAP 238 (PAGE 162)
Carta general de quanto asta hoy se ha descubierto y examinado por los Espanoles en la Costa Septentrional de California, formada . . . por D. Juan Francisco de la Bodega y Quadra Ano de 1791
Juan Francisco de la Bodega y Quadra, 1791
Museo Naval

MAP 239 (PAGE 162)
Carta Reducida de la Costa Septentrional de California . . .
Juan Francisco de la Bodega y Quadra, 1791 or 1792
LC: G3351.P5 1799.C vault, Map 1

MAP 240 (PAGE 162)
Carta de los Descubrimientos hechos en la Costa N.O. America Septentrional
Juan Francisco de la Bodega y Quadra, 1792
LC: G3350 1792.B6 TIL vault

MAP 241 (PAGE 163)
[Preliminary chart of the Northwest Coast of America from George Vancouver's landfall to Cape Mudge]
George Vancouver, 1792
PRO: MPG 557 (4), removed from CO 5/187

MAP 242 (PAGE 163)
[Survey of Johnstone Strait and Loughborough Inlet]
James Johnstone, 1792
UKHO: 231/4 Ac 1

MAP 243 (PAGE 163)
Chart of the Coast of N W America and islands adjacent north Westward of the Gulf of Georgia as explored by His Majesty's ships Discovery & Chatham in the months of July & August 1792
George Vancouver, 1792
PRO: MPG 557 (3), removed from CO 5/187

MAP 244 (PAGE 164)
A Chart shewing part of the Western Coast of N. America in which the continental shore from the Latde. of 42° 30' N and Longde. 230° 30' E. to the latde. 52° 15' N and longde 288° 03'; E. has been finally traced and determined by His Majesty's Sloop Discovery and armed tender Chatham under the Command of George Vancouver Esqr. in the Summer of 1792. The parts of the Coast red, are copied from Spanish Charts constructed by the Officers under the order of Senres. Quadra and Malaspina. Prepared by Lieut. Jos. Baker, under the immediate inspection of Captn. Vancouver.
Joseph Baker and George Vancouver, 1792
UKHO: 228 on 82

MAP 245 (PAGE 165)
A Chart shewing part of the N.W. Coast of North America with the Tracks of His Majesty's Sloop Discovery and Armed Tender Chatham . . .
Joseph Baker and George Vancouver, 1798
From: *A Voyage of Discovery to the North Pacific Ocean and Around the World*, Plate 14 of atlas, George Vancouver, 1798

MAP 246 (PAGES 166–67)
Map of the North-West Territory of the Province of Canada from actual survey during the years 1782 to 1812. This map, made for the North West Company in 1813 and 1814 embraces the region lying between 45 and 60 degrees North latitude and 84 and 124 West longitude comprising the surveys and discoveries of 20 years, namely the discovery and survey of the Oregon Territory to the

Pacific Ocean, the survey of the Athabasca Lake, Slave River and Lake from which flows Mackenzie's River to the Arctic Sea by Mr. Phillip Turner the route of Sir Alexander Mackenzie in 1792 down part of Frasers River together with the survey of this river to the Pacific Ocean by the late John Stewart of the North West Company, by David Thompson, Astronomer and Surveyor. Sgd. David Thompson
David Thompson, 1814
AO 1541

MAP 247 (PAGE 168)
[Survey of the international boundary along the St. Lawrence River]
David Thompson, 1820
NMC 16863

MAP 248 (PAGE 168)
[Lake of the Woods showing the international boundary proposals]
David Thompson and Anthony Barclay, 1824
NMC 6851

MAP 249 (PAGE 169)
[Map of Lake Ontario]
Anon., c1675
SHM

MAP 250 (PAGE 169)
Plan of Toronto [showing proposal for a town]
Alexander Aitken, 1788
AO 5161

MAP 251 (PAGE 169)
Plan of Toronto Harbour with the proposed Town and part of the Settlement
Gother Mann, 1788
NMC 4434

MAP 252 (PAGE 169)
[The Toronto carrying place]
Elizabeth Simcoe, c1793
AO 1352

MAP 253 (PAGE 170)
[Untitled map called the "Toronto Purchase" map, with signatures on the reverse side]
William Chewett, 1805
National Archives of Canada:
RG 10, Vol. 1841, IT 039

MAP 254 (PAGE 170)
[Map of Lake Erie to Montréal, part showing site of Toronto]
Anon., c1790
AO 1363

MAP 255 (PAGE 171)
Plan of York
George Phillpotts, 1818 (1823)
NMC 17026

MAP 256 (PAGE 171)
A Map of the Province of Upper Canada and the Adjacent Territories in North America
James G. Chewett, 1825 or 1826
NMC 113165

MAP 257 (PAGE 172)
Plan of Old Fort Frontenac and Town of Kingston
Anon., 1784
AO 1380

MAP 258 (PAGE 172)
[Plan of York Redoubt at the entrance to Halifax Harbour]
Anon., c1800
PANS: H16/250, REO No. N15

MAP 259 (PAGE 172)
[Lake Erie to Montréal showing proposed fort at Kingston (Fort Henry)]
Anon., c1790
AO 1363

MAP 260 (PAGE 173)
Map of Part of Lower Canada. Compiled by Messrs Gale and Duberger in 1794 and 1795 By Order of His Excellency Guy Lord Dorchester
Samuel Gale and John B. Duberger, 1794–95
NMC 57718 (in three sections)

MAP 261 (PAGE 174)
[Amherstburg and the Detroit River]
Anon., 1817
NMC 21693

MAP 262 (PAGE 174)
Plan of the Town and Harbour of York
George Williams, 1814
NMC 21771

MAP 263 (PAGE 174)
[Queenston Heights]
Anon., 1817
NMC 21729

MAP 264 (PAGE 175)
[Map of the Niagara Frontier]
Anon., 1810
NMC 19551 (2)

MAP 265 (PAGE 175)
View of the Country Around the Falls of Niagara
John Melish, 1826
Lundy's Lane Historical Museum, Niagara Falls

MAP 266 (PAGE 176)
No. 1 Part of River Thames Upper Canada
Anon., 1813–14
NMC 21814

MAP 267 (PAGE 176)
Sketch of the Battle of la Fourche or Chateauguay Oct 26th 1813
J. Walker, 1815
SMM

MAP 268 (PAGE 176)
No. 4 Upper Canada: Plan of Niagara River
Anon., 1817
NMC 21729

MAP 269 (PAGE 177)
Sketch of an action fought on the night of 25 July 1814 near the Falls of Niagara between a British force under Genl Drummond & an American force under Major Genl Brown by G. A. Eliott D:A:2. M.G^l
G. A. Eliott, 1814
Inset in: *Part of the Niagara Frontier*
NMC 21586

MAP 270 (PAGE 177)
[Site of the battlefield of Lundy's Lane]
Part of the Niagara Frontier
Anon., 1814
NMC 18559

MAP 271 (PAGE 177)
Fort Erie as left by the Enemy
Anon., 1814
NMC 70956

MAP 272 (PAGE 178)
[Map attached to the deed conveying Assiniboia from the Hudson's Bay Company to the Earl of Selkirk]
[Aaron Arrowsmith], 1811
Deed dated 12 June 1811
HBCA: E8/1 folio 6

MAP 273 (PAGE 178)
[Map attached to the deed conveying land along the Red and Assiniboine Rivers from native chiefs to the Earl of Selkirk]
Deed dated 18 July 1817
HBCA: E8/1 folio 11

MAP 274 (PAGE 179)
A Map of Red River District
Peter Fidler, 1819
HBCA: B22/e/1, folio 1

MAP 275 (PAGE 180)
[Survey of the international boundary at Red River]
David Thompson, 1840
NMC 24773-1

MAP 276 (PAGE 180)
Map of North America
Inset in:
Map of the United States partly from new survey Dedicated to the citizens thereof by their humble servant Chas Varle Engineer & Geographer, 1817
Charles Varle, 1817
BCA: CM W47,2/2

MAP 277 (PAGE 180)
[Map of western Canada showing boundary line claimed by the United States]
Anon., 1818
NMC 6852

MAP 278 (PAGE 181)
Eastern End of Route of Rideau Canal
Thomas Burrowes, 1830
From: Burrowes' watercolour sketchbook
AO 5517

MAP 279 (PAGE 182)
Plan of the Line of the Rideau Canal
John By, 1829
NMC 21972

MAP 280 (PAGE 182)
Huron Tract belonging to the Canada Company
Anon., 1832
NMC 2860

MAP 281 (PAGES 182–83)
A Map of the Province of Upper Canada and the Adjacent Territories in North America
James G. Chewett, 1825 or 1826
NMC 113165, sheets 1 and 2

MAP 282 (PAGE 184)
Chart of the World on Mercator's Projection
Aaron Arrowsmith, 1794 (dated 1790)

MAP 283 (PAGE 184)
[Map of the polar regions illustrating John Barrow's theories]
From: *Quarterly Review*, London, 1817

MAP 284 (PAGE 184)
Track of H.M. Ships Isabella & Alexander from 29th August to the 1st September 1818
John Ross, 1819
From: Ross, 1819

MAP 285 (PAGE 185)
Survey of Winter Harbour Melville Island June 1820
William Edward Parry, 1821
From: Parry, 1821

MAP 286 (PAGE 185)
General Chart shewing the track of H.M. Ships Hecla & Griper from the Orkneys to Melville Island, North Georgia
William Edward Parry, 1821
From: Parry, 1821

MAP 287 (PAGES 186–87)
Lancaster Sound by Capt. W. H. Parry (sic)
No. 43 C [title on back of map]
[Parry's map of his discoveries, Baffin Bay to Melville Island.]
William Edward Parry, 1819–20
BL: Maps.188.0.1 (3)

MAP 288 (PAGES 186–87)
North America [northern coast]
Aaron Arrowsmith, 1824, with MS additions and patches by the Hudson's Bay Company
HBCA: G4/31

MAP 289 (PAGE 188)
Route From Lake Athapescow, to the Coppermine River, North America Surveyed by the Northern Land Expedition under the command of Lieu^t Franklin, R.N.
John Franklin, 1820–21
PRO: CO 700 Canada 79, Map 1

MAP 290 (PAGE 188)
Eskimaux Chart No. 2 The shaded parts drawn by Iligliuk at Winter Island 1822. The Original in the Possession of Cap.ⁿ Parry
Iligliuk and William Edward Parry, 1822
From: Parry, 1824

MAP 291 (PAGE 189)
Chart of Part of the North Eastern Coast of America and its adjacent Islands shewing the Track and Discoveries of His Majesty's Ships Fury and Hecla in search of a North West Passage under the Command of Capt.ⁿ W. E. Parry in the Years 1822–23
J. Bushnan and William Edward Parry, 1822–23
From: Parry, 1824

MAP 292 (PAGE 189)
Route of the Land Arctic Expedition under the command of Lieutenant [?] J. Franklin R.N. from Great Bear Lake River to the Polar Sea Surveyed and drawn by Mr. E. A. Kendall R.N., Assistant Surveyor
Edward Kendall, John Richardson, and John Franklin, 1825
PRO: MPG 386

MAP 293 (PAGES 190–91)
A Chart of the Discoveries of Captains Ross, Parry & Franklin in the Arctic Regions In the Years 1818, 1819, 1820, 1821 & 1822
With Inset: *Capt. Franklin's Journey from Coppermine River to the head of Bathurst Inlet & Return by Hood's River*
John Thomson, 1827
NMC 24922

MAP 294 (PAGE 191)
Chart Drawn by the Natives
Anon. [Ikmalick and Apelaglu?], 1829–30
From: Ross, 1835

MAP 295 (PAGE 192)
To His Most Excellent majesty William IVth King of Great Britain Ireland &c This Chart of the Discoveries made in The Arctic Regions, in 1829, 30, 31, 32, & 33 is Dedicated with his Majesty's gracious permission to His Majesty's Loyal and devoted Subjects John Ross, Captain Royal Navy. James Clark Ross, Commander Royal Navy.
John Ross, 1834
From: Ross, 1835

MAP 296 (PAGE 193)
Chart of Part of the Arctic Regions as known in 1845, being a copy of the Chart supplied to the Franklin Expedition
A. G. Findlay, 1858
From: *The North-West Passage and the Search for John Franklin*, John Browne, E. Stanford, London, 1860

MAP 297 (PAGE 193)
[Map of the Arctic Coast showing the discoveries of Thomas Simpson and Peter Warren Dease, 1838–39]
Anon., 1839
HBCA: G1/5

MAP 298 (PAGE 194)
Chart showing the North West Passage Discovered by H. M. Ship Investigator *Also the Coast Explored in Search of Sir J. Franklin. Drawn by W. H. Fawckner, 2nd Master.*
W. H. Fawckner, 1853
UKHO: L9311 Shelf Tt
Reproduced from the original by permission of the Controller of Her Majesty's Stationery Office and the UK Hydrographic Office.

MAP 299 (PAGE 194)
[Map of Committee Bay]
John Rae, 1847
HBCA: G1/177

MAP 300 (PAGE 195)
Map of a Portion of the Arctic Shores of America to Accompany Capt.ⁿ M.cClintock's Narrative
John Arrowsmith, 1859
From: M'Clintock, 1859

MAP 301 (PAGE 195)
Arctic Seas Shewing the North-West Passage, The Coasts explored by the several Searching Expeditions, and the spot where the remains of Sir John Franklin have been discovered
W. & A. K. Johnston, 1854, with MS additions
NMC 6296

MAP 302 (PAGE 196)
Explorations in Northern Canada and Adjacent portions of Greenland and Alaska 1904
Department of the Interior, Canada, 1904
NMC 17629

MAP 303 (PAGE 197)
[Map of the Liard River]
Murdoch McPherson, 1824
HBCA: B116/a/2, folio 26

MAP 304 (PAGE 198)
North America [British Columbia region]
Aaron Arrowsmith, 1824, with MS additions and patches by the Hudson's Bay Company
HBCA: G4/31

MAP 305 (PAGE 198)
Sketch Map of Peel River
Alexander K. Isbister, 1841–42
From: *Journal of the Royal Geographical Society*, Vol. 15, 1845

MAP 306 (PAGE 199)
British North America [Yukon River system]
John Arrowsmith, 1857
HBCA: G3/9

MAP 307 (PAGE 199)
A Sketch of the course of the West Branch of the Liard River and Pelly's River so far discovered By Your obedient Humble Servant, R. Campbell
Robert Campbell, 1844
HBCA: G1/71

MAP 308 (PAGE 200)
[Navy Island] No. 4 Upper Canada Plan of the Niagara River
Anon., 1810
NMC 21729

MAP 309 (PAGE 200)
Sketch Plan of the Village of Sᵗ Eustache After the Action Decʳ 16th 1837
Anon., 1837
NMC 6260

MAP 310 (PAGE 200)
Sketch of Proposed Improvements for Kingston
Robert G. Gourlay, 1841
NMC 22432

MAP 311 (PAGE 201)
A Plan of the Erie and Ontario Junction or Welland Canal
Anon., 1826
NMC 3005

MAP 312 (PAGE 201)
Plan of the Niagara Frontier shewing the General Line of the Welland Canal To Accompany Lt Colonel Phillpotts Report on the Inland Navigation of the Canadas With letter to the Inspector General dated 19th Febʸ 1840
George Phillpotts, 1840
NMC 29139

MAP 313 (PAGE 201)
Plan of part of the line of the Welland Canal showing the intended deviation between St. Catherines and Thorold
George Phillpotts, 1841
NMC 34150

MAP 314 (PAGE 202)
British North America
John Thomson, 1814
From: *Thomson's New General Atlas*, 1817

MAP 315 (PAGE 202)
To His most Excellent Majesty King William VIth This Map of the Provinces of Upper & Lower Canada Nova Scotia, New Brunswick, Newfoundland & Prince Edward Island . . .
Joseph Bouchette, 1831
NMC 113504-3

MAP 316 (PAGE 202)
Sketch of the North Eastern Boundary Disputed between Great Britain and the United States as Settled by Treaty Augᵗ 9th 1842
James Wyld, 1842
NMC 6846

MAP 317 (PAGE 203)
Ground Plan of Portion of Vancouvers Island Selected for New Establishment Taken by James Douglas Esqʳ
James Douglas and Adolphus Lee Lewes, 1842
HBCA: G2/25

MAP 318 (PAGE 203)
Map of Vancouver Island with the adjacent coast, to illustrate a description of the Island, by Lt. Col. W. C. Grant, 1856.
John Arrowsmith, 1856
Published for the *Journal of the Royal Geographical Society* by J. Murray, London, 1857

MAP 319 (PAGE 204)
Disputed Territory of Columbia or Oregon Showing its limits as settled by different treaties and the Boundaries proposed by England and America. From the large map of M. Duflot de Mofras and other recent & authentic sources.
W. and A. K. Johnston, 1846
BCA: CM A156

MAP 320 (PAGE 204)
Map of the Gold Regions of the Frazer River and the Washington Territory on the Western Coast of America
James Wyld, 1858
PRO 925 1650, 32

MAP 321 (PAGE 205)
Map of the Principal Communications in Canada West
Baron de Rottenburg, c1850
NMC 21437

MAP 322 (PAGE 206)
New Westminster British Columbia Lithographed at the Royal Engineers Camp, New Westminster, May 1861, by order of Col. R.C. Moody R.E. 1861
Anon., 1861
PRO: CO 700 British Columbia 11, 8

MAP 323 (PAGE 206)
[Albert City (New Westminster)]
Detail from MAP 320

MAP 324 (PAGE 206)
British Columbia (New Caledonia)
From: *Weekly Dispatch Atlas*, Supplement to *Weekly Dispatch* for Sunday, 29 August 1858
Edward Weller, 1858
BCA: CM A1575

MAP 325 (PAGE 206)
Sketch of Part of British Columbia by Lieut. R.C. Mayne RN of HMS Plumper. [Fort Hope and gold workings, Fraser River]
Richard Charles Mayne, c1860
PRO: CO 700 British Columbia 8, 2

MAP 326 (PAGE 207)
The Fertile Belt
Henry Youle Hind, 1860
From: Hind, 1860

MAP 327 (PAGE 207)
Lake Superior to Lake Winnipeg. Map to Accompany Report of the Canadian Red River Exploring Expedition
Printed map with MS additions by Henry Youle Hind, 1858
NMC 113510

MAP 328 (PAGE 208)
A General Map of the Routes in British North America Explored by the Expedition under Captain Palliser, During the Years 1857, 1858, 1859, 1860.
Stanford's Geographical Establishment, 1865

MAP 329 (PAGE 209)
British North America Exploring Expedition Under the Command of Captain John Palliser Map of the Country explored from October 1857 to Dᵒ [ditto] 1858 From field Sketches by Captain Jⁿ Palliser, Doctor Hector and Mr Sullivan.
James Hector, with John Palliser and James Sullivan, 1858
NMC 15953

MAP 330 (PAGE 210)
A Geological Map of Nova Scotia, Cape Breton, and Prince Edward Island
Abraham Gesner, 1849
PANS: 202-1849 Nova Scotia, N-476

MAP 331 and MAP 332 (PAGE 210)
Parts of:
Environs of Montreal shewing the Railway Communications with the City. Compiled and Drawn by George Horatio Smith, Montreal 1851
George Horatio Smith, 1851
BNQ: G3453 M65 1851 S55 CAR

MAP 333 (PAGE 211)
Map of the Townships in the Province of Upper Canada (printed map with MS additions): Great Northern and Great Western Railways & Plank Roads 1843
Anon., 1843[?]
NMC 2872

MAP 334 (PAGE 211)
Kingston: Extension of Grand Trunk Railway into the City
Signed: Arthur J. Storer Lieut. R.E. 17th Decʳ 1858
NMC 26613

MAP 335 (PAGE 211)
[Southern Ontario showing railways and MacAdamized and Plank Roads]
D. W. Greany, 1866 [?]
NMC 2924

MAP 336 (PAGE 212)
General Map to Accompany Report on the Intercolonial Railway:- Exploratory Survey
Sandford Fleming, 1864
NMC 11751

MAP 337 (PAGE 212)
Eastern Part of the Dominion of Canada
W. and A. K. Johnston, 1876

MAP 338 (PAGE 213)
Rough Diagram Based on Hind's Map, intended to illustrate Report of this date on Township Surveys—Red River Territory, Ottawa, February 12th 1870
John Stoughton Dennis, 1870
NMC 7064

MAP 339 (PAGE 214)
Map of the Province of Manitoba
Alexander Lord Russell, 1871
NMC 17551

MAP 340 (PAGE 214)
Map of the Red River Territory Published by Dawson Brothers, Montreal, 1870
E. H. Charles Lionais, 1870
NMC 26753

MAP 341 (PAGE 215)
Map of British Columbia to the 56th Parallel, North Latitude Compiled and drawn at the Lands and Works Office, Victoria, B.C., under the direction of the Honble J. W. Trutch.
Dated 9 May 1870, with additions to January 1871
James Benjamin Launders, 1871
BCA: CM A1557

MAP 342 (PAGE 216)
Bishop's North West War Map
"George Bishop Eng. Ptg. Co.," c1885
NMC 15955

MAP 343 (PAGE 216)
Map of the Seat of Riel's Insurrection Showing the Connection of Prince Albert with Other Points in the North West
W. H. Holland, 1885
NMC 24373

MAP 344 (PAGE 217)
Winnipeg to District of Riel's Rebellion
"Alexander, Clare & Cable," 1885
NMC 24374

MAP 345 (PAGE 218)
Plan of the Attack on Batoche By the North West Field Force
George F. Cole, 1885
NMC 19793

MAP 346 (PAGE 218)
Map from the Pacific Ocean across the Rocky Mountain Zone to accompany Report on the Exploratory Survey Canadian Pacific Railway January 1874 Sheet No. 8
From: *Report of Progress on the Explorations and Surveys up to January 1874*, Sandford Fleming, Ottawa, MacLean Roger and Co., 1874
LC

MAP 347 (PAGE 219)
Map of the Dominion of Canada Shewing the Extent and Situation of its Public Lands [it does not], also its Geographical Relation to the British Isles.
John Macoun, 1882
From: *Manitoba and the Great North-West*, John Macoun, 1882

MAP 348 (PAGE 220)
Dominion of Canada General Map of Part of the North-West Territories Including the Province of Manitoba Shewing Dominion Land Surveys to 31ˢᵗ December 1882
Lindsay A. Russell, 1882
NMC 11621

MAP 349 (PAGE 221)
[Map showing Prof. Macoun's route for 1880]
John Macoun, 1880
NMC 17678

MAP 350 (PAGE 221)
Regina
Canadian Pacific Railway Lands Department, 1882
Glenbow

MAP 351 (PAGE 222)
General Map of Part of the North-West Territory and of Manitoba
John Macoun, 1882
From: *Manitoba and the Great North-West*, John Macoun, 1882

MAP 352 (PAGE 222)
Map of the Canadian Pacific Railway
Anon., 1881
From: Railway tariff, June, 1881
CPRA: RG31

MAP 353 (PAGE 222)
Topographical map of part of the Selkirk Range, British Columbia
Arthur O. Wheeler and Morrison P. Bridgland, 1902
NMC 44265, sheet 3

MAP 354 (PAGE 223)
[Telegraph in Western Canada]
Dominion of Canada Telegraph and Signal Services, c1880
NMC 13190, sheet 1

MAP 355 (PAGE 223)
Medicine Hat
Canadian Pacific Railway Lands Department, 1883, with MS additions, January 1888
Glenbow

Map 356 (page 223)
Manitoba and the North West Territories of Canada showing the Line and Land Grant of the Canadian Pacific Railway
Canadian Pacific Railway, 1886
Glenbow

Map 357 (page 224)
New Westminster District B.C. 1876
[Province of British Columbia, printed map]
With MS additions *Reserved Railway Land the Property of the Dominion Gov* coloured red, c1876
CPRA MP21, ID 5464

Map 358 (page 224)
Map of the Province of Manitoba and Part of the District of Keewatin and North West Territory Shewing the Townships & Settlements Drawn from the Latest Gov. Maps, Surveys & Reports for "The Prairie Province"
A. G. E. Westmacott, 1876
From: *The Prairie Province*, J. C. Hamilton, Belford Bros., Toronto, 1876
NMC 98197

Map 359 (pages 224–225)
The Canadian Pacific Railway. Traversing the Great Wheat Region of the Canadian Northwest
Canadian Pacific Railway 1883–85
NMC 11868

Map 360 (page 226)
Treaty No. 8 N.W.T. Plan of Sucker Creek Reserve No. 150A Situated on the South shore of Lesser Slave Lake surveyed for Councillor Moosloos and a portion of Chief Kinoosayos band
A. W. Ponton, 1901
NMC 23781

Map 361 (page 226)
Map of Manitoba Shewing Provincial Government Lands for Sale
Bulman Bros., Winnipeg, 1900
NMC 18781

Map 362 (page 227)
Plan of River Lots, in the parishes of St. John, St. James, and St. Boniface, Province of Manitoba
Duncan Sinclair and George McPhillips, November 1873, Surveys Branch, Manitoba Department of Mines and Natural Resources, Winnipeg, 1874
NMC 23464

Map 363 (page 227)
Plan of the City of Winnipeg and its vicinity Province of Manitoba Compiled and Drawn by John D. Parr
John D. Parr, 1874
NMC23816

Map 364 (page 228)
Plan of Fort Edmonton on the Saskatchewan River
Mervin Vavasour, 1846
PRO: MPK 59 (20)

Map 365 (pages 228–29)
Plan of Edmonton Settlement N.W.T.
Department of Interior, Dominion Lands Office, 25 May 1883
M. Deane, 1882; signed A. Russell, 1883
Glenbow: G3504 E24 1883a C212

Map 366 (page 229)
[Telegraph in Western Canada]
Dominion of Canada Telegraph and Signal Services, c1880
NMC 13190, sheet 1

Map 367 (page 230)
Map Shewing Mounted Police Stations and Patrols Throughout the North-West Territories During the Year 1886
Anon., 1886
Glenbow

Map 368 (page 230)
Calgary Subdivision of a Part of Section 15, Township 24, Range 1, W5
A[rchibald] W. McVittie, Canadian Pacific Railway Company. Lands Department, Winnipeg, 1 January 1884
Glenbow

Map 369 (page 231)
Plan of Township No. 24 Range 1 West of Fifth Meridian
Chs. Eug. [Charles Eugene?] Larue; signed E. [Édouard-Gaston] Deville, Dominion Lands Office, 8 March 1884
Glenbow

Map 370 (page 232)
[Map of the Turner Valley]
Anon., 1914, with MS additions, 1914–15
UA

Map 371 (page 232)
World's Highest Grade Oil Calgary-Alberta Oil Fields Map Showing Southern Portion
Theodore Seyler, 1914
Glenbow: G3502 S728 H8 1914 S521

Map 372 (page 233)
[Bird's eye map of] *Winnipeg, Manitoba 1880*
Thaddeus Fowler. Published by J. J. Stoner, 1880
NMC 15026

Map 373 (page 233)
[Bird's eye map of] *Chatham, Ontario*
Anon., c1880
LC: G3464 .C4A3 1880 .B5

Map 374 (page 234–35)
[Bird's eye map of] *Halifax, Nova Scotia 1890*
Published by D. D. Currie, 1890
LC: G3424 .H2A3 1890 .C8

Map 375 (page 234)
[Bird's eye map of] *Winnipeg 1894*
W. G. Fonseca, published by Mortimer & Co., 1884
LC: G3484 .W5A3 1884 .F6 vault: oversize

Map 376 (page 235)
Bird's Eye View of London, Ontario, Canada, 1878
E. S. Glover, 1878; 1932 reproduction
LC: G3464.L6 A3 1872 .G6 1932

Map 377 (page 236)
[Detail of *Carta que comprehende* showing Vancouver area]
(Map 235, pages 160–61)
LC: G3351.P5 1799.C vault, Map 12

Map 378 (page 236)
Plan of the City of Vancouver Western Terminus of the Canadian Pacific Railway. Published by Rand Brothers. 1887
Inset: *Index Plan of Vancouver B.C. Terminus*
CPR 1887
PRO: CO 700 British Columbia 17

Map 379 (page 237)
Panoramic View of the City of Vancouver, British Columbia 1898 J. C. McLagan. Printed by Toronto Lithographic Co. Published by the Vancouver World Printing and Publishing Co. Ltd.
J. C. McLagan, 1898
CVA: Map 547

Map 380 (page 238)
[Bytown and the eastern end of the Rideau Canal]
Detail of Map 278 (page 181)
AO 5517

Map 381 (page 238)
[Map attached to deed dated 18 June 1823, transferring land from Hugh Fraser to the Crown]
Anon., 1823
NMC 79949

Map 382 (page 239)
[Bird's-eye view of] *City of Ottawa, Canada, with views of principal business buildings*
Toronto Lithographing Company, 1895
LC: G3464.O8A3 1895 .T6 Oversize

Map 383 (page 240)
Topographical Plan of the City of Toronto
Sandford Fleming, 1851, from a survey by J. Stoughton Dennis
NMC 44116

Map 384 (page 240)
Toronto Plan to Accompany the Returns
Copied by William Mahony from a Royal Engineers plan, 1851
NMC 43216

Map 385 (page 241)
Birds eye view of Toronto, 1876
P. A. Gross, 1876
NMC 17628

Map 386 (pages 240–41)
[Bird's-eye view of Toronto, 1893]
Chromolithograph in three parts, printed by Barclay, Clark & Co., 1893
MTL: 916-2-1 to 3, T18147

Map 387 (page 242)
Plan of the Town and Fortifications of Montreal or Ville Marie in Canada
Thomas Jefferys [?], 1759
NMC 27649

Map 388 (page 243)
[Bird's-eye map of Montréal]
Anon., 1889
NMC 11075

Map 389 (page 243)
Plan of the frontier of Canada East From St. Regis to Canaan, surveyed in the year 1839
Under direction of Charles Gore; zincographed by British War Office, 1863
BNQ: G3451 F2 1863 P53 CAR

Map 390 (page 244)
"The Province" Map of the Klondyke And the Canadian Yukon and Routes Thereto
Province Publishing Co., 1897
NMC 44324

Map 391 (page 244)
Birdseye View of Dawson, Yukon Ter., 1903
M. Epting, 1903
NMC 24503

Map 392 (page 245)
Map of the Alaskan Gold Fields
T. S. Lee, 1897
LC: G4371.H2 1897 .L4 TIL

Map 393 (page 245)
Millroy's Map of Alaska and the Klondyke Gold Fields
J. J. Millroy, 1897
LC: G4371.H2 1897 .M5 TIL

Map 394 (page 245)
To the Land of Gold [poster]
Anon., c1897

Map 395 (page 246–47)
British America Showing also the British Empire
Dominion Publishing Company, 1902
NMC 17931

Map 396 (page 248)
Kart Over Kong Haakon VII's Kyst og Dronning Mauds Hav, Samt over Løitnant Hansens og Sergent Ristvedts Slæde-Ekspedition 1905
From: *Nordvest-Passagen: Beretning om Gjøa-Ekspeditionen 1903–1907*, Roald Amundsen, 1908

Map 397 (page 248)
[Map of the Ringnes Islands]
Otto Sverdrup, 1905
From: *Sverdrup*, 1905

Map 398 (page 249)
North America
From: *The Century Atlas*, 1897

Map 399 (page 249)
North Polar Chart
John Bartholomew & Co., 1905
From: *Century Atlas*, 1905

Map 400 (page 249)
Gjøahavn Med Nærmest Omgivelser
From: *Nordvest-Passagen: Beretning om Gjøa-Ekspeditionen 1903–1907*, Roald Amundsen, 1908

Map 401 (page 249)
Discoveries in the Arctic Sea 1916
Vilhjalmur Stefansson, 1916
From: *Stefansson*, 1921

Map 402 (page 250)
Plan of Arctic Bay, Baffin Island
Joseph-Elzéar Bernier, 1911
From: *Bernier*, n.d. (1911–12)

Map 403 (page 250)
Surveys and Discoveries in the Arctic Regions with additions and changes to 1911 on Coast of Baffin Island by J. T. E. Lavoie, C.E. Capt. J. Bernier's Arctic Expedition, 1910-11
J. T. E. Lavoie, 1911
From: *Bernier*, n.d., (1911–12)

Map 404 (page 250)
Discoveries in the Arctic Sea
Vilhjalmur Stefansson, 1916
From: *Stefansson*, 1921

Map 405 (page 251)
William Dow & Co. Brewery & Malthouse
Charles E. Goad, 1903
NMC 10582

Map 406 (page 251)
Map 5, from: *Fire Map of Vancouver, B.C. Issued by the Dakin Publishing Co. Of San Francisco to Messrs. Majors and Pearson* [real estate and insurance brokers]
Dakin Publishing, November 1889
Don Stewart, MacLeod's Books, Vancouver

Map 407 (page 252)
[Map of Russian America]
Grigorii Shelikov, 1796

Map 408 (page 252)
[Proposals for the Alaska boundary]
Anon., 1886
NMC 25126

Map 409 (page 252)
Map of the Canadian Pacific Railway and Connections showing routes to the Yukon Gold Fields, Alaska, Klondike and the Northwestern Mining Territories of Canada
Poole Brothers, Chicago, 1898
LC

Map 410 (page 253)
Dominion of Canada
J. Bartholomew, c1875
Atlas, Blackie & Son, c1876

Map 411 (page 253)
Map of the Dominion of Canada, Western Part
From: *Eclectic Series of Geographies*, A. von Steinwehr, 1878

Map 412 (page 253)
[Dominion of Canada]
George F. Cram, 1881
From: *Atlas*, 1887

Map 413 (page 254)
Dominion of Canada Western Part
James Monteith, 1885

Map 414 (page 254)
Map of the British Provinces of North America
Anon., 1868
From: *The Common-School Geography*, D. M. Warren, Cowperthwait & Co., Philadelphia, 1868

Map 415 (page 254)
Manitoba and the North West
John Bartholomew & Co., 1905
From: *Century Atlas*, 1905

Map 416 (page 255)
Sketch Map of Quebec. Showing the whole extent of the Province
The Century Co., 1897
Inset in: *Quebec*
From: *Century Atlas*, the Century Co., New York, 1897

Map 417 (page 255)
Dominion of Canada (Eastern Provinces)
John Bartholomew & Co., 1905
From: *Century Atlas*, 1905

Map 418 (page 256)
The Rand-McNally New Commercial Atlas Map of Dominion of Canada
Rand-McNally, 1912
From: *Commercial Atlas of America*, 1912

Map 419 (page 256)
[Newfoundland and Labrador]
Atlas map, 1947

Map 420 (page 256)
The Century Atlas. Dominion of Canada and Newfoundland
The Century Atlas Co., 1897

Map 421 (page 267)
Detail of Map 39 (page 34)
William Borough, 1575 or 1576, with additions by Martin Frobisher of his discoveries, 1576
Hatfield House, *Courtesy The Marquess of Salisbury*

Map 422 (page 271)
[Map of North America and the Pacific Ocean]
Gerard Van Keulen, 1728
BL: Maps.13.TAB.2, Map No. 87

Notes

References are to page numbers.

9 The details of the Severin voyage are from *National Geographic*, vol. 152, no. 6, p. 769, December 1977.

10 The information about Norse map tradition is from Seaver, 1996.

10 The Chegoggin River Vinland claim was from the *Vancouver Sun*, 4 November 1999.

11 Apparent evidence of ongoing Norse voyages: Patricia Sutherland, Canadian Museum of Civilization; *National Post*, 2 December 1999.

11 Settlement claim for Albans: Mowat, 1999, p. 334.

14 Wytfliet's atlas is *Descriptionis Ptolemaicæ Augmentum* (1597). An excellent original is in the manuscripts department at the British Library.

15 Cabot petition: PRO Treaty Roll 178, membr. 8, in Latin; translation by Harrisse, 1892 (1961), p. 5.

15 The Spanish archive was Archivo Generale de Simancas (Estado de Castilla, leg. 2, fol. 6).

15 "To hym that found the New Isle": *Excerpta Historica*, p. 113, quoted Harrisse 1892 (1961), p. 28.

15 "Messer Zoane" quoted by Morison, 1971.

16 "The stopping of the English": Archivo Generale de Simancas, Cedulas, No. 5; English translation from James A. Williamson, *Cabot Voyages and Bristol Discovery under Henry VII*, Cambridge University Press, 1962.

18 A date for the Juan de la Cosa map of 1505 is not supported by a number of authorities, notably Williamson, Skelton, and Quinn.

18 "Founde his new lands only on the ocean's bottom" is from Polydore Vergil, *Anglia Historia of Polydore Vergil*, Liber 24 of a manuscript copy in the Bibliotheca Apostolica, Rome, translated by Williamson, 1962 (see 16, above).

20 The historian referred to in the first paragraph is Samuel Morison, 1971, p. 215.

20 "Formerly did make great efforts . . ." is quoted in Harrisse, 1892 (1961), p. 59.

25 Cartier's first voyage is documented in his own book, *La premier Relation, or The first relation of Iaques Carthier of S. Malo, of the new land called New France, newly discoured in the yere of our Lord 1534*, published in English by the Hakluyt Society, as part of the *Principal Navigations*, 1903–05. The original French manuscript is in the Bibliothèque nationale de France.

27 Cartier's second voyage is documented in *Bref récit et succincte narration de la navigation faite en 1535 et 1536 parle capitaine Jacques Cartier aux îles de Canada, Hochelaga, Saguenay et autres Relation originale de Jacques Cartier Voyage au Canada*, published in Paris by Librairie Tross, 1863. See also the translation by H. P. Biggar (new edition, 1993).

32 On Sebastian Cabot's map, M.CCCC.XCIII (1494) was an engraver's error for MCCCCXCVII (1497).

32 Identification of the features on the Alphonce map is as Winsor, 1884. Alphonce labelled Anticosti *L'Ascention*, a mistake for Cartier's *Assomption*. An edition of *La Cosmographie* was published in Paris in 1904, G. Musset (ed.); this is in the National Library of Canada. However, the maps are redrawings.

34–35 Best's quotes and Frobisher's accounts were published in a report of the Commisssioners on the Public Records, 1837, and were reprinted in the Collinson edition of George Best's book.

37 There is some confusion as to the authorship of Map 44. It is clearly based on Emery Molyneaux's 1589 globe, and the map was at one time attributed to him with the same date (Morison, 1971, p. 608), but it is now thought to date from 1599 rather than 1589, at which date, according to Schwartz and Ehrenberg (1980), Molyneaux was not in England. Nordenskiöld (1889), from which the facsimile comes, gives 1599 as the date of the edition of Hakluyt's book, *The*

principall navigations, voiages, and discoveries of the English nations, but to add to the confusion, there is also a 1589 edition. I have followed Schwartz and Ehrenberg in attributing the map to mathematician Edward Wright, but as a copy of the Molyneaux globe.

45 One reason put forward as to why Newfoundland became English rather than French has been said to be that England had no source of salt of its own, whereas France did. Thus the English had a vested interest in using the drying method of preserving fish—which required stages on land—while the French could more cheaply use the "wet" method of throwing their catch into a ship's hold, where it was salted.

49 Most of the Champlain documents are reproduced in the Champlain Society's *Works of Samuel de Champlain*, by far the most valuable book on the subject.

59 Du Creux's work, *Historiæ Canadensis* (1660), has been republished as *The History of Canada, or New France* by the Champlain Society, 1951–52.

74 An excellent modern map reconstructing the Acadian ownership of the *marais* is available at Fort Anne (*Au Coeur de l'Acadie: Acadian Settlement on the Annapolis River, 1707*, Annapolis Ventures, n.d.).

79 The quote about Henry Kelsey was in a letter from the Committee to Governor George Geyer in 1688, quoted in Rich, 1958, vol. 1, p. 296.

79 The quote "slept at the edge of a frozen sea" was coined by John Robson, a somewhat disgruntled ex-employee of the Hudson's Bay Company, in his book, *Account of Six Years Residence in Hudsons Bay*, published in 1752. A mason who went on to supervise and survey buildings, he was at the Bay from 1733 to 1736 and 1745 to 1748.

86 The La Vérendrye quotes are from Kavanagh, 1967.

88 J. S. McLennan's book, *Louisbourg: From Its Foundation to Its Fall, 1713–1758*, originally published in 1918, is still the best English source for documents pertaining to Louisbourg. The partially reconstructed town of Louisbourg is a must-see for all interested in Canadian history.

97 Another original of the Samuel Holland map of Louisbourg is held by the Royal Ontario Museum.

120 The obituary was in the *Acadian Reporter*, 6 November 1824.

124 Richard Oswald was a wealthy Scottish merchant with American trade connections, and, lacking diplomatic experience, an unlikely candidate for treaty negotiations. He was selected by the government only because of its desire to restore good relations with the Americans.

139 Hearne quote is from his book *A Journey from Prince of Wales's Fort in Hudson's Bay to the Northern Ocean* (1795); Richard Glover, editor, Macmillan, Toronto, 1972.

140 Pond journal quote is from the "Journal of 'Sir' Peter Pond—Born in Milford, Connecticut, in 1740," introduction by Mrs. Nathan Gillett Pond, *Connecticut Magazine*, 1906, facsimile edition, n.d.

140 It is likely that Pond used Ledyard's book rather than the official publication by James Cook for his coastal information, because Ledyard's book, published in 1781, used the name *King George's Sound*, whereas by the time Cook's book was published in 1784, the Admiralty had changed the name to *Nootka Sound*, and this name is the one used in Cook's book. Pond, however, uses *King George's Sound* on all his maps but the last one (1790).

140 The only extant Pond map variant not shown here is one copied by Ezra Stiles, the president of Yale University, whom Pond visited in 1790. It shows Samuel Hearne's route to the Arctic Ocean but adds his name and the date, July 1771. Pond's previous maps had always attributed it to "Indian report," and so this map shows that somehow Pond found out about the specifics of Hearne's explorations even though Hearne worked for the rival company. Information on Hearne only became general knowledge in 1795, when his book was published, posthumously.

143 The "Chart called Mackenzie's map" was found by Charles Davidson in the British Colonial Office before 1918 and mentioned, though not illustrated, in his book *The North West Company* (1918).

143–44 Mackenzie quotes are from his 1801 book. See Lamb (ed.), 1970

150 The "nudge of necessity" quote is from J. G. MacGregor, 1998.

158 Cook made all of his coastal longitude calculations using astronomical observations. Chronometers were used to cross-check, and at sea, when astronomical observations could not be taken due to the requirement of a stable surface on which to set a telescope. Chronometers could be used constantly, whereas astronomical observations, because of their complexity, and the time they took, were only used very occasionally.

163 George Vancouver's map of Alaska, drawn in 1778, is reproduced as Map 80 in Hayes, 1999.

165 J. C. Beaglehole quote is from *The Exploration of the Pacific*, A. & C. Black, London, 1966.

166 Quote from David Thompson's *Narrative*. The writer quoted is Richard Glover, in the introduction to the 1967 edition of the *Narrative*.

167 A copy of the Thomas Devine map is in the Archives of Ontario, but it could not be reproduced here for conservation reasons.

184 John Barrow's theory of an open Polar Sea was published in the *Quarterly Review* in 1817; William Scoresby's treatise *On the Greenland or polar ice* had been published in 1815, and his ideas were incorporated into his *Account of the Arctic Regions*, published in 1820.

185 Parry's 1818 quote is from his report to the Admiralty, quoted in *Parry of the Arctic: The Life Story of Admiral Sir Edward Parry 1790–1855*, by Ann Parry, Chatto & Windus, London, 1963.

185 Parry's 1819–20 quotes are from his book (Parry, 1821).

188 "Roof on the map of Canada" is from Cameron, 1980.

188 Iligliuk's map shown here is the engraved version, published in Ross's book. There also exists a manuscript version, held at the Liverpool Museum in Britain. However, even this is not the original, which, according to Ross's own narrative, was drawn on a number of sheets of paper. It appears lost.

202 The newspaper quote is from the *Morning Chronicle*, 19 September 1842, quoted by Carroll, 2001.

205 It seems likely that Baron de Rottenburg who drew the road map was related to Major General Baron Francis de Rottenburg, who was military commander and civil administrator of Upper Canada from June to December 1813, and who died in 1832.

219 The John Macoun quote is from Macoun, *Manitoba and the Great North-West*, 1882, p. 144.

231 Édouard-Gaston Deville, signer of Map 369, page 231, became Canada's surveyor general in 1885. In 1889 he published *Photographic Surveying*, and it was he who initiated photogrammetric survey in Canada.

244 Dawson City had been founded in 1896, within a few days of Carmack's announcement of his gold finds. A town was staked out by Joseph Ladue, anticipating a rush of miners to the region. It was named after George Mercer Dawson, government geologist and explorer.

249 Technically, Amundsen named but did not discover the Royal Geographical Society Islands, as they had been seen from a distance from Victoria Island by John Rae in 1851.

Bibliography

Amundsen, Roald
Nordvest-Passagen: Beretning om Gjøa-Ekspeditionen 1903–1907
Aschehoug, Kristiania (Oslo), 1908

Anon.
Sir Thomas Button
Manitoba Culture, Heritage and Recreation, Historic Resources Branch, Winnipeg, 1984

Bacon, Edgar Mayhew
Henry Hudson: His Times and His Voyages
G. P. Putnam's Sons, New York, 1907

Barrow, John
A Chronological History of Voyages into the Arctic Regions, undertaken chiefly for the purpose of discovering a north-east, north-west, or polar passage between the Atlantic and the Pacific
John Murray, 1818

Beck, E. Boyde, et al.
Atlantic Canada at the Dawn of a New Nation: An Illustrated History
Windsor Publications, Burlington, Ontario, 1990

Belyea, Barbara (ed.)
A Year Inland: The Journal of a Hudson's Bay Company Winterer [Anthony Henday]
Wilfred Laurier University Press, Waterloo, 2000

Bernier, Joseph-Elzéar
Report on the Dominion Government Expedition to the Northern Waters and Arctic Archipelago of the D.G.S "Arctic" in 1910, under the command of J. E. Bernier.
Government Printing Bureau, Ottawa, n.d. (1911–12)

Berton, Pierre
The Arctic Grail: The Quest for the Northwest Passage and the North Pole, 1818–1909
McClelland & Stewart, Toronto, 1988

Best, George
The Three Voyages of Martin Frobisher, in Search of a Passage to Cathaia and India by the North-West, A.D. 1576–8
Reprint of edition edited by Richard Collinson, n.d., Burt Franklin, New York, n.d. (1963?)

Biggar, H.P. (trans. and ed.)
The Voyages of Jacques Cartier
With an introduction by Ramsay Cook.
University of Toronto Press, Toronto, 1993

Bishop, R.P.
Lessons of the Gilbert Map
Geographical Journal, 72, pages 235–43, 1928

Blacker, Irwin (ed.)
Hakluyt's Voyages: The Principal Navigations, Voyages, Traffiques & Discoveries of the English Nation. Selections from Richard Hakluyt's book published in 1600
Viking Press, New York, 1965

Bolotenko, George
The Future Defined: Canada from 1849 to 1873
Records of Our History series,
National Archives of Canada, Ottawa, 1992

Bond, Courtney C. J.
Surveyors of Canada 1867–1967
Canadian Institute of Surveying, Ottawa, 1966
Also: *The Canadian Surveyor*, No. 5, Vol. 20

Boudreau, Claude
La Cartographie au Québec 1760–1840
Les Presses de l'Université Laval, Sainte-Foy, 1994

Boudreau, Claude, Serge Courville, and Normand Séguin
Atlas Historique du Québec: Le Territoire
Les Presses de l'Université Laval, Sainte-Foy, 1997

Bruce, Harry
An Illustrated History of Nova Scotia
Nimbus/Province of Nova Scotia, Halifax, 1997

Buck, George H.
From Summit to Sea: An Illustrated History of Railroads in British Columbia and Alberta
Fifth House, Calgary, 1997

Buisseret, David
Mapping the French Empire in North America: An Interpretive Guide to the Exhibition Mounted at The Newberry Library
Newberry Library, Chicago, 1991

Cameron, Ian
To the Farthest Ends of the Earth: The History of the Royal Geographical Society 1830–1980
Macdonald and Jane's, London, 1980

Careless, J. M. S.
Toronto to 1918: An Illustrated History
James Lorimer/National Museum of Man, Toronto, 1984

Carroll, Francis M.
A Good and Wise Measure: The Search for the Canadian-American Boundary, 1783–1842
University of Toronto Press, Toronto, 2001

Cell, Gillian T.
Newfoundland Discovered: English Attempts at Colonisation 1610–1630
Hakluyt Society, London, 1982

Champlain, Samuel de (with various editors)
The Works of Samuel de Champlain (6 volumes)
Champlain Society, Toronto, 1922–26

Collins, Gilbert
Guidebook to the Historic Sites of the War of 1812
Dundurn, Toronto, 1998

Conrad, Margaret R., and James K. Hiller
Atlantic Canada: A Region in the Making
The Illustrated History of Canada,
Oxford University Press, Toronto, 2001

Cook, Ramsay (general editor)
Dictionary of Canadian Biography
14 volumes on CD-ROM, University of Toronto Press, 2000

Cooke, Alan, and Clive Holland
The Exploration of Northern Canada: 500 to 1920 A Chronology
Arctic History Press, Toronto, 1978

Costain, Thomas
The White and the Gold: The French Regime in Canada
Doubleday, Toronto, 1954

Craig, Gerald M.
Upper Canada: The Formative Years 1784–1841
McClelland & Stewart, Toronto, 1988

Crouse, Nellis M.
La Vérendrye: Fur Trader and Explorer
Cornell University Press, Ithaca, 1956

Davidson, Gordon Charles
The North West Company
University of California Press, Berkeley, 1918

Dawson, Joan
The Mapmaker's Eye: Nova Scotia Through Early Maps
Nimbus/Nova Scotia Museum, Halifax, 1988

De Costa, Benjamin F.
"Jacques Cartier and His Successors"
In Winsor, Justin (ed.), *Narrative and Critical History of America*, Volume 4, pages 47–80.
Houghton Mifflin, Boston, 1884.

Delgado, James P.
Across the Top of the World: The Quest for the Northwest Passage
Douglas & McIntyre, Vancouver, 1999

[Drage, T. S.]
An Account of a Voyage For the Discovery of a North-West Passage by Hudson's Streights. to the Western and Southern Ocean of America Performed in the Year 1746 and 1747, in the Ship California, *Capt. Francis Smith, Commander*
By the Clerk of the *California*, London, 1749

Dunbar, Moira, and Keith Greenaway
Arctic Canada from the Air
Canada Defence Research Board, Ottawa, 1956

Dunbarin, J. P. D.
"Red Lines on Maps: The Impact of Cartographical Errors on the Border between the United States and British North America, 1782–1842"
Imago Mundi, 50, pages 105–24, 1998

Eccles, W. J.
Frontenac: The Courtier Governor
McClelland & Stewart, Toronto, 1959

Eccles, W. J.
Canada under Louis XIV 1663–1701
McClelland & Stewart, Toronto, 1964

Eccles, W. J.
The Canadian Frontier 1534–1760
University of New Mexico Press, Albuquerque, revised edition, 1983

Eccles, W. J.
Essays on New France
Oxford University Press, Toronto, 1987

Fingard, Judith, et al.
Halifax: The First 250 Years
Formac, Halifax, 1999

Firstbrook, Peter
The Voyage of the Matthew: John Cabot and the Discovery of North America
McClelland & Stewart Inc., Toronto, 1997

[Fisher, A.]
Journal of a Voyage of Discovery to the Arctic Regions (William Edward Parry, 1818)
Richard Phillips, London, 1819

Franklin, John
Narrative of a Journey to the Shores of the Polar Sea, in the Years 1819, 20, 21, and 22
John Murray, London, 1823

Franklin, John
Narrative of a Second Expedition to the Shores of the Polar Sea, in the Years 1825, 1826, and 1827
John Murray, London, 1828

Gentilcore, R. Louis, and C. Grant Head
Ontario's History in Maps
University of Toronto Press, Toronto, 1984

Gentilcore, R. Louis (ed.)
Historical Atlas of Canada, Vol. 2: The Land Transformed, 1800–1891
University of Toronto Press, Toronto, 1993

Glover, Richard (ed.)
David Thompson's Narrative, 1784–1812
Champlain Society, Toronto, 1962

Goetzmann, William H., and Glyndwr Williams
The Atlas of North American Exploration: From the Norse Voyages to the Race to the Pole
Prentice Hall, New York, 1992

Guillet, Edwin C.
The Story of Canadian Roads
University of Toronto Press, Toronto, 1967

Harris, R. Cole (ed.)
Historical Atlas of Canada, Vol. 1: From the Beginning to 1800
University of Toronto Press, Toronto, 1987

Harrisse, Henry
The Discovery of North America : A Critical, Documentary, and Historic Investigation
N. Israel, Amsterdam, 1961. Facsimile reprint of edition originally published in London and Paris in 1892.

Hayes, Derek
Historical Atlas of British Columbia and the Pacific Northwest
Cavendish Books, Vancouver, 1999

Hayes, Derek
First Crossing: Alexander Mackenzie, His Expedition Across North America, and the Opening of the Continent
Douglas & McIntyre, Vancouver, 2001

Hayes, Derek
Historical Atlas of the North Pacific Ocean:
Maps of Discovery and Scientific Exploration 1500–2000
Douglas & McIntyre, Vancouver, 2001

Hébert, John R., and Patrick E. Dempsey
Panoramic Maps of Cities in the United States and Canada
Library of Congress, Washington, 1984

Heidenreich, Conrad E., and Edward H. Dahl
"The French Mapping of North America
in the Seventeenth Century"
Map Collector, 13, pages 2–11, 1981

Heidenreich, Conrad E., and Edward H. Dahl
"The French Mapping of North America, 1700–1760"
Map Collector, 19, pages 21–20, 1982

Henry, Alexander ("the elder")
Travels and Adventures In Canada and the Indian
Territories Between the Years 1760 and 1776
Riley, New York, 1809; also Hurtig, Edmonton, 1969

Hind, Henry Youle
Narrative of the Canadian Red River Exploring Expedition
of 1857 and of the Assinniboine and Saskatchewan
Exploring Expedition of 1858 (2 volumes)
Longmans Green, Longmans, and Roberts, London, 1860

Hitsman, J. Mackay
Safeguarding Canada 1763–1871
University of Toronto Press, Toronto, 1968

Hitsman, J. Mackay
The Incredible War of 1812: A Military History
Edition updated by Donald E. Graves.
Robin Brass Studio, Toronto, 1999

Hoehn, R. Philip
Union List of Sanborn Fire Insurance Maps Held
by Institutions in the United States and Canada
Western Association of Map Libraries, Santa Cruz,
California, c1976

Imperial Oil
The Discovery That Made History: The Legacy of Leduc
Imperial Oil, Toronto, 1997

James, Thomas (ed. W. A. Kenyon)
The Strange and Dangerous Voyage of
Capt. Thomas James (1633)
Royal Ontario Museum, Toronto, 1975

Karamanski, Theodore J.
Fur Trade and Exploration: Opening the Far Northwest,
1821–1852
University of Oklahoma Press, Norman, 1988

Kavanagh, Martin
La Vérendrye: His Life and Times
Martin Kavanagh, Brandon, 1967

Kerr, D. G. G.
Historical Atlas of Canada
Thomas Nelson, Don Mills, Ontario, 1975

Lamb, W. Kaye
Canada's Five Centuries: From Discovery to Present Day
McGraw Hill Company of Canada, Toronto, 1971

Lamb, W. Kaye
History of the Canadian Pacific Railway
Macmillan, New York, 1977

Lamb, W. Kaye (ed.)
The Letters and Journals of Sir Alexander Mackenzie
Cambridge University Press/Hakluyt Society, Cambridge/
London, 1970

Lass, William E.
Minnesota's Boundary with Canada:
Its Evolution Since 1783
Minnesota Historical Society, St. Paul, 1980

Lavallée, Omer
Van Horne's Road: An Illustrated Account of the
Construction and First Years of Operation of the
Canadian Pacific Transcontinental Railway
Railfare, Montreal, 1974

Legget, Robert F.
Canals of Canada
Douglas, David and Charles, Vancouver, 1976

Legget, Robert F.
Railways of Canada
Douglas & McIntyre, Vancouver, 1987

Lemon, Donald P.
Theatre of Empire: Three Hundred Years of Maps of the
Maritimes/Ambitions impérialists: Trois cents années de
cartographie dans les Maritimes
New Brunswick Museum/Musée du Nouveau-Brunswick,
1987

M'Clintock, Francis Leopold
The Voyage of the 'Fox' in Arctic Seas:
A Narrative of the Discovery of the Fate of Sir John
Franklin and his Companions
John Murray, London, 1859

M'Clure, Robert
The Discovery of the North-West Passage
Edited by Sherard Osborn.
Longman, Brown, Green, Longmans & Roberts, London,
1856

Macdonald, Bruce
Vancouver: A Visual History
Talonbooks, Vancouver, 1992

McGhee, Robert
Canada Rediscovered
Canadian Museum of Civilization/Libre Expression, 1991

MacGregor, J. G.
Edmonton: A History
Hurtig Publishers, Edmonton, 1975

MacGregor, J. G.
Peter Fidler: Canada's Forgotten Explorer 1769–1822
Fifth House, Calgary, 1998

McLennan, J. S.
Louisbourg: From Its Foundation to Its Fall, 1713–1758
The Book Room, Halifax, 1979

Macoun, John
Manitoba and the Great North-West
Ontario World Publishing, Guelph, 1882

Macoun, John
Autobiography of John Macoun:
Canadian Explorer and Naturalist 1831–1920
Ottawa Field-Naturalists' Club, Ottawa, 1922 and 1979

Malcomson, Robert
Lords of the Lake:
The Naval War on Lake Ontario, 1812–1814
Robin Brass Studio, Toronto, 1998

Manitoba Culture, Heritage and Recreation
Peter Fidler
Winnipeg, 1984

Marsh, James H. (editor in chief)
Canadian Encyclopedia Year 2000 Edition
McClelland & Stewart, Toronto, 1999

Marshall, Ingeborg
A History and Ethnography of the Beothuk
McGill-Queens University Press, Montréal, 1996

Masters, D. C.
The Rise of Toronto 1850–1890
University of Toronto Press, Toronto, 1947

Mealing, S. R. (ed.)
The Jesuit Relations and Allied Documents: A Selection
Carleton University Press, Ottawa, 1990

Mika, Nick and Helma
Bytown: The Early Days of Ottawa
Mika Publishing, Belleville, Ontario, 1982

Miquelon, Dale
New France 1701–1744
McClelland & Stewart, Toronto, 1987

Morison, Samuel Eliot
The European Discovery of America:
The Northern Voyages A.D. 500–1600
Oxford University Press, New York, 1971

Morison, Samuel Eliot
Samuel de Champlain: Father of New France
Atlantic Monthly Press, Little Brown, Boston, 1972

Morrison, William R.
True North: The Yukon and Northwest Territories
The Illustrated History of Canada,
Oxford University Press, Toronto, 1998

Morton, W. L.
The Critical Years:
The Union of British North America, 1857–1873
McClelland & Stewart, Toronto, 1964

Mowat, Farley
The Farfarers: Before the Norse
Seal Books, Toronto, 1999

Nagy, Thomas L.
Ottawa in Maps: A Brief Cartographical History of Ottawa/
Ottawa par les cartes: Brève histoire cartographique de la
ville d'Ottawa, 1825–1973
Public Archives of Canada, Ottawa, 1974

National Archives of Canada
Treasures of the National Archives of Canada
University of Toronto Press, Toronto, 1992

Neatby, L. H.
In Quest of the North West Passage
Longmans, Green, Toronto, 1958

Neatby, Hilda
Quebec: The Revolutionary Age, 1760–1791
McClelland & Stewart, Toronto, 1966

Nelson, Paul David
General Sir Guy Carleton, Lord Dorchester:
Soldier-Staresman of Early British Canada
Fairleigh Dickinson University Press, Madison, 2000

Nicholson, Norman L.
The Boundaries of Canada, Its Provinces and Territories
Canada Department of Mines and Technical Surveys,
Geographical Branch, Memoir 2, Ottawa, 1954

Nicholson, Norman L.
The Boundaries of the Canadian Confederation
Macmillan, Toronto, 1979

Nordenskiöld, A. E.
Facsimile-Atlas to the Early History of Cartography
Stockholm, 1889; Dover reprint, New York, 1973

Normandeau-Jones, Léa
French Forts in New France
Heritage, Ottawa, 1998

O'Dea, Fabian
The 17th Century Cartography of Newfoundland
Cartographica Monograph No. 1
B. V. Gutsell, Toronto, 1971

Oppen, William A.
The Riel Rebellions: A Cartographic History/
Le Récit cartographique des affaires Riel
University of Toronto Press, Toronto, 1979

Parry, William Edward
Journal of a Voyage for the Discovery of a North-West
Passage from the Atlantic to the Pacific Performed in the
Years 1819–20 in His Majesty's Ships Hecla *and* Griper
John Murray, London, 1821

Parry, William Edward
Journal of a Second Voyage for the Discovery of a North-
West Passage from the Atlantic to the Pacific Performed
in the Years 1821–22–23 in His Majesty's Ships
Fury *and* Hecla
John Murray, London, 1824

Parsons, John
On the Way to Cipango: John Cabot's Voyage of 1498
Creative Publishers, St. John's, 1998

Penlington, Norman
The Alaska Boundary Dispute: A Critical Reappraisal
McGraw Hill-Ryerson, Toronto, 1972

Pole, Graeme
The Spiral Tunnels and the Big Hill:
A Canadian Railway Adventure
Altitude, Canmore, Alberta, 1995

Pope, Peter E.
The Many Landfalls of John Cabot
University of Toronto Press, Toronto, 1997

Prévost, Robert
Montreal: A History
McClelland & Stewart, Toronto, 1993

Quinn, David B.
European Approaches to North America, 1450–1640
Variorum, Brookfield, Vermont, 1998

Raddall, Thomas H.
The Path of Destiny: Canada from the British Conquest
to Home Rule: 1763–1850
Doubleday Canada, Toronto, 1957

Rae, John
*Narrative of an Expedition to the Shores
of the Arctic Sea in 1847 and 1848*
Boone, London, 1850

Rawlyk, George A.
Yankees at Louisbourg: The Story of the First Siege, 1745
Breton Books, Wreck Cove, Nova Scotia, 1999

Rayburn, Alan
Dictionary of Canadian Place Names
Oxford University Press, Don Mills, Ontario, 1999

Rich, E. E.
The History of the Hudson's Bay Company 1670–1870
(2 volumes)
Hudson's Bay Record Society, London, 1958

Robinson, Percy J.
Toronto during the French Regime, 1615–1793
University of Toronto Press, Toronto, 1965
Originally published in 1933.

Ross, John
*Voyage of Discovery, Made Under the Orders of the
Admiralty, in His Majesty's Ships* Isabella and Alexander,
*for the Purpose of Exploring Baffin's Bay, and Inquiring
into the Probability of a North-West Passage*
John Murray, London, 1819

Ross, John
*Narrative of a Second Voyage in Search of a North-West
Passage, and of a Residence in the Arctic regions During
the Years 1829, 1830, 1831, 1832, 1833*
A. W. Webster, London, 1835

Roy, Patricia E.
Vancouver: An Illustrated History
James Lorimer/National Museum of Man, Toronto, 1980

Ruggles, Richard
*A Country So Interesting: The Hudson's Bay Company
and Two Centuries of Mapping, 1670–1870*
McGill-Queen's University Press, Montréal, 1991

Savours, Ann
The Search for the North West Passage
St. Martin's Press, New York, 1999

Seaver, Kirsten
*The Frozen Echo: Greenland and the Exploration
of North America ca. 1000–1500*
Stanford University Press, Stanford, 1996

Schull, Joseph
Rebellion: The Rising in French Canada, 1837
Macmillan, Toronto, 1996

Schwartz, Seymour I., and Ralph E. Ehrenberg
The Mapping of America
Harry N. Abrams, New York, 1980

Shirley, Rodney
*The Mapping of the World:
Early Printed World Maps, 1472–1700*
New Holland, London, 1993

Skelton, R. A.
Explorer's Maps
Praeger, New York, 1958

Skelton, R. A., Thomas E. Marston, and George Painter
The Vinland Map and the Tartar Relation
Yale University Press, New Haven, 1965. New edition 1996.

Skelton, R. A., and R. V. Tooley
*The Marine Surveys of James Cook in North America,
1758–1768, Particularly the Survey of Newfoundland.
A Bibliography of Printed Charts and Sailing Directions*
Map Collectors' Circle, London, 1967

Smith, G. Hubert
*The Explorations of the La Vérendryes in the
Northern Plains, 1738–43*
University of Nebraska Press, Lincoln, 1980

Spink, John
Eskimo Maps from the Canadian Eastern Arctic
Cartographica Monograph No. 5
B. V. Gutsell, Toronto, 1972

Spry, Irene M.
*The Palliser Expedition: The Dramatic Story
of Western Canadian Exploration 1857–1860*
Fifth House, Calgary, 1995

Spry, Irene M. (ed.)
The Papers of the Palliser Expedition 1857–1860
Champlain Society, Toronto, 1968

Stanley, George F. G.
New France: The Last Phase, 1744–1760
McClelland & Stewart, Toronto, 1968

Stefansson, Vilhjalmur
The Friendly Arctic
Macmillan, New York, 1921

Sterne, Netta
Fraser Gold 1858: The Founding of British Columbia
Washington State University Press,
Pullman, Washington, 1998

Suárez, Thomas
*Shedding the Veil: Mapping the European Discovery
of America and the World*
World Scientific Publishing, Singapore, 1992

Suthren, Victor
The War of 1812
McClelland & Stewart, Toronto, 1999

Suthren, Victor
*To Go Upon Discovery: James Cook and Canada,
from 1758 to 1779*
Dundurn Press, Toronto, 2000

Sverdrup, Otto
New Land: Four Years in the Arctic Regions
Longmans, London, 1905

Taylor, John H.
Ottawa: An Illustrated History
James Lorimer and Canadian Museum of Civilization,
National Museums of Canada, Toronto, 1986

Thomson, Don W.
*Men and Meridians: The History of Surveying
and Mapping in Canada* (3 volumes)
Department of Mines and Technical Surveys, Ottawa, 1966

Trudel, Marcel
Atlas de la Nouvelle-France/Atlas of New France
Les Presses de l'Université Laval, Laval, 1968

Turner, Robert D.
*West of the Great Divide: An Illustrated History of the
Canadian Pacific Railway in British Columbia, 1880–1986*
Sono Nis, Victoria, 1987

Turner, Wesley B.
The War of 1812: The War That Both Sides Won
Dundurn, Toronto, 2000

Tyrrell, J. B. (ed.)
The Journals of Samuel Hearne and Philip Turnor
Champlain Society, Toronto, 1934

Vancouver, George
*A Voyage of Discovery to the North Pacific Ocean
and Round the World 1791–1795* (4 volumes)
Edited by W. Kaye Lamb, Hakluyt Society, London, 1984.
Also original edition, London, 1798.

Vashon, André, et al.
Dreams of Empire: Canada before 1700
Records of Our History series,
Public Archives of Canada, Ottawa, 1982

Vashon, André, et al.
Taking Root: Canada from 1700 to 1760
Records of Our History series,
Public Archives of Canada, Ottawa, 1985

Verner, Coolie
Explorers' Maps of the Canadian Arctic 1818–1860
Cartographica Monograph No. 6
B. V. Gutsell, Toronto, 1972

Verner, Coolie, and Basil Stuart-Stubbs
The Northpart of America
Academic Press, Toronto, 1979

Waite, P. B.
Canada 1874–1896: Arduous Destiny
McClelland & Stewart, Toronto, 1971

Walker, Elizabeth
Street Names of Vancouver
Vancouver Historical Society, 1999

Warhus, Mark
*Another America: Native American Maps
and the History of Our Land*
St. Martin's Griffin, New York, 1997

Washburn, Wilcomb E. (ed.)
Proceedings of the Vinland Map Conference
University of Chicago Press, Chicago, 1971

Warkentin, John, and Richard I. Ruggles
*Historical Atlas of Manitoba: A Selection of Facsimile Maps,
Plans and Sketches from 1612 to 1969*
The Historical and Scientific Society of Manitoba,
Winnipeg, 1970

Whitfield, Peter
Charting the Oceans: Ten Centuries of Maritime Maps
Pomegranate Artbooks, Rohnert Park, California, 1996

Whitfield, Peter
New Found Lands: Maps in the History of Exploration
Routledge, New York, 1998

Williamson, James A. (ed.)
*The Voyages of the Cabots and the Discovery of North
America Under Henry VII and Henry VIII*
Argonaut Press, London, 1929; reprinted by N. Israel,
Amsterdam, and Da Capo Press, New York, 1970

Wilson, Bruce
Colonial Identities: Canada from 1760 to 1815
Records of Our History series,
National Archives of Canada, Ottawa, 1988

Winsor, Justin
"Maps of the Eastern Coast of North America, 1500–1535"
In Winsor, Justin (ed.), *Narrative and Critical History of
America*, Volume 4, pages 81–102.
Houghton Mifflin, Boston, 1884

Winsor, Justin
"The Cartography of the Northeast Coast of
North America, 1535–1600"
In Winsor, Justin (ed.), op. cit., pages 33–46.

Wohler, J. Patrick
*Charles de Salaberry: Soldier of Empire,
Defender of Quebec*
Dundurn, Toronto, 1984

Wolff, Hans
America: Early Maps of the New World
Prestel, Munich, 1992

Woodward, David, and G. Malcolm Lewis
*Cartography in the Traditional African, American, Arctic,
Australian, and Pacific Societies
History of Cartography*, Volume 2.
University of Chicago Press, Chicago, 1998

Woodward, Frances, with assistance from Robert J. Hayward
*Fire Insurance Plans of British Columbia
Municipalities: A Checklist*
University of British Columbia Library, 1974

Zaslow, Morris
The Opening of the Canadian North, 1870–1914
McClelland & Stewart, Toronto, 1971

Zaslow, Morris
The Northward Expansion of Canada, 1914–1967
McClelland & Stewart, Toronto, 1988

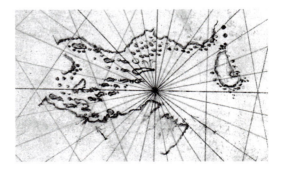

MAP 421.
Martin Frobisher's map of his "strait"—actually Frobisher Bay
on Baffin Island, drawn in 1576 on a base map provided by
William Borough. A larger part of this map is shown as MAP
39, page 34. This is the first map of any part of Canada drawn
by the person who explored it.

Index

A

Abercromby, James 96
Aberdeen, Lord 204
Abitibi River 66, 67
Ac ko mok ki (Blackfoot chief) 153, 155
Acadia 47, 49, 50, 51, 56, 71, 72, 73, 85, 90, 95
Acadian deportation 95
Account of a Voyage For the Discovery of a North-West Passage (Drage, 1749) 83
Act of Parliament (reward for finding Northwest Passage), 1745 81
Act of Union (Province of Canada, 1841) 200
Adam of Bremen 13
Adams Sound 250
Adams, W. (whaling captain) 250
Adelaide Peninsula 193
Admiralty Inlet 250
Agona (Laurentian Iroquois chief) 31
Agricultural potential on the Prairies 219
Air Force Island (Foxe Basin) 256
Aitken, Alexander 169
Ak ko wee a ka (Blackfoot chief) 153
Alaska boundary dispute 252
Alaska Highway, building of 229
Alaska purchased by United States 213
Albanel, Charles 62, 66, 67
Albany River 78
Albert City (New Westminster) 206
Alberta (District/Province) 209, 246, 254, 255
Albion Mines (Stellarton, NS) 210
Alderman Jones Sound 41
Alexander (John Ross) 184
Alexander, Sir William 46, 47
Alfonce, Jean 31
Algonkin (native group) 53, 58, 61
Allan, Sir Hugh 218
Allen, Ethan (American commander) 116–17
Allouez, Father Claude 61
Allumette Island 52, 53
Alneau, Father Jean-Pierre 86
American attack on Québec 116
American Revolution 89, 114, 126
Amherst, Sir Jeffrey 96, 102, 242
Amherstburg 174, 176
Amisk Lake 138
Amund Ringnes Island 248, 249
Amundsen Gulf 249
Amundsen, Roald 191, 194, 248
Angle Inlet 168
Angle, Northwest 180
Anglo-Azorean syndicate 20, 23
Ango, Jean (merchant/financier) 26
Annapolis Basin and River 50, 51, 73, 74
Annapolis Royal, Nova Scotia 74, 89, 95
Anse-au-Foulon 99
Anticosti Island 26, 32, 75
Apelaglu (Inuit mapmaker) 191
Arathapescow Lake (Great Slave Lake) 137
Arbitration of San Juan boundary by German kaiser, 1872 204
Arbitration of international boundary by king of Netherlands/Holland, 1831 202
Arctic Archipelago claimed for Canada 250
Arctic Bay, Baffin Island 250
Arctic exploration 1818–1859 184–96
Arctic islands 248, 256
Arctic Ocean 136, 143, 186, 189
Arnold, Benedict (American commander) 16, 152
Arrowsmith, Aaron 145, 147, 151, 155, 168, 178, 184, 186, 198
Arrowsmith, John 194, 199, 208, 209
Asshehurst, Thomas 21
Assiniboia (grant/District) 179, 254
Assiniboine River 86, 138, 178, 179, 207, 213, 227
Assistance (Erasmus Ohmmanney) 194, 195
Astor, John Jacob 166
Astoria, Oregon 168
Athabasca (District) 254
Athabasca country 138
Athabasca Pass 166
Athabasca River 138, 148, 153
Atlantic Neptune (Des Barres) 120
Aubert, Thomas 24

Austin, Horatio 194
Avalon Peninsula 46
Axel Heiberg Island 248, 249

B

Babine Lake 198
Back, Sir George 186, 189, 192
Back River 192
Bad River (James Creek) 144
Baffin Bay 36, 41, 184, 186
Baffin Island 36, 190, 248, 249, 256
Baffin, William 40, 41, 184, 185
Bagot, Charles 177
Baie des Chaleurs 26
Bainbrigge, Captain 152
Baltimore, Baron (George Calvert) 45–47
Bank of Commerce 240
Bank of Montreal 219, 240
Bank of Toronto 240
Banks Island (Baring Island) 186, 194, 195
Banks, Sir Joseph 186
Barclay, Anthony 168, 180
Barclay, Robert 175
Baring, Alexander (Baron Ashburton) 202
Barkley, Charles 133, 159
Barrow, Sir John 184, 194
Barrow Strait 185, 193
Bathurst Inlet 193
Batoche (battle, Saskatchewan) 216, 217
Battle of Châteauguay 173, 176
Battle of Lundy's Lane 177
Battle of Montmorency 100, 102
Battle of Moraviantown 176, 177
Battle of Québec/Plains of Abraham 103
Battle of Sainte-Foy 102, 103, 112
"Battle of the Windmill" 200
Battle of Trafalgar 172
Battle River 151
Battleford 217
Bay of Fundy 50, 73, 74, 85, 127
Bay of Quinte 170
Baye Françoise 51, 73
Bayfield, Henry Wolsey 182
Bayly, Charles 66, 79
Beare, James 35
Beauharnois, Marquis de 86
Beauport 99, 101, 103
Beaver Dams (battle, War of 1812) 175
"Beaver Map" (Nicolas de Fer) 66
Beaver River 197, 203, 222, 225
Beechey, Frederick 188
Beechey Island 193, 194, 248
Belcher, Edward 195
Bell, John 198
Bell River 199
Bella Coola, BC 144, 165
Bellin, Jacques-Nicolas 87, 90, 135
Bellot Strait 195
Beothuk of Newfoundland 122, 123
Bering Strait 184, 249
Bering, Vitus 135
Bernier, Joseph-Elzéar 249
Bernizet, Gérault-Sébastien 159
Best, George 34, 35
Big Bear (Cree chief) 217
"Big Hill" (on Canadian Pacific Railway) 222
Biogeographic information on maps 137, 154
Birchbark canoe 207
Birchbark, maps on 116, 152
Bird's-eye maps (panoramic maps) 42, 93, 233–35, 237, 239, 240–41, 243, 244, 251
Black, Samuel 197, 198, 199
Blackfoot 152, 154
"Blackfoot Treaty" (Treaty 7) 226
Blakiston, Thomas 208
Bligh Island, Nootka Sound 158
Bockoune (French admiral) 4, 97
Bodega y Quadra, Juan Francisco de 156, 160, 161, 162, 164
Boke of Idrography (Jean Rotz, 1542) 27
Bonanza Creek 244
Bonfield, Ontario (railway terminus) 218
Booth, Felix (expedition sponsor) 191
Boothia Peninsula 191, 193, 194, 195
Borden Island 250
Borden Peninsula 250
Borden, Robert 249, 250
Borough, William 34
Boscawen, Admiral Edward 95, 96
Bouchette, Joseph 202
Bougainville, Louis-Antoine de 101, 102
Boullé, Hélène 53

Boundary Bay 224
Boundary, international 124, 180, 202, 204
Boundary surveyed by David Thompson 168
Boundary with Alaska 252
Bourdon, Jean 52, 57
Bourgeau, Eugène 208
Bow River 151, 221
Bradstreet, John 96
Brandon House 179
Brandon, Manitoba 179
Brant, Joseph 127, 128
Brantford 127, 128
Breadalbane (supply ship) 194
Brébeuf, Father Jean de 59, 61
Brendan (Tim Severin) 9
Brendan, Saint 9
Bressani, Father Francesco Giuseppe 61
Briefe Discourse of the New-found-land (John Mason, 1620) 45
Briggs, Henry 40, 42
Brighouse, Samuel 236
Bristol Society of Merchant Adventurers 46
Bristol's Hope, Newfoundland 46
British Columbia 134, 157, 158, 159, 161, 162, 163, 198, 203, 204, 206, 218, 219, 236, 246, 253
British Columbia joins Confederation 206, 215
British Empire 35, 246
British North America Act, 1867 212, 213
Brock, Isaac 174
Brock Island 250
Brodeur Peninsula 250
Brouckner, Isaac 135
Broughton, William 160, 164, 165
Brown, Jacob 177
Brûlé, Étienne 55, 169
Buache, Philippe 82
Buchan, David 122, 184
Burgoyne, John 117
Burney, James 158
Burrard Inlet 161, 224, 236, 237
Burrowes, Thomas 181, 238
Buss (fictional island) 39
Button, Sir Thomas 39, 40
By, John 181, 238
Bylot, Robert 39, 41
Bylot Island 188
Bytown (Ottawa) 139, 181, 238, 239

C

Caamaño, Jacinto 160
Cabot, John 15
Cabot, Sebastian 4, 21, 32, 38
Cadillac, Antoine Laumet de Lamothe 68, 72
Calgary 228–29, 230
Calgary Natural Gas Company 232
California (Francis Smith) 82
Calvert, George *See* Baltimore, Baron
Cambridge Bay 194
Cameron, Duncan 178, 179
Campbell, John 96
Campbell, Robert 127, 198, 199
Campbellton, NB 212
Camsell Bend (on Mackenzie River) 143
Canada, Dominion of *See* Dominion of Canada
Canada as an island 8
Canada Central Railway 222
Canada Company 182
Canada East (1841-67) 200, 218
Canada West (1841-67) 200, 207, 218
Canadian Arctic Expedition (1913–18) 250
Canadian National Railways 211
Canadian Northern Railway 228, 237
Canadian Pacific Railway 207, 208, 209, 211, 216, 217, 218–226, 228, 230, 237, 242, 252
Canadian Pacific Railway Act, 1874 219
Canadian Pacific Railway Lands Department 220, 221, 223, 230
Canadian Red River Exploring Expedition 207
Cañizarez, Josef de 156, 157
Cantino "planisphere" (1502) 21
Cape Breton Island 17, 22, 25, 30, 75, 88, 97, 118, 120, 127, 130
Cape Muzon 156
Capitulation of New France 99–105
Cariboo goldfields 215
Carignan Salières regiment 70, 71, 76
Carleton, Guy (Baron Dorchester) 114, 116, 173
Carmack, George Washington 244
Caroline (rebel ship) 200
Carolinople (proposed Newfoundland city) 46
Carrasco, Juan 160, 236

Carta que comprehende 161, 236
Cartier, George-Étienne 215
Cartier, Jacques 6, 8, 25–33, 57
Cartwright, John 122, 123
Cary, Henry 46
Catalogne, Gédéon de 76
Cator, John 194
Cedar Lake 87
Censitaires 76
Cent-Associés, Compagnie des 55, 58, 70
Centurion (British warship) 100, 102
Chambly, Fort 70, 112, 116
Chambly, Jacques de 70
Chambon, Louis Du 89
Champlain and St. Lawrence Railroad 210, 243
Champlain, Samuel de 39, 47, 49, 57, 58, 238
Chantrey Inlet 192
Charles (Luke Foxe) 42
Charles Fort 66
Charlesbourg-Royal 31
Charlottetown 118, 212
Charlton Island 43, 78
Chaste, Aymar de 49
Châteauguay River 173, 177 *See also* Battle of Châteauguay
Chatelain, Henri 85
Chatham (William Broughton) 160, 163–165
Chatham, Ontario 233
Chaudière River 116, 173, 239
Chauncey, Isaac 174
Chaussegros de Léry, Gaspard-Joseph 57, 98
Chauvin, Pierre 49
Chebucto 92
Chesapeake (American ship) 172
Chesterfield House 151, 153, 154, 155
Chesterfield Inlet 81, 82, 83, 154
Chevalier (François La Vérendrye) 86
Chewett, James 171, 182
Chewett, William 128, 170
Chignecto Bay 95
Chilkat 199
Chipewyan 154
Chiputneticook River 202
Chomedey, Paul de 57
Chronometers 158
Churchill River 42, 78, 138, 155
Chynk y es cum ("Bungee" chief) 153
Clarence Strait 160
Claus, William 170
Clayoquot Sound 161
Clearwater River 138
Cleveland, Grover (US President) 252
Cnoyen, Jacob 13
Coal Harbour (Vancouver) 236
Coal, discovery on the Prairies 151
Cocking, Matthew 146
Colbert, Jean-Baptiste 61
Colen, Joseph 146, 166
Collins, John 128, 170
Collinson, Richard 194
Colnett, James 159
Colony of Vancouver Island 203
Columbia Department 203, 204
Columbia River 166, 203, 204
Columbus (Columbo), Bartolomeo 15
Colville River 199
Come By Chance (Newfoundland) 45
Committee Bay 191, 194
Compagnie de la Nouvelle France 55
Compagnie des Cent-Associés 55, 58, 70
Compagnie des Indes occidentales 70
Compagnie du Nord 66
Company of Adventurers 42
Company of Adventurers into the New Found Lands 21
Company of Cathay 34, 35
Company of the Merchants Discoverers of the North-West Passage (Northwest Company) 39
Conception Bay 45, 46
Confederation 212, 253, 254, 256
"Congress Map" (Peter Pond) 141
Connaught Tunnel 222
Constitution Act of 1982 114
Constitutional Act of 1791 115
Contarini, Giovanni 9, 16
Continental Divide 221
Convention of 1818 177, 180, 204
Cook, Frederick 249
Cook, James 99, 106, 140, 156, 158, 163
Cook's River (Inlet) 140, 165
Coppermine River 4, 136, 137, 185, 186, 188, 189, 193

Cormack, William Epps 122
Cormorant Cove 96
Cornwall, Ontario 129
Cornwallis, Edward 92
Coronelli, Vincenzo 48, 62
Corte-Real, Gaspar 15, 20, 21, 22
Corte-Real, João Vaz 14, 21
Corte-Real, Michael 14
Cosa, Juan de la 16; map 18–19
Couagne, Jean-Baptiste de 76
Countess of Warwick's (Kodlunarn) Island 34
Coureurs de bois 61, 62, 85
Covens, Jean and Corneille Mortier 132
Craigellachie (completion of Canadian Pacific
     Railway) 225
Cree 77, 217
Cresswell, Samuel Gurney 194, 195
Crèvecoeur, J. Hector St. John de 141
Croker, John 186
Croker's Bay/Mountains 184, 186
Crown Point 116
Crozier, Francis 193
Crysler's Farm (battle, War of 1812) 177
Cumberland House 138, 147, 151, 166
Cumberland Sound 36, 37, 248
Cupids (Newfoundland) 45
Cut Knife Hill 216, 217

D

Dablon, Father Claude 61
Dagelet, Joseph Lapaute 159
Dakin Company, fire insurance maps 251
Dalhousie 212
Darnley Bay 189
Davis, John 11, 36
Davis Strait 36, 39, 184
Dawson (City) 244
Day, John 15
De Fonte, Bartholemew 81, 82, 132
De Fonte's Strait 160
De Haven, Edwin 194
De L'Isle, Guillaume 66, 68
De L'Isle, Joseph-Nicolas 82, 133
De Meuron Regiment 179
Dean Channel 144
Dearborn, Henry 174
Dease Lake 198
Dease, Peter Warren 193, 199
Dease River 198
Dee, John 9, 35, 36, 37
Deed granting Assinniboia to Lord Selkirk 178
Deerfield (Massachusetts) 73
Deighton, John "Gassy Jack" 237
Demasduit (Mary March) 122
Dennis, John Stoughton 213
Denonville, Jacques-René de Brisay de 71
Derby (proposed town) 206
Des Barres, Joseph Frédéric Wallet 58, 120
Desceliers, Pierre 26, 29
Desliens, Nicolas 6, 27, 32
Detroit 68, 72
Détroit Jacques-Cartier 27
Detroit River 174
Devine, Thomas 167
Devon Island 193, 248
Dickens, Francis 217
Dieppe school of mapmakers 6, 22, 25, 26,
     27, 29, 32–33
Dingman, Archibald 232
Discourse of a Discoverie for a New Passage to
     Cathay (Humfrey Gilbert, 1566/1576) 34
Discovery (Hudson/Bylot/Baffin) 39, 41
Discovery (William Moor) 80
Discovery (George Vancouver) 163
Divers Voyages touching the discouerie of
     America (Richard Hakluyt, 1582) 23
Dixon Entrance 156
Dobbs, Arthur 79, 80, 81, 83, 132
Dobbs Galley (William Moor) 82
Dolphin (boat: Richardson/Kendall) 189
Dolphin and Union Strait 189
Domagaya (son of Donnacona) 27
Dominion Lands Survey 216, 220, 224, 226,
     228, 230
Dominion of Canada 212, 218, 239, 240, 246,
     253
Dominion Parliament 212
Donnacona (Laurentian Iroquois chief) 27, 30
Dorothea (David Buchan) 184
Douglas, James 203, 206
Drage, T. S. 82, 83
Drucourt, Chevalier Augustine de 96
Drumheller Coalfield 151
Drummond, Gordon 177

Du Chambon, Louis, Governor of Île Royale 89
Du Creux, François 59, 77
Du Gua, Pierre, Sieur de Monts 49
Du Lhut, Sieur, Daniel Greysolon 61, 62
Duberger, Thomas 173
Duck Lake 216, 217
Dudley, Robert 47
Dufrost de La Jemerais, Christophe 86
Dumont, Gabriel 216, 217
Dundas Street 130
Durham, Lord (John George Lambton, first
     earl of Durham) 200, 212
Durham Report (1839) 200
Dutch East India Company 39, 41

E

Eagle Hills 146
Eagle Pass 218, 225
Eaglet (Radisson/Groseilliers) 77, 79
Eastern Townships 76
Eaton, Timothy 240
Edmonton House 228
Egmont, Lord, First Lord of the Admiralty 109
Eiriksson, Leif 10
Elbow, Saskatchewan 220
Eliza, Francisco de 160
Ellef Ringnes Island 248, 249
Ellesmere Island 248, 249
Ellis, Henry 82, 84
Elyot, Hugh 11, 23
Empress of India (Canadian Pacific Railway) 237
"Empress of Russia" map 140
Encouragement to Colonies, An
     (William Alexander, 1624) 46, 47
English Bay 237
English Coast (Juan de La Cosa map) 18
English colonization in Newfoundland 45
English Pilot (Henry Southwood, 1716) 48
Enterprise (James Clark Ross) 193, 194
Erebus (John Franklin) 193
Erie Canal 201
Etobicoke River 171
Exploits River 122

F

Faden, William 117, 130
Fagundes, João Alvares 21, 24
Falls of Montmorency 99
False Creek 237
Fawckner, William 194
Felix (John Ross) 194
Felix Harbour 191
Fer, Nicolas de 66
Fernandes, Francisco 21
Fernandes, João 20
Ferryland, Newfoundland 45, 48
Fertile belt 207
Fidler, Peter 147, 148, 150, 151, 152, 154,
     178
Field, BC 221
"Fifty-four forty or fight!" 204
Finlay River (Finlay Branch) 144, 197, 198
Fire insurance maps 251
Fire ships, used in battle for Québec 100
First Nations treaties 226
Fish Creek 216, 217
Five Nations of the Mohawks 71
Fleming, Sandford 212, 218, 219, 224, 240,
     242
Foley Island (Foxe Basin) 256
Forlani, Paolo 31
Forsyth, Charles 194
Forts:
     Fort Albany 66, 67
     Fort Amherst 118
     Fort Anne 74, 95
     Fort Chouaguen 98
     Fort Beauséjour 95
     Fort Brisebois 230
     Fort Calgary 230
     Fort Carillon (Ticonderoga) 96
     Fort Carlton 216, 217
     Fort Cataraqui 172
     Fort Chambly 112, 116
     Charles Fort 66
     Fort Chipewyan 143, 144, 145
     Fort Chouaguen (Oswego) 96
     Fort Conti 73
     Fort Dauphin 86
     Fort de Richelieu 70
     Fort Detroit 174
     Fort Douglas 179
     Fort du Port Royal 73

Fort Edmonton 209, 228
Fort Enterprise 186
Fort Erie 177
Fort Fork 144, 145
Fort Franklin (Déline) 189
Fort Frontenac 71, 85, 96, 98
Fort Garry 213, 218, 227
Fort George 175, 176, 177
Fort Gibraltar 178, 179
Fort Halkett 199
Fort Henry 172
Fort Kaministiquia 87
Fort Kilmaurs 198
Fort La Reine 86, 135, 138
Fort Langley 198, 203, 236
Fort Lawrence 95
Fort Liard 197
Fort Mackinac 178
Fort Malden 174, 176
Fort Maurepas 86, 87
Fort McHenry 177
Fort McPherson 198
Fort Mississauga 176
Fort Monsoni 66
Fort Nelson 85
Fort Niagara 73, 85, 98, 176
Fort Oswego 96
Fort Paskoya (or Paskoyac) 87
Fort Pitt 217
Fort Providence 186, 188
Fort Quichichouane 66
Fort Rouge 86
Fort Rouillé 169
Fort St. Joseph 174
Fort Saint-Louis 70
Fort St. Pierre 86
Fort Saskatchewan 228
Fort Selkirk 199
Fort Simpson 197
Fort Toronto 240
Fort Vancouver 203, 228
Fort Victoria 203, 204, 228
Fort Whoop-Up 230
Fort William 86, 87, 167, 168, 179
Fort William Henry 96
Fort York 174, 240
Fort Yukon 199
Forty-ninth parallel boundary 180, 204
Fou-Sang (British Columbia coast) 134, 156
Fowler, Thaddeus 233
Fox (Francis Leopold M'Clintock) 195
Foxe Basin 43, 188, 256
Foxe, Luke 42, 43, 77
Fram (Fridtjof Nansen) 248
France-Roy 31
Frances Lake 198, 199
Frances River 197, 198
Franklin (District) 246, 248, 254
Franklin Bay 189
Franklin, Benjamin 116, 124
Franklin, demise of 195, 248
Franklin, Lady Jane 194
Franklin, Sir John 184, 186, 189, 193
Franklin, search for 193
Franquelin, Jean-Baptiste-Louis 64
Franquet, Louis 95, 96, 118
Fraser River 144, 145, 160, 166, 206, 236
Fraser, Simon 144, 166, 167, 179, 198, 236
Fraser Valley 224, 237
Fredericton (St. Annes) 96, 127
French and Indian War 92, 96
French exploration to 1700 24, 58–69
French fur trade 85
French River 53, 54, 58
Friendly Arctic (Vilhjalmur Stefansson, 1921) 250
Friendly Cove (Yuquot, Nootka Sound) 160
Frisland (mythical island) 35, 39
Frobisher Bay/Straight 35, 36, 37, 256
Frobisher, Martin 34, 37, 49, 250
Frontenac et de Palluau, Louis de Buade,
     Comte de 61, 71
Fur trade 85, 138, 197, 252
Furnace (Christopher Middleton) 80, 83
Fury (Edward Parry; Henry Hoppner) 188, 189
Fury and Hecla Strait 188, 190
Fury Beach 189, 192

G

Gabarus Bay 4, 89, 96
Gabriel (Martin Frobisher) 34
Galaup, Jean-François, Comte de La Pérouse 159
Gale, Samuel 173
Galiano, Dionisio Alcalá 160–162, 236
Gallatin, Albert 180

Galt (Cambridge, Ontario) 182
Galt, John 182
Garry Island 143, 189 See also Whale Island
Gaspé 25, 96
Gaspé Bay 106
Gastaldi, Giacomo 15, 25, 28
Gaultier de Varennes et de La Vérendrye,
     Pierre 86
Georgian Bay 53, 171
Gerritz, Hessel 39, 41, 52, 53
Gibbons, William 40
Gibraltar Point 174
Gilbert, Humfrey 34, 35, 36, 45
Gjøa (Roald Amundsen) 191, 194, 248, 249
Gjoa Haven 249
Gladman, George 207
Goad Company (Charles E. Goad)
     fire insurance maps 251
Goderich, Ontario 182
Gold rush, British Columbia 206
Gold rush, Klondike 244–45
Gomez, Estévan 22
Gonsalves, João 21
Goulburn, Henry 180
Gourlay, Robert 200
"Governor and Adventurers of England
     tradeing into Hudson's Bay" 79
Graham, Andrew 146
Grand Banks 48
Grand Falls–Windsor 122
Grand Portage 62, 138
Grand River 127
Grand Trunk Railway 210, 211
Grant, Cuthbert 179
Grant, Walter Colquhoun 203
Granville (Gastown), Vancouver 237
Graves, Thomas 109
"Great American Desert" 207, 209
Great Bear Lake 189
Great Lakes 59, 60, 61
Great Peace of Montréal 72
Great Slave Lake 138, 140, 141, 142, 143,
     147, 148, 150, 151, 152, 154, 186, 192
Great Western Railway 210, 240
Grenville (James Cook) 109
Greysolon, Daniel, Sieur Du Lhut 61, 62
Grinnell, Henry 194
Griper (Matthew Liddon) 185
Groseilliers, Médart Chouart de 61, 62, 66, 77
Gudmonson, Jón 11
Guelph, Ontario 182
Gulf of Boothia 191
Guy, John 45

H

Habitation (Samuel de Champlain) 51, 52, 53
Haida 156
Hailstone, William 237
Hakluyt, Richard 11, 23, 36
Haldimand, Frederick 127, 128
Halifax 92, 94, 109, 120, 172, 212, 234
Hall, Charles 248
Hall, Christopher 34
Hamilton, Henry 142
Hamilton, Ontario 240
Hampshire (John Fletcher) 66
Hampton, Wade 173, 177
Harbour Grace, Newfoundland 46
"Harleian" map (Harleian Mappemonde) 23,
     26, 27
Harrison, William 176
Hastings (Vancouver) 237
Hay Lakes 229
Hayes River 136
Hayman, Robert 46
Hazen, Moses 96
Hearne, Samuel 4, 136, 137, 146, 151, 152,
     155, 158, 185, 186, 190
Hecla (Edward Parry) 185, 188
Hector, James 208
Heiltsuk 144
Helluland 11
Henday, Anthony 136, 146
Hennipin, Louis 66
Henrietta Maria (Thomas James) 43
Henry, Alexander "the elder" 138, 140, 155
     map of the West 138
Henry, Alexander, "the younger" 138
Herald (Henry Kellett) 193
Herjolfsson, Bjarni 10
Herron, William 232
Herschel Island, Yukon 249
Highwood River 151
Hill, James J. 219

Hind expedition 207
Hind, Henry Youle 207, 218
Historiæ Canadensis (François Du Creux, 1664) 77
History of New France (Marc Lescarbot, 1609) 56
Hochelaga (Montréal) 6, 8, 27, 28
Hojeda, Alonso de 16
Holland River 171
Holland, Samuel 106, 112, 118
Holmes, Charles 99
Hondius, Joducus 39
Hood, Robert 186
Hooper, William 193
Howe Sound 161
Howse, Joseph 208
Howse Pass 166, 208
Hudson Bay 42, 49, 61, 62, 78, 79, 81, 136, 146, 155
   French attack in 66
Hudson, Henry 35, 38, 39, 271
Hudson Hope, British Columbia 144
Hudson House 147
Hudson Strait 41, 44
Hudson's Bay Company 61, 77, 80, 83, 136, 138, 146, 147, 152, 166, 178, 186, 197, 203, 204, 207, 209, 213, 216, 218, 219, 227, 228, 236, 252, 253
Hull, Québec 238
Hull, William 174
Hundred Associates, Company of the 55
Hunt, Wilson Price 168
Huron 53, 58
"Huron Map" 58
Huron Tract 182
Hydrographic surveys, Lake Huron 182

I

Iberville *See* Le Moyne d'Iberville, Pierre
Idotlyazee (Cree mapmaker) 152
Igloolik Island 188, 189
Ikmalick (Inuit mapmaker) 191
Île d'Anticosti 114
Île d'Orléans 27, 99
Île Royale 75, 88, 89, 118
Île Sainte-Hélène 53
Île St. Jean 88, 118
Îles de la Madeleine 25, 30, 114
Iligliut (Inuit mapmaker) 188
Illecillewaet River 222, 225
Immigration, 1901 246
Imperial Bank 240
Imperial Oil 232
Intercolonial Railway 211, 212, 218
International boundary 124, 180, 202, 204
Intrepid (John Cator; Francis M'Clintock) 194, 195
Inuit maps/mapmakers 155, 188, 191
Inventio Fortunata (Nicholas of Lynn? c1360) 13
Investigator (Edward Bird; Robert M'Clure) 193, 194
Iqaluit, Nunavut 34, 256
Iroquois 53, 70, 71, 72
Isabella (John Ross) 184, 192
Isbister, Alexander Kennedy 198, 199
Isham, James 136
Isometric three-dimensional views 251

J

Jaillot, Alexis Hubert 66, 67
James Bay 43, 44, 67, 73, 79
James Creek 144
James, Thomas 43, 44, 78
Jasper, Alberta 166
Jefferson, Thomas 172
Jefferys, Thomas 92, 99, 101, 109, 111, 130, 134, 156
Jemerais *See* Dufrost de La Jemerais, Christophe
Jesuits 58–69
John Barrow (sledge) 194
Johnson, Sir John 129
Johnstone, James 163, 165
Johnstone Strait 163
Johnstown 128
Joint occupancy, Oregon 180, 204
Jolliet, Adrien 61
Jolliet, Louis 61, 62, 64, 66

K

Kahnawake 243
Kaministiquia 86
Kamloops 224

Kechika River 197, 199
Keenooshayoo, Chief 226
Keewatin (District) 253, 254, 255
Kellett, Henry 193, 195
Kelsey, Henry 79
Kendall, Edward 189
Kennebec River 116
Kennington Cove 89
Ki oo cus (Blackfoot chief) 154
Kicking Horse Pass 208, 209, 219, 221
King George's Sound (Nootka Sound) 158
King George's War 88–89
King Point 249
King William Island 191, 192, 193, 248, 249
"King-Hamy" map 20
Kingston 71, 98, 172, 174, 177, 181, 200, 240
Kirke family 55
Kittson, Norman 219
Kjipuktuk 92
Klondike gold rush 244, 245, 246, 252, 256
Klondike River 244
Knight, James 79, 80, 152
Kodlunarn (Countess of Warwick's) Island 34, 35
Kwomais Point 236

L

La Dauphine (Giovanni Verrazano) 24
La France, Joseph 81
La Grande Hermine (Jacques Cartier) 27
La Hontan, Baron 66, 68
La Pensée (Thomas Aubert) 24
La Pérouse, Comte de, Jean-François Galaup 159
La Petite Hermine (Jacques Cartier) 27
La Prairie 112, 210, 243
La Roque, Marguerite de 31
La Salle, René Robert Cavelier, Sieur de 61, 62, 71
La Vérendrye, Pierre Gaultier Varennes et de 86, 87, 138
Labat, Sieur De 92
Labrador 8, 108, 110, 255
Labrador Peninsula 255
Lac Bourbon 87
Lac des Prairies 86
Lac Île-à-la-Crosse 138, 139
Lac La Loche 140
Lac Mistassini 66, 67
Lac Saint-Jean 66
L'Acadia 24
Lachine Canal 57, 71, 210, 242, 243
Lachine raid 71
Lachine Rapids 31, 53
Lacolle River 177
Lacombe, Albert 228
Lake Abitibi 67
Lake Athabasca 138, 141, 143, 147, 150, 151
Lake Bennett 244
Lake, Sir Bibye 79
Lake Champlain 53, 71, 96, 116, 177
Lake Dauphin 86
Lake Diefenbaker 220
Lake Erie 174, 175, 176, 201
Lake Huron 59, 202, 210
Lake Manitoba 87, 219
Lake Nipigon 77, 85
Lake Nipissing 54, 139, 222
Lake of the Woods 62, 86, 87, 124, 135, 138, 168, 178, 202, 207
Lake Ontario 59, 60, 71, 96, 98, 169, 175, 176, 201
Lake Simcoe 59, 85, 169, 171
Lake Superior 60, 61, 85, 138, 207, 217, 219
Lake Timiskaming 67
Lake Winnipeg 64, 79, 85, 86, 87, 138, 146, 147
Lake Winnipegosis 87
Lalemant, Father Gabriel 61
Lancaster Sound 36, 41, 184, 185, 186, 190, 191
Lands Department, Canadian Pacific Railway 230
Lane, Michael 111
Langara Island 156
Langdon and Shepard (contractors) 221
L'Anse aux Meadows 10
Larue, Jean-Baptiste 76
Launders, James 215
Laurier, Wilfrid 255
Lawrence (Oliver Hazard Perry) 176
Lawrence, Charles 95, 127
Le Bocage-Boissaie 48
Le Moyne d'Iberville, Pierre 66, 69, 79
Leduc oil strike 229, 232

Ledyard, John 140
L'Émerillon (Jacques Cartier) 27
Leopard (British warship) 172
Lescarbot, Marc 56
Lesser Slave Lake 153
Lethbridge 230
Lewes, Adolphus Lee 203
Lewes River 199
Lewis, Meriwether, and William Clark 86, 32, 151
Lewis, Thomas 95
L'Havre Anglais (Louisbourg) 75
Liard River 197, 198, 199
Liddon, Matthew 185
Lion (boat; Franklin/Back) 189
Little Bell River 199
Liverpool (name for Vancouver) 237
Liverpool Bay 189
Loche River 138
Lok, Michael 14
London Confederation conference, 1866–67 212
London, Ontario 127, 234
Long River 68
Longueuil 210, 243
Lotter, Conrad Tobias 94
Louisbourg 4, 75, 88, 89, 92, 96, 97, 106
Louisiana 72, 102
Louisiana Purchase 180
Low, Albert Peter 249
Lower Bytown 239
Lower Canada 115, 128, 173, 200
Lowestoft (British frigate) 102
Loyalists 115, 126, 171, 172, 182, 200
Lyon, George 188
Lyon Inlet 188
Lytton, Edward Bulwer 206

M

McAdam, John 205
Macadamized roads 205, 211
M'Clintock, Francis Leopold 191, 194, 195
M'Clure, Robert 194
M'Clure Strait 194
Macdonald, Sir John A. 212, 213, 215, 216, 218, 219, 252
Macdonald Tunnel 222
Macdonell, Miles 178
McDougall, William 213
McGillivray, William 179
McKee, Alexander 127
Mackenzie, Alexander (explorer) 4, 87, 133, 140, 143, 147, 150, 154, 155, 158, 165, 178, 189, 197, 242
Mackenzie, Alexander (prime minister) 218
Mackenzie Delta 143, 189, 249
Mackenzie King Island 250
Mackenzie River 4, 138, 143, 188, 189, 197
Mackenzie Rock 144
Mackenzie, William Lyon 171, 200, 240
Macleod, Archibald 179
Macleod, James 230
McLeod, John 197
McLoughlin, John 179, 203
McMillan, James 198
McNeill, William 203
McNiff, Patrick 130
Macoun, John 209, 219, 220, 222
McPherson, Murdoch 197
McVittie, Archibald 230
Madison, James 172, 177
Magellan, Ferdinand 20
Maisonneuve, Paul de Chomedy, Sieur de 57
Manitoba 178, 214, 219, 227, 246, 253, 254, 255, 256
Manitoba Act 214
Manitoba-Ontario boundary dispute 255
Mann, Gother 169
Marais (marshlands) 74
Marble Island 80
March, Mary (Demasduit) 122
Markland 11
Marquette, Father Jacques 61, 62
Martínez, Estéban José 156
Mary (John Ross) 194
Mason, John 45, 46
Massacre Island 86
Matonabbee (Chipewyan chief) 136, 152
Matonabbee and Idotlyazee's map 155
Mattawa River 54, 58, 61, 139
Matthew (John Cabot) 15
Maurepas, Jean-Frédéric Phélypeaux de 86

Mayne, Richard Charles 206
Medicine Hat 221
Meighen, Arthur 249
Meighen Island 249, 250
Melish, John 175, 180
Melville Island 185, 186, 190, 195, 250
Melville Peninsula 188, 190, 192
Memoirs for the Curious (Anon., 1708) 82
Menzies, Archibald 165
Mer Douce 54, 55
Mercator, Gerard 13, 30, 37
Mercator, Rumold 36
Mercy Bay 194, 195
Merritt, WilliamHamilton 201
Methye Portage 138, 140
Métis 179, 198, 213, 216, 217
Mexicana (Cayetano Valdes) 160
Michael (Gryffyn Owen) 34
Michel (voyageur) 186
Michilimackinac 174
Michipicoten 86
Middleton, Christopher 79, 80, 81, 83
Middleton, Frederick 216
Midland, Ontario 59
Miramichi 96
Mississauga (native group) 171
Mississippi River's mistaken source 124
Mistaken Straightes (Frobisher) 35
Mitchell, John, 1755 map of America, 1775 edition 124–25
Mitchell, Thomas 83
Mohawk 70
Molyneaux, Emery 36, 37
Monashee Mountains 225
Monbeton de Brouillan, Jacques-François de 69
Monckton, Robert 95, 100, 116
Mont Réal 28, 57
Mont-Royal 243
Montagnais 53
Montcalm, Louis-Joseph, Marquis de 96, 99, 101
Montgomery, Richard 116
Montgomery's Tavern (Toronto) 200
Montréal 6, 8, 28, 49, 53, 57, 72, 96, 112, 116, 124, 138, 177, 181, 201, 210, 242, 251
Montréal and Lachine Railroad 210
Montressor, John 58, 112
Moody, Richard Clement 206
Moodyville 237
Mooneshine (John Davis) 36
Moor, William 80, 81
Moore, Thomas 193
Moose River 78
Moose Fort 66, 67
Moose Jaw Creek 222
Morris, Charles 118, 127
Morton, John 236
Munk, Jens 42, 43
Murray, Alexander 199
Murray, James 100, 102, 112, 114, 118
Muscovy Company 38
Musgrave, Anthony 215
Musqueam village (Vancouver) 236
Myths, geographical 132

N

Nansen, Fridtjof 248
Nares, George 248
Narrative (David Thompson) 168
Nárvaez, José María 160, 236
Native land purchase maps 127, 170, 178
Native maps 152–155
Navigatio (Anon.) 9
Navy Hall 175
Navy Island 200
Nelson, Horatio 172
New Brunswick 130, 202, 212, 246, 253
New Caledonia (British Columbia) 206
New France 49, 54, 56, 70, 73, 90
New Land (Otto Sverdrup, 1905) 248
New Westminster 206, 236
Newark *See* Niagara-on-the-Lake
Newfoundland 8, 15, 17, 18, 20, 21, 22, 23, 30, 33, 45, 46, 47, 69, 75, 88, 90, 102, 108, 110, 111, 122, 246, 255, 256
Newfoundland and Labrador 256
Newfoundland Company 45
Niagara Falls 210
Niagara Frontier 171, 174, 177
Niagara Peninsula 174, 205
Niagara River 175, 200
Niagara-on-the-Lake (Newark) 171, 175
Nicholas of Lynn 13

Nicholson, Francis 73
Nicollet de Belleborne, Jean 58
Nipigon, Lake 62, 86
Nolin, Jean Baptiste 62
Nonsuch (Radisson/Groseilliers) 77, 79
Nootka Convention 165
Nootka Sound 140, 156, 157, 158, 160, 162
Norse voyages 10
North American Railway Contracting Company 221
North Bentinck Arm 144
North Pole 248
North Pole, Canada reaches to 256
North Saskatchewan River 209
North Star (William Pullen) 195
North West Company (1770s–1821) 4, 79, 138, 39, 140, 142–44, 146, 147, 166, 168, 178, 186, 197, 198, 203, 242
Northeast Passage 38
Northumberland (James Cook, Halifax) 109
Northwest Company (1612) 39, 41
North-West Mounted Police 216, 220, 226, 228, 230, 244
Northwest Passage 23, 34, 35, 36, 39, 41, 42, 44, 66, 79, 80, 81, 82, 84, 132, 136, 160, 162, 163, 165, 184, 186, 188, 191, 194, 195, 236, 248, 249, 250
North-West Rebellion, 1885 216, 222
North-West Territories 213, 216, 217, 220, 221, 244, 246, 253–255
Northwest Territories 256
North-Western Territory 253
Norton, Moses 136, 152, 155
Notre-Dame-de-la-Victoire (church) 72, 75
Notre-Dame-des-Victoires (church) 53, 75
Nottingham House 151
Nova Scotia 15, 22–25, 46, 47, 49, 50, 75, 88, 89, 90, 95, 120, 126, 127, 130, 210, 212, 246, 253
Noyan, Sieur de 97
Noyon, Jacques de 62
Nunavut 256
Núñez de, Vasco Balboa 20
Nuxalk 144

O

Observatory Inlet 198
Ogden, Isaac 140, 142
Oil discovery in Alberta 229, 230, 232
Ommanney, Erasmus 194
Onondaga 71
Onderdonk, Andrew 219, 224
Ontario 212, 246, 253, 254, 255
Ontario, Simcoe and Huron Railway 210, 240
Open Polar Sea 184
Opuntia (Prickly pear) 151
Oregon Country 203, 204, 206
Oregon Treaty (Treaty of Washington), 1846 204
Orillia, Ontario 169
Ortelius, Abraham 8, 38
Osborn, Sherard 194, 195
Oswald, Richard 124, 125
Oswald, W. R. 224
Ottawa 54, 58, 61, 139, 181, 212, 239
Ottawa River 52, 53, 67, 139, 181
Ottawa Valley 130, 222, 238
Otter, William 217
Outaouais 54
Overwintering in the Arctic 185

P

Pacific Fur Company 166
Pacific railway surveys 218
Pacific Scandal 218
Pack River 144
Palliser expedition 208
Palliser, Hugh 109, 122
Palliser, John 207, 208, 215, 218, 220, 255
Palliser's Triangle 209, 219
Panoramic maps *See* Bird's-eye maps
Papineau, Louis-Joseph 200
Parliament Buildings 238
Parr, John 127
Parry Channel 185, 191
Parry Peninsula 189
Parry, Sir William Edward (Edward) 155, 184, 185, 189, 190, 249
    first voyage 185–87
    second voyage 188
    third voyage 188–89
Parsnip River 144, 197
Parti Patriote (Patriotes) 200
Peace of Montréal 72

Peace River 138, 141, 144, 150
Peace River Canyon 144
Peary, Robert E. 248
Peel River 198
Peel River Post 198
Peel Strait 193
Peguis (Saulteaux chief) 179
Pelee Island 176, 200
Pélican (Pierre Le Moyne d'Iberville) 66
Pelly River 199
Pemaquid 71
Pembina 213
Pembroke 106
Pemmican Proclamation 151, 178
Penny, William 194
Pepperrell, William 88
Peré, Jean 61
Pérez Hernández, Juan Josef 156, 157
Perry, Hazard 175
Peter Pond Lake 138
Phillpotts, George 171, 201
Phips, William 71, 72, 99

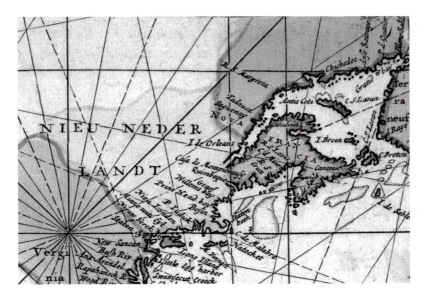

MAP 422

An atlas map by the Dutch mapmaker Gerard Van Keulen, dated 1728. Dutch territory—New Netherlands—covers much of eastern Canada. The Dutch laid claim to the Hudson River and its hinterlands following the 1609 voyage of Henry Hudson, at the time in the employ of the Dutch East India Company. Searching for a Northwest Passage after being foiled in an attempt to sail towards the Northeast Passage, Hudson found himself in the river now named after him (see page 39). In 1625, the Dutch established New Amsterdam at the mouth of the Hudson River, but in 1664 the English took control, so by the time this map was published *Nieu Neder Landt* was no longer Dutch territory, despite Van Keulen's wishful thinking.

Phoenix (Edward Inglefield) 194, 195
Pictou Harbour 210
Pierre, South Dakota 86
Pig War (San Juan dispute) 204
Pigeon River 62
Pike, Zebulon 174
Pim, Bedford 194, 195
Pioneer (Sherard Osborn) 194, 195
Pitt, William 96
Placentia (Plaisance) 33, 69, 75, 88
Placentia Bay 45
Plains of Abraham 99, 100, 101, 172
Plancius, Peter 39
Plank roads 205, 211
Plattsburgh, New York 174
Plover (Thomas Moore) 193
Point Atkinson 161, 236
Point Conclusion 165
Point Douglas 178, 179
Point Grey 161, 236
Point Lévis 100, 103
Point Menzies, North Bentinck Arm 165
Point Roberts 161
Point Separation 189
Point Turnagain 186, 188, 192
Pointe-à-Callière Museum (Montréal) 57, 243
Polk, James (U.S. president) 204
Polonus, Johannes Scolvus 14
Pond Inlet 188
Pond, Peter 4, 135, 138, 140, 141, 142, 143, 155
Pont-Gravé, François 49, 53

Population, 1901 246
Porcupine River 199
Port Arthur 221
Port Colborne 201
Port La Joie (Prince Edward Island) 118
Port Moody 224, 225, 237
Port Robinson 201
Port Roseway (Shelburne) 126, 127
Port Royal 50, 51, 71, 72, 73, 74
Port Weller 201
Portage and Main, Winnipeg 227
Portage La Prairie 86, 135, 138, 219
Poundmaker (Cree chief) 217
Pre-Columbian apocryphal voyages 13
Prescott 200
Prevost, George 177
Prince Albert 194
Prince Albert, Saskatchewan 147, 194, 216–17
Prince Charles Island (Foxe Basin) 256
Prince Edward Island 22, 88, 118, 130, 178, 212, 246, 253, 254
Prince of Wales Fort 78, 79, 136, 137, 155

Prince of Wales Strait 194
Prince Regent Inlet 185, 186, 189, 191, 193, 194
Princess Royal Islands 194
Principal meridian 226
Principall Navigations (Richard Hakluyt, 1589) 36
Proctor, Henry 176
Province of British Columbia 215
Province of Canada 212, 218
Province of Manitoba 214, 227
Province of Newfoundland 256
Provincial boundaries 253
Provincial District of Yukon 256
Provisional government, Louis Riel, 1869 213
Provisional government, Louis Riel, 1885 217
Prudhoe Bay, Alaska 189
Puget, Peter 164
Puget Sound 165, 204
Pullen, William 193, 195
Purchas, Samuel 39, 40, 41
Put-in-Bay, Bass Islands (U.S.) 175

Q

Quadra *See* Bodega y Quadra, Juan Francisco de
Quadra and Vancouver's Island 165
Qu'Appelle 216
Québec (City) 50, 52, 53, 55, 72, 86, 96, 98, 99, 101, 106, 114, 116, 127, 172, 173, 202, 212
Québec Act, 1774 114

Québec (Province) 112, 212, 246, 253, 254, 255, 256
Québec Conference, 1864 212
Québec-Labrador boundary 256
Queen Charlotte Islands 156, 159, 160
Queen Victoria 206, 212, 213
Queene Elizabeth's Forlande 34
Queenston Heights 174
Quen, Father Jean de 62
Quimper, Manuel 160

R

Rabbit Creek (later Bonanza Creek) 244
Radisson, Pierre Esprit 61, 62, 66, 77
Rae, John 191, 194, 195
Railways 205, 210–11, 212, 218–26
Rainy Lake 86, 87, 138
Rainy River 168
Rat Portage 168
Rat River 198
Rebellions of 1837 200
Récollet friars 58
Red Deer, Alberta 136, 151
Red Deer River 150, 151, 153, 154
Red Indian Lake (Lieutenant's Lake) 122
Red River 86, 138, 178, 179, 207, 213, 221, 227
Red River Exploring Expedition (Hind, 1857) 207
Red River Rebellion (Riel, 1869) 213
Red River Settlement/Colony 178, 179, 207, 213, 227, 255
"Red-lined map" (Mitchell/Oswald) 125
Reform Party 200
Regina 217, 220, 221
Reinel, Pedro 21, 22
Relación (Spanish, anon., 1802) 160
Relations, Jesuit 59
Reliance (boat; Franklin and Back) 189
Renews, Newfoundland 46
Republic of Upper Canada 200
Repulse Bay 84, 188, 192
Resen, Bishop Hans Poulsen 12
Resolute (Austin; Kellett) 194, 195
Resolution (Thomas Button) 39
Resolution Cove, Nootka Sound 158
Resolution Island 34
Return Reef 189
Revelstoke 225
Ribiero, Diogo 22
Richards, Henry 215
Richardson, John 186, 189, 194
Richelieu, Cardinal 59
Richelieu River 70, 96, 116, 173, 177, 210
Rideau Canal 181, 238
Rideau Falls 239
Ridout, Thomas 182
Riel, Louis 213, 216–17, 222
Rigaud de Vaudreuil, François-Pierre de 92, 102, 242
Rimouski 212
River of the West 86, 132, 133, 135
Rivière des Rochers 150
Rivière du Loup 212
Rivière St. Pierre 57, 242
Roads 112, 171, 205
Robert Campbell Highway 199
Roberts, Henry 158, 163
Robertson, Colin 178
Roberval, Jean-François de La Rocque, Sieur de 29, 31
Robinson, Frederick 180
Rocky Mountain House 209
Rocky Mountain Portage 197
Rocky Mountains 140, 150, 153, 166, 206, 207, 221
Roes Welcome Sound 43, 77, 84
Rogers, Albert B., Major 219, 225
Rogers Pass 222, 225
Roque, John 135
Ross, Sir James Clark 191, 192, 193, 222, 225, 249
Ross, Sir John 41, 155, 184, 189, 190, 194
Ross, Malcolm 166
Rosselli, Francesco 16
Rottenburg, Baron de 205
Rotz, Jean 25, 26, 27
Royal Botanical Gardens, Kew 208
Royal Canadian Air Force 408 Photo Squadron 256
Royal Engineers 206, 215, 236
Royal Geographical Society 198, 208
Royal Geographical Society Islands 249
Royal George (British warship) 174

Royal Proclamation, 1763 114, 124, 256
Royal Society 111
Rupert House (Charles Fort) 66
Rupert's Land 78, 79, 178, 207, 213, 218, 219, 253, 254
Rush, Richard 177, 180
Russell, Alexander Lord 214
Russell, Lindsay 214, 220
Russell Point 194
Russian-American Company 197
Rut, John 23
Ruysch, Johann 17

S

Sackets Harbor 174, 177
Saguenay, Kingdom of 30, 31
Saguenay River 27, 29, 32, 49, 62, 66
St. Albert, Saskatchewan 228
St. Anne's/St. Anns (Fredericton, NB) 96, 127
Saint Brendan 9
St. Catharines, Ontario 201
Saint-Charles 200
St. Charles River 101
St. Croix River 50, 202
Saint-Denis-sur-Richelieu 200
Saint-Eustache 200
Saint-Germain-en-Laye 55
Saint-Jean 112, 116, 210
Saint John 51, 121, 127
St. John, Island of 118
Saint John River 127
Saint John Valley 130
St. John's 35, 47, 109, 256
St. Joseph Island 60
St. Joseph mission 58, 60
St. Lawrence, River 49, 53, 71, 75, 76, 85, 90, 98, 99, 106, 111, 114, 129, 130, 168, 173, 181, 200, 202, 212, 242
St. Lawrence Seaway 242
St. Louis Rapids 210, 242
Ste. Marie mission (Sainte-Marie among the Hurons) 58, 59
St. Pierre (island) 33
St. Pierre and Miquelon 21, 30, 102, 109
St. Pierre River 53
Saint-Simon, Paul Denis de 62
Salaberry, Charles-Michel d'Irumberry de 173, 176
Salteaux 179
Samson (railway locomotive) 210
San Juan Islands 204
Sanborn Map and Publishing Company 251
Sanderson, William 36
Sanson d'Abbeville, Nicolas 60
Santa Saturnina (José María Nárvaez) 161, 236
Santiago (Juan Pérez) 156
Saratoga 117
Sarnia, Ontario 240
Saskatchewan, District/Province 207, 246, 254, 255
Saskatchewan River 87, 138, 146, 147, 166
Saskatoon 146
Sault Ste. Marie, Ontario 174
Saunders, Charles 99, 106
Saurel, Pierre de 70
Savona, British Columbia 224
Sayer, Robert 124, 125
"Schadzue" (Stikine) River 197
Schenectady New York 71
Schwatka, Frederick 248
Scoresby, William 184
Scott, Thomas 213, 214
Scott, Winfield 177
Sea of the West 132, 133, 135, 136
Seale, Richard 83
Seigneurial system 71, 76, 115
Selkirk, Earl of 151, 178, 179, 227
Selkirk grant 178–179, 180
Selkirk, Manitoba 219
Selkirk Mountains 221, 222
Seller, John 44
Semple, Robert 179
Seutter, Matthias 94
Seven Oaks Massacre (1816) 179
Seven Years War (French and Indian War) 96–98
Seyler, Theodore 232
Shanawdithit (Beothuk) 122
Shaughnessy, Thomas 221, 237
Sheaffe, Roger Hale 174
Shelburne (Port Roseway) 126, 127
Shelikov, Grigorii 252
Shew ditha da (Chipewyan) 154
Shirley, William 88, 95

Simcoe, Elizabeth 139, 169
Simcoe, John Graves 130, 139, 169, 171
Simpson, George 197, 203
Simpson Lake (Simpson's Lake) 197, 198
Simpson, Robert 240
Simpson, Thomas 193, 194, 199
"Simpson's River" 206
Sinclair, Prince Henry 14
Sinus St. Laurentii (Gulf of St. Lawrence) 30
Sir James Lancaster's Sound 41, 44
        See also Lancaster Sound
Sir Thomas Roe's Welcome 40, 84
        See also Roes Welcome Sound
Six Nations 127, 128
Skagway, Alaska 244
Skeena River 198
Skookum Jim 244
Slave River 138, 143, 150
Smallpox 60
Smallwood, Joseph 256
Smith, Donald A. 218, 219, 225
Smith, Francis 82, 83
Smith Sound 248
Smoky River 144, 145
Société de Notre Dame de Montréal 57
Somerset Island 185, 189
Sophia (Alexander Stewart) 194
Sorel, Québec 70, 71, 112, 210
South Nahanni River 197
South Saskatchewan River 146, 151, 153, 154, 216, 220
South Surrey 236
South Vancouver 237
Southampton Island 43, 81, 84
Southwood, Henry 48
Sovereignty, over Arctic 248
Spanish Banks (Vancouver) 160
Spanish explorations of the West Coast 160–62
Spanish maps 156–57, 160–62, 236
Spiral Tunnels 222
Squirrel (Martin Frobisher) 35
Stadaconé (Québec) 6, 27, 28, 31, 49
Stanford, Edward 208
Starvation Cove 193
Stefánsson, Sigurdur 11
Stefansson, Vilhjalmur 249, 250
Stellarton, Nova Scotia 210
Stephen, George 219, 221, 222, 226
Stephens, Philip 158
Stewart, Alexander 194
Stickeen Territory 253
Stikine River 197, 198
Stoney Creek (battle, War of 1812) 175
Strait of Belle Isle 108, 110
Strait of Georgia 160, 163, 236
Strait of Juan de Fuca 133, 135, 159, 160, 162, 224
Strange and Dangerous Voyage of Capitaine Thomas James, 1633) 44
Strathcona (South Edonton) 228
Subercase, Daniel d'Auger de 73
Sucker Creek 226
Sullivan, James 208
Sunneshine (John Davis) 36
Sutil (Dionisio Galiano) 160
Sverdrup Islands 248
Sverdrup, Otto 248, 249
Swift Current, Saskatchewan 221

T

Taché, Alexandre-Antonin, Bishop 214
Tacoutche Tesse (Fraser River) 145
Tadoussac, Québec 49, 62
Tagish Charlie 244
Tahltan River 198
Taignogny (Donnacona's son) 27
Talon, Jean, Intendant 61, 62, 70
Tecumseh 174, 176, 177
Terror (Francis Crozier) 193
Texada Island 160, 236
Thames River 127, 177
Thomson, John 190
Thorne, Nicholas 23
Thorne, Robert 23
Thornton, John 77, 78
Thornton, Samuel 78
Thorold, Ontario 201
"Three greenhorns" 237
Thunder Bay, Ontario 86, 87, 221
Thutade Lake 197
Tiarks, Johann 168, 180

Ticonderoga, New York 53, 116
Times, The (newspaper) 249
Tordesillas, Treaty/demarcation line 25
Toronto 98, 169, 170, 174, 200, 210, 240
"Toronto Purchase" map 170
Toronto River 169
Toronto Stock Exchange 240
Townshend, Charles 100
Townships 213, 216, 226
Tracy, Alexandre de Prouville, Sieur de 61, 70
Trans-Canada Highway 208, 209
Traverse (on St. Lawrence RIver) 107, 111
Treaties, native (1–9) 226
Treaty of Aix-la-Chapelle, 1748 89, 92, 118
Treaty of Ghent, 1814 177, 180, 202
Treaty of Paris, 1763 102, 109, 114, 168
Treaty of Paris, 1783 180, 202
Treaty of Ryswick, 1697 72, 79
Treaty of Saint-Germain-en-Laye, 1632 55, 99
Treaty of Utrecht, 1713 66, 75, 78, 79, 80, 85, 86, 88, 90, 95, 118
Treaty of Washington (Oregon Treaty), 1846 204
Trent (John Franklin) 184
Triangulation 168
Trinity Bay, Newfoundland 45
Troyes, Pierre de 66, 79
Truro, Nova Scotia 212
Trutch, Joseph 215
Tuktoyaktuk, North West Territories 189
Tupper, Charles 219
Turnagain River 197, 198
Turner Valley 232
Turnor, Philip 146, 147, 148, 150, 151, 154, 166
Twelve Mile Creek 201
Twillingate, Newfoundland 122

U

Ungava (District) 248, 255, 256
Union (boat; Richardson and Kendall) 189
United Province of Canada 181, 200
Upper Bytown 239
Upper Canada (Ontario) 115, 128, 169, 171, 172, 182, 200

V

Val, Pierre du 54, 56
Valdes, Cayetano 160, 162, 165
Vallard, Nicolas 33
Van Horne, William Cornelius 219, 221, 237
Van Keulen, Gerard 271
Vancouver (city) 160, 224, 227, 236, 237, 245, 251, 263
Vancouver, George 4, 133, 145, 159, 160, 163–65, 188, 236
Vancouver Island 157, 161, 162, 165, 203, 204, 206
Vaudreuil *See* Rigaud de Vaudreuil, François-Pierre de
Vaughan, William 45, 46
Vaugondy, Didier Robert de 82, 132
Vavasour, Mervin 228
Verdía, José 160
Vérendrye *See* La Vérendrye, Pierre Gaultier Varennes et de
Verrazano, Giovanni 15, 22, 24, 37
Verrazano Narrows 24
Vetch, Samuel 73, 75
Victoria Bridge, Montréal 243
Victoria, British Columbia 161, 203, 215, 245
Victoria Island 189, 193, 194
Victoria Strait 249
Victory (John Ross) 191, 192
Vigilant (French warship) 89
Ville-Marie (Montréal) 57, 243
Vimont, Father Barthélemy 57
Vincent, John 175
Vinland 10, 11
Virginia Falls 197
Viscount Melville Sound 185
Voltigeurs (regiment) 177
Voyage of Discovery to the North Pacific Ocean (George Vancouver, 1798) 165
Voyage to Hudson's-Bay by the Dobbs Galley *and* California (Henry Ellis, 1748) 84
Voyages du Sieur de Champlain, Les (Samuel de Champlain, 1613) 53
Voyages from Montreal (Alexander Mackenzie, 1801) 168, 242

W

Wager Bay/River/ Strait 81, 82, 83
Wager, Charles 80
Wakeham, William 248
Waldseemüller, Martin 15
Walker, Sir Hovenden 75, 99
Walter, John 228
Wapta Lake 221
War of 1812 172–177, 178
War of American Independence 172
Warren, Admiral Peter 89
Watson Lake 197
Waymouth, George 38
Webb, A. C. (surveyor) 213
Webster, Daniel 202
Webster-Ashburton Treaty, 1842 202
Welland Canal 201
Welland Canal Company 201
Welland River 201
Wellington Channel 193
West Road River 144
Western Sea 80, 86, 132
Whale Island (Garry Island) 143, 144, 189
Whitbourne, Richard 46
White Pass and Yukon Railway 244
Whitehorse, Yukon 244
Width of Canada, determining the 158
Wigate, John 83
Wilkes, Charles 204
Wilkinson, James 177
Williams, George 174
Windsor, Ontario 210
Winnebago (tribe) 58
Winnipeg 86, 179, 218, 219, 221, 226, 227, 233, 234
Winter Harbour, Melville Island 185, 186, 250
Winter Island 188
Winter Lake (Fort Franklin) 186
Wolfe, James 96, 99
Wollaston Peninsula 189
Wolseley, Garnet 213
Wrangell Island, Russia 250
Wright, Edward 37, 45
Wrightsville (Hull, Québec) 239
Wye River 58
Wyld, James 202, 204
Wytfliet, Cornelius 14, 38, 39

Y

Yellowhead Pass 219
Yellowknife, North West Territories 256
Yeo, Commodore James Lucas 175
Yonge Street 130, 171, 200
York (Toronto) 169, 171, 174, 240
York Fort (est. 1684, Nelson River) 78, 79, 80, 136, 146, 147, 166, 186
York Harbour (Toronto) 108, 110
Yukon District 244
Yukon River 198, 199, 244, 245
Yukon Territory 199, 244, 248, 254, 255, 256
Yukon Territory Act 244

Z

Zeno map 11, 14, 34, 35, 36, 37

A MAP OF AMERICA,

between Latitudes 40 and 70 NORTH, and Longitudes 45 and

EXHIBITING MACKENZIE'S TRACK

From Montreal *to* Fort Chipewyan & *from thence to the* Nor

In 1789, & *to the* Weft Pacific Ocean *in* 1793.

THE SEA

THE SEA
Seen by Mr Hearne in 1771

Coppermine Rr

COPPER

Buffaloe Lake

Stoney Mountain

INDIANS

This River by Indian report
Joins the Sea

Congecathewhachaga

Great Bear R.

Great Bear L.

Very high Hills

NATHANA IND.

Grand Lake

Theye Check L.

Theye kye lyned L.

HARE IND.

A Minitee

Small River

Chesterfield Inlet
Fresh Water

MOUNTAIN
IND

Bakers Lake

Point L.

Theye hore kred L.

INDIANS

Nipschish Lake

Yath Kyed
Lake

Rankins Inlet

Mackenzies Rr

Martin

INLAND IND.

Doobaunt
Lake

Corbet Inlet

Whale Cove

STRONGHOW
INDIANS

River

BEAVER
IND.

Very Hills

and Stoney

Cassandgad
Lake

Ana-nethai-bed

Titmos L.

Knights I.

Mt St Elias

Horn Mountain
river

Methye I.

Anawi I.

Clowey

Magnasse and R.

Nevills Bay

Esquimeaux

SLAVE LAKE

Clowey
River

Thoo-bel-Kre

Dear River

Knape

Observatory
Inlet

River of the Mountains

Buffaloe

Slave River

This way are York

Wholdyackuck I.

Northline L.

Lake

Bearabau

Egg River

Churchill Fort

River

Salt Springs

Hesh Rocks

Rocky Hills

Shethani R.

Seal R.

Cape

Finlays Br.

Old Establishment

Unjigah or Peace R.

Fort Chipewyan

Elk River

Rain Deer
Lake

Churchill R.

Split L.

Port Nelson R.

Steel River

New Establishment

Red Willow River

Pelican Rr

Lake

Sinking L.

Mc Leods Fort

The Fork

Lake

Prince Lake

Black Bear
Lake

3 Points L.

Fox L.

Fork
Fort

Lesser
Slave Lake

Carry I.

Buffalo
Lake

Ia la Cross
& Lake

Burntwood River

Carrying place

Burntwood L.

Setting Lake

Red Deer Ir.

Swan or L.

Moon L.

Beaver River

Rapids

Beaver Lake

Pine Island L.

Sturgeon L.

Reed L.

BLOOD IND.

BLACKFOOT
IND.

Manchester
House

Hudsons Ho.

Cumberland House

Cedar
Lake

LAKE
WINNIPIC

Kikanoo R.

Red River

St Buffaloe L.

Saskashawin R.

South Branch House

Elbow we mak mo R.

Swan Lake

Semonet House

FALL IND.

great quantity of Goal
in this Creek

Edge Goal Creek

South Branch

Eagle hill Creek

Carlton House

Red River

Kisow or Bad River

Morlboro House

CATTENAHOWES

OxStrait
Cat Head

Grants Ho.

Thorburne Ho.

Mc Donells Ho.

Stone Indian R.

Pembina R.

Goose R.

Red Lake R.

Quadra & Vancouvers I.

Nootka

Breakers Point

Queen Charlottes Sound

Supposed Strait or Juan de Fuca

Pinnacle

Queen Ho.

Whidbeys Harb

Saddle Hill

C. Mizaria

Quick Sand Bay

C. Feabweather

C. Perpetua

C. Gregory

Cape Blanco

Pt St George

Red River

Prince Village

Leech Lake

Otter Tail L.